Introduction to
Economic Reasoning

Introduction to Economic Reasoning

THIRD EDITION

William D. Rohlf, Jr.

Drury College

ADDISON-WESLEY PUBLISHING COMPANY

Reading, Massachusetts • Menlo Park, California • New York
Don Mills, Ontario • Wokingham, England • Amsterdam
Bonn • Sydney • Singapore • Tokyo • Madrid
San Juan • Milan • Paris

Senior Editor: Denise Clinton
Associate Editor: Lena Buonanno
Editorial Assistant: Amy Folsom
Production Supervisor: Patsy DuMoulin
Editorial and Production Services: Barbara Pendergast
Text Designer: Sally Bindari, Designworks
Cover Designer: Peter Blaiwas
Illustrator: Tech-Graphics
Photo Research: Sarah Evertson/Image Quest
Manufacturing Supervisor: Hugh Crawford
Marketing Manager: Craig Bleyer

Library of Congress Cataloging-in-Publication Data

Rohlf, William D.
Introduction to economic reasoning / by William D. Rohlf, Jr.—3rd ed.
    p.   cm.
Includes index.
ISBN 0-201-60994-0
1.–Economics.   2.–United States—Economic conditions.   I.–Title.
HB171.5.R73   1995
330   dc20   95-9341
                                                                                        CIP

Photo Credits   Page 13, Peter Southwick/Stock Boston; page 16, Tony Freeman/PhotoEdit; page 42, Wide World Photos; page 51, AP/Wide World Photos; page 137, Spencer Grant/Stock Boston; page 169, Ellis Herwig/Stock Boston; pages 187, 222, 312, Wide World Photos; page 211, Phil Matt; page 238, Alan Oddie/PhotoEdit; page 272, Tom Hollyman/Photo Researchers; page 285, N.R. Rowan/Stock Boston; page 401, John Ficara/Woodfin Camp & Associates; page 407, Paul Hosefros/NYT Pictures; page 490, UPI/Bettmann; pages 459, 474, 498, Paul Conklin/PhotoEdit; page 522, John Coletti/Stock Boston; page 531, Brown Brothers

1 2 3 4 5 6 7 8 9 10   DOC   9998979695

To my parents, who helped me learn the value of persistence

Preface

Almost one hundred years ago, Alfred Marshall defined economics as "the study of mankind in the ordinary business of life." Today, the ordinary business of life has become incredibly complex. The purpose of this textbook is to help prepare students for that life.

Introduction to Economic Reasoning is intended for students taking the one-term course in introductory economics. Many of these students, perhaps a majority, will take only one course in economics. They have a variety of interests and educational objectives. Some are enrolled in preprofessional programs; others will pursue majors in areas such as business, psychology, or the liberal arts. At a number of institutions, the one-term course also enrolls first-year students in MBA programs and other graduate business programs. Many of these students pursued nonbusiness majors as undergraduates and did not elect to take an economics course. Others desire to review economics before entering the graduate program. Although the students enrolling in the one-term course have diverse objectives and interests, they can all benefit from a course that prepares them to understand economic issues better and helps them to become better decision makers.

The Focus of the Book

How do we prepare students to understand economic issues and help them become better decision makers? I am convinced that we cannot accomplish these objectives by focusing solely on economic issues and short-cutting a discussion of economic concepts. This approach might provide students with ready answers to existing problems, but it would do little to prepare students for coping with new social problems and little to refine their decision-making skills. To accomplish those objectives, we must teach students something about economic reasoning.

Economists are fond of saying that economics is a way of thinking, or a way of reasoning about problems. The essence of economic reasoning is the ability to use theories or models to make sense out of the real world and devise policy solutions to economic problems. If we want students to use economic reasoning, we have to help them to learn and understand the basic economic theories. Without an understanding of economic theory, a course in economics can leave the student with little more than memorized solutions to current economic problems.

The Need to Make Choices

Obviously, we can't do everything in a one-term course in introductory economics. And unless we can keep the student's interest and show the relevance of economics, we can't accomplish anything. So the instructor in a one-term course (and the author of a one-term text) must make choices. He or she must decide what to include and what to exclude, how to balance theory with application, and how to motivate the student without sounding too much like a cheerleader. This textbook attempts to bridge these extremes.

Because economists use theories or models in problem solving, the core of this text is economic theory. No essential micro or macro concept is omitted. Many refinements are omitted, however, so that more time can be devoted to the careful development of the most important concepts. This is one of the distinctive features of the text: a very careful development of the core ideas in economic theory.

Making Economics Relevant

Today's student wants to know why he or she should be studying economics. What problems or issues will it help to clarify? What decisions will it help to improve? In *Introduction to Economic Reasoning*, the relevance of economics is illustrated by the use of examples in the text and through special features entitled "Use Your Economic Reasoning." These features, which are listed in a separate table of contents on pages xxv–xxvii, contain current news articles that have been carefully selected to illustrate the relevance of the economic principles being discussed and to provide the student with an opportunity to test his or her knowledge of those principles. Each article is accompanied by a set of questions to ensure that the student gains the maximum benefit from the article, and the features themselves have been designed to make them easy to locate.

Writing Style

In writing this text, my overriding objective has been to make economics accessible to the average student. I have been careful to avoid unnecessarily sophisticated vocabulary and needlessly long sentences. Most important, I have worked to ensure that my explanations of economic concepts are carefully and clearly developed. While professors may adopt a text for a wide variety of reasons, I am convinced that the most common reason for discontinuing its use is because students can't understand it. Your students will be able to read this text and understand it.

Aids in Learning

In addition to a clear writing style, the text contains a number of additional learning aids:

1. Learning objectives are stated at the beginning of each chapter.
2. New terms are presented in boldface italic type and are always defined when they are introduced.
3. "Use Your Economic Reasoning" news article selections not only generate student interest but also give the student an opportunity to apply the concepts that have been presented and thereby reinforce learning.
4. Careful summaries highlight the contents of the chapter.
5. A glossary of new terms appears at the end of each chapter so that a student can easily review definitions.
6. A study guide including fill-in-the-blank and multiple-choice questions (with answers) and problems and questions for discussion appears at the end of each chapter. This increases the likelihood that the study guide will be used, and encourages the student to review the chapter to correct deficiencies.

Additional Features

1. The demand and supply model (the core of micro theory) is more fully developed than in other one-semester texts, and the student is given numerous opportunities to test his or her understanding of the model.

2. The organization of the macroeconomics chapters provides for maximum flexibility in use. Instructors wishing to employ only the aggregate demand–aggregate supply framework can do so, while those desiring to integrate the Keynesian total expenditures model have that option.

3. Modern developments in macroeconomic theory, such as the theory of rational expectations, are presented in a manner that is accessible to the beginning student.

4. The student is exposed to important areas of debate among economists (the activist-nonactivist debate in macroeconomics, for example) without being left with the impression that economic analysis is solely a matter of opinion.

Third Edition Changes

International economics receives increased attention in this third edition. The benefits of trade are introduced in the first chapter, and international examples and issues have been integrated throughout the text. Chapter 16 (International Trade) has been updated with expanded coverage of nontariff/nonquota barriers to trade and up-to-date coverage of the GATT and NAFTA agreements. In addition, Chapter 17 (International Finance) has been completely rewritten to simplify and update the coverage.

Additional changes in the third edition include an expanded discussion of common property resources and the contributions of Nobel laureate Ronald Coase, new coverage of price discrimination, game theory, and public choice economics, and modifications to make it possible for instructors to bypass the Keynesian model completely and concentrate on the aggregate demand–aggregate supply framework if they choose to do so. The third edition also contains almost thirty new "Use Your Economic Reasoning" selections drawn from such publications as the *Wall Street Journal*, *Forbes*, *Fortune*, and the *New York Times*.

Strategies for Using the Text

Introduction to Economic Reasoning provides balanced coverage of microeconomics and macroeconomics. The book is divided into four parts. A two-chapter introduction (Part 1) examines the basic economic problem and economic systems. This is followed by six chapters on microeconomics (Part 2), seven chapters on macroeconomics (Part 3), and two chapters on international economics (Part 4).

The chapters in the text are arranged in micro-macro sequence, but an instructor could easily reverse this order by covering Chapters 1, 2, and 3 and then moving directly to Part 3. The remaining micro chapters and Part 4 could then be covered in sequence.

If an instructor desired to shorten the micro portion of the course, Chapter 4 ("The Elasticity of Demand and Supply") and Chapter 8 ("Market Failure") could be omitted with no loss in continuity. Chapter 7 ("Industry Structure and Public Policy") extends the analysis presented in Chapter 6 and could also be skipped if necessary.

The macro coverage can also be reduced. Instructors wishing to omit the Keynesian model and concentrate on the aggregate demand–aggregate supply framework can skip Chapter 11 and the first part of Chapter 12 with no loss in continuity. Coverage can be further reduced by omitting Chapter 14 (which develops the model of a self-correcting economy) and Chapter 15 (the activist-nonactivist debate). The remaining chapters would provide an introduction to the *AD-AS* model (Chapter 10), along with coverage of both fiscal policy (Chapter 12) and monetary policy (Chapter 13).

International economics is the last part of the book. This material has traditionally been the first to be omitted whenever an instructor found it necessary to shorten his or her course. Today, the growing importance of this subject matter may call for a different strategy. As a compromise course of action, an instructor might cover Chapter 16 ("International Trade") and omit Chapter 17 ("International Finance").

The Instructor's Manual, Test Bank, and Transparency Masters

The instructor's manual that accompanies this book is intended to make the instructor's job easier. New instructors may benefit from the teaching tips provided for each chapter. The manual also contains answers to the "Use Your Economic Reasoning" questions, answers to the "Problems and Questions for Discussion" at the end of each chapter, and a test bank of essay, multiple-choice, and true-false questions. Transparency masters of text images are located in the back of the instructor's manual. A computerized test bank is also available.

Acknowledgments

One author is listed on the cover of this textbook, but there are many people who have helped in its preparation and to whom I owe my thanks.

First I would like to thank those who reviewed the third edition proposal and/or manuscript:

Carlos Aguilar
El Paso Community College

Jeffrey Blais
Rhode Island College

James E. Clark
Wichita State University

Jane H. Crouch
Pittsburgh State University

Price Fishback
University of Arizona

David T. Geithman
New Jersey Institute of Technology

Tommy Georgiades Jr.
DeVry Institute of Technology

Richard J. Gosselin
Houston Community College

Stanley Reynolds
University of Arizona

Bruce Roberts
Highline Community College

Duane L. Sorensen
Indiana State University

Donald A. Wells
University of Arizona

Their comments and suggestions have been immensely helpful to me and are reflected in the content of this revision.

As with the previous editions, I owe a particular debt of thanks to Steve Mullins, my colleague at Drury College. He was often called upon to help me interpret reviewer comments and decide between conflicting opinions. His good judgment and ready assistance have made a major difference in the quality of this edition.

I would also like to thank those with whom I have worked at Addison-Wesley: Denise Clinton, Lena Buonanno, Barbara Pendergast, Patsy DuMoulin, and Mary Dyer. Their attention to detail and their personal encouragement have been very much appreciated.

Finally, I would like to thank my wife, Bev. In our first year of marriage she has had to endure too many boring evenings and weekends alone. Without her patience and support this edition would never have been completed.

Springfield, MO   W.D.R.

Brief Contents

Detailed Contents

Use Your Economic Reasoning News Articles

"Use Your Economic Reasoning" is a news article spread that builds critical thinking skills by illustrating and reinforcing the economic concepts of each chapter.

Introduction to
Economic Reasoning

PART 1

Introduction: Scarcity and the Economic System

CHAPTER 1 explains what the study of economics is about and how the knowledge you gain from this course may affect your thinking in many ways. Here you will be introduced to the concept of "opportunity cost"—one of the most important concepts in economics and in everyday living. You will learn about the role of economic theory in helping us make sense out of the things we observe in the world around us. In Chapter 2 you will discover what an economic system is and how economic systems differ from country to country.

With that introductory material behind you, you can begin exploring economics in more detail. Part 2 of the text examines microeconomics: the study of individual markets and individual business firms. Part 3 explores macroeconomics: the study of the economy as a whole and the factors that influence the economy's overall performance. Part 4 considers international economics: the study of economic exchanges between nations.

The Study of Economics

1. State the fundamental economic problem and provide a definition of economics.
2. Identify the four categories of economic resources.
3. Explain the concept of opportunity cost.
4. Draw a production possibilities curve and use it to illustrate opportunity cost, economic growth, and the benefits from trade.
5. Discuss the three fundamental economic problems.
6. Identify five common goals of economic systems and illustrate how they may conflict.
7. Define economic theories and discuss their role.
8. Explain why economists sometimes disagree.

Beginning a subject you haven't explored before is something like starting out on a blind date: You always hope for the best but anticipate the worst. This time, be reassured. No course you take in college is likely to be more relevant to your future—whatever your interests—than this one. An understanding of economic principles is valuable because so many of the questions and decisions that touch our lives have an economic aspect. This is true whether you are evaluating something as personal as your decision to attend college or attempting to grapple with one of today's fundamental social issues: the debate about the proper role of government in the United States, for example, or the future of nuclear power or the advisability of protecting U.S. businesses and workers from foreign competition. Each of these issues has important implications for your welfare and mine, yet they are just a few of the many complex questions that confront us as consumers, workers, and citizens. To understand and evaluate what economists, politicians, and others are saying about these issues, we need a knowledge of economics. Then we can do a better job of separating the "sense" from the "nonsense" and forming intelligent opinions.

Obviously you won't learn all there is to know about economics from one short textbook. But here is your opportunity to build a solid understanding of basic economic principles and discover how economists interpret data and analyze economic problems. That is especially important because economics is as much a way of reasoning as it is a body of knowledge. Once you have learned what it means to "consider the opportunity costs," to "compare the costs and benefits," and to "think marginally," nothing will ever look quite the same again. You'll find yourself making better decisions about everything from how to use your time more effectively to whom to support in the next presidential election. Watching the TV news and reading newspapers and magazines will become more meaningful and enjoyable. You will begin to notice the economic dimension of virtually every problem confronting society—pollution, crime, health care, higher education, and so on. Your knowledge of economics will help you understand and deal better with all these problems.

The Economic Problem

The fundamental economic problem facing individuals and societies alike is the fact that our wants exceed our capacity for satisfying those wants. Consider, for example, one of your personal economic problems: how to use your limited income—your limited financial resources. With the possible exception of the very rich, none of us can afford to buy everything we'd like to have. Each of us can think of a virtually limitless number of products we want or "need": food, shelter, clothing, membership at a health club, new tires for the car, a personal computer. We really won't tax our brains if we continue. Economist and social critic John Kenneth Galbraith has suggested that the satisfaction of a want through the purchase of a product not only fails to reduce our wants but in fact creates new ones. Purchase an audio system, for instance, and soon you will want compact discs, headphones, storage cabinets, and the like.

Societies face essentially the same dilemma: The wants of their members exceed the societies' capacities for satisfying those wants. In order to satisfy human wants, societies or nations require the use of **economic resources,** the scarce inputs that are used in the process of creating a good or providing a service. Traditionally economists divide these resources into four categories: land, labor, capital, and entrepreneurship. **Land** signifies more than earth or acreage; it includes all raw materials—timber, water, minerals, and other production inputs—that are created by nature. **Labor** denotes the work—both physical and mental—that goes into the production process. **Capital** refers to the human-made aids to production, such as factories, machinery, and tools. **Entrepreneurship** is the managerial function that combines all these economic resources in an effective way and uncovers new opportunities to earn a profit—for example, through new products or processes. Entrepreneurship is characterized by a willingness to take the risks associated with a business venture.

Every society's stock of economic resources is limited, or *scarce,* in relation to the infinite wants of its members. At any given time even the world's richest economies have available only so much raw material, labor, equipment, and managerial talent to use in producing goods and services. Consequently an economy's ability to produce goods and services is limited, just as an individual's ability to satisfy his or her personal wants is limited.

The inability to satisfy all our wants forces us to make choices about how we can best use our limited resources. That is what economics is all about: making wise choices about how to use scarce resources. Therefore we define **economics** as the study of how to use our limited resources to satisfy our unlimited wants as fully as possible. When individuals, businesses, or nations try to make the most of what they have, they are "economizing."

Choice and Opportunity Cost

In order to make wise choices, we must compare the costs and benefits associated with each alternative or option we consider. A particular decision or choice will improve our well-being only if the benefits associated with that decision exceed the costs, if what we gain is worth more to us than what we lose.

One of the fundamental lessons of economics is that all our choices entail costs: There is no "free lunch." Whenever you make a decision to do or have one thing, you sacrifice the opportunity to do or have some other thing. The best, or *most valued,* alternative you must sacrifice in order to take a particular action is the **opportunity cost** of that action. What opportunity are you sacrificing by reading this chapter? Perhaps you could be studying for another class or watching your favorite TV show. The opportunity cost of reading this chapter is whatever you wanted to do most. When your city council or town meeting allocates tax dollars to install sidewalks, it may sacrifice books for the public library, street lights for a residential area, or tennis courts for a local park. Whatever that body would have chosen to do if it hadn't installed sidewalks is the opportunity cost of the sidewalks.

When Congress debates the size of the defense budget, the outcome of that debate affects each of us. If a nation's resources are fully employed, an increase in the output of military goods and services requires a reduction in the output of something else. An increase in military spending may mean a cut in welfare, road construction, or aid to education; it may mean an increase in taxes, which in turn will lead to a reduction in private consumer spending and the output of consumer goods.

Either way, more military output means less civilian output because at any given time there is a limit to the amount of total output the economy can produce. This doesn't necessarily mean that we shouldn't spend more on military goods if there are sound reasons for doing so. It does mean that we should be aware of what that spending costs us in terms of private goods and services or other government programs. The economist's point here is that we can't make the best decisions about how to use our scarce resources unless we know the true costs and benefits of our decisions. (See "For High School Graduates, a Job Market of Dead Ends," on page 8, for a discussion of the costs and benefits of a college education.)

The Production Possibilities Curve

We can illustrate the concept of opportunity cost with a simple graph called a production possibilities curve. (The appendix at the end of this chapter explains how graphs are constructed and interpreted.) A **production possibilities curve** shows the combinations of goods that the economy is capable of producing with its present stock of economic resources and its existing techniques of production. Because it outlines the boundaries, or limits, of the economy's ability to produce output, it is sometimes called a *production possibilities frontier.* Any point along or inside the frontier represents a combination of goods that the economy can produce; any point above the curve is beyond the economy's present production capacity.

Exhibit 1.1 shows the production capabilities of a hypothetical economy. The economy's output of civilian goods is measured on the vertical axis and its output of military goods on the horizontal axis. According to this exhibit, if all the economy's resources were used to produce civilian goods, 80 million units of civilian goods could be produced each year (point *A*). On the other hand, if the economy were to use all its economic resources to produce military goods, 50 million units of military goods could be produced each year (point *D*). Between these extremes lie other production possibilities—combined outputs of military and civilian goods that the economy is capable of producing. For example, the economy might choose to produce 70 million

EXHIBIT 1.1

The Production Possibilities Curve

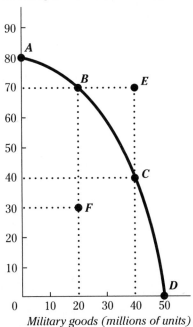

Civilian goods (millions of units)

Military goods (millions of units)

The production possibilities curve, *ABCD*, shows the combinations of civilian goods and military goods that the economy is capable of producing with its present stock of economic resources and the existing techniques of production. Any point on or below the curve is possible. Any point above the curve is ruled out (impossible).

units of civilian goods and 20 million units of military goods (point *B*). Or it might choose to produce 40 million units of civilian goods and 40 million units of military goods (point *C*). We can see, then, that the curve *ABCD* outlines the boundaries of our hypothetical economy's production abilities. Point *E*, which lies above the curve, represents a combination of products that is beyond the economy's present capacity.

Unfortunately economies do not always live up to their production capabilities. Whenever an economy is operating at a point inside its production possibilities curve, we know that economic resources are not being fully employed. For example, at point *F* in Exh. 1.1, our hypothetical economy is producing 30 million units of civilian goods and 20 million units of military goods each year. But according to the production possibilities curve, the economy could do much better. For example, it could increase its output of civilian goods to 70 million units a year without sacrificing any military goods (point *B*). Or it could expand its output of civilian goods to 40 million units while

Use Your Economic Reasoning

New York Times

May 30, 1994

For High School Graduates, a Job Market of Dead Ends

MEMPHIS

For hundreds of thousands of people graduating from high school this spring, the diploma is a one-way ticket to low-paying, part-time jobs at best.

Most graduates who are planning to go straight to work are offered the same low wages, the same part-time hours and the same assignments in the restaurants, supermarkets, motels and gasoline stations where they worked in after-school jobs they held as students.

And they might consider themselves lucky. In 1993, the Bureau of Labor Statistics reports, nearly a quarter of high school graduates who did not go on to college and wanted jobs were still unemployed in October, compared with 21 percent of each year's new graduates in the 1980's and 16 percent in the 1970's. For the first time, unemployment grew among graduates while the economy was growing.

"The market is fraught with dead ends," said Alison Bernstein, the head of education programs at the Ford Foundation. "Unless they have certain kinds of skills they can get locked on a path that doesn't take them anywhere. They could be among the working poor very early."

Not long ago, a graduate of Craigmont High and Middle School in Memphis could walk from graduation into the factory of International Harvester or Firestone Tire and Rubber and start earning real money.

"If you could hit a nail every time one went by on an assembly line," Ada Jane Walters, the principal, said, "you got a job that in today's market would pay $12 or $13 an hour."

But Harvester and Firestone, like many other manufacturers, have flown, leaving behind fast-growing, lower-wage industries. Today, Federal Express, the biggest employer in Memphis, offers high school graduates 20-hour-a-week jobs for $8 an hour.

"We try to be very up front about it," said Chuck W. Thomson, a vice president for personnel at Federal Express. "We tell them they should take this job with the understanding that it will be part time indefinitely."

Kroger supermarkets here offer $4.50 an hour for entry-level jobs like stock clerks.

Jack Overbrook, the head of personnel, said promotion to full time and a wage of $7 or $8 "could take three or four years."

So it goes around the nation.

Adjusted for inflation, the starting pay of people with at least four-year college degrees has slipped a bit in two decades, said Lawrence Mishel, an economist at the Economic Policy Institute in Washington. But in the same period, wages have plunged 25 percent to 30 percent for men with only high school diplomas and 15 percent to 18 percent for women in that category.

The nation's economy is producing two million new jobs a year, but they come with wages typically below $8 an hour, or about $16,000 a year, and without health benefits, much opportunity for promotion or promises that the jobs will last.

Many students have taken the statistics to heart by going to college and vocational schools. The Labor Department said on May 20 that 63 percent of last year's 2.3 million high school graduates had entered two- or four-year colleges by October, compared with 50 percent in 1980. . . .

But even college degrees, good attitudes and skills do not guarantee a decent job. The growth of low-paid, low-skilled jobs is outpacing the growth of more-skilled jobs in fields like health care and data processing.

At the same time, industry is shedding layers of middle-management jobs held by college graduates, creating an additional challenge for high school graduates: People with college degrees have invaded their blue-collar turf. As a result, of last year's 736,000 new high school graduates who joined the labor force a year ago, 24 percent—nearly four times the rate for all workers—were still unemployed in October.

Aware of the Realities

Students at Craigmont, a three-story yellow brick building on the working-class fringe of north Memphis, are well aware of the world that awaits them. . . .

But of Craigmont's 214 graduating seniors, less than the national average of 63 percent will go straight to two- or four-year colleges.

The guidance counselor, Mary Beth Yates, said 142 seniors, or 66 percent, say they would like to go, but for lack of money or ambition or adequate grades and test scores, only 80 have been admitted to colleges in the fall.

Some students are considering six months or a year of trade school or plan to join

the armed forces. But around half of the seniors will be heading straight for the job market the day after the graduation on June 6.

Goals and Wanderlust

The realities of the job market have taken a psychological toll. "For some reason," Ms. Yates said, "our kids are not real adventuresome.". . .

They want the security of homes and wages that pay the rent, not adventures and risks.

"This is the era of lowered expectations," said Harold Hodgkinson, an expert in American education who is

director of the Center for Demographic Policy in Washington. "For this group of kids, lowered expectations is a mentally healthy way for some of them to go. You can't get hurt if your expectations are low.". . .

—*Peter T. Kilborn*

Use Your Economic Reasoning

1. How should an individual decide whether a college education is worth pursuing; what comparison should he or she make?

2. The wages of high school graduates have declined (after adjusting for inflation) by 15 to 30 percent over the last two decades. Ignoring other changes, what does this mean has happened to the opportunity cost of attending college; has the opportunity cost increased or decreased?

3. How would you expect high school graduates to respond to this change in the opportunity cost of attending college? Does the article suggest that they have reacted in the expected manner?

4. Even college recruiters say that the costs and benefits of attending college will differ from one individual to the next. Why? Why, for instance, will the opportunity cost of attending college be higher for some individuals than for others?

also expanding its production of military goods to 40 million units (point C). In short, when an economy has unemployed resources, it is not satisfying as many of the society's unlimited wants as it could if it used its full potential.

Opportunity Costs along the Curve

We have seen that the production possibilities curve graphically represents the concept of opportunity cost. When an economy's resources are fully employed—that is, when it is operating on the production possibilities curve rather than inside it—larger amounts of one product can be obtained only by producing smaller amounts of the other product. The production possibilities curve slopes downward to the right to illustrate opportunity cost: More of one thing means less of the other thing. We can see opportunity costs changing as we move from one point on the production possibilities curve to another. For example, suppose that the society is operating at point A on the production possibilities curve in Exh. 1.1, producing 80 million units of civilian goods and no military goods. If the society decides that it would prefer to operate at point B, the opportunity cost of acquiring the first 20 million units of military goods would be the loss of 10 million units of civilian goods. The economy can move from point A to point B only by transferring resources from the production of civilian goods to the production of military goods.

Suppose that the society would like to have even more military goods—for example, 40 million units of military goods produced each year. According to the production possibilities curve, the opportunity cost of acquiring the next 20 million units of military goods (and moving from point B to point C) would be a loss of 30 million units of civilian goods—three times what it cost the society to acquire the first 20 million units of military goods. Moving from point C to point D would be even more expensive. In order to acquire the last 10 million units of military goods, the society would have to sacrifice 40 million units of civilian goods.

The Law of Increasing Costs

Our hypothetical production possibilities curve illustrates an important principle known as the **law of increasing costs:** As more of a particular product is produced, its opportunity cost per unit will increase. How do we explain the law of increasing costs? Why does our hypothetical society have to sacrifice larger and larger amounts of civilian output in order to obtain each additional increment of military output?

The explanation is fairly simple. Not all resources are alike; some economic resources—skilled labor and specialized machinery, for instance—are better suited to the production of one product than another. In our example some resources are better suited to the production of civilian goods and services, others to the production of military products. Consequently when the society attempts to expand its output of military goods and services, it must eventually use resources that are not well suited to producing those military products.

To illustrate that problem, let's examine the process of transferring resources from the production of civilian products to the production of military products. Suppose that initially our hypothetical economy is not producing any military output. At first it will not be difficult for the economy to increase its military output. Some of the existing capital resources, including factories, can be converted to the production of military products with relative ease, and many members of the labor force will have skills that are readily transferable to the production of military products. For example, it would be relatively easy to convert a clothing factory to the production of uniforms or to convert an awning factory to the production of tents. Since these conversions are relatively easy, the society will gain just about as much in military output as it will lose in civilian output.

But to continue expanding the output of military products, it will be necessary to use resources that are increasingly less suitable. For instance, consider the difficulty that might be encountered in converting an amusement park to a missile-manufacturing facility, or a toy factory to an explosives plant. Much of the equipment that was useful in producing civilian output will be of no use in producing military output. Therefore although the conversion of these facilities will require society to give up a large quantity of civilian output (many rides at the amusement park and thousands of toys), it will not result in very many additional units of military output.

The point is that because some resources are better suited to the production of civilian goods than to the production of military products, increasing amounts of civilian goods and services will have to be sacrificed to obtain each additional increment of military output. It is this principle (the law of increasing costs) that causes the production possibilities frontier to have the curved shape depicted in Exhs. 1.1 and 1.2. (If resources were equally well suited to the production of both products, what would the production possibilities curve look like?)

Economic Growth and the Benefits of Trade

As we have seen, it is important for economies to operate on rather than inside their production possibilities curves. But even when an economy fully employs its resources, it cannot satisfy all of a society's wants. Any point *above* the production possibilities frontier exceeds the economy's current production capabilities. For instance, point *E* in Exh. 1.2, which combines 70 million units of civilian goods and 40 million units of military goods, is beyond the in-

EXHIBIT 1.2

Illustrating Economic Growth

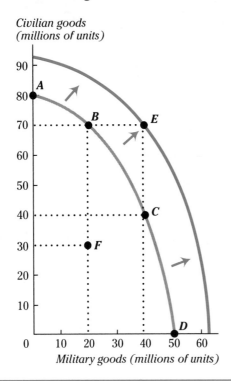

Civilian goods (millions of units)

Military goods (millions of units)

If the quantity of economic resources were to increase or better production methods were discovered, the economy's ability to produce goods and services would expand. Such economic growth can be illustrated by shifting the production possibilities curve to the right.

side production possibilities curve representing the existing capacity of this hypothetical economy. Society clearly would prefer that combination of products to the combination represented by, say, point *C*, but it can't obtain it.

Of course, the economy's production capacity is not permanently fixed. If the quantity of economic resources were to increase or if better production methods were discovered, the economy could produce more goods and services. Such an increase in production capacity is usually described as *economic growth* and is illustrated by shifting the production possibilities curve to the right. The outside curve in Exh. 1.2 represents economic growth sufficient to take point *E* within the economy's production possibilities frontier.

Trade between nations can provide benefits that are very similar to those that result from economic growth—increased amounts of goods and services. To illustrate, suppose that our hypothetical economy is operating at point *A* on the inside production possibilities curve in Exh. 1.2, producing 80 units of civilian goods and no military goods. According to the production possibili-

Like economic growth, free trade can increase the goods and services available for consumption.

ties curve, the economy could acquire 40 million units of military goods (and move to point C) only if it were willing to give up 40 million units of military goods; the cost of acquiring each additional unit of military goods would be the sacrifice of one unit of civilian goods. But suppose that through trade with other nations, this economy could acquire a unit of military goods by sacrificing only one-fourth of a unit of civilian goods. That would permit the economy to acquire the 40 million units of military goods it desires by giving up (trading) only 10 million units of civilian goods. The economy could move to point E, a point well beyond its own production capabilities.[1]

The ability to acquire goods at a lower opportunity cost (and thereby increase the total amount of goods and services available for consumption) is why **free trade**—trade that is not hindered by artificial restrictions or trade barriers—is generally supported by economists. Chapter 16 explores the theoretical basis for trade in much greater detail.

As you can see, the production possibilities curve is a useful tool for thinking about our economy. It shows that an economy with fully employed resources cannot produce more of one thing without sacrificing something else. Equally important, the production possibilities model can be used to

---

[1] Unlike economic growth, trade does not shift an economy's production possibilities curve but instead merely permits a nation to consume a combination of products beyond its own production capabilities.

illustrate the benefits of economic growth and free trade. Of course, neither economic growth nor free trade eliminates the need to make choices about how to use our scarce resources. The next section explores the nature of those choices in more detail.

The Three Fundamental Questions

The choice between military goods and civilian goods is only one of the broad decisions that the United States and other nations face. The dilemma of unlimited wants and limited economic resources forces each society to make three basic choices, to answer the "three fundamental questions" of economics: (1) What goods and services will we produce and in what quantities? (2) How will these goods and services be produced? (3) For whom will these products be produced—that is, how will the output be distributed?

What to Produce?

Because no society can produce everything its members desire, each society must sort through and assess its various wants and then decide which goods and services to produce in what quantities. Deciding the relative value of military products against civilian goods is only one part of the picture, because each society must determine precisely which civilian and military products it will produce. For example, it must decide whether to produce clothing or to conserve its scarce resources for some other use. Next, it must decide what types of clothing to produce—how many shirts, dresses, pairs of slacks, overcoats, and so on. Finally, it must decide in what sizes to produce these items of clothing and determine the quantities of each size. Only after considering all such alternatives can a society decide which goods and services to produce.

How to Produce?

After deciding which products to produce, each society must also decide what materials and methods to use in their production. In most cases a given good or service can be produced in more than one way. For instance, a shirt can be made of cotton, wool, or acrylic fibers. It can be sewn entirely by hand, partly by hand, or entirely by machine. It can be packaged in paper, cardboard, plastic, or some combination of materials. It can be shipped by truck, train, boat, or plane. In short, the producer must choose among many options with regard to materials, production methods, and means of shipment.

For Whom to Produce?

Finally, each society must decide how to distribute or divide up its limited output among those who desire to receive it. Should everyone receive equal shares of society's output? Should those who produce more receive more? What about those who don't produce at all, either because they can't work or because they don't want to work? How much of society's output should *they* receive? In deciding how to distribute output—how output will be shared— different societies are influenced by their traditions and cultural values.

Whether a society is rich or poor, simple or complex, democratic or authoritarian, it must have some *economic system* through which it addresses the three fundamental questions. Chapter 2 examines a variety of economic systems and discusses how they respond to these questions.

Five Economic Goals

A given economic system's answers to the three fundamental questions are not always satisfactory to either the nation's citizens or its leaders. For example, if an economy is operating inside its production possibilities curve, it is not using all its production capabilities and is therefore not satisfying as many human wants as possible. A society with unemployed resources may want to take steps to improve the economy's performance so that it does a better job of fulfilling citizen expectations or, in some cases, the expectations of those in power.

What should a society expect from its economic system? Before a society can attempt to improve its economic performance, it must have a set of goals, objectives, or standards by which to judge that performance. Although there is room for debate about precisely what constitutes "good performance" from an economic system, many societies recognize five essential goals:

1. *Full employment of economic resources.* If a society is to obtain maximum benefit from its scarce resources, it must utilize them fully. Whenever resources are unemployed—when factories stand idle, laborers lack work, or farmland lies untilled—the society is sacrificing the goods and services that those resources could have produced. Therefore it is doing a less than optimal job of satisfying the unlimited wants of its members.
2. *Efficiency.* Economic efficiency means getting the most benefit out of limited resources. This goal has two separate elements: (a) production of the goods and services that consumers desire the most and (b) realization of

When labor or other economic resources are unemployed, society must do without the goods and services those resources could have produced.

this production at the lowest cost in terms of scarce resources. Economic efficiency is the very essence of economics. If an economic system fully employs its resources but uses them to produce relatively unwanted products, the society cannot hope to achieve maximum satisfaction from its resources. By the same token, if an economy does not minimize the amount of resources used in producing *each* product, it will not be able to produce as many products; consequently fewer wants will be satisfied.

3. *Economic growth.* Because most people want and expect their standard of living to improve continually, economic growth—expansion in the economy's output of goods and services—is an important objective. If population is increasing, some economic growth is necessary just to maintain the existing standard of material welfare. When a nation's population is stable or is increasing less rapidly than output, economic growth results in more goods and services per person, contributing to a higher standard of living.

4. *A fair distribution of income.* Distribution of income means the way income is divided among the members of a society. In modern economies the income distribution is the primary factor determining how output will be shared. (In primitive economies, such as Ethiopia or Burundi, custom or tradition plays a major role in deciding how output is divided.) People with larger incomes receive larger shares of their economy's output. Is this a fair distri-

bution of output? Some contend that it is. Others call for redistribution of income to eliminate poverty in the society. Still others argue that nothing less than an equal distribution is truly fair.

5. *A stable price level.* A major goal of most economies is a stable price level. Societies fear inflation—that is, a rise in the general level of prices. Inflation redistributes income arbitrarily: Some people's incomes rise more rapidly than inflation, whereas other people find that their incomes can't keep pace. The former group emerges with a larger share of the economy's output, while the latter group must make do with less than before. The demoralizing effect of this redistribution can lead to social unrest.

In pursuing the five economic goals, societies strive to maintain compatibility with their noneconomic, or sociopolitical, objectives. Americans, for example, want to achieve these economic goals without harming the environment or sacrificing the rights of people to select their occupations, own property, and spend their incomes as they choose. Societies that place high value on tradition, such as Japan, may strive to pursue these economic goals without violating the customs of the past. Insofar as the cultural, political, religious, and other noneconomic values of societies differ, the relative importance of each of the five economic goals and the methods of meeting those goals will also differ.

Conflicts and Trade-offs

Defining economic goals is only the first step in attempting to improve our economy's performance. The next step is to decide how to achieve these goals. Often the pursuit of one goal forces us to sacrifice at least part of some other economic or noneconomic goal. That is what economists call a *trade-off*—society gets more of one thing only by giving up, or trading off, something else. This is another way of stating the problem of opportunity cost. The opportunity cost of achieving a particular goal is whatever other goal has to be sacrificed or compromised. Let's consider three problems societies face in pursuing economic goals.

Full Employment versus Stable Prices

The goal of achieving full employment may conflict with the goal of maintaining a stable price level. Experience has taught us that attempting to reduce unemployment generally results in a higher rate of inflation. By the same token, attempts to reduce the rate of inflation often lead to higher unemployment. Frequently it becomes necessary to sacrifice part of one goal in favor of the other. For instance, society may accept some unemployment to maintain a lower inflation rate. The trade-off each society makes depends partly on economic analysis but is also influenced by societal values.[2]

Economic Growth versus Environmental Protection

Conflict frequently occurs between the goals of economic growth and a clean environment. Although most Americans support these two goals, it has become apparent that expansion of the economy's output takes a toll on the environment. For instance, our attempts to expand agricultural output by using pesticides and chemical fertilizers have been partially responsible for the pollution of our rivers and streams. We make trade-offs between economic growth and environmental preservation, trade-offs that reflect prevailing national values.

Equality versus Efficiency

Consider now the potential conflict between income equality and economic efficiency. Suppose that a society decided that fair income distribution demanded greater equality of income than presently exists. Many economists would point out that efforts to achieve greater equality tend to have a negative impact on economic efficiency. Remember, efficiency means producing the most wanted products in the least costly way. To accomplish this, the economy must be able to direct labor to the areas where it is most needed, often by making wages and salaries in these areas more attractive than those in other areas. For example, if a society needs to increase its number of computer programmers more rapidly than its number of teachers or nurses, it can encourage people to become computer programmers by making that occupation more rewarding financially than teaching or nursing.[3] If pay differentials are reduced in order to meet the goal of equality, a society will sacrifice economic efficiency, because it will be more difficult to direct the flow of labor.

Choosing between Objectives

When our society's goals conflict and demand that we choose between them, it is not the function of economists to determine the best trade-off. The choice between equality and efficiency, for example, is a **normative issue,** involving judgments about what "should be" rather than what is. Setting goals is the job of the society or its representatives. The function of the economist is to make

---

[2] Most economists agree that there is a short-run trade-off between unemployment and inflation that may not exist in the long run. This issue is discussed in Chapter 14.

[3] In some economic systems these adjustments in wages and salaries would occur automatically; in others deliberate action would be required. Chapter 2 has more to say about how specific economic systems direct or allocate labor.

sure that those in charge of setting goals (or devising policies to achieve goals) are aware of the alternatives available to them and the sacrifices each alternative requires. When economists stop talking about how things are and start talking about how they should be, they have entered the realm of values, an arena in which they have no more expertise than anyone else. (See "Oregon's New Health Rationing Means More Care for Some but Less for Others," on page 20, for a discussion of economics and ethics.)

Economic Theory and Policy

Before economists can recommend policies for dealing with economic problems or achieving goals, they must understand thoroughly how the economic system operates. This is where economic theory comes into play.

Economic theories are generalizations about causal relationships between economic variables; through theories, economists attempt to explain what causes what in economics. Theories are also referred to as laws, principles, and models. When in later chapters you encounter the *law* of demand, the *principle* of comparative advantage, and the *model* of command socialism, bear in mind that each of these tools is a theory. Economic theories help economists understand the real world by simplifying reality. In fact theories or models are sometimes described as simplified pictures of the real world. By leaving out extraneous details and complexities, theories help us see the essential relationships more clearly—much as a map clarifies the shape and layout of a city by excluding unnecessary detail.

When you read the evening newspaper or tune in the news on television, you are exposed to a deluge of facts and figures about everything from housing construction to foreign trade. Without theories to help you interpret them, however, these data are of little value. As an example, suppose we observe that per capita gasoline consumption in the United States is declining. In order to explain this fact, we need a theory. Suppose that after studying the relevant data—number of cars on the road, availability of gasoline and its price—we discover what seems to be a relationship between two facts: As gasoline prices have risen, gasoline consumption has declined. We might "theorize" from this that rising gasoline prices have caused gasoline consumption to decrease.

Testing Economic Theories

We could test our theory by gathering data for a number of different time periods to see if in fact gasoline consumption has increased and decreased consistently in accordance with changes in its price. But this test would not include other significant elements. Even if the price of gasoline is a major

Oregon's New Health Rationing Means More Care for Some but Less for Others

When Oregon doctors Leigh Dolin and Rick Wopat go to work next week, it won't be health care as usual for them. Or for their patients.

After years of statewide debate and federal scrutiny, Oregon will on Feb. 1 launch a radical redesign of its federally funded Medicaid program in the nation's most serious attempt at health-care rationing.

Oregon's new health plan will extend Medicaid coverage to many working poor people who have, until now, been uninsured. It will also phase current Medicaid recipients into cost-conscious managed-care plans. Most radically, Oregon will limit its coverage to a priority list of 606 medical procedures, stressing prevention and basic care and trimming what the state deems unnecessary or futile, from cosmetic surgery to heroic measures for the terminally ill. . . .

Oregon was ripe for a new health-care system. Many of the state's 3 million residents depend on cyclical industries such as timber and agricul-ture—and far too many Oregonians fell through the cracks in the health-care system. In 1992, about 479,000 people, or 16.1%, of Oregon's population were uninsured, well above the national average of 13.9%.

Now about 120,000 of uninsured Oregonians who live at the poverty level will become newly eligible for Medicaid. In addition, about 180,000 of the 250,000 people already enrolled in Medicaid will be embraced by the new plan. (The remainder of Oregon's poor and uninsured will be phased in over the next five years. Elderly and disabled people and children in foster care are scheduled to enter the plan in 1995. An additional 300,000 of the working poor are scheduled to enter the plan in 1997 and 1998, when an employer-based coverage law kicks in.)

Despite Oregon's fiscal woes–it expects a $1 billion budget shortfall in 1995–97—the state was able to fund the expansion of its Medicaid rolls and enhance services like adult dental care by imposing cigarette taxes of 10 cents a pack in recent months.

"The most exciting thing," says Jean Thorne, head of Oregon Medicaid, is that "we'll newly entitle 120,000 people who haven't had care." Also, she expects new monthly capitation fees, where doctors receive payment per patient instead of for specific services, will offer striking improvements on the old Medicaid reimbursement rates, under which doctors often complained they lost money caring for the poor.

Oregon's insistence on managed care means a primary-care doctor will coordinate care and keep patients from falling into expensive and inefficient emergency rooms as their provider-of-last-resort. . . .

Still, the plan's designers faced hard choices and imposed strict—sometimes severe—limits on what care can be funded by the public purse.

Though the plan pays for many lifesaving treatments—liver or kidney transplants for people with cirrhosis or renal failure, for example—it draws a line where the data don't promise a cure.

Among routine procedures no longer covered are treatment for many benign or self-limited illnesses: common colds, simple sprains and basic food poisoning. Nonessential or controversial surgery is also out: circumcision of newborns or gastric bypass operations for the obese, both formerly covered.

"Somebody who thinks their nose is too big won't be covered," says Dr. Dolin. More important, neither will a poor woman who seeks reconstructive breast surgery after mastectomy. The affluent, of course, can continue to purchase such services in Oregon as elsewhere.

Most wrenching of these limits is the lack of coverage for curative treatments for people with terminal illnesses such as endstage cancer or AIDS. Instead, the state emphasizes early diagnosis and treatment at the beginning of serious illness, medical treatments as long as they can prolong life and "comfort care"—including pain medication and hospice services—when the odds of cure fall below 5%.

"That's the most impossible issue to deal with," concedes Dr. Dolin. "Doctors and insurance plans can't solve that problem. Society needs to say everybody can't have everything they want at the end of life."

Groups like the American Cancer Society tentatively applaud the plan for its coverage of early diagnostic procedures, like mammography. "We're rather pleased," says a spokeswoman. Still, "Those [providers and patients] who want to fight to the bitter end are going to have a battle under the new system."

Rick Wopat, a physician in the rural logging town of Lebanon, was one of the drafters of "the List" of covered procedures. He says there is only enough money to pay for what medicine knows will work, not enough to finance costly experiments with little chance of success.

"The state shouldn't spend its resources on things not clearly shown to be effective," he says. . . .

—*Marilyn Chase*

SOURCE: Marilyn Chase, "Oregon's New Health Rationing Means More Care for Some but Less for Others," January 28, 1994. Reprinted by permission of *The Wall Street Journal*, © 1994 Dow Jones & Co., Inc. All Rights Reserved Worldwide.

Use Your Economic Reasoning

1. What statements in this article indicate that the provision of health care involves an economic problem?

2. Oregon's plan will provide basic health benefits to 120,000 additional Oregonians by refusing to pay for some high-cost procedures and by taxing cigarettes. What are the opportunity costs of providing benefits to these previously ineligible residents?

3. Under Oregon's new plan, the state will not pay for "curative treatments for people with terminal diseases." Why? What is the opportunity cost of providing such treatments?

4. Oregon's health-care program clearly involves normative issues. Explain.

factor influencing the amount consumed, it is clearly not the *only* factor. It seems likely that over a given period, personal income also affects gasoline consumption. If the incomes of car owners remain constant while gasoline prices rise, gasoline consumption may well decline. But if incomes increase during the same period, offsetting the rise in gasoline prices, gasoline consumption will probably remain the same; it may even increase.

To determine whether the consumption of gasoline is in fact related to the price of gasoline, economists have to be able to hold constant personal income and any other nonprice factors that might influence the amount of gasoline consumed. Unfortunately economists cannot control these other factors as precisely as chemists or physicists can control variables in their experiments. So economists do the next best thing. They *assume* that everything else remains the same; that is, they assume other factors, such as personal incomes, remain constant. This is the assumption of **ceteris paribus,** which literally means "other things being equal." In a sense what economists are doing is stating the conditions under which they expect a theory to be valid. To illustrate, our theory about the consumption of gasoline might be restated this way: "Consumers will buy less gasoline at higher prices than at lower prices, ceteris paribus—other things being equal." Economists then compare what actually happens to what they expected, on the basis of the theory, to happen. If the facts are not consistent with the theory, we must determine whether it is because the theory is invalid or because the assumption of ceteris paribus has been violated (that is, because something other than the price of gasoline changed).

Policies and Predictions

Once a theory has been tested and accepted, it can be used as a basis for making predictions and as a guide to formulating economic policy. On the basis of our gas-price theory, for example, we would predict that if gasoline prices go up, consumption will decline and that if prices fall, consumption will increase. We could also use this theory as the basis for devising policies for influencing the level of gasoline consumption. In order to reduce domestic gasoline consumption, for instance, we might recommend an increase in the federal tax on gasoline.

The formulation of policies for dealing with economic problems is the most important use of economic theory and the most important function of economists. In considering this function, it is important to remember that usually there is more than one way to achieve a given objective. A society wants to select the policy option that will permit it to achieve its objective at the lowest "cost" in terms of its other goals.

Economists and Conclusions

If you listen to the TV news or read the newspaper, you know that economists do not always agree on matters of economic policy. "You can lay all economists end to end and never reach a conclusion" is a popular saying about the inability of economists to agree on the best economic policy for specific social problems. Laypersons therefore may be skeptical about the contribution that economics can make toward solving society's problems. Because you are going to spend the next few months studying economics, it seems appropriate to take a few minutes now to consider the reasons why economists disagree. Economists may disagree either because they have different views about what *should be* or because they have different views of what *is*.

We've already explained that economists possess no special expertise in choosing goals, in deciding *how things ought to be*. Yet like all thinking people, economists hold individual values and opinions about which of society's economic goals are the most important. Obviously economists with different philosophies about what the society should be attempting to achieve will have different recommendations with respect to economic policy. Economists attempt to avoid this source of disagreement by asking political leaders and other decision makers to specify their economic goals; then the economists can suggest policies to achieve those goals.

Economists may also disagree about the proper policy for achieving a chosen goal or combating an economic problem because they disagree about how things *are*—about how the economy works or how a particular policy would work. Suppose, for example, that the challenge is to eliminate inflation. Some economists conclude that the major cause of virtually every outbreak of inflation is a too-rapid growth of the money supply. Not surprisingly the remedy they suggest is a reduction in the growth rate of the money supply. Other economists argue that inflation springs from a variety of causes: too much government spending; "shocks," such as steep OPEC oil-price increases and bad crop harvests; the wage-price spiral, wherein higher wage costs push up prices, and higher prices lead to demands for higher wages. These economists call for a variety of policies to deal with what they see as a multidimensional problem. In the absence of controlled testing, each economic theory retains its supporters, and the debate continues about the merits of one explanation and the limitations of the other.

The fact that economists, like all social scientists, are intensely interested in exploring and debating issues on which they disagree does not mean that they can never reach a conclusion. There are many issues and answers on which economists are in general agreement, so don't let the disagreements about particular policy questions mislead you. The study of economics has a great deal to contribute to your understanding of the world and its many social problems. Approach that study with an open mind, and it will help you to make sense out of facts and events you never before understood.

The Organization of the Text

Now that you have some sense of what the study of economics is about, let's take a brief look at the organization of this book. It is composed of four major parts. Part 1 forms the introduction and lays the conceptual groundwork for the rest of the text. Part 2 takes up **microeconomics,** the study of the individual units of the economy. These chapters examine how the prices of particular goods and services are determined and how individual consumers and businesses function. True to its name, microeconomics looks at the small units that make up the whole economy. Part 3 examines **macroeconomics,** the study of the economy's overall performance and the factors influencing that performance. These chapters address such problems as unemployment and inflation and examine the role of government in combating these economic ills. Through macroeconomics you will begin to view the economy in terms of the big picture. Part 4 turns to **international economics,** the study of international trade and finance. These chapters explore the reasons for trade and how transactions between nations are financed.

As you can see, economics embraces several specialized areas. Because these areas are interrelated, what you learn in Part 1 will help you understand problems taken up in Part 4. In fact to a large extent the chapters in this text build on one another. So please take the time to understand each one thoroughly for an easier and more rewarding trip through economic theory and practice.

Summary

The fundamental economic problem facing both individuals and societies is the fact that our wants exceed our capacity for satisfying those wants. No society has enough *economic resources* (*land, labor, capital,* and *entrepreneurship*) to satisfy its members fully. Consequently individuals and societies must make choices about how best to use their limited resources. *Economics* is the study of how to use our limited resources to satisfy our unlimited wants as fully as possible.

One of the principal lessons of economics is that all choices entail costs, that there is no "free lunch." Whenever you make a decision to do or have one thing, you are sacrificing the opportunity to do or have some other thing. The most valued alternative you must sacrifice in order to take a given action is the *opportunity cost* of that action.

A *production possibilities curve* illustrates the concept of opportunity cost by showing the combinations of goods that an economy is capable of producing with its present stock of economic resources and existing techniques of production. It shows that unless there are unemployed resources, producing more of one thing means producing less of something else.

The dilemma of unlimited wants and limited resources forces each society to make three basic choices, to answer the three fundamental questions of economics: (1) What goods and services will the society produce and in what quantities? (2) How will these goods and services be produced? (3) For whom will these products be produced?

In order to determine how well it is answering the three fundamental questions, a society must establish goals or objectives against which it compares its performance. Full employment, economic efficiency, economic growth, a fair distribution of income, and a stable price level are widely accepted goals. When these goals are in conflict, as they often are, the pursuit of one goal commonly requires a trade-off, some sacrifice in terms of fulfilling another goal.

Before economists can recommend policies for dealing with economic problems or achieving specific objectives, they must develop economic theories, generalizations about causal relationships between economic variables. Testing economic theories can be tricky because the assumption of *ceteris paribus* ("other things being equal") is often violated. This makes it difficult to determine when a theory is flawed, since the results of an experiment could be biased by changes in uncontrolled factors.

Once a theory has been tested and accepted, it can be used as a basis for making predictions and as a guide to formulating economic policy. When it comes to making policy recommendations, economists do not always agree. They may disagree for one or both of two distinct reasons: because they have different views about what *should be* or because they have have different views about what *is*.

Glossary

Capital. Human-made aids to the production process; for example, factories, machinery, and tools.

Ceteris paribus. "Other things being equal"; the assumption that other variables remain constant.

Economics. The study of how to use our limited resources to satisfy our unlimited wants as fully as possible.

Economic resources. The scarce inputs used in the process of creating a good or providing a service; specifically, land, labor, capital, and entrepreneurship.

Economic theories. Generalizations about causal relationships between economic variables.

Entrepreneurship. The managerial function that combines land, labor, and capital in a cost-effective way and uncovers new opportunities to earn profit; includes willingness to take the risks associated with a business venture.

Free trade. Trade that is not hindered by artificial restrictions or trade barriers of any type.

International economics. The study of international trade and finance: why nations trade and how their transactions are financed.

Labor. The mental and physical work of those employed in the production process.

Land. All the natural resources or raw materials used in production; for example, acreage, timber, water, iron ore.

Law of increasing costs. As more of a particular product is produced, the opportunity cost per unit will increase.

Macroeconomics. The study of the economy's overall performance and the factors influencing that performance.

Microeconomics. The study of the behavior of individual economic units.

Normative issue. A question that calls for a value judgment about how things ought to be.

Opportunity cost. The best, or most valued, alternative that is sacrificed when a particular action is taken.

Production possibilities curve. A curve that shows the combinations of goods that an economy is capable of producing with its present stock of economic resources and existing techniques of production.

Study Questions

Fill in the Blanks

1. Land, labor, and capital are examples of _____.

2. The dilemma of _____ wants and _____ resources is referred to as the economic problem.

3. _____ are combiners, innovators, and risk takers.

4. The term _____ is used by economists to describe the economic resources created by nature.

5. When we sacrifice one alternative for another, the alternative forgone is called the _____ of that action.

6. A _____ shows the combinations of goods that an economy is capable of producing.

7. Economists use economic _____ to make sense out of the facts they observe.

8. When the pursuit of one objective forces society to sacrifice or compromise some other objective, economists say that a _____ exists.

9. Issues involving what "should be" rather than what "is" are referred to as _____ issues.

10. Because economists cannot conduct controlled experiments, they often make the assumption of _____ to state the conditions under which they expect their theory to hold.

Multiple Choice

1. Economics is the study of how to
   a) completely satisfy our unlimited wants.
   b) do the best we can with what we have.
   c) reduce our unlimited wants.
   d) expand our stock of economic resources.

2. The opportunity cost of attending summer school is
   a) whatever you could have purchased with the money spent for tuition and books.
   b) negative, because you will finish college more rapidly by attending summer school.
   c) the income you could have earned over the summer.
   d) the products, income, and recreational opportunities that must be forgone.

3. If something has an opportunity cost, we should
   a) avoid that action.

b) take that action.

c) be sure that the benefit of the action exceeds the cost.

d) be sure that the cost of the action exceeds the benefit.

4. Producing the most-wanted products in the least costly way is

a) full employment.

b) economic growth.

c) a fair income distribution.

d) economic efficiency.

5. Economists have trouble testing their theories because

a) people are unpredictable.

b) the real world is too complicated to be explained.

c) they can't hold constant the "other factors" that might influence the outcome of the experiment.

d) the necessary economic data are almost never available.

6. Economists should not be permitted to

a) devise policies to achieve economic goals.

b) determine society's economic goals.

c) explain how the economy works.

d) explain how particular economic goals conflict.

7. Economists sometimes reach different conclusions on a given issue because

a) they disagree about goals.

b) they disagree about the way the economy works.

c) a and b

d) neither a nor b

8. Macroeconomics deals with the study of

a) international trade.

b) individual economic units.

c) production possibilities.

d) the economy's overall performance.

9. Of the three fundamental questions, the "distribution" question has to do with

a) who will receive the output.

b) how the output will be shipped from the place of production to the consumer.

c) how economic resources are distributed to producers.

d) what products will be produced.

10. Suppose that you have just found $5.00 on the street and are thinking of using it to buy a ticket to the movies. The opportunity cost of going to the show would be

a) nothing—since you found the money, you are sacrificing nothing to spend it.

b) whatever you would have bought with the money if you hadn't used it to go to the show.

c) the other activities you would have to sacrifice to attend the show.

d) b and c

Use the following production possibilities curve in answering questions 11 and 12.

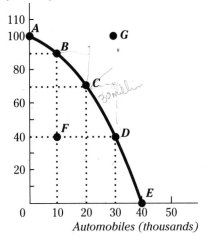

Bushels of wheat (millions)

Automobiles (thousands)

11. If the economy is operating at point *C*, the opportunity cost of producing an additional 10,000 automobiles will be

 a) 10 million bushels of wheat.

 b) 20 million bushels of wheat.

 c) 30 million bushels of wheat.

 d) 40 million bushels of wheat.

12. Point *G* on the diagram represents

 a) an optimal use of the society's resources.

 b) a combination of outputs beyond the economy's productive capacity.

 c) a situation in which some of the economy's resources are unemployed.

 d) the same output combination as point *B*.

13. Foreign trade permits an economy to

 a) eliminate the problem of scarcity.

 b) operate inside its production possibilities curve.

 c) shift its production possibilities curve inward.

 d) consume a combination of products beyond its own production possibilities.

Problems and Questions for Discussion

1. List the four categories of economic resources and explain each.

2. Define economics. Why is economics sometimes called the "study of choice"?

3. List and explain the three fundamental choices that each society is forced to make.

4. What is meant when we say that a secretary is efficient? What about a sales clerk? Why is economic efficiency an important performance objective for an economy?

5. Airline personnel are often allowed to make a certain number of free flights each year. How would you compute the opportunity cost to the airlines of these free trips? Might this cost vary from route to route? Might the cost be different at different times of the year? Explain.

6. List and briefly explain the economic objectives recognized as worthwhile by many societies.

7. What are trade-offs? Give some examples.

8. A theory that has been around for quite some time says, "Better-educated people earn higher incomes than less-educated people, ceteris paribus." If we know a high school dropout who earns $200,000 a year, does this mean that we should discard the theory? Explain.

9. Suppose that we accept the theory given in problem 8 and decide to use it to formulate policies for reducing poverty. Apply this theory by suggesting three policies to reduce poverty.

10. Why is it important to separate the process of setting economic goals from the process of devising policies for achieving these goals? In which process is the economist more expert? Explain.

Answer Key

Fill in the Blanks

1. economic resources
2. unlimited, limited
3. Entrepreneurs
4. land
5. opportunity cost
6. production possibilities curve
7. theories (or models)
8. trade-off
9. normative
10. ceteris paribus

Multiple Choice

1. b	4. d	7. c	10. d	12. b
2. d	5. c	8. d	11. c	13. d
3. c	6. b	9. a		

APPENDIX: Working with Graphs

Economists frequently use graphs to illustrate economic concepts. This appendix provides a brief review of graphing and offers some practice problems to help you become more comfortable working with graphs.

The Purpose of Graphs

The basic purpose of a graph is to represent the relationship between two variables. A *variable* is any quantity that can take on different numeric values. Suppose, for example, that a university has conducted a survey to determine the relationship between two variables: the number of hours its students study and their grade-point averages. The results of that hypothetical survey could be shown in table, or schedule, form, as in panel (a) of Exh. A.1, or they could be represented graphically, as in panel (b) of Exh. A.1. Notice the difference: The graph reveals the relationship between the variables at a glance; you don't have to compare data as you do when reading the table.

Constructing a Graph

The first step in constructing a graph is to draw two perpendicular lines. These lines are called *axes.* In our example the vertical axis is used to measure the first variable, the grade-point average; the horizontal axis is used to measure the second variable, hours of study. The place where the two axes meet is called the *origin* because it is the starting point for measuring each of the variables; in our example the origin is zero. Once the axes are in place, we are ready to draw, or *plot,* the points that represent the relationship between the variables. Let's begin with the students who study 32 hours a week. According to the table in panel (a), these students typically earn a grade-point average of 4.0. To show this relationship graphically, we find the point on the horizontal axis that represents 32 hours of study per week. Next we move directly upward from that point until we reach a height of 4.0 grade points. This point, which we will label *A,* represents a combination of two values; it tells us at a glance that the typical student who studies 32 hours a week will earn a 4.0 grade-point average.

We plot the rest of the information found in panel (a) in the same way. To represent the typical, or average, grade of the student who studies 24 hours a week, all we need to do is locate the number 24 on the horizontal axis and then move up vertically from that point to a distance of 3.0 grade points (point *B*). We plot all the remaining points on the graph in the same way.

Once we have plotted all the points, we can connect them to form a curve. Economists use the term "curve" to describe any graphical relationship be-

EXHIBIT A.1

The Hypothetical Relationship between Grades and Study Time

HOURS OF STUDY (PER WEEK)	GRADE-POINT AVERAGE
32	4.0
28	3.5
24	3.0
20	2.5
16	2.0
12	1.5
8	1.0
4	0.4
0	0.0

(a) Relationship with Table

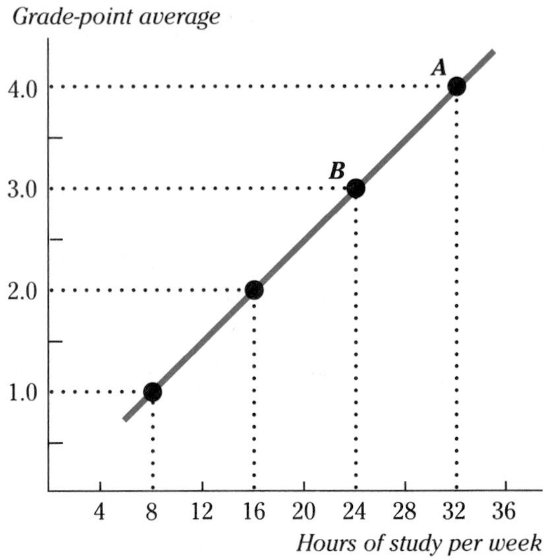

(b) Relationship with Graph

Both (a) and (b) illustrate the relationship between hours of study and grades. Panel (a) uses a table to show this relationship; panel (b), a graph. Both illustrations show that the relationship between the two variables is direct; more hours of study tend to be associated with a higher grade-point average.

tween two variables, so don't be surprised when you discover a straight line referred to as a curve. You can see that the resulting curve slopes upward and to the right. This indicates that there is a positive, or *direct*, relationship between the two variables—as one variable (study time) increases, the other (grade-point average) does also. If the resulting curve had sloped downward and to the right, it would have indicated a negative, or *inverse*, relationship between the two variables—as one variable increased, the other would decrease. We would be surprised to find an inverse relationship between these particular variables; that would suggest the unlikely possibility that increased study time lowers the grade-point average!

Practice in Graphing

All graphs are basically the same, so if you understand the one we just considered, you should be able to master all the graphs in this textbook and in library sources. If you want some practice, take a few minutes to graph the three sets of data at the end of this appendix.

The first step is to draw and label the vertical and horizontal axes and mark them off in units that are convenient to work with. As you probably know, mathematicians always measure the *independent* variable (the variable that causes the other to change) along the horizontal axis and the *dependent* variable (the variable that responds to changes) along the vertical axis. Economists are less strict in deciding which variable to place on which axis, so don't be alarmed if occasionally you see the dependent variable on the horizontal axis.

Once you have decided which variable to place on which axis, the next step is to plot the information from the table as points and connect them. Then see if you can interpret your graph. What does it tell you about the relationship between the two variables? Are they directly or inversely related? (It's possible that they are not related at all. For example, there is probably no relationship between a student's weight and his or her grade-point average.) Does the relationship change somewhere along the graph? The way to become comfortable with graphs is to work with them. Try drawing these graphs to see how easy it is.

1. Graph the relationship between the hourly wage rate paid by the school and the number of students desiring to work in the school cafeteria. Is the relationship direct or inverse?

POINT	WAGE RATE (PER HOUR)	NUMBER OF STUDENT WORKERS
A	$2.50	5
B	3.00	10
C	3.50	15
D	4.00	20
E	4.50	25
F	5.00	30

2. Graph the relationship between the average daily temperature and the average number of students playing tennis on the school tennis courts. How does this relationship change?

POINT	TEMPERATURE (IN DEGREES FAHRENHEIT)	NUMBER OF TENNIS PLAYERS
A	60	20
B	70	30
C	80	40
D	90	30
E	100	20

3. Graph the relationship between the price of gasoline and the quantity of gasoline purchased by consumers. Is the relationship direct or inverse?

POINT	PRICE (PER GALLON)	QUANTITY PURCHASED (IN GALLONS)
A	$ .50	15 million
B	1.00	12 million
C	1.50	9 million
D	2.00	6 million
E	2.50	3 million

Economic Systems

LEARNING OBJECTIVES

1. Explain the concept of an economic system.
2. Describe how economic systems differ from one another.
3. Identify the elements of pure capitalism.
4. Draw and explain the circular-flow model of pure capitalism.
5. Explain how pure capitalism answers the three fundamental questions.
6. Discuss the strengths and weaknesses of pure capitalism.
7. Identify the elements of command socialism.
8. Draw and explain the pyramid model of command socialism.
9. Explain how command socialism answers the three fundamental questions.
10. Discuss the strengths and weaknesses of command socialism.
11. Explain why all real-world economies are mixed economies.

Every nation, from the richest to the poorest, faces the same economic dilemma: how to satisfy people's unlimited wants with its limited economic resources. Each society must decide which products and services to produce, how to produce them, and for whom to produce them; in other words, it must establish an economic system. An **economic system** is a set of procedures for answering the three fundamental questions of economics—what, how, and for whom to produce. We will identify different economic systems according to the following criteria:

Who owns the means of production?

Who makes the economic choices that determine what, how, and for whom to produce?

What mechanism is used to ensure that these decisions are carried out?[1]

The variety of real-world economic systems is probably as great as the number of world nations, but all economic systems lie somewhere between two divergent models. At one extreme the means of production are privately owned, economic choices are made by individuals, and implementation occurs through markets. At the other extreme the means of production are owned publicly, by the state; economic choices are made collectively, and implementation occurs through commands from a central authority.

The purpose of this chapter is to give you an overview of how economic systems function. First, we examine the two divergent models—pure capitalism and pure command socialism. Recall from Chapter 1 that models simplify reality, making it possible for us to see more clearly how the parts of a system function and interact. Once we have become familiar with these theoretical models, we can compare the economies of the United States and the former Soviet Union against them to discover how they conform and how they deviate from the models.

The Model of Pure Capitalism

Our model of pure capitalism describes a hypothetical economy. As you work through the following sections, remember that you are learning about a theoretical model, not an existing system. As you will see later in the chapter, the United States and other real-world economies don't conform perfectly to either of the two divergent models. Here we will examine the elements of pure capitalism, diagram the operation (or functioning) of the system, see how it answers the three fundamental questions, and conclude by assessing its strengths and weaknesses.

Elements of Capitalism

By definition **capitalism** is an economic system in which the means of production are privately owned, and fundamental economic choices are made by individuals and implemented through the market mechanism—the interaction of buyers and sellers. The model of pure capitalism is entirely consistent with our definition and contains five basic elements, which we will describe briefly.

---

[1] This is the classification system adopted by Gary M. and Joyce E. Pickersgill in *Contemporary Economic Systems* (Englewood Cliffs, N.J.: Prentice-Hall, 1974), p. 10.

Private Property and Freedom of Choice. One of the principal features of capitalism is private property. In a capitalist economy private individuals and groups are the owners of the **means of production:** the raw materials, factories, farms, and other economic resources used to produce goods and services. These resource owners may sell or use their resources, including their own labor, as they see fit. Businesses are free to decide what products they will produce and to purchase the necessary economic resources from whomever they choose. Consumers, in turn, are free to spend their incomes any way they like. They can purchase whatever products they choose, and they can decide what fraction of their incomes to save and what fraction to spend.

Self-Interest. Self-interest is the driving force of capitalism. In 1776 Adam Smith, the founder of modern economics, described a capitalist economy as one in which the primary concern of each player—of each producer, worker, and consumer—was to promote his or her own welfare.[2]

Smith introduced the **invisible hand** doctrine, which held that as individuals pursued their own interests, they would be led as if by an invisible hand to promote the good of the society as a whole. In order to earn the highest profits, predicted Smith, producers would generate the products consumers wanted the most. Workers would offer their services where they were most needed, because wages would be highest in those sectors. Consumers would favor producers who offered superior products and/or lower prices, because they would seek the best value for their money. The result would be an economy that produced the goods and services desired by the society, without the need for any central direction by government.

Markets and Prices. Capitalism is often described as a market system. This is because a capitalist economy contains numerous interdependent markets through which the functioning of the economy is coordinated and directed. A **market** consists of all actual or potential buyers and sellers of a particular item and can be local, regional, national, or international. For example, there are numerous local and regional markets for used automobiles, each consisting of all buyers and sellers of such vehicles in that particular area. Similar markets exist for all other goods and services and for all economic resources as well.

Market prices are determined by the interaction of buyers and sellers and serve three important functions. First, prices signal information to prospective buyers and sellers, telling buyers the relative costs of the various products on the market and telling producers how much they can expect to receive by producing a particular product. Second, prices motivate businesses to pro-

---

[2] Adam Smith's description of the functioning of a capitalist economy appeared in *An Inquiry into the Nature and Causes of the Wealth of Nations,* published in 1776.

duce more of some products and less of others. Businesses generally want to supply products that yield the highest profits, the ones with the highest prices in relation to their costs of production. Third, prices help to divide up, or ration, the society's limited output of goods and services. Only those consumers who are willing and able to pay the market price receive the product.

Competition. Adam Smith recognized that for the invisible hand to work—for individuals seeking their own interests to promote the good of all—the pursuit of self-interest had to be guided and restrained by competition. Competition ensures that producers remain responsive to consumers and that prices remain reasonable.

Pure capitalism requires **pure competition,** a situation in which a large number of relatively small buyers and sellers interact to determine prices.[3] Under conditions of pure competition, no individual buyer or seller can set—or even significantly influence—the prevailing price of a product or resource. Prices are thus determined by market forces, not by powerful buyers or sellers, and change only when market conditions change.

Limited Government Intervention. Pure capitalism is above all a **laissez-faire economy.** (Laissez-faire is a French phrase that in this context means "let the people do as they choose.") The model describes no role for government in making economic decisions. Through pricing, the market determines all production and distribution decisions—what, how, and for whom to produce—and competition ensures that consumers will be charged reasonable prices. The only role of government is to provide the kind of environment in which a market economy can function well. For example, government must define and enforce the private-property rights that enable individuals to own and use property.

The Circular-Flow Model

We can represent the operation of a capitalist economy in a diagram called the circular-flow model. Exhibit 2.1 models an economy composed of only two sectors: households and businesses. You can see that these two sectors are connected through transactions, or flows, that occur continuously between them. We'll examine how each sector processes the flow it receives and returns it to the other sector.

The Household and Business Sectors. The household sector is shown at the right in Exh. 2.1. A **household** is both a living unit and an economic unit. Whether it consists of a single person or numerous people, each household

---

[3] Further assumptions relating to pure competition are described in Chapter 5.

EXHIBIT 2.1

The Circular Flow of Pure Capitalism

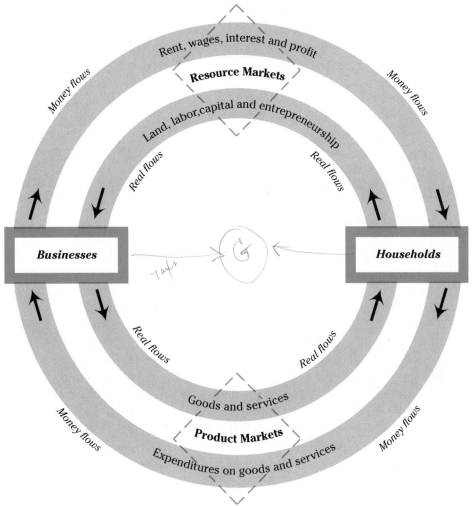

will have a source of income and will spend that income. The household sector is composed of all the individual households in the economy. Because households own the land, labor, capital, and entrepreneurship that businesses need to produce goods and services, this sector is the source of all economic resources in the model of pure capitalism. It is also the source of consumer spending for the goods and services produced.

The business sector, on the left, is composed of all the businesses in the economy. The business sector purchases economic resources from households, converts those resources into products, and sells the products to the households.

Real Flows and Money Flows. You can see in the diagram that two types of flows circle in opposite directions. In the outside circle *money flows*—in the form of rent, wages, interest, and profit—go from businesses to households to pay for economic resources. These flows return to businesses as households pay for products. *Real flows* involve the physical movement of the resources and products. The inner flow in the diagram shows economic resources in the form of land, labor, capital, and entrepreneurship flowing from the household sector to the business sector, where they are used to produce goods and services. The unbroken arrows in the diagram show that these circular flows proceed endlessly.

The Resource and Product Markets. Markets are the key to the operation of a capitalist system because they hold together its decentralized economy of millions of individual buyers and sellers. The interaction of these buyers and sellers ensures that the right products (the ones desired by consumers) are produced and that economic resources flow to the right producers (the ones producing the most-wanted products at the lowest prices).

In the resource markets, depicted in the upper portion of Exh. 2.1, the interaction of buyers and sellers determines the prices of the various economic resources. For example, in the labor market for accountants an accountant's salary is determined by the interaction of employers seeking to hire accountants (the buyers) and accountants seeking employment (the sellers). Changes in resource prices guide and motivate resource suppliers to provide the type and quantity of resources producers need the most. Using our example of labor, suppose that the number of businesses desiring accountants is expanding more rapidly than new accountants are being trained. What will happen to the salaries of accountants? They will tend to increase. As a result, we can expect more people in the household sector to invest the time and money necessary to become accountants. You can see how the price mechanism ensures that (1) the types of labor, equipment, and other resources most needed by businesses will be supplied and (2) these resources will be supplied in the proper quantities.

In the product markets, depicted in the lower portion of Exh. 2.1, the prices of all products—from eggs and overcoats to haircuts and airline tickets—again are determined by the interaction of buyers and sellers. Prices serve the same function here as they do in the resource market: They make it possible to divide up, or ration, the limited amount of output among all those who wish to receive it. Only those consumers who are willing and able to pay the market price can obtain the product. When prices change, this informs producers about desired changes in the amount they are producing and motivates them to supply the new quantity. For example, when consumers want more of a product than is available, they tend to bid up its price. Producers, getting a clear signal that consumers like that item, thus have an incentive to supply more of it.

How Capitalism Answers the Three Fundamental Questions

Now that we have discussed the elements of pure capitalism and have a general idea of the role of markets in such an economy, we can determine more easily how this system answers the three fundamental questions.

What to Produce? One feature of pure capitalism is **consumer sovereignty,** an economic condition in which consumers dictate which goods and services businesses will produce. Because producers are motivated by profits and because the most profitable products tend to be the ones consumers desire most, producers must be responsive to consumer preferences. To illustrate consumer sovereignty in action, let's consider how automobile manufacturers in a pure capitalist economy would respond if consumer preferences suddenly took a dramatic turn away from standard-sized cars in favor of small ones. If people began to buy more compacts or subcompacts and fewer full-sized cars, the price of small cars would rise and they would become more profitable, whereas full-sized cars would decline in price and become less profitable. Therefore automobile manufacturers would produce more compacts and fewer full-sized cars: just what consumers want.

Because consumers are free to spend their incomes as they choose, producers who wish to earn profits must be responsive to consumers' desires. As a result, pure capitalism might be described as a system in which the consumer is the ruler and the producer an obedient servant.

How to Produce? Automobile producers have a number of options available for manufacturing compact cars and other vehicles that consumers desire. They can produce these automobiles through highly mechanized techniques, or they can rely primarily on skilled labor and simpler tools. They can manufacture car bodies from steel, aluminum, fiberglass, or some combination of the three. In selecting which production technique and combination of resources to use, the capitalist manufacturers will minimize the cost of production; they will adopt the *least-cost* approach because lower costs contribute to higher profits.

In a capitalist economy, highly mechanized production methods—such as those utilizing robots—may be selected if labor is expensive.

The search for the least-cost approach is guided by the market prices of the various economic resources. Because the scarcest resources cost the most, producers use them only when they cannot substitute less expensive resources. For example, if steel is very expensive, automobile makers will tend to use it only where other materials would be inadequate, perhaps in the frame or in other parts of the car that require great strength. Thus the prices of resources help to ensure that resources are used to their best advantage in a capitalist economy. Abundant, cheaper resources are used when they will suffice; scarcer, more costly resources are conserved.

For Whom to Produce? Finally, we consider the task of distributing our hypothetical economy's output of automobiles. We know that only those who can afford to buy automobiles will receive them. The ability to pay, however, is only half the picture; the other half is willingness to purchase, which takes into account consumer preferences. Some of those who can afford a new car will prefer to spend their money elsewhere: remodeling their homes, perhaps, or sending their children to college. Some who seemingly cannot afford a new car may be able to purchase one by doing without other things—new clothes or a larger apartment, for example. Of course, consumers with low incomes will face less attractive choices than those earning high incomes. A low-income consumer may sacrifice basic necessities in order to afford an automobile, whereas a wealthy consumer need choose only between the new car and some luxury item, such as a sailboat or a winter vacation. In the final analysis those with higher incomes will always have more choices than those with lower incomes and will receive a larger share of the economy's total output.

Capitalism: Strengths and Weaknesses

Before moving on from our discussion of pure capitalism, we will describe briefly some of the strengths and weaknesses inherent in such a system. One of the major strengths of pure capitalism is *economic efficiency.* In a market economy businesses are encouraged to produce the products that consumers want most and to produce those products at the lowest cost in terms of scarce resources. A system that accomplishes those objectives goes a long way toward ensuring that a society achieves the maximum benefit possible from its limited resources.

A second positive feature of capitalism is *economic freedom.* Under pure capitalism consumers, workers, and producers are free to make decisions based on self-interest. To many people this economic freedom is the overwhelming virtue of the capitalist model.

Economist Milton Friedman, a vocal advocate of competitive capitalism, notes a third strength of the system: It promotes *political freedom* by separating economic and political power. The existence of private ownership of the means of production ensures that government officials are not in a position to deny jobs or goods and services to individuals whose political views conflict with their own.[4]

Pure capitalism also has some shortcomings. First, people are not uniformly equal in ability, and some will succeed to a greater extent than others. In a capitalist system the result is the unequal distribution of income and output. This inequality tends to be perpetuated because the children of the rich usually have access to better educational opportunities and often inherit the income-producing assets of their parents. Such inequality weakens capitalism's claim that it produces the goods and services that the *society* wants the most. It is more the case that capitalism produces the products that the consumers *who have the money* want most.

A second, closely related criticism was voiced by the late Arthur Okun, chairman of the Council of Economic Advisors during the Johnson administration. In a capitalist economy, observed Okun, money can buy a great many things that are not supposed to be for sale:

> Money buys legal services that can obtain preferred treatment before the law; it buys platforms that give extra weight to the owner's freedom of speech; it buys influence with elected officials and thus compromises the principle of one person, one vote. . . . Even though money generally cannot buy extra helpings of rights directly, it can buy services that, in effect, produce more or better rights.[5]

Third, pure capitalism may be criticized for encouraging the destruction of the environment. Because air, rivers, lakes, and streams are **common-**

[4] Milton Friedman, *Capitalism and Freedom* (Chicago: The University of Chicago Press, 1962), p. 9.
[5] Arthur M. Okun, *Equality and Efficiency: The Big Tradeoff* (Washington: The Brookings Institution, 1975), p. 22.

property resources belonging to the society as a whole, they tend to be seen as free—available to be used or abused without charge or concern. The pursuit of self-interest would cause producers to dump their wastes into nearby rivers to avoid the cost of disposing of those wastes in an environmentally acceptable manner. Farmers would select pesticides according to their favorable impact on output and without regard to their undesirable effects on wildlife and water supplies. In this case Adam Smith's invisible hand fails. The pursuit of self-interest by individuals may not promote the good of all but may instead lead to environmental destruction.

The Model of Pure Command Socialism

The opposite of the model of pure capitalism is the model of pure command socialism. The socialist command economy described in this section represents no existing economic system. Like the model of pure capitalism, the model of pure command socialism is simply a tool to help us understand how command economies operate. Again we will examine the basic elements of the model, diagram how the hypothetical economy operates, and see how the system decides what, how, and for whom to produce. Then we will examine the strengths and weaknesses of pure command socialism.

Elements of Command Socialism

We define **command socialism** as an economic system in which the means of production are publicly owned, the fundamental economic choices are made by a central authority, and commands are used to ensure that these decisions are implemented. Four basic elements of pure command socialism support this definition.

Public Ownership. A socialist economy is characterized by state, or public, ownership of the means of production. In the model of pure command socialism state ownership is complete. The factories, farms, mines, hospitals, and other forms of capital are publicly owned. Even labor is publicly owned in the sense that workers and managers do not select their own employment but are assigned their jobs by the state.

Centralized Decision Making. One of the most distinctive features of command socialism is that economic choices are made by a central authority. This central authority may be either responsive to the feelings of the people (democratic socialism) or unresponsive to their wishes (authoritarian socialism or communism). In either case this authority makes the fundamental production and distribution decisions and then takes the necessary actions to see that these decisions are carried out.

Economic Planning. In the model of command socialism economic planning replaces the market as the method for coordinating economic decisions. The central authority, or central planning board, gathers information about existing production capacities, supplies of raw materials, and labor force capabilities. It then draws up a master plan specifying production objectives for each sector or industry in the economy. Industrywide objectives are translated into specific production targets for each factory, farm, mine, or other kind of producing unit. Central planning ensures that specific production objectives agree so that automobile manufacturers will not produce one million cars, for example, while tire manufacturers produce only two million tires.

Allocation by Command. In command socialism resources and products are allocated by directive, or command, and the central authority uses its power to enforce these decisions. Once it determines production and distribution objectives, the central planning board dictates to each producing unit the quantity and assortment of goods the unit is to produce and the combination of resources it is to use. Commands are also issued to producers of raw materials and other production inputs to supply these inputs to the producing units that need them. Further commands direct individuals to places of employment—wherever the central planning board determines that their services are needed—and dictate distribution of the economy's output of goods and services. All the allocative functions that a capitalist economy leaves to the market and the pursuit of self-interest are accomplished in pure command socialism through planning and allocation by directive.

The Pyramid Model

Exhibit 2.2 represents a socialist command economy as a pyramid, with the central planning board at the top and the various producing and consuming units below it. This diagram emphasizes the primary feature of a command economy: centralization of economic decision making.

The outer arrow at the right in Exh. 2.2 shows how information about production capacities, raw materials supplies, and labor capabilities flows up from the producing units in the middle of the pyramid to the central planning board at the top. Information, if requested, about which goods and services consumers desire also flows up from the consuming units at the base of the pyramid (outer left arrow). Production objectives, or targets, are transmitted

EXHIBIT 2.2

The Command Pyramid

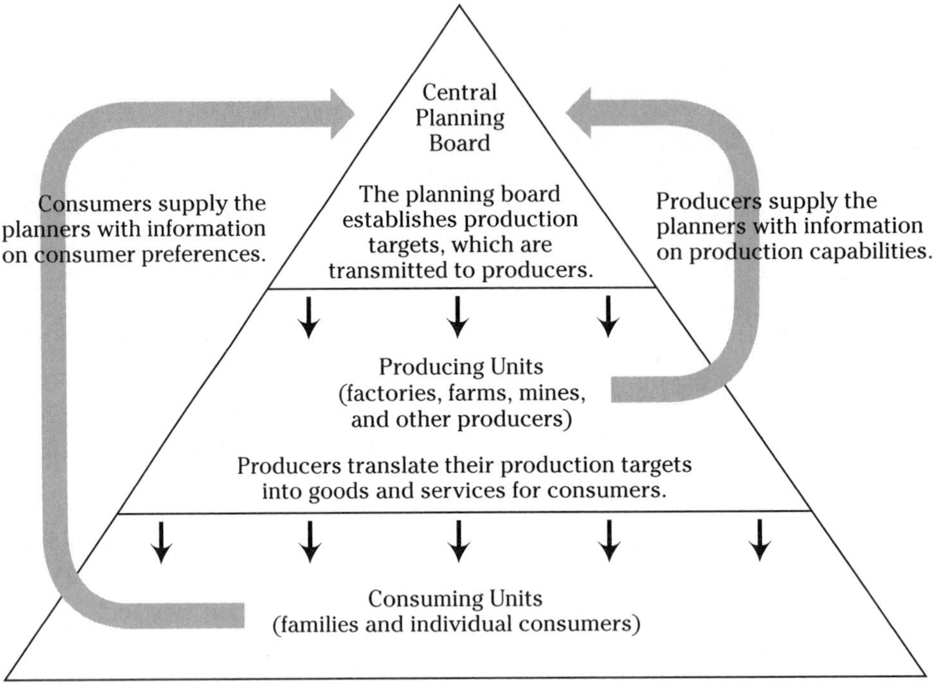

Central Planning Board

Consumers supply the planners with information on consumer preferences.

The planning board establishes production targets, which are transmitted to producers.

Producers supply the planners with information on production capabilities.

Producing Units
(factories, farms, mines, and other producers)

Producers translate their production targets into goods and services for consumers.

Consuming Units
(families and individual consumers)

back to the individual producing units, which then supply the targeted quantity and assortment of products and produce them as specified. Finally, the output is distributed to consumers in accordance with the plan.

How Command Socialism Answers the Three Fundamental Questions

In many respects the operation of a socialist command economy is easier to understand than the functioning of a capitalist economy. The answers to the three fundamental questions are decided by the central planning board, which then uses its authority to ensure that all directives are carried out.

The central planners can select any output targets, any mix of products within the limits set by the economy's production capacity. Of course, the planners will have to gather an abundance of information before they have a good picture of the economy's capabilities. They must determine the size of the labor force and the skills it possesses, for example, as well as how many factories exist and what they are capable of producing. Until the central planners have this kind of information, they cannot establish realistic output targets. And even then they will face some tough decisions because, as you already know, more of one thing means less of something else. So if they decide to produce more automobiles, they won't be able to manufacture as many refrigerators and military weapons and other products.

In deciding how to produce each product, central planners must try to stretch the economy's limited resources as far as possible. This requires that each resource be used efficiently—where it makes the greatest contribution to the economy's output. If some resource is particularly scarce, planners must be careful to use it only where no other input will suffice; otherwise they won't be able to maximize the economy's output.

Even with the best of planning, an economy's resources will stretch only so far. The central planning board can allocate the economy's limited output in accordance with any objective it has set. If the planning board's primary objective is equality, it can develop a method of rationing, dividing up the society's output in equal shares to each member. If it wants to promote loyalty to the government, the central authority can give supporters extra shares while penalizing dissenters. Whatever its objectives, the central planning board can use distribution as a method to further them.

Command Socialism: Strengths and Weaknesses

Like pure capitalism, the economy of pure command socialism has certain strengths and certain weaknesses. Some people argue that a major strength of command socialism is its ability to promote a high degree of equality in the distribution of income and output. Because the central planners control the distribution of goods and services, they can elect to distribute output in ways that achieve whatever degree of equality in living standard they consider appropriate. Thus it is theoretically possible for command socialism to avoid the extremely unequal income and output distribution that characterizes pure capitalism.

Another major strength of command socialism is its potential for achieving economic objectives in a relatively short period of time. As an example, consider the power of the planners to foster more rapid economic growth. If a society wants to increase its capacity for producing goods and services, it must devote more of its resources to producing capital goods (factories and equipment) and fewer resources to producing consumer goods. In other words, society must consume less *now* in order to be able to produce and consume more *later*. Because the central authority has the power to dictate the fraction of the society's resources that will be devoted to capital goods production, in effect it can force the society to make the sacrifices necessary to increase the rate of economic growth.

You probably recognize that the power to bring about rapid economic changes is not necessarily a good thing. The major shortcoming of command socialism, in fact, is the possibility that the central planning board may pursue goals that do not reflect the needs or desires of the majority. If the socialist government is not democratically elected, its goals may bear no relationship to the needs of the general population.

A second weakness in the model of command socialism is its inefficient information network. The system we have described needs more information than it can reasonably expect to acquire and process to ensure efficient use of the economy's resources. The system must not only have a substantial organizational network to acquire information about consumer preferences and production capabilities but also use that network to transmit the decisions of central planners to millions of economic units. Moreover, the central planners have to be able to process all the acquired information and return it in the form of a consistent plan—a staggering task, considering that the output of one industry is often the production input required by some other industry. Finally, they must see that each product is produced efficiently. This complex and cumbersome process is bound to result in breakdowns in communication and decision making. When these occur, the wrong products may be produced or the right ones produced using the wrong combinations of resources. In either case inefficiency means that the society does not achieve maximum benefit from its limited resources.

Mixed Economies: The Real-World Solution

No existing economic system adheres strictly to either pure capitalism or pure command socialism. All real-world economies are **mixed economies;** they represent a blending of the two models. To illustrate the diversity among economic systems, we will consider two existing economies that are distinctly different from each other: the United States and the former Soviet Union. Our discussion will begin with the U.S. economy, the system that will occupy most of our attention throughout this text.

The U.S. Economic System

Because the U.S. economic system is marked by such a high degree of private ownership and individual decision making, American children learn early from their teachers, the news media, and others that they live in a capitalist economy. And certainly there is ample evidence to support that viewpoint. Most U.S. businesses, from industrial giants like General Motors and IBM to small firms like your neighborhood barbershop or hair salon, are private operations, not government-owned enterprises. The U.S. economy is coordinated and directed largely by the market mechanism, the interaction of buyers and sellers in thousands of interdependent markets. Each of those buyers and sellers is guided by self-interest, which among producers takes the form of profit seeking. Fortunately for consumers, the drive for profits is usually kept in check by another feature of pure capitalism: competition. In most American industries competition, though not pure, is adequate to keep prices reasonable and to ensure that consumers receive fair treatment.

Given these elements of pure capitalism, why do we call the United States a "mixed economy"? There are several reasons. First, let us consider the degree of public ownership in our economic system. Although most American businesses are privately owned, some very important and visible producers are publicly owned enterprises. For example, the electricity on which we rely to heat and cool our homes and run our appliances is supplied in part by municipal, state, or county power companies. With few exceptions, we attend public elementary and secondary schools. When we apply for admission to college, we mail those applications via the U.S. Postal Service, often to state universities. If we ride the bus in the morning, that bus is probably the property of a public transit system. In short, although public ownership is by no means the dominant feature of the American economy, it cannot be ignored.

Nor is public ownership the lone feature our predominantly capitalist economy "borrows" from command socialism. Many of our basic economic choices are made or influenced by powerful economic units—government, labor, and business—rather than by individuals, and often these decisions are implemented by commands rather than through markets.

Regulations and restrictions are two means through which the government exerts influence on businesses and consumers. Think of the regulations imposed on automobile manufacturers, for example. They must produce cars that (1) meet specified mileage requirements; (2) conform to certain exhaust-emission standards; (3) can sustain a front- or rear-end crash of a specified force without serious injury to passengers; and (4) include seat belts and other safety features. In addition to complying with these directives or commands, automobile producers must conform to the plant health and safety regulations set by the Occupational Safety and Health Administration, and their factories must operate within the various pollution-control standards set by the Environmental Protection Agency. To a greater or lesser extent, most American industries are subject to government regulations.

Government spending and taxing decisions constitute another significant influence on the mixture of goods and services that the economy produces and the distribution of those goods and services among the members of the society. Through its tax policies, for example, the federal government encourages investment in certain industries and discourages investment in others. Our tax system requires that people who earn higher incomes pay a greater fraction of their incomes in taxes, thus altering the distribution of output. Government expenditures for education, national defense, and aid to the poor also have a significant impact on what our economy produces and who will receive that output.

Government is not the only powerful economic unit in our economy. Labor organizations and large businesses have a substantial impact on the way our economy operates. In many industries labor unions influence market forces and use their bargaining power to force wage increases and negotiate work rules that maximize employment and reduce the likelihood of layoffs. Unions use their political clout and considerable financial resources to lobby for government policies—minimum wage laws and import bans, for example—that enhance their own economic position. Indeed, it is the business of the labor union to attempt to influence to its advantage any market force that has an impact on wages and working conditions.

Powerful businesses exert their own influence on market forces. Under pure capitalism all businesses would respond to prices dictated by the market, but businesses in our economy often use their size to influence the prices of both the resources they buy and the products they sell. They use advertising in an attempt to influence consumer spending patterns and convince prospective buyers that their product is worth more than the ones offered by competitors. They also use their financial resources and their status as major employers to influence government policies. Like labor unions, powerful businesses use every tool at their disposal to try to alter the economic environment to their advantage.

In summary, the U.S. economy diverges from the model of pure capitalism in a variety of ways. Publicly owned enterprises make an important contribution to the economy; laws and government regulations significantly influence economic decisions; and powerful labor unions and businesses are able to influence the economic environment rather than simply respond to it. Whether these modifications of pure capitalism are good or bad is a matter for debate. What is clear is that the U.S. economic system is really a mixed economy. Rather than adhering strictly to the capitalist model, it combines elements of capitalism and command socialism.

The Soviet Economic System

The Soviet Union was dissolved in 1991 and was replaced by the Commonwealth of Independent States, a federation of former Soviet republics. Al-

The Soviet Union has been declared dead, but the ghost of the Soviet economic system will haunt the newly independent states for many years to come.

though the Soviet Union has passed into history, much can be learned from examining the Soviet economic system. For decades the Soviet economy was the economic system that most closely approximated the model of pure command socialism. By studying the Soviet system, we will see just how different an economic system can be from our own and still share the designation "mixed economy." We will also gain insights into the economies of China and Cuba, since these systems duplicate in many ways the old Soviet system. Finally, an understanding of the Soviet system is essential if we are to appreciate the problems confronting the new Commonwealth states as they attempt to construct their own economic systems from the ruins of the Soviet economy. Although the Soviet Union has been declared dead, the ghost of the Soviet economic system will haunt the Commonwealth states for a long time to come.

The Soviet economic system had much in common with the model of pure command socialism. Most factories, farms, and other enterprises were owned and operated by the state rather than by private citizens. The fundamental choices about what, how, and for whom to produce were made by the State Planning Committee (GOSPLAN), and GOSPLAN's decisions were implemented mainly by command.

However, even prior to market reforms (which will be discussed later), the Soviet economy deviated significantly from the model of command socialism; distinct strands of capitalism were woven into the economy's socialist fabric. Consider Soviet agriculture, for example, which operated at three levels: state farms, collective farms, and private plots. Soviet state farms were run the same as other state enterprises; they received commands from the planning authority and were expected to meet their production objectives. But collective farms, at least in theory, operated by and for the benefit of their members. (In practice, however, a significant portion of a collective farm's output had to be sold to the state at prices dictated by the state.) The private sector was made up of small plots that peasants farmed in addition to the work they did on collective farms. Although these small plots occupied less than 2 percent of the nation's farmland, they were cultivated intensively and produced roughly one-third of the nation's agricultural output. Part of this output was consumed by the owners, but the major portion was sold in open markets at prices dictated by market forces.

Further elements of capitalism were evident in the labor sector of the Soviet economy; planners attempted to duplicate some of the wage adjustments that would occur naturally in a free market. Although Soviet planners dictated production goals, they did not adhere to the model of command socialism by issuing directives about who would work at which occupations. Instead, they manipulated wages to bring about the changes they desired. For example, if too few people wanted to become electricians, wages for electricians were increased in order to attract more individuals to this occupation. If there were too many electricians, wages were either reduced or simply not increased when other wage increases were ordered.

Consumer prices were managed in a similar fashion. Rather than command which consumer goods each household would receive, central planners set the prices for each consumer good and allowed households to make their own choices based on their reactions to those prices. Although planners kept some prices artificially low as a matter of policy—the prices of basic food items, for example—they manipulated most prices in an attempt to equalize the amounts available and the amounts consumers desired. Whereas free competitive markets automatically produce this result, Soviet pricing was never flexible enough to precisely duplicate the market process. That is, Soviet prices never changed quickly enough or often enough to ensure that the amounts desired by consumers would exactly duplicate the amounts available.

In addition to manipulating wages and prices, Soviet planners used market-related incentives to achieve their goals. Successful managers, for example, were rewarded with bonuses that might amount to a substantial fraction of their annual income. Payments in kind—a chance for a better apartment or a nice vacation, for instance—also provided incentive for good performance.

As you can see, the economy of the Soviet Union combined elements of capitalism and command socialism. The capitalist elements began to take on even greater weight when Mikhail Gorbachev became supreme leader of the Soviet Union in 1985. Calling the Soviet economic system rigid and inefficient, he introduced measures to correct these problems. State-owned enterprises were given more freedom in pricing their products and were given permission to buy inputs and sell their products abroad, without going through the planning board. Individuals were allowed to sell services (house painting and home and auto repair, for example), and some private enterprises, such as restaurants, were permitted. Political reforms were also undertaken when Gorbachev became convinced that economic reform could be accomplished only if accompanied by democratization of the political system.

Although Gorbachev's moves to reform the economy were accorded much attention in the press, they were in fact modest and piecemeal changes. Gorbachev clearly recognized the failures of the Soviet Union, but he was unwilling to accept some basic tenets of capitalism—the concept of private property, for instance. This ambivalence led to conflicting policy moves. Measures to promote free markets were passed one day, only to be revoked or somehow neutralized on the next. This resulted in chaos for producers and a substantial disruption in the supplies of goods and services. In short, Gorbachev succeeded in discrediting and disrupting the Soviet economic system without really moving the economy closer to capitalism.

Gorbachev's efforts toward democratization were seen by Communist Party officials and those in the military as a greater threat than his economic reforms. Several Soviet republics had declared their intention to seek independence, and Soviet citizens were openly criticizing policies of the central government. In August 1991 a handful of Soviet hardliners staged a coup against Gorbachev. But the coup was poorly planned and met unexpected resistance. As a consequence, the coup failed, and Gorbachev was returned to power after only a few days' absence.

The failure of the coup contributed to further disintegration of the central government. The Communist Party collapsed, and most of the Soviet republics declared their independence. Gorbachev's power waned, and Russian President Boris Yeltsin—who had achieved prominence by resisting the coup—moved to center stage. In December 1991 the Soviet Union was officially dissolved and replaced with the Commonwealth of Independent States, a loose federation of former Soviet republics.

In Ukraine, Barren Ground for Farm Reform

ZVENYGOROD, UKRAINE

Marija and Ivan Olishchuk, a middle-aged couple with faces worn beyond their years and hands creased from working the soil, should represent the future of farming in the former Soviet Union. They understand the concept of profit and know the imperative of private land. They hold about 50 acres of their own.

But for the last two years, as the couple have coaxed higher yields of potatoes and carrots and wheat from their earth, they have been blocked at every turn by the state.

"The attitude is very hostile," Mrs. Olishchuk said, explaining how the local state farm manager refused to sell the family equipment and spread rumors to undermine them. And farm workers refused offers of employment from the Olishchuks, she said.

"Communism killed the mentality of the people," Mrs. Olishchuk said. "People are not willing to sell their labor and work for us. If they work for nothing on a state farm that's O.K., but they say they won't be exploited for money."

Ukraine is blessed with some of the world's richest soil. One-third of all the world's black soil lies within its borders. And this country, which is the size of France and has a population of 52 million, is also endowed with a strategic location and access to ports that give it a better chance at fast integration with the world economy than most of the other republics of the former Soviet Union, according to a World Bank assessment.

Despite these advantages, Ukraine, more than two years into its independence, has proved a recalcitrant reformer to a market economy, especially in agriculture.

President Leonid M. Kravchuk's policies perpetuate state farms, even as many of them disintegrate, and Parliament has refused to consider legislation that would allow farmers to sell their land or leave it to their children.

Whether the breadbasket of the former Soviet Union can be turned into an efficient food producer will depend on how well privatization pioneers like the Olishchuks fare, and their success may depend on how many ob-

structions the old-line Communists in the Ukranian Government put in their way. The roadblocks have been organized and deliberate.

Managers Form a Lobby

So far a handful of farmers scattered across Ukraine are trying to persevere against the odds. In the east, where the former Communists are stronger, surveys of farm workers show they have only a faint understanding of private ownership. But in the west, where the Olishchuks live, traditions of land ownership linger from the days when the region belonged to Poland, . . .

Ukraine was by far the most important agricultural component of the Soviet Union, with higher productivity in crops and animals than Russia and a higher percentage of people on the land, and vestiges of the Soviet days linger.

Managers of the large state farms, like the man who has opposed the Olishchuks, have formed a powerful nationwide lobby, said Bogdan Pankevitch, a regional representative of the Government's Council of Ministers, who oversees agriculture in the west. Fearful that private farmers will succeed and eventually supplant them, the managers, mostly stalwarts of the old Communist Party, are doing everything they can to preserve their power, Mr. Pankevitch said. . . .

For the Olishchuks, breaking away from the state farm has been an odyssey of willpower backed by a fundamental grasp of market mechanisms and political possibilities.

An agricultural engineer, Mr. Olishchuk, 53, became chairman of his village in 1990, the year villagers first became eligible to apply for plots of the "reserve" land of the local state farm. Mr. Olishchuk and his son-in-law, Ivan, who had been successfully growing flowers in hothouses for many years, were among a handful of villagers who obtained land to work for themselves. The year after they got the land, the local state farm manager banned private holdings bigger than about 7.5 acres.

Help from the Dutch

They spent the winter of 1990 using Mr. Olishchuk's mechanical expertise to rebuild an old tractor that had been smashed in a car accident. The local state farm management took the family's payment for some old machinery but never released the equipment. They then took a loan when interest rates were still manageable at 10 percent and 20 percent to buy another tractor, a small combine and potato planting and digging machinery.

The determination of the Olishchuks drew the attention of a Dutch Government agricultural aid program to encourage privatization of the land, and they were allowed to use, with four other private farmers, even more sophisticated machinery donated by the Dutch.

To get fuel for the tractors was a major problem. The Olishchuks managed to exchange some wheat for fuel from the state farm. To get labor was another hurdle.

"We got the worst rap because we had the most land," Mr. Olishchuk said. Because local laborers were discouraged from working on their farm, they paid higher wages for laborers outside the district. . . .

Survival of the Fittest

Mr. Olishchuk said he knew that if Parliament passed a law allowing the privatization of land, production would increase and prices would drop. But this was fine with him, he said.

"The market will be flooded," Mr. Olishchuk said. "But we are not worried. The fittest will survive.". . .

—*Jane Perlez*

SOURCE: Jane Perlez, "In Ukraine, Barren Ground for Farm Reform," June 12, 1994. Copyright © 1994 by The New York Times Company. Reprinted with permission.

Use Your Economic Reasoning

1. Some analysts believe that capitalist reforms are likely to fail because many citizens of the former Soviet Union lack the work ethic and entrepreneurial spirit that such reforms demand. What statements in the article support that viewpoint? What statements conflict with it?

2. The Olishchuks clearly embrace the concepts of private property and profit, although other farmers in Ukraine seem unfamiliar and uncomfortable with these concepts. Why do these different viewpoints exist?

3. Old-line communists in the Ukrainian government may pose a greater threat to reform efforts than do the attitudes of the general population. Why are these individuals opposing efforts to reform the economy?

A major reason for Yeltsin's emergence as a leader was his advocacy of more rapid economic change. As Gorbachev vacillated, Yeltsin criticized and called for quickening the pace of market reforms. Reforms have indeed occurred under Yeltsin's leadership. By the end of 1993 about one-third of Russian industry had been "privatized"—the ownership transferred from government to private individuals and groups. The Yeltsin government also eliminated most price regulation, an important step in allowing markets to work properly. But many problems remain. Some big industries—particularly those related to the military—continue to receive government subsidies or loans that permit them to stay in business even though they are unprofitable. These subsidies contribute to inflation, which is now a major problem throughout the Commonwealth. In addition, the banking system is very primitive, making it difficult to funnel funds to promising businesses. A more fundamental problem is that there is little general understanding of the profit motive or the value of competition, two essential ingredients of capitalism. As a consequence, successful entrepreneurs are often likened to criminals rather than being respected for the jobs they create.

Can Russia and the other Commonwealth states overcome these problems and move closer to the capitalist model, or will the citizens become frustrated and demand a return to something like the old command system? Will the new independent states be able to cooperate, or will economic or ethnic rivalries cause the Commonwealth to fail? No one can answer these questions. Reformers throughout the Commonwealth believe that market reforms can raise living standards, but the transition to a more market-oriented economy will be slow and painful, and success is by no means certain. ("In Ukraine, Barren Ground for Farm Reform," on page 54, considers some of the problems that must be overcome for reform efforts to succeed.)

The Diversity of Real-World Economies

Compared to the United States and the former Soviet Union, most of the world's economies are characterized by a more thorough blending of capitalism and command socialism. Few, if any, approximate the model of pure capitalism better than the United States, and none matches the model of command socialism better than the former Soviet Union. Exhibit 2.3 summarizes the characteristics of nine national economies. Although this summary is by no means a refined analysis of the cited economies, it captures the diversity of organization of these real-world systems. As you can see, a high degree of public ownership usually corresponds with a high degree of central direction and command implementation. But there is no hard-and-

EXHIBIT 2.3

Characteristics of Some Selected Economies

COUNTRY	DEGREE OF PUBLIC OWNERSHIP	DEGREE OF CENTRAL DIRECTION	DEGREE OF COMMAND IMPLEMENTATION
Brazil	Moderate	Moderate	Minimal
China	Extensive	Extensive	Extensive
France	Moderate	Moderate	Minimal
Germany	Moderate	Minimal	Minimal
Great Britain	Moderate	Minimal	Minimal
Japan	Minimal	Moderate	Minimal
former Soviet Union	Extensive	Extensive	Extensive
Sweden	Moderate	Moderate	Moderate
United States	Minimal	Minimal	Minimal

fast rule. The nations appear to mix and match these three features as if they were experimenting to find the best combination for their particular situations.

In recent years many countries that we have come to think of as socialist have shown an increased interest in the market mechanism. We have already mentioned the changes in the former Soviet Union, but there are other examples. Hungary, Czechoslovakia, Poland, and China are among the nations experimenting with a greater role for markets.

Even if the market mechanism continues to win converts, we should not expect to see a world populated by precise copies of the model of pure capitalism. Each national economic system will remain unique, its own blend of public and private ownership, individual and collective decision making, and command and market implementation. The principles we have explored in this chapter provide a framework for understanding the more than 150 unique economies in the world.

In the remaining chapters of this text we will examine the operation of the U.S. economy in more detail. To better understand our economy, however, we need to know more about how markets work and how government influences economic choices in our system. In Chapter 3 we begin to broaden our understanding of markets.

Summary

An *economic system* is a set of established procedures by which a society answers the three fundamental questions of what, how, and for whom to produce. Although economic systems differ significantly, all can be described according to three criteria: Who owns the *means of production*? Who makes the economic choices about what, how, and for whom to produce? What method is used to ensure that these economic choices are carried out?

Economists commonly use theoretical models to explain the operation of economic systems. At one extreme the model of *pure capitalism* describes an economic system in which the means of production are privately owned, and fundamental economic choices are made by individuals and are implemented through markets. The principal features of pure capitalism include private property and freedom of choice, with self-interest as the driving force (held in check by *pure competition*); price determination through markets; and a *laissez-faire* condition of minimum government intervention.

In a capitalist economy *consumer sovereignty* dictates which goods and services will be produced. If consumers want more of a particular product, its price will tend to rise, encouraging profit-seeking businesses to produce more of it. To produce these products, businesses buy economic resources (e.g., labor) from households, thereby providing households with the money needed to purchase the output of businesses. The circular-flow model of capitalism diagrams this process by showing how the flows of money (money flows) and of resources and products (real flows) circulate between the household and business sectors and operate through product and resource markets.

At the other extreme the model of *command socialism* describes an economic system in which the means of production are owned by the public or the state, decisions on the three fundamental questions are made by a central authority, and implementation of these decisions occurs through command. The principal features of command socialism include public ownership, centralized decision making, economic planning, and allocation by command.

In command socialism the central planning authority gathers information on production capabilities and consumer preference (if the latter is a concern) and establishes production targets for the producing units, such as factories and farms. These units are required to produce the products dictated by the central authority in the manner specified. Output is then distributed according to the central authority's goals. Command socialism is depicted as a pyramid with the central planning board at the top and the producing and consuming units below. The producing and consuming units supply information to the central planners, who use this information to develop production targets and decide how the limited output will be distributed among the potential consumers.

No existing economic system fits neatly into either model. All real-world economies are *mixed* because they represent some blending of the two models. For example, the U.S. economy, commonly described as a capitalist system, contains some elements of a socialist command economy. Public ownership is not uncommon in the United States, and powerful economic units—government, business, and labor—influence many of the fundamental economic choices. And the former Soviet economy, the system thought to exemplify command socialism, contained some elements of capitalism. Free markets existed for certain products, and market-related incentives were sometimes used instead of commands. Most of the world's economies represent more complete blendings of capitalism and command socialism.

Glossary

Capitalism. An economic system in which the means of production are privately owned and fundamental economic choices are made by individuals and implemented through the market mechanism—the interaction of buyers and sellers.

Command socialism. An economic system in which the means of production are publicly owned, the fundamental economic choices are made by a central authority, and commands are used to ensure that these decisions are implemented.

Common-property resources. Resources that belong to society as a whole rather than to particular individuals.

Consumer sovereignty. An economic condition in which consumers dictate which goods and services will be produced by businesses.

Economic system. The set of established procedures by which a society provides answers to the three fundamental questions.

Household. A living unit that also functions as an economic unit. Whether it consists of a single person or a large family, each household has a source of income and responsibility for spending that income.

Invisible hand. A doctrine introduced by Adam Smith in 1776 holding that individuals pursuing their self-interest will be guided (as if by an invisible hand) to achieve objectives that are also in the best interest of society as a whole.

Laissez-faire economy. An economy in which the degree of government intervention is minimal.

Market. All actual or potential buyers and sellers of a particular item. Markets can be international, national, regional, or local.

Means of production. The raw materials, factories, farms, and other economic resources used to produce goods and services.

> ***Mixed economies.*** Economies that represent a blending of capitalism and command socialism. All real-world economies are mixed economies.
>
> ***Pure competition.*** A situation in which a large number of relatively small buyers and sellers interact.

Study Questions

Fill in the Blanks

1. The driving force or engine of capitalism is _____.

2. The functioning of a capitalist economy is coordinated and directed through _____ in which _____ are determined by the interaction of buyers and sellers.

3. In the model of pure capitalism the pursuit of self-interest by producers is kept in check by _____. The model of pure capitalism requires _____, a situation in which there are a large number of buyers and sellers of each product.

4. Because businesspeople in a capitalist economy are motivated by self-interest, they want to produce the goods and services that will allow them to earn the highest _____. Those products tend to be the ones that are most desired by _____.

5. According to Milton Friedman, competitive capitalism promotes _____ _____ by separating economic and political power.

6. In pure command socialism the fundamental economic decisions are made by the _____ and implemented through _____.

7. In pure command socialism _____ replaces the market as the method of coordinating the various economic decisions.

8. It is possible to represent a socialist command economy as a _____ with the _____ at the top and producing and consuming units at the bottom.

9. One weakness of command socialism is its inefficient _____

   network.

10. The United States and the former Soviet Union are both examples of _____

    _____ economies.

Multiple Choice

1. Which of the following is _not_ a characteristic of pure capitalism?
   a) Public ownership of the means of production
   b) The pursuit of self-interest
   c) Markets and prices
   d) Pure competition
   e) Limited government

2. In a market economy the scarcest resources will be used very conservatively because
   a) central planners will allocate such resources only where they are most needed.
   b) the scarcest resources will tend to have the highest prices.
   c) government officials will not permit their use.
   d) the scarcest resources will tend to have the lowest prices.

3. In a capitalist economy
   a) businesses are free to produce whatever products they choose.
   b) consumers are free to utilize their incomes as they see fit.
   c) resource owners have the freedom to sell their resources to whomever they choose.
   d) All of the above
   e) None of the above

4. Consumer sovereignty means that
   a) consumers dictate which goods and services will be produced by the way they spend their money.
   b) central planners allocate a major share of society's resources to the production of consumer goods.
   c) the role of government in the economy is very limited.
   d) all economic resources are used efficiently.

5. Which of the following best describes command socialism?
   a) An economic system characterized by private ownership of the means of production, centralized decision making, and command implementation
   b) An economic system characterized by public ownership of the means of production, centralized decision making, and market implementation
   c) An economic system characterized by public ownership of the means of production, individual decision making, and command implementation
   d) An economic system characterized by public ownership of the means of production, centralized decision making, and command implementation.

6. Which of the following is correct?
   a) In command socialism the basic economic choices are made by individuals.
   b) In pure capitalism powerful economic units have a substantial impact on the way economic choices are made.
   c) In command socialism producers are required to produce whatever products central planners dictate.
   d) In pure capitalism economic planning ensures that the various production decisions will be consistent with one another.

7. In deciding what products to produce, the central planners in a socialist command economy need not consider
   a) the size of the economy's labor force.
   b) the production capabilities of the economy's factories.
   c) consumer preferences.
   d) the economy's stock of raw materials.

8. Which of the following is a true statement about the economic system of the former Soviet Union?
   a) All prices were set by market forces.
   b) Workers were free to make their own choices about jobs, based on their reactions to wages set by central planners.
   c) Bonuses of all forms were illegal.
   d) All agricultural output was produced on state farms.

9. One reason the United States is not an example of pure capitalism is that
   a) most producing units are publicly owned.
   b) commands are used to implement some economic decisions.
   c) the pursuit of self-interest is a powerful force.
   d) markets are used to coordinate most economic decisions.

10. Which of the following was *not* an accomplishment of Mikhail Gorbachev?
    a) Discrediting the Soviet economic system.
    b) Introducing greater political freedom.
    c) Eliminating most price regulation.
    d) Permitting some small private enterprises.

Problems and Questions for Discussion

1. What is an economic system? Why is it valid to say that no two real-world economic systems are exactly alike?

2. List the characteristics or elements of pure capitalism and explain each. Are any of these elements absent from the U.S. economy? Explain.

3. How would a socialist command economy answer the three fundamental questions? What elements of command socialism exist in the U.S. economy?

4. Explain the role of economic planning in command socialism. Who is in charge of economic planning in a capitalist economy?

5. Try to draw the circular-flow diagram without looking back in the text. Now label all the parts of the diagram and indicate which flows are money flows and which are real flows. Use the diagram to explain how a capitalist economy works.

6. Draw the command pyramid and label the parts. What does the command pyramid tell us about the way that a socialist command economy functions?

7. If all real-world economies are mixed economies, why is the U.S. economy commonly described as a market economy and that of the former Soviet economy a command system?

8. Why might a centrally planned economy, such as the former Soviet economy, use economic incentives rather than commands to accomplish some objectives? If the leadership is willing to rely on incentives and markets to some extent, why does it restrict their use?

9. Soviet factory managers were known to deliberately understate their factories' production capabilities when reporting to central planners. How was such understatement to their advantage?

10. The development of high-speed computers might be a more important breakthrough for a socialist command economy than for a capitalist economy. Why?

Answer Key

Fill in the Blanks

1. self-interest
2. markets, prices
3. competition, pure competition
4. profits, consumers
5. political freedom
6. central authority, commands
7. economic planning
8. pyramid, planning board
9. information
10. mixed

Multiple Choice

1. a	3. d	5. d	7. c	9. b
2. b	4. a	6. c	8. b	10. c

PART 2

Microeconomics: Markets, Prices, and the Role of Competition

I N CHAPTER 3 we begin our study of microeconomics by investigating how prices are determined in competitive markets. You will learn the precise meaning of "supply" and "demand" and how the interaction of these forces determines prices. You will examine how prices can change and will learn the functions that price changes perform in a market economy. In Chapter 4 you will investigate the degree of consumer and producer responsiveness to price changes.

Chapter 5 examines the behavior of the purely competitive firm and explores how firms determine the amount of output to produce in order to maximize profit. You will discover the characteristics of a competitive industry and will see why competition is beneficial for consumers. Chapter 6 examines how firms acquire pricing discretion, or market power, and how the behavior of firms that possess market power differs from that of purely competitive firms. This chapter also examines the pricing techniques employed by businesses and compares them to the theoretical techniques suggested by economists. Chapter 7 considers the "degrees" of competition that exist in different industry structures and explores the impact of those different industry structures on the well-being of consumers. Chapter 8 looks at some of the inherent limitations of a market economy by examining external costs and the origin of problems such as pollution.

Demand and Supply: Price Determination in Competitive Markets

1. Define demand and supply and represent these concepts graphically.
2. State the "laws" of demand and supply.
3. Identify the determinants of demand and supply.
4. Recognize the difference between a change in demand (supply) and a change in the quantity demanded (supplied).
5. Explain and illustrate graphically how the equilibrium price and quantity are determined.
6. Describe the rationing, signaling, and motivating functions of prices.
7. Identify the factors that can cause the equilibrium price to change.
8. Use demand and supply curves to predict changes in the equilibrium price and quantity.
9. Discuss the impact of government-established maximum and minimum prices.

How do markets work? A market economy is governed by the forces of demand and supply—the interaction of buyers and sellers in thousands of different product and resource markets. These forces determine *prices.* The prevailing prices of goods and services tell producers which products consumers want most. Resource prices tell producers which resources to use to produce those products profitably. Resource prices not only affect consumers' incomes but also influence the distribution of goods and services. For example, workers whose skills are particularly scarce can command higher salaries and thereby claim a larger share of the society's limited output.

A competitive market is composed of many independent buyers and sellers, each small enough in relation to the size of the total market so that no single buyer or seller can significantly affect the market demand or supply. In this chapter you will see how the forces of demand and supply interact to determine prices in competitive markets. Later in the text we will explore the meaning of competition in greater detail and examine the behavior of the purely competitive firm (Chapter 5). But for now just remember that in competitive markets prices are determined by the impersonal forces of demand and supply—not by the manipulations of powerful buyers and sellers.

After you study this chapter, you will have a greater appreciation of the role that prices play in a market economy. You'll understand why the price of gold fluctuates and why salaries are higher in some occupations than in others. You'll understand why antique cars often command higher prices than this year's models and why a poor wheat harvest in Canada or Ukraine can mean higher bread prices in the United States. You will also understand how prices both direct the actions of producers and determine the distribution of society's limited output of goods and services. The material in this chapter will give you a clearer comprehension of the role of markets and prices in our economy.

Demand

In a market economy consumers are sovereign; that is, consumers dictate which goods and services will be produced. But it is consumer *demand* rather than consumer desire that makes the actual determination. We have already noted that human wants are unlimited. However, wanting an item and being willing and able to pay for it are two distinctly different things. If the item we want carries a price tag, we may have to do without it: We may lack the money to pay, or we may prefer to spend that money on something else.

People who are both *willing and able* to make purchases are the consumers who determine which products a market economy will produce. When consumers lack either the willingness or the ability to spend their dollars, producers do not respond. Thus the concept of demand includes the willingness and ability of potential buyers to purchase a product. We define **demand** as a schedule (or table) showing the quantities of a good or service that consumers are willing and able to purchase at various prices during a given time period, when all factors other than the product's price remain unchanged.

Exhibit 3.1 illustrates the concept of demand through a simple example. The schedule shows the yearly demand for jogging shoes of a given quality in the hypothetical community of Hometown, U.S.A. You can see that the number of pairs of jogging shoes that Hometown consumers are willing and able to purchase each year depends on the selling price. If jogging shoes sell for $50 a pair, Hometowners will purchase 2,000 pairs a year, assuming that other factors remain the same—their incomes, for example, and their present jogging routines.

EXHIBIT 3.1

Hometown Demand for Jogging Shoes

PRICE (per pair)	QUANTITY (pairs per year)
$50	2,000
40	4,000
30	6,000
20	8,000
10	10,000

Demand Curves

Economists usually represent schedules in the form of graphs. To graph the demand for jogging shoes, we first plot the information in Exh. 3.1 and then connect the points to form a demand curve, as shown in Exh. 3.2. A **demand curve** is simply a graphical representation of demand. By convention we measure price on the vertical axis and quantity on the horizontal axis. Each point on the curve represents a price and the quantity that consumers would de-

EXHIBIT 3.2

The Demand Curve for Jogging Shoes in Hometown, U.S.A.

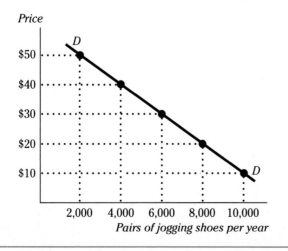

A demand curve is a graphical representation of demand. It demonstrates the inverse relationship between price and quantity demanded.

mand per year at that price. For example, we can see in Exh. 3.2 that at a price of $40, Hometown joggers would demand 4,000 pairs; at a price of $30, the quantity demanded would increase to 6,000 pairs.

The Law of Demand

Our hypothetical demand schedule and demand curve for jogging shoes demonstrate clearly what economists call the **law of demand,** which holds that the quantity demanded of a product is *negatively, or inversely, related* to its price. This simply means that consumers will purchase more of a product at lower prices than at higher prices. That's why demand curves always slope downward and to the right.

Economists believe that two factors explain the inverse relationship between price and quantity demanded:

1. When prices are lower, consumers can afford to purchase a larger quantity of the product out of any given income. Economists refer to this *ability* to purchase more as the **income effect** of a price reduction.
2. At lower prices the product becomes more attractive relative to other items serving the same function. This **substitution effect** explains the *willingness* of consumers to substitute for other products the product that has declined in price.

To illustrate the income and substitution effects, let's return to our Hometown consumers. Why will they purchase more jogging shoes at $10 than at $50? Because of the income effect, their incomes will now buy more: If the price of jogging shoes declines and other prices don't change, consumers will be able to buy more goods and services with their fixed incomes. It's almost as though each consumer had received a raise. And because of the substitution effect, consumers will buy jogging shoes instead of tennis shoes, sandals, or moccasins because jogging shoes have become a better footwear buy. Because of both the income effect and the substitution effect, we all, like these hypothetical consumers, tend to purchase more of a product at a lower price than at a higher price.

Determinants of Demand

The demand curve and the law of demand emphasize the relationship between the price of a product and the quantity demanded, but price is not the only factor that determines how much of a product consumers will buy. A variety of other factors underlie the demand schedule and determine the precise position of the demand curve. These **determinants of demand** include income, tastes and preferences, expectations regarding future prices, the price of related goods, and the number of buyers in the market. Any demand curve is based on the assumption that these factors are held constant. Changes in one or more of these determinants cause the entire demand curve to shift to a new position.

Income

The most obvious determinant of demand is income. Consumers' incomes influence their *ability* to purchase goods and services. For what economists call **normal goods,** an increase in income will cause consumers to purchase more of a product than before at each possible price. For example, an increase in per capita income (income per person) will probably cause consumers to buy more steak than before at whatever price exists. We would show this by shifting the demand curve to the right, as illustrated in Exh. 3.3.

Not all products are normal goods, however. An increase in income will cause consumers to purchase less of an **inferior good,** thus shifting the demand curve to the left. Powdered milk, generic macaroni and cheese, and

---

EXHIBIT 3.3

Income as a Determinant of Demand

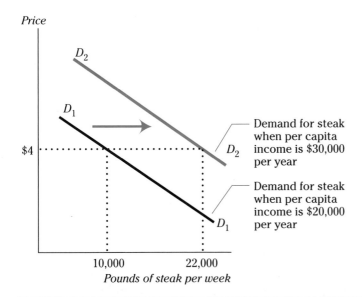

An increase in per capita income will shift the demand curve for a normal good to the right. Consumers will purchase more of the product at each price.

cheap wine are examples of products that might be inferior goods. When their incomes increase, consumers may choose to buy less of these products in favor of more appetizing grocery items.

Tastes and Preferences

Consumers' tastes and preferences—how well they like the product relative to other products—are also important determinants of demand. A change in tastes and preferences will affect the demand for products. For example, the desire to limit cholesterol intake has altered consumer tastes and preferences for various food products. Today consumers demand less red meat and fewer eggs than in times past but demand more fish and chicken. In other words this change in tastes and preferences has caused the demand curves for red meat and eggs to shift to the left and the demand curves for fish and chicken to shift to the right.

Expectations about Prices

Expectations may also influence consumer behavior. For example, the expectation that the price of an item will rise in the future usually encourages consumers to buy it now. We would represent this by shifting the entire demand curve to the right to show that more would be demanded now at whatever price prevailed. Similarly the expectation that a product will decline in price is a good incentive to postpone buying it; the present demand curve for the product would shift to the left.

Price of Related Goods

A somewhat less obvious determinant of demand is the price of related goods. Although all goods compete for a consumer's income, the price of substitutes and complements may be particularly important in explaining consumer behavior. **Substitutes** are simply products that can be used in place of other products because, to a greater or lesser extent, they satisfy the same consumer wants. Hot dogs are a typical substitute for hamburgers, and tennis shoes may substitute for jogging shoes unless one is a serious jogger. **Complements** are products normally purchased along with or in conjunction with another product. For example, pickle relish and hot dogs are complements, as are lettuce and salad dressing.

If the price of hamburgers increased and the price of hot dogs remained unchanged, consumers might be expected to buy fewer hamburgers and more hot dogs. The demand curve for hot dogs would shift to the right. By the same token an increase in the price of lettuce is likely to have an adverse effect on the sale of salad dressing. Because people buy salad dressing as a complement to salad vegetables, anything that causes consumers to eat fewer salads causes them to demand less salad dressing. The demand curve for salad dressing would shift to the left.

The Number of Consumers in the Market

The final determinant of demand is the number of consumers in the market. The more consumers who demand a particular product, the greater the total demand for the product. When the number of consumers increases, the demand curve for the product shifts to the right to show that a greater quantity is now demanded at each price. If the number of consumers declines, the demand curve shifts to the left.

As we think about the demand for a particular product, we need to remember the five determinants we have listed and how changes in these factors will affect the demand curve. We also need to recognize that more and more U.S. firms are selling their products to consumers in Mexico, Europe, and other locations outside the United States. As a consequence, the position of the demand curve for many products is determined not solely by local or national factors but by international factors as well. For instance, rising incomes in Mexico are certain to shift the demand curve for U.S. automobiles to the right, whereas the increased availability of cheap Chilean wines will probably shift the demand curve for many California wines to the left. The point is that markets are often international in scope, so we need to look beyond national boundaries to determine the level of demand.

Change in Quantity Demanded versus Change in Demand

In analyzing the factors that cause consumers to increase or decrease their purchases of a particular product, it is helpful to distinguish between the impact of a change (1) in the price of the product and (2) in one or more of the determinants of demand.

A change in the price of the product results in a **change in quantity demanded** and is represented graphically by movement along a stationary demand curve. For example, if the price of steak declines from $6 a pound to $4 a pound, consumers will move from point A to point B on demand curve D_1 in Exh. 3.4. Note that the consumers will now choose to purchase a greater quantity of the product because its price is lower. This is an increase in the quantity demanded. If, on the other hand, the price rises from $2 a pound to $4 a pound, the consumers will move from point C to point B on the demand curve. Here a price increase will cause a reduction in the quantity demanded.

EXHIBIT 3.4

Distinguishing Change in Demand from Change in Quantity Demanded

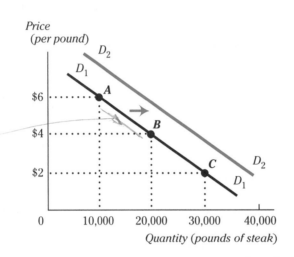

A change in the price of steak will cause a *change in the quantity demanded.* When the price of steak declines from $6 to $2 a pound, the quantity demanded increases from 10,000 to 30,000 pounds; consumers move from *A* to *C* along demand curve D_1.

A change in a determinant of demand will cause a *change in demand:* the entire curve will shift. The movement from D_1 to D_2 is an increase in demand.

When any of the determinants of demand changes, the result is a **change in demand**—an entirely new demand schedule represented graphically by a shift of the demand curve to a new position. If consumers develop a stronger preference for steak, for instance, or if the prices of substitutes for steak rise, the entire demand curve for steak will shift to the right—an increase in demand. This shift is depicted in Exh. 3.4. An entire demand curve shift to the left would denote a decrease in demand. See "Accelerating Prices on the Hottest Cars," on page 75, to test your understanding of the difference between a change in demand and a change in the quantity demanded.

Supply

A knowledge of demand is essential to an understanding of how prices are determined, but it is only half the picture. Now we turn to the supply side of the market.

When we use the term "supply" in our everyday language, usually we are referring to a fixed quantity. That's what the owner of the local sporting-

Accelerating Car Prices

Get out your calculators, You're going to need them to keep up with rising car prices, especially on hot-selling cars and trucks.

Take the 1994 Chevrolet Camaro. When the car was introduced last fall, it carried a base price of $13,399. By Jan. 10 this year, that price rose to $13,499. On May 9, the price went up $250 to $13,749.

Yet, the sporty Camaro and its companion Pontiac Firebird continue to sell at a brisk pace. Current sales are almost four times what they were in 1993—42,353 Camaro models sold so far in 1994 vs. 9,099 at this time last year.

So what's going on here?

Partly it's the end of recession. People are buying cars again and that's creating high demand, which is leading to higher prices. Partly it's manufacturers such as General Motors Corp. scrambling to find money and ways to expand production. And partly it's shifting exchange rates putting pressure on Japanese companies to raise prices.

"We're having the opposite side of the problem that we had two years ago, when we were shutting down plants because we couldn't sell enough cars," said John F. Maciarz, GM's marketing spokesman. "Now our de-mand is so high, we can't build enough cars and trucks."

Oddly enough, Japanese automakers with their factories of legendary efficiency are experiencing similar capacity problems, even though their prices are rising faster than those of their American rivals.

Yet, the Japanese share of the car and truck market in the United States for the first four months of this year stood at 23.1 percent, up two-tenths of a percentage point over its 1993 level. . . .

"That sort of pokes a hole in the argument that higher prices necessarily mean lower market share," said Joel Pitcoff, an industry analyst for Ford. "In spite of their higher prices [and] our increases in quality, in spite of the fact that more Americans are beginning to buy our cars, the Japanese are still making gains; and we're not taking them lightly."

—*Warren Brown*

SOURCE: Warren Brown, "Accelerating Prices on the Hottest Cars," *The Washington Post*, May 28, 1994. Reprinted with permission.

Use Your Economic Reasoning

1. How do you explain the fact that sales of the Chevrolet Camaro increased during a period when the price of the Camaro was raised two times; how would you represent this phenomenon graphically?

2. Why would you expect the end of a recession (a period of reduced economic activity and relatively high unemployment) to bring increased automobile sales? Which determinant of demand has changed?

3. If the prices of Japanese autos have increased more rapidly than the prices of U.S. models, how do you explain the fact that the Japanese share of the U.S. auto market has increased?

EXHIBIT 3.5

Hometown Supply of Jogging Shoes

PRICE (per pair)	QUANTITY (pairs per year)
$50	10,000
40	8,000
30	6,000
20	4,000
10	2,000

goods store means when advertising a *limited supply* of Fleet Feet tennis shoes or SuperFit swimsuits. But that's not what economists mean when they talk about supply. To economists supply is a schedule—just as demand is. **Supply** is a schedule (or table) showing the quantities of a good or service that producers are willing and able to offer for sale at various prices during a given time period, when all factors other than the product's price remain unchanged.

Exhibit 3.5 represents the annual supply of jogging shoes in the Hometown market area. As the schedule shows, the number of pairs of jogging shoes that suppliers will make available for sale depends on the price of jogging shoes. At a price of $50 a pair suppliers are willing to produce 10,000 pairs of jogging shoes a year; at a price of $30 they would offer only 6,000 pairs. Because supply is a schedule, we can't determine the quantity supplied unless we know the selling price.

The Supply Curve

To transform our supply schedule into a supply curve, we follow the same procedure we used in constructing a demand curve. Here we graph the information in Exh. 3.5, measuring price on the vertical axis and quantity on the horizontal axis. When we've finished graphing the points from the schedule, we connect them to get a **supply curve**—a graphical representation of supply (Exh. 3.6).

Interpreting a supply curve is basically the same as interpreting a demand curve. Each point on the curve represents a price and the quantity of jogging shoes that producers will supply at that price. You can see, for example, that producers will supply 4,000 pairs of shoes at a price of $20 per pair or 8,000 pairs at a price of $40 per pair.

EXHIBIT 3.6

The Supply Curve of Jogging Shoes in Hometown, U.S.A.

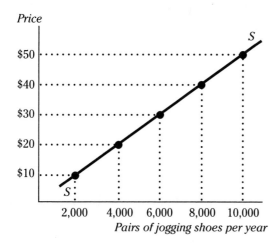

A supply curve is a graphical representation of supply. It demonstrates the direct relationship between price and quantity supplied.

The Law of Supply

You've probably noticed that the supply curve slopes upward and to the right. The supply curve slopes upward because the **law of supply** holds that price and quantity supplied are *positively, or directly, related.* Producers will supply a larger quantity at higher prices than at lower prices.

Why would producers supply more jogging shoes at a higher price than at a lower price? The major reason is that the higher price allows them to cover the higher unit costs associated with producing the additional output. It probably costs more to produce the thousandth pair of jogging shoes than it did to produce the five hundredth pair. It's also likely that it would cost even more to produce the two thousandth pair, and so on. Producers are willing to supply a greater quantity at a higher price because the higher price enables businesses to cover the higher cost of producing the additional units—units that would not have been profitable at lower prices.

Costs per unit tend to increase with output because some of a business's resources, such as its production plant and equipment, cannot be expanded in a short period of time. Therefore as the business increases output by hiring more labor and employing more raw materials, it eventually begins to overutilize its factory and equipment. This leads to congestion, workers waiting to use equipment, more frequent breakdowns of equipment, and production bottlenecks—situations in which one stage of the production process is slowing down the entire operation. These problems increase the cost of producing additional units. Producers will supply the additional units only if they can obtain a price high enough to justify paying the higher costs. Thus the supply curve is upward sloping because a higher price is *necessary* to call forth additional output from suppliers.

Determinants of Supply

The supply curve shows the relationship between the price of a product and the quantity supplied when other factors remain unchanged. However, price is not the only factor that influences the amount producers will offer for sale. Three major **determinants of supply** underlie the supply schedule and determine the position of the supply curve: technology, prices of the resources used in producing the product, and the number of producers in the market. Each supply curve is based on the assumption that these factors are held constant. Changes in any of the determinants will shift the entire supply curve to a new position.

Technology

Each supply curve is based on the existing technology. **Technology** is our state of knowledge about how to produce products. It influences the types of machines we use and the combinations of other resources we select to produce goods and services. A **technological advance** is the discovery of a better way to produce a product—a method that uses fewer resources to produce each unit of output or that produces more output from a given amount of resources. Because a technological advance allows producers to supply a higher quantity at any given price, it is represented by shifting the supply curve to the right, as depicted in Exh. 3.7. As you can see, the development of a better method for producing personal computers will allow computer producers to supply a higher quantity at each price.

Resource Prices

Businesses must purchase economic resources in order to produce their products. Each supply curve assumes that the prices of resources remain unchanged. An increase in the price of labor, materials, or some other production input will increase producers' costs and cause them to supply less at any given price. The supply curve will shift to the left. A reduction in resource prices will have the opposite effect; the supply curve will shift to the right, because producers will be able to supply a higher quantity at each price.

EXHIBIT 3.7

The Impact of a Technological Advance on the Supply of Personal Computers

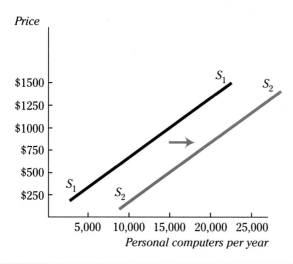

A technological advance will allow producers to supply a higher quantity at any given price.

The Number of Producers in the Market

A third determinant of supply is the number of producers in the particular market: the more producers, the greater the supply. Each supply curve assumes that the number of producers is unchanged. If additional producers enter the market, the supply curve will shift to the right; if some producers leave, the supply curve will shift left.

Many other changes have essentially the same impact on supply as an increase or decrease in the number of producers. A severe frost destroys half the orange crop, decreasing supply; a good growing season enlarges the wheat harvest, increasing supply; trade barriers are lowered and additional beef enters the United States, increasing supply. With each of these changes, the supply curve shifts as it would if the number of suppliers had increased or decreased.

As with demand, we need to recognize that the three determinants of supply—technology, resource prices, and the number of producers in the market—may be subject to international influences. For instance, the need to compete with foreign rivals has been a major factor spurring U.S. producers to search for and implement cost-reducing technological advances. In the furniture industry, for example, pressure from foreign producers has resulted in innovations that increase the amount of furniture produced from a given amount of wood. These innovations will cause the supply curve for furniture to shift to the right. At the same time, the supply curve of aluminum has shifted to the right for a very different reason. In the wake of the collapse of the Soviet Union, Russia has been supplying the world with massive amounts of aluminum—aluminum that once would have gone to military uses in the USSR. As you can see, we cannot ignore international factors as we attempt to determine the level of supply.

Change in Supply versus Change in Quantity Supplied

Earlier in this chapter you learned the difference between a change in demand and a change in *quantity* demanded. Economists make the same distinction for supply. A **change in the quantity supplied** results from a change in the price of the product, with factors other than price held constant. It is represented graphically by movement along a stationary supply curve. According to Exh. 3.8, if the price of personal computers declines from $1,000 to $500, the quantity supplied will decrease from 20,000 units to only 10,000 units a year,

---

EXHIBIT 3.8

**Distinguishing Change in Supply
from Change in Quantity Supplied**

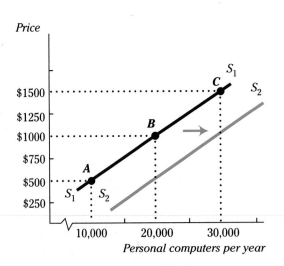

A change in the price of computers will cause a *change in the quantity supplied*. When price increases from $500 to $1,500, the quantity supplied increases from 10,000 to 30,000 computers per year; we move from A to C along supply curve S_1.

A change in a determinant of supply will cause a *change in supply*: the entire curve will shift. The movement from S_1 to S_2 is an increase in supply.

as suppliers move from point B to point A along supply curve S_1. But if the price of computers increases from $1,000 to $1,500, producers will move from point B to point C, and the quantity supplied will expand from 20,000 to 30,000 computers a year.

A **change in supply** is an increase or decrease in the amount of a product supplied at each and every price. A change in supply is caused by a change in one of the determinants of supply and is represented graphically by a shift of the entire supply curve, as depicted in Exh. 3.8. If the supply curve shifts to the right (from S_1 to S_2), it denotes an increase in supply; a shift to the left indicates a decrease in supply. (To test your ability to distinguish between a change in supply and a change in quantity supplied, read the article "On the Cutting Edge," page 82, and answer the questions.)

The Process of Price Determination

Now that you understand the basics of demand and supply, let's put those two pieces of the puzzle together and examine how prices are determined. To do that, we'll consider again the market for jogging shoes. Exhibit 3.9 displays hypothetical demand and supply schedules for that product. As you already know, the demand schedule shows the quantities of jogging shoes that will be demanded at various prices, and the supply schedule reveals the quantities that will be supplied at those prices. But which of these possible prices will prevail in the market? And what quantity of jogging shoes will be exchanged between buyers and sellers? To answer those questions, let's compare the reactions of buyers and sellers to each possible price.

What would happen in the market if jogging shoes were selling for $10 a pair? Because the $10 price would be attractive to consumers but not to pro-

EXHIBIT 3.9

The Demand and Supply of Jogging Shoes in Hometown, U.S.A.

PRICE (per pair)	QUANTITY DEMANDED (pairs per year)	QUANTITY SUPPLIED (pairs per year)
$50	2,000	10,000
40	4,000	8,000
30	6,000	6,000
20	8,000	4,000
10	10,000	2,000

On the Cutting Edge

Sharp new technology helps the woodworking industry compete

If you think it doesn't take a rocket scientist to cut a piece of wood, you obviously haven't met aerospace engineer and former NASA trainee John Stewart.

In a warehouselike building on the campus of North Carolina State University that is a cross between a machine shop and a physics lab, Stewart uses lasers, electron microscopes, vibration detectors, electronic strain gauges and computer models to study exactly what happens, sometimes down to a millionth of a meter, when a metal tool meets a piece of wood. He and his colleagues delve into such mysteries as why green oak lumber is hell on carbide-tipped saws (tannic acid in the wood eats away the microscopic layer of cobalt that glues the carbide to the blade) or why spindles in high-speed routers self-destruct with such alarming frequency (a router bit unbalanced by imperfections as tiny as a few grams a millimeter off center can make the whole shaft vibrate violently).

Wizardry

The remarkable thing is not so much the scientific wizardry going on here. The remarkable thing is that the American woodworking industry is actually paying attention to what Stewart is up to. One of the last bastions of 19th-century seat-of-the-pants engineering, America's wood-machinery and furniture-making companies are now fighting for their lives. Foreign competition in the past decade has cut into a third of the domestic furniture market and as much as 90 percent of some segments of the wood-machinery business. And soaring lumber prices—most wood has doubled in price in the past four years—have created an urgent demand for technology that can squeeze even an extra fraction of an inch out of each piece. As a result, America's machinery makers and machinery users have come to the belated conclusion that the venerable tobacco-spitting shop foreman could use more than a little help from the white-coated scientist.

Many of the scientific problems that Stewart and his co-workers are now being called upon to solve for the industry arise directly from this competitive push for speed and efficiency. In the days of cheap lumber and low-speed machinery, saws that wasted material or bits that vibrated a little didn't matter. But routers that ran at 8,000 revolutions per minute 10 years ago are now turning at 20,000 or even 30,000 rpm. A higher turning speed means wood can be fed through faster—and time is definitely money—but it also means that stresses and imbalances are hugely multiplied. The margins for error are becoming literally microscopic.

One practical product of the research at N.C. State has been guidelines that tell operators at what speed they can safely run their machines for a given degree of tool unbalance. Ultimately, the research could lead to automatic technical fixes. Vibration sensors on machines, and even lasers that scan the surface of the wood as it is machined, checking for roughness, could send a feedback signal that adjusts the rpm of the machine or the feed rate of the stock.

Waking Up

The rising price of lumber has proved to be the real wake-up call to a long-somnolent industry. Although some of the price rise reflects the economic expansion, forestry economists note that a fundamental restructuring of the supply side of the business is underway. As recently as 1987, loggers were cutting nearly 12 billion board feet of timber a year from old-growth forests on public lands in Washington and Oregon; last year it was down to 2.6 billion, and the figure is likely to fall to a billion or less if the Clinton administration's compromise plan for protecting spotted owl habitat goes into effect. Total U.S. softwood production was 33.5 billion board feet last year a 12 percent drop since 1987.

Protecting habitat for the red-cockaded woodpecker and other environmental concerns in the East have led to a similar crunch in supplies of Appalachian hardwoods important for the furniture industry.

Improving Yield

Cutting waste in the manufacturing process has thus become a top priority. Several major North Carolina furniture makers are anticipating losses this year as a result of rising lumber costs; improving yield by a small percent can make a difference

of hundreds of thousands of dollars on the bottom line. There's a lot of room for improvement. As much as 85 percent of a saw log is wasted; up to 25 percent is lost planing the boards to smooth them, and 6 to 7 percent is lost just as a result of the thickness of the saw blades used to cut boards into furniture parts. "Every time we run a saw through a board, we lose yield," says Nicholas Weidhaas, another N.C. State faculty member, who feels so passionately about the subject that he calls saw-cut losses "a national tragedy."

The technology exists to reduce saw blades from the current standard of $\frac{3}{16}$ or $\frac{1}{4}$ of an inch to 0.100 inch or even less. But thin blades are less able to withstand stress, so cutting edges must be extremely sharp. They are much more susceptible to vi-

bration, too—a thin blade can act almost like a drumhead, flexing and vibrating in complex patterns—which can cause the blade to wobble and make a sloppy cut, defeating the purpose. Studying these vibration modes involves complex physics and computer modeling.

"Fifty years ago," says Stewart, "you could hire a mechanical engineer and he could take care of all your problems. Today, you've got computer problems, electronic problems, dynamics problems, materials science problems." Sounds like a job for a rocket scientist.

—*Stephen Budiansky*

SOURCE: Stephen Budiansky, "On the Cutting Edge," May 31, 1994. Copyright © 1994 U.S. News & World Report. Reprinted with permission.

Use Your Economic Reasoning

1. The article mentions two factors that have played a role in convincing U.S. furniture manufacturers to search for new technology. What are the two factors and why have they hastened the search for improved technology?

2. A technological advance generally reduces the cost of producing a given level of output. How might improved woodworking technology reduce the cost of producing furniture?

3. Will improved woodworking technology increase the supply of furniture or the quantity supplied? How should this change be represented graphically?

ducers, 10,000 pairs of jogging shoes would be demanded, but only 2,000 pairs would be supplied. At the $10 price there would be a **shortage**—an excess of quantity demanded over quantity supplied—of 8,000 pairs of jogging shoes. Therefore some potential buyers would offer to pay a higher price in order to obtain the product. Competition among these buyers would tend to push the price to a higher level, and the higher price of jogging shoes would tend to reduce the quantity demanded while encouraging producers to expand the quantity supplied. In this way price increases would tend to reduce the shortage of jogging shoes.

Suppose that the price of jogging shoes rose to $20 a pair. At that price 8,000 pairs of jogging shoes would be demanded and 4,000 pairs supplied. Once again there would be a shortage, but this time it would amount to only 4,000 pairs of jogging shoes (8,000 pairs demanded minus 4,000 pairs supplied). Competition among potential buyers again would bid up the price of jogging shoes. The higher price would lead to a reduction in the quantity demanded and an increase in the quantity supplied, which would reduce the shortage still further.

You can probably see what happens as we move from lower to higher prices. Now let's reverse the process, beginning with the highest price in Exh. 3.9. A price of $50 would tend to encourage production and discourage consumption. Producers would be willing to supply 10,000 pairs of jogging shoes a year, but consumers would demand only 2,000 pairs. The result would be a **surplus**—an excess of quantity supplied over quantity demanded—of 8,000 pairs of jogging shoes a year. How do producers react to a surplus? They begin to cut the price of the product in order to compete for existing customers and lure additional customers into the market. The lower price of jogging shoes tends to increase the quantity demanded and decrease the quantity supplied, thus reducing the surplus. If the price fell to $40, there would still be a surplus of 4,000 pairs of jogging shoes (8,000 pairs supplied minus the 4,000 pairs demanded). Price cutting would then continue, and the surplus would continue to shrink.

Equilibrium Price and Quantity

In our example $30 is the market-clearing, or equilibrium, price, and 6,000 units is the equilibrium quantity. The **equilibrium price** is the price that brings about an equality between the quantity demanded and the quantity supplied. The **equilibrium quantity** is the quantity demanded and supplied at the equilibrium price. Equilibrium essentially means stability; once established, the equilibrium price will be maintained so long as the basic supply and demand conditions remain unchanged.

In a competitive market the actual, or prevailing, price will tend toward equilibrium. As you saw in Exh. 3.9, when the price of jogging shoes is above or below equilibrium, market pressures tend to push it down or up toward the equilibrium level. Only when the existing price is at the equilibrium level will there be neither a shortage nor a surplus and no pressure for price to change.

We use supply and demand curves to represent the process of price determination. By graphing the demand and supply schedules in Exh. 3.9, we can construct the demand and supply curves found in Exh. 3.10. These curves intersect at the equilibrium price ($30) and the equilibrium quantity (6,000 pairs of jogging shoes). At any price *above* equilibrium (say, $40), we can measure

EXHIBIT 3.10

Demand and Supply Curves or Jogging Shoes in Hometown, U.S.A.

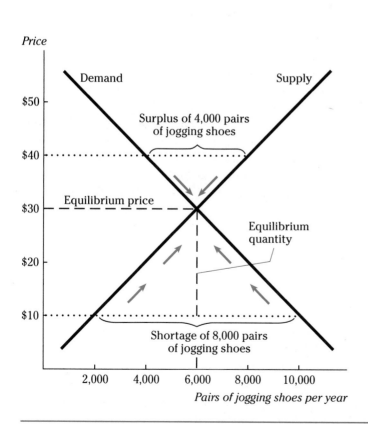

The equilibrium price is the price that equates the quantity supplied and the quantity demanded. In our example the equilibrium price is $30. Whenever the existing price is above or below equilibrium, pressure exists to push it toward the equilibrium level. For example, at a price of $40 there would be a surplus, and price cutting would take place. At a price of $10 there would be a shortage, and the price would tend to rise in order to eliminate the shortage. The arrows indicate the direction of the adjustments in price and quantity.

the amount of the surplus as the horizontal distance between the demand curve and the supply curve. For any price *below* equilibrium ($10, for example), the horizontal distance between the curves tells us the amount of the shortage. As we noted earlier, the shortage or surplus tends to shrink as price approaches the equilibrium level. The graph visually represents these shrinking amounts in the diminishing distance between the demand curve and the supply curve. When price finally achieves equilibrium, the curves intersect. At that point quantity demanded equals quantity supplied, and there is neither shortage nor surplus.

The Rationing, Signaling, and Motivating Functions of Prices

In the preceding example the equilibrium price succeeds in matching up the quantity supplied and the quantity demanded because it performs three important functions. First, the equilibrium price rations jogging shoes perfectly among the various possible users; at a price of $30, 6,000 pairs are demanded—exactly the quantity made available by producers. Second, it signals or guides producers to supply the correct quantity, the quantity consumers are willing to purchase at $30. Finally, it motivates producers to supply that quantity because it makes it profitable for them to do so.

You may recall from Chapter 1 that because every society faces the basic economic problem of unlimited wants and limited resources, some system must exist for **rationing**—that is, dividing up or allocating the scarce items among those who want them. In the United States and other economies that rely heavily on markets, price is the dominant rationing device. Rationing in a market economy works hand in hand with **signaling**—providing information to producers about how much to supply—and **motivating**—providing incentives to produce the desired output. Let's use Exh. 3.10 to examine this process further, first from the perspective of the consumers demanding jogging shoes and then from the perspective of the producers supplying them.

How does the price of a product ration the supply of it among users? Prices ration because they influence our ability and willingness to purchase the product. The higher the price of jogging shoes, the more of our income it takes to buy them (which means a greater sacrifice in terms of other goods and services we must do without), and the less attractive jogging shoes become in relation to substitute products (tennis shoes, for instance).

To illustrate how price rations, let's begin with a relatively low price for jogging shoes—$10. If jogging shoes were selling for $10 (a price well below equilibrium), consumers would be willing and able to purchase a relatively high quantity—10,000 pairs. But as we learned earlier, producers are willing to supply only 2,000 pairs at that price, so there will be a shortage, and price will tend to rise. As the price of jogging shoes rises toward its equilibrium level, the quantity demanded is reduced—fewer consumers are willing and able to pay the higher price. By discouraging consumers from purchasing the product, the higher price of jogging shoes helps to bring the quantity demanded into line with the number of jogging shoes available; it *rations* jogging shoes. By the same token, at a price initially above equilibrium—for example, $40—the quantity demanded would be too low. But price will tend to decline, and the falling price will encourage consumers to purchase more of the product. Thus higher prices ration by reducing the quantity demanded, and lower prices ration by increasing it.

But changing prices do more than reduce or increase the quantity demanded: They also signal producers to expand or shrink production and motivate them to supply the new quantity. We know from the law of supply that more will be supplied at higher prices than at lower prices. Thus when the price of jogging shoes increases from $10 to $30, the quantity of jogging shoes supplied will increase from 2,000 pairs to 6,000 pairs. At the same time, the quantity of jogging shoes is being rationed among consumers; the quantity demanded is declining from 10,000 pairs to 6,000 pairs. This is how the rationing, signaling, and motivating functions of price work together to balance the desires of consumers and producers and prevent a shortage or surplus. Every consumer who values jogging shoes enough to pay $30 will have them, and every producer that is willing to supply jogging shoes at that price will be able to sell its entire output.

Changes in the Equilibrium Price

You have seen that in the absence of artificial restrictions, prices in competitive markets tend toward equilibrium. Once established, the equilibrium price will hold as long as the underlying demand and supply conditions remain unchanged. Of course, such conditions don't remain unchanged forever, often not even for a short time. Anything that causes a change in either demand or supply will bring about a new equilibrium price.

The Impact of a Change in Demand

Recall from earlier in this chapter that the determinants of demand are all the factors that underlie the demand schedule and determine the precise position of the demand curve. These include consumer tastes and preferences, consumer income, the prices of substitutes and complements, expectations regarding future prices, and the number of buyers in the market. Changes in any of these factors will cause a change in demand—a shift of the entire demand curve.

The housing market provides a good example. Increased demand for new houses in your city or town could result from any of several factors: heightened desire for single-family dwellings instead of apartments, an increase in residents' incomes, rent hikes in the area, expectations of higher housing prices in the near future, or a local population expansion. Any of these changes will cause the demand curve for new homes to shift to the right, as depicted in Exh. 3.11.

You can see that 8,000 new houses are demanded and supplied at the initial equilibrium price of $120,000. However, as demand increases from D_1 to D_2, perhaps because of an increased number of buyers in the market, there is a shortage of 4,000 houses (12,000 minus 8,000) at the $120,000 price. This shortage will lead to competition among prospective home buyers, which in turn will push the average price upward toward the new equilibrium level of $130,000. The higher price will perform three functions: ration new houses by reducing the quantity demanded and both signal and motivate builders to increase the quantity supplied from 8,000 to 10,000. Note here that the increase in demand (the shift of the entire demand curve) causes an increase in the *quantity* supplied (movement along the stationary supply curve). In other words, a *shift* in one curve causes movement *along* the other curve. Thus an in-

EXHIBIT 3.11

The Effect of an Increase in Demand on the Equilibrium Price

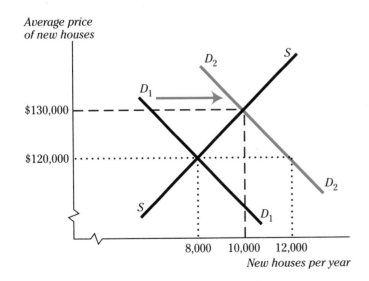

Average price of new houses

D_2

S

D_1

$130,000

$120,000

S

D_2

D_1

8,000   10,000   12,000

New houses per year

An increase in the demand for new houses will cause the equilibrium price of new homes to rise.

crease in demand leads to a higher equilibrium in both price ($130,000) and quantity (10,000 new homes per year).

Now suppose that any of the conditions that might have increased the demand for new houses is reversed, causing demand to decline. As shown in Exh. 3.12, the demand curve will shift to the left, from D_1 to D_2. As demand declines, a surplus of houses develops at the old price of $120,000 (only 4,000 homes will be demanded, but 8,000 will be supplied). This surplus will lead to price cutting as builders compete for buyers and as customers shop around for the best buys. Once again the price change performs three functions. The falling price convinces home buyers to purchase more than 4,000 homes per year, and it signals and motivates builders to supply fewer than 8,000 homes. Price will continue to decline until the quantity of new houses demanded is exactly equal to the quantity supplied at that price. In our example the new equilibrium price is $110,000, and the new equilibrium quantity is 6,000 new homes per year.

The Impact of a Change in Supply

Price changes also can be initiated on the supply side. Recall the three determinants of supply: technology, prices of economic resources, and the number of suppliers in the market. Changes in any of these factors that underlie the

---

EXHIBIT 3.12

The Effect of a Decrease in Demand on the Equilibrium Price

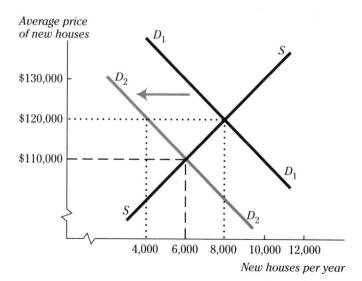

A decrease in the demand for new houses will cause the equilibrium price of new homes to fall.

supply schedule will cause a change in supply. In our example the supply of housing might be increased by any of the following: (1) the development of new construction methods that enable builders to produce more houses from a given amount of resources; (2) decreases in the cost of land, labor, or materials used in home construction; (3) an increase in the number of builders, enabling the market to produce more houses than before at each possible price.

An increase in the supply of new houses is represented by shifting the supply curve to the right, as shown in Exh. 3.13. When the supply of housing increases from S_1 to S_2, 12,000 new homes will be supplied at a price of $120,000, but only 8,000 will be demanded. As before, the surplus will lead to price cutting downward toward the new equilibrium level of $110,000. Note that here the increase in supply (the shift of the entire supply curve) causes an increase in the *quantity* demanded (movement along the stationary demand curve). As we saw earlier, a shift in one curve causes movement *along* the other. This is the process that results in the lower price and the higher equilibrium quantity. A *decrease* in the supply of housing would have the opposite effect; it would raise the equilibrium price and lower the equilibrium quantity.

EXHIBIT 3.13

Effect of an Increase in Supply on Equilibrium Price

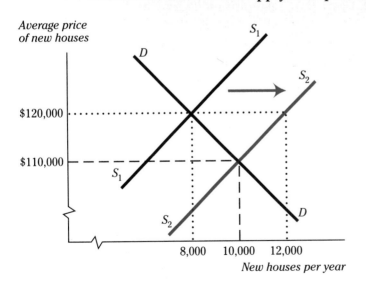

An increase in the supply of new houses will cause the equilibrium price of new homes to fall.

The Impact of Simultaneous Changes in Demand and Supply

All the price changes we have explored so far have resulted from a single cause: either a change in demand while supply remained constant, or a change in supply while demand remained constant. But in many real-world situations simultaneous changes occur in demand and supply. Let's consider two examples in the housing market. In the first case we find an area undergoing a population expansion (a source of increased demand for new houses) at the same time that building-material costs are rising (causing a decrease in supply). In the second case a period of high unemployment is causing the incomes of area residents to decline (less demand for new houses), while new production methods are reducing the cost of new-home construction (increased supply).

In these two examples the forces of demand and supply are pulling in opposite directions—the demand curve is shifting one way while the supply curve is shifting the other. Under these conditions it is relatively easy to determine what will happen to the equilibrium price. In the first example demand increases while supply decreases, so the equilibrium price tends to rise. In the second example demand decreases while supply increases, so the equilibrium price tends to fall. Take a minute to draw the diagrams and convince yourself of these results.

Predicting the impact of simultaneous changes in demand and supply becomes a little trickier when both the demand curve and the supply curve are shifting in the same direction. As you can see from Exh. 3.14, when demand and supply are both increasing, the effect on price depends on how much demand increases relative to supply. If demand and supply increase by the same amounts, equilibrium price will not change. If demand increases more than supply, equilibrium price will rise. If supply increases more than demand, equilibrium price will fall. (See if you can predict what would happen to price if demand and supply both *decreased* by the same amount, if demand decreased more than supply, and if supply decreased more than demand.)

In summary, the price of a product can change because of a change in demand, a change in supply, or simultaneous changes in demand and supply. In all cases the basic principle is the same: Whenever demand increases in relation to supply, the equilibrium price will rise; whenever supply increases in relation to demand, the equilibrium price will fall. By keeping that principle in mind, we can predict what is going to happen to the price of cattle or wheat or any other product whose price is determined in a competitive market. Read "U.S. Aluminum Makers Hit Downside of Going Global," on page 92, and try to explain why aluminum prices have fallen in spite of rising U.S. demand.

U.S. Aluminum Makers Hit Downside of Going Global

American aluminum producers built an empire across the world even before "going global" became popular. But these days, this pioneering industry is feeling a bit homesick.

As other U.S. industries roar back to health, the aluminum business is entering the third year of its deepest slump ever, with little prospect for much improvement in 1993. With real aluminum prices at their lowest in history, virtually all major producers have dipped into the red. . . .

The worst part is that, because of the industry's international nature, the North Americans are largely powerless to fix the problem. Despite record shipments in the U.S., weak economies in Europe and Japan and a surge in exports from the former Soviet Union are depressing prices on world markets, which dictate U.S. prices.

"We're doing whatever we can to compete against the rest of the world, and it's an uphill fight," says Emmett Boyle, chief executive of Oralco Inc., a Wheeling, W.Va., aluminum company. "The United States has already taken a tremendous

beating." Mr. Boyle says the U.S. has shut down 10 of its 32 aluminum smelters in the last 15 years and sold technology to foreign producers that benefit from lower energy and labor costs.

While American companies in many industries, from chemicals to consumer products, have been affected recently by troubles overseas, aluminum makers have a bigger problem because they have more international exposure. Alcoa had 40'% of its sales and 43% of its identifiable assets in foreign lands in 1992. The percentages for Reynolds Metals were 25% and 36%.

And while more parochial industries such as American steel have been able to ratchet up prices domestically in part because of protection from foreign steel, aluminum makers have no such luxury. Since 1978, aluminum prices have been set on the London Metal Exchange, putting U.S. producers at the whim of overseas traders. . . .

Rising U.S. Demand

U.S. aluminum demand was actually up some 10% last year and continues to climb to record levels, as

American producers gain market share in new products. At the same time, U.S. production will drop about 8.5% this year, Lehman Brothers analyst Thomas M. Van Leeuwen predicts, because of cutbacks forced by drought in the Pacific Northwest.

That should mean higher prices for U.S. producers—but it doesn't. While U.S. producers cut production, output is rising in Canada, Europe and the Middle East. And because of slack demand in Japan and Europe, world-wide aluminum growth is flat. As a result, Mr. Van Leeuwen says, "This industry is up to its eyeballs in inventory.". . .

Aggravating the situation is the flow of metal from the former Soviet Union. Because of deflated demand at home and a need for cash to prop up the economy, these countries, beginning in late 1990, have boosted exports from under 300,000 tons annually to some 1.2 million tons—equivalent to 8% of Western production. . . .

"Collective Lunacy"

At the same time, Western European producers have shown little appetite for cutbacks. Unprofitable, state-owned producers such as Italy's Aluminio SpA and Spain's Aluminio Espanol SA and Inespal continue to pump out metal. The Norwegian producer, Norsk Hydro, has returned to its previous output after calling for cutbacks.

Stewart Spector, an analyst who writes the Spector Report, calls the situation "collective lunacy." Virtually every smelter in the world lost money in 1992, dragging down fabricated prices and dropping margins for can sheet, the industry's biggest product, near all-time lows.

Aluminum producers believe that their cost-cutting and marketing efforts will help them outlast their international troubles. In the end, they believe, most aluminum growth will come from abroad. But they have also learned the perils of going global. "The U.S. industry didn't understand [international developments] would keep hitting us with problems one after another," Reynolds's Mr. O'Carroll says. "The international nature of the business makes the entire cycle more volatile."

—*Dana Milbank*

SOURCE : Dana Milbank, "U.S. Aluminum Makers Hit Downside of Going Global," March 22, 1993. Reprinted by permission of *The Wall Street Journal*, ©1993 Dow Jones & Co., Inc. All Rights Reserved Worldwide.

Use Your Economic Reasoning

1. According to the article, the U.S. demand for aluminum has been increasing and "continues to climb to record levels." Why, then, is the price of aluminum falling? Graph this result and explain your graph.

2. How would you expect weak economies in Europe and Japan to affect the price of aluminum? What impact would the "surge in exports" from the former Soviet Union have on price?

3. Suppose that the U.S. market were protected by trade barriers that prevented foreign aluminum from entering the country. What would be happening to the price of aluminum in the United States and why? Show graphically.

4. Congress is continually being lobbied to erect trade barriers to keep out foreign products. What impact would such barriers have on the prices we pay for products such as aluminum?

EXHIBIT 3.14

**Effect of Simultaneous Increases in Demand
and Supply on Equilibrium Price**

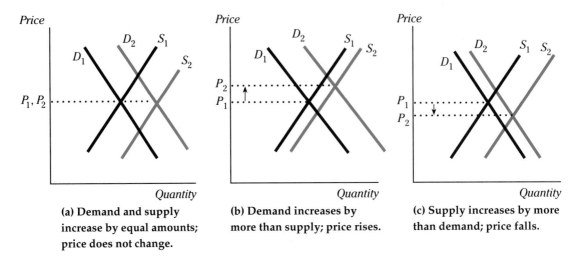

(a) Demand and supply
increase by equal amounts;
price does not change.

(b) Demand increases by
more than supply; price rises.

(c) Supply increases by more
than demand; price falls.

Intervention in Price Determination: Supports and Ceilings

Sometimes the prices that result from the interaction of demand and supply may cause hardship for producers or consumers and therefore be perceived as "unfair" by the injured group. Producers may feel that prevailing market prices are too low to provide them with adequate incomes. Consumers may believe that market prices are too high and thus place an unreasonable burden on households—particularly low-income households. To protect their various interests, both consumers and producers form pressure groups and lobby the government to intervene in the process of price determination. Agricultural price supports, minimum-wage laws, interest-rate ceilings, and rent controls are just a few examples that illustrate the success of these campaigns.

Price Supports

Government usually intervenes in pricing by establishing maximum or minimum prices. A **price support** is a legally established minimum price above the

EXHIBIT 3.15

Price Supports and Surpluses

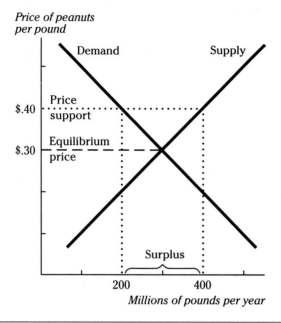

Price of peanuts per pound

Millions of pounds per year

equilibrium price.[1] In the 1930s, for example, the federal government initiated a program of agricultural price supports designed to raise the income of farmers. Under this program the government "supports" the price of the product by agreeing to purchase, at the legally established price, whatever output the farmer is unable to sell at that price.

Exhibit 3.15 shows a hypothetical situation in which the government has established a price support (or support price) for peanuts at $.40, ten cents above the equilibrium price of $.30 per pound. At $.40 a pound customers are willing to purchase only 200 million pounds a year, but producers are eager to supply 400 million pounds. We know that in a free or unregulated market, sellers of peanuts would deal with the surplus of 200 million pounds by cutting prices down to the equilibrium level of $.30, at which the equilibrium quantity of 300 million pounds would be supplied. However, once the gov-

---

[1] When established, price supports are usually above the equilibrium price. However, over time the equilibrium price may rise above the support level, causing the price support to become ineffective. For instance, at $4.25 an hour, the minimum wage (a form of support price) is probably below the equilibrium wage for unskilled labor in most parts of the country.

ernment establishes a price support of $.40, the market remains in disequilibrium, with surpluses continuing to accumulate. The government is then required to buy these surplus peanuts, store them, and dispose of them, all at the expense of taxpayers. It usually distributes part of the surplus through such enterprises as supplying peanut butter, cheese, and other commodities to school lunch programs and food pantries that aid low-income families.

Similar problems occur with other price-support programs—the minimum wage, for example. By law most employers are required to pay their employees at least the government-established minimum wage ($4.25 an hour in 1994). Because this wage is generally above the equilibrium wage for unskilled labor, there are more people willing to work at that wage than employers are willing to hire at that wage. Of course, those who can find jobs are better off because of the minimum wage. But some unskilled workers who would have been able to find jobs at the equilibrium wage will be unemployed at the minimum wage; this occurs because employers simply do not believe that these workers will be able to contribute enough to the production process to justify that high a wage. Just as the support price for peanuts created a surplus of that product, the minimum wage creates a surplus of workers. To the extent that the minimum wage increases unemployment, it conflicts with our objective of raising the incomes of low-income Americans.

Price Ceilings

Government may also intervene in the pricing process when it is convinced that prevailing prices are either too high or are increasing too rapidly. In such cases the government will set **price ceilings,** maximum prices that are established below the equilibrium price. During World War II, for example, price ceilings were placed on most nonfarm prices in order to prevent them from being pushed to exorbitant levels by the demands of the war effort. Price ceilings (or ceiling prices) also have been used during peacetime as a technique both for combating inflation (a general rise in the level of prices) and for controlling specific prices. For instance, in 1971 President Nixon "froze" virtually all wages and prices for a period of 90 days in an attempt to slow the rate of inflation. In the same decade, the federal government used price ceilings selectively to limit the prices of beef, pork, gasoline, and natural gas, among other products.

Because price ceilings are designed to hold prices below equilibrium, they tend to produce shortages. Consider, for example, the problems that result when interest rates are restricted to artificially low levels. Until 1982 the state of Arkansas did not permit lenders to charge more than 10 percent interest on loans to consumers. Although interest-rate ceilings may seem to be in the best interest of consumers, they frequently create problems for borrowers. Because the interest rate is fixed at an artificially low level, more people will want to

EXHIBIT 3.16

Price Ceilings and Shortages

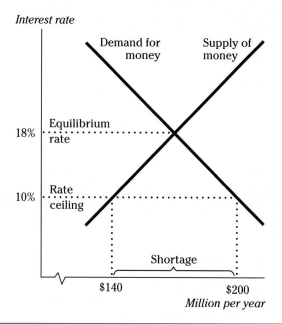

A price ceiling will tend to produce a shortage, since price is legally fixed below the equilibrium level. In this example an interest-rate ceiling of 10 percent leads to a shortage of $60 million in loans.

borrow money than would desire to do so at the equilibrium rate. In addition, the low rate will make consumer loans less attractive to lenders, who consequently will make available less money than they would provide at the equilibrium rate. The result will be a number of unsatisfied customers, some of whom may borrow from loan sharks—individuals who violate the law by lending money at interest rates above the ceiling.

Exhibit 3.16 illustrates the plight of the Arkansas consumer prior to 1982. As you can see from the diagram, 18 percent is the interest rate at which the amount of money consumers are willing to borrow is exactly equal to the quantity lenders are willing to make available. When the interest rate is held below this equilibrium level, problems occur. At the 10 percent ceiling rate consumers want to borrow $200 million a year, but lenders are willing to loan only $140 million. There is a shortage of $60 million in loans.[2]

---

[2] The 10 percent interest-rate ceiling was repealed in November 1982 but was replaced by a floating interest-rate ceiling that permits lenders to charge no more than 5 percent above the discount rate determined by the Federal Reserve, the agency that regulates the nation's money supply. Although the new ceiling is more flexible, it continues to discourage lenders from making certain loans—particularly loans to less credit-worthy customers. Thus the floating interest-rate ceiling probably reduces the magnitude of the loan shortage but does not eliminate it.

A Model for Destroying a City

Next week marks the 50th anniversary of the passage of the Emergency Wartime Residential Rent Control Act. Designed to prevent transient, well-paid, wartime workers from outbidding local residents for apartments in industrial cities, the law was eventually extended to New York City—which had few wartime industries and reasonably high vacancy rates.

After the war, rent controls were abandoned everywhere except New York, where they have been extended by state law ever since. During the inflationary 1970s, a second wave of rent control ordinances captured Boston, Cambridge, and Brookline, Mass.; Newark; much of suburban Long Island and New Jersey; Washington; and more than half the population of California. Today more than 200 cities, containing about a fifth of the rental units in the country, are under rent control. The results have been disastrous. . . .

Dilapidated Housing

Today, most New Yorkers have become accustomed to the idea that finding an apartment requires Eastern European-style guile and duplicity. A few years ago, New York magazine recommended "joining a church or synagogue" as a good way of meeting people who might provide leads on a new apartment.

After 50 years of rent control, New York, which once had arguably the most beautiful housing stock in the world, now has the most dilapidated housing in America. Beautiful brownstones from the turn of the century now stand shuttered with window decals that feature drawings of curtains and flowerpots, designed to make it *appear* that someone is living in them. Over 70% of central Harlem has been taken for back taxes. . . .

What has happened is fairly predictable from economic theory, which forecasts supply shortages, disinvestment and deterioration of the product when price controls go into effect. What has been less explored is the "nomenklatura" phenomenon—the emergence of an elite capable of turning the regulations to its advantage.

Although rent control is always advertised as "helping the poor," the rich and well-connected have been the clear winners. In New York, rents in Harlem and the outer boroughs are at market levels, while all the "great deals" are on the Upper East Side, the Upper West Side and Greenwich Village—home of the cultural and financial elite.

Such luminaries as Deputy Mayor Barbara Fife, City Council President, Ruth Messinger, former Mayor Ed Koch, James Levine, music director of the Metropolitan Opera, Alistair Cooke and ballerina Suzanne Farrell have all spent years benefiting from rent control.

The same pattern is beginning to emerge in other cities that adopted rent control during the "second wave" of the 1970s. In recent months, independent studies in Cambridge, Mass., and Berkeley, Calif., have found that the major benefits of rent control have gone to upper-income professionals who use their mastery of the bureaucracy and their superior networks of friends and connections to exploit the system.

In Cambridge, Rolf Goetze, a highly respected housing consultant, compiled statistics on residents' age and occupation from the city's 71,000-person voter registration records. He then compared the characteristics of tenants in rent-controlled housing with those of tenants and homeowners in the uncontrolled sector.

Despite the tendency of high-income people to own

their own homes, Mr. Goetze found rent-controlled apartments to be more densely populated with professional people in their prime earning years. Over 52% of rent-controlled tenants are age 30 to 49, compared with 34.4% in the noncontrolled sector. Senior citizens make up only 7.7% of the rent-controlled sector but 16.6% in unregulated housing. Also underrepresented in rent-controlled apartments are young people, age 18 to 29, who are 32.3% of the unregulated population but only 24.5% of those in controlled housing. . . .

"The largest concentration of people in rent-controlled apartments seems to be white-collar professionals in their 30s and 40s," says Mr. Goetze. "Rent-controlled units are not concentrated in any particular neighborhood. It's just that, wherever they are, professional people seem to be more skillful at ferreting them out.". . .

In Berkeley, Michael St. John, a Ph.D. in economics who has consulted for landlords for many years, is just completing a study for the Pacific Legal Foundation that reaches almost identical conclusions. "We've compared the population of Berkeley in 1980, just after rent control was instituted [1979], with the population of Berkeley today," says Mr. St. John. "It's already obvious that there has been an enormous shift toward the professional and white-collar classes. Welfare mothers form a much smaller portion of the population today, as do several other categories of older and poorer people. Berkeley probably would have gentrified anyway—the same thing has happened in neighboring towns—but rent control seems to have accelerated the process."

Revenge Backfires

Ironically, even though rent control was adopted in both Berkeley and Cambridge with the help of vast student voter populations taking revenge on their "townie" landlords, today's college students do not seem to be getting any of the benefits.

Eva Floystrup, who with her carpenter husband has owned a building in Berkeley for 20 years, still rents to the six thirtysomething professionals who came to her as Berkeley students 15 years ago. "I can't get rid of them," she says. "I have students coming up to me all the time saying, 'Why can't I find anyplace to live in Berkeley?' I tell them, 'We're still taking care of the Class of '79. If they ever leave, I'll have room for you.' "

—*William Tucker*

SOURCE: William Tucker, "A Model for Destroying a City," March 12, 1993. Reprinted by permission of *The Wall Street Journal,* © 1993 Dow Jones & Co., Inc. All Rights Reserved Worldwide.

Use Your Economic Reasoning

1. Why is it necessary to use "guile and duplicity" to find an apartment in New York City? How can this be related to rent controls?

2. The article suggests that rent controls have been responsible for the deterioration of the housing stock in New York City. Why might we expect rent controls to produce this result?

3. Because rent controls keep apartment rents below their equilibrium levels, landlords are faced with more potential renters than they can satisfy. If you were faced with 20 applicants for every vacated apartment, how would you choose among them? Why might you choose white-collar professionals rather than blue-collar workers or students?

4. The article suggests that rent controls have produced a class of people who have learned to take advantage of the system. Who is in this class and why are these people in a better position than others to profit from the system?

We know that in the market a shortage of any item, including loan money, will lead to a price increase, which signals businesses to supply more of it and consumers to demand less. A ceiling prevents the interest rate from rising to its equilibrium level, so lenders are faced with more potential borrowers than they can satisfy. Consequently they must use some secondary rationing device to decide which consumers will receive loans.

A **secondary rationing device** is a nonprice condition that supplements the primary rationing device, price. The consumer in our example must not only be willing to pay 10 percent interest to get the loan but also be able to satisfy some supplementary requirement imposed by lenders. Perhaps lenders will grant loans only on the basis of first come, first served. They may choose instead to lend money only to customers with the very best credit ratings. Or lenders may decide to make loans only to "preferred" customers. In this final situation the definition of "preferred" is seldom precise. It may mean certain customers whom the lender wants to keep; it may mean influential people whom the lender doesn't want to offend; it may include all friends of the bank president or the owner of the business. Whether the use of a secondary, nonprice rationing device is preferable to higher interest rates is a matter for you to decide. It is clear, however, that price ceilings do not eliminate the need to ration; they simply force sellers to use secondary rationing devices.

Price ceilings result in shortages in a number of markets. In New York City, for example, where ceilings on rents (rent controls) are enforced to keep rents within the reach of low-income citizens, finding an apartment is a major problem. Because rents are kept below their equilibrium level, New Yorkers face a perpetual shortage of rental housing. To some extent existing housing is rationed on a first-come, first-served basis, and would-be renters spend countless hours in vain attempts to find a vacant apartment. Some frustrated searchers resort to checking obituaries in hope of zeroing in on a newly available rental before anyone else hears of it. Others make secret payments to landlords for the privilege of a new lease. Low rents not only produce a shortage but also prevent the supply of housing from expanding. In fact landlords may allow some rental units to deteriorate. If rental income cannot rise, owners cannot profit from money spent on improvements or even break even on money invested in maintenance. In summary, although rent controls succeed in maintaining low rents for those lucky enough to find apartments, they create shortages and prevent expansion, problems that would be eliminated if rents were allowed to rise to their equilibrium level. See "A Model for Destroying a City," on page 98, to learn why rent control may help the rich and well connected rather than the poor.

Economic Efficiency and the Role of Prices

The automatic response of price changes to changes in demand and supply conditions is an important feature of a market economy. As increasing consumer demand pushes the price of a product upward, the higher price rations some consumers out of the market and simultaneously signals and motivates producers to expand their production of the product. Because these producers are receiving a higher price for their product, they will be able to outbid producers of less-valued items for the resources needed to expand production. In this way price changes help to ensure that businesses produce the goods and services that consumers value the most, in the quantities they desire.

Price changes also help ensure that each product is produced with as few of society's scarce resources as possible. As a particular resource becomes scarcer (due to increased demand or reduced supply), its price tends to rise. This higher cost encourages producers to economize on its use by substituting cheaper resources whenever possible. The end result is the efficient use of society's scarce resources: Producers supply the most-wanted products in the least-costly way in terms of scarce resources.[3] The way that competitive markets promote the efficient use of resources is explored in greater detail in Chapter 5. Later chapters examine how such factors as inadequate competition and the ability of firms to ignore the "cost" of the pollution they create can interfere with the ability of markets to achieve this optimal result.

Summary

In a competitive market prices are determined by the interaction of demand and supply. *Demand* is a schedule showing the quantities of a good or service that consumers are willing and able to purchase at various prices during some given time period, when all factors other than the product's price remain unchanged. Demand may be represented graphically in a *demand curve*, which slopes downward and to the right because the *law of demand* holds that consumers will purchase more of a product at a lower price than at a higher price. *Supply* is a schedule showing the quantities of a good or service that producers are willing and able to offer for sale at various prices during a given time

---

[3] Note that the fewer the resources an economy needs to produce each product, the more goods and services it can produce with its limited resource stock. Thus an economy that is operating efficiently is producing the goods and services that consumers value the most *and* producing as many of those goods and sevices as possible from the society's scarce resources.

period when all factors other than the product's price remain unchanged. Supply may be represented graphically as a *supply curve.* The supply curve slopes upward and to the right because the *law of supply* states that price and quantity supplied are positively related; that is, a greater quantity will be supplied at higher prices than at lower prices.

The demand curve will shift to a new position if there is a change in any of the *determinants of demand:* consumer income, tastes and preferences, expectations regarding future prices, the prices of substitute and complementary goods, and the number of consumers in the market. By the same token, the supply curve will shift if there is a change in one or more of the *determinants of supply:* technology, the prices of resources, or the number of producers in the market.

Economists are careful to distinguish between a change in the quantity demanded and a change in demand. A change in the amount purchased due to a change in the price of the product, while other factors are held constant, is a *change in the quantity demanded* and is represented by movement up or down a stationary demand curve. A change in any of the determinants of demand, while price is held constant, will cause consumers to purchase more or less of a product at each possible price. This is described as a *change in demand* and is represented by a shift of the entire demand curve to the right (in the case of increased demand) or to the left (in the case of decreased demand).

A similar distinction is necessary on the supply side of the market. A *change in the quantity supplied* results from a change in the price of the product and is represented graphically by a movement along a stationary supply curve. A *change in supply* results from a change in one of the determinants of supply and is represented by a shift of the entire supply curve to a new position.

The *equilibrium price* is the price that brings about an equality between the quantity demanded and the quantity supplied, which we call the *equilibrium quantity.* The equilibrium price can be identified by the intersection of the demand and supply curves. If the prevailing price is above equilibrium, a *surplus*—an excess of quantity supplied over quantity demanded—will occur, and sellers will be forced to reduce price to eliminate the surplus. If the prevailing price is below equilibrium, a *shortage*—an excess of quantity demanded over quantity supplied—occurs, and buyers will bid up the price as they compete for the product. Only when the existing price is at the equilibrium level will there be neither a shortage nor a surplus and no pressure for price to change.

Prices perform three important functions: They (1) *ration,* or divide, the limited amount of available output among possible buyers; (2) *signal* producers about how much to supply; and (3) *motivate* producers to supply the desired quantity. Higher prices ration by discouraging consumers from purchasing a product; they also signal and motivate producers to increase the quantity supplied. Lower prices have the opposite effect. They encourage consumers to purchase more of the product and simultaneously signal and motivate producers to reduce the quantity supplied. The equilibrium price succeeds in matching the quantity demanded with the quantity supplied because it balances the desires of consumers and producers. Every consumer who values the product enough to pay the equilibrium price will have it, and every producer that is willing to supply the product at that price will be able to sell its entire output.

In the absence of artificial restrictions, prices will rise and fall in response to changes in demand and supply. Whenever demand increases in relation to supply, the equilibrium price will tend to rise; whenever supply increases in relation to demand, the equilibrium price will fall. These price changes help to ensure that producers not only supply the goods and services consumers value the most but also use as few scarce resources as possible in the production of those goods and services.

Price supports (minimum prices above the equilibrium price) and *price ceilings* (maximum prices below the equilibrium price) prevent price from reaching its equilibrium level in the market. Because these restrictions interfere with the rationing and signaling functions of price, they give rise to surpluses (supports) and shortages (ceilings). Price ceilings also create the need for *secondary rationing devices*—nonprice conditions that supplement the primary rationing device, price.

Glossary

Change in demand. An increase or decrease in the quantity demanded at each possible price, caused by a change in the determinants of demand; represented graphically by a shift of the entire demand curve to a new position.

Change in quantity demanded. An increase or decrease in the amount of a product demanded as a result of a change in its price, with factors other than price held constant; represented graphically by movement along a stationary demand curve.

Change in quantity supplied. An increase or decrease in the amount of a product supplied as a result of a change in its price, with factors other than price held constant; represented graphically by movement along a stationary supply curve.

Change in supply. An increase or decrease in the amount of a product supplied at each and every price, caused by a change in the determinants of supply; represented graphically by a shift of the entire supply curve.

Complement. A product that is normally purchased along with another good or in conjunction with another good.

Demand. A schedule showing the quantities of a good or service that consumers are willing and able to purchase at various prices during a given time period, when all factors other than the product's price remain unchanged.

Demand curve. A graphical representation of demand, showing the quantities of a good or service that consumers are willing and able to purchase at various prices during a given time period, ceteris paribus.

Determinants of demand. The factors that underlie the demand schedule and determine the precise position of the demand curve: income, tastes and preferences, expectations regarding prices, and the prices of related goods.

Determinants of supply. The factors that underlie the supply schedule and determine the precise position of the supply curve: technology, resource prices, and number of producers in the market.

Equilibrium price. The price that brings about an equality between the quantity demanded and the quantity supplied.

Equilibrium quantity. The quantity demanded and supplied at the equilibrium price.

Income effect. Consumer ability to purchase greater quantities of a product that has declined in price.

Inferior good. A product for which demand decreases as income increases and increases as income decreases.

Law of demand. The quantity demanded of a product is negatively, or inversely, related to its price. Consumers will purchase more of a product at lower prices than at higher prices.

Law of supply. The quantity supplied of a product is positively, or directly, related to its price. Producers will supply a larger quantity at higher prices than at lower prices.

Motivating. The function of providing incentives to supply the proper quantities of demanded products.

Normal good. A product for which demand either increases as income increases or decreases as income decreases.

Price ceiling. A legally established maximum price below the equilibrium price.

Price support. A legally established minimum price above the equilibrium price.

> *Rationing.* The function of dividing up or allocating a society's scarce items among those who want them.
>
> *Secondary rationing device.* A nonprice condition that supplements the primary rationing device, price.
>
> *Shortage.* An excess of quantity demanded over quantity supplied.
>
> *Signaling.* The function of providing information to producers about how much to supply.
>
> *Substitute.* A product that can be used in place of some other product because to a greater or lesser extent it satisfies the same consumer wants.
>
> *Substitution effect.* Consumers' willingness to substitute for other products the product that has declined in price.
>
> *Supply.* A schedule showing the quantities of a good or service that producers are willing and able to offer for sale at various prices during a given time period, when all factors other than the product's price remain unchanged.
>
> *Supply curve.* A graphical representation of supply.
>
> *Surplus.* An excess of quantity supplied over quantity demanded.
>
> *Technology.* The state of knowledge about how to produce products.
>
> *Technological advance.* The discovery of a better way to produce a product, a method that uses fewer resources to produce each unit of output or that produces more output from a given amount of resources.

Study Questions

Fill in the Blanks

1. If the entire demand curve shifts to a new position, we describe this as a change in _____.

2. If a product is a normal good, an increase in income will cause the demand curve for a product to shift to the _____.

3. Movement along a stationary supply curve due to a change in price is called a change in _____.

4. The function of dividing up or allocating scarce items among those who desire to receive them is called _____.

5. The price that exactly clears the market is called the _____ price.

6. Whenever the prevailing price is above equilibrium, a _____ will exist.

7. Prices perform three important functions: They ration scarce items among the consumers who desire to receive them; they _____ producers about the proper quantity to produce; and they _____ producers to supply that quantity.

8. If supply rises and demand declines, we would expect the equilibrium price to _____.

9. If supply increases more than demand, the equilibrium price will _____ _____.

10. We would expect a price ceiling to lead to a _____.

Multiple Choice

1. If the price of automobiles increases and all other factors remain unchanged, it will be reasonable to expect
   a) an increase in the demand for automobiles.
   b) a decrease in the demand for automobiles.
   c) an increase in the quantity of automobiles demanded.
   d) a decrease in the quantity of automobiles demanded.

2. If the demand curve for Heavy Beer shifts to the left, this could be due to
   a) an increase in the price of Heavy Beer.
   b) an increase in consumer income.
   c) an increase in the price of other beers.
   d) a shift in tastes and preferences to light beers.

3. An increase in the price of apples is likely to cause
   a) a decrease in the demand for apples.
   b) an increase in the quantity demanded of apples.
   c) an increase in the demand for other types of fruit.
   d) an increase in the quantity demanded of other types of fruit.

4. If the price of black walnuts increases and other factors remain unchanged, it is reasonable to expect
   a) an increase in the quantity supplied.
   b) a decrease in the quantity supplied.
   c) an increase in supply.
   d) a decrease in supply.

5. A new labor settlement that increases a firm's costs will probably cause
   a) a decrease in supply.
   b) an increase in supply.
   c) a reduction in the quantity supplied.
   d) the supply curve to shift to the right.

6. If grasshoppers destroy half of the wheat crop, the result will be
   a) a decrease in the quantity supplied.
   b) a rightward shift of the wheat supply curve.
   c) a leftward shift of the wheat supply curve.
   d) None of the above

7. If demand increases and supply declines,
   a) the equilibrium price and quantity will both increase.
   b) the equilibrium price will rise, but the quantity will fall.
   c) the equilibrium price will fall, but the quantity will rise.
   d) the equilibrium price and quantity will both fall.
   e) the equilibrium price will rise; quantity will be indeterminate.

8. If the U.S. government were to artificially restrict the price of beef below the equilibrium level, the result would be
   a) a shortage.
   b) a surplus.
   c) an excess of quantity supplied over quantity demanded.
   d) None of the above

9. If the demand for used cars declines, the likely result will be
   a) a reduction in equilibrium price.
   b) an increase in equilibrium price.
   c) an increase in the supply of used cars.
   d) no change in equilibrium price.

10. If the price of cattle feed increases, the result will probably be
    a) an increase in the supply of cattle and lower cattle prices.
    b) a decrease in the supply of cattle and higher cattle prices.
    c) an increase in the demand for cattle and higher cattle prices.
    d) a decrease in the demand for cattle and lower cattle prices.

11. If a shortage exists, it indicates that the existing price is
    a) the equilibrium price.
    b) below the equilibrium price.
    c) above the equilibrium price.

12. If the price of coffee increases, the probable result will be
    a) a decrease in the demand for coffee.
    b) a decrease in the price of substitutes for coffee.
    c) an increase in the price of substitutes for coffee.
    d) a decrease in the supply of coffee.

13. Which of the following statements is *incorrect*?
    a) If demand increases and supply remains constant, the equilibrium price will rise.
    b) If supply rises and demand remains constant, the equilibrium price will fall.
    c) If demand rises and supply falls, the equilibrium price will rise.
    d) If supply increases and demand decreases, the equilibrium price will rise.

14. If additional farmers enter the hog-producing industry, the result will be
    a) lower prices but a higher equilibrium quantity.
    b) higher prices but a lower equilibrium quantity.
    c) lower prices but the same equilibrium quantity.
    d) lower prices and a lower equilibrium quantity.

15. If the supply of cattle is increasing more rapidly than the demand,
    a) cattle prices will rise.
    b) cattle prices will fall.
    c) cattle prices will not change.
    d) any of the above is possible.

Problems and Questions for Discussion

1. My eldest daughter says that she really "needs" a new sweatshirt, but she won't use her allowance to buy it. ("I don't need it *that* badly.") How can a "need" evaporate like that? What is the difference between "need" and "demand"?

2. Podunk College experienced a substantial drop in enrollment last year. As an economist, what possible explanations can you offer for what happened? Try to list all possibilities.

3. Why does the supply curve slope upward and to the right? In other words why will producers supply a higher quantity at higher prices?

4. Which of the following events would cause movement along a stationary supply curve for wheat, and which would cause the supply curve to shift? Explain each situation from the producer's point of view.
    a) The price of wheat declines.
    b) The cost of fertilizer rises.
    c) Wheat blight destroys half the wheat crop.
    d) New combines make it possible for one person to do the work of three.

5. Explain the economic reasoning behind the following newspaper headlines: *decrease in supply, increase in demand*
   a) "Weather Slows Fishing: Seafood Prices Double"
   b) "Sugar: Crisis of Plenty" *excess of supply, prices will decrease*
   c) "Minimum Wage Costs Jobs" *Increased wage employer less likely to hire*
   d) "Bountiful Wheat Crop Is Hurting Growers"
      excess of supply drives price down if steady demand

6. If the supply of oranges in a competitive market decreases due to severe weather, will there be a shortage of oranges? Why or why not? (*Hint:* Use graphs to help answer this question.)

7. Suppose that your local tennis courts are very crowded and your city is considering charging a fee to ration their use. Who would like to have a fee charged? Would only wealthy individuals feel this way? Why might someone be in favor of a fee?

8. People, including news reporters, often use the terms "supply" and "demand" incorrectly. For example, you will often read that "supply exceeds demand" or "demand exceeds supply." What is wrong with these statements? What does the writer probably mean to say?

9. Why is it important that prices in a market economy be allowed to change in response to changing demand and supply conditions? What functions do these changing prices perform? *Market balance*

10. Assume that consumers are buying equal numbers of hamburgers and hot dogs when these products are selling at the same price. If the supply of hamburger declines, what will happen to the price of hamburgers? What about the price of hot dogs? Graph your conclusions.

Answer Key

Fill in the Blanks

1. demand	5. equilibrium	8. fall
2. right	6. surplus	9. fall
3. quantity supplied	7. signal (or inform); motivate	10. shortage
4. rationing		

Multiple Choice

1. d	4. a	7. e	10. b	13. d
2. d	5. a	8. a	11. b	14. a
3. c	6. c	9. a	12. c	15. b

CHAPTER 4

The Elasticity of Demand and Supply

1. Define price elasticity of demand.
2. Compute and interpret the coefficient of demand elasticity.
3. Describe the degrees of price elasticity.
4. Explain the relationship between the price elasticity of demand and the total revenue received by a firm.
5. Identify the factors that influence the price elasticity of demand.
6. Define the price elasticity of supply.
7. Compute and interpret the coefficient of supply elasticity.
8. Describe the relationship between time and the price elasticity of supply.

In Chapter 3 we considered how demand and supply interact to determine prices, and we discovered how changes in demand or supply cause prices to change. In this chapter we investigate the degree of consumer and producer responsiveness to increases or decreases in prices. Economists refer to this degree of responsiveness as the price "elasticity." As you will see, the concept of price elasticity is extremely important and has many applications in the world around you.

Elasticity of Demand

The law of demand tells producers that if they raise their prices, consumers will buy less and that if producers lower their prices, consumers will buy more. But the law of demand doesn't tell them anything about the size of the response to a given change in price. If a professional football team decides to raise the price of season tickets by $50, how many fewer tickets will fans buy? If a local health club doubles its rates, how many customers will it lose? To answer these questions, we need some knowledge of how responsive consumers are to changes in the price of a particular product—we need to know something about the price elasticity of demand.

The **price elasticity of demand** is a measure of the responsiveness of the quantity demanded of a product to a change in its price. If the quantity demanded expands or contracts a great deal in response to a price change, demand is said to be very responsive or *"elastic"*; if the quantity demanded doesn't change very much, demand is described as not very responsive or *"inelastic."*

In gauging the responsiveness of consumers, the absolute size of the changes in price and quantity is not very meaningful. Suppose that a $5 price reduction causes consumers to demand an additional 1,000 units of some product. Should we describe the demand for this product as elastic or inelastic? We can't tell unless we know the starting point, the initial price and quantity. To illustrate, suppose the firm had cut price from $10 to $5 and this price reduction caused the quantity demanded to increase from 100,000 units to 101,000 units. Would you describe demand as elastic (very responsive to the price change) under those conditions? Probably not; a 50 percent price reduction only led to a 1 percent increase in the quantity demanded! But if the price reduction had been from $100 to $95 (the same $5, but in this case only 5 percent of the original price) and the increase in quantity demanded had been from 1,000 to 2,000 units (a 100 percent increase), you would probably agree that consumers were quite responsive to the change in price; demand is elastic.

The point is that when we describe the responsiveness of consumers we need to think in terms of percentages—the percent change in price and the percent change in the quantity demanded. This approach adjusts for the initial prices and quantities and gives us a much more meaningful comparison.

The Coefficient of Demand Elasticity

We can measure the degree of elasticity or inelasticity by calculating a value called the **coefficient of demand elasticity.** We compute the coefficient of elasticity by dividing the percentage change in quantity demanded by the percentage change in price:

$$\text{Coefficient of elasticity} = \frac{\dfrac{\Delta Q}{Q}}{\dfrac{\Delta P}{P}} = \frac{\text{Percentage change in quantity demanded}}{\text{Percentage change in price}}.$$

In this formula for the coefficient, Q stands for quantity, P stands for price, and the Greek letter delta (Δ) stands for "change in." $\Delta Q/Q$ is the percentage change in quantity demanded, and $\Delta P/P$ is the percentage change in price.

Let's apply this formula to the elasticity of demand for Fantastic Cola after a price hike. We'll say that after the price per six-pack rises from $2.50 to $3.00, weekly sales decline from 1,000 six-packs to 900. What is the price elasticity of demand for Fantastic Cola? If the change in quantity demanded (ΔQ) is 100 fewer six-packs per week and the original quantity demanded (Q) is 1,000 six-packs, the percentage change in quantity demanded ($-100/1,000$) is -10 percent. And if the change in price (ΔP) is 50 cents and the original price (P) is $2.50, the percentage change in price ($\$.50/\$2.50$) is 20 percent. If we divide the 10 percent reduction in quantity by the 20 percent increase in price, we arrive at an elasticity coefficient of -0.5.[1]

$$\text{Coefficient of elasticity} = \frac{\dfrac{-100}{1000}}{\dfrac{\$0.50}{\$2.50}} = \frac{-10\%}{20\%} = -0.5.$$

An elasticity coefficient of 0.5 means that for every 1 percent change in price, the quantity demanded will change by 0.5 percent. Thus if the price of Fantastic Cola goes up by 10 percent, we would expect a 5 percent reduction in the quantity demanded. If it increases by 20 percent, we would expect a 10 per-

---

[1] The simple formula we are using to compute the elasticity coefficient produces somewhat ambiguous results. If the sellers of Fantastic Cola raise the price from $2.50 to $3.00, the value of the elasticity coefficient is 0.5. But if the sellers lower their price from $3.00 to $2.50, the coefficient will be 0.67, because the initial price and quantity are different.

Economic theory does not suggest any reason why these two coefficients should be different, so we might argue that they should be the same. This can be accomplished by using the average of the two prices and the average of the two quantities as the base values for computing percentages. When this approach is used, the value of the coefficient will be the same regardless of whether the initial price is the higher price or the lower price. In the Fantastic Cola example the value of the elasticity coefficient would be 0.58. In the modified formula below, we add the two quantities, Q_1 and Q_2, and divide by 2 to arrive at the average quantity. Average price is determined the same way.

$$\frac{\Delta Q/[(Q_1 + Q_2)/2]}{\Delta P/[(P_1 + P_2)/2]} = \frac{100/(1,900/2)}{\$0.50/(\$5.50/2)} = \frac{100/950}{\$0.50/\$2.75} = \frac{10.5\%}{18.2\%} = 0.58.$$

cent reduction in quantity demanded. However, if the elasticity coefficient were 2.0 instead of 0.5, each 1 percent change in price would cause a 2 percent change in quantity demanded. For example, a 10 percent increase in price would cause a 20 percent decrease in quantity demanded.

You will note that in our formula the elasticity coefficient (-0.5) carries a negative sign. We know from the law of demand that changes in price normally cause the quantity demanded to change in the opposite direction. Thus price increases cause reductions in the quantity demanded, whereas price reductions cause increases in the quantity demanded. In either case the sign is negative and is usually ignored in referring to price elasticity values.

Degrees of Elasticity

Economists use the coefficient of elasticity to define precisely the terms elastic and inelastic. *Elastic* demand exists when the coefficient of elasticity is greater than one, when a given percentage change in price brings about a larger percentage change in the quantity demanded. When the elasticity coefficient is less than one, demand is *inelastic*; a given percentage change in price brings about a smaller percentage change in the quantity demanded. If the coefficient is exactly one, *unitary elasticity* prevails; a given percentage change in price results in an identical percentage change in quantity demanded. The elasticity coefficient can vary from zero to infinity, where zero represents the least elastic demand imaginable, and infinity represents the most elastic demand imaginable.

If the coefficient of elasticity were zero, a change in price would bring no change at all in the quantity demanded. Demand would be described as *perfectly inelastic*, and the demand curve would be a vertical straight line. For example, over some range of prices the demand for lifesaving drugs, such as insulin, may be perfectly inelastic. Another example would be the demand for dialysis treatment by those suffering from kidney failure.

If the coefficient of elasticity approached infinity, a very small change in price would lead to an enormous change in the quantity demanded. Demand would be described as *perfectly elastic* and would be graphed as a horizontal straight line. Perfectly inelastic and perfectly elastic demand curves are depicted in Exh. 4.1. The individual apple farmer faces a situation that illustrates perfectly elastic demand. If the market price of apples is $10 a bushel, the farmer can sell as much as desired at that price. But a farmer who attempts to charge more than $10 will sell nothing; consumers will simply buy their apples from someone else. This is the type of situation we represent with a perfectly elastic demand curve. In Chapter 5 we will have much more to say about perfectly elastic demand curves.

EXHIBIT 4.1

Perfectly Inelastic and Perfectly Elastic Demand Curves

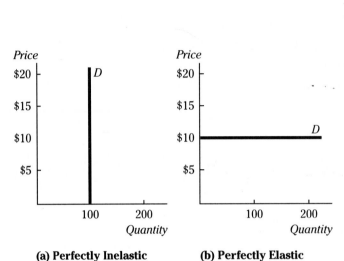

(a) Despite an increase or decrease in price, consumers buy exactly the same quantity. The demand curve for insulin may look like this over some price range. (b) A very small increase in price would cause consumers to reduce their purchases to zero. The individual apple farmer may face a demand curve like this one.

(a) Perfectly Inelastic Demand

(b) Perfectly Elastic Demand

Elasticity along a Straight-Line Demand Curve

In most instances demand curves do not show just one degree of elasticity; they show several. All linear, downward-sloping demand curves show unitary elasticity midway on the curve, with elastic demand above the midpoint and inelastic demand below it. Exhibit 4.2 depicts such a demand curve.

In Exh. 4.2 note that because the demand curve is a straight line, it has a constant inclination, or "slope." Therefore a price change of a given size will always bring the same quantity change. In this hypothetical example each $.60 drop in price brings a 60 million-gallon increase in the quantity demanded, regardless of whether we are at the upper or the lower end of the curve. (Look, for example, at what happens to the quantity demanded when price declines from $2.40 to $1.80 or from $1.80 to $1.20; in both instances quantity increases by 60 million gallons.) That would seem to suggest that consumers are equally responsive to price changes at either end of the curve. But that's not true! We have to remember that the responsiveness, or elasticity of demand, deals with percentage changes, not with absolute quantities.

If you remember that fact, you will recognize that the responsiveness of consumers changes quite dramatically as we move along this demand curve.

EXHIBIT 4.2

How Elasticity Changes along a Hypothetical Demand Curve for Gasoline

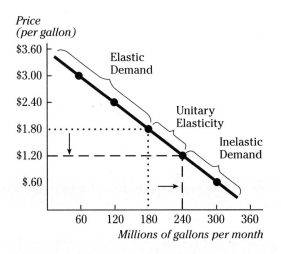

Every straight-line demand curve that is downward sloping displays unitary elasticity at its midpoint, elastic demand above it, and inelastic demand below it.

For instance, when price drops from $3.00 to $2.40 (a 20 percent decline), quantity demanded increases from 60 million to 120 million gallons (a 100 percent increase). Since the percentage change in quantity is greater than the percentage change in price, demand is elastic at this upper end of the curve. At the other end the same *absolute* changes in price and quantity represent different percentage changes and consequently produce different elasticities. For instance, when price declines from $1.20 to $.60 (a 50 percent change), the quantity demanded increases from 240 million to 300 million gallons (a 25 percent change). The coefficient of elasticity is 0.5; demand is inelastic. We want to remember, then, that the slope of a demand curve is not the same as its elasticity. A linear demand curve has a constant slope, but it displays many different degrees of elasticity.

Elasticity and Total Revenue

Knowing how responsive consumers will be to price changes is of vital interest to businesses. The elasticity of demand determines what happens to a business's **total revenue**—the total receipts from the sale of its product—when it alters the price of the product it is selling. (Total revenue is equal to the price of the product multiplied by the quantity sold: $TR = P \times Q$.)

To better understand total revenue and the importance of the degree of elasticity, put yourself in the place of the seller making a pricing decision.

Suppose that you're a college president contemplating an increase in tuition from, say, $1,500 to $1,600 a semester. The basic question you face is whether the gain in revenue due to the higher tuition per student will be offset by the loss in revenue due to the smaller number of students who are willing and able to pay that higher tuition. To answer that question, you must know how responsive students will be to changes in tuition. In other words you must have some estimate of the elasticity of demand for an education at your college.[2]

Case 1: Elastic Demand. Suppose that demand is highly elastic, that is, very responsive to price changes. If tuition is increased, the college will receive more money from each student, but it will enroll considerably fewer students; the percentage change downward in quantity demanded will be greater than the percentage change upward in price. As a result, the college will take in less total revenue than it did before the tuition hike. In the face of elastic demand, the logical action for the college to take—assuming there are vacant dormitory rooms and unfilled classes—would be to lower, not raise, tuition. The college will receive less from each student who enrolls, but it will enroll many more students, and total revenue will increase.

Case 2: Inelastic Demand. Suppose that demand for an education at your college is inelastic, that is, not very responsive to price changes. If the college increases tuition, it will lose some students but not very many, and the percentage change in quantity demanded will be less than the percentage change in price. Because each student will pay more than before, the result will be an increase in total revenue. If you decided to reduce tuition under these inelastic conditions, you would probably be fired. The tuition reduction wouldn't attract many new students, and all the students would pay a lower rate than before. As a result, total revenue would be lower than it was before the tuition reduction.

Case 3: Unitary Elasticity. If the demand for an education at your college is of unitary elasticity, any change in price will be offset exactly by a proportional change in the quantity demanded (enrollment). If you institute a 10 percent tuition increase, 10 percent fewer students will enroll, and total revenue will be unchanged. If you put into effect a 5 percent tuition reduction, 5 per-

---

[2] In reality the question faced by a college president or a businessperson would be somewhat more complicated, because any pricing decision may also have an indirect impact on the firm's costs. For example, because a higher price will cause a firm to sell less of its product, the firm may also incur lower costs, since it will not need to produce as much output. Before making any pricing decision, a wise entrepreneur considers its impact on costs as well as on revenues. (The nature and behavior of a firm's costs are discussed in Chapter 5.)

cent more students will enroll, and total revenue will be unchanged. As long as demand is of unitary elasticity, total revenue is unaffected by the seller's pricing decision.

The relationship among price changes, elasticity, and total revenue (*TR*) for each of the three cases is summarized in Exh. 4.3. Before continuing, take the time to work through the exhibit. You will see that if demand is inelastic, a price reduction will lead to a decline in total revenue, and a price increase will cause total revenue to increase. If demand is elastic, a price reduction will lead to an increase in total revenue, and a price increase will cause total revenue to decline. With unitary elasticity, a price change up or down is offset by a proportional change in quantity demanded, and total revenue remains unchanged. (Is price cutting a sensible response to sagging magazine sales? See if you can answer that question after reading "A Dying Business?" on page 118.)

EXHIBIT 4.3

Elasticity and Total Revenue

DEGREE OF ELASTICITY	PRICE INCREASE			PRICE DECREASE		
Case 1: Elastic Demand. (The coefficient of elasticity is greater than 1.)	↑	↓	↓	↓	↑	↑
	$P \times Q = TR$			$P \times Q = TR$		
Case 2: Inelastic Demand. (The coefficient of elasticity is less than 1.)	↑	↓	↑	↓	↑	↓
	$P \times Q = TR$			$P \times Q = TR$		
Case 3: Unitary Elasticity (The coefficient of elasticity is equal to 1.)	↑	↓	No change	↓	↑	No change
	$P \times Q = TR$			$P \times Q = TR$		

Symbols: ↑ increase, ↓ decrease

The elasticity of demand for a firm's product dictates what will happen to total revenue (price × quantity) when the firm alters price. When demand is elastic, a price increase results in a *significantly lower* quantity demanded and therefore in lower total revenue, whereas a price decrease leads to a *significantly higher* quantity demanded and therefore results in higher total revenue. When demand is inelastic, a price increase results in a lower quantity demanded, *but not much lower,* so that total revenue increases; a price decrease results in a higher quantity demanded, *but not much higher,* so that total revenue decreases. If demand is of unitary elasticity, any change in price will be exactly offset by the change in quantity demanded, so total revenue will not change.

A Dying Business?

U.S. News & World Report *is experimenting with cutting its cover price. But will lower prices boost the newsweekly's newsstand sales?*

Mitchell Ratliff, a 39-year-old marketing executive at Chase Manhattan Bank, used to be a good customer at his local newsstand. He'd buy a sports magazine one day, an antiques or wine hobbyist magazine another, maybe a newsweekly. But now he visits the newsstand near his office for one reason only: to buy his weekly lottery ticket.

Ratliff reads more magazines than he used to, but he gets them all through subscriptions rather than through single-copy purchases. "As far as I'm concerned," he says, "the neighborhood newsstand is pretty much a relic."

People like Ratliff are making publishers of mass-market magazines, which typically rely for 20% or more of their circulation on newsstand sales, very nervous. In March *U.S. News & World Report* stopped hand-wringing and did something almost unheard of in the business: The newsweekly began testing lower cover prices in parts of the country. It cut its $2.50 cover price to $1.50 in some regions and to $1 in others, in hopes that it can stem a nasty decline in single-copy sales— down 12.7% last year, to 63,730 copies. *U.S. News* has a total circulation of 2.2 million.

Magazine cover prices go up all the time; they almost never go down. Which is why the entire U.S. magazine business is watching the *U.S. News* test and holding its breath. Virtually everybody's in the same leaky boat. Over the past 12 years, single-copy sales for the top 572 magazines fell by 24%. Other surveys show higher drops.

"It's a dangerous trend," says Michael Pashby, senior vice president at the Magazine Publishers of America. Among the hardest-hit: *Family Circle*, whose newsstand sales dropped from 7.2 million in 1982 to 2.8 million last year; *TV Guide*, 9.7 million to 5.6 million; *Woman's Day*, 7 million to 3 million; and *Penthouse*, 3.8 million to 919,000. . . .

Why keep pushing on the single-copy string? Several reasons. Single-copy sales are still the cheapest way to acquaint raders with a magazine. Any publisher would rather get a subscription from a magazine purchsaed at full price than hector insomniacs with offers of free calculators on late-night television.

And even at moneylosing levels, single-copy sales still prop up the number of readers guaranteed to advertisers. Another, less tangible reason to keep the racks stocked: Advertisers like to see the magazines they use on the newsstand. It's a matter of ego, but in the magazine business the advertiser's ego is not to be ignored.

The industry, spearheaded by the Magazine Publishers of America, is mounting a lobbying effort— mostly videotapes and sales presentations—to prod newsstand owners and supermarkets into making room for more magazines. There are now 3,300 magazines available through retailers, up from about 1,800 in 1982, crammed into space that hasn't grown.

But the publishers are likely to be disappointed. Companies like Coke and Pepsi can easily outbid publishers for valuable space by the supermarkets' checkout counters. At some point, says Vos, Gruppo Managing Director E. Daniel Capell, magazines may start giving up on single-copy sales altogether. Says Capell: "I believe the newsstand will be a thing of the past."

—*Joshua Levine*

SOURCE: Joshua Levine, "A Dying Business?" Reprinted by permission of *Forbes* magazine, May 23, 1994. © Forbes, Inc., 1994.

Use Your Economic Reasoning

1. What theory tells us to expect newsstand sales to increase when a magazine's cover price is reduced? Is this expectation dependent on the price elasticity of demand? For instance, must demand be elastic for this to occur?

2. By lowering price, *U.S. News & World Report* may succeed in increasing newsstand sales but at a cost of reducing the amount of total revenue generated by those sales. Explain this possibility.

3. If management's objective is to increase total revenue from newsstand sales, under what elasticity conditions would a price reduction be the proper strategy?

The Determinants of Elasticity

As you saw in the preceding discussion, producers need to know whether the demand for their services and products is elastic or inelastic before they can make intelligent pricing decisions. But how can sellers know? Often they can gain insight into the elasticity of demand by considering two major factors that dictate the degree of elasticity: the number of good substitutes available and the importance of the product in consumers' budgets. As you examine these factors, recall our earlier discussion of the *income* and *substitution effects* that underlie the law of demand.

The Number of Available Substitutes for the Product. The primary factor in determining the price elasticity of demand is the number of good substitutes available. Recall that a substitute is a product that can be used in place of another product because to a greater or lesser extent it satisfies the same consumer wants. Some people consider chicken a good substitute for fish, for example; many people would acknowledge that a Ford automobile is an acceptable substitute for a Chevrolet with the same features.

When a large number of good substitutes exist, demand for a product tends to be elastic because consumers have alternatives—they can buy something else if the price of the product becomes too high. But if a product has few good substitutes, demand tends to be inelastic because consumers have few options; they must buy the product even at the higher price. Movie tickets, pond-raised catfish, and women's hats have elastic demand because there are a large number of substitutes for each of these items. Cigarettes, electricity, local telephone service, and gasoline tend to have relatively inelastic demand because of the limited options available to consumers.[3]

The Importance of the Product in Consumers' Budgets. The second factor influencing the elasticity of demand for a product is the importance of the product in consumers' budgets. If consumers are spending a significant portion of their income on a particular item (rent or long-distance phone service, for example), a price hike for that item will force a vigorous search for less-expensive substitutes. Demand will tend to be elastic. But if expenditures on the product are relatively small (the average family's annual outlay for lemon juice or soy sauce, for instance), consumers are more likely to ignore the price increase. Demand will tend to be inelastic.

---

[3] The elasticity of demand for a product tends to increase over time. When the price of a product increases, consumers may not be aware of substitutes for that product, so demand initially may be inelastic. But the more time that elapses after the price change, the more opportunities consumers have to discover substitutes and to develop new tastes and new habits. As consumers discover more substitutes, demand tends to become more elastic.

Some major budget items persist in having relatively inelastic demand. For example, even though many smokers spend a significant fraction of their incomes on cigarettes, statistical research shows that the demand for cigarettes by adults is quite inelastic. In this case demand is inelastic because the more important determinant of elasticity is the number of good substitutes. If, like cigarettes, a product has few good substitutes, the fact that it is a major expense item is generally less important to consumers. The article on page 123, "Elasticity, It's Wonderful," reveals some interesting and useful facts about the elasticity of demand for cigarettes.

Elasticity of Supply

Thus far we have considered only how the quantity demanded responds to price changes. Now we explore the supply side of the market. The price elasticity of supply describes the responsiveness of producers to price changes. More precisely, the **price elasticity of supply** is a measure of the responsiveness of the quantity supplied of a product to a change in its price.

The Coefficient of Supply Elasticity

Individual producers of goods and services display varying degrees of response when the price of a product changes. Some are able to expand or contract their supply of the product significantly in a short period of time; others are able to make only minimal adjustments. The more responsive producers are to a change in price, the more elastic their supply.

We measure the elasticity of supply by calculating the **coefficient of supply elasticity,** a value that indicates the degree to which the quantity supplied will change in response to a price change. The coefficient of supply elasticity is computed by dividing the percentage change in quantity supplied by the percentage change in price:

$$\text{Coefficient of elasticity} = \frac{\dfrac{\Delta Q}{Q}}{\dfrac{\Delta P}{P}} = \frac{\text{Percentage change in quantity supplied}}{\text{Percentage change in price}}.$$

Suppose that the price of coal rises from $40 to $50 a ton and that coal production in the United States therefore increases from 600 to 900 million tons a year. To compute the coefficient of supply elasticity, we first determine the percentage change in quantity supplied: If the change in quantity supplied (ΔQ) is 300 million tons and the original quantity supplied (Q) is 600 million tons, the percentage change in quantity supplied (300/600) is 50 percent. Next we take the percentage change in price: If the change in price (ΔP) is $10 and the original price is $40, the percentage change in price ($10/$40) is 25 percent. When we divide the 50 percent increase in quantity supplied by the 25 percent increase in price, we arrive at an elasticity coefficient of 2.[4]

$$\text{Coefficient of elasticity} = \frac{\dfrac{300}{600}}{\dfrac{\$10}{\$40}} = \frac{50\%}{25\%} = 2.$$

Note that whereas the coefficient of demand elasticity is negative, the coefficient of supply elasticity usually is positive: Because of the law of supply, an increase in price leads to an increase in the quantity supplied.

Interpreting the Elasticity Coefficient

We interpret coefficients of supply elasticity in essentially the same way we interpret coefficients of demand elasticity. A supply elasticity of 2 means that for every 1 percent change in price, the quantity supplied will change by 2 percent. For example, a 10 percent increase in price would lead to a 20 percent increase in the quantity supplied, and a 20 percent increase in price would lead to a 40 percent increase in the quantity supplied. Of course, reductions in price will have the opposite effect. A 10 percent decrease in price would lead to a 20 percent reduction in the quantity supplied.

An elasticity coefficient greater than one means that supply is elastic, or very responsive to price changes; a given percentage change in price results in a larger percentage change in quantity supplied. When the elasticity coefficient is less than one, supply is inelastic; a given percentage change in price results in a smaller percentage change in quantity supplied. If the coefficient is exactly one, supply is of unitary elasticity; a given percentage change in price results in an identical percentage change in the quantity supplied.

Using Supply Elasticity in Policy Decisions

An understanding of the elasticity of supply can be useful to government policymakers and others seeking solutions to economic problems. Consider, for example, the energy-policy debate that occurred in the late 1970s, a time when the United States was heavily dependent on foreign oil to meet its energy needs. During this period, the price of domestically produced oil was regu-

---

[4] As with the elasticity of demand, the more precise formula for calculating the elasticity of supply involves using the average of the two prices and the average of the two quantities as the base values for computing percentages.

Elasticity, It's Wonderful

More than any of its predecessors, the Surgeon General's latest report on smoking is a treasure trove of nicotinic esoterica. Flipping randomly through the pages, one learns, for example, that the heaviest-smoking ethnic group in America is Alaskan Natives, 56% of whom were recently on the weed. Estimates for miscellaneous other groups: Mexican-American men, 43%; Puerto Rican men, 40%; all blacks, 34%; all whites, 29%; college graduates, 16%. . . . Proportion of all regular smokers expected to die of smoking-related diseases: about 25%. . . .

What might turn the situation around? . . . Huge chunks of text are given to the need for still more educational programs, more federally funded research, more regulation of smokers' behavior, more restrictions on tobacco advertising. In other words, more of the same. The report also includes an excellent, but maddeningly abbreviated, report on the possible use of economic incentives (a.k.a. taxes) to reduce smoking.

Anyone focusing hard on these incentives could conclude rapidly that excise taxes represent the one available strategy that might curtail smoking sharply. The report includes a summary of "price elasticity" studies, i.e., studies estimating the effects of higher prices on demand for cigarettes in the U.S. As has long been known, the elasticities are highest for young people, who are both less habituated and less affluent than the middle-aged. One study shows, for example, that among beginners in the 12–17 age zone, a 10% increase in prices results in a 14% decline in smoking. But even for older smokers, the effects of price increases are nonnegligible. Looking at a range of elasticity studies, you get the sense that for smokers as a whole, consumption has typically declined by around 6% to 7% when prices rose by 10%.

Next question (not considered in the report): What if federal excise taxes pushed up prices by a lot more than 10%? By, say, 50% or 100%? Nobody knows exactly what would happen, since all extant elasticity studies have been based on much smaller tax increases. But we could be pretty sure of this much: A diet of steady price increases could move far beyond 10% while continuing to (a) substantially reduce smoking, especially among young people and (b) substantially increase federal tax revenues. . . .

—*Daniel Seligman*

SOURCE: Daniel Seligman, "Elasticity, It's Wonderful," FORTUNE, February 13, 1989. © 1989 Time Inc. All rights reserved.

Use Your Economic Reasoning

1. Compute the coefficient of demand elasticity for cigarettes among beginning smokers and for smokers as a whole.

2. How would you explain the fact that younger smokers seem to be more responsive to price hikes than older smokers?

3. Recall how price elasticity changes along a linear demand curve. As we increase cigarette prices (through higher taxes), will the elasticity coefficient rise or fall?

lated; it could not rise above the government-dictated price. Imported oil was beyond government control, however, and in the mid-1970s it skyrocketed in price. To reduce dependence on foreign oil, some politicians and policy-makers began to argue for the deregulation of domestic oil prices, so that U.S. producers would have incentive for increased exploration and production. Deregulation began in 1978–1979 and, in conjunction with consumer conservation (brought about by higher prices), helped to reduce substantially our dependence on foreign oil.

Suppose that the United States would like to increase domestic oil production by 50 percent to reduce its dependence on foreign oil. How much would the price of domestic oil have to rise to make that possible? Since the supply elasticity of oil is about one (actually it's slightly less than one), the price of oil would have to rise by 50 percent. (Remember, when the coefficient is 1, each 1 percent change in price brings a 1 percent change in quantity supplied.) Of course, if supply were more elastic—if producers were more sensitive to price changes—a smaller price hike would accomplish the same result. For example, if the coefficient were 2, the price of oil would have to rise by only 25 percent in order to increase the quantity supplied by 50 percent.

As you can see, the elasticity of supply allows us to determine how much price has to rise to convince suppliers to increase their output by a given amount. That kind of information is very important in making sound decisions about energy policy and addressing a host of other questions.

Time and the Elasticity of Supply

The responsiveness of suppliers to a change in the price of their product depends on the amount of time they are given to adjust their output to the new price. As a general rule, the longer producers are given to adapt to a price change, the greater the elasticity of supply. We can see the importance of time as a determinant of elasticity by comparing the kinds of adjustments suppliers facing a price change can make in the short run with the changes they can make in the long run.

The Short Run. In economics the **short run** is defined as the period of time during which at least one of a business's inputs (usually plant and equipment) is fixed—that is, incapable of being changed. Therefore short-run adjustments to a change in price are limited. Producers must use their existing plants and equipment more or less intensively, adding or eliminating a work shift or using a larger or smaller work force on existing shifts.

The short-run supply curve in Exh. 4.4 shows an increase in the price of oil from $20 to $25 a barrel ($5 equals a 25 percent increase) bringing an increase in the quantity of oil supplied from 800 to 900 million barrels (100 mil-

EXHIBIT 4.4

The Effect of Time on the Elasticity of Supply

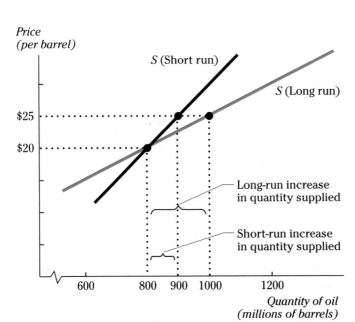

The more time a firm or industry is given to respond to a change in price, the larger the increase or decrease in the quantity supplied and the greater the elasticity of supply. Suppose, for example, that the price of oil rises from $20 to $25 a barrel. In the short run the quantity supplied can be increased from 800 million barrels per year to 900 million barrels; in the long run it is possible to increase the quantity supplied from 800 million barrels to 1,000 million barrels per year.

lion barrels equals an increase of 12.5 percent). Thus the coefficient of supply elasticity is 0.50 (12.5%/25%); supply is quite inelastic in the short run.

The Long Run. The **long run** is defined as the period of time during which all of a business's inputs, including plant and equipment, can be changed. The long run provides sufficient time for firms to build new production facilities and to expand or contract existing facilities. New firms can enter the industry and existing firms can leave. These kinds of adjustments make it possible to alter output significantly in response to a price change.

Note that the long-run response to an increase in the price of oil from $20 to $25 a barrel (a 25 percent increase) is an increase in the quantity of oil supplied from 800 million to 1,000 million barrels (200 million barrels equals a 25 percent increase). The coefficient of supply elasticity in this case is 1.0 (25%/25%), so supply is of unitary elasticity in the long run.

As you can see from our example, the elasticity of supply may vary substantially from the short run to the long run for a given product. Both the short-run and the long-run elasticities of supply also vary from industry to industry and even from firm to firm. What is certain for any particular firm or industry, however, is that the elasticity of supply will increase directly in relationship to the length of time that firm or industry is given to adjust to the price change. The response of petroleum producers to higher oil prices illustrates the important role that price changes can play in informing and motivating producers.

Summary

To know how much more consumers will purchase at lower prices or how much less they will purchase at higher prices, we need to know how responsive consumers are to price changes. The *price elasticity of demand* is a measure of the responsiveness of the quantity demanded to a change in price. If a given percentage change in price brings about a larger percentage change in quantity demanded (a coefficient of elasticity greater than one), demand is described as *elastic*. If a given percentage change in price brings about a smaller percentage change in quantity demanded (a coefficient less than one), demand is said to be *inelastic*. If a given percentage change in price brings an equal percentage change in quantity demanded (a coefficient equal to one), *unitary elasticity* prevails.

If demand is perfectly inelastic (the coefficient of elasticity is zero), a very large change in price will bring no change in the quantity demanded; the demand curve will be a vertical straight line. If demand is perfectly elastic (the coefficient approaches infinity), a very small change in price will bring an extremely large change in the quantity demanded; the demand curve will be a horizontal straight line. Most demand curves, however, do not show just one degree of elasticity; they show several. All linear, downward-sloping demand curves will show unitary elasticity in the middle, elastic demand at the upper end, and inelastic demand at the lower end.

The degree of elasticity is important to businesses because it determines what happens to *total revenue*, or total receipts from sales, when a business alters the price of its product. If demand is elastic, a price reduction will lead to an increase in total revenue, and a price increase will cause total revenue to decline. If demand is inelastic, a price reduction will lead to a decline in total revenue, and a price hike will cause total revenue to increase. With unitary elastic demand, any change in price will be offset exactly by a proportional change in the quantity demanded, and total revenue will be unchanged.

The major determinants of the elasticity of demand are the number of good substitutes that exist and the importance of the product in consumers' budgets. The greater the number of substitutes for a product and the more important the item in the budgets of consumers, the greater the elasticity of demand for the product.

Suppliers as well as consumers respond to price changes. The measure of suppliers' responsiveness to a change in the price of their product is called the *price elasticity of supply*. Economists use the *coefficient of supply elasticity* to determine the degree of responsiveness. The formula for the coefficient is the percentage change in quantity supplied divided by the percentage change in price. Supply is elastic if the coefficient is greater than one, inelastic if it is less than one, and unitary if it is equal to one.

As a general rule, the more time a firm or industry is given to adapt to a specified price change, the larger the change in quantity supplied and the greater the elasticity of supply. The *short run* is a time during which at least one input is fixed. In the short run, output can be expanded by employing additional units of labor and raw materials, but time does not permit plant and equipment expansion. Producers have additional options in the *long run,* a period of time sufficient to change all inputs. In the long run new production facilities can be built and existing facilities can be expanded. As a consequence, output can be increased much more in the long run than in the short run.

Glossary

Coefficient of demand elasticity. A value that indicates the degree to which quantity demanded will change in response to a price change.

Coefficient of supply elasticity. A value that indicates the degree to which the quantity supplied will change in response to a price change.

Long run. The period of time during which all of a business's inputs, including plant and equipment, can be changed.

Price elasticity of demand. A measure of the responsiveness of the quantity demanded of a product to a change in its price.

Price elasticity of supply. A measure of the responsiveness of the quantity supplied of a product to a change in its price.

Short run. The period of time during which at least one of a business's inputs (usually plant and equipment) is fixed—that is, incapable of being changed.

Total revenue. The total receipts of a business from the sale of its product. Total revenue is determined by multiplying the selling price of the product by the number of units sold.

Study Questions

Fill in the Blanks

1. If a decrease in the price of the product leads to a decrease in total revenue, demand must be (elastic/inelastic/unitary) _____.

2. If a 10 percent reduction in price leads to a 20 percent increase in quantity demanded, the coefficient of elasticity would be equal to _____.

3. If the coefficient of elasticity is greater than one, demand is _____; if it is less than one, demand is _____; if it is equal to one, demand is _____.

4. The major determinant of the elasticity of demand for a product is the number of good _____ that exist for the product.

5. The greater the fraction of the family budget spent for a particular product, the (greater/smaller) _____ the elasticity of demand for that product.

6. A perfectly inelastic demand curve would be a (vertical/horizontal) _____ straight line.

7. Along a downward-sloping linear demand curve, the elasticity of demand is the greatest at the (upper/lower) _____ end of the curve.

8. The degree of responsiveness of suppliers to a price change depends in part on the amount of _____ they are given to adapt to the change.

9. The time period during which all resources or inputs are variable is called the _____.

10. In general the greater the period of time producers are given to adjust to a change in price, the (greater/smaller) _____ the elasticity of supply.

Multiple Choice

1. If a seller reduces the price of a product and this leads to an increase in the quantity sold, what can be concluded?
   a) Demand is elastic.
   b) Demand is inelastic.
   c) Demand is of unitary elasticity.
   d) Nothing can be concluded about the degree of elasticity.

2. If the demand curve for a product is a vertical straight line, the coefficient of elasticity would be
   a) zero.
   b) one.
   c) infinity.
   d) different between any two points on the curve.

3. If an increase in price causes total revenue to fall, what can be concluded?
   a) Demand is elastic.
   b) Demand is inelastic.
   c) Unitary elasticity prevails.

4. On a downward-sloping demand curve, demand is more elastic
   a) at the upper end.
   b) at the lower end.
   c) in the middle.

5. In general demand for a product is more elastic
   a) the fewer the substitutes and the larger the fraction of the family budget spent on that product.
   b) the greater the number of substitutes and the larger the fraction of the family budget spent on that product.
   c) the fewer the substitutes and the smaller the fraction of the family budget spent on that product.
   d) the greater the number of substitutes and the smaller the fraction of the family budget spent on that product.

6. The local transit company is contemplating an increase in bus fares in order to expand revenues. A local senior-citizens group, Seniors for Fair Fares, argues that a rate increase would lead to lower revenues. This disagreement suggests that
   a) the transit company does not believe that the rate increase would reduce the number of riders, but the SFF believes that it would.
   b) the transit company believes that the demand for bus service is elastic, but the SFF believes that it is inelastic.
   c) the transit company believes that the demand for bus service is inelastic, but the SFF believes that it is elastic.

7. If the supply curve for a product were a vertical straight line,
    a) the quantity supplied would not depend on price.
    b) supply would be a fixed quantity.
    c) supply would be perfectly inelastic; that is, the elasticity coefficient would be equal to zero.
    d) All of the above

8. Which of the following is _not_ a short-run adjustment?
    a) The purchase of additional raw materials
    b) The construction of a new factory building
    c) The hiring of additional workers
    d) The addition of a second production shift

9. If the coefficient of supply elasticity for widgets is equal to 4, a 20 percent increase in the price of widgets would cause the quantity supplied to expand by
    a) 80 percent.
    b) 5 percent.
    c) 40 percent.
    d) 4 percent.

10. In general we can say that supply is more elastic
    a) in the short run than in the long run.
    b) in the long run than in the short run.

Problems and Questions for Discussion

1. If a college increases tuition as a method of increasing total revenue, what assumption is it making about the elasticity of demand for its service? Do you think that assumption is valid for your college? Why or why not?

2. If the price of Wrinkled jeans is reduced from $10 to $8 a pair and the quantity demanded increases from 5,000 to 10,000 pairs a month, what is the coefficient of demand elasticity?

3. According to Mark Moore of Harvard's Kennedy School of Government, the ideal demand-side drug policy would make illegal drugs cheap for addicts and expensive for neophytes. What logic can you see for such a policy, and how would it be related to the elasticity of demand for illegal drugs?

4. Which would tend to be more elastic, the demand for automobiles or the demand for Ford automobiles? Why?

5. Suppose that the price elasticity of demand for water is 2.0 and that the government wants to reduce the quantity of water demanded by 40 percent. By how much must the price of water be raised to accomplish this objective?

6. Sales taxes are a major source of revenue for many state governments. But higher taxes mean higher prices, which mean lower quantities sold by merchants. If the government wants to expand its tax revenue yet inflict minimum damage on the sales of merchants, should it tax products with elastic

tax inelastic demand

demand or inelastic demand? Why? Can you see any drawbacks to focusing taxes on these products?

7. Suppose that the coefficient of supply elasticity is equal to 2.5 for a particular product. If the price of that product increases by 10 percent, how much will the quantity supplied increase?

8. If price declines by 5 percent and quantity supplied declines by 20 percent, what is the coefficient of supply elasticity?

9. Why do we expect supply to be more elastic in the long run than in the short run?

10. Suppose that the coefficient of supply elasticity for housing were equal to 1.5. How much would the price of housing need to rise in order to expand the quantity of housing supplied by 30 percent?

Answer Key

Fill in the Blanks

1. inelastic	4. substitutes	8. time
2. 2.0	5. greater	9. long run
3. elastic, inelastic, unitary	6. vertical	10. greater
	7. upper	

Multiple Choice

1. d	3. a	5. b	7. d	9. a
2. a	4. a	6. c	8. b	10. b

The Purely Competitive Firm

In Chapter 3 we discussed how demand and supply interact to determine prices in competitive markets. To fully understand the operation of competitive markets, we need to step behind the scenes and examine the decision-making processes of the individual supplier, commonly known as the *firm.*

The **firm** is the basic producing unit in a market economy. It buys economic resources—land, labor, capital, and entrepreneurship—and combines them to produce goods and services. A group of firms that produce identical or similar products is called an **industry.** Exxon, Phillips Petroleum, and Texaco are firms in the petroleum industry; McDonald's, KFC (Kentucky Fried Chicken), and your local pizzeria are firms in the fast-food industry.

Economists argue that the performance of firms—how effectively they serve consumers—depends on the degree of competition within the industry; the greater the competition, the better the performance. As we have seen in earlier chapters, performing well in a market economy means producing the goods and services that consumers desire the most and selling those goods and services at the lowest possible prices. We begin this chapter by examining the assumptions that underlie the model of pure competition. Then we investigate the types of production costs the firm incurs and discover how it decides on the level of output that will maximize its profits. Finally, we examine the factors that cause firms to enter or leave an industry, explaining why this behavior is thought to be in the best interest of consumers.

The Nature of Pure Competition

Since the time of Adam Smith, economists have recognized that a market economy will serve consumers well only if competition exists to protect their interests. The competition economists have in mind, however, is more than mere rivalry among a few sellers. By definition, pure competition must satisfy three basic assumptions:

1. *There must be a large number of sellers, each producing a relatively small fraction of the total industry supply.* This rules out the possibility that a single firm could affect price by altering its level of output.
2. *The firms in the industry must sell identical products.* This condition excludes the possibility of there being any product differences, including those created through advertising, and ensures that consumers will view the products of different firms as perfect substitutes.
3. *There can be no substantial barriers (obstacles) to entering or leaving the industry.* Examples of barriers to entry include patent restrictions, large investment requirements, and restrictive licensing regulations.

If you find these conditions somewhat unrealistic, don't be alarmed. No industries in the United States or any other economy meet all of those conditions perfectly. Pure competition is not an attempt to describe any existing industry but rather an economic *model* that will allow us to see how an industry would function if it conformed to certain assumptions. In later chapters we will relax these assumptions and see how the performance of industries will change when they are no longer satisfied.

By using the benefits of pure competition as our standard, or yardstick, we can better understand the problems that may emerge when industries are less competitive. The competitive model also will offer insights into the behavior of industries that come reasonably close to meeting the assumptions of pure competition. These highly competitive industries include building construction, lumber manufacturing, limestone and gravel mining, and the agricultural industries, such as hog and dairy-product production.[1]

The Firm under Pure Competition

In a purely competitive industry the individual firm is best described as a **price taker;** it must accept price as a given that is beyond its control. This description follows from two of the basic assumptions of our model. First, because each firm produces such a small fraction of the total industry's supply, no single firm can influence the market price by altering its level of production. Even if a firm withheld its entire output from the market, the industry supply curve would not shift significantly to the left, and the equilibrium price would be essentially unchanged. Second, because all firms sell identical products, no one firm can charge a higher price for its product without losing all its customers; consumers would simply buy cheaper identical products from other firms. As a consequence of both these conditions, the firm must accept, or *take,* the price that is determined by the impersonal forces of supply and demand.

To illustrate how a firm operates under pure competition, we'll consider a producer of pine lumber, an important component in the construction of new homes. Several thousand sawmills in the United States produce pine lumber, and they produce virtually identical products. We will assume that the individual lumber producer is such a small part of the total industry that it cannot influence the market price. Whether that price means a profit or a loss, the firm can do nothing to alter it. The firm can't charge more than the prevailing price, because its product is identical to that of all other producers. Withholding the firm's output from the market in an attempt to drive up prices would be fruitless, because its output is just a "drop in the bucket" and would never be missed.

The price the firm receives for its product can change, of course, but price changes under pure competition are due to changes in *industry* demand and supply conditions, not to any actions the firm may take. Price is a given, and the demand curve facing the individual firm is therefore a horizontal line at the equilibrium price. A horizontal demand curve in Exh. 5.1 indicates that the firm can sell as much output as it wishes at the market price but no output

---

[1] Although most agricultural industries conform fairly well to the competitive model, price supports and other forms of government intervention in agriculture reduce the usefulness of the model in describing the performance of agricultural producers.

EXHIBIT 5.1

The Firm as a Price Taker

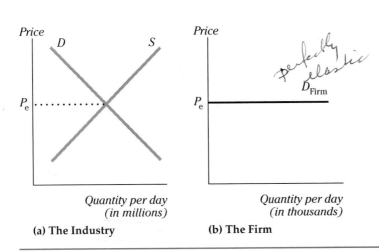

In a purely competitive industry market forces determine the equilibrium price, and the individual firm is unable to influence that price. The demand curve facing the firm is a horizontal line at the height of the market price, because the firm can sell as much output as it desires at the prevailing price but nothing at a higher price. Note that the industry's quantity is measured in millions, whereas the firm's is measured in thousands.

at a higher price. Under conditions of pure competition a firm's demand curve is perfectly, or infinitely, elastic. Recall from Chapter 4 that a high degree of elasticity means that a small change in price will lead to a large change in the quantity demanded. Here a very small change in price leads to an infinitely large change in the quantity demanded, because our lumber mill would lose *all* its customers if it were to raise its price even slightly.

Profit Maximization and Price Takers

The model of pure competition assumes that firms are *profit maximizers;* that is, they are always attempting to earn the most profit possible. *Profit* is the excess of a firm's total revenue over its total cost. When a firm's total costs exceed its total revenue, the firm is incurring a *loss.* (Profit and loss are simple accounting terms; the next section explains why economists need special terms for different kinds of profits.)

A firm's **total revenue (TR)** is the amount of money it takes in from the sale of its product. *TR* is calculated by multiplying the selling price of the product by the number of units sold. **Total cost (TC)** refers to the sum of all the costs incurred by a business in producing its product and making it available for sale. The behavior of total cost—how rapidly it increases when output is expanded—helps to determine which level of output will maximize a firm's profit. If producing an additional unit of output adds more to a firm's revenue than it adds to cost, the additional unit should be produced. If the unit adds more to cost than it adds to revenue, it should not be produced. In other words if an extra unit of output is profitable, it should be produced. We'll explore this profit-maximizing rule in greater detail after we discuss the types of costs a firm incurs and how they vary with output.

Short-Run Costs of Production

All firms must incur costs in order to produce the goods or services that they offer in the marketplace. Although this chapter concentrates on the purely competitive firm, the discussion of production costs that is presented here applies to all firms, regardless of the competitive setting in which they operate.

Our discussion of production costs will focus on the short run. The short run, as you learned in Chapter 4, is a time period during which at least one of a business's inputs (usually its plant and equipment) is incapable of being changed. In the short run a business must expand output by using its fixed production plant more intensively, since it does not have sufficient time to build a new plant or expand its existing facilities. In the long run, you will recall, all inputs can be varied, including plant and equipment. Firms have sufficient time to build new production facilities and to expand or contract existing ones. We'll have more to say about the firm's long-run adjustments later in the chapter.

Total Costs: Fixed and Variable

Short-run production costs can be classified as either fixed or variable. Total cost *(TC)* is simply the sum of the fixed and variable costs incurred by the firm.

Fixed Costs. **Fixed costs** are costs that do not vary with the level of output. They neither increase when the firm produces more nor decrease when the firm produces less. Fixed costs are often referred to as *overhead* and include such expenditures as insurance payments, rent on the production plant, fees for business licenses, salaries of managers, and property taxes.

The salaries of security guards are fixed costs because they must be paid even if a firm decides not to produce any output.

The distinguishing feature of fixed costs is that they have to be paid whether or not the firm is producing anything. If our hypothetical sawmill were forced to shut down because of a strike, the firm would still have to pay the salaries of its managers in order to avoid losing them to other companies. It would still have to make interest payments on loans it had taken to purchase the production plant and equipment. It would continue making payments for damage and accident insurance, and it would still require the services of security guards (an expense that might even increase).

Economists also include a normal profit as a fixed cost. **Normal profit** is the amount that the owners of a business could have earned if the money, time, and other resources they have invested in the business were invested elsewhere, in the next best alternative. In other words normal profit is the opportunity cost of owner-supplied resources. As an example, suppose that the owner of our sawmill had been earning $30,000 a year working for another lumber producer before he decided to buy his own mill. When he quit his job, he withdrew $20,000 from his savings account, which had been earning 10 percent interest per year, and used the money as a down payment to buy the sawmill. Since the earnings he is giving up to launch this venture are his $30,000 supervisor's salary plus $2,000 interest (10 percent of $20,000) on his savings, he will have to make $32,000 in his business (after subtracting all other costs) in order to earn a normal profit.

A normal profit is a fixed cost of keeping a business going. In fact, a firm that is earning a normal profit is said to be *breaking even*. Although some individuals may be willing to work for less than normal profit—perhaps because of the sense of independence they gain by being their own bosses—most owners will keep their resources employed only where they can expect at least a normal return.

Any profit above a normal profit is called an **economic profit.** If, for example, our lumber mill has total revenues of $75,000 and total costs of $57,000 (including $32,000 normal profit), the remaining $18,000 is economic profit. Economic profit is not considered a cost, because the owners would remain in the business even at zero economic profit, where the firm would be breaking even.

Variable Costs. **Variable costs** are costs that change with the level of output. They tend to increase when the level of output increases and to decline when output declines. Many of a business's costs are variable costs: payments for raw materials, such as timber, iron ore, and crude oil, and the manufactured inputs transformed from such materials (lumber, sheet steel, paint); wages and salaries of production workers; payments for electricity and water; and shipping expenses.

In many instances a specific element of cost may be partly a fixed cost and partly a variable cost. For example, although a firm's electricity bill increases as it expands production, some fraction of that bill should be considered a fixed cost because it relates to security lights, running the air conditioners in administrative offices, and other functions that are independent of the rate of output. Payments for raw materials and other inputs can also have a fixed-cost element if the firm has agreed to purchase some minimum amount of these inputs or to make some minimum payment to suppliers each year. Perhaps our sawmill operator has contracted to purchase a minimum of 100,000 pine logs per year in return for a guaranteed price or an assured source of supply. In that case the cost of the 100,000 logs will be a fixed cost, even though it is a payment for raw materials. Because each business is unique, we cannot determine to what extent a particular cost is fixed or variable without knowing quite a bit about the nature of the business and the firm's specific contractual obligations.

Total Cost. Each firm's total cost *(TC)* of production is the sum of its total fixed cost *(TFC)* and its total variable cost *(TVC).* The first four columns of Exh. 5.2 illustrate how these costs respond to changes in the level of output. The figures in column 2 show that the firm's total fixed cost (the sum of its expenditures for insurance payments, management salaries, and other fixed expenses) is constant, whereas column 3 shows the firm's total variable cost (total expenditures for gasoline, oil, labor, and other variable expenses)

EXHIBIT 5.2

Daily Costs of Manufacturing Pine Lumber

OUTPUT (thousands of feet of lumber)*	TOTAL FIXED COST (*TFC*)	TOTAL VARIABLE COST (*TVC*)	TOTAL COST (*TC*)	AVERAGE FIXED COST (*AFC*)	AVERAGE VARIABLE COST (*AVC*)	AVERAGE TOTAL COST (*ATC*)
0	$180	$ 0	$ 180	—	—	—
1	180	270	450	$180.00	$270.00	$450.00
2	180	510	690	90.00	255.00	345.00
3	180	720	900	60.00	240.00	300.00
4	180	900	1080	45.00	225.00	270.00
5	180	1110	1290	36.00	222.00	258.00
6	180	1350	1530	30.00	225.00	255.00
7	180	1620	1800	25.71	231.43	257.14
8	180	1950	2130	22.50	243.75	266.25
9	180	2340	2520	20.00	260.00	280.00
10	180	2790	2970	18.00	279.00	297.00

*Large quantities of lumber are generally sold in increments of 1000 *board feet*; a board foot measures 12 × 12 × 1 inches.

increasing as the level of output increases. Because total cost (column 4) includes this variable-cost component, it also increases with the level of production.

Average Costs: Fixed, Variable, and Total

Producers are often more interested in the average cost of producing a unit of output than they are in any of the total-cost concepts we've examined. By comparing average, or per unit, costs with those of other firms in the industry, a producer can judge how efficient (or inefficient) its own operation is.

Average-cost functions are of three types: average fixed cost, average variable cost, and average total cost. **Average fixed cost (AFC)** is computed by dividing total fixed cost by the firm's output. For example, if the firm were producing seven units of output, the *AFC* would be $180/7 = $25.71. As you can see in column 5 of Exh. 5.2, average fixed cost declines as output expands. This must be true because we are dividing a constant—total fixed cost—by larger and larger amounts of output. The decline in *AFC* is what a business means when it talks about "spreading its overhead" over more units of output.

The figures in column 6 describe the behavior of the firm's average variable cost. **Average variable cost (AVC)** is calculated by dividing the total variable cost at a given output level by the amount of output produced. For instance, if our lumber mill were producing six units of output (6,000 feet of lumber), its *AVC* would be $1,350/6 = $225. As you can see from the table, average variable cost declines initially and then rises as output continues to expand. The reason for this behavior will be provided a little later.

Average total cost (ATC) is always equal to average fixed cost plus average variable cost. For instance, the average total cost of producing four units of output is equal to the average fixed cost of $45 *plus* the average variable cost of $225; that means that *ATC* is equal to $270. Average total cost can also be computed by dividing the total cost at a particular level of output by the number of units of output. Using that technique, we find that the average to-

---

EXHIBIT 5.3

The Marginal Cost of Manufacturing Pine Lumber

OUTPUT PER DAY (thousands of feet of lumber)	TOTAL COST (*TC*)	MARGINAL COST (*MC*)
0	$ 180	—
1	450	$270
2	690	240
3	900	210
4	1,080	180
5	1,290	210
6	1,530	240
7	1,800	270
8	2,130	330
9	2,520	390
10	2,970	450

Marginal cost is the additional cost of producing one more unit of output. For example, if it costs the firm $1,290 to produce five units of lumber and $1,530 to produce six units of lumber, the marginal cost of the sixth unit of lumber is $240.

tal cost of producing four units of output is $1,080/4 = $270, the same answer as before. As you can see from column 7, average total cost declines initially and then rises.

Marginal Cost

Average total cost is useful in gauging a firm's efficiency in production, but the concept of marginal cost plays the more important role in guiding production decisions. The term *marginal* means extra or additional. Thus **marginal cost (MC)** is the additional cost of producing one more unit of output. It is equal to the change in total cost from one unit of output to the next. Consider, for example, the marginal cost of the first unit of output—the first thousand feet of lumber—in Exh. 5.3. If it costs the firm $180 to produce zero output (remember fixed costs) and $450 to produce one unit of output, the marginal cost of the first unit of lumber is $270. The *MC* of the second unit of output is $240, the difference between *TC* $450 and *TC* $690. Take a few moments to compute the marginal costs for the remaining units of output, using the total-cost column in Exh. 5.3. Then check your answers against the marginal-cost column in that exhibit.

The Cost Curves

The information scheduled in Exh. 5.2 and Exh. 5.3 is depicted as cost curves in Exh. 5.4. We read cost curves in much the same way we read the demand and supply curves presented in Chapter 3. If we are interested in knowing the average total cost of producing three units of output, for example, we find three units on the horizontal axis, move directly up from that quantity to the *ATC* curve (point *A*), move across to the vertical axis, and read $300. The *ATC* of producing three units of output is $300 per unit. To determine the *AVC* when six units are being produced, we find that quantity on the horizontal axis, move directly up to the *AVC* curve (point *B*), move across to the vertical axis, and read $225. The *AVC* of producing six units of output is $225. The other cost curves are read in the same way.

Cost curves help us see how a particular cost behaves as the level of output changes. Note that *AFC* declines as output increases, reflecting the spreading of fixed costs over more units of output. The marginal cost curve and the average cost curves (*AVC* and *ATC*) decline initially and then begin to increase as output expands, giving them a U-shape. As you read the following sections, you will see why the curves behave this way.

EXHIBIT 5.4

A Graphic Look at Costs

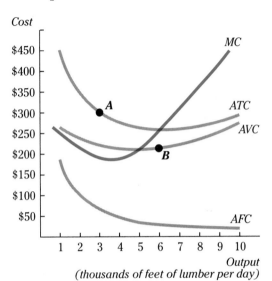

Cost curves show the way that a particular type of cost is related to the level of output. Average fixed cost *(AFC)* declines as output increases. Marginal cost *(MC)*, average variable cost *(AVC)*, and average total cost *(ATC)* graph as U-shaped curves; that is, these types of costs decline initially and then rise.

The Marginal Cost Curve

Why does marginal cost first decline and then increase? As you've already learned, marginal cost is the additional cost of producing one more unit of output. It is a variable cost because it changes as output changes. The shape of the marginal cost curve, therefore, must be related to some specific variable cost—often the cost of labor.

Let's see how changing labor costs can account for the U-shaped curve in Exh. 5.4. The labor cost of producing an additional unit of output depends on the amount of labor time it takes to produce that unit. If our firm is paying its workers $10 per hour and it takes eight hours of labor to produce the additional unit, the labor cost of that unit is $80. Keep in mind that the amount of labor time it takes to produce each additional unit of output is not constant. It depends on the degree of *specialization* of labor: the extent to which workers perform a single task rather than several. Workers who specialize do their jobs better, which means lower *MC*.

When a firm is producing relatively little output, the labor cost of producing an additional unit tends to be high, because the low volume permits little specialization. To illustrate, let's think about the variety of tasks you would need to perform if you wanted to run our hypothetical sawmill alone. You would be required to roll the logs onto the saws and cut them into lumber. Then you would have to smooth the rough surface of the boards with a tool known as a plane. Next you would need to stack the lumber for drying. And of course you'd be the one who cleaned and serviced the equipment so that it would continue to operate properly. Many additional tasks would be required, but probably by now you get the point. If you were trying to run the mill by yourself, you would spend a great deal of time moving from one task to the next, and it's likely that you wouldn't become very proficient at any of them. As a consequence, more hours would be required to accomplish each task than would be needed if you were allowed to specialize in one job (or a few jobs) and become more skilled. This is why the marginal cost of producing the first unit of lumber is relatively high ($270).

As output expands, opportunities for specialization increase. For example, if the lumber mill needs to hire two workers to keep up with demand, one of them might do all the sawing while the other planes the boards and stacks them for drying. This greater specialization permits workers to become better at their jobs and reduces the time wasted in moving from one task to another. The result is a lower marginal cost for the second unit of output ($240) and an even lower cost for the third ($210) and fourth ($180), because the amount of labor time required to produce these additional units of output is reduced. Remember, this is a hypothetical example; the numbers are not precise but rather are meant only to illustrate a principle. In some businesses specialization can result in significant reductions in marginal cost; in others the savings may be minimal.

Marginal cost will not decline infinitely. If the firm continues to expand output, eventually it will start to overutilize its plant and equipment, causing marginal cost to rise. Remember that in the short run the firm must operate with a fixed amount of plant and equipment. If the firm continues to hire additional workers in order to increase output, at some point it will experience congestion, workers waiting for machines, and high breakdown rates as overused machines begin to fail. Then the marginal cost of producing an additional unit of output will rise, as it does in our example when the output is expanded from four to five units of lumber.[2]

---

[2] The fixed factor need not be plant and equipment; in agriculture it might be land. As a farmer adds units of fertilizer (or some other variable input such as labor, irrigation water, or insecticide) to a fixed plot of land, the second unit of fertilizer may increase the output of corn by more than the first unit, and the third unit of fertilizer may increase output by more than the second. Thus the cost of producing each additional bushel of corn declines initially because it takes less fertilizer (and therefore less expenditure on fertilizer) to produce it.

Again, this process can't continue indefinitely. Eventually it will reach the point where the fixed land is being overutilized, the point where the next unit of fertilizer applied to the land will yield less additional output than the unit before it. When that happens, the marginal cost of producing the next bushel of corn will rise. In other words the marginal cost curve will turn upward.

In summary, if a firm continues to expand output in the short run, eventually it will overutilize its fixed plant and equipment, causing marginal cost to rise. This principle is simply an extension of the law of increasing costs introduced in Chapter 1.

The Relationship between Marginal and Average Costs

Marginal cost is related to average variable cost and average total cost in a very precise way. In Exh. 5.4 you'll notice that the *MC* curve intersects the *AVC* curve at the lowest point, or minimum, of the *AVC* curve. This point is not a chance intersection but is due to the relationship between marginal and average cost values. A simple example will help clarify this relationship. Let's assume that you want to know the average weight of the students in your class. To determine the class average, you coax each student onto the scales, add up the individual weights, and then divide by the number of students in the class. If an additional (marginal) student who weighs more than the average joins the class, the average will be pulled up. If the additional student weighs less than the previous class average, the average will be pulled down. As you can see, the marginal value determines what happens to the average.

Essentially the same logic applies to the cost curves. Notice that so long as the *MC* curve is below the *AVC* curve, the *AVC* is falling; the marginal value is pulling down the average, just as the thin student pulled down the class average. However, when *MC* is above *AVC*, *AVC* is rising; the marginal value is pulling the average up. When *MC* = *AVC*—that is, when *MC* and *AVC* intersect—the average will remain unchanged. As you can see, the shape of the *AVC* curve depends largely on the behavior of marginal cost. Thus if *MC* declines initially and then increases as output continues to expand, *AVC* must display the same general behavior.

The shape of the *ATC* curve is also influenced by marginal cost but in a somewhat more complex manner. Recall that average total cost is the sum of average fixed cost and average variable cost. Initially both *AVC* and *AFC* decline, so *ATC* declines as well. But note that *ATC* continues to decline after *AVC* has turned upward. This occurs because *AFC* is continuing to decline, and for a while the downward pull of *AFC* outweighs the upward pull of *AVC*. Eventually the increase in *AVC* will more than offset the decrease in *AFC*, and *ATC* will begin to rise. Thus *ATC* will have the same basic shape as *AVC*, but the minimum point on the curve will occur at a somewhat higher output. (An increase in the cost of inputs—higher wage rates or raw materials prices, for instance—would shift the cost curves upward without altering the basic relationship between the curves. A reduction in input costs would have the opposite effect; it would shift the curves downward.)

In summary, the marginal cost curve plays a major role in determining the shape of both the average variable and the average total cost curves. As you will see in a moment, marginal cost also plays a major role in guiding the production decisions of the competitive firm.

Profit Maximization in the Short Run

Because the purely competitive firm is a price taker, in effect bound to the price determined by the market, the only variable it can control to maximize its profit (when market conditions permit a profit) or minimize its loss (when a loss is unavoidable) is the level of output.

In the short run the purely competitive firm can produce any level of output within the capacity of its existing plant and equipment. It adjusts its output by altering the amount of variable resources (labor and raw materials, for example) that it employs in conjunction with its fixed plant and equipment. In the long run, of course, the firm has additional options for expanding or contracting production.

Determining the Profit-Maximizing Output

The profit-maximizing (loss-minimizing) level of output in the short run can be determined by comparing marginal cost with marginal revenue. We have seen that marginal cost is the additional cost of producing one more unit of output. **Marginal revenue (MR)** is the additional revenue to be gained by selling one more unit of output. When the firm is a price taker, MR equals price, because the additional revenue to be gained by selling one more unit is exactly the market price.

A firm seeking to achieve the profit-maximizing output will continue to increase production so long as marginal revenue exceeds marginal cost. When MR > MC, each additional unit "pays its own way," because it adds more to revenue than to cost. In Exh. 5.5 the market price of the product is $270, so each additional unit produced will add $270 to revenue. You can see that the marginal cost of producing the fifth unit is $210 and that the firm will be $60 "better off" for producing that unit. In the case of the sixth unit, the company will be only $30 better off, because the marginal cost of that unit is $240. It is important to recognize that although the sixth unit adds less to profit than the fifth unit, it continues to enlarge the firm's *total* profit, so it should be produced.[3]

---

[3] With the information provided thus far, we cannot determine whether this firm is earning a profit or incurring a loss. But we can say that by producing the sixth unit, the firm will either enlarge its total profit *or* reduce its total loss. You'll see how to determine the profit *or* loss in just a moment.

EXHIBIT 5.5

The Profit-Maximizing Output

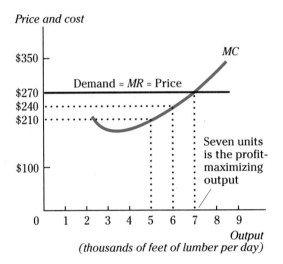

Price and cost

The profit-maximizing firm should continue to expand output until *MR = MC*. In this case profit maximization (or loss minimization) occurs at an output of seven units (7,000 feet) of lumber per day.

*Output
(thousands of feet of lumber per day)*

The seventh unit of output is a little trickier to evaluate. It brings in no more revenue ($270) than it costs to produce ($270), so the firm should be neutral, or indifferent, toward its production. Economists generally assume, however, that the firm will go ahead and produce that unit.

This assumption provides us with a rule for selecting the profit-maximizing output: Produce the level of output where *MC = MR*, the output that corresponds to the point where the *MC* and *MR* curves intersect. In instances when there is no whole-number unit of output for which *MC* is exactly equal to *MR*, the firm should produce all the units for which *MR > MC* but no unit for which *MC > MR*.

Evaluating Profit or Loss

By producing where marginal revenue is equal to marginal cost, the purely competitive firm is doing the best it can; it is either maximizing its profit or minimizing its loss. Marginal values alone, however, will not tell us exactly how well the firm is doing; they will not tell us whether the firm is earning a profit or incurring a loss, and they will not tell us the amount of the profit or loss.

To answer those questions, we need to calculate and compare the firm's total revenue and total cost. You already know that total revenue is computed by multiplying the selling price of the product by the number of units sold. To compute total cost, we need the information provided by the average total cost curve. Multiplying the *ATC* by the number of units of output produced gives us the total cost of producing that output level. (Recall that we get our per unit, or *ATC,* cost by performing the reverse operation: dividing *TC* at a particular level of output by the number of units.) By comparing total revenue with total cost, we can determine the profit or loss of the firm. Some examples should help clarify this procedure.

Profits, Losses, and Breaking Even. Exhibit 5.6 shows a purely competitive firm in three different short-run situations. As you study the three cases, keep in mind that market price equals *MR* under conditions of pure competition. And the *MR = P* curve is the demand curve for the purely competitive firm. In each case, the firm is producing where the *MC* curve intersects the demand curve, where *MC = MR,* but it is experiencing different degrees of success in these three situations. In part (a), the firm is enjoying an above normal, or economic, profit. The amount of this profit can be determined by comparing total revenue with total cost. Total revenue is equal to $1,890 (the $270 sell-

EXHIBIT 5.6

Finding the Profit or Loss

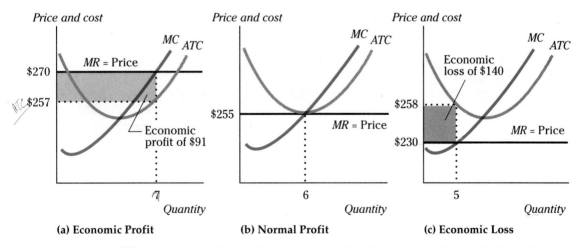

(a) Economic Profit   **(b) Normal Profit**   **(c) Economic Loss**

All firms maximize their profits or minimize their losses by producing the level of output at which marginal revenue is equal to marginal cost. In some instances a firm will be able to earn an above-normal, or *economic*, profit. In other instances only a normal profit—zero economic profit—will be possible. Finally, in some cases an economic loss—less than a normal profit—will be the best that the firm can do.

ing price × 7 units), whereas total cost is only $1,799 (*ATC* of $257 × 7 units). Therefore the firm is earning an economic profit of $91. (Alternatively, we could determine the firm's profit by multiplying the average, or per-unit profit by the number of units sold. Here the firm is earning a profit of $13 per unit ($270 − $257 = $13) and selling 7 units; total profit is $13 × 7 = $91.)

In part (b) the firm isn't doing as well. Its total revenue of $1,530 ($255 × 6 units) exactly matches its total cost, so the firm is breaking even; it is earning zero economic profit. Remember, zero economic profit is the same as normal profit, the amount the owners of the business could expect to earn if they invested their resources elsewhere. In part (c) the firm has fallen on hard times. Price is now so low that it will no longer cover average total cost. Indeed, the firm will be earning less than a normal profit and therefore facing an *economic loss:* total cost, including all opportunity cost, will exceed total revenue. In our example the total cost is $1,290 ($258 × 5 units), whereas its total revenue is only $1,150 (*ATC* of $230 × 5 units), a loss of $140. (Note that if we multiply the per-unit loss of $28 × 5 units we arrive at the same $140 figure for the firm's total loss.)

Operating with a Loss. Why would the company continue to produce in part (c)? Why not simply close down the business and not reopen until conditions improve? The answer has to do with fixed costs, or overhead, which must be paid whether or not any output is produced. If a firm shuts down temporarily—if it stays in the industry but stops producing output—its loss will equal its total fixed costs. But if the price the firm can get for its product is high enough to allow the firm to cover its variable costs (costs that would not exist if the firm shut down) and pay *some* of its fixed costs, the firm will be better off if it continues to operate. This is why U.S. wheat farmers continued to produce in the mid-1980s, despite substantial losses. Doing so resulted in smaller losses than the farmers would have incurred by shutting down. When price reaches so low a level that the firm can no longer recover the variable costs of producing, it will shut down and wait for better times.

Exhibit 5.7 illustrates these two situations. In part (a) the selling price of $200 is greater than the average variable cost of $180, so each unit that the firm produces (up to the point where *MR* = *MC*) provides it with $20 ($200 − $180 = $20) to help pay its fixed costs. Although the firm will still incur a loss, continued operation will make the loss smaller than it would be if the firm shut down and paid its fixed costs. In part (b) the $150 price is less than the *AVC* of $175, so each unit the firm produces increases its total loss by $25. This firm would be better off to shut down, accept its fixed-cost loss, and wait for business conditions to improve. Of course, if losses continue period after period, eventually the firm will be forced out of business. In summary, when *P* >

EXHIBIT 5.7

Minimizing a Loss

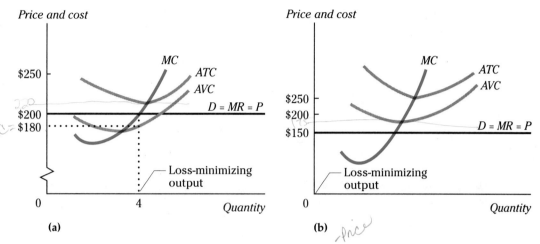

Whenever price exceeds average variable cost $(P > AVC)$, the firm will minimize its loss by continuing to operate. This is the situation represented in part (a), where the firm will continue to produce despite an economic loss. When price is less than average variable cost $(P < AVC)$, the firm will minimize its loss by shutting down. This situation is represented in part (b).

AVC, the firm will minimize its loss by continuing to operate; when $P < AVC$, the firm should shut down. (Some critics of President Clinton's plan for national health insurance have argued that it would impose short-run losses on firms. Companies facing foreign competition might even be forced out of business. Read Peter Passell's article on page 150, to find out how the Clinton plan would affect U.S. businesses.)

Profit Maximization in the Long Run

In the short run the purely competitive firm must do the best it can with fixed plant and equipment, but in the long run the firm has many more options; all costs are variable in the long run. If the industry has been profitable, the firm may decide to expand the size of its production plant or otherwise increase its productive capacity. If losses have been common, it can sell out and invest in another industry, one in which the prospects for profits appear brighter. In the

Companies Will Meet Health Costs with Higher Prices and Lower Pay

Who will pay for national health insurance? Why business, of course, President Clinton assured the nation. Under the White House plan, most employers would be required to write checks for 80 percent of the cost of a generous package of medical benefits for employees and families.

But many economists think the President has it exactly backward: Of all the possible candidates, corporate America is least likely to be stuck for the buck. One way or another, they say, the cost of employer-mandated health premiums will either be passed forward to consumers in the form of higher prices, or backward to workers in the form of lower wages.

And while there may be admirable political reasons for preserving what Uwe Reinhardt of Princeton University calls "the myth that someone else will pay," linking insurance to employment is likely to have side-effects that range from irritating complexity to flagrant inefficiency.

The plan calls for employers to cover 80 cents on the premium dollar charged to members of each "regional health alliance." This premium would be "community rated"—that is, unrelated to age, medical history or health-threatening personal habits. It would vary only with the size of the worker's family and the number of family members who are employed.

How then would it be possible for employers to dodge their legal share of the bill? One route, suggests Barry Bosworth of the Brookings Institution, would be for corporations to raise their prices. This, he argues, is what happens when business costs are broadly (and uniformly) increased by a government mandate like an increase in Social Security taxes.

Forward shifting may not work, though. If, for example, producers compete directly with importers who are unaffected by the insurance mandate or if consumers are unwilling to buy as much at the higher price, some of the extra costs must come from another pocket.

Thus stockholders may initially suffer a squeeze on profits. But the mobility of capital, the global flow of funds to investment with the highest returns, makes it virtually impossible to trap capital for long: Either jobs must be pared, or labor must pick up the tab. In the 1980's, Mr. Bosworth says, much of the increase in employer-paid health insurance costs came out of pension benefits.

Where mandated cost increases hit businesses more selectively (as may prove the case with the Clinton plan) employers are apt to go directly to labor for the extra money. Jonathan Gruber, an economist at the Massachusetts Institute of Technology, found that maternity benefits mandated in the 1970's were matched "roughly dollar for dollar" with cuts in wages for the young, married employees likely to claim the benefits. Over all, researchers believe that about three-quarters of mandated labor benefits are passed back to workers, with the rest passed forward to consumers. . . .

An appealing alternative to employer mandates is individual mandates. Washington could oblige everyone to buy community-rated private health insurance, or pay an equivalent income tax surcharge. Those who could not afford the full premium could be subsidized by Uncle Sam.

The political catch is that Americans would be confronted with the reality that people, not corporations, pay for health insurance. "With health care reform," Mr. Gruber reluctantly concludes, "the best may be the enemy of the good."

—*Peter Passell*

SOURCE: Peter Passell, "Companies Will Meet Health Costs with Higher Prices and Lower Pay," September 20, 1993. Copyright © 1993 by The New York Times Company. Reprinted with permission.

Use Your Economic Reasoning

1. Suppose that the sandal industry is purely competitive on a worldwide basis and that both foreign and U.S. firms have identical costs as represented below. Assume also that the U.S. firms produce an insignificant share of total world output. According to the exhibit, how much profit is each U.S. firm making? Each foreign firm?

2. Now suppose that only U.S. firms are required to pay for health insurance for their employees. How would the exhibit change? What would happen to the profitability of U.S. firms? (*Hint:* U.S. firms can't raise prices when their costs increase. Why?)

3. Why would firms facing foreign competition feel compelled to cut wage rates (or other benefits, such as vacation pay) if they were required to pay for health care? What if employees refused to accept wage cuts?

4. Why do may economists favor "individual mandates" to "employer mandates" as a method of paying for health care?

5. Answer this question after reading the next section, "Profit Maximization in the Long Run." Suppose that the firms were initially earning economic profits. Would that alter your answer to question 3?

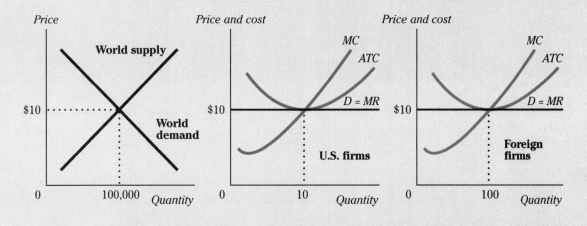

short run the number of firms in an industry remains constant—time is inadequate for firms to enter or leave. But in the long run there is time for these adjustments to occur, and the industry can expand or contract. In this section we examine how firms in a purely competitive industry adjust to the presence or absence of short-run profits and how this adjustment process eventually leads to long-run equilibrium for the industry. **Long-run equilibrium** is a situation in which the size of an industry is stable: There is no incentive for additional firms to enter the industry and no pressure for existing firms to leave.

Setting the Stage: The Short-Run Picture

In Exh. 5.8 we follow the path by which a purely competitive firm and industry arrive at long-run equilibrium. Each panel shows the demand and supply curves for the industry on the left and the diagram for a representative firm on the right. In part (a) the industry demand and supply curves establish a price of $300. The representative firm takes that price as a given and maximizes its profits (or minimizes its losses) by producing where $MC = MR$. Here the representative firm is earning an economic profit in the short run, and as a consequence, additional firms will be attracted to this industry in the long run.

The Entrance of Firms: Attraction of Profits

The entrance of additional firms is made possible by one of the assumptions of the purely competitive model—the absence of significant barriers to entry. As additional firms enter the industry, they will increase the industry supply and depress the market price. This adjustment is represented in the left-hand graph of part (b), where supply has increased to S_1 and intersects with the demand curve to establish a new price of $270. Note that at the new price the firms in the industry still are able to earn economic profits; ATC is still below $MR = P$. As a consequence, firms will continue to enter the industry until the price falls to $255, where the demand curve and S_2 intersect in part (c), and price is consistent with normal profits.

Once the price of $255 is established, both the firm and the industry are in long-run equilibrium: They have achieved a state of balance, a situation in which there is no tendency for further change. The industry is in long-run equilibrium because at zero economic profit, there is no incentive for additional firms to enter it and no incentive for established firms to leave it. The individual firms are in equilibrium because they have no incentive to alter their level of output so long as the market price remains at $255. (The personal computer industry was once highly profitable. Now profits are falling and some firms are being forced from the industry. Read "Crashing Prices," on page 156 to learn about the competitive nature of the computer industry.)

EXHIBIT 5.8

The Long-Run Adjustment Process

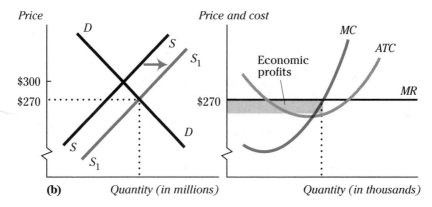

The Industry   **The Firm**

(a)   At a price of $300, the firms in the industry will be able to earn an economic profit. Since above-normal profits are being earned, additional firms will be attracted to the industry. This development is reflected in (b).

(b)   As additional firms enter the industry, the industry supply curve will shift from S to S_1 and price will be forced down to $270. However, since that price still permits an economic profit to be earned, additional firms will enter the industry, as revealed in (c), on the next page.

The Exit of Firms: Looking for Greener Pastures

If a purely competitive industry undergoes short-run economic losses, a similar adjustment process is likely to result. In the long run some firms will respond to the short-run losses (less than normal profits) by leaving the industry to search for a better opportunity elsewhere. As these firms exit, in-

EXHIBIT 5.8 (*Cont.*)

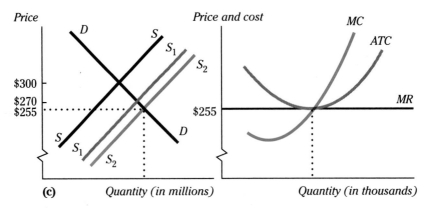

(c)   *Quantity (in millions)*   *Quantity (in thousands)*

(c) The entrance of additional firms will shift the supply curve to S_2 and depress market price to $255. At that price the firms in the industry will be able to earn only a normal profit. There will be no incentive for additional firms to enter the industry, and the industry will be in long-run equilibrium.

dustry supply decreases and the market price rises. Firms will continue to leave the industry until the market price has risen sufficiently to afford the re-maining firms exactly a normal profit. When that happens, the exodus will cease; the firms and the industry will be in long-run equilibrium.

The Benefits of Pure Competition

As we noted at the beginning of this chapter, economists often use the model of pure competition as an ideal by which to judge other, less competitive in-dustry structures. Economists hold pure competition in such high esteem pri-marily because it would lead to an efficient use of our scarce resources.

Production Efficiency

One of the most important features of pure competition is its tendency to pro-mote **production efficiency:** production at the lowest possible average total cost, or minimum *ATC*. As you look at Exh. 5.9, you'll see that the purely com-petitive firm is in long-run equilibrium when it is producing at the level where its *ATC* curve is tangent to, or barely touching, its demand curve. This tangency occurs at the lowest point on the firm's *ATC* curve, showing that the firm is producing at the lowest possible average cost. In essence this means that the product is being produced with as few scarce resources as possible.

EXHIBIT 5.9

The Competitive Firm in Long-Run Equilibrium

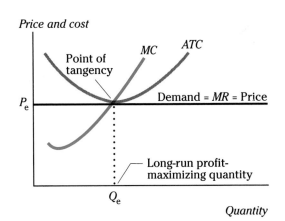

Price and cost

Point of tangency

MC   ATC

P_e

Demand = MR = Price

Long-run profit-maximizing quantity

Q_e

Quantity

In long-run equilibrium the competitive firm will earn only a normal profit. This is indicated in the graph by the tangency between the demand curve, or price line, and the *ATC* curve at the profit-maximizing output (where *MR(P) = MC*). The equality of price and minimum *ATC* indicates that the firm is achieving *production efficiency*. The equality of price and marginal cost signals that the firm is also achieving *allocative efficiency*.

Production efficiency is a benefit of pure competition; it allows us to spread our scarce resources across more products, and in so doing it enables us to satisfy more of society's unlimited wants.

Note also that in long-run equilibrium consumers are able to purchase the product at a price equal to this minimum *ATC*. This must be true, because at the tangency point in Exh. 5.9, Price *(MR) = ATC*. Thus we can see that the benefits of production efficiency are passed on to consumers. They receive the lowest possible price, given the cost conditions that exist in the industry.

Allocative Efficiency

If pure competition resulted in the efficient production of millions of buggy whips or other products that were not in much demand, consumers obviously would not be pleased. However, pure competition also leads to **allocative efficiency:** Producers use society's scarce resources to provide consumers with the proper quantities of the goods and services they desire the most. Economists argue that if pure competition prevailed throughout the economy, all of our scarce resources would be allocated or distributed so as to produce the precise mix of products that consumers desire the most.

Crashing Prices

It is the best of times in the personal-computer market. Prices are in free fall. Options that were once prohibitively expensive are now packaged at rock-bottom prices. The fastest chips and the biggest hard drives are cheap and plentiful. For consumers who have often had to wait years to buy the latest, most powerful machines at affordable prices, the market has entered what seems to be a golden age.

It is also the worst of times. For most of the companies that make those computers, that market has suddenly become a lethal place. Once successful companies such as IBM, Compaq, Dell and Apple are floundering; profits are plunging, margins squeezed. Last month one of the personal-computer industry's leading lights—the pioneering Tandy Corp.—became a prominent casualty. Faced with $52 million in losses in the past year and an even bloodier future, Tandy decided to abandon the PC business, which accounted for 10% of its sales last year. The company simply could not survive the intense price competition.

Tandy has been swept up in the personal-computer industry's most savage shake-out ever. . . . PC makers are realizing their worst night-mare: their once exotic, high-technology products have become little more than cheap, interchangeable commodities. Since the PCs all use basically identical hardware, consumers are no longer picky about what brand of computer they buy so long as the price is right. The result: retail prices are falling an average of 8% *every three months.* . . .

So far this year the price war has claimed as many as two dozen firms, including CompuAdd Computer, a big mail-order firm based in Austin, Texas, that filed for bankruptcy in June, and Everex Systems Inc., a PC manufacturer located in Fremont, California. It has also left many others gravely wounded. Dell Computer is expected to report losses of $68 million this week, its first quarterly deficit ever. Ironically, Dell, which built a $2 billion-a-year business by selling cheap, reliable computers by mail, is being done in by copycat mail-order firms offering bigger discounts. . . .

But . . . . the industry's . . . woes are just beginning. By the time the dust settles, analysts predict that fewer than 100 of the 350 PC makers in business today will be left standing. Says Richard Shaffer, editor of the *Computer Letter:* "What's going to happen to the personal-computer industry in the next few years won't be a pretty sight."

The primary instigators of the price war have been new small companies that function more as assembly lines than as manufacturers. Many of these firms, such as Zeos, Graystar and PC Brand, don't invest in costly research or development, nor do they own expensive manufacturing plants. Instead they operate out of factories and garages. Rather than make PCs from scratch, they buy everything from circuit boards, displays and disk drives to entire computers from foreign firms that largely copy American PC designs. Says Brad Smith, vice president of PC research at Dataquest: "All you need to start a PC company today is a fax machine to take orders and a Black & Decker screwdriver to assemble the parts."

The price war, though, is only a symptom of more fundamental transformation taking place in the industry, not all of which will be to the advantage of the U.S. As the PC has changed from a magic black box to a run-of-the-mill commodity like a television set or a radio, so has the economics of the business. Since there is no mystery to the technology, PCs can be manufactured as well as priced like any other commodity. That fact has helped make computers a more global business, but it has also played into the hands of copycat, low-cost producers: up to 75% of the internal components are imported.

Ironically, the price war may have strengthened U.S. computer leadership in some key markets. American firms, which feared a takeover by Japanese firms during the 1980s, have exported their cut-throat pricing to Tokyo with stunning success. Led by IBM, Dell and Compaq, U.S. companies sent shock waves through the Japanese PC establishment by trimming prices up to 30%. While Japanese domestic manufacturers, such as Gujitsu and NEC, have responded with deep discounts of their own, they have been unable to shake off the Americans, much to the delight of Japanese consumers.

Still, more victims than victors are expected as falling prices and changing economics force many U.S. PC makers to reevaluate the market. To compete in the future, say analysts, PC makers must bring unique products to market in order to stand out from the pack. As a result, many companies are placing big bets on such emerging technologies as pen-based

computing, hand-held PCs and multimedia. Says John McCarthy, director of technology at Forrester Research: "If you're just a boxmaker, with nothing else to offer, your days may be numbered.". . .

—*Thomas McCarroll*

Use Your Economic Reasoning

1. In order for the personal computer industry to be purely competitive, the firms in the industry must sell identical products. Is that the case? Support your conclusion with statements from the article.

2. Are there substantial barriers to entering the personal computer industry?

3. The article suggests that personal computer makers were once very successful but that now profits are falling. Use the competitive model to explain what has happened. Supplement your explanation with the appropriate graphs.

4. To the extent that computer manufacturers can bring out personal computers with unique features (that are not elsewhere available), they may be able to continue earning profits. Why? Would this segment of the computer industry be described as purely competitive? Why or why not?

How do we know when the correct amount of a product is being produced? Allocative efficiency requires that price equals marginal cost ($P = MC$). To understand why this is true, it is necessary to reexamine the concepts of price and marginal cost. The price of a product reflects the value that consumers place on an additional unit of the item. Marginal cost, on the other hand, represents the opportunity cost of the resources that are used up in producing that additional unit. For instance, if the marginal cost of an additional unit of lumber were $200, society would have to do without $200 worth of alternative goods—whatever products the same amount of raw materials, labor, and capital could have produced—in order to obtain this unit of lumber. When $P = MC$, the value that consumers place on an additional unit of the product is exactly equal to the value of the other things they must give up in order to produce that product.

To illustrate why allocative efficiency is important, consider a situation in which resources are being allocated *in*efficiently. Suppose that lumber is selling for $300 a unit and that the marginal cost of producing another unit is $270. The production of an additional unit of lumber would allow consumers to receive something valued at $300 while sacrificing alternative products valued at only $270. Clearly society would be better off if these resources were allocated to the production of lumber rather than to alternative goods.

Next consider a situation in which lumber is selling for $300 a unit, but the marginal cost of producing another unit is $330. Here the production of another unit of lumber would require consumers to sacrifice alternative products valued at $330 in order to obtain lumber worth only $300. Society would be better off if these resources were allocated to the production of things other than additional lumber.

Our point is that an efficient allocation of resources requires that each product be produced up to the point at which price is equal to marginal cost. When that occurs, the value of the last unit of output produced is exactly equal to the value of the alternative goods that must be sacrificed for its production. Pure competition ensures this outcome. In order to maximize profits, the purely competitive firm must produce where MR $(P) = MC$ (see Exh. 5.9). Therefore pure competition would ensure the efficient allocation of resources.

Let's synthesize what we have just discussed: Under conditions of pure competition, producers seeking their own self-interest are guided by the presence or absence of profits to produce the right amounts of the products that consumers desire the most. The forces of competition also lead to long-run equilibrium, whereby all firms in the industry operate at the lowest possible average cost (minimum ATC) and receive a price just equal to that cost. Thus in the long run consumers are able to purchase their most-desired products at the lowest possible prices.

Summary

A *firm* is the basic producing unit in a market economy, and an *industry* is a group of firms that produce similar or identical products. A purely competitive industry is one in which (1) a large number of sellers (firms) each produce a small fraction of the total industry supply; (2) the products offered by the different sellers are identical in the minds of consumers; and (3) no substantial barriers exist to prevent firms from entering or leaving the industry. Although no industries fully meet these conditions, the model of pure competition provides a standard by which to judge the performance of less competitive industries and helps us to predict price and output behavior in industries that come reasonably close to meeting the assumptions of the model.

The model of pure competition assumes that firms are profit maximizers; that is, they are always attempting to earn the most profit possible. *Profit* is the excess of a firm's total revenue over its total cost. When a firm's total costs exceed its total revenue, the firm is incurring a *loss*.

All costs can be classified as either fixed or variable. *Fixed costs* are costs that do not vary with the level of output. *Variable costs* are costs that do change with the level of output. *Total cost* is simply the sum of the fixed and variable costs incurred by the firm.

The purely competitive firm may be described as a *price taker;* it accepts the price determined by market forces. The only variable that a purely competitive firm can control in order to influence its profit position is the level of output. In order to reach its profit-maximizing level of output, a firm should produce at the point where marginal revenue equals marginal cost. For the purely competitive firm, the price taker, *marginal revenue (MR)* is equal to price, or average revenue per unit sold. *MR* is the revenue earned from selling one more unit of output. *Marginal cost (MC)* is the additional cost of producing one more unit. *MC* is a more important concept than *average total cost (ATC)* because *MC* determines the level of output that earns maximum profit.

In the long run firms in a purely competitive industry tend to earn a *normal profit,* the amount that the owners' resources could earn elsewhere; earning normal profit means breaking even. Above-normal profits are called *economic profits,* and below-normal profits are called *economic losses.* If economic profits exist in the short run, the entrance of additional firms will cause an increase in supply and drive down the market price to the level of zero economic profits, where all firms are breaking even at normal profit. If losses exist, firms will exit the industry until price has risen to a level consistent with normal profits.

When *long-run equilibrium* is finally established, the purely competitive firm will be producing at minimum *ATC,* the point at which its *ATC* curve is tangent to its demand curve. When firms operate at minimum *ATC, production efficiency* exists. This is a desirable outcome because it indicates that the fewest possible scarce resources are being used to produce the product, and therefore more of society's unlimited wants are being met. In addition to production efficiency, pure competition leads to *allocative efficiency:* the production of the goods and services consumers want the most in the quantities they desire. An efficient allocation of resources requires that each product be produced up to the point at which price is equal to marginal cost. Pure competition ensures this outcome. Thus we can say that the purely competitive firm achieves both production efficiency and allocative efficiency in long-run equilibrium.

Glossary

Allocative efficiency. Using society's scarce resources to produce in the proper quantities the products that consumers value the most.

Average fixed cost (AFC). Total fixed cost divided by the number of units being produced.

Average total cost (ATC). Total cost divided by the number of units being produced.

Average variable cost (AVC). Total variable cost divided by the number of units being produced.

Economic loss. The amount by which total cost, including all opportunity costs, exceeds total revenue.

Economic profit. The amount by which total revenue exceeds total cost, including the opportunity cost of owner-supplied resources. (Also called an above-normal profit.)

Firm. The basic producing unit in a market economy. It buys economic resources and combines them to produce goods and services.

Fixed costs. Costs that do not vary with the level of output.

Industry. A group of firms that produce identical or similar products.

Long-run equilibrium. A situation in which the size of an industry is stable: There is no incentive for additional firms to enter the industry and no pressure for established firms to leave it.

Marginal cost (MC). The additional cost of producing one more unit of output.

Marginal revenue (MR). The additional revenue to be gained by selling one more unit of output.

Normal profit. An amount equal to what the owners of a business could have earned had their resources been employed elsewhere; the opportunity cost of owner-supplied resources.

Price taker. A firm that must accept price as a given that is beyond its control.

> ***Production efficiency.*** Producing a product at the lowest possible average total cost. The essence of production efficiency is that each product be produced with as few scarce resources as possible.
>
> ***Total cost (TC).*** Total fixed cost plus total variable cost.
>
> ***Total revenue (TR).*** The total receipts of a business from the sale of its product. Total revenue is calculated by multiplying the selling price of the product times the number of units sold.
>
> ***Variable costs.*** Costs that change with the level of output, tending to increase when output increases and decrease when output declines.

Study Questions

Fill in the Blanks

1. A purely competitive firm is sometimes described as a _____ _____ because it must accept the price dictated by the market.

2. The demand curve of the purely competitive firm is a _____ _____ line at the price determined in the market.

3. Costs that don't vary with output are called _____ costs; costs that vary with output are called _____ costs.

4. A business that has no output must still pay its _____ costs.

5. _____ cost is the additional cost of producing one more unit of output.

6. Average total cost, _____ cost, and _____ cost all graph as U-shaped curves.

7. If a competitive firm wants to maximize its profits, it should continue to produce additional units so long as _____ is greater than or equal to _____.

8. If economic profits exist in the short run, they will tend to be _____ _____ in the long run as firms _____ the industry and depress market price.

9. If losses exist in the short run, firms will tend to _____ the industry in the long run. This will reduce market _____ and help to
push price back up.

10. When $P = MC$, _____ efficiency exists; when a firm produces its
product at minimum ATC, _____ efficiency exists.

Multiple Choice

1. Which of the following is not characteristic of a purely competitive industry?
   a) A large number of sellers
   b) Identical products
   c) Substantial barriers to entry
   d) Relatively small firms

2. Which of the following is the best example of a price taker?
   a) General Motors
   b) Big Bob's Burger Barn
   c) IBM
   d) An average wheat farmer

Answer questions 3, 4, and 5 on the basis of the following information:

QUANTITY	TOTAL COST
0	$10
1	18
2	23
3	30
4	42

3. The firm's fixed cost is
   a) $5.
   b) $42.
   c) $23.
   d) $10.

4. The marginal cost of the third unit would be
   a) $30.
   b) $7.
   c) $10.
   d) $5.

5. If the firm produced three units, average total cost would be
   a) $10.
   b) $30.

c) $7.

d) None of the above.

6. Which of the following is <u>least</u> likely to be a variable cost?

a) The cost of raw materials

b) Insurance payments

c) The wages of production workers   ✓

d) Shipping expenses   ✓

7. *Price and cost*

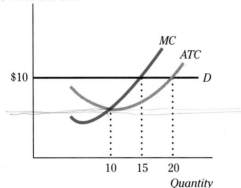

The firm depicted should

a) produce 10 units and maximize its profits.

b) produce 15 units and maximize its profits. —

c) produce 10 units and minimize its losses.

d) produce 15 units and minimize its losses.

e) shut down.

8. *Price and cost*

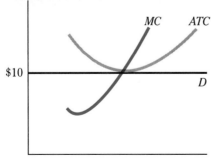

Quantity

The firm depicted is

a) facing a loss.

b) making an economic profit.

c) making a normal profit.

d) about to go out of business.

9. *Price and cost*

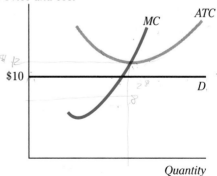

Quantity

The firm represented is

a) earning a profit.

b) facing a loss.

c) not a competitive firm.

d) breaking even.

10. If the firms in an industry are earning economic profits,
    a) additional firms will enter the industry, and the supply curve will shift to the left.
    b) some firms will decide to leave the industry, and the supply curve will shift to the left.
    c) additional firms will enter the industry, and the supply curve will shift to the right.
    d) some firms will leave the industry, and the supply curve will shift to the right.

Problems and Questions for Discussion

1. Even when an industry does not meet the first two requirements of pure competition, consumers will still benefit if barriers to entry are low. Why?

2. Complete the following:

QUANTITY	TC	TVC	TFC	MC	ATC
0	$ 50				
1	100				
2	130				
3	180				
4	260				
5	380				

3. One reason for the declining prices of hand-held calculators may be the fat profits earned by early producers. Explain.

4. Can you think of any undesirable aspects of pure competition? From the consumer's standpoint? From the producer's standpoint?

5. Why would a firm continue to operate even though it is incurring a loss? When should it decide to shut down?

6.
QUANTITY	TOTAL COST
0	$ 50
1	100
2	130
3	180
4	260
5	380

If the prevailing price of this firm's product is $50, how many units of output should it produce? Would it earn a profit or incur a loss? How much profit or loss?

7.

QUANTITY	MARGINAL COST
1	$20
2	10
3	30
4	40
5	50

If the prevailing price of our product is $35 and our total fixed costs are $15, how many units of output should we produce? What will be the amount of our profit or loss?

8. Draw the diagrams necessary to show the purely competitive firm and industry in long-run equilibrium.

9. In long-run equilibrium the purely competitive firm is forced to produce where price equals minimum *ATC*. Why is that good news for consumers?

10. What is meant by allocative efficiency? Why must a firm produce where $P = MC$ in order for allocative efficiency to exist?

Answer Key

Fill in the Blanks

1. price taker
2. horizontal
3. fixed, variable
4. fixed
5. Marginal
6. average variable, marginal
7. marginal revenue, marginal cost
8. eliminated, enter
9. exit, supply
10. allocative, production

Multiple Choice

1. c
2. d
3. d
4. b
5. a
6. b
7. b
8. c
9. b
10. c

CHAPTER 6

The Firm with Market Power

1. Define "market power" and discuss its sources.
2. Distinguish between a price searcher and a price taker.
3. Describe a price searcher's demand and marginal revenue curves.
4. Describe how a price searcher determines the profit-maximizing price and output.
5. Define "price discrimination" and explain why some firms employ the practice while others do not.
6. Evaluate, graphically, the extent of a price searcher's profit or loss.
7. Discuss the impact of barriers to entry on the long-run profitability of price searchers.
8. Explain why price searchers distort the allocation of scarce resources.
9. Describe the day-to-day pricing techniques employed by businesses and the limitations of these techniques.

In the world of pure competition the individual firm is a price taker—it has no pricing discretion of its own, because price is determined by the impersonal forces of supply and demand. The individual seller manipulates only production output, deciding how much or how little to offer for sale at the given price.

We saw in Chapter 5 that lumber manufacturers, wheat farmers, cattle ranchers, and some other agricultural producers are price takers. However, most sellers in the U.S. economy possess a degree of pricing discretion or **market power:** some ability to influence the market price of their products. Chapter 6 examines the process through which firms with pricing discretion select their prices and considers how the existence of market power can distort the allocation of scarce resources. The chapter goes on to explore some pricing techniques employed by businesses and to evaluate the extent to which these techniques make use of economic theory.

The Acquisition of Market Power

A firm may acquire market power in two basic ways: (1) through **product differentiation,** distinguishing its product from similar products offered by other sellers, and (2) by gaining control of a significant fraction of total industry output. Sellers with either or both of these abilities can exert some influence on the market price of their product; sellers that possess neither ability are powerless to influence price.

Product Differentiation as a Source of Market Power

Product differentiation promotes market power by convincing buyers that a particular firm's product is unique or superior and therefore worth a higher price than the products offered by competitors. By claiming superiority, manufacturers of brand-name aspirin tablets manage to obtain prices that are substantially higher than those charged by sellers of generic and store-brand analgesics. By associating uniqueness with status, the makers of designer-label jeans are able to sell their product at prices much higher than nameless jeans can command.

Sellers can differentiate their products in a wide variety of ways. Some product differentiation is based on real, albeit slight, product differences; in other cases the essential differentiation is created by advertising and promotional efforts. Both types of product differentiation allow the seller to distinguish its product from the competition and thereby acquire pricing discretion that is not available to the purely competitive firm.

Control over Supply as a Source of Market Power

Firms that cannot differentiate their products successfully must turn elsewhere to acquire market power. Sellers of standardized commodities, such as steel and oil, can gain pricing discretion by controlling a significant share of the industry output of that product. In the 1970s, for example, the Organization of Petroleum Exporting Countries (OPEC) cartel had substantial market power. (A **cartel** is a group of producers acting together to control output and the price of their product.) Since the cartel controlled a substantial fraction of the world's oil production, it was able to drive up price simply by cutting back on production. The reduced supply created a shortage at the existing price, and users bid up the price as they competed for the available supplies. United States steel-producing firms have also cooperated to restrict supply and maintain high prices, though the market power of these firms has declined substantially in recent years due to foreign competition. Sometimes firms elicit government help to control the supply of a product. For instance, U.S. automakers successfully lobbied Congress for restrictions limiting the number of new foreign automobiles permitted into the United States. By limiting supply, these restrictions help domestic producers maintain high prices. The article on page 170 examines the methods that the DeBeer's diamond cartel has used to restrict the supply of diamonds and how new sources of supply may be undermining its control.

Degrees of Market Power

It stands to reason that all firms would like to possess as much market power as possible. But some firms succeed to a greater extent than others. The local telephone company and the local producer of electric power are obvious examples of firms with substantial market power. Here a single firm is the entire industry and has complete control over the industry's output, giving it substantial pricing discretion. Because of the potentially exploitive market power these firms possess, their rates are commonly regulated by state or local government agencies in an attempt to protect the public from unreasonable prices.

Few firms possess the potential market power enjoyed by the local phone company. The neighborhood dry-cleaning establishment and the nearby pizzeria also have market power, but not very much. These establishments can charge somewhat higher prices than their competitors because they offer convenient locations and/or slightly different products. But their prices cannot be much higher than those of other firms, because their products are very similar. In Chapter 7 we'll take a closer look at the degrees of market power that exist in different types of industries. For now the important thing to remember is that most firms possess at least some pricing discretion; they are not price takers.

Price Searching

Firms with pricing discretion are sometimes described as **price searchers,** which means that although they have some freedom in setting prices, they still must search for the profit-maximizing price. A price searcher may possess substantial market power (as does the local telephone company) or very little (as does the local pizzeria), but all price searchers have one thing in common: Unlike price takers, which will lose all their customers if they raise their

The local utility company possesses substantial market power, since it is generally the only source of electricity.

prices, price searchers can charge more and still retain some customers. Conversely, although price takers can sell any quantity they desire at the market price, price searchers must reduce price to sell more.

Consider as a hypothetical example Woodstuff Inc., a small manufacturer of executive desks. Although a number of firms produce such office furniture, we can be sure that if Woodstuff raises the price of its desks, it won't lose all its customers so long as it keeps its price within reason. Some customers will prefer the quality or design of the Woodstuff desks to those offered by other sellers. Other customers may be swayed by the firm's product warranty or by its record for prompt delivery. Still others may be influenced by the firm's policy of accepting old desks in trade or by the variety of payment plans it offers. For all these reasons and others, Woodstuff will still sell some desks despite a price increase. But it won't be able to sell the same quantity; it will have to choose between selling more desks at a lower price or fewer desks at a higher price. That's the fundamental dilemma faced by all price searchers.

The Price Searcher's Demand Curve

Since price searchers have to reduce their prices in order to sell a higher quantity, they must face downward-sloping demand curves, not the horizontal demand curves confronting price takers. Exhibit 6.1 depicts the demand curve

De Beers's Control of Diamonds Softens

Commodities

LONDON

A diamond may be forever, but maybe not the international diamond cartel run by **De Beers Centenary AG.**

After six decades of dominance over world-wide diamond sales, the London-based Central Selling Organization, which De Beers controls, appears to be splintering under the pressures of a persistent market glut and a Russian rebellion within the ranks of its own producing members. (Swiss-based De Beers Centenary is itself controlled by South Africa's Oppenheimer family.) If De Beers fails to pacify the Russians, the cartel could crumble, triggering sharp cuts in gem prices and in diamond-mining profits.

Russia is the most serious threat right now, as it is the world's second-largest diamond producer after South Africa and a leading member of the CSO cartel. The Russian government is pushing aggressively to circumvent De Beers's grip and sell more of its gems directly on the open market. To raise much-needed hard currency, and challenge De Beers at the bargaining table, Russia has been leaking large quantities of rough, uncut diamonds onto the world market.

"This is brinkmanship to extract the best possible agreement from De Beers," as Russia negotiates a new five-year marketing agreement with the cartel, said Martyn Marriott, a director of Diamond Counsellor International, consultants and valuers of gems. But such behavior not only undermines De Beers's efforts to support diamond prices amid the current glut, but also could open irreparable cracks in the cartel itself.

Under the current agreement that expires next year, De Beers is supposed to control 95% of Russia's diamond exports, an allocation that amounts to roughly a quarter of its cartel's total sales. But Russia is flexing its independence in hopes of expanding its selling quota under a new agreement to be hammered out by the end of 1995.

The results of those negotiations will set the tone for other producers' contracts, dealers said. And if the Russians are allowed to sell more diamonds outside the cartel, Botswana, Australia and other members would certainly demand similar concessions, they warned. . . .

De Beers has dominated the diamond industry since the dawn of South African diamond mining in the 1880s. The CSO cartel was established in the 1930s by De Beers patriarch Sir Ernest Oppenheimer in response to the economic chaos of the Great Depression. By monopolizing the channels through which diamonds are sold, De Beers has maintained an iron grip on supplies and prices ever since.

The cartel buys diamonds not only from De Beers's own African mines (which account for about half of the value of world output), but also from Russia, Australia and other producers. The stones are then sold to 165 select dealers from Antwerp and Tel Aviv to Bombay and New York. Meanwhile, to promote the allure of diamonds, De Beers spends around $170 million a year on glossy advertising, company officials said.

But increasingly, "diamond fields are being discovered outside De Beers's direct South African sphere of influence," said Geoffrey Leggett, a director of IDC (Holdings) Ltd., a London diamond dealer. Barring a surge in world-wide demand, such new competition means it's inevitable that the cartel's hold on the market will slip, he added.

In the past decade, world diamond output has more than doubled to 103 million carats a year—about 55% of which are stones of "gem" or "near-gem" quality to be cut for jewelry, dealers say. (A carat weighs one fifth of a gram.) Despite the cartel's record $2.58 billion gem sales in the first half of the year, supplies are so abundant that De Beers has had to stockpile more and more diamonds to keep prices stable, dealers said. . . .

Russian diamond experts argue that De Beers enriches itself unfairly at the expense of other cartel members. "Depending on the quality, the market pays 13% to 35% more for our diamonds than De Beers," said the Precious Metals and Gems Committee's Mr. Gurevich.

De Beers officials vigorously reject such arguments, saying that the company's commission on purchases is only around 10%. Nor do such criticisms account for De Beers's advertising expenses and other costs of promoting diamonds, which directly benefit Russian ex-

porters, they added. Moreover, De Beers guarantees the Russians a stable sales outlet through the cartel, the officials said.

Indeed, "dealers in Tel Aviv, New York and Bombay are complaining that Russain sales are de-stabilizing the market and hurting business," said Marcel Pruwer, consultant to Rappaport International, New York diamond brokers that publishes prices of gems. Both Mr. Pruwer, and Mr. Marriott of Diamond Counsellor International fear that Russian tactics could backfire by roiling

the market's fragile price structure, ultimately hurting the Russians themselves.

But others are more sanguine. "The Russians were wily traders even under the old Communist regime," said Jacques Zucker, a director of Beldiamex BVBA.

—*Neil Behrmann*

SOURCE: Neil Behrmann, "De Beers's Control of Diamonds Softens," October 31, 1994. Reprinted by permission of *The Wall Street Journal*, © 1994 Dow Jones & Co., Inc. All Rights Reserved Worldwide.

Use Your Economic Reasoning

De Beers is the largest producer of diamonds in the world. It also runs the Central Selling Organization (CSO), which is the middleman between diamond-producing nations and dealers. The CSO buys diamonds from producers and then resells them to dealers.

1. According to the article, De Beers has maintained "an iron grip on [diamond] supplies and prices" ever since forming the CSO in the 1930s. Why is the control of supplies essential to maintaining high prices?

2. Why does the discovery of diamonds "outside De Beers's direct South African sphere of influence" create problems for the CSO? Why is it particularly concerned about maintaining the exclusive

right to market Russia's diamonds.

3. Why has De Beers been stockpiling diamonds? What would happen to diamond prices if they stopped this practice?

4. Diamond producers are unhappy because the CSO charges "a commission" on the diamonds it resells for them. But if producers start to bypass the CSO in order to avoid paying this commission, they may be cutting their own throats. Why?

EXHIBIT 6.1

The Price Searcher's Demand Curve

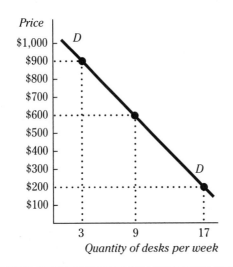

A price searcher can select any price it wants, but it must accept the quantity that results from that price. For example, Woodstuff can charge $900 per desk and sell three desks each week; it can charge $600 per desk and sell nine desks a week; or it can charge $200 and sell seventeen desks per week.

facing our hypothetical desk manufacturer. It shows that at $900 a desk, Woodstuff will sell only three desks each week. At $600 it will sell nine desks a week. Of course, at $200 a desk, sales will be even higher—seventeen desks a week. Although the price searcher can select any price it wants, it cannot choose a high price ($900 a desk) and expect to sell a high quantity (seventeen desks a week), because that's not a point on the demand curve. Thus even a price searcher finds that its actions are constrained by its demand curve; it cannot choose a price without being locked into a quantity. The firm's task, then, is to decide which of the price-quantity combinations it prefers in order to maximize its profit.

The Profit-Maximization Rule

For a price searcher the profit-maximization rule is essentially the same as it is for a price taker: Produce where marginal revenue equals marginal cost. The difference between a price searcher and a price taker is not in the logic used to maximize profits but in the environment confronting the seller. The price taker has no control over price, so it uses the profit-maximization rule solely to determine the optimal level of output. The price searcher, on the other hand, uses this rule to determine both output and price.

Calculating Marginal Revenue

The first step in determining the profit-maximizing price and quantity is finding the price searcher's marginal revenue curve. Because a price searcher faces a downward-sloping demand curve, it must reduce price to sell more. Consequently the marginal revenue that the price searcher gains by selling an additional unit of output will always be *less* than the selling price of the product (not equal to the price, as under pure competition), and the firm's marginal revenue curve will lie inside its demand curve. Since this idea is conveyed best with an example, let's consider Exh. 6.2.

The first two columns of Exh. 6.2 represent the demand schedule for desks that was graphed in Exh. 6.1. You can see that at a price of $1,000, only one desk will be sold each week. At a price of $950, two desks will be sold each week, and total revenue would increase to $1,900. What will be the marginal revenue from selling a second desk? (Remember, marginal revenue is the additional revenue gained by selling one more unit.) The correct answer is $900 ($1,900 − $1,000 = $900), $50 less than the $950 selling price. This rela-

---

EXHIBIT 6.2

Marginal Revenue for a Price Searcher

PRICE PER UNIT	QUANTITY DEMANDED	TOTAL REVENUE	MARGINAL REVENUE
$1,050	0	$ 0	
1,000	1	1,000	$1,000
950	2	1,900	900
900	3	2,700	800
850	4	3,400	700
800	5	4,000	600
750	6	4,500	500
700	7	4,900	400
650	8	5,200	300
600	9	5,400	200
550	10	5,500	100
500	11	5,500	0
450	12	5,400	−100

tionship—marginal revenue being less than price—holds at all price levels.[1] To understand why, we need to consider the price reduction in more detail.

When Woodstuff reduces the price of executive desks from $1,000 to $950, it allows the first customer—the one who would have paid $1,000—to acquire the product for $950. In return the seller manages to attract an additional customer who is willing to pay $950 but wouldn't pay $1,000. The marginal revenue from the second desk is $900—the $950 the firm gains by selling one more unit *minus* the $50 lost by having to reduce the price on the first unit. Because marginal revenue is less than price, a price searcher's marginal revenue curve will always lie inside its demand curve (Exh. 6.3).

The Profit-Maximizing Price and Quantity

To maximize its profit (or minimize its loss), Woodstuff must produce at the output where marginal revenue is equal to marginal cost. This rule permits the firm to continue producing additional units only so long as those units add more to revenue than to costs. Exhibit 6.3 graphs Woodstuff's demand and marginal revenue curves along with its marginal cost curve. Note that the marginal cost curve has the U-shape introduced in Chapter 5; marginal cost declines initially and then rises as output is increased.

How many desks should Woodstuff produce and sell in order to maximize its profits? You can tell by studying the graph (or the table accompanying it) that the profit-maximizing (loss-minimizing) output is seven units per week. When output is less than seven units a week, marginal revenue exceeds marginal cost. For instance, the marginal revenue from the fifth unit of output is $600, and the marginal cost of that unit is only $300. Thus Woodstuff will be $300 better off if it produces and sells that unit. The sixth unit doesn't make as great a contribution to the firm, but the marginal revenue of $500 still exceeds the marginal cost of $340, so the unit should be produced. The seventh unit adds $400 to revenue and $400 to cost, so seven units represents the profit-maximizing (loss-minimizing) output: the output where $MR = MC$. All subsequent units would add more to cost than to revenue, so their sale would either reduce the firm's profit or increase its loss.[2]

Once the profit-maximizing output has been determined, the profit-maximizing price can be discovered by drawing a line directly up to the firm's demand curve and over to the vertical axis. Remember, the demand curve shows the amount that consumers are willing to purchase at various prices. If we

---

[1] Note that marginal revenue will always be equal to price for the first unit of output. For all subsequent units, marginal revenue will be less than price.
[2] In this example the firm will earn the same profit (or incur the same loss) whether it sells six or seven units of output. The firm wants to operate where $MR = MC$ not because it benefits from the last unit sold but because it benefits from each unit up to that point.

EXHIBIT 6.3

Determining the Profit-Maximizing Price

PRICE PER UNIT	QUANTITY OF DESKS	MARGINAL REVENUE	MARGINAL COST
:	:	:	:
$800	5	$600	$300
750	6	500	340
700	7	400	400
650	8	300	480
600	9	200	580
:	:	:	:

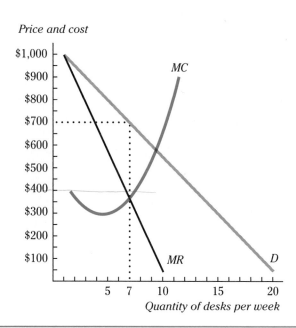

Price and cost

Quantity of desks per week

All firms maximize their profits (or minimize their losses) by producing at the output where marginal revenue is equal to marginal cost. In this example the profit-maximizing output is seven units. Once the profit-maximizing output has been determined, the profit-maximizing price can be discovered by drawing a line directly up to the firm's demand curve and over to the vertical axis. In our example the profit-maximizing price is $700 per desk.

know the price, we can tell how much will be purchased. Conversely if we know the quantity (output), we can use the demand curve to determine the maximum price that the firm can charge and still sell that amount of output. In our example Woodstuff should charge a price of $700 per desk. That's the firm's profit-maximizing price.

Pricing Videos: A Rental-or-Sales Gamble

After weeks of speculation. Paramount Home Video is expected to announce on Thursday that "Ghost," one of the largest box-office hits of last year, will be released as a videocassette on March 21. Paramount sets no retail price on its videos, but using an industry formula based on the wholesale price that Paramount will probably charge distributors, "Ghost" should cost about $100.

The high prices raises a question heard frequently in video stores. Why are some new hit movies priced low when they are first released and others priced four or five times as high? Why does "Pretty Woman," nearly as big a hit as "Ghost," cost $19.99 and "Total Recall," $24.99, when "Dick Tracy" is priced at $92.99 and "The Hunt for Red October" at $99.50?

"Customers are confused about prices," said Jack Messer, president of the Video Software Dealers Association. "They're particularly confused when two or three movies come out at the same time. How can one be $19 and the others $90?"

The answer, of course, has to do with profit, or rather potential profit. By offering a videocassette at a lower price, a studio is gambling that income from sales direct to consumers will exceed income from sales to rental outlets. Studios normally sell several hundred thousand cassettes to rental dealers at wholesale. . . .

By offering the film at the lower retail price, the studios are hoping that sales to the public will reach into the millions. . . .

Based on its performance in theaters, "Ghost," which many compare to "Pretty Woman" in its audience appeal, would seem a likely candidate for a lower sale price. Officials at Paramount won't comment on the coming release. . . .

. . . while rentals still dominate video, industry figures show that sales of hit movies—along with sales of older films and nontheatrical titles of all kinds—are the fastest-growing area of the industry.

Children's films, animated or otherwise, generally make the strongest candidates for sales. "The things that do best have great kid appeal because kids are the audience that will repeat them over and over," said Ron Castell, a senior vice president at Blockbuster, the nation's largest chain of video stores. Disney, for instance, has had many sales successes with its animated films—"Bambi," "Peter Pan," "The Little Mermaid"—as well as such theatrical titles as "Honey, I Shrunk the Kids," which was released early last year. Each of those films carried a lower price tag.

"Pretty Woman" a Best Seller
But other types of films also sell well. One notable example is "Pretty Woman," which has been at or near the top of many best-seller lists since its release last October by Touchstone, a Disney company. The sales success of "Pretty Woman" is linked to its popularity among women and its musical score, among other reasons.

Action-adventure also sells strongly—"Indiana Jones and the Last Crusade," "Lethal Weapon 2" and "Total Recall," all released last year, are examples—provided that their helpings of sex and violence aren't objectionable to either consumers or outlets, particularly mass merchandisers anxious to preserve a family image. These films all sold for about $25.

Other sales titles perform well for reasons ranging from their stars to their collectibility as a genre or as part of a series ("Indiana Jones," for example), or suitability as gifts.

But many of those in the video business say it's a rare movie—a "Batman," "E.T.," "Top Gun," "Honey, I Shrunk the Kids," "Peter Pan," to name a few examples—that has sufficient mass appeal to make it more profitable for a studio to sell it than to make it a rental title. . . .

—*Peter M. Nichols*

SOURCE: Peter M. Nichols, "Pricing Videos: A Rental-or-Sales Gamble," January 29, 1991. Copyright © 1991 by The New York Times Company. Reprinted with permission.

Use Your Economic Reasoning

1. What comments in the article suggest that Paramount and other producers of videos are price searchers rather than price takers?

2. How do studios decide which films to target for the rental market (with higher prices) and which to aim at the retail market? Can this be related to the price elasticity of demand?

3. Suppose that Paramount determines that it will maximize its profit on a new video by charging a price of $25 and selling one million units. Will the marginal revenue gained from the sale of the millionth unit be greater than, equal to, or less than $25? What can we say about the marginal *cost* of the millionth unit? (*Hint:* Try to picture this situation graphically.)

The article on page 176, "Pricing Videos: A Rental-or-Sales Gamble," illustrates that the search for the profit-maximizing price involves some uncertainty. We'll have more to say about that issue later in the chapter.

A Digression on Price Discrimination

In the preceding example we have assumed that there is a single profit-maximizing price, and we'll return to that assumption in just a moment. But in some instances, there is more than one profit-maximizing price. *Price discrimination* exists when firms charge different consumers different prices for the same product.

Surgeons and lawyers and car dealers often practice "individual" price discrimination. They charge virtually every customer a different price, a price based largely on the customer's ability to pay (but limited, at least in the case of automobiles, by how much that customer has "shopped around" and become informed about the prices charged elsewhere). To illustrate, suppose that Honest John's Autos is selling the RAMPAGE automobile. Assume also that the following represents a portion of the demand schedule for Honest John's automobiles.

PRICE	QUANTITY
$20,000	1
19,000	2
18,000	3
17,000	4
16,000	5

As you can see, only one consumer is willing to pay Honest John $20,000 for a RAMPAGE. A second consumer won't pay $20,000 but is willing to pay $19,000. (Note that two consumers are willing to buy automobiles at a price of $19,000. One of those individuals is the first consumer, the one who would have paid $20,000.[3]) A third consumer won't pay $19,000 but would pay $18,000.

Car dealers that practice price discrimination want their sales personnel to obtain the highest price that each consumer will pay. So the salesperson would try to extract $20,000 from the first customer, $19,000 from the second, $18,000 from the third, and so on. Honest John would be willing to continue selling additional units as long as the price he could obtain was at least equal to the marginal cost of an additional vehicle. (Notice that when firms discriminate, the marginal revenue the firm receives from the sale of an additional

---

[3] This assumes that each consumer buys only one automobile.

unit is *equal* to its selling price, not less than its selling price as it was for the nondiscriminating price searcher.) For instance, if the marginal cost of an additional RAMPAGE is $16,500, Honest John would be willing to sell the fourth vehicle (which adds $17,000 to his revenue) but not the fifth (which contributes only $16,000).

It is unlikely that the salesperson would actually be able to obtain the maximum price a consumer would be willing to pay. But effective sales personnel may come close. If the sales rep started at the sticker price on the vehicle and then haggled, giving in only when necessary, he or she might approximate this solution. And, of course, that would mean more profit for the dealer than could be obtained by selling all four of these vehicles at a price low enough to convince the fourth buyer to participate.

Another form of price discrimination is "group" price discrimination. This is a situation in which a firm charges different prices to different *categories* of consumers. For example, movie theaters commonly charge different ticket prices to adults, students, and senior citizens. And we'd all like to order from the Kiddie menu when we're short on cash. Even telephone companies practice price discrimination, charging one price for long distance service during the day (when most calls are business related) and a lower price in the evening (when we make our personal calls).

The purpose of group price discrimination is similar to the purpose of individual price discrimination—to obtain the highest price possible from each category of consumer. Consider, for instance, the different ticket prices that airlines charge business and vacation travelers. The airlines recognize that the business traveler usually *must* travel by air. He or she cannot afford the time involved in a lengthy automobile trip. In addition, many of these trips arise on short notice, so the business executive has no other alternative. These factors mean that the business traveler's demand curve for plane travel is less elastic—less price sensitive—than the vacation traveler, who usually has a more flexible time schedule. By charging business travelers higher fares, the airlines maximize their profits from that group without discouraging travel by vacationers.[4]

Why doesn't everyone practice price discrimination? There are two primary reasons. First, it takes time, and time is money. Think about our car dealer again. It can take hours for the salesperson to negotiate with a customer and arrive at the price that particular customer will pay. That time expenditure makes sense in the case of big-ticket items such as cars and motor

---

[4] Airlines separate business and vacation travelers by requiring that the lower priced tickets (intended for vacationers) be purchased well in advance and/or that the traveler stay over at least one Saturday night before returning. These are requirements that most business travelers are unable or unwilling to meet.

homes and boats. But it doesn't make sense for milk and clothing and most of the items we buy every day.

A second reason firms may not practice price discrimination is that they may be unable to prevent consumers from reselling items that they can buy cheaper than other customers. For instance, suppose that the AJAX TV Center was charging regular customers $300 for a TV set, but allowing senior citizens to buy the same set for $250. Under these circumstances we might expect to see some seniors buying TV sets in large quantities and reselling them at a profit. That would be a nice way for those senior citizens to earn extra cash, but it would make it very difficult for AJAX to sell any television sets at the higher price. The point is that when we can't prevent a product's resale, we generally offer that product at the same price to everyone. Because most markets are characterized by uniform pricing, we will now return to our single-price model.

Evaluating the Short-Run Profit or Loss

As we discovered in Chapter 5, producing where $MR = MC$ does not ensure a profit. It ensures only that the firm will do as well as possible in any short-run situation. Recall that we find profits by subtracting total costs from total revenue. In our present example we can't tell whether Woodstuff Inc. is earning a profit or incurring a loss, because we've focused entirely on marginal values.

To compute Woodstuff's short-run profit or loss, we need to know the firm's total revenue and its total costs. Exhibit 6.4 shows our hypothetical price searcher in three different situations. In case (a) the firm is earning a profit. As in the previous chapter, the amount of the profit can be determined by comparing total revenue with total cost. Total revenue is equal to $4,900 (the $700 selling price × 7 units—the profit-maximizing output). Total cost is equal to $4,200 (the ATC of $600 × 7 units). This leaves the firm with an economic profit of $700 ($4,900 − $4,200 = $700).

Case (b) finds our price searcher earning only a normal profit. You can see in the diagram that the MC curve intersects the MR curve at an output of six desks. At that output the profit-maximizing price would be $600, so total revenue would be $3,600 ($600 × 6 units). Since the ATC curve is tangent to the demand curve at $600, ATC must also be $600 when the firm is producing six desks. Therefore the firm's total cost is $3,600 (the ATC of $600 × 6 units). This means that the firm is earning zero economic profit ($3,600 − $3,600 = $0), or a normal profit. Recall that a normal profit is acceptable; the owners of the business are earning as much as they could expect to earn if they invested their time and money elsewhere.

Case (c) depicts the price searcher facing a short-run economic loss (earning less than a normal profit). At the profit-maximizing (loss-minimizing)

EXHIBIT 6.4

Calculating the Short-Run Profit or Loss

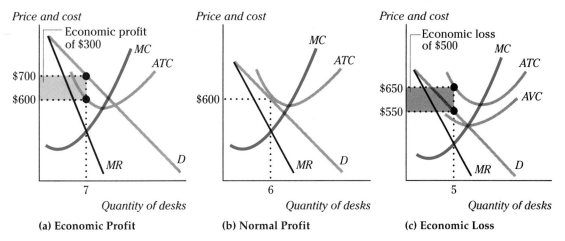

(a) Economic Profit   **(b) Normal Profit**   **(c) Economic Loss**

Case (a): When the profit-maximizing price is above *ATC*, the price searcher will earn an economic profit. Case (b): When the price is exactly equal to *ATC*, the price searcher will earn a zero economic profit, or a normal profit. Case (c): When the price is less than *ATC*, the firm will incur an economic loss—it will earn less than a normal profit.

output of five desks, the firm's total cost of $3,250 (*ATC* of $650 × 5 units) exceeds its total revenue of $2,750 (the $550 selling price × 5 units). This results in a loss of $500 ($3,250 − $2,750 = $500). Note, however, that the selling price of $550 exceeds the firm's average variable cost of approximately $500, so the firm should continue to operate rather than shut down. Since *P* exceeds *AVC* by $50, each of the five units produced will contribute $50 toward paying the firm's fixed costs. Through continued operation, the firm reduces its loss by $250. Of course, if *AVC* exceeded price (for example, if the average variable cost curve were positioned where the *ATC* curve is presently located), the firm would minimize its loss by shutting down.

Barriers to Entry and Long-Run Profits

We've seen that in the short run price searchers may gain economic profits, may earn a normal profit, may even sustain a loss. But how do they do in the long run? Is it possible for price searchers to earn economic profits in the long run, or is a normal profit the best that can be expected? (All firms, whether price searchers or price takers, must earn at least a normal profit in the long run, or the owners will sell out and reinvest their money where a normal return is possible.)

If a price searcher is earning an economic profit in the short run, its ability to continue earning that profit in the long run depends on the extent of the barriers to entering that industry. Some price searchers exist in industries with substantial entry barriers—automobile and aircraft manufacturing, for example. Others exist in industries with very modest barriers—shoe retailing, fast photo processing, and dry-cleaning establishments, to cite a few. Because entry barriers differ from industry to industry, we can't generalize about the long-run fate of price searchers as we could about the fate of price takers. (Recall that a normal profit is the *best* that a price taker can expect in the long run. Because there are no significant barriers to entering purely competitive industries, any short-run profits will be eliminated in the long run, as additional firms enter and drive down prices.)

If price searchers are protected by substantial barriers to entry, short-run profits can turn into long-run profits. For instance, it is estimated that Hoffman-La Roche of Switzerland earned multi*billion* dollar profits from the worldwide sale of its Valium and Librium tranquilizers, drugs that were protected by patents and therefore could not be duplicated by competitors.[5] Although profits of this magnitude are clearly exceptional, they indicate the impact of entry barriers. In the absence of substantial barriers, we expect economic profits to attract additional sellers into the market. This leads to price cutting and other forms of competition that have the potential to eliminate economic profits in the long run.

Thus the fact that a price searcher earns above-normal profits in the short run is no assurance that it will be able to do so in the long run. Unless entry barriers exist, the entrance of additional firms will result in added competition for consumers' dollars and subsequent elimination of all economic profits.

Price Searchers and Resource Allocation

Although the price searcher maximizes its profit by producing the output at which marginal revenue is equal to marginal cost, such a firm actually produces too little output from a societal standpoint.

Recall from Chapter 5 that an efficient allocation of resources requires that firms continue to produce each product up to the precise point where its selling price *(P)* is equal to its marginal cost *(MC)*. This is desirable because *P* is a reflection of the value consumers place on an additional unit of the product in

---

[5] F. M. Scherer, *Industrial Market Structure and Economic Performance,* 2d ed. (Chicago: Rand McNally, 1980), p. 449.

question, whereas *MC* represents the value of the alternative goods that must be sacrificed to produce the additional unit. If firms produce at the output where $P = MC$, the value of the last unit produced is exactly equal to the value of the alternative products sacrificed to obtain that unit. Alternatively the benefit that consumers expect to derive from an additional unit of this product is exactly equal to the cost of producing that additional unit.

Price searchers distort the allocation of resources because they will not allow output to expand up to the point where $P = MC$. To do so would cause them to earn a smaller profit (or suffer a larger loss) than they earn by operating where $MR = MC$.

Consider Exh. 6.5. The profit-maximizing price searcher will produce where $MR = MC$, at seven units in this example. At that output marginal revenue and marginal cost are equal. But if you move upward in the exhibit from seven units of output to the demand curve, you find that when *MR* and *MC* are equal to $400, price is equal to $700. Therefore price exceeds marginal cost at the profit-maximizing output. This tells us that society values an additional unit of this product more highly than the alternative products that could be produced with the same resources. In short, the price searcher is producing

EXHIBIT 6.5

Price Searchers and Resource Misallocation

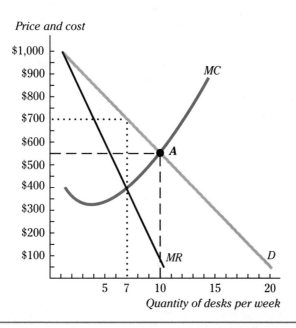

Quantity of desks per week

Allocative efficiency requires that production take place at the output where $P = MC$, an output of ten units in this example. But the profit-maximizing price searcher will produce where $MR = MC$, an output of seven units. By restricting output, price searchers fail to provide consumers with the optimal quantity of this product and misdirect resources to the production of less-valued goods and services.

too little output; fewer resources are being allocated to the production of this product than is socially desirable.

An efficient allocation of resources would require the price searcher to produce at the output where the marginal cost curve intersects the demand curve (see point *A* in Exh. 6.5). If our hypothetical price searcher produced ten units of output and charged a price of $550 (so that $P = MC$), resources would be allocated efficiently. But that won't happen, because expanding output in this manner would cause the firm to earn a smaller profit. Note that for each unit beyond seven (the profit-maximizing output), marginal cost *exceeds* marginal revenue. Production of these additional units would lower the firm's total profit.

Thus price searchers distort the allocation of scarce resources by producing too little output and thereby forcing resources to be used in the production of less-valued products. In response to this resource misallocation, the federal government has employed a variety of means to encourage competition or to correct for the negative impact of market power. (These efforts are discussed in Chapter 7.)

Pricing in Practice

A firm's day-to-day pricing techniques may differ somewhat from the theoretically correct pricing practices that we have discussed thus far. This difference stems in part from the fact that firms are frequently guided by motives other than profit maximization. Ethical considerations, for example, may result in the pursuit of a "satisfactory" profit rather than a maximum profit. The quest for prestige is another motive that may cause the firm or its managers to maximize sales or market share, subject to some minimum profit constraint.[6] Firms pursuing objectives such as these will not select the price where $MR = MC$. For instance, if a firm wants to maximize sales, it will choose a lower price (than the one that maximizes profit) to encourage additional customers to buy the product.

Even those firms motivated by the pursuit of maximum profit may find it difficult to employ the $MR = MC$ rule in precisely the manner we've described. In most real-world situations pricing takes place in an environment beset with uncertainty. Firms seldom possess precise information about their demand and cost curves. These deficiencies force sellers to rely on other methods for determining price.

---

[6] Although firms may choose to pursue objectives other than profit maximization, they must strive to achieve at least a normal profit in the long run. Otherwise they won't be able to attract the economic resources they need in order to remain in business. Thus, although some firms may not choose to pursue profit *maximization,* no firm can ignore profitability entirely.

Cost-Plus Pricing

The most common technique for determining selling price is probably **cost-plus pricing** (or full-cost pricing, as it is sometimes called). In its simplest form the cost-plus method involves adding some percentage, or markup, to the cost of the goods acquired for sale. For example, a furniture store may pay $100 for a chair, mark it up 150 percent, and attempt to sell it for $250.

Firms using this method do not consider all their costs in arriving at the selling price. They assume that the markup on the **cost of goods sold** (the cost of the items they buy for resale) will be sufficient to cover all other costs—rent, utilities, wages, and salaries—and leave something for profit.

A more sophisticated version of the cost-plus technique attempts to ensure that *all* costs are recovered by building them into the price. Here the seller arrives at a price by determining first the average total cost *(ATC)* of producing the product or offering the service and then adding some margin for profit.

A Cost-Plus Example: Building a Boat. Let's assume that we have just purchased a boat-manufacturing facility for $200,000. It has an expected useful life of twenty years and was designed with a production capacity of 1,000 boats per year. The estimated cost of materials is $150 per boat, and estimated direct labor cost (the cost of the labor directly involved in the manufacture of the boat) is $200 per boat. Besides these variable costs, we have a variety of fixed costs—everything from utility payments to the salaries of security guards—that amount to $125,000 per year. Since our factory cost $200,000 and has a useful life of twenty years, we must also add $10,000 per year ($200,000/20 years) for **depreciation**—the reduction in the value of the production plant due to wear and tear and obsolescence.

Assuming that we expect to sell 1,000 boats this year, which would mean that we would be able to operate the plant at its designed capacity, we arrive at the following costs per boat:

Direct labor	$200.00
Materials	150.00
Depreciation on plant and equipment ($10,000 per year, or $10 per boat—i.e., $10,000 divided by 1,000 boats)	10.00
Fixed costs ($125,000 per year, or $125 per boat—i.e., $125,000 divided by 1,000 boats)	125.00
Total cost per boat (average total cost)	**$485.00**

Now that we have the average total cost of producing a boat, the final step in determining the selling price is adding on the markup that provides our profit margin. A number of factors seem to influence the size of the markup that firms strive to achieve. For instance, executives commonly mention the firm's assessment of what is a "fair" or "reasonable" profit margin.

Custom is another factor that seems to play a major role in some industries. Retailers, for example, often use a particular percentage markup simply because they have always used it or because it is the accepted, therefore "normal," markup in the industry. Obviously a markup that endures long enough to become customary must be somewhat successful in allowing firms to meet their profit objectives. In fact it may indicate that these firms have discovered through informal means the price and output levels that would have emerged had they applied the theoretical $MR = MC$ rule.

A final factor influencing the size of the markup is the impact of competition. Although a firm may desire high profit margins, ultimately the degree of actual and potential competition determines what margins the firm will be able to achieve. The more competitive the industry, the lower the profit margin.

Let's assume that we've considered all these factors and have decided to use a 10 percent markup on cost in determining our selling price. Our final step, then, is to add the 10 percent markup to the average total cost calculated earlier. The resulting value is the firm's selling price as determined by the cost-plus technique:

Total cost per boat (average total cost)	$485.00
Markup on cost (10 percent × $485)	48.50
Selling price	**$533.50**

Cost-Plus Pricing in Action. Cost-plus pricing has been criticized by economists as a naive pricing technique that ignores demand and competition and bases price solely on cost considerations. When the cost-plus technique is used in a mechanical or unthinking way, these criticisms are certainly valid. But that's seldom the case. Most businesses consider carefully the strength of demand and the degree of competition before selecting their markup or profit margin. In addition, the cost-plus price generally is viewed as a preliminary estimate, or starting point, rather than as the final price. Since demand and competition seldom can be measured with precision, the firm must be willing to adjust its price if it has misjudged market conditions. It is through these subjective adjustments that the firm gropes its way closer to the profit-maximizing price. A few examples may help to illustrate this point.

Example 1: The Department Store. A local department store receives its shipment of Nifty Popcorn Poppers just in time for the Christmas gift-buying season. It prices the item at $19.50 in order to earn a 30 percent markup on the popper's cost.

Competition—like the competition among the fast-food retailers on this New York street corner—limits the profit margins that firms can achieve.

Two weeks later the store has sold 50 percent of the shipment, and Christmas is still six weeks away. The manager realizes that he has a "hot" selling item and that he won't be able to get any more from the manufacturer in time for Christmas. He decides to increase his markup (and consequently the product's selling price) in order to take advantage of the product's strong demand.

Example 2: The Car Dealer. A car dealer in a large metropolitan area has found that in the past several years she has been able to average a 15 percent profit margin on the cost of the automobiles she sells. Her experience has taught her that it is much easier to sell a car at a high markup early in the season, when people will pay to be among the first to own the new model, than later, when the next year's model is about to be announced. So the dealer instructs her sales personnel to strive for a 20–25 percent markup early in the year and to settle for a 5–10 percent margin toward the end of the season.

Example 3: The Appliance Manufacturer. Acme Appliance manufactures refrigerators for sale to a regional market. In response to consumers' different

Final Final Sale! Stores Unload Buyers' Errors

Approaching the cashier, Susanne Lemberger can hardly carry all the designer dresses, jackets and shoes she has picked out. But the price is light—about $200. "It almost seems like a mistake," she says.

It is, and Dillard Department Stores Inc. is paying for it.

Ms. Lemberger, a real-estate agent, is shopping in what some department-store executives call a repository of mistakes: the Dillard clearance center in Kansas City, Kan. One of the oldest kinds of discount stores, it is the ignoble home of merchandise that failed to sell—even at 50% off—in Dillard Department Stores. At its half-dozen clearance centers, Dillard unloads some merchandise for less than wholesale. The full retail price of Ms. Lemberger's booty exceeded $1,000.

The existence of these centers shows that department-store retailing remains an art—despite predictions that technology would make it a science. Dillard's computer system tracks every purchase and informs company officials which items aren't selling and need promotion and which are selling out and need replenishing. But as yet, computers can't predict consumer tastes.

Not long ago, Dillard bet on an American Film Classics necktie, featuring illustrations from "Gone With the Wind"; on a polka-dot sweatshirt for teenage girls; and on a dark-brown all-cotton Claiborne lady's jacket. Today, dozens—even hundreds—of these items fill the Dillard clearance center in Arlington, Texas.

"This isn't retailing—it's getting some money out of the goods and washing your hands of it," says Sidney Doolittle, a Chicago retail consultant.

That's a fine distinction for customers who find a Ralph Lauren sweater just as handsome at $29.99 as at $165—and who are willing to buy it in August. "It's the only Dillard's I'll shop," says Jeanne Young, a Missouri schoolteacher who drove 40 miles to Kansas to shop at the Dillard clearance center, past full-price Dillards as well as factory-outlet centers.

Few discount stores or factory outlets can beat the clearance centers' prices. On a recent trip, Ms. Young and two companions "bought $2,200 worth of merchandise—I mean names like Ellen Tracy and Liz Claiborne—for $300," she says.

Predicting consumer behavior is the job of retail buyers; for them, clearance centers are halls of shame. "Walking in and seeing those 1,000 green sweaters you bought isn't pleasant," says Kay Winzenried, a Dallas retail consultant whose 17-year career at the Neiman Marcus chain included a stint as buyer.

At Neiman Marcus, whose clearance centers are named Last Call, buyers are required to "visit their mistakes" twice a year, says Ms. Winzenried, adding that any buyer whose goods consistently land there won't survive. But she and others say that any buyer whose choices never enter a clearance center may be buying too little. "Not having what the customer wants is the biggest mistake," Ms. Winzenried says.

Nor should a buyer apologize, she and others say, for taking risks. In an age of complaints about department-store homogeneity, "buyers should be encouraged to seek novelties, and novelty makes the gamble greater," says Stanley Marcus, the former chief executive of Neiman Marcus who advises retailers on buying matters. . . .

Dillard has placed its centers in unattractive sites that it gained as part of acquisitions. The Kansas City store, once a Macy's, sits in a half-abandoned mall, the store itself half closed. The license plates outside indicate that word has spread far beyond Kansas. Savvy shoppers know when to come, for pickings are slim between shipments. "My daughter-in-law works at Dillard and tells me when new stuff is coming," says Ms. Young, the teacher from Missouri.

For the uninformed, the store can be a shock. With no sign out front distinguishing it from any other Dillard, Robert Adoki, a federal-government worker, pulled off the interstate expecting a full-price department store. "What is this?" he asks, entering what resembles a garage sale. "I thought this was a Dillard."

—*Kevin Helliker*

Use Your Economic Reasoning

1. The article describes 1,000 green sweaters that Dillard's was unable to sell, even at 50 percent of their original price. What theory leads us to believe that further price reductions will allow the firm to sell them?

2. Dillard's can't get back what it paid for the 1,000 sweaters described above; those costs are "sunk." Should what Dillard's paid for the sweaters influence the minimum price Dillard's is willing to accept for them?

3. Dillard's could simply give away merchandise it is unable to sell in its regular stores. Instead, it has opted to run six "clearance centers." How should Dillard's decide if these clearance centers are a wise investment? Can marginal reasoning help them here?

budgets and "needs" in terms of optional features, the company offers two models: a basic model that is available only in white and a deluxe model that offers additional features and comes in a variety of colors.

In pricing its product, Acme feels that a 10 percent markup on average cost will produce the desired rate of return on its investment. Rather than use a single markup percentage, however, Acme has decided to apply a 5 percent markup to the basic model and a 15 percent markup to the deluxe model, for an average markup of 10 percent. This decision was made because previous sales experience indicated that low-income customers are substantially more sensitive to price than are intermediate- and high-income customers.

Although the cost-plus technique is essentially straightforward, its application requires management personnel to make subjective judgments about the strength of demand and the degree of competition, as these examples illustrate. Both factors are difficult to evaluate and impossible to quantify. As a consequence, pricing remains more an art than a science.

Marginal Analysis and Managerial Decisions

As the foregoing examples indicate, firms that desire to maximize profits must adjust their cost-plus prices to reflect market conditions; they cannot use the technique mechanically. Learning to "think marginally" can also lead to better decisions and greater profits.

The major limitation of the cost-plus technique is the fact that it doesn't rely on **marginal analysis:** a comparison of the additional revenue and the additional cost associated with a contemplated action. It concentrates instead on average values, stressing the need to recover all costs plus some markup. That can lead to smaller profits (or larger losses) than necessary, since (as we will see in a moment) marginal costs are the only relevant costs for many business decisions.

Although firms commonly lack the information required to use the $MR = MC$ approach to price determination, they generally have some knowledge of marginal values. For instance, even though a firm probably does not know the marginal cost of producing the two hundred thousandth unit of output, usually it can determine the additional cost of producing some block of units— another 10,000 cars, for example. And probably it can discover the additional cost of some contemplated course of action, such as adding or discontinuing a product line. This information will allow a firm to improve the quality of many of its decisions.

To illustrate, suppose that you own a chain of fast-food restaurants that has traditionally opened for business at 11:00 A.M. What costs would you consider in deciding whether it would be profitable to open earlier in order to serve breakfast?

The cost-plus approach implies that the decision should be based on the full cost (or **fully allocated cost,** as it is sometimes called) of the new project—on the project's share of the firm's total costs. In other words, the breakfast meal would be expected to generate enough revenue to pay for the labor, utilities, and food used in the morning meal, plus a share of the firm's overhead costs (rent, insurance, equipment depreciation) and some profit margin. If you anticipate enough business to achieve that objective, you should open for business. Otherwise you would remain closed.

Marginal analysis yields a different conclusion. According to marginal analysis, the only costs relevant to a decision are those that are influenced by the decision. In deciding whether to open for breakfast, you should *ignore* such costs as rent and insurance because these fixed costs will have to be paid whether or not the restaurants are open for breakfast. The only true cost of serving breakfast is the marginal cost: the increase in the restaurant's total cost that results from the breakfast meal. If the marginal revenue derived from serving breakfast is expected to exceed the marginal cost, you should open earlier. If not, you should continue to serve only the noon and evening meals. Does it make sense for businesses to run clearance centers to get rid of unwanted merchandise? Can firms justify selling product for less than 25 percent of their original price? Read "Final Final Sale . . ." on page 188 and decide for yourself.

Marginal analysis can often improve the quality of managerial decisions. Many projects that don't appear to be profitable when evaluated on the basis of their fully allocated costs look quite appealing when analyzed in terms of their marginal costs and revenues. By using marginal analysis and applying judgment to cost-plus prices, firms may be able to approximate the profit levels that would be achieved by using the $MR = MC$ rule.

Summary

In most U.S. industries individual firms have some pricing discretion, or *market power.* A firm may acquire market power either through *product differentiation*—distinguishing its product from similar products offered by other sellers—or by gaining control of a significant fraction of total industry output. Firms with either or both of these abilities can exert some influence on the market price of their product.

Sellers with pricing discretion are described as *price searchers* because they must search for the profit-maximizing price. All price searchers face demand curves that slope downward and to the right. Unlike the price taker, which can sell as much as it desires at the market price, the price searcher has to reduce price to sell more. Therefore the price searcher is forced to choose between selling a low quantity at a high price or selling a high quantity at a low price.

Because price must be reduced in order to sell more, the marginal revenue the price searcher obtains from selling an additional unit of output is always less than the unit's selling price, and the price searcher's marginal revenue curve lies inside its demand curve. The price searcher can determine the profit-maximizing (loss-minimizing) level of output by equating marginal revenue and marginal cost. The profit-maximizing price can then be discovered by drawing a line directly up from the quantity to the firm's demand curve and over to the vertical (price) axis.

Some price searchers are able to enlarge their profits by practicing price discrimination. *Price discrimination* is charging different consumers different prices for the same product. When firms engage in individual price discrimination, they attempt to charge each consumer the maximum price he or she will pay. Group price discrimination results when firms charge different prices to different categories of consumers.

Like price takers, price searchers must determine the amount of their profit or loss by comparing total revenue and total cost. If total revenue exceeds total cost, the price searcher is earning an economic profit; if total cost exceeds total revenue, the firm is incurring an economic loss. When total revenue is exactly equal to total cost, a normal profit is being earned.

Although a normal profit is the most that a price taker can hope to earn in the long run, a price searcher may be able to do better. When price searchers are protected by substantial barriers to entry, they may continue to earn long-run economic profits.

The possibility of long-run profits is not the only outcome that distinguishes price searchers from price takers. In addition, price searchers fail to achieve allocative efficiency. Allocative efficiency requires that producers expand output up to the point where $P = MC$. Although price takers do produce at this level, price searchers stop short of it. In other words, price searchers produce less output than is socially desirable.

The pricing techniques employed by businesses often differ from the theoretically correct procedures described by economists. Although the $MR = MC$ approach would enable the firm to maximize its profits, the seller seldom has sufficient information to use this approach in the manner described. As a consequence, most price searchers resort to some other method for determining price. The most common technique is *cost-plus pricing*.

With cost-plus pricing, the seller arrives at the price by determining the average total cost *(ATC)* of producing a product and adding to this figure some margin for profit. Although this technique seems quite straightforward, its application requires managers to make subjective judgments regarding strength of demand and degree of competition.

The major limitation of the cost-plus approach is the fact that it doesn't rely on *marginal analysis*. Although firms seldom know precisely what their marginal cost and revenue curves look like, they generally have some knowledge of their marginal values. By undertaking activities that are expected to more than cover their marginal costs, firms can enlarge their profits or reduce their losses.

Glossary

Cartel. A group of producers acting together to control output and the price of their product.

Cost of goods sold. The cost of items purchased by a firm for resale.

Cost-plus pricing. The technique of determining price by adding some percentage or markup to the average total cost *(ATC)* of producing an item or acquiring it for sale.

Depreciation. The reduction in the value of a fixed asset (plant or equipment) because of physical deterioration and/or obsolescence.

Fully allocated cost. The full cost of a project or activity; the project's share of the firm's total cost.

Marginal analysis. A comparison of the additional revenue and the additional cost associated with a contemplated action.

Market power. Pricing discretion; the ability of a firm to influence the market price of its product.

Price discrimination. Charging different consumers different prices for the same product.

Price searcher. A firm that possesses pricing discretion.

Product differentiation. Distinguishing a product from similar products offered by other sellers in the industry; accomplished through advertising, packaging, or physical product differences.

Study Questions

Fill in the Blanks

1. Firms that possess pricing discretion are sometimes described as _____ _____.

2. _____ creates market power by convincing buyers that a particular product is unique and superior.

3. A price searcher maximizes profit by equating _____ and _____ .

4. For a price searcher, marginal revenue is (greater/less) _____ _____ than price.

5. In the short run, a price searcher that is incurring a loss will continue to operate rather than shut down, provided that price is greater than _____ _____ cost.

6. A price searcher will not be able to earn economic profits in the long run unless _____ exist.

7. It is difficult to apply the $MR = MC$ technique because firms seldom possess precise information about _____ and _____ _____ .

8. One common method by which firms determine price is the _____ _____ technique.

9. In the final analysis the markup used in the cost-plus technique is probably determined primarily by the degree of _____ in a market.

10. A major limitation of the cost-plus technique is the fact that it does not utilize _____ analysis.

Multiple Choice

1. Which of the following would probably *not* be a price searcher?
   a) The local utility company
   b) A Kansas wheat farmer
   c) General Motors
   d) A local movie theater

2. All price searchers
   a) face downward-sloping demand curves.
   b) must reduce price to sell more.
   c) can raise their prices without losing all their customers.
   d) possess some pricing discretion.
   e) All of the above

3. Both price searchers and price takers
  a) must produce homogeneous products.
  b) produce where $MR = MC$ to maximize profits.
  c) face horizontal demand curves.
  d) must earn normal profits in the long run.

4. If a price searcher is operating where MR exceeds MC,
  a) it is producing the profit-maximizing output.
  b) it is producing too much to maximize profits.
  c) it is producing too little to maximize profits.
  d) None of the above is true.

Use the following exhibit to answer questions 5–7.

Price and cost

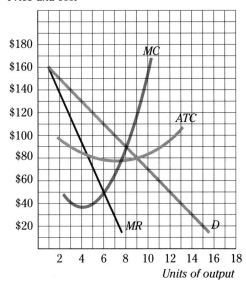

Units of output

5. To maximize its profit or minimize its loss, this price searcher should
  a) produce six units and charge a price of $50.
  b) produce six units and charge a price of $110.
  c) produce eight units and charge a price of $90.
  d) produce nine units and charge a price of $80.

6. This price searcher is
  a) incurring a loss of $180.
  b) earning a normal profit.
  c) earning a profit of $360.
  d) earning a profit of $180.

7. Allocative efficiency would require this firm to
   a) produce seven and one-half units of output and charge a price of $78.
   b) produce eight units and charge a price of $90.
   c) produce six units and charge a price of $50.
   d) None of the above

8. If a price searcher's fixed costs have increased,
   a) the firm's profit-maximizing quantity will increase.
   b) the firm's profit-maximizing quantity will not change.
   c) the firm's profit-maximizing quantity will decline.
   d) the firm will operate at a loss.

9. Sonic Waterbeds faces a traditional downward-sloping demand curve (included below), but its marginal cost curve is a horizontal straight line at a height of $600. In other words marginal costs are constant at $600. How many units should Sonic sell, and what price should it charge to maximize profit?

PRICE (per bed)	QUANTITY (per day)
$1,000	1
900	2
800	3
700	4
600	5
500	6

   a) One unit at $1,000
   b) Two units at $900
   c) Three units at $800
   d) Four units at $700
   e) Five units at $600

10. If the waterbed retailer described in question 9 were able to practice individual price discrimination, it would sell _____ waterbeds and earn a profit of _____ dollars on the last waterbed sold.
    a) 3, 200
    b) 4, 200
    c) 5, 0
    d) 6, 0

11. When firms practice group price discrimination, they tend to charge higher prices to consumers
    a) whose demand is more elastic.
    b) who are more price sensitive.
    c) whose demand is less elastic.
    d) who do comparison shopping.

12. Last week you purchased a bowling ball for $40. This week you've decided to give up bowling. Marginal analysis would suggest that you sell the bowling ball for

a) whatever you can get.

b) anything over $40.

c) $40.

d) $40 plus a normal profit.

Problems and Questions for Discussion

1. The price searcher's price and output decisions are one and the same. Explain.

2. Why is marginal revenue less than price for a price searcher? Illustrate with an example.

3. Why should consumers be concerned about the existence of barriers to entry?

4. Explain the cost-plus pricing technique.

5. Why is it often necessary to modify a result determined by the cost-plus method?

6. If a firm includes all its costs in its price by using the cost-plus method, will it ever show a loss? Explain.

7. The Springfield Bouncers, a new professional basketball team, want to rent the high school gymnasium on Sunday afternoons. How would you determine an appropriate rent? If they rejected your first offer, how would you determine the *minimum* acceptable rent?

8. Bland Manufacturing Company manufactures men's suits for sale throughout the Midwest. For the past five years, Bland has operated with about 20 percent unused capacity. Last month a retailer on the West Coast offered to buy as many suits as Bland could supply as long as the price did not exceed $45 per suit. This price is substantially below the price Bland charges its regular customers. Given the information presented below, should Bland accept the offer? Why or why not?

> *ATC* at present output level (80,000 units) = $55
>
> *ATC* at capacity output (100,000 units) = $50
>
> Normal markup = 40% on *ATC*

9. Both price searchers and price takers produce at the output where $MR = MC$. Yet price takers achieve allocative efficiency, whereas price searchers do not. Explain.

10. Suppose that a price searcher finds itself incurring a short-run loss. How should it decide whether to shut down or continue to operate? What would the price searcher's graph look like if it were in a shut-down situation?

Answer Key

Fill in the Blanks

1. price searchers
2. Product differentiation
3. marginal cost, marginal revenue
4. less
5. average variable
6. barriers to entry
7. demand conditions, cost conditions (or *MR* and *MC*)
8. cost-plus
9. competition
10. marginal (or incremental)

Multiple Choice

1. b	4. c	7. b	9. c	11. c
2. e	5. b	8. b	10. c	12. a
3. b	6. d			

Industry Structure and Public Policy

Nearly all the firms in our economy enjoy some pricing discretion, or market power. In Chapter 6 we saw how these firms determine their prices, and we considered the impact of market power on the allocation of scarce resources. Chapter 7 takes a closer look at the degrees of market power that exist in different industries and considers how the makeup, or structure, of an industry influences the amount of pricing discretion enjoyed by its individual firms. This chapter also explores the impact of market power on consumer welfare and examines the role of antitrust enforcement and government regulation in limiting that power.

Industry Structure and Market Power

You have learned that a firm may acquire market power either through product differentiation—distinguishing its product from similar products offered by other sellers—or by gaining control of a significant fraction of total industry output. The degree of product differentiation and the extent to which a firm is able to control industry output are related to the structure of the industry in which the firm operates. **Industry structure** is the makeup of an industry as determined by certain factors: (1) the number of sellers and their size distribution (all sellers approximately the same size as opposed to some much larger than others); (2) the nature of the product; (3) the extent of barriers to entering or leaving the industry. Note that these factors correspond to the three assumptions of the competitive model discussed early in Chapter 5.

There are four basic industry structures: pure competition, monopolistic competition, oligopoly, and pure monopoly. Their characteristics are summa-

EXHIBIT 7.1

Industry Structure: A Preview

PURE COMPETITION (No pricing discretion)	MONOPOLISTIC COMPETITION (Modest pricing discretion)	OLIGOPOLY (Modest to substantial pricing discretion)	PURE MONOPOLY (Substantial pricing discretion)
1. Many sellers, each small in relation to the industry	1. Many sellers, each small in relation to the industry	1. Few sellers, large in relation to the to the industry	1. One firm the sole supplier
2. Identical products	2. Somewhat differentiated products	2. Identical or differentiated products	2. Unique product; no close substitutes
3. No substantial barriers to entry	3. No substantial barriers to entry	3. Substantial barriers to entry	3. Substantial barriers to entry
Examples: Many agricultural industries and a few manufacturing industries (cotton weaving) come close.	*Examples:* Retail trade (hair salons, restaurants, gas stations) and a few manufacturing industries (men's suits and women's dresses)	*Examples:* Steel and aluminum manufacturing (identical products); automobile and cigarette manufacturing (differentiated) products)	*Examples:* Local telephone and utility companies

rized in Exh. 7.1. You are already familiar with pure competition, so we will use that model to open our discussion of the relationship between industry structure and market power.

Pure Competition

As you learned in Chapter 5, firms that operate in a purely competitive industry are price takers and lack market power for two reasons. First, because they produce and sell identical products, no one firm can expect consumers to pay a higher price than they would pay elsewhere. Such firms must be content with the price dictated by the market. Second, because the purely competitive firm is quite small in relation to the industry, it cannot affect the total industry supply enough to alter the market price. It cannot, for instance, push up prices the way the OPEC oil cartel did in the 1970s.

That cannot happen in wheat or corn production or any other industry that approximates pure competition. In these industries the individual seller supplies such a small fraction of total industry output that the firm is not in a position to alter the market price by reducing production. Once again, the purely competitive firm has no choice but to accept the price that is dictated by the market.

Monopolistic Competition

Few industries in the U.S. economy approximate pure competition. Monopolistic competition is a much more common industry structure. Most of the retailers with which you do business each week are firms in monopolistically competitive industries: restaurants, day-care centers, grocery stores, hair salons, and photo processors, to name just a few examples. In addition, some manufacturers, such as those making wooden furniture, women's dresses, and men's suits, operate in monopolistically competitive industries.

Like pure competition, **monopolistic competition** is characterized by a large number of relatively small sellers and by modest barriers to entering the industry. The feature that distinguishes monopolistic competition from pure competition is product differentiation. Each monopolistically competitive firm sells a product that is slightly different from those of other firms in the industry. Firms compete on price *and* through product differentiation. Products are differentiated by style, quality, packaging, the location of the seller, advertising, the services offered by the firm (free delivery, for example), and other real or imagined characteristics.

As the term suggests, a monopolistically competitive firm is part monopolist and part competitor. It is a monopolist because it is the only firm selling its unique product; it is competitive because of the large number of firms selling products that are close substitutes. We all have a favorite pizza parlor. It is a monopolist in the limited sense that no other restaurant offers exactly the same food, service, atmosphere, and location. On the other hand, our pizza parlor is in competition with dozens, perhaps hundreds, of other restaurants that sell pizza and substitutes for pizza as well. Your neighborhood hardware store and clothing retailer are in a similar situation. They may have convenient locations and offer some brand names that are not available elsewhere, but they face substantial competition from other sellers of similar products.

Monopolistic Competition and Market Power

Insofar as it sells a unique product, each monopolistically competitive firm has some pricing discretion. In other words it is a price searcher rather than a price taker. If a monopolistic competitor raises the price of its product, it will lose some customers but not all of them. Some will still prefer the product because they believe it to be superior to that of competitors. We can infer, then, that the firm faces a downward-sloping demand curve, not the horizontal or perfectly elastic demand curve facing competitive firms. However, with many substitute products available, the demand for the monopolistically competitive firm's product will be quite elastic, so consumers will be very responsive to price changes. As a consequence, the market power of the firm is limited; no monopolistically competitive firm can raise its price very much without losing an injuriously large number of customers.

The low entry barriers also function as a check on market power. Additional firms can easily enter a monopolistically competitive industry to take advantage of short-run economic profits. Consider the monopolistically competitive firm represented in Exh. 7.2. In case (a) the firm is earning a short-run profit (price exceeds *ATC* at the output where *MR = MC*). However, in the long run this profit will be eliminated by the entrance of additional firms selling similar but slightly differentiated products. As the new firms enter the industry, the demand curve facing our hypothetical firm will begin to shift to the left because each firm's share of total industry demand will become smaller. If there are now twenty pizza restaurants instead of ten, the typical restaurant will have fewer customers than before. Additional firms will continue to enter the industry (and the individual firm's demand curve will continue to shift leftward) until the typical firm is earning just a normal profit. This situation is depicted in case (b). In long-run equilibrium, then, the monopolistically competitive firm will do no better than a purely competitive

EXHIBIT 7.2

The Long-Run Adjustment Process in Monopolistic Competition

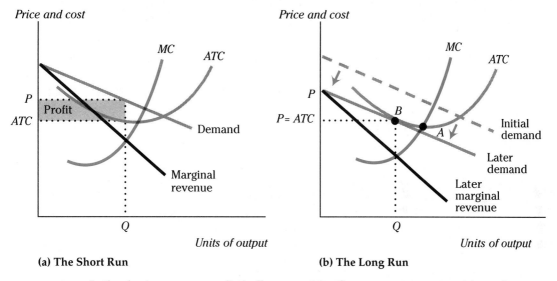

(a) The Short Run

(b) The Long Run

In the short run a monopolistically competitive firm may earn an economic profit, as represented in case (a). In the long run, however, the presence of the above-normal profit will cause additional firms to enter the industry, reducing each firm's share of the industry demand and eventually eliminating all economic profit, as in case (b). In long-run equilibrium the typical monopolistically competitive firm will earn just a normal profit.

firm; it will just break even. (The article on page 204, "After Frantic Growth, Blockbuster Faces Host of Video-Rental Rivals," illustrates the long-run adjustment process in a monopolistically competitive industry.)

Evaluating Monopolistic Competition

We discovered in Chapter 6 that price searchers misallocate resources because they fail to produce up to the point where $P = MC$. An examination of Exh. 7.2 confirms that monopolistically competitive firms behave this way. Note that in long-run equilibrium (case b) price exceeds marginal cost, which indicates that society values an additional unit of this product more highly than the alternative products that could be produced with the same resources. In other words, monopolistically competitive firms produce less output than is socially desirable.

After Frantic Growth, Blockbuster Faces Host of Video-Rental Rivals

FORT LAUDERDALE, FLA. During a recent roast here for H. Wayne Huizenga, the chairman of Blockbuster Video, Jane Fonda appeared (on tape, of course) to applaud his success and to suggest a joint dieting venture called "Bellybuster."

It's true, Mr. Huizenga has done very well indeed for a guy who got his start driving a garbage truck, who still uses the R-rated language of the refuse trade, and who just four years ago was running a modest little video chain that has since burgeoned into Blockbuster Entertainment Corp., a company that owns and franchises video-rental stores with annual sales of $633 million.

Blockbuster is to the video trade what McDonald's is to fast food: a company that created an industry. Blockbuster took a business typified by seedy little mom-and-pop neighborhood rental shops and went national. Its stores are more like supermarkets, they don't have a porno section and they have gobbled up competitors right and left. Blockbuster claims to open a new store, somewhere, every 17 hours. . . .

But is Blockbuster living on borrowed time?

Since the beginning of last year, Blockbuster's year-over-year store revenue growth has slowed each quarter—from a 79% rise in the first three months to a 55% gain in the final quarter, even as the company aggressively opened and acquired stores. (At the end of last year, Blockbuster owned 787 stores itself, and franchised another 795). Then, last week, Blockbuster officials said they expect first-quarter earnings growth to be in the range of 10% to 20%—much less than heretofore and roughly half what analysts had been predicting.

Blockbuster executives claim to be unfazed. "Growth to us is limitless at this point," says Steven R. Berrard, vice chairman and chief financial officer. Blockbuster, big as it is, still has just 11% of the video market, so there's room to bloom. . . .

Attracting Giants

But . . . Blockbuster's growth has made the industry attractive to competitors. Everyone has always expected a shakeout in the in-

dustry, but now it's likely to be a clash of titans. . . .

Evidence of that abounds. Qualities that once set Blockbuster apart have been successfully copied by others. With 8,000 titles, Blockbuster used to offer the ultimate in choice. But in some markets, competitors offer even more. Tower Video, based in West Sacramento, Calif., sells the latest in home-movie technology, including 8-mm videos and laser disks, which Blockbuster largely ignores. It sticks pretty much to VHS cassettes.

Blockbuster touted service—longer hours, speedy, computerized checkout. Now it has rivals like the Video Factory in Buffalo, N.Y., where clerks in tuxedos escort shoppers to their cars under umbrellas when it rains. But when Blockbuster was unique, it could charge $3 per tape, against an industry average of more like $2 for an overnight rental. The extra buck contributed to earnings growth.

Lately, Blockbuster has been drawn into price wars. When some Blockbuster stores dropped their rental price to $2 in San Antonio in February, competing HEB

Video Central stores dropped their charge for new movies to $1.50 and offers 99-cent specials.

The nation is littered with video stores—28,000, by one count. The biggest and best markets are saturated. In the Pacific and mid-Atlantic states, according to Video Store magazine, a given video store is likely to have six rivals within a three-mile radius. "There is very little key real estate left in the business," says Steve Apple, executive editor of Video Insider magazine. . . .

The crowded field might not matter so much if it weren't for signs that the fast-forward days are over for the video business. Since the mid-'80s, the growth of movie rentals has paralleled sales of videocassette recorders. As hardware prices fell, consumers snapped up 65 million VCRs in six years and surged into video stores. But with the machines now in about 70% of U.S. households, growth in the rental market last year slipped into single digits for the first time—just 7%. . . .

. . . The continuing evolution of pay-per-view television is the ultimate cloud over Blockbuster. Making a trip to the store to rent a film is inherently inconvenient. Ordering it up in your living room is the essence of convenience. Though technology and pricing are problems, pay-per-view appears to be marching inexorably forward, particularly if 150-channel cable systems become a reality for most households.

"I think Blockbuster will do just fine for the next several years," says Robert Wussler, president of Comsat Video Enterprises, a pay-per-view company. "Whether they will still be around 10 to 12 years from now, that's another question."
—*Michael J. McCarthy*

SOURCE: Michael J. McCarthy, "After Frantic Growth, Blockbuster Faces Host of Video-Rental Rivals," March 22, 1991. Reprinted by permission of *The Wall Street Journal,* © 1991 Dow Jones & Co., Inc. All rights Reserved Worldwide.

Use Your Economic Reasoning

1. New monopolistically competitive industries may remain profitable for quite some time. Why? Has the video-rental business followed this pattern?

2. As a monopolistically competitive industry matures, it becomes increasingly necessary for firms to differentiate themselves from their rivals. Why? How has Blockbuster attempted to differentiate its outlets from other video-rental stores?

3. What evidence is there that the video-rental business is less profitable than it once was? Use the model of monopolistic competition to explain this outcome.

In addition to distorting the allocation of resources, monopolistically competitive firms are somewhat less efficient at producing their products and charge slightly higher prices than purely competitive firms with the same costs. These outcomes are at least in part the result of the overcrowding that characterizes most monopolistically competitive industries.

The crowded nature of monopolistically competitive industries is illustrated by the large number of clothing stores, video-rental establishments, convenience groceries, and fast-food restaurants that exist in your city or town. By differentiating its product, each of these firms is able to capture a small share of the market. But often so many firms share that market that it is difficult for any one of them to attract enough customers to use its facilities efficiently—to permit it to operate at minimum *ATC*.

Because the monopolistically competitive firm underutilizes its production facilities, its average cost of production will be higher than the *ATC* of a purely competitive firm with identical cost curves.[1] For example, consider the *ATC* curve in case (b) of Exh. 7.2. In long-run equilibrium a purely competitive firm would earn zero economic profit and produce its product at minimum *ATC* (point *A*), whereas we've seen that monopolistically competitive firms will operate at a somewhat higher *ATC* (point *B*). As a consequence, the monopolistically competitive firm must charge a higher price than the purely competitive firm in order to earn a normal profit in the long run.

Fortunately for consumers, the difference in price is probably not substantial. Furthermore, consumers gain something for the additional dollars they pay. Remember, purely competitive firms sell products that are identical in the minds of consumers, whereas monopolistic competitors aim for product differentiation. Many of us are willing to pay a little more to obtain the product variety that monopolistic competition provides.

Oligopoly

Millions of firms in hundreds of U.S. retail industries match the model of monopolistic competition reasonably well. However, most manufacturing industries—steel, aluminum, automobiles, and prescription drugs, for example—are more accurately described as oligopolistic. An **oligopoly** is an industry dominated by a few relatively large sellers that are protected by substantial barriers to entry. The distinguishing feature of all oligopolistic in-

---

[1] This analysis assumes that the monopolistic competitor has cost curves that are identical to those of the pure competitor. In fact, the monopolistic competitor probably has higher costs due to advertising expense and other product differentiation efforts. Thus there are two reasons to expect its selling price to be higher: It does not operate at the minimum on its *ATC* curve (whereas a pure competitor does), *and* its *ATC* curve is higher than that of a pure competitor.

dustries is the high degree of interdependence among the sellers and the very personal nature of the rivalry that results from that interdependence.

Oligopolists and Market Power

Because oligopolistic firms enjoy a large share of their market, their production decisions have a significant impact on market price. A substantial increase in production by any one of them would cause downward pressure on price; a significant decrease would tend to push price upward. Suppose, for instance, that the Aluminum Company of America (Alcoa) decided to increase production by 50 percent. Since Alcoa is a major producer, this increase in output would expand industry supply significantly and thereby depress the industry price. A substantial reduction in Alcoa's output would tend to have the opposite effect; it would push price upward.

We have seen that soybean farmers, hog producers, and others in purely competitive industries cannot influence price by manipulating industry output: They're not big enough and they don't control a large enough share of the market. In addition, the large number of firms in these competitive industries makes it virtually impossible for them to coordinate their actions—to agree to limit production, for example. As a consequence, changes in the output of a competitive industry are always the unplanned results of independent actions by thousands of producers. Output in an oligopolistic industry, on the other hand, is often carefully controlled by the few large firms that dominate production. This control is one of the keys to the pricing discretion of the oligopolists.

Some oligopolists also acquire market power through product differentiation. Although producers of such commodities as aluminum ingots, steel sheet, and heating oil sell virtually identical products, many oligopolists sell differentiated products. Producers of automobiles, pet food, greeting cards, cigarettes, breakfast cereals, and washers and dryers belong in this category. Oligopolistic sellers of differentiated products possess market power both because they are large in relation to the total industry *and* because their product is somewhat unique.

Mutual Interdependence and Game Theory

Since oligopolistic firms have pricing discretion, they are price searchers rather than price takers. But the high degree of interdependence among oligopolists tends to restrict the pricing discretion of the individual firm and complicate its search for the profit-maximizing price.

Because there are only a few large sellers, each firm must consider the reactions of its rivals before taking any action. For instance, before altering the price of its product, Ford Motor Company must consider the reactions of General Motors, Toyota, and the other firms in the industry. Raising its prices may be ill advised unless the other firms can be counted on to match the price hike. Price reductions may be an equally poor strategy if other firms respond with matching price cuts or with deeper cuts that lead to continuing price warfare.

Game theory is the study of the strategies employed by interdependent firms such as Ford and General Motors. Economists often use game theory to try to understand how oligopolists make decisions about price, advertising, and other competitive variables. While game theory is quite complex, a simple example should illustrate the main points revealed by the model.

Imagine a hypothetical industry dominated by two firms (A and B) selling differentiated products. Let's assume that these two firms are trying to decide whether to charge $30 or $35 for their products. In making this decision, each firm recognizes that its profits depend not only on the price it selects, but also on the price selected by its rival. The different possible outcomes are contained in the payoffs matrix presented in Exh. 7.3.

The payoffs matrix shows the amount of profit that will be earned by each of the firms under the two pricing strategies being considered. For example, if firm A selects a price of $35 and firm B chooses the same price, each firm will earn a profit of $50,000 (see the upper left-hand cell of the matrix).

EXHIBIT 7.3

Profit Payoffs for Two Oligopolists

Firm A's price strategies

		$35	$30
Firm B's price strategies	$35	Each firm earns a $50,000 profit.	A earns $60,000. B earns $20,000.
	$30	A earns $20,000. B earns $60,000.	Each firm earns a $35,000 profit.

The payoffs matrix shows that each firm's profits depend not only on its actions but also on the actions of its rivals. For instance, if firm A charges a price of $35, it will earn a profit of $50,000 if firm B matches that price, but only $20,000 if firm B opts to undercut it and charge a price of $30.

The problem with this strategy is that neither firm can be certain that its rival will decide to charge $35. In fact, as the matrix reveals, each firm has incentive to undercut its rival. If firm A selects the $35 price and firm B counters with a $30 price, firm B will earn a $60,000 profit (see the lower left-hand cell) while firm A will earn only $20,000. If firm B selected the $35 price and firm A opted to charge $30, the outcomes would be reversed; firm A would earn a $60,000 profit and firm B would earn only $20,000 (see the upper right-hand cell). The remaining possibility is that both firms will decide to charge $30. In that case, each firm will earn a profit of $35,000. While this is not the best that the firms could do, it is not the worst either, since it avoids the possibility of earning only a $20,000 profit.

According to game theorists, both oligopolists will see the $30 price as particularly attractive. There are two reasons for this attraction: First, if a firm decides to charge $30 and its rival opts to charge $35, the firm charging the lower ($30) price will earn a $60,000 profit, the highest amount possible. Second, charging $30 eliminates the possibility that a firm will be undercut by its rival and find itself able to earn only a $20,000 profit (the lowest profit outcome in the matrix).

If both firms select a price of $30, they will have reached a "Nash equilibrium" (after John Nash, the 1994 Nobel prize-winning economist who discovered the concept). Remember that equilibrium means stability, a situation that tends to be maintained. A **Nash equilibrium** exists when each firm's strategy is the best it can choose, given the strategy chosen by the other firm. In our example, $30 is the equilibrium or stable solution because, given firm A's price, firm B can do no better, and given firm B's price, firm A can do no better. Thus each firm will tend to charge the same price next period.

One interesting point about the Nash equilibrium is that neither firm earns as much profit as it could if they both decided to charge $35. But each firm is reluctant to select this price for fear of being undercut by its rival. This points to the incentive that oligopolists have to cooperate (rather than compete) and mutually raise prices in order to earn greater profits. We turn next to the methods that they might employ to facilitate cooperation.

Tactics for Cooperating

Oligopolists may respond to their interdependence by employing tactics that allow them to cooperate and make mutually advantageous decisions. One tactic is **collusion**, agreement among sellers to fix prices, divide up the market, or in some other way limit competition. Collusive agreements result in cartels such as the OPEC oil cartel and the DeBeers diamond cartel. Although collusive agreements are legal in some countries, they are illegal in the United States and punishable by fine and imprisonment. (As a consequence, firms attempt to keep them secret.) In spite of the penalties, some U.S. firms continue to engage in collusion. Dozens of violators are prosecuted each year and many others probably go undetected. The fact that business executives are willing to risk prison sentences to engage in collusion is testimony both to the potential financial gains and to the problems posed by interdependence.

A more subtle form of cooperation (and communication) is price leadership. **Price leadership** is much like a game of follow-the-leader. One firm— perhaps the biggest, the most efficient, or simply the most trusted—initiates all increases or decreases in prices. The remaining firms in the industry follow the leader. This leader-follower behavior is generally reinforced by indirect forms of communication (rather than the direct communication involved in collusion). For example, price leaders usually signal their intent to raise prices through press releases or through public speeches. This lets the follower firms know that a price increase is coming so that they will not be taken by surprise. (If the price leader hikes its price and no one follows, it will probably have to back down, creating confusion for the industry.) This tactic allows the firms in the industry to accomplish price changes legally, without collusion.

Neither collusive agreements nor price leadership may be necessary when an industry is dominated by firms that recognize their interdependence. **Conscious parallelism** occurs when, without any communication whatsoever, firms adopt similar policies. For instance, even without meeting or signaling each other, firms may come to recognize that price cutting, because it invites retaliation, leaves all firms worse off. They may therefore shun this practice as long as their rivals reciprocate. Conscious parallelism may also explain why all firms in an industry provide the same discounts to larger buyers and why they all raise prices at the same time of year.

Collusion, price leadership, and conscious parallelism all tend to result in an avoidance of price competition. Instead, oligopolists channel their competitive instincts into *nonprice competition*—advertising, packaging, and new product development. This form of rivalry has two significant advantages over price competition. First, a new product or a successful advertising campaign is more difficult for a competitor to match than is a price cut, so an oligopolist may gain a more permanent advantage over its rivals. Second, rivalry through product differentiation or new product development is less likely than price competition to get out of control and severely damage the profits of all firms in the industry. Thus nonprice competition is seen as a more promising strategy than price competition.

Factors Limiting Cooperation

Although oligopolists strive to avoid price warfare and confine their rivalry to nonprice competition, these efforts are not always successful. Collusion and price leadership often break down because of the strong temptation to

Oligopolists often channel their competitive instincts into nonprice competition: advertising, packaging, and new product development.

cheat (price cut) in order to steal customers. Even conscious parallelism can give way to price cutting if firms believe their actions may be undetected. To understand this temptation, look back at Exh. 7.3 for a moment. Suppose that firms A and B have agreed, either informally or through collusion, to charge a price of $35. Each firm recognizes that if it undercuts the other firm by charging $30, it can expand its profits. And if the firm is not too greedy—if the price cutting is limited to a small fraction of the industry sales, for example—the practice may go undiscovered and the rival may not retaliate.

The likelihood of cheating is greatest in markets in which prices tend to be secret (so that price cutting may go undetected) and in which long contracts may delay the impact of retaliation. Cheating also becomes more common-place as the number of firms in the industry increases, since it becomes more difficult for the firms to agree on the best price. In addition, the state of the economy clearly influences the likelihood of cheating. History shows that price cutting is particularly common in periods of weak demand, when firms have substantial excess capacity that they would like to put to work. During such periods, firms will be tempted to undercut their rivals in order to expand sales.

In truth the success of oligopolists in avoiding price competition varies significantly from industry to industry. Some industries—the breakfast cereal industry, for example—have demonstrated a marked ability to avoid price competition; others, steel, for instance, experience recurring bouts of price warfare. Because the behavior of oligopolists is so varied, it is difficult to generalize about the impact of oligopoly of social welfare. We will attempt some cautious observations after discussing the final industry structure, pure monopoly.

Monopoly

Although both monopolistic competitors and oligopolists have some pricing discretion, the classic example of a firm with market power is the monopolist.

Monopoly is an industry structure in which a single firm sells a product for which there are no close substitutes. (Monopoly is sometimes called *pure monopoly* to emphasize that it is the industry structure farthest removed from pure competition.) A firm can become a monopolist in a variety of ways but can remain a monopolist only if barriers prevent other firms from entering the industry. One barrier to entry is exclusive control of some critical input—a basic raw material needed in the production process, for instance. A second way a firm may enjoy a monopoly is through sheer size, when larger size brings with it greater efficiency and lower production costs. Entry into the industry is effectively blocked by the large capital investment a rival would require to begin operating at competitive size. A possible third source of monopoly is government policies. For instance, the U.S. government issues patents that provide a firm with the exclusive right to control a new product for a period of seventeen years. The government franchise is another example of government policies promoting monopoly. A **government franchise** is an exclusive license to provide a product or service. Government franchises account for the presence of only one restaurant chain on the interstate highway and the single boat-rental establishment in a state park. National governments can also create or preserve monopolies through their trade policies. By erecting trade barriers, governments can prevent foreign products from entering their countries, thereby reserving the market for domestic firms.

Monopoly and Market Power

Monopolists enjoy substantial pricing discretion because they are the sole suppliers of their products. This enables the monopolist to manipulate industry output and thereby alter the market price. The monopolist's control over output does not provide it with complete or unlimited pricing discretion, however. Complete pricing discretion would result in a vertical, perfectly inelastic demand curve, signifying the ability to increase price without losing *any* customers. This condition would represent the true opposite to the purely competitive firm, which possesses no market power and faces a horizontal, perfectly elastic demand curve.

But a monopolist does stand to lose some customers when it raises its price, because monopolists face a certain amount of competition from rivals in *other* industries. Think about your local telephone and utility companies, for example. These sellers fit the description of a monopolist fairly well, yet neither is without competition. If the telephone company were to charge exorbitant rates for its service, we could communicate by letter or by CB radio or by personal visit. If the utility company were to effect a drastic rate increase for electricity, we could begin by reducing our use of electricity. We could insulate our homes and install energy-saving appliances; ultimately we could even purchase our own electricity generator.

In the face of increasing fuel and electricity costs, many U.S. consumers have already insulated their homes and demanded energy-saving devices. And although none of us wants to resort to a CB radio as a substitute for local telephone service, some customers might choose to do just that if rates become high enough. The availability of substitutes, however imperfect, constrains the monopolist's pricing discretion.

Monopoly and Profit Maximization

Because a monopolist stands to lose some customers when it raises its price, the demand curve it faces must be downward sloping like that of other price searchers. This tells us that the monopolist must restrict output to charge a high price; conversely it must reduce price to sell more. The monopolist will select the profit-maximizing output and price in exactly the same way as other price searchers do; it will produce at the output where $MR = MC$ and find its price by going up to the demand curve. The difference between a monopolist and other price searchers is found not in the rules used to determine their price but in the competitive situation. Monopolistically competitive firms and oligopolists face some degree of competition from other firms in the industry. The monopolist *is* the industry, so its only competition comes from firms in other industries.

Because monopolists enjoy substantial pricing discretion, it is commonly believed that they must earn economic profits. But that need not be the case. In the short run monopolists, like other producers, may experience economic profits, normal profits, or even losses. How well a monopolist will fare depends on the demand and cost conditions that it faces. Imagine, for instance, a firm that has patented a medicine for a very rare disease—an average diagnosis of ten cases a year. This monopolist has substantial pricing discretion with these unfortunate victims, but the demand is so limited that the product probably will be unprofitable to produce. Or consider the boat-rental concession at an isolated state park. The owner enjoys a government-granted monopoly, but if few vacationers frequent the lake, it won't be a very profitable monopoly. The point is that even a monopolist can't earn a profit if the demand for its product is very limited. High production costs can signal a similar problem. Exhibit 7.4 depicts a monopolist incurring a short-run economic loss.

When monopolists are able to earn short-run profits, substantial entry barriers help them to continue earning those profits in the long run. But the long run does not mean forever! Ultimately the development of new products, the introduction of new technologies, and/or the elimination of legal barriers to entry tend to undermine the monopolist's position. For example, at one time Atlantic Telephone and Telegraph (AT&T) enjoyed a monopoly in providing long distance telephone service. But new technology ultimately destroyed its monopoly status (this will be discussed in greater detail in a moment). Or consider the monopoly presently enjoyed by Burroughs Wellcome in the manufacture of AZT, the drug used to treat AIDS patients. Burroughs Wellcome obtained a monopoly in AZT by developing the drug and then obtaining a patent to prevent other firms from duplicating it. But the substantial profits the firm is earning from the drug ensure that other companies will go to great lengths to develop a substitute. And even if they are not successful,

---

EXHIBIT 7.4

A Monopolist Incurring a Loss

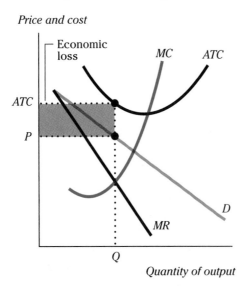

Price and cost

Even a monopolist can incur a loss if there is little demand for its product or if its costs are high.

patent protection will ultimately expire and consumers will be flooded with "generic" forms of AZT which will substantially lower its price and Burroughs Wellcome's profits. (Your local cable TV firm may soon find its monopoly status threatened. Read "Kamikaze Satellites" on page 216 to find out why.)

None of this is intended to make you feel sorry for monopolists. Technological progress is hard to predict and generally occurs slowly. And patent protection is currently granted for a period of seventeen years. The point is that change is inevitable and eventually most monopolists find their status eroded by forces that are largely beyond their control.

The Consequences of Monopoly or Oligopoly

The presence of monopoly can have a significant effect on consumer well-being. Monopolists tend to produce too little output and sometimes charge prices that are inflated by economic profits. These negative effects may be partially offset by lower production costs or greater innovation. Oligopoly can have a similar impact on consumer welfare, though it is much more difficult to generalize about the consequences of this industry structure.

The Problems of Misallocation of Resources and Redistribution of Income

Economists generally agree that monopolists distort the allocation of scarce resources. Like monopolistically competitive firms, monopolists fail to produce up to the point where price is equal to marginal cost—the point where resources would be allocated efficiently. As a consequence, too few resources are devoted to the production of the goods and services produced by monopolists, and too many resources are left over to be used in the more competitive sectors of the economy. For example, if there were only two industries in the economy, a monopolized computer industry and a purely competitive farming industry, society probably would receive too few computers and too many agricultural products.

The redistribution of income is another problem caused by monopolies. Because entrance into these industries is blocked, consumers may be required to pay higher prices than necessary, prices that include economic profits on top of the normal profits that are necessary to convince firms to continue operation. These higher prices redistribute income from consumers (who will be made worse off) to monopolists (who will be made better off).

Kamikaze Satellites?

Sometime near the summer solstice, if all went according to plan, a GM Hughes satellite broke open local cable monopolies all across the continent. From its position 22,300 miles over the center of the U.S., the high-power satellite can beam 75 television channels directly to subscribers' homes. The satellite is shared by DirecTV, an arm of General Motors, and U.S. Satellite Broadcasting, a company founded by entrepreneur Stanley S. Hubbard. A sister satellite to be installed alongside it later this year will double the channel capacity.

The satellites' content will be similar to what cable television offers but with more choices: Home Box Office, ESPN, the Disney Channel and CNN, plus about 55 channels of pay-per-view movies. Pricing: about the same as cable, at least to start.

There's more trouble for cable where this came from. By the fall of 1995 Englewood, Colo.-based EchoStar Communications Corp. plans to provide a similar satellite service from a different slot in the sky. Initial pricing: a bit lower than the going rates for cable.

And then? There's no telling what will happen.

Fiber-optic cabling by telephone companies represents a fourth potential vendor in what is now a market pretty much monopolized by cable systems; signal-splitting by broadcast stations is a fifth potential threat. But even if these technologies' day is a long way off, an unsettling question arises: What's to stop a price war between cable and satellite deliverers of TV signals?

Faced with competition from EchoStar, the Hughes/Hubbard operation might abandon the sort of gentlemanly competition it has in mind now. It might respond with crass price discounting. That would greatly expand its market. Instead of appealing primarily to prosperous viewers willing to pay extra for a few new channels, it would be reaching out to average Americans who just don't like $30 monthly cable bills.

Once the customer-stealing starts, there is little to stop it. Cable operators would presumably retaliate with price cuts of their own. Then the satellite owners might cut prices some more. The TV signal business could start to look like the airline industry.

Running an airline and distributing television shows have this in common: Fixed costs are high and marginal costs are low. For the airline, the big fixed cost is the plane; it costs about as much to fly a plane empty as with all the seats filled. For a cable operator, the big cost is either in stringing wires or in buying (at up to $2,500 per subscriber) an existing system. For the Hughes/Hubbard and EchoStar ventures, the fixed cost is the $500 million to $1 billion it costs to loft satellites and set up ground transmitters.

Airlines constantly offer cut-rate deals because anything they can get for an otherwise empty seat is found money. So, too, with TV signals, with one difference: A distributor of television shows does pay a fee to the owner of the show based on the number of sets that watch the show. . . .

In a price war, a distributor desperate for business might be willing to take any price that covers its marginal cost. Once you've got the satellite up in the sky, any revenue at all (beyond the program fees) is better than nothing, even if it falls far short of what you need to pay off the loan you took out for the launch. Such economics, at any rate, explains why a lot of airlines went bust.

Alfred Kahn, a retired professor of economics at Cornell, witnessed the airline mess firsthand as chairman of the former Civil Aeronautics Board. Once the CAB stopped setting minimums for airline fares, price wars broke out. Eventually, they got out of hand. They continued until the industry was in dire straits. Kahn's view of the coming cable/satellite competition: "There could be unstable and extreme price wars." . . .

—*Nikhil Hutheesing*

SOURCE: Nikhil Hutheesing, "Kamikaze Satellites?" Reprinted by permission of *Forbes* magazine, July 4, 1994. © Forbes, Inc. 1994.

Use Your Economic Reasoning

1. How do satellites threaten the monopoly presently enjoyed by many local cable television operators?

2. If we end up with each community being served by one cable company and two or three satellite providers of TV programming, which model would best describe the structure of the industry?

3. Satellite customers would need to purchase a small (18-inch) antenna costing about $500 to receive the satellite's signal. Would this requirement have any impact on the monthly fee satellite broadcasters can charge for their service? Why or why not?

4. Once the satellite is up, the marginal cost of serving an additional customer is quite low. Why might that fact lead to price warfare? What techniques might these rivals employ to prevent or eliminate price warfare?

Although economists are fairly confident in generalizing about the consequences of monopoly, they find it more difficult to make blanket statements regarding the impact of oligopoly. This is primarily because the behavior of oligopolists is so varied. To the extent that oligopolists cooperate and avoid price competition, the welfare effects of oligopoly probably are very similar to the effects of pure monopoly. When cooperation breaks down, consumer welfare is enhanced and the negative effects of oligopoly are reduced. Since it is clear that oligopolists do not always succeed in avoiding price competition, the impact of oligopoly on consumer well-being probably lies somewhere between the impacts of monopoly and pure competition.

The Possible Benefits of Size

Although monopoly and oligopoly often have undesirable effects on consumer welfare, this is not always the case. Under certain conditions these market structures may benefit society. For example, if a monopolist's/oligopolist's greater size means that it produces at a lower *ATC* because it can afford more specialized equipment and greater specialization of labor, it may use fewer resources per unit of output and charge a lower price than a competitive firm even as it earns an economic profit. And because monopolists and oligopolists are often able to earn economic profits in the long run, they can afford the investment necessary to develop new products and cost-reducing production techniques. Thus in the long run society may receive better products and lower prices from monopolists and oligopolists than from competitive firms.

Studies of the U.S. economy provide limited support for these arguments. For example, in the refrigerator-manufacturing industry a firm needs 15 to 20 percent of the market in order to achieve production efficiency, or minimum *ATC*. This means that for optimal efficiency, room exists for only five or six firms in that industry. The efficient manufacture and distribution of beer requires a somewhat smaller but nevertheless substantial market share: 10 to 14 percent. Fortunately, in more than half the manufacturing industries surveyed, firms with 3 percent or less of the market were large enough to operate at minimum *ATC*. Thus generally it is not necessary for industries to be dominated by one or a few firms in order to achieve production efficiency.[2]

Evidence on business research and development efforts leads to a similar conclusion. Firms in highly competitive industries are not particularly innovative, perhaps because they are unable to earn the profits necessary to finance research and development efforts. But neither do firms in "tightly" oligopolis-

---

[2] F. M. Scherer, *Industrial Market Structure and Economic Performance* (Chicago: Rand McNally, 1980), p. 119.

tic industries (wherein a very few firms closely coordinate their actions) tend to be innovative. These firms often have the money but seem to lack the incentive from competitive pressure to invest in research and development. The most innovative tend to be medium-sized firms in "loosely" oligopolistic industries—industries composed of several firms (perhaps ten or twenty) with no single dominant firm. Because some competitive pressure exists, it may be harder for the firms in these industries to coordinate their actions, but because they have some pricing discretion, such firms often earn the economic profits necessary to support research and development efforts.[3]

In summary lower production costs and greater innovation may compensate for the resource misallocation and income redistribution caused by oligopolists and monopolists. In some cases we may even be able to justify a monopoly on the basis of greater production efficiency or other technical considerations, a possibility that will be discussed shortly. However, even when we take these benefits into consideration, we find that manufacturing industries have fewer and larger firms than necessary to achieve the advantages of greater production efficiency and increased innovation. In general U.S. consumers would be better off if the existing industry structure were more, not less, competitive.

Antitrust and Regulation

Because the exercise of market power by monopolists and oligopolists can distort the allocation of scarce resources and redistribute income, the federal government pursues policies designed to promote competition and restrict the actions of firms with market power. The primary weapons used in the battle against market power are antitrust laws and industry regulation. As you will see, these two approaches to the problem differ significantly in both their philosophies and the remedies they propose.

Antitrust Enforcement

Antitrust laws have as their objective the maintenance and promotion of competition. These laws (1) outlaw collusion, (2) make it illegal for a firm to attempt to achieve a monopoly, and (3) ban **mergers,** the union of two or more companies into a single firm, when such mergers are likely to result in substantially less competition.

Virtually all antitrust enforcement in the United States is based on three fundamental statutes enacted around the turn of the century: the Sherman

---

[3] Douglas F. Greer, *Industrial Organization and Public Policy* (New York: Macmillan, 1980), p. 598.

Antitrust Act of 1890, the Clayton Antitrust Act of 1914, and the Federal Trade Commission Act, also passed in 1914. Exhibit 7.5 offers a brief comparison of these laws.

The Sherman Antitrust Act. The Sherman Act, the first of the big three, was a response to the monopolistic exploitation that occurred in the latter half of the nineteenth century, when trusts had become commonplace. **Trusts** are combinations of firms organized for the purpose of restraining price competition and thereby gaining economic profit. (For our purposes, a trust is the same thing as a cartel.) So many companies were merging at this time that competitors were disappearing at an alarming rate! Du Pont, for example, achieved a near monopoly in the manufacture of explosives by either merging with or acquiring some 100 rival firms between 1872 and 1912.[4] Monopolies and monopolistic practices translated into higher prices for consumers and inspired a strong political movement that led to the passage of the Sherman Antitrust Act in 1890.

The Sherman Act declared illegal all agreements between competing firms to fix prices, limit output, or otherwise restrict the forces of competition. It also declared illegal all monopolies or "attempts to monopolize any part of trade or commerce among the several states, or with foreign nations." The law was not applied with much force until 1904, when it was used to dissolve the Northern Securities Company, a firm that had been formed to monopolize railroad transportation in certain northern states. Later, in 1911, the law became the basis for the antitrust suit that resulted in the breakup of Standard Oil, a trust that controlled some 90 percent of the petroleum industry.

As a result of the limits laid down by the courts in the Standard Oil case, businesses became somewhat less aggressive in their monopolistic practices. Rather than strive for monopoly, they were content to become the dominant firms in their respective oligopolistic industries. However, many firms gained dominion not by abandoning practices but by pursuing them in disguised and subtle ways. This led Congress in 1914 to pass two more bills aimed at curbing anticompetitive practices: the Clayton Antitrust Act and the Federal Trade Commission Act.

The Clayton Antitrust Act. The Clayton Act was designed primarily to stem the tide of mergers that had already reduced competition significantly in a number of important industries, such as steel production, petroleum refining, and electrical equipment manufacture. The act prohibited mergers between competing firms if the impact of their union would be to "substantially

---

[4] F. M. Scherer, *Industrial Market Structure and Economic Performance* (Chicago: Rand McNally, 1980), p. 121.

EXHIBIT 7.5

The Antitrust Laws and What They Do

The Sherman Antitrust Act (1890)	Outlawed agreements to fix prices, limit output, or share the market. Also declared that monopolies and attempts to monopolize are illegal.
The Clayton Antitrust Act (1914)	Forbade competitors to merge if the impact of merger would be to substantially lessen competition. Also outlawed certain practices, such as tying contracts.
The Federal Trade Commission Act (1914)	Created the Federal Trade Commissioni and empowered it to initiate and decide cases involving "unfair competition." Also declared that deceptive practices and unfair methods of competition are illegal.

---

lessen competition or to tend to create a monopoly." The act also outlawed other practices if they lessened competition. "Other practices" included **tying contracts**—agreements specifying that the purchaser would, as a condition of sale for a given product, also buy some other product offered by the seller. Once again enforcement was a problem, because the courts interpreted this law in ways that permitted mergers between competing firms to continue. Finally, in 1950, the Cellar-Kefauver Act amended the Clayton Act by closing a major loophole, thus effectively eliminating the possibility of mergers involving major competitors.

During the Reagan administration, the government relaxed its restriction against mergers involving major competitors. This more permissive attitude was at least partially responsible for a wave of merger activity in the 1980s. The Clinton administration has taken a somewhat tougher stance on antitrust enforcement, including stricter merger guidelines.

The Federal Trade Commission Act. The last of the three major antitrust statutes, the Federal Trade Commission Act, was also passed in 1914. Its primary purpose was to establish a special agency, the Federal Trade Commission, empowered to investigate allegations of "unfair methods of competi-

Under the leadership of John D. Rockefeller, the Standard Oil trust acquired a virtual monopoly in petroleum refining.

tion" and to command businesses in violation of FTC regulations to cease those practices. Although the FTC Act did not specify the precise meaning of "unfair methods of competition," the phrase has been interpreted by the commission to include practices prohibited under the Sherman and Clayton Acts—price fixing and tying contracts, for example—and any other practices that can be shown to limit competition or damage the consuming public. For instance, the FTC has deemed it unfair for a funeral home to fail to provide, in advance, an itemized price list for funeral services and merchandise or to furnish embalming without first informing customers about alternatives.

The Federal Trade Commission is one of the two federal agencies charged with the enforcement of the antitrust statutes. The other agency is the Antitrust Division of the Justice Department. The Antitrust Division is responsible for enforcing the Sherman and Clayton Acts and lesser pieces of antitrust legislation. The FTC is also charged with antitrust enforcement, including civil actions against violators of either the Sherman or Clayton Acts, but its responsibilities are somewhat broader. About half its resources are devoted to combating deception and misrepresentation: improper labeling and misleading advertisements, for example. The overlapping responsibilities of the FTC and the Antitrust Division have posed some problems of coordination, but these are at least partially offset by the fact that one agency's oversights may be picked up by the other.

Industry Regulation

Government regulation of industry approaches the problem of market power from a different perspective and therefore provides a different solution.[5] The basic assumption is that certain industries cannot or should not be made competitive. Hence the role of government is to provide a framework whereby the actions of these less-than-competitive firms can be constrained in a manner consistent with the public interest. This is accomplished by establishing regulatory agencies empowered to control the prices such firms can charge, the quality of service they must provide, and the conditions under which additional firms will be allowed to enter the industry.

The reason that certain industries should not be made competitive is because they are natural monopolies. A **natural monopoly** exists when technical or cost conditions make it unfeasible or inadvisable to have more than one firm in a particular industry. A fairly good example is the telephone industry, where the presence of competing local phone companies would mean not only a duplication of investment—telephone poles, cables, and switching stations—but also considerable inconvenience to consumers, who would have to subscribe to the services of each company if they wanted to be able to reach all parties living in the community. Rather than permit duplication, the government allows a single company to become a monopoly but imposes certain restrictions on its actions. Similar justification is often offered for the existence of a single local utility company. (Local utilities and phone companies are regulated by state commissions rather than by the federal government.)

At one time, long-distance phone service was also regarded as a natural monopoly because it was necessary to string expensive copper wire from city to city. Today microwave communications make it possible to avoid that expense, thus opening the way for competition and eliminating the justification for natural monopoly status. The *Federal Communications Commission (FCC)* continues to regulate the rates charged by AT&T (the former monopolist provider of long-distance service), but it is clear that rates will be fully deregulated after AT&T's new rivals have established themselves.

One criticism of federal industry regulation is that it has not been confined to natural monopolies. Over the years numerous industries—including airlines, trucking, radio and television, and water carriers (ships and barges)—have been thought to be sufficiently "clothed with the public interest" to justify regulation. In recent years, that justification has been ques-

---

[5] Regulation designed to deal with the problems posed by market power is sometimes described as "price and entry regulation" to distinguish it from "health and safety regulation."

tioned and virtually all federal regulatory agencies have seen their rate-setting powers either eliminated or substantially reduced. The reason for this trend toward deregulation is discussed below.

Criticisms of Government Regulation and Antitrust Policies

Neither antitrust policies nor government regulation has been totally success-ful in dealing with the problem of market power. In fact it can be argued that consumers would be better off if fewer industries were subject to regulation and fewer antitrust laws were on the books. We'll explore the basis for that ar-gument as we consider criticism against regulation.

What's Wrong with Regulation?

You have seen why there is a fairly strong case for industry regulation of clear-cut natural monopolies—local telephone and utility companies, for ex-ample. However, critics argue that regulation outside this arena too often be-comes a device for restricting entry and raising prices in industries that might otherwise be reasonably competitive. The railroad and trucking industries stand out as examples.

Both railroads and interstate trucking are regulated by the *Interstate Commerce Commission (ICC)*. The ICC was created in 1887 to oversee the railroads, which were believed to have substantial market power. Research suggests, however, that although the railroads clearly enjoyed some pricing discretion, they faced much more price competition than they desired. In fact the rail-roads themselves were in favor of regulation as a way of stabilizing price-fix-ing agreements in the industry.[6] The railroads hoped that the ICC would be able to do for them what they had been unable to do for themselves: restrain price competition.

In 1935, at least partly in response to pressure from the railroads, the in-terstate trucking industry was brought under the ICC's control. Although the trucking industry at that time was in its infancy, the railroads recognized that competition from trucking might harm them, and they believed that regula-tion would limit that competition. Available evidence suggests that they were correct; regulated industries are often protected from competition.

---

[6] Almarin Phillips, *Promoting Competition In Regulated Markets* (Washington, D.C.: The Brookings Institution, 1975), p. 77.

Under the ICC regulation, competition within the trucking industry and between trucking and railroads was significantly restricted. Until recently the commission strictly limited the number of trucking firms that could operate between any two cities. In addition, it regulated the routes each firm's trucks were permitted to travel and the number of products each firm could carry. Most important, the commission permitted the trucklines to agree on minimum rates.

Defenders of industry regulation argued that these restrictions were needed to prevent "destructive and wasteful" competition—too many firms serving a particular market, for example. Critics contended that these regulations resulted in much higher shipping charges than would have been possible in a more competitive environment.

These and similar criticisms of other regulatory agencies resulted in a great deal of pressure for the deregulation of the transportation and shipping industries. In 1978 these pressures led to the passage of legislation to deregulate the airline industry. This process was completed in 1985, when the *Civil Aeronautics Board (CAB),* the agency that regulated the airline industry, was dissolved. Airlines are now free to compete in whichever markets they choose and to set their own ticket prices. The Motor Carriers Act of 1980 accomplished essentially the same thing in the trucking industry. Trucking firms are now permitted to decide what markets to serve, what prices to charge, and what products to haul.

Similar legislation related to other forms of surface transportation has drastically reduced the Interstate Commerce Commission's control over the rates and practices of railroads, buses, freight forwarders, and the other carriers it supervises. Other regulatory agencies have experienced similar reductions in their powers.[7]

What's Wrong with Antitrust Policies?

Critics of antitrust policies show less consensus than exists among critics of regulation. At one extreme, economists believe that the antitrust laws are weak and ineffective. At the other, they view these laws as unnecessarily restrictive and counterproductive.

The first group of economists argues that our existing antitrust laws are virtually useless in a world of oligopolies. These statutes, passed at the turn of the century, were designed to prosecute "attempts to monopolize" and vari-

---

[7] The 1992 Cable TV Consumer Protection and Competition Act, which re-regulated some cable television rates, clearly runs counter to this trend. The Federal Communications Commission is charged with implementing this act.

ous forms of collusion. But the modern-day antitrust problem is one of oligopoly, not monopoly. As we have seen, oligopolists don't need to resort to collusion to achieve their objectives; they rely instead on price leadership and conscious parallelism to achieve the same results without violating the antitrust laws.

Some economists believe that the solution to this problem is to pass legislation that will make "bigness" itself a violation of the antitrust laws. For example, the law might define any firm producing more than 50 percent of an industry's output as being too big and thus subject to being divided into several smaller firms.

The second group of economists, which includes Lester Thurow of MIT, argues that the advantages of bigness—lower production costs and more rapid development of new products—far outweigh the disadvantages. In Thurow's opinion our antitrust laws force U.S. firms to spend millions of dollars a year defending themselves against government lawsuits, dollars that could be better spent on research and development.

More important, Thurow believes that increased foreign competition has made these antitrust efforts unnecessary and probably even counterproductive. Firms that seem large relative to the U.S. economy are not so large when viewed in the context of the world economy; therefore they possess less market power than is commonly assumed. According to Thurow, even some of the largest U.S. firms are now in danger of being driven out of business by foreign rivals.

> Think, for example, about General Motors. For many years it was the largest industrial firm in the world. Today, even if it were the only American auto manufacturer, it would still be in a competitive fight for its life.[8]

U.S. antitrust laws may in fact handicap domestic producers in this competitive struggle. Consider, for example, the Japanese *keiretsu,* or "group of companies." This arrangement joins together rival producers, their suppliers, banks, and government agencies in order to share knowledge and gain efficiency. These structures, although legal in Japan, would probably be illegal in the United States under present antitrust laws. Critics argue that by prohibiting such joint ventures, we tie the hands of our domestic producers and put them at a competitive disadvantage relative to their foreign rivals.[9]

In our discussion of antitrust and regulation we have tried to remain objective. Some economists believe that our antitrust laws are far too weak; others argue that they are counterproductive. Both sides probably overstate their

---

[8] Lester C. Thurow, "An Era of New Competition," *Newsweek,* January 18, 1982, p. 63.
[9] Patrick M. Boarman, "Antitrust Laws in a Global Market," *Challenge,* January-February, 1993, pages 30–36.

cases. Even though the antitrust laws may deal ineffectively with price leadership, they succeed in discouraging price fixing and other forms of collusive behavior. This effect may be more important than critics believe. Firms in oligopolistic industries may have a difficult time avoiding price competition, particularly when profits are threatened by a recession or by overcapacity in the industry. In such situations oligopolists are tempted to collude in order to ensure cooperation and avoid price warfare. Vigorous antitrust enforcement can deter such collusion and thereby enhance consumer well-being.

Those who argue that antitrust laws are unnecessary also exaggerate. Although competition from foreign firms has changed the economic environment for many U.S. businesses, other industries do not face significant competitive pressure from abroad. Some industries that do have already convinced Congress to erect trade barriers to reduce the inflow of foreign products and protect them from foreign competition. Furthermore, statistical studies suggest that most U.S. firms can compete effectively with their foreign rivals. There probably are exceptions to this generalization, however, and the *keiretsu* and similar foreign alliances of companies may require that similar alliances be permitted in the United States. In short, although international competition does not justify an abandonment of our antitrust statutes, it may require some rethinking so that we can promote competition without sacrificing efficiency.

Summary

In the U.S. economy most firms have some market power, or pricing discretion. Market power is exercised through product differentiation or by altering total industry output. The extent of the firm's market power depends on the structure, or makeup, of the industry in which it operates. The definitive characteristics of *industry structure* are the number of sellers in the industry and their size distribution, the nature of the product, and the extent of barriers to entry. The four basic industry structures are pure competition, monopolistic competition, oligopoly, and pure monopoly.

At one end of the spectrum lie purely competitive firms, which are totally without market power. Because the competitive industry is characterized by a large number of relatively small firms selling undifferentiated products, each firm is powerless to influence price. The absence of significant barriers to entry prevents purely competitive firms from earning economic profits in the long run.

Monopolistic competition is the market structure most closely resembling pure competition; the difference is that monopolistically competitive firms sell differentiated products. The ability to differentiate its product allows the monopolistically competitive firm some pricing discretion, although that discretion is limited by the availability of close substitutes offered by competing firms. Monopolistically competitive firms misallocate resources because they fail to produce up to the point where $P = MC$. They also are somewhat less efficient at producing their products than are purely competitive firms with identical cost curves. These disadvantages are at least partially offset by the product variety offered by these sellers.

The third market structure, *oligopoly*, is characterized by a small number of relatively large firms that are protected by significant barriers to entry. Although these firms may enjoy substantial pricing discretion, their market power is constrained by the high degree of interdependence that exists among oligopolistic firms. Oligopolists use *collusion*, secret agreements to fix prices, and *price leadership*, informal agreements to follow the price changes of one firm, as tactics to reduce competition. Even in the absence of collusion or price leadership, oligopolists may choose to avoid price competition because it tends to invite retaliation. Instead these firms tend to channel their competitive instincts into *nonprice competition*—advertising, packaging, and new product development.

The market structure farthest removed from pure competition is monopoly, or *pure monopoly*. The monopolist enjoys substantial pricing discretion and dictates the level of output. The monopoly *is* the industry because it is the sole seller of a product for which there are no close substitutes. Unlike that of the purely competitive firm, the monopolist's position is protected by substantial barriers to entry, which may enable monopolistic firms to earn economic profits in the long run.

Like monopolistically competitive firms, monopolists tend to distort the allocation of resources by halting production short of the point where $P = MC$. Monopolists may charge higher prices than necessary—prices that include economic profits. These higher prices redistribute income from consumers to the monopolists. Oligopoly can have a similar impact on consumer welfare, but it is more difficult to generalize about the consequences of that market structure. In some industries the negative consequences of monopoly or oligopoly may be offset by the lower production costs that result from their greater size or by greater innovation due to their ability to invest economic profits in research and development.

Because monopolists and oligopolists may misallocate resources and redistribute income, the U.S. Congress has passed antitrust laws and created regulatory agencies. Enacted in response to the formation of *trusts* (combinations of firms organized to restrain competition), *antitrust laws* prohibit certain kinds of behavior: price fixing, tying contracts, and *mergers* entered into for the purpose of limiting competition. The major antitrust statutes are the Sherman Antitrust Act of 1890, the Clayton Antitrust Act of 1914, and the Federal Trade Commission Act, also passed in 1914. Industry regulation, the other approach to dealing with potentially exploitive market power, is designed to establish and police rules of behavior for *natural monopolies,* industries in which competition cannot or should not develop, because of technical or cost considerations. Unfortunately regulation has been extended to some industries in which there is little evidence of natural monopoly status—transportation, for example. In recent years, many of those industries have been deregulated.

Both regulation and antitrust laws have been subject to criticism. Critics argue that regulation too often becomes a device for restricting entry and raising prices in industries that might otherwise be reasonably competitive. Antitrust laws are criticized from two perspectives. Some hold that they are too weak to constrain the behavior of oligopolists. Others contend that such laws are unnecessary because foreign competition provides adequate protection against abuses of firms with market power. Most economists see some truth in each of these criticisms but argue that antitrust is neither as weak nor as counterproductive as critics suggest.

Glossary

Antitrust laws. Laws that have as their objective the maintenance and promotion of competition.

Collusion. Agreement among sellers to fix prices or in some other way restrict competition.

Conscious parallelism. A situation in which firms adopt similar policies even though they have had no communication whatsoever.

Game theory. The study of the strategies employed by interdependent firms.

Government franchise. An exclusive license to provide some product or service.

Industry structure. The makeup of an industry: its number of sellers and their size distribution; the nature of the product; the extent of barriers to entry.

Merger. The union of two or more companies into a single firm.

Monopolistic competition. An industry structure characterized by a large number of small sellers of slightly differentiated products and by modest barriers to entry.

Monopoly. An industry structure characterized by a single firm selling a product for which there are no close substitutes and by substantial barriers to entry.

Nash equilibrium. A situation in which each firm's strategy is the best it can choose, given the strategies chosen by the other firms in the industry.

Natural monopoly. An industry in which it is not feasible or advisable to have more than one firm due to technical or cost considerations.

Oligopoly. An industry structure characterized by a few relatively large sellers and substantial barriers to entry.

Price leadership. An informal arrangement whereby a single firm takes the lead in all price changes in the industry.

Trusts. Combinations of firms organized for the purpose of restraining competition and thereby gaining economic profit.

Tying contract. An agreement specifying that the purchaser will, as a condition of sale for some product, also buy some other product offered by the seller.

Study Questions

Fill in the Blanks

1. Firms that can influence the price of their product are said to possess _____ _____ .

2. An industry dominated by a few relatively large sellers is an _____ _____ .

3. The closest market structure to pure competition is _____ .

4. In long-run equilibrium purely competitive firms and _____ firms can earn only a normal profit.

5. The distinguishing feature of oligopoly is the high degree of _____ _____ that exists among sellers.

6. A _____ is the sole seller of a product for which there are no good substitutes.

7. _____ is agreement between sellers to fix prices or limit competition.

8. Monopolists distort the allocation of scarce resources because they produce (more/less) _____ of their product than is socially desirable.

9. The first major antitrust law, the _____ Act, was passed in 1890.

10. Both oligopolists and monopolists may earn economic profits in the long run because they are protected by substantial _____ .

11. The study of the strategies employed by interdependent firms is known as

_____ .

12. _____ refers to oligopolists adopting similar policies without any communication whatsoever.

Multiple Choice

1. Which of the following is *not* an element of industry structure?
   a) The number of sellers in the industry
   b) The extent of barriers to entry
   c) The existence of economic profits
   d) The size distribution of sellers

2. Which of the following statements about unregulated monopolists is *false*?
   a) They may incur an economic loss in the short run.
   b) They maximize their profit (or minimize their loss) by producing at the output where $MR = MC$.
   c) They sell their product at a price equal to marginal cost.
   d) They face competition from rivals in other industries.

3. Which of the following is *not* a characteristic of monopolistic competition?
   a) Substantial barriers to entry
   b) Differentiated products
   c) A large number of sellers
   d) Small firms

4. Which of the following is probably *not* a monopolistically competitive firm?
   a) A barber shop
   b) A wheat farm
   c) A hardware store
   d) A furniture store

5. American Airlines will not raise prices without first considering how United will behave. This is probably evidence of their
   a) cutthroat competition.
   b) collusion.
   c) interdependence.
   d) price fixing.

6. Which of the following is *not* a characteristic of oligopolistic industries?
   a) Mutual interdependence
   b) Substantial barriers to entry
   c) Relatively large sellers
   d) Fierce price competition

7. Which of the following do monopolistically competitive firms, oligopolists, and monopolists have in common?
   a) All are relatively large.
   b) All have some market power.
   c) All are protected by substantial barriers to entry.
   d) All are concerned about the reactions of rivals to any actions they take.

8. Which of the following statutes outlawed mergers that would substantially lessen competition?
   a) The Sherman Act
   b) The Clayton Act
   c) The Merger Act
   d) The Federal Trade Commission Act

9. What is the primary difference between antitrust enforcement and industry regulation?
   a) Antitrust enforcement attempts to promote competition; regulation does not.
   b) Antitrust enforcement has some critics; industry regulation does not.
   c) Antitrust enforcement is concerned about the public interest; industry regulation attempts to protect the regulated firms.
   d) Industry regulation deals only with natural monopolies; antitrust does not.

10. The concept of conscious parallelism suggests that oligopolists
    a) will always collude.
    b) can adopt similar policies without any communication.
    c) use price leadership to coordinate their pricing policies.
    d) prefer price competition to nonprice competition.

Use the following payoffs matrix in answering questions 11 and 12.

Firm X's price strategies

		$15	$20
Firm Y's price strategies	**$15**	Each firm earns a $20,000 profit.	X earns $10,000. Y earns $40,000.
	$20	X earns $40,000. Y earns $10,000.	Each firm earns a $30,000 profit.

11. A Nash equilibrium would result if
   a) firm X selected a price of $20 and Y selected $15.
   b) firm Y selected a price of $15 and X selected $20.
   c) both firms selected the $15 price.
   d) both firms selected the $20 price.

12. If both firms charge $15,
   a) each firm will earn a profit of $30,000.
   b) there will be incentive to collude and raise price to $20.
   c) firm X will earn $40,000.
   d) firm Y will earn $40,000.

13. Cheating on collusive agreements is more likely when
   a) there are very few firms in the industry.
   b) the economy is weak and firms have excess capacity.
   c) each firm's prices are readily known.
   d) cheaters can expect swift retaliation.

14. Which of the following is not an example of a barrier to entry?
   a) a government franchise
   b) exclusive control of a critical input
   c) the presence of a small number of firms in the industry
   d) the requirement of a large investment to begin production

15. Firms that are monopolists
   a) always earn economic profits in the short run.
   b) always earn economic profits in the long run.
   c) can see their monopoly status eroded by technological progress.
   d) all of the above

Problems and Questions for Discussion

1. What constrains a monopolist's pricing discretion?

2. What problems might be associated with monopolistic or oligopolistic market structures? That is, how might they harm consumer well-being?

3. How do firms acquire market power? What impact do barriers to entry have on a firm's market power?

4. Why would we expect prices to be somewhat higher under monopolistic competition than under pure competition?

5. Suppose that there is only one grocery store in your neighborhood. What limits its market power? If your neighborhood were more isolated, would that increase or decrease the grocery store's market power?

6. In some communities grocery stores may act as oligopolists, whereas in other communities they may act as monopolistically competitive firms. How is this possible? How would you distinguish the first situation from the second?

7. Under what circumstances might consumers be better off with monopoly or oligopoly than with a competitive structure?

8. What is meant by a *natural monopoly,* and how can its existence justify regulation?

9. As a group, economists have been critical of regulation. Why?

10. Why might our existing antitrust laws be ineffective against oligopolistic firms?

Answer Key

Fill in the Blanks

1. market power	5. interdependence	10. barriers to entry
2. oligopoly	6. monopoly	11. game theory
3. monopolistic competition	7. Collusion	12. Conscious parallelism
4. monopolistically competitive	8. less	
	9. Sherman	

Multiple Choice

1. c	4. b	7. b	10. b	13. b
2. c	5. c	8. b	11. c	14. c
3. a	6. d	9. a	12. b	15. c

Market Failure

1. Define market failure and identify its sources.
2. Distinguish between internal and external costs (and benefits).
3. Describe how externalities distort the allocation of scarce resources.
4. Explain pollution as the result of poorly defined property rights.
5. Discuss why pollution taxes are superior to emissions standards.
6. Explain why government should encourage the production of products yielding significant external benefits.
7. Distinguish between private and public goods.
8. Explain the free-rider problem and its consequences.
9. Describe the income distribution and the extent of poverty in the U.S. economy.
10. Discuss the views of public choice economists and the concept of government failure.

At times a market economy may produce too much or too little of certain products and thus fail to make the most efficient use of society's limited resources. This, as you might expect, is referred to as **market failure.** In *The Affluent Society*, John Kenneth Galbraith describes numerous instances of market failure:

. . . The family which takes its mauve and cerise, air-conditioned, power-steered, and power-braked automobile out for a tour passes through cities that are badly paved, made hideous by litter, blighted buildings, billboards, and posts for wires that should long since have been put underground. They pass on into a countryside that has been rendered largely invisible by commercial art. . . . They picnic on exquisitely packaged food from a portable icebox by a polluted stream and go on to spend the night at a park which is a menace to public health and morals. Just before dozing off on an air mattress, beneath a nylon tent, amid the stench of decaying refuse, they may reflect vaguely on the curious unevenness of their blessings. Is this, indeed, the American genius?[1]

In Galbraith's view the American economy has produced an abundance of consumer goods—automobiles, appliances, sporting goods, and numerous other items—but far too little of other goods that Americans desire: clean air and water, parks, and well-paved roads, for example. Why do such market failures occur? As you will learn in this chapter, there are three major sources of market failure: market power, externalities, and public goods. The passage from Professor Galbraith's book points at two of these: externalities and public goods. In this chapter we explore those two sources of market failure in some detail. Because the impact of market power has been examined at length in Chapters 6 and 7, we will review it only briefly here.

Market Power Revisited

As we all know, the American economy does not function in the idealized manner envisioned by the model of pure capitalism; that is, businesses do not always serve the best interests of society as a whole. In part this is because our industries are less competitive than the model requires them to be. Very few U.S. industries are purely competitive; most are monopolistically competitive or oligopolistic. And the less competitive an industry, the greater the market power (pricing discretion) of its firms.

Because firms with market power tend to restrict output in order to force up prices, too few of society's resources are allocated to the goods and services they produce. In simplified terms this means that because firms such as IBM and General Electric have market power, fewer of society's resources are devoted to producing computers and appliances, and too few Americans will be able to own these products. Markets are "failing" in the sense that they are not allocating resources in the most efficient way—the allocation that would occur under pure competition.

Although virtually all economists agree that this form of market failure exists, clearly it is not what Galbraith was describing when he wrote the words we quoted. Galbraith seems to believe that Americans have done quite well in the area of consumer goods. How, then, do we explain his criticism of our economy's performance? The answer lies beyond the problems caused by market power, in some shortcomings of the market mechanism itself.

---

[1] John Kenneth Galbraith, *The Affluent Society* (New York: New American Library, 1958), pp. 199–200.

Externalities as a Source of Market Failure

Considerable resource misallocation results from the failure of private, or un-regulated, markets to take into account all the costs and benefits associated with the production and consumption of a good or service.

When producers are deciding what production techniques to use and what resources to purchase, they tend to consider only **internal costs,** or **private costs**—the costs borne by the firm. They do not take into account any ex-ternal costs that are borne by (or spill over on) other parties. Consumers behave in a similar manner; they tend to consider only **private benefits**—the benefits that accrue to the person or persons purchasing the product—and ig-nore any external benefits that might be received by others.

If businesses and consumers are permitted to ignore these external costs and benefits, or **externalities,** the result will be an inefficient use of our scarce resources: We will produce too much of some items because we do not con-sider the full costs; we will produce too little of others because we do not con-sider the full benefits.

Externalities: The Case of External Costs

It's not difficult to think of personal situations in which external costs have come into play. Perhaps you've planned to savor a quiet dinner at your fa-vorite restaurant, only to have a shrieking baby seated with its harried par-ents at the next table. Think about the movie you might have enjoyed if that rambunctious five-year-old hadn't been using the back of your seat as a bongo drum. Why do parents bring young children to these places, knowing that they will probably disturb the people around them? According to the teachings of Adam Smith, they are pursuing their own self-interest—in this case by minimizing the monetary cost of an evening's entertainment. But their actions are imposing different kinds of costs on everyone around them. The frazzled nerves, poorly digested meals, and generally spoiled evenings expe-rienced by you and your fellow diners or moviegoers are examples of **exter-nal costs:** the costs created by one party or group and imposed, or *spilled over,* onto some other (nonconsenting) party or group.

Pollution as an External Cost. The classic example of external costs is pol-lution: the contamination of our land, air, and water caused by the litter that lines our streets and highways, the noxious fumes emitted into our atmo-sphere, and the wastes dumped into our rivers, lakes, and streams. Why does pollution exist? The answer is really quite obvious. It's less expensive for a manufacturer to dispose of its wastes in a nearby river, for example, than to haul that material to a so-called safe area. But it is a low-cost method of disposal only in terms of the private costs borne by the manufacturing firm. If we consider the social cost, there may well be a cheaper method of disposal.

Social cost refers to the total cost to a society of the production and/or consumption of a product. The term includes not only private, or internal, costs but also external costs. To illustrate, let's consider the misuse of our water resources. Polluted water means less fishing and fewer people enjoying water sports. It also means less income for the people who rent boats and cottages and sell fishing bait, for example. It further affects the people living downstream, who need water for drinking and bathing; they will have to pay—through taxes—to purify the water. Finally, it may have a deadly effect on the birds and animals that live off the fish and other creatures in the water. Thus water pollution may create numerous external costs that are ignored by polluters.

External Costs and Resource Misallocation. When the act of producing or consuming a product creates external costs, an exclusive reliance on private markets and the pursuit of self-interest will result in a misallocation of society's resources. We can illustrate why this is so by investigating a single, hypothetical, purely competitive industry.

Dumping wastes into a river may minimize private costs, but it can create substantial external costs.

For the purpose of our investigation, let's assume that the paint industry is purely competitive. In Exh. 8.1 demand curve D shows the quantity of
paint that would be demanded at each possible price. Supply curve S_1 shows
the quantity of paint the industry would supply at each price if all firms considered only their private costs and disposed of their wastes by dumping
them into local rivers. As you can see, these demand and supply curves reveal
an equilibrium price of $8 per can and an equilibrium quantity of 120,000 cans
per year.

Now suppose that the firms are forced to eliminate the external costs
they are creating; that is, they must develop production techniques that eliminate the pollution. This will increase their internal (private) costs of production, which in turn will cause them to reduce their supply to S_2. With this
supply reduction will come a higher equilibrium price and a lower equilibrium quantity.

So long as paint suppliers were allowed to shift some of their production
costs to society as a whole (or to some portion of society), the price of paint
was artificially low; that is, it did not reflect the true social cost of producing
the product. Consumers responded to this low price by purchasing an artificially high quantity of the product—more than they would have purchased if

EXHIBIT 8.1

The Impact of External Costs

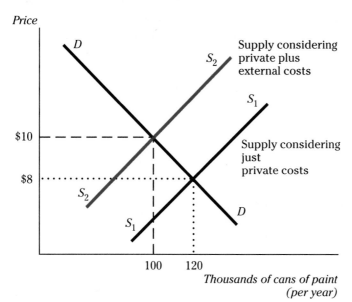

*Thousands of cans of paint
(per year)*

the price reflected the true social cost of production. As a consequence, more of society's scarce resources were allocated to the production of paint than was socially optimal.

When paint suppliers are forced to internalize all costs—that is, when they are forced to consider external as well as internal costs—they must charge a higher price in order to recover these additional costs. To the extent that this higher price reflects accurately the true social cost of production, it will lead to the socially optimal level of output. As you can see from Exh. 8.1, the higher price of paint results in a reduction in the quantity demanded from 120,000 to 100,000 cans per year. Resources must have been misallocated initially, for when consumers are required to pay the true cost of production, their preferences are to use fewer resources in producing paint and to allocate more resources to the production of other things.

Poorly Defined Property Rights. Our paint example points out that when manufacturers create external costs, the private market does not record the true costs of production and thereby fails to provide the proper signals to ensure that our resources are used optimally. Why is the private market unable to communicate the true cost of production? In many instances the problem is poorly defined property rights. **Property rights** are the legal rights to use goods, services, or resources. For example, you have the right to use your car and lawnmower and barbeque grill; your neighbor does not. But who owns the Mississippi River and the Atlantic Ocean and the air we breathe? As you probably recognize, no one owns these natural resources. And therein lies the problem. Because no one owns these resources, no one has the right to charge for their use. And because no one has the right to charge for their use, individuals assume that they are available to be used (and abused) for free. Remember, individuals and businesses respond only to private, or internal, costs and benefits; if private markets don't register the cost, people may act as if there is none.

Correcting for External Costs. How do we force businesses and individuals to consider all of the costs of their actions, to internalize all costs? One possibility is for government to assign property rights to unowned resources so that some individual will be in a position to charge for their use. Another possibility is for Congress to pass laws that forbid (or limit) activities that impose external costs (such as dumping wastes into lakes and streams). A third possibility is for government agencies to harness market incentives in an effort to compensate for external costs. Let's consider those alternatives.

Assigning property rights. Because the source of the pollution problem is poorly defined property rights, one possible solution is for government to clarify the ownership of the resources that are being abused. Think about our hypothetical example involving the polluting paint company. Suppose that the state legislature gave the legal ownership of the river to the paint company. Suppose also that the only use of the river was as the water supply for a small city downstream. Once the ownership of the river is established, we might expect the city to attempt to bargain with the paint company to stop dumping its wastes into the river. Assume, for example, that the next cheapest disposal technique would cost the company $100,000 a year. Suppose also that it would cost the city $200,000 a year to purchase water from a neighboring community. Since the river is worth more as a source of drinking water than as a method of waste disposal, the city should be able to negotiate with the paint company to stop dumping its wastes in the river. For example, if the city were to offer the paint company $150,000 to stop discharging its wastes, the paint company would probably agree. The paint company will stop dumping its wastes into the river, because it will no longer see the use of the river as free. If it dumps its wastes into the river, it will have to forgo the $150,000 payment from the city. Since the cost of alternative disposal is only $100,000, the firm will choose the alternative method and pocket the $50,000 difference.

Suppose that the legislature had assigned the ownership of the river to the city. Would the outcome have been different? This time the company would need to approach the city to get permission to dump into the river. The company would be willing to pay up to $100,000 a year to use the river, since that is the cost of alternative disposal. But since an alternative water supply would cost the city $200,000, it would not be willing to deal; the river would again be used as a water supply.

The preceding example illustrates two important points. First, when property rights are clearly defined, resources are put to their most valued use; that is, they are used efficiently. In this case the river will be used as a water supply, but in some instances its most valued use might be for waste disposal.[2] Second, the resources will be used efficiently regardless of who is assigned their ownership. (Note that either way, the river was used as a water supply.) The idea of solving externality problems by assigning property rights and encouraging negotiation is based on the work of Nobel prize-winning economist Ronald Coase. In our society many cases involving externalities are resolved by negotiation after the courts have clarified property rights. The assignment of property rights has even been proposed as a solution to the overfishing of our oceans (see "Not Enough Fish in the Stormy Sea," on page 242). However, as Professor Coase has recognized, this solution works only in situ-

---

[2] Suppose, for example, that alternative disposal would cost the paint company $250,000 a year. In that case the paint company would be willing to bid up to $250,000 to use the river for waste disposal. If it offered the city $225,000, the city would probably agree (since it can purchase water for $200,000 a year), and the river would be used for waste disposal.

Not Enough Fish in the Stormy Sea

Lawmakers Consider Property Rights for Fishers to Protect the Nation's Dwindling Stocks

The pair of U.S. trawlers had set out for sea scallops, but instead, they themselves became the catch of the day. Wielding guns, Canadian fisheries enforcement officers seized the U.S. vessels and escorted them to Newfoundland. The alleged crime? Infringing on Canada's fishing grounds on the Grand Banks. The humble scallop scarcely seems significant enough to provoke such gunboat diplomacy. But the Canadian seizure two weeks ago is one more instance of growing tensions on the high seas as the world's oceans run out of fish.

Now a new battle is being fought not on the water but in the halls of Congress over how to preserve this resource once thought to be virtually inexhaustible. Lawmakers are now reauthorizing the Magnuson Act, which governs ocean fishing in U.S. waters and under which fish stocks have dwindled. Between 1977 and 1987, for instance, stocks of haddock, cod, flounder and other groundfish off New England's shores plunged a stunning 65 percent. Fishing communities around the country are reeling as tens of thousands are put out of work. . . .

The problem is that the Magnuson Act was fundamentally flawed. Passed to promote the U.S. fishing industry at a time when U.S. waters were heavily fished by foreign fleets, it established a 200-mile territorial zone around the U.S. coastline and empowered eight regional councils to regulate catches. Other laws enacted around the same time provided federal subsidies for buying and upgrading boats and equipment. As a result, the industry grew too large for the resource. Fishers went to sea in ever bigger boats equipped with more sophisticated hunting technologies. Domestic catches soared but fish stocks dropped.

The industry-dominated regional councils generally responded by limiting the length of the fishing seasons for various species. But this created a host of new problems. As more fishers have chased ever fewer fish, seasons that once stretched for most of the year have been cut to a couple of months or even days. In the North Pacific, for instance, halibut fishers must haul in their total annual catch within one or two frantic 24-hour periods. "It's a completely irrational business environment," says Joe Blum of the Seattle-based American Factory Trawler Association. Dumping millions of pounds of fish into the market at one time slashes prices, he asserts. Short seasons create pressure to fish even when the weather is unsafe and boats should not leave harbor.

Disastrous Results

Critics say this derby-style system also encourages wasteful practices. Fishers scoop up everything in sight and then toss overboard fish that are the wrong size or not the right species. In Alaskan waters alone, an estimated 560 million pounds of dead and dying whole fish are dumped overboard each year during fishing operations.

In response to these problems, some experts are advocating a plan that in essence privatizes the nation's fisheries. In this market-based system, boat owners no longer would have to race for fish during short seasons but instead would be granted a share of the total catch. These shares—called "individual transferable quotas," or ITQs—would be allocated in proportion to the amount of fish a boat has caught in the past. Fishers could then harvest when and where they wanted, and if they opted to leave the fishery, they could sell their shares to the highest bidder. Already, two small fisheries, the South Atlantic wreckfish fishery and the Atlantic surf clam and ocean quahog fishery, are under ITQ plans. In 1995, Alaska halibut and sablefish fisheries are slated to convert to ITQs as well.

Advocates of the new system assert that ITQs streamline now bloated fishing fleets. In areas where ITQs have been used, the more marginal fishers typically sell out almost immediately, says Doug Hopkins, a senior attorney at the Environmental Defense Fund in New York. In the wreckfish fishery, for instance, only 39 fishers remain of the 51 who were initially granted ITQ shares. The new system also can give fishers an incentive to conserve the natural resource, since they own a piece of it. After ITQs were implemented in the wreckfish fishery, fishers dropped their opposition to reducing the total annual catch.

Unfair Reward

But critics argue that ITQ regimes favor big industry boats and will eventually squeeze out small fishers. . . .

Others charge that the system enriches the very people who created the problem in the first place. The big fishing operators "had no morals," says Alaska fisher John Petraborg. "They put out too much gear, they didn't care about waste, and now they are being rewarded." . . .

SOURCE: "Not Enough Fish in the Stormy Sea," August 15, 1994. Copyright © 1994 U.S. News & World Report. Reprinted with permission.

Use Your Economic Reasoning

1. Why are the oceans being overfished; why are individuals and companies unwilling to voluntarily limit their catches?

2. Short fishing seasons have helped to reduce overfishing but have created other problems. Discuss.

3. What are ITQs, and how might their use help to prevent overfishing?

4. Critics argue that resorting to ITQs would mean giving a public resource to private industry. Why would anyone support such a move?

ations in which the transactions costs—the costs of striking a bargain between the parties—are relatively low and in which the number of people involved is relatively small. When the assignment of property rights does not work, another method must be sought to solve the problem.

Emissions Standards. The U.S. government has attempted to limit pollution by establishing *emissions standards*—laws that specify the maximum amounts of various wastes that each firm will be allowed to emit into the air or water. To meet these emissions standards, firms have to install pollution-control devices, hire additional personnel to monitor these devices, and take other steps that tend to increase the cost of production and lead to higher product prices. When consumers are required to pay a price that more fully reflects the true cost of production, they purchase fewer units of the formerly underpriced items. Therefore resources can be reallocated to the production of other items whose prices more accurately reflect the full social costs of production.

Although government emissions standards have helped reduce pollution, fulfilling their requirements and limiting the discharge of industrial waste to less than some permitted maximum amount can be very costly. Since the polluting firms come from a wide range of industries and employ vastly different production methods, some firms find it much more expensive than others to reduce their discharges. As a consequence, some firms are able to meet their standards at relatively low cost, whereas others face severe financial burdens. The total cost to society of achieving any given level of environmental quality is the sum of the costs incurred by the various firms.

Pollution Taxes. Many economists contend that it would be less expensive to create a *pollution tax* whereby firms would be required to pay a fee for each unit of waste they discharge into the air or water. Under a system of pollution taxes, firms could discharge as much waste into the environment as they chose, but they would have to pay a specified levy—say, $50—for each unit emitted. Ideally this tax would bring about the desired reduction in pollution. If not, it would be raised to whatever dollar amount would convince firms to reduce pollution to acceptable levels.

A major advantage of a pollution tax is that it would allow the firms themselves to decide which ones could cut back on emissions (the discharges of wastes) at the lowest cost. For example, given a fee of $50 for each ton of wastes emitted into the environment, those firms that could reduce their emissions for less than $50 per ton would do so; other firms would continue to pollute and pay the tax. As a result, pollution would be reduced by the firms that could do so most easily and at the lowest cost. Society would then have achieved a given level of environmental quality at the lowest cost in terms of its scarce resources.

A simple example may help to illustrate why the pollution tax is a less expensive approach. Assume that the economy is made up of firms A and B and that each firm is discharging four tons of waste a year. Assume also that it costs firm A $30 per ton to reduce emissions and firm B $160 per ton.

Suppose that society wants to reduce the discharge of wastes by four tons a year. An emissions standard that required each firm to limit its emissions to two tons a year would cost society $380 ($60 for firm A and $320 for firm B). A pollution tax of $50 a ton would accomplish the same objective at a cost of $120, since it would cause firm A to reduce its emissions from four tons to zero. (Firm A would opt to reduce its emissions because this approach is less costly than paying the pollution tax. If the firm paid the pollution tax; it would be billed $50 × 4 tons = $200. But it can reduce emissions at a cost of $30 × 4 tons = $120. Thus it would prefer to reduce its emissions rather than to pay the pollution tax.) Note that firm B will prefer to pay the tax; thus government will receive $200 in pollution tax revenue. This $200 should not be considered a cost of reducing pollution, since it can be used to build roads or schools or be spent in any other way society chooses.

As we noted earlier, the United States has relied on emissions standards to reduce pollution; pollution taxes have been used very sparingly and primarily in an experimental way. But the Clean Air Act of 1990 contains provisions that, like pollution taxes, encourage businesses to reduce pollution in the least costly way. The Clean Air Act encourages businesses to reduce their emissions by more than the law requires; they are given the right to sell pollution "credits" to other businesses that find it very costly to reduce their emissions. By giving firms the option of buying credits or reducing emissions, the act hopes to achieve its air quality standards at the lowest possible cost.

The Optimal Level of Pollution. Although emissions standards and pollution taxes are both designed to reduce pollution, neither system is designed to eliminate pollution entirely. The total elimination of pollution would not be in society's best interest, since it requires the use of scarce resources that have alternative uses. Economists support reducing pollution only so long as the benefits of added pollution controls exceed their costs. For example, it makes no sense to force firms to pay an additional $300,000 to reduce pollution if the added benefits to society amount to only $100,000. For that reason, any rational system of pollution control—whether based on emissions standards or pollution taxes—will permit some level of pollution. Unfortunately, because it is difficult to measure the costs and benefits of pollution control in an exact manner, it is also difficult to determine whether efforts to control pollution have been carried too far or not far enough.

Externalities: The Case of External Benefits

Not all externalities are harmful. Sometimes the actions of individuals or businesses create **external benefits**—benefits that are paid for by one party but spill over to other parties. One example is the flowers your neighbors plant in their yard each year. You can enjoy their beauty without contributing to the cost of their planting and upkeep. Another example is flu shots. You pay for them, and they help protect you from the flu. But they also help protect everyone else; if you don't come down with the flu, you can't pass it on to others.

Businesses also can create external benefits. For example, most firms put their workers—particularly their young and/or inexperienced workers—through some sort of training program. Of course, the sponsoring firm gains a more productive, more valuable employee. But most people do not stay with one employer for their entire working careers; when trained employees decide to move on, other employers will benefit from the training they have received.

External Benefits and Resource Allocation.

In a pure market economy individuals would tend to demand too small a quantity of those products that generate external benefits. To understand why this is so, consider your own consumption decisions for a moment. When you are deciding whether to purchase a product (or how much of a product to purchase), you compare the product's benefits with its price. If you value a unit of the product more than the other items you could purchase with the same money, you buy it. If not, you spend your money on the product you value more highly. In effect you are deciding which product delivers the most benefits for the money. But whose benefits are you considering? Your own, of course! In other words, you respond to private rather than external benefits. Most consumption decisions are made this way. As a result, consumers purchase too small a quantity of the products that create external benefits, and our scarce resources are misallocated. That is to say, fewer resources are devoted to producing these products than is justified by their **social benefits**—the sum of the private benefits received by those who purchase the product and the external benefits received by others.[3]

---

[3] As we learned earlier, when property rights are clearly defined, the existence of external benefits need not lead to resource misallocation. To illustrate, suppose that a restaurant owner notices higher sales on weekends when a neighboring pub has live entertainment. The restaurant owner may entice the pub into more frequent entertainment by agreeing to share its cost. This bargaining solution can lead to an optimal level of entertainment.

Adjusting for External Benefits. To illustrate the underproduction of products that carry external benefits, let's examine what would happen if elementary education were left to the discretion of the private market. Reading, writing, and arithmetic are basic skills that have obvious benefits for the individual, but they also benefit society as a whole. In his prize-winning book *Capitalism and Freedom,* economist Milton Friedman makes the case as follows:

> A stable and democratic society is impossible without a minimum amount of literacy and knowledge on the part of most citizens and without widespread acceptance of some common set of values. Education can contribute to both. In consequence, the gain from the education of a child accrues not only to the child or to his parents but also to other members of the society. . . .[4]

For the sake of our example, let's suppose that all elementary education in the United States is provided through private schools on a voluntary basis. In such a situation the number of children enrolled in these schools would be determined by the forces of demand and supply. As shown in Exh. 8.2, the market would establish a price of $500 per student, and at that price three million students would attend elementary school each year. The market demand curve (D_1) provides an incomplete picture, however. It considers private benefits—the benefits received by the students and their parents—but ignores external benefits. If we include the external benefits of education, society would want even more children to be educated. Demand curve D_2 shows that society would choose to educate five million students a year at an equilibrium price of $700 per student.

As you can see from Exh. 8.2, individuals pursuing their own self-interests would choose to purchase less education than could be justified on the basis of the full social benefits. An obvious solution to this problem would be to require that each child attend school for some minimum number of years, allowing the family to select the school and find the money to pay for it. The U.S. government has taken a different approach, however. That is, most elementary and secondary schools are operated by local governments and financed through taxes rather than through fees charged to parents. This spreads the financial burden for education among all taxpayers rather than just the parents of school-aged children. In effect, taxpayers without children "subsidize" taxpayers with children. The rationale for this approach is fairly clear-cut. Since all taxpayers share in the benefits of education (the external benefits, at least), they should share in the costs as well.

In a variety of circumstances subsidies can be used to encourage the consumption of products that carry external benefits. Consider the flu shots

---

[4] Milton Friedman, *Capitalism and Freedom* (Chicago: The University of Chicago Press, 1962), p. 86.

EXHIBIT 8.2

The Impact of External Benefits

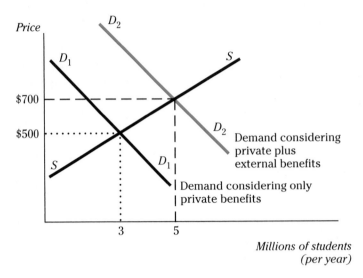

again. They protect not only the people inoculated but also those in contact with them. Still, many people will not pay to receive a flu shot. So if we want more people to get flu shots (but we don't want to pass laws requiring such shots), we could have the government subsidize all or part of the cost. The lower the price of flu shots, the more people who will agree to get them. (Should government subsidize measles vaccinations? Read "Return of a Childhood Killer," on page 250 before you decide.)

There is no reason why subsidized flu shots would have to be provided by government doctors; the government could simply agree to pay private doctors for each flu shot administered. It is precisely this approach that Milton Friedman would like to see implemented in education. Rather than continuing to subsidize public schools, Friedman would prefer a system that permitted students to select their own privately run schools.

> Government could require a minimum level of schooling financed by giving parents vouchers redeemable for a specified maximum sum per child per year if spent on "approved" educational services. Parents would then be free to spend this sum and any additional sum they themselves provided on purchasing educational services from an "approved" institution of their own choice. . . . The role of government would be limited to insuring that the schools met certain minimum standards. . . .[5]

[5] Milton Friedman, *Capitalism and Freedom* (Chicago: The University of Chicago Press, 1962), p. 86.

Whether or not you agree with Friedman's particular approach, it should be clear to you by now that subsidies can be useful in correcting for market failure. By encouraging the production and consumption of products yielding external benefits, subsidies help ensure that society's resources are used to produce the optimal assortment of goods and services.

Market Failure and the Provision of Public Goods

Market power and the existence of externalities are not the only sources of market failure. Markets may also fail to produce optimal results because some products are simply not well suited to sale by private firms. These products must be provided by government, or they will not be provided at all.

Private Goods versus Public Goods

In order to understand this problem, we must think first about the types of goods and services our economy produces. Those goods and services fall into three categories: pure private goods, private goods that yield external benefits, and public goods.

Pure private goods are products that convey their benefits only to the purchaser.[6] The hamburger you had for lunch falls in that category, as does the jacket you wore to class. Most of the products we purchase in the marketplace are pure private goods.

Some products convey most of their benefits to the person making the purchase but also create substantial external benefits for others. These are **private goods that yield significant external benefits.** We have talked about education and flu shots, but there are numerous other examples—fire protection, police protection, and driver's training, to name just a few.

The third category, **public goods,** consists of products that convey their benefits equally to paying and nonpaying members of society. National defense is probably the best example of a public good. If a business attempted to sell "units" of national defense through the marketplace, what problems would arise? The major problem would be that nonpayers would receive virtually the same protection from foreign invasion as those who paid for the protection. There's no way to protect your house from foreign invasion with-

---

[6] Note that although pure private goods convey their benefits only to the purchaser, the purchaser may *choose* to share those benefits with others. For instance, you may decide to share your hamburger with another person or allow someone else to wear your jacket. But if others share in the benefits of a pure private good, it is because the purchaser allows them to share those benefits, not because the benefits automatically spilled over to them.

Return of a Childhood Killer

Two trips to the doctor, two relatively painless shots: Measles prevention is that simple. Yet the virus that in 1983 seemed all but extinct has doctors and public-health officials seriously worried. In Dallas, Los Angeles and Chicago, measles has turned into an epidemic. Some 17,850 people got measles last year, and officials at the federal Centers of Disease Control (CDC) in Atlanta expect to see 25,000 cases by the end of 1990, up from 1,500 in 1983. At least 80 people have died of the disease this year; seven years ago, not one person did. "It's shameful that a country as wealthy as ours has fallen so far behind in fighting a virus we know how to stop," says Dr. Leonard Plotkin, chairman of the American Academy of Pediatrics (AAP) committee on infectious diseases.

The reasons for the flagging fight are hardly mysterious. Before 1963, when the measles vaccine was introduced, 400,000 people a year became ill. Recent outbreaks have seemed so insignificant by comparison that many parents, especially those who rely on public health clinics, dismiss the risk and don't have children inoculated when they should; instead, they wait until they have to, when the kids enter school. Sometimes those who do get a shot are not protected, since the vaccine fails to "take" in 5 of every 100 people, according to Dr. William Atkinson, an epidemiologist in charge of measles surveillance at the CDC. Some scientists put the number at 8 in 100. . . .

Because all states now require entering kindergarteners to have been vaccinated, school-age children, once hardest hit, are relatively safe this time. Instead, the profoundly contagious virus has grown virulent in two new groups: Children under 5, especially inner-city preschoolers, and adults age 19 to 33 who never had the disease. Seventy percent of the current cases occur in unvaccinated infants and preschoolers, who then spread the virus in day care, in shopping malls, on elevators, in hospital waiting rooms. Because of their immature immune systems, very young children are at a higher risk than other age groups of developing potentially fatal complications such as pneumonia. . . .

In the wake of the 1989 outbreaks, the medical community last year tightened its recommendations on administration of the measles vaccine. The longstanding practice of giving children their first vaccination at the age of 15 months stands. That's the earliest a shot will be effective; in younger infants, antibodies received from the mother through the placenta may prevent the vaccine from causing the mild infection that induces the immune system to produce its own antibodies.

Once an outbreak hits a community, children 12 months old or even younger should get a shot; vaccination within three days of exposure greatly reduces chances of getting sick. . . .

A Double Shield
Virtually everyone who receives a second shot is assured immunity, which prompted the medical community's announcement last year that every child should be vaccinated twice. . . .

Many adults would be wise to head for the doctor's office, too. The American College of Physicians now recommends one dose of the vaccine for any adult age 33 or under who has neither had measles nor been vaccinated. . . .

Unless you belong to a health maintenance organization, which normally absorbs all or most of the cost of vaccination, the $35-to-$50 office visit and measles shot will come from your pocket.

In theory, at least, public-health clinics will vaccinate any child, usually for free. But many urban clinics are overburdened because doctors are referring more patients to public facilities. The clinics have often had to turn people away. Once inconvenienced, many people fail to return. In Texas, where officials report a 700 percent rise in referrals from private doctors to public clinics since 1980, there has been nowhere near a corresponding rise in funds to extend clinic hours and add nurses. Last year, Southern California public clinics saw demand for vaccine services jump 24 percent, more than triple the normal 7 percent annual rise. The AAP thinks the federal budget for next year should include $236 million for childhood-immunization programs, compared with $156 million this year; the President is asking for $153 million. "We're chasing the epidemic, rather than trying to stop it," complains Jackie Noyes, a lobbyist for the AAP.

Measles is here to stay, at least for a few more years. But preventing it in your own family demands no more than checking a few records and, if necessary, a trip to get a shot. That's hardly a high price to pay.

—Scott Minerbrook and Francesca Lunzer Kritz

SOURCE: Scott Minerbrook and Francesca Lunzer Kritz, "Return of a Childhood Killer," August 20, 1990. Copyright © 1990 U.S. News & World Report. Reprinted with permission.

Use Your Economic Reasoning

1. The article seems to suggest that there are external benefits associated with measle vaccinations. What are those external benefits?

2. If individuals are purchasing too few measles vaccinations (or are waiting too long to have their children vaccinated), how can government attack the problem?

3. Suppose that the only action taken by government was to require that parents have their children inoculated at 15 months. Would this solve the problem? Why or why not?

out simultaneously protecting your neighbor's. The inability to exclude non-payers from receiving the same benefits as those who have paid for the product is what economists call the *free-rider problem.*

The Free-Rider Problem

Why does the inability to exclude certain individuals from receiving benefits constitute a problem? Think about national defense for just a moment. How would you feel if you were paying for national defense and your neighbor received exactly the same protection for nothing? Very likely, you would decide to become a free rider yourself, as would many other people. Products such as national defense, flood-control dams, and tornado warning systems cannot be offered so as to restrict their benefits to payers alone. Therefore no private business can expect to earn a profit by offering such goods and services, and private markets cannot be relied on to produce these products, no matter how important they are for the well-being of the society. Unless the government intervenes, they simply will not be provided at all.

Of course, we're not willing to let that happen. That's why a substantial amount of our tax money pays for national defense and other public goods. (Not all publicly *provided* goods are public goods. Our tax dollars are used to pay for education and public swimming pools and a host of other goods and services that do not meet the characteristics of public goods.) As we have emphasized, the ultimate objective of government intervention is to improve the allocation of society's scarce resources so that the economy will do a better job of satisfying our unlimited wants. To the extent that government intervention contributes to that result, it succeeds in correcting for market failure and in improving our social welfare.

Poverty, Equality, and Trends in the Income Distribution

As we've seen, market failure results when a market economy fails to use its scarce resources in an optimal way; when it produces too much or too little of certain products. But even if a market system were able to achieve an optimal allocation of resources, if it distributed income in a way that a majority of the population saw as inequitable or unfair, we might judge that to be a shortcoming of the system.

In a market system, a person's income depends on what he or she has to sell. Those with greater innate abilities and more assets (land and capital) earn higher incomes; those with fewer abilities and fewer assets earn lower incomes. These differences are often compounded by differences in training and education and by differences in the levels of inherited wealth. As a consequence, a total reliance on the market mechanism can produce substantial inequality in the income distribution. Some people have less while others have much more.

How unequal is the income distribution in the United States? As you can see from Exhibit 8.3, there is a significant amount of inequality. In 1993, the households in the lowest quintile (the lowest fifth) of the income distribution received less than 4 percent of total money income in the United States, while the households in the upper fifth received more than 48 percent of total income. In fact, the households in the upper fifth of the income distribution actually received more total income than all the households in the bottom three-fifths of the distribution. Moreover, the income distribution in the United States seems to be growing somewhat less equal. As you can see in the exhibit, the fraction of aggregate income going to the richest fifth of U.S. households has increased over the last twenty years, while the share going to the remaining four-fifths of households has declined.

The existence of inequality may not concern us very much if everyone—including the households in the bottom fifth of the income distribution—is earning enough income to live comfortably. What most of us are really concerned about is households that are living in poverty—those with incomes that are insufficient to provide for their basic needs (according to some standard established by society).

In the United States we have adopted income standards by which we judge the extent of poverty. For example, in 1993, a family of four was classi-

EXHIBIT 8.3

Percent of Aggregate Income Received by Each Fifth of Households in the United States*

	1973	1983	1993
Lowest fifth	4.2%	4.0%	3.6%
Second fifth	10.5	9.9	9.1
Third fifth	17.1	16.4	15.3
Fourth fifth	24.6	24.6	23.8
Highest fifth	43.6	45.1	48.2

*Source: *Preliminary report from the Bureau of the Census, Housing and Household Economic Statistics Division,* 1994.

fied as "poor" if it had an annual income of less than $14,763. By that definition, there were 39.3 million poor people in the United States in 1993—a little less than 15 percent of the population.

Most people would probably agree that if 15 percent of our population— one person out of every seven—is living in poverty we have some cause for concern. The U.S. government has attempted to address the problem of poverty in a variety of ways, primarily by enacting programs designed to address the source of poverty: the inability of the family to earn an adequate income. Examples include government-subsidized training programs for unemployed workers and policies designed to reduce discrimination in hiring. In addition, the minimum wage is intended to lift the earnings of unskilled workers.

Other government programs are designed to reduce the misery of the poor, even if they do not address the cause of poverty. Social Security, for example, provides financial assistance to the old, the disabled, the unemployed, and families that are experiencing financial difficulty because of the death of a breadwinner. Aid to Families with Dependent Children (a federal-state program) provides aid to poor families, often with the stipulation that there is no able-bodied man in the house. In addition to these cash-assistance programs, there are a variety of in-kind assistance programs that provide the poor with some type of good or service. Food stamps and subsidized public housing are two examples. All of these programs are designed to improve the status of the poor and in this way moderate the income distribution dictated by the market.

While there is widespread agreement with the objective of helping the poor, disagreements exist concerning the costs and benefits of particular policies. For example, many economists believe that the minimum wage does more harm than good, since it tends to reduce employment (at the higher wage, employers hire fewer workers). And the welfare program (Aid to Families with Dependent Children) has been criticized both for discouraging work and for encouraging illegitimacy. These criticisms suggest that government intervention may not improve on market outcomes. The next section explores that possibility.

Government Failure: The Theory of Public Choice

The existence of market failures and poverty suggests that market economies do not always use resources efficiently or distribute income fairly. But whether government can be relied upon to improve either the allocation of scarce resources or the income distribution is open to debate. In fact, public choice economists point out that **government failure**—the enactment of government policies that produce inefficient and/or inequitable results—is also a possibility.

Public choice is the study of how government makes economic decisions. This area of economics was developed by James Buchanan, a professor at Virginia Polytechnic Institute and the 1986 recipient of the Nobel Prize in economics. Although many of us would like to think of government as an altruistic body concerned with the public interest, public choice economists advise us to think of government as a collection of individuals each pursuing his or her own self-interest. Just as business executives are interested in maximizing profits, politicians are interested in maximizing their ability to get votes. And government bureaucrats are interested in maximizing their income, power, and longevity. In short, the people who make up government are no different than the rest of us, and we need to remember that if we want to understand their behavior.

Recognizing that politicians are merely "vote maximizers" can help us to understand why special-interest groups exert a disproportionate influence on political outcomes. Consider, for example, the efforts of farmers to maintain price supports. The farm lobby represents a relatively small group of people who are intensely interested in the fate of this program. If price supports are repealed, each of these individuals will be significantly harmed. So farm lobbyists make it clear that their primary interest in selecting a senator or representative is his or her position on this one issue. And they reward those who support their position with significant financial contributions. The reward for opposing price supports is likely to be nonexistent! Because the cost of price supports to any one consumer is relatively small, few voters are likely to choose their next senator or representative on the basis of how they voted on this issue. As a consequence, public choice theory predicts that members of Congress will vote in favor of price supports even though this program leads to the overproduction of agricultural products (is inefficient) and benefits people with incomes greater than the national average (is inequitable).

It is not just special-interest groups that can distort the spending decisions of government. The voting mechanism itself may lead to inefficient outcomes. One problem is that there is no way for voters to reflect the strength of their preferences. They can vote in favor of an issue, or against it, but they cannot indicate the strength of their favor or opposition. Consider, for example, a vote regarding the building of a flood-control dam. Even if the benefits of the dam vastly outweigh its costs, majority voting may prevent its construction. While voters living near the dam stand to benefit in a major way from its construction, most voters will see little reason to help pay for it. As a consequence, the project is likely to be rejected even though it represents an efficient use of society's resources.

Another problem stems from the logrolling efforts that are commonplace in Congress. **Logrolling** is trading votes to gain support for a proposal; politicians agree to vote for a project they oppose in order to gain votes for a project they support. For example, a senator from Missouri might agree to vote in favor of a bill that would expand the federal highway system in Florida in return for a Florida senator's favorable vote on a bill appropriating more money for Missouri's military bases. In many instances, logrolling can lead to efficient outcomes. But in others, it can lead to the approval of projects or programs whose costs exceed their benefits.

In addition to the problems posed by special-interest groups and the voting process itself, public choice economists point to the problems posed by government bureaucrats. Many of the spending decisions that are made by our local, state, and federal governments are not made by elected officials, they are made by the bureaucrats who run our various government agencies. Public choice economists argue that these individuals, like the rest of us, pursue their own self-interest. In other words, they seek to increase their salaries, their longevity, and their influence. Rather than attempting to run lean, efficient agencies, their goal is to expand their power and resist all efforts to restrict their agencies' growth or influence. As a consequence, these agencies may become larger than justified and require tax support in excess of the benefits they provide to citizens.

As you can see, public choice economists are not optimistic that government will make decisions that improve either efficiency or equity. Instead, they see politicians and bureaucrats making decisions intended largely to benefit themselves. While public choice economists make important observations, they might overstate their case. In recent years, significant strides have been made in reducing trade barriers and some agricultural subsidies, despite howls of protest from those adversely affected. These reforms indicate that government action can lead to a more efficient use of society's scarce resources. In addition, while majority voting can lead to inefficient results, it can also lead to outcomes that are closer to the efficient one than those produced by private markets. This is likely to be true, for example, in the case of public goods, where private markets may fail to provide the product at all.

The real message of public choice economics is not that government action always leads to inefficiency or inequity. Rather, it is that we need to be just as alert to the possibility of government failure as we are to the possibility of market failure.

Summary

Market failure occurs when a market economy produces too much or too little of certain products and thus fails to make the most efficient use of society's limited resources.

There are three major sources of market failure: market power, externalities, and public goods. The exercise of market power can lead to a misuse of society's resources because firms with market power tend to restrict output in order to force up prices. As a consequence, too few of society's resources will be allocated to the production of the goods and services provided by firms with market power.

Another source of market failure is the market's inability to reflect all costs and benefits. In some instances the act of producing or consuming a product creates *externalities*—costs or benefits not borne by either buyers or sellers but that spill over onto third parties. When this happens, the market has no way of taking those costs and benefits into account and adjusting production and consumption decisions accordingly. As a consequence, the market fails to give us optimal results; our resources are not used as well as they could be. We produce too much of some things because we do not consider all costs; we produce too little of other things because we do not consider all benefits. To correct these problems, government must pursue policies that force firms to pay the full social cost of the products they create and encourage the production and consumption of products with external benefits.

Markets may also fail to produce optimal results simply because some products are not well suited for sale by private firms. Public goods fall into that category. *Public goods* are products that convey their benefits equally to all members of society, whether or not all members have paid for those products. National defense is probably the best example. It is virtually impossible to sell national defense through markets, because there is no way to exclude nonpayers from receiving the same benefits as payers. Since there is no way for a private businessperson to earn a profit by selling such products, private markets cannot be relied on to produce these goods or services, no matter how important they are to the well-being of the society.

Even if a market system uses its resources efficiently, if income is distributed unfairly, we may judge that to be a shortcoming of the system. There is significant income inequality in the U.S. economy. In 1993, the lowest quintile of the income distribution received less than 4 percent of total money income, while the highest quintile received approximately 48 percent of total income. In addition, almost 15 percent of the population was living in poverty. A variety of programs have been adopted to attack the problem of poverty and moderate the income distribution. These include training programs for the unemployed and programs to provide direct financial assistance to the poor: Aid to Families with Dependent Children and Social Security, for example.

Although market economies may fail to use resources efficiently and distribute income fairly, public choice economists are not convinced that government can be counted on to improve either of these outcomes. *Public choice* is the study of how government makes economic decisions. According to public choice economists, government is a collection of individuals each pursuing his or her own self-interest. Because politicians and government bureaucrats make decisions largely to benefit themselves, we cannot count on them to pursue policies that further the public interest. In fact, *government failure*—the enactment of government policies that produce inefficient and/or inequitable results—is also a possible consequence.

Glossary

External benefits. Benefits paid for by one party or group that spill over to other parties or groups; also referred to as spillover benefits.

External costs. Costs created by one party or group and imposed on other (unconsenting) parties or groups; also referred to as spillover costs.

Externalities. Costs or benefits that are not borne by either buyers or sellers but that spill over onto third parties.

Government failure. The enactment of government policies that produce inefficient and/or inequitable results.

Internal costs. The costs borne by the firm that produces the good or service; also referred to as private costs.

Logrolling. The trading of votes to gain support for a proposal.

Market failure. Situations in which a market economy produces too much or too little of certain products and thus does not make the most efficient use of society's limited resources.

Private benefits. The benefits accruing to the person or persons purchasing a good or service; also referred to as internal benefits.

Private costs. The costs borne by the firm that produces the good or service; also referred to as internal costs.

Private goods that yield significant external benefits. Products that convey most of their benefits to the person making the purchase but also create substantial external benefits for other individuals or groups.

Property rights. The legal rights to use goods, services, or resources.

Public choice. The study of how government makes economic decisions.

Public goods. Products that convey their benefits equally to paying and non-paying members of society.

Pure private goods. Products that convey their benefits only to the purchaser.

Social benefits. The total benefits received by all the members of society; the sum of private benefits and external benefits.

Social cost. The total cost to a society of the production and/or consumption of a product; the sum of private, or internal, costs and external costs.

Study Questions

Fill in the Blanks

1. _____ are instances in which a market economy fails to make the most efficient use of society's limited resources.

2. The term _____ is used to describe costs borne or benefits received by parties other than those involved in the transaction.

3. Social costs are the sum of _____ and _____ .

4. One way to encourage the consumption of products with external benefits would be to _____ their purchase.

5. _____ are products that convey their benefits only to the buyer.

6. National defense is an example of a _____ .

7. Another word for "private" costs and benefits is _____ costs and benefits.

8. _____ are benefits that are paid for by one party but spill over to other parties.

9. The major reason our rivers and streams have been used as disposal sites is that this approach minimized the firm's _____ costs of production.

10. If an action creates no external costs or benefits, private costs will equal _____ costs.

11. _____ is the study of how government makes economic decisions.

12. When politicians trade votes to gain support for a proposal, they are engaging in _____ .

Multiple Choice

1. A market economy will tend to underproduce products that create
   a) social benefits.
   b) social costs.
   c) external benefits.
   d) external costs.

2. Which of the following is an example of a pure private good?
   a) A desk
   b) Education
   c) A fence between neighbors
   d) A park

3. Which of the following is most likely to produce external costs?
   a) Liquor
   b) A steak
   c) A flower garden
   d) A storm warning system

4. If the firms in an industry have been creating pollution and are forced to find a method of waste disposal that does not damage the environment, the result will probably be
   a) a lower price for the product offered by the firms.
   b) a higher product price and a higher equilibrium quantity.
   c) a lower product price and a higher equilibrium quantity.
   d) a higher product price and a lower equilibrium quantity.

5. Which of the following is the best example of a pure public good?
   a) A cigarette
   b) A bus
   c) A lighthouse
   d) An automobile

6. If a product creates external benefits, the demand curve that reflects all social benefits
   a) will be to the left of the demand curve that reflects only private benefits
   b) will be to the right of the demand curve that reflects only private benefits.

    c) will not be downward sloping.

    d) will be the same as the demand curve that reflects private benefits.

7. Public goods can lead to market failure because they

    a) create external costs.

    b) create social costs.

    c) cannot be sold easily in markets.

    d) cannot be paid for through taxes.

8. Banning all pollution may not be the optimal strategy, because

    a) the costs may exceed the benefits.

    b) the benefits of this approach are probably limited.

    c) the harm caused by pollution is generally overestimated.

    d) the benefits of a clean environment are generally overestimated.

9. Which of the following is *not* true?

    a) If social costs exceed private costs, external costs are present.

    b) If a product creates external costs, society should devote fewer resources to its production.

    c) If a society fails to consider externalities, it will not use its resources optimally.

    d) Consumers tend to purchase too much of products that create external benefits.

10. Which of the following best describes the free-rider problem?

    a) Your brother always rides home with you but never pays for the gas.

    b) Some private goods create external benefits for those who have not paid.

    c) Some people think that the environment is a free resource and therefore abuse it.

    d) Some goods cannot be sold in markets because the benefits they confer are available to all—whether they have paid or not.

11. Public choice economists argue that

    a) majority voting always leads to efficient outcomes.

    b) government bureaucrats tend to act in the public interest.

    c) politicians generally find it in their self-interest to oppose special-interest groups.

    d) self-interest is the motivation of both business executives and politicians.

12. Suppose that a proposed government project would cost $50,000 and convey benefits worth $100 to 1,000 people, and benefits worth $5 to the remaining 9,000 people in the community. If each person would be assessed a $50 tax to pay for this project, the theory of public choice predicts that it would be

    a) rejected because the project's total costs exceed its total benefits.

    b) approved because the project's total benefits exceed its total costs.

    c) rejected because voters are unable to reflect the strength of their preferences.

    d) approved because voters recognize that it is an efficient use of society's limited resources.

Problems and Questions for Discussion

1. Why should you and I be concerned about whether our society's resources are used optimally?

2. What is market failure, and what are the sources of this problem?

3. How can fines and subsidies be used to correct market failure?

4. Most businesses are concerned about our environment, but they may be reluctant to stop polluting unless all other firms in their industry are also forced to stop. Why?

5. If we force firms to stop polluting, the result will probably be higher product prices. Is that good or bad? Why?

6. Why is it important (from society's viewpoint) to encourage the production and consumption of products that yield external benefits?

7. If we're really concerned about external costs, there would be some logic in fining any spectator who insisted on standing up to cheer at football games. What would be the logic? What practical considerations make this an impractical solution?

8. Why is a tornado warning system a public good? What about a flood-control dam? Why does it fall into that category?

9. Milton Friedman suggests that although it makes sense to subsidize a general education in the liberal arts, it makes much less sense to subsidize purely vocational training. What do you suppose is the logic behind that distinction?

10. Explain how the free-rider problem leads to market failure.

11. How can the absence of clearly defined property rights lead to the abuse or misuse of a resource?

12. According to Ronald Coase, the assignment of property rights can help to resolve externality problems if the number of parties involved is relatively small. Why is this solution unworkable when a large number of people are involved, as when a firm's pollution affects thousands of people?

Answer Key

Fill in the Blanks

1. Market failures
2. externalities or spillovers
3. private costs, external costs
4. subsidize
5. Private goods
6. public good
7. internal
8. External benefits
9. private or internal
10. social
11. public choice
12. logrolling

Multiple Choice

1. c	4. d	7. c	9. d	11. d
2. a	5. c	8. a	10. d	12. c
3. a	6. b			

PART 3

Macroeconomics:
The Economy as a Whole

MACROECONOMICS is the study of the economy as a whole and the factors that influence the economy's overall performance. (If you have a hard time remembering the difference between microeconomics and macroeconomics, just remember that *micro* means small—microcomputer, microfilm, microsurgery—whereas *macro* means large.) Macroeconomics addresses a number of important questions: What determines the level of total output and total employment in the economy? What causes unemployment? What causes inflation? What can be done to eliminate these problems or at least to reduce their severity? These and many other considerations relating to the economy's overall performance are the domain of macroeconomics.

In Chapter 9 we begin our study of macroeconomics by examining some indicators, or measures, that economists watch in order to determine how well the economy is performing. Chapter 10 introduces aggregate demand and aggregate supply and considers how these twin forces interact to determine the levels of prices, output, and employment in the economy. The chapter then uses the aggregate demand and supply framework to examine the views of the classical economists—the earliest macroeconomists—and why their views were challenged in the Keynesian revolution. Chapter 11 takes a closer look at the Keynesian model of income and output determination. It investigates the determinants of consumption and investment spending and the way in which consumption, investment, and saving interact to determine the equilibrium level of output. The possibility of unemployment or inflation is also explored. Chapter 12 takes a detailed look at *fiscal policy*—government spending and taxation policy designed to combat unemployment or inflation. This chapter also considers some of the problems that may be encountered in applying these policies.

Chapter 13 examines how depository institutions—commercial banks, savings and loan associations, mutual savings banks and credit unions—"create" money and how the Federal Reserve attempts to control the money supply. Chapter 14 takes a detailed look at the concepts of aggregate demand and supply that were briefly introduced in Chapter 10 and uses the aggregate demand and supply framework to examine the possibility that the economy is self-correcting—that it tends to automatically eliminate unemployment. Chapter 15 concludes the macroeconomics section of the textbook by exploring the debate between "activists," who believe that government should attempt to manage the economy's overall performance, and "nonactivists," who believe that such attempts are ill-advised.

Measuring Aggregate Performance

Of the economic problems we've talked about so far, which one do you think Americans are most concerned about: The market power of large corporations and labor unions? The distortions caused by agricultural price supports or minimum-wage laws? Environmental pollution?

According to national surveys, none of these problems are foremost in the minds of Americans. Throughout most of the last decade, the major concerns voiced by Americans have been two macroeconomic problems: unemployment and inflation. In the next few chapters we'll be examining the factors that influence the economy's *aggregate*, or overall, performance and how problems such as unemployment and inflation arise. We will also consider policies to combat unemployment and inflation and the difficulties that may be encountered in applying these policies.

This chapter sets the stage for that discussion by examining some **economic indicators**—signals, or measures, that tell us how well the economy is performing. After all, policymakers can't take actions that lead to better performance unless they know when problems exist. Economic indicators provide that information. The economic indicators we will discuss in this chapter include the unemployment rate, the Consumer Price Index, and the gross domestic product (GDP)—the indicator that many economists believe is the most important single measure of the economy's performance.

Measuring Unemployment

One dimension of our economy's performance is its ability to provide jobs for those who desire to work. For most of us, that's an extremely important aspect of the economy's performance, because we value work not only as a source of income but also to maintain our sense of personal worth. The most highly publicized indicator of performance in this area is the unemployment rate. The **unemployment rate** traditionally reported is the percentage of the civilian labor force that is unemployed. The **civilian labor force** is made up of all persons over the age of sixteen who are not in the armed forces and who are either employed or actively seeking employment. The Bureau of Labor Statistics (BLS), the agency responsible for gathering and analyzing labor force and employment data, surveys some 60,000 households throughout the United States monthly to determine the employment status of the residents. It uses the statistics gathered from this sample (a sample scientifically designed to be representative of the entire U.S. population) to estimate the total size of the labor force and the rate of unemployment.

Counting the Unemployed

How does the Bureau of Labor Statistics decide whether a particular person should be classified as unemployed? First, it determines whether or not the person has a job. As far as the BLS is concerned, you are employed if you did *any* work for pay in the week of the survey. It doesn't matter how long you worked, provided that you worked for pay. You are also counted as employed if you worked fifteen hours or more (during the survey week) as an unpaid worker in a family-operated business.

Even if you didn't have a job during the survey week, you are not recognized as unemployed unless you were actively seeking employment. To be "actively seeking employment," you must have done something to try to find a job—filled out applications, responded to want ads, or at least registered at an employment agency. If you did any of those things and failed to find a job, you are officially unemployed. If you didn't look for work, you're considered as "not participating" in the civilian labor force, and consequently you won't be counted as unemployed.

The purpose of the BLS monthly survey is to estimate the size of the civilian labor force (the number employed plus those actively seeking employment) and the number of unemployed. Then the bureau computes the unemployment rate by dividing the total number of unemployed persons by the total number of people in the civilian labor force. In 1994, for example, there were 131 million people in the civilian labor force; 8.0 million were unemployed. These figures represent averages—the average number of people in the civilian labor force and the average number of people unemployed—for 1994. This means that the average **civilian unemployment rate** for 1994 was 6.1 percent.

$$\text{Unemployment rate} = \frac{\text{Total number of unemployed persons}}{\substack{\text{Total number of persons} \\ \text{in the civilian labor force}}}$$

$$\text{Unemployment rate (1994)} = \frac{\text{8.0 million unemployed persons}}{\substack{\text{131 million persons in} \\ \text{the civilian labor force}}}$$

$$= 6.1 \text{ percent.}$$

As you can see from Exhibit 9.1, our unemployment rate compares quite favorably with those of other industrialized nations. In 1994 the average unemployment rate in the seven nations surveyed was 8.5 percent, well above our 6.1 percent. When we look at the figures for the last decade, our perfor-

---

EXHIBIT 9.1

Unemployment Rates in Major Industrialized Countries

	UNITED STATES	CANADA	JAPAN	FRANCE	GERMANY	ITALY	UNITED KINGDOM	7-NATION AVERAGE
Unemployment rate 1994	6.1%	10.3%	2.9%	12.4%	6.5%	11.6%	9.5%	8.5%
Average unemployment rate 1985–1994	6.4%	9.5%	2.5%	10.5%	5.8%	8.0%	9.4%	7.4%

Source: *Economic Report of the President*, 1995.

mance still looks relatively good; the seven-nation average was 7.4 percent, whereas our average unemployment rate was 6.5 percent. But is 6.5 percent the best that the U.S. economy can hope to achieve, or can we do better still? Let's turn to that question.

Types of Unemployment

In general a high unemployment rate is interpreted as a sign of a weak economy, whereas a low rate is seen as a sign of strength. But in order to recognize a low rate of unemployment when we see it, we have to know what we are aiming for, what is possible or realistic. That in turn requires knowledge of the three basic types of unemployment—frictional, cyclical, and structural—and the extent to which these types of unemployment are unavoidable.

Frictional Unemployment. Even when plenty of jobs are available, there are always some people out of work because they are changing jobs or searching for their first job. Economists call this **frictional unemployment,** to describe the fact that labor-market adjustments involve time lags, or "friction." A certain amount of frictional unemployment is unavoidable and probably even desirable. It is a sign that employers are looking for the most-qualified workers and that workers are searching for the best jobs. Neither party is willing to settle for the first thing that comes along. That's good for the economy because it means that the right people are more likely to be matched with the right jobs. But it takes time for workers and employers to find each other, and meanwhile the job seekers are adding to the nation's unemployment rate.

Cyclical Unemployment. **Cyclical unemployment** is joblessness caused by a reduction in the economy's total demand for goods and services. When such a reduction occurs, perhaps because consumers have decided to save more and spend less, businesses that are not able to sell as much output as before usually must cut back on production. This means that some of their workers will become unemployed. We call this unemployment cyclical because we recognize that the economy goes through cycles of economic activity. For a while the economy expands and unemployment declines; then economic activity slows and unemployment rises. You can see this pattern clearly in Exh. 9.2.

When people are cyclically unemployed, the economy is losing the output these workers could have produced, and of course the workers are losing the income they could have earned. Many economists argue that it is possible to reduce the amount of cyclical unemployment by using government policies to stimulate the total demand for goods and services.

EXHIBIT 9.2

The Unemployment Rate: 1929–1994

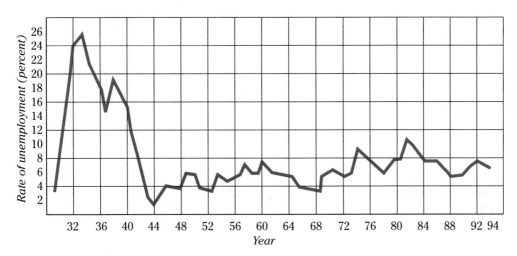

This exhibit shows that the unemployment rate varies significantly from year to year. But even though the unemployment rate is not a constant, there is a pattern to that variation, an up-and-down cycle that keeps repeating itself. For example, we can see that the unemployment rate dropped from a high of about 25 percent in 1933 to approximately 14 percent in 1937. Then the unemployment rate jumped back up to 19 percent in 1938 and started a steady decline that continued until 1944. The same sort of pattern is evident over other time periods, although the magnitude of the changes certainly is not as great.

The rate reported is the civilian unemployment rate. Sources for these statistics were *Historical Statistics of the United States* (Bureau of the Census) and *Economic Report of the President*, 1995.

Structural Unemployment. **Structural unemployment** is caused by changes in the makeup, or structure, of the economy that render certain skills obsolete or in less demand. The economy is always changing. New products are introduced and old ones are dropped; businesses continually develop new production methods. These kinds of changes can have a profound effect on the demand for labor. Skills that were very much in demand ten or twenty years ago may be virtually obsolete today. Computerized photocomposition machines have virtually eliminated the need for newspaper typesetters, for example, and robots have begun to replace semiskilled workers in automobile manufacturing plants. Further automation will signal a similar fate for workers in many other manufacturing industries.

Structurally unemployed workers may need to be retrained before they can find jobs.

The Bureau of Labor Statistics predicts that by the year 2000, the number of jobs in manufacturing will decrease to 18.2 million, from about 19 million in 1990. Moreover, the nature of manufacturing work will change so that many of today's manufacturing workers will find themselves unqualified for the jobs of the future—jobs that will require more education and the ability to work with programmable machines.[1]

The changing skill requirements for the workplace are not the only source of structural unemployment. Some people cannot hold a job in the modern economy because they never received much education or training in the first place. This is the case with many members of inner-city minorities, who often are educated in second-rate school systems that have a high dropout rate. It is also possible for people to be structurally unemployed even though they have marketable skills. For example, unemployed construction workers in the Midwest (where economic growth has slowed) may have skills that are very much in demand. But if the available construction jobs are in New England or the South Atlantic region of the United States, the Midwestern workers remain structurally unemployed.

All structurally unemployed workers have one thing in common: If they are to find jobs, they must make drastic changes. They will have to acquire new skills or move to a different part of the country. They may even find it necessary to do both. Since such changes cannot be made overnight, economists

---

[1] Doron P. Levin, "Smart Machines, Smart Workers," *New York Times,* October 17, 1988, p. D1.

see structural unemployment as a longer-term problem than frictional or cyclical unemployment. This is also the reason why many social scientists view structural unemployment as one of the most serious problems of our time.

Full Employment versus Zero Unemployment

Since a certain amount of frictional and structural unemployment is unavoidable, economists consider zero unemployment an unattainable goal. Although no one knows precisely how much unemployment is of the frictional and structural varieties, a common estimate is $5\frac{1}{2}$ to 6 percent. This is considered to be the **natural rate of unemployment**—the minimum level of unemployment that our economy can achieve in normal times. (Note that this is the rate that would exist in the absence of cyclical unemployment.) When the actual unemployment rate is equal to the natural rate, the economy has achieved **full employment.**

A Closer Look at Unemployment Rates

Recognizing that full employment doesn't mean zero unemployment is an important step in learning how to interpret unemployment statistics. The next step is learning to look beyond the overall unemployment rate to see how various groups in our society are being affected. Although we all talk about "the" unemployment rate, in reality the rate of unemployment varies substantially among different subcategories of the American labor force. Historically, blacks have been about twice as likely to be unemployed as whites, in part because they have lower levels of education and training. For the last decade, women have enjoyed slightly lower unemployment rates than men, due largely to the fact that a higher proportion of women are employed in the service sector—the fastest-growing segment of the economy. Teenagers, who are often unskilled and lacking in good work habits, have unemployment rates about $2\frac{1}{2}$ to 3 times the overall rate for their racial group.

Exhibit 9.3 shows the unemployment rates for 1994. Note that in 1994 the overall unemployment rate for all civilian workers—that is, "the" unemployment rate—was 6.1 percent. During the same time period, the overall rate for blacks (11.5 percent) was more than twice the rate for white workers (5.3 percent), and this relationship held for each of the subcategories: men, women, and teenagers. The rates for teens and women were also within the expected ranges: White and black women had slightly lower rates than their male counterparts, and teenagers had unemployment rates roughly 3 times the rate for their race.

As you can see, the overall unemployment rate conceals a great deal of variation across particular groups. Even when the overall rate is low, the un-

EXHIBIT 9.3

Unemployment Rates for 1994

WORKER CATEGORY	RATE	WORKER CATEGORY	RATE	WORKER CATEGORY	RATE
All civilian workers	6.1%	*White*	5.3%	*Black*	11.5%
Men (20 and over)	5.4	Men (20 and over)	4.8	Men (20 and over)	10.3
Women (20 and over)	5.4	Women (20 and over)	4.6	Women (20 and over)	9.8
Teenagers (16–19)	17.6	Teenagers (16–19)	15.1	Teenagers (16–19)	35.2

Source: *Economic Report of the President,* 1995.

employment rate among certain subcategories of our population may be unacceptably high. For that reason, those who rely on unemployment statistics for devising policies to combat unemployment or for helping the unemployed in other ways must be willing to look beyond the overall rate to gain a clearer picture of the nature and severity of the unemployment problem.

Unemployment Rates: A Word of Caution

Before we leave this section on unemployment statistics, a few words of caution are appropriate. Watching the unemployment rate can help you understand whether the economy is growing weaker or stronger. But changes in the unemployment rate from one month to the next may not be very meaningful and in fact can sometimes send misleading signals about the state of the economy.

To illustrate that point, suppose that the economy is in the midst of a deep *recession*—a period of reduced economic activity and relatively high unemployment—when the Bureau of Labor Statistics reports a small drop in the unemployment rate. Should that drop be taken as a sign that the economy is growing stronger? Not necessarily. When the economy has been in a recession for quite a while, some unemployed workers become discouraged in their search for jobs and stop looking. Since these "discouraged workers" are no longer actively seeking employment, they are no longer counted as unemployed. That makes the unemployment rate look better, but it's really not a sign that the economy has improved. In fact, it may be a sign that labor-market conditions have become even worse. (The article on page 276, "Urban Teen-Agers, Who Often Live Isolated from the World of Work, Shun the Job Market," looks at the discouraged-worker phenomenon as it affects teens in our country's major cities.)

Of course, we can be misled in the other direction just as easily. Suppose that the economy has begun to recover from a recession and that the unemployment rate is falling. Suddenly the monthly survey shows an increase. Does that mean that the economy is headed back toward recession? It may, but a more likely interpretation is that the economy's improved condition has attracted a lot of additional job seekers who have swelled the labor force and pushed up the unemployment rate. Here the unemployment rate has risen not because the economy is worse but because it is better: People are more confident about their prospects for finding jobs.

Because changes in the unemployment rate can send misleading signals about the strength of the economy, they should be interpreted with caution. But even when the unemployment rate seems to be sending clear signals (for instance, when it has risen for several consecutive months), we must be careful not to base our evaluation of the economy's health solely on this statistic. After all, the unemployment rate looks at only one dimension of the economy's performance—its ability to provide jobs for the growing labor force. Other dimensions are equally important. To obtain an accurate picture of our economy's performance, we must consider each of these dimensions by examining several different economic indicators.

Measuring Inflation

Another important dimension of our economy's performance is its success or failure in avoiding inflation. **Inflation** is defined as a rise in the general level of prices. (The existence of inflation does not necessarily mean that *all* prices are rising but rather that *more* prices are going up than are coming down.) Inflation means that our dollars won't buy as much as they would before. In general this means that it will take more money to pay the grocery bill, buy clothes, go out for an evening, or do almost anything else.

Unanticipated Inflation and Income Redistribution

Each of us tends to believe that we are being hurt by inflation, but that is not necessarily the case. We forget that at the same time that prices are rising, our money incomes are also likely to be rising, sometimes at a faster rate than the increase in prices. Instead of focusing solely on prices, then, we ought to be concerned about what economists call real income. **Real income** is the pur-

Urban Teen-Agers, Who Often Live Isolated from the World of Work, Shun the Job Market

NEW YORK

Alex Perez, a Puerto Rico-born 19-year-old on this city's Lower East Side, looks for a job—sometimes.

Much of the time lately, though, the high school dropout has been so discouraged at the prospects that he hasn't even bothered to try. And that makes Alex Perez, unskilled and unsure what to do with himself, one more part of a growing problem in big cities.

There are hundreds of thousands of teen-agers like Mr. Perez, "hanging out," as he says, on city streets and only desultorily looking for work. Nationally, about half of those age 16 to 19 are working or say they are looking for work. But in many of the country's major cities, the labor force includes far fewer teen-agers, reflecting the fact that growing numbers of teens, particularly minorities, not only don't have jobs but aren't looking.

Big City Problem

In Philadelphia, Chicago and Detroit, fewer than 40% of teen-agers are in the labor force. The situation in New York is even worse. In the first half of the year, only one in five teen-agers had work or were looking for it. Officials say the rate is even a few points lower for Hispanic youths like Alex and for black youths.

"It means many thousands of youngsters don't get the kind of understanding that comes from work experience," says Samuel Ehrenhalt, New York regional commissioner of the Bureau of Labor Statistics. "It affects their understanding of how education relates to your work life and makes it better."

"We haven't even begun to feel the real impact of this on the city," says Josephine Nieves, New York City's commissioner of employment. "We are in for dire things if we have ever more kids on the street who have no knowledge of the working world."

Sociologists and economists aren't completely sure what is causing the problem. Part of it appears to be a decline in demand for teen-age labor as laid-off white collar workers enter the job market and skill requirements grow.

In New York at least, part of it is caused by the fact that the types of industries predominant here tend to create fewer part-time jobs. Discrimination is another important factor. So are overly high salary expectations. Then there's the lure of working in the illegal but lucrative drug industry.

But perhaps the most significant factor that emerges from a number of days spent talking with teen-agers and social workers in New York is the sense of isolation many minority kids feel from the world of work.

Unfamiliar Territory

For instance, the Henry Street Settlement, a Lower East Side social services agency, is only a few minutes away by subway from bustling Wall Street or midtown Manhattan, yet many teen-agers in the area seem frightened by and unfamiliar with those nearby-but-foreign territories. It's an important factor, notes Mr. Ehrenhalt, because of "the simple fact that the places where most black and Hispanic youngsters live don't have that many jobs."

Most kids seem to make at least a perfunctory search for a job. But it is a huge, difficult leap to the working world for teen-agers from the disadvantaged and often troubled families that live in the housing projects.

"A lot of kids from around here don't know where Madison and 42nd Street is," says Carlos Gonzalez, a job counselor at Henry Street. "They've never been there. If I send someone on a job interview in midtown they'll often arrange for a friend to drive them rather than take the subway, which they don't realize is a lot faster."

Mr. Perez, the 19-year-old, is isolated from the working world in more ways than one. A sincere, soft-spoken young man, he lives with his disabled mother in public housing on nearby Delancey Street. His mother can't afford a phone, so he has to list his girlfriend's parents' number when he fills out job applications.

Finding Their Way

Basic job-finding tactics are in short supply. One day, Henry Street social worker Rafael Jaquez suggests Mr. Perez try to get a day construction job at a site in Brooklyn the next morning at 6:30. Mr. Perez is eager to try, but he doesn't know which subway stop would be closest. He says he will guess where it is, go an hour early and hope for the best. Mr. Jaquez has to suggest that Mr. Perez check a street map

that shows cross streets, rather than a subway map, to find out.

With so few good role models in the neighborhood, city agencies and social workers find themselves not just scaring up jobs and placing teens but also teaching elemental rules of the working world. "I have a thing about hats," says Nilsa Pietri, head of youth services at Henry Street. "I always have to tell the kids to take their hats off. Employers will write them off if they wear them."

Bill Tomlinson, another Henry Street counselor, leads a session for 20 teen-agers in New York's summer youth employment program. Many are from poor families and seem dumbfounded by his questions about how to act in a job interview. One kid wears a T-shirt that says, "2 Cool 4 School." The gregarious Mr. Tomlinson tells the

kids to shake hands firmly, make eye contact, then keep their hands in their laps.. . .

Peter Kleinbard, who runs a training and educational program for high school dropouts in Spanish Harlem, says one of his biggest problems is getting kids to show up for job interviews. He attributes the problem less to irresponsibility than to fear. "Minority youth live in such isolation from the culture of work," he says. "Many of the kids I see have never been in an office or a factory.". . .

—*Paul Duke, Jr.*

SOURCE: Paul Duke, Jr. "Urban Teen-Agers, Who Often Live Isolated from the World of Work, Shun the Job Market," August 14, 1991. Reprinted by permission of The Wall Street Journal, © 1991 Down Jones & Co., Inc. All Rights Reserved Worldwide.

Use Your Economic Reasoning

1. Based on the second paragraph of the article, would you classify Alex Perez as "unemployed"? Why or why not?

2. Nationally, about 50 percent of all teenagers are in the labor force. But in Philadelphia, Chicago, and Detroit the figure is less than 40 percent; in New York, only about 20 percent. Explain this discrepancy. Why are fewer teenagers working or seeking work in our major cities?

3. What problems do you foresee for cities if the trend described continues?

chasing power of your income—the amount of goods and services it will buy. Economists argue that unanticipated inflation is essentially an income redistribution problem: It takes real income away from some people and gives it to others. (As you will see later, when people anticipate inflation, they tend to prepare for it and thereby reduce its redistributive effects.)

Keeping Pace with Inflation. The people hurt by unanticipated inflation are ones whose money incomes (the number of *dollars* they earn) don't keep pace with rising prices. If prices rise by 10 percent but your money income increases by only 5 percent, your real income will have fallen. The amount of goods and services that you can buy with your income will be 5 percent less than before.

Whether your money keeps pace with inflation depends on a variety of factors. The most important is how flexible your income is, that is, how easily it can be adjusted. Professional people—doctors, lawyers, dentists, and so on—often can adjust the prices they charge their customers and thereby stay abreast (or ahead) of inflation. People who own their own businesses—their own hardware store or motel or janitorial service—may be able to adjust their prices similarly. Of course, whether professional people and businesses can successfully increase prices and stay abreast of inflation depends on the degree of the market power they possess. If a seller faces very little competition and therefore has significant market power, it may be able to increase its prices to offset inflation. If it operates in a highly competitive environment, it may not be able to do so.

Workers who are represented by strong unions also may do reasonably well during periods of inflation. Often these unions are able to negotiate cost-of-living adjustment (COLA) clauses, which provide for automatic wage and salary adjustments to compensate for inflation. Other workers may have the forces of demand and supply operating to their advantage. When the demand for workers with a particular skill is strong relative to their supply, those workers often are able to obtain wage or salary increases that more than offset the impact of inflation. Unskilled workers and others in oversupplied fields—those in which there are several prospective employees for each job opening—usually find it more difficult to gain wage increases that match the rate of inflation.

Savers and People on Fixed Incomes. Hardest hit by inflation are people on fixed incomes, whose incomes are by definition inflexible. The classic example is a retired person living on a fixed pension or perhaps on his or her accumulated savings. (Of course, many retired persons are not dependent on fixed pensions. For example, Social Security payments are automatically adjusted for increases in the cost of living.)

Savers can also be hurt by inflation. Whether you are relying on your savings to provide retirement income, to make a down payment on a home some day, or to buy a car next summer, inflation can eat away at the value of your savings account and make your saving objective more difficult to achieve. For example, if your savings account is paying 6 percent interest and the inflation rate is 10 percent, the purchasing power of your savings is declining by 4 percent a year. After you pay taxes on the interest, you're even further behind.

Creditors versus Debtors. Unanticipated inflation can also hurt banks and other creditors, since borrowers will be able to repay their loans with dollars that are worth less than those that were borrowed. As the largest debtor of all, the federal government is probably the biggest gainer from such inflation. Other gainers include families with home mortgages and businesses that borrowed money to purchase factories or equipment.

When Inflation Is Anticipated

The redistributive effects of inflation occur because inflation is unforeseen or unanticipated. To the extent that inflation is anticipated, the redistributive effects will tend to be reduced, because individuals and businesses will take actions to protect themselves from inflation.

COLA clauses are one way that we attempt to insulate ourselves from inflation, but there are others. For example, banks try to protect themselves from anticipated inflation by working the inflation rate into the interest rates they set for loans. If a bank wants to earn 5 percent interest on a loan and expects the inflation rate to be 4 percent, the bank will charge 9 percent interest to get the desired return. If the inflation rate turns out to be 4 percent, neither the bank nor the customer will be harmed by inflation. Of course, the bank's inflation forecast won't always be correct. Forecasting inflation has proved very difficult, so bankers and others will make mistakes. As a consequence, inflation is likely to benefit some and hurt others.

Consequences of inflation extend beyond its effect on the income distribution. When inflation is anticipated, individuals and businesses waste resources in their attempts to protect themselves from its impact. Labor time and energy are expended shopping around and shifting money from one financial institution to another in pursuit of the highest interest rate. Restaurant menus and business price lists must be continually revised, and sales personnel must be kept informed of the most recent price information. In short, efforts to stay ahead of inflation use up resources that could be used to produce other things.

In addition to wasting resources, inflation (whether anticipated or unanticipated) can lead to inefficiency through its tendency to distort the information provided by the price system. To illustrate, suppose that the price of portable computers increases. Does the higher price indicate greater demand for the product, or does it merely reflect an increase in the overall price level? Because computer manufacturers are uncertain, they may be reluctant to invest in new production capacity. Thus inflation may slow investment spending and retard the economy's rate of economic growth.

In summary, both anticipated and unanticipated inflation impose costs on society. Unanticipated inflation causes income redistribution; anticipated inflation causes scarce resources to be wasted and used inefficiently.

Calculating a Price Index

Bankers, union leaders, business executives, and most other people in our society are keenly interested in changes in the general level of prices because they want to try to compensate for those changes; they'd like to build them into the prices they charge their customers and the wages they negotiate from their employers. Government policymakers also want to know what is happening to the price level in order to know when inflation-fighting policies may be necessary.

Economists attempt to measure inflation by using a **price index.** A price index is really nothing more than a ratio of two prices: the price of an item in a base period that serves as a reference point, divided into the price of that item in a period we wish to compare to the base period. For example, if the price of steak was $3.75 a pound in 1989 and $6.00 a pound in 1994, the price index for steak in 1994 would be 160 if 1989 were used as the base year:

$$\text{Price index} = \frac{\text{Price in any given period}}{\text{Price in the base period}}$$

$$= \frac{\$6.00}{\$3.75}$$

$$= 1.60 \text{ or } 160 \text{ percent or } 160.$$

(Note that although the price index is in fact a percentage, by convention it is written without the percent sign.)

The price index tells us how much the price of the item in question has increased or decreased since the base period. Since the price index in the base period is always 100, an index of 160 means that a price has increased by 60 percent since the base period.[2] By the same logic, an index of 75 would indicate that a price had decreased by 25 percent since the base period. Although

---

[2] The price index in the base period is always 100 because the numbers in the numerator and denominator of the price-index formula must be the same. For example, if we want to calculate the price index for steak in 1989 using 1989 as the base period, we would have $3.75/$3.75 = 1.00 or 100 percent.

price indexes can be used to determine how much prices have risen or fallen since the base period, their most common use is to determine the annual rate of inflation for a particular product or group of products. The **annual infla-tion rate** is the percent change in a price index from one year to the next. For example, if the price index for steak increased from 160 in 1994 to 170 in 1995, the rate of inflation for steak between 1994 and 1995 would be 6.3 percent (10/160 = 0.063). Exhibit 9.4 provides another example of how to compute the annual inflation rate.

Three basic price indexes are used in the United States: the Consumer Price Index, the Producer Price Index, and the Implicit Price Deflator. Each in-dex surveys a particular range of goods and services in order to determine the rate of inflation among those items. Each computes an overall index showing the average rate of price change for its assortment (or "basket") of commodi-ties and presents individual price indexes for each major class of items in the survey. This makes it possible to determine which products are most responsi-ble for any change in the overall index.

The Consumer Price Index

The best-known index is the Consumer Price Index (CPI). The CPI looks at the prices of some 400 goods and services that have been chosen to represent the kinds of products typically purchased by urban consumers. The CPI measures the purchasing power of consumers' dollars by comparing the current cost of this so-called basket of goods and services with the cost of the same basket at an earlier date.

EXHIBIT 9.4

Computing the Annual Rate of Inflation for Medical Care

The price index for medical care was 201.4 in 1993 and 211.0 in 1994, using 1984 as the base year. Thus the price of medical care increased by 101.4 percent between 1984 and 1993. But what was the rate of inflation in medical care between 1993 and 1994?

$$\text{Annual rate of inflation} = \frac{\text{Change in the price index from one year to the next}}{\text{Price index in the initial year}}$$

$$= \frac{211.0 - 201.4}{201.4}$$

$$= \frac{9.6}{201.4}$$

$$= 0.048 \text{ or } 4.8 \text{ percent.}$$

Exhibit 9.5 shows the kinds of items that are included in the Consumer Price Index survey. You can see how the rate of inflation differs from one class of items to another. The top line—the all-items index—is the CPI usually referred to by economists and the media. It tells us the average rate of price increase for all the items in the market basket. According to the exhibit, the all-items index stood at 148.2 in 1994. Because the most recent CPI uses the average level of prices between 1982 and 1984 as the base, prices increased approximately 48 percent between the period 1982–1984 and 1994. More precisely, in 1994 it cost $148.20 to purchase a basket of goods and services that sold for $100 in 1982–1984. As you can see, some items increased even more than that. For example, medical care rose to an index of 211.0; the cost of medical care increased more than 100 percent (more than doubled) between 1982–1984 and 1994.

Because consumers spend greater percentages of their incomes on certain index items—more, say, on food and beverages than on entertainment—merely averaging all the indexes at face value to arrive at the all-items index would be misleading. Therefore the all-items index is computed as a *weighted average* of the individual indexes. That is, the things for which consumers spend more of their incomes are counted more heavily in determining the all-items index. For example, if consumers spend twice as much on food and beverages as they do on entertainment, food and beverage prices will be twice as important in computing the all-items index.

By comparing the 1993 and 1994 consumer price indexes, we can compute the annual rate of inflation for consumer goods. Recall that the annual inflation rate is the percent change in a price index from one year to the next. The

---

EXHIBIT 9.5

Consumer Price Indexes, 1994 (1982–1984=100)

ALL ITEMS	148.2		
Food and beverages	144.9	Apparel and upkeep	133.4
Housing	144.8	Transportation	134.3
Shelter	160.5	Medical care	211.0
Fuel & other utilities	122.8	Entertainment	150.1
Furnishings & operating	121.0	Other goods and services	198.5

Source: *Economic Report of the President*, 1995.

CPI was 144.5 in 1993 and 148.2 in 1994, so the inflation rate between 1993 and 1994 was 2.6 percent (3.7/144.5 = 0.026).

How does our 3 percent inflation rate compare with the rates experienced by other major industrialized nations? As you can see from Exhibit 9.6, our 1994 inflation rate was higher than in most of the countries surveyed; only Germany and Italy experienced greater inflation. Over the past decade, however, the U.S. inflation rate is virtually identical to the average rate for the seven nations.

The rates of inflation reported in this table reflect inflation on consumer goods; the U.S. rates are based on the CPI, and the foreign rates are based on similar indexes. But in some instances we may be more interested in inflation at the wholesale level, or the rate of inflation in government services or capital goods (factories and equipment). For these purposes we need to turn to other price indexes.

The Producer Price Index and the Implicit Price Deflator

The Producer Price Index (PPI) and the Implicit Price Deflator (IPD) don't receive as much publicity as the Consumer Price Index, which is closely watched because it is used for cost-of-living adjustments in labor contracts and Social Security payments. Nevertheless, they have their particular uses and advantages. The PPI and the IPD are interpreted precisely the same as the CPI. That is, an index of 170 means that prices have risen by 70 percent since the base period.

EXHIBIT 9.6

Inflation Rates in Major Industrialized Countries

	UNITED STATES	CANADA	JAPAN	FRANCE	GERMANY	ITALY	UNITED KINGDOM	7-NATION AVERAGE
Inflation rate 1994	2.6%	0.2%	0.7%	1.6%	3.0%	3.9%	2.4%	2.1%
Average inflation rate 1985–1994	3.7%	3.7%	1.2%	2.0%	2.3%	6.0%	5.4%	3.5%

Source: *Economic Report of the President*, 1995.

The Producer Price Index is sometimes called the Wholesale Price Index.[3] It reflects the rate of inflation in the wholesale prices of finished products—both consumer goods and capital goods. Economists pay particular attention to the PPI because they think that it provides an indication of what will happen to consumer prices in the months to come. The logic here is fairly simple. Any increases in wholesale prices are eventually going to be passed on to consumers.

The broadest measure of inflation is the Implicit Price Deflator. This index examines the rate of increase in prices for all of the items included in the gross domestic product (GDP) and is also used to adjust GDP figures for inflation so that we can compare GDP from one year to the next without having that comparison distorted by changes in the price level. But before we say any more about the Implicit Price Deflator, we need to understand what gross domestic product is and how it functions as an economic indicator.

Measuring Total Output

The fundamental purpose of every economic system is to produce output in order to satisfy human wants. Therefore, many economists argue that gross domestic product (GDP) is the most important single indicator of our economy's performance. **Gross domestic product** is the total monetary value of all final goods and services produced within a nation in one year. In other words, it is a measure of the economy's annual production or output.[4]

Calculating GDP: A Sneak Preview

Because GDP is measured in monetary units rather than units of output, we can add apples and oranges, so to speak; we can sum the economy's output of eggs, stereos, houses, tractors, and other products to produce a meaningful statistic. The procedure is quite simple: The output of each product is valued at its selling price, and these values are added to arrive at a figure for GDP.

---

[3] Actually, there are three separate Producer Price Indexes: one for finished goods, one for semifinished goods, and one for raw materials. The index for finished goods is the one referred to as the Wholesale Price Index. It's also the one commonly referred to in the news.

[4] Until recently, the most commonly reported measure of the U.S. economy's aggregate output was gross national product (GNP). However, in 1991 the Department of Commerce began to use GDP as its basic measure, primarily for comparability with other nations.

Gross national product, by contrast, is the monetary value of all final goods and services produced by domestically owned factors of production in one year. U.S. GNP includes the value of final output produced by the resources owned by U.S. citizens, wherever those resources are located. (GDP includes the value of output produced in the United States by foreign-owned factories and foreign workers but excludes the value of output produced in other countries by U.S. workers and factories owned by U.S. companies.) For the United States, GDP and GNP are virtually identical; for other countries the difference can be quite large.

Although GDP is a measure of output, you should note that only the output of final goods and services is permitted to enter the GDP calculation. *Final goods* are those that are purchased for final use rather than for further processing or resale. For example, a new pair of jeans is a final good, but the thread, cloth, zippers, and snaps that are used in manufacturing the jeans are *intermediate goods.* Since the value of the jeans already includes the value of the thread and other intermediate goods, only the value of the jeans should count in GDP. If the value of intermediate goods were to be included in the calculation, the result would be double counting, which would overstate the value of the economy's annual production.

GDP and the Circular Flow

There are two ways to measure gross domestic product: the expenditures approach and the income approach. The *expenditures approach* measures how much money is spent in purchasing final goods and services; the *income ap-*

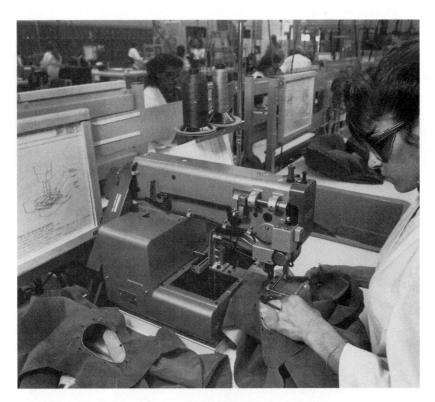

The cloth and thread used in manufacturing clothing are intermediate goods, whereas finished product is a final good.

proach measures the income that is created in producing these goods and services. Since one person's expenditure becomes another person's income, the two approaches must arrive at the same amount. In dollar terms, total output *must* equal total income.

The equality between total output and total income is reflected in the circular-flow diagram in Exh. 9.7, which is simplified to show the interaction of only the household and business sectors. The expenditures approach measures GDP by summing the various expenditures that make up the flow depicted at the bottom of the diagram. The income approach computes GDP by adding the various categories of income contained in the flow at the top of the diagram. The circular nature of the diagram indicates that all income spent on final goods and services must be received by someone as income; thus total output must equal total income.

EXHIBIT 9.7

Total Output = GDP = Total Income

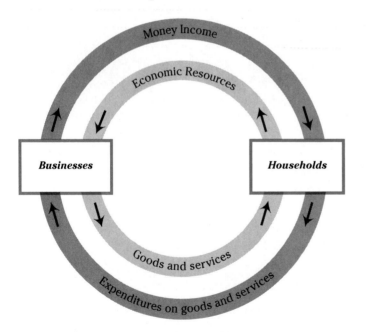

This simplified model of the economy (which ignores government and foreign trade) illustrates that there are two ways to calculate gross domestic product. The total expenditures made by households on final goods and services (the bottom flow) must equal the sum of the income received by the various economic resources (rent + wages + interest + profits)—the uppermost flow in the diagram. Both the total income received by the economic resources and the total household expenditures must equal GDP.

The Expenditures Approach

As you know, the U.S. economy is much more complex than the system depicted in Exh. 9.7. In our economy it's not only households that make expenditures for goods and services but also businesses, various levels of government, and foreign consumers. The categories of expenditures made by these groups are as follows:

1. *Personal consumption expenditures.* The total amount spent by consumers for goods and services includes both the purchase of consumer *durables,* such as automobiles, refrigerators, and stereos, and the purchase of *nondurables,* such as food, clothing, and entertainment.

2. *Gross private domestic investment.*[5] This category includes all types of expenditures on capital goods, including business expenditures for new factories and equipment and household expenditures for new homes and major home improvements. (For accounting purposes, new homes are classified as an investment.) This category also includes changes in firms' inventories.[6]

3. *Government purchases.* This category covers federal, state, and local governments' purchases of all kinds of goods and services—for example, purchases of government vehicles, office supplies, weapons, concrete for roads, and even the consulting services of private firms hired to advise various government departments. This category excludes transfer payments such as welfare and Social Security, which do not represent the purchase of newly produced goods and services.

4. *Net exports.* Some of the output of American businesses is sold in foreign countries, so it doesn't show up in our domestic sales. At the same time, some of the final goods and services sold in the United States were produced in foreign countries. To adjust for this situation, we subtract the value of imported goods from the value of our exports. The resulting fig-

---

[5] The term *domestic* means "limited to our own country"; for example, domestic investment takes place within the boundaries of the United States.
[6] Counting changes in inventories as part of investment also ensures that total expenditures will equal the value of total output. If a business produces something this year but doesn't sell it this year, that production goes into inventory and is not recorded in total expenditures. So if we just add up the various types of expenditures, we'll miss the portion of GDP that was not sold. To adjust for this problem, we add any additions to inventory that occur from one year to the next in order to make sure that all production is counted. (Decreases in inventories represent the sale of items produced in previous years. Since those items were included in GDP figures for previous years, they must be subtracted from this year's total expenditures if GDP is to reflect current production accurately.)

ure, called *net exports,* is then added to our domestic sales. The formula for net exports is

Net exports = total exports − total imports.

The net exports total will be positive when exports exceed imports and negative when imports exceed exports.

To calculate gross domestic product by the expenditure approach, we add these four categories of expenditures. This procedure is illustrated in Exh. 9.8, which shows the U.S. GDP for 1994 as measured by both the expenditures approach and the income approach.

The Income Approach

Calculating GDP by the income approach is somewhat more complicated than the circular-flow diagram would make it appear. In addition to the various forms of income that are created in the process of producing final goods and services (wages and salaries, rent, interest, and profits) are two *nonincome payments* (indirect business taxes and capital consumption allowances) that account for a portion of the money received by businesses. The categories of

EXHIBIT 9.8

Gross Domestic Product in 1994 (in billions)

EXPENDITURES APPROACH		INCOME APPROACH	
Personal consumption expenditures	$4,628.4	Employee compensation	$4,004.6
		Rental income	27.7
Gross private domestic investment	1,032.9	Net interest	409.7
		Corporate profits	542.7
Government purchases of goods and services	1,175.3	Proprietors' income	473.7
		Indirect business taxes	564.7
Net exports of goods and services	−98.3	Capital consumption allowances	715.3
Gross Domestic Product	$6,738.4	Gross Domestic Product	$6,738.4

Source: Developed from the March 1995 edition of the *Survey of Current Business,* published by the U.S. Department of Commerce.

income received by the economic resources and the types of nonincome payments are as follows:

1. *Compensation of employees.* In addition to wages and salaries, this income category includes such things as payroll taxes and employer contributions to health plans.

2. *Rental income.* This is the income earned by households from the rental of property, such as buildings and land.

3. *Net interest.* This category includes the interest earned by households on the money they lend to businesses to finance inventories, build plant additions, and purchase new machinery.

4. *Corporate profits.* The before-tax profit of corporations, this category has three components, representing the three things that corporations can do with their profits: (a) *corporate profits tax liability*—profits used to pay federal and state taxes; (b) *dividends*—profits paid out to stockholders; and (c) *retained earnings*—profits kept by businesses for reinvestment (also called *undistributed corporate profits*).

5. *Proprietors' income.* This category includes the income earned by unincorporated businesses, such as proprietorships, partnerships, and cooperatives.

6. *Indirect business taxes.* Indirect business taxes include sales taxes and excise taxes. The important thing about such taxes is that they are collected *by* businesses *for* government. Therefore a portion of the money received by businesses must be passed on directly to government; it is not available as a payment to the owners of economic resources. Such taxes are described as *nonincome payments.*

7. *Capital consumption allowances.* Also called *allowances for depreciation,* these are funds set aside for the eventual replacement of worn-out factories and equipment. Like indirect business taxes, they represent a nonincome payment.

To measure gross domestic product by the income approach, we add the five types of income and the two nonincome payments. As you can see in Exh. 9.8, the answer we get is the same as the one generated earlier by the expenditures approach.[7] Again, that result is necessary because every dollar spent on output must be received by someone as income or as a nonincome payment.

---

[7] In fact, the GDP calculated by the income approach never turns out to be exactly the same as the GDP calculated by the expenditures approach. The difference is what the Department of Commerce calls the *statistical discrepancy.* In Exh. 9.8 the entry for indirect business taxes has been adjusted to incorporate the statistical discrepancy.

Interpreting GDP Statistics

Now that we know what gross domestic product means and how it is measured, we need to note two facts before interpreting GDP statistics. An increase in GDP does not always mean that we're better off. Similarly, a decrease in GDP is not always a cause for concern and corrective action.

Real GDP versus Money GDP. From 1970 to 1980, gross domestic product in the United States increased from $993 billion to $2,632 billion (or $2.6 trillion). That's an increase of 165 percent in ten years. On the surface, that seems like a pretty good performance, particularly when you realize that our population increased less than 10 percent in that period. It looks as though the average American had a lot more goods and services at his or her disposal in 1980 than in 1970.

But numbers can be misleading. Because GDP is the physical output of a given year valued at the prices that prevailed in that year, it can increase from one year to another because of increased output, increased prices, or a combination of the two. (To underscore the fact that GDP can change simply due to a change in prices, economists often refer to GDP as *money GDP* or *nominal GDP*.) Therefore if we want to know how much *physical* output has increased, we have to calculate the **real gross domestic product**—that is, the GDP that has been adjusted to eliminate the impact of changes in the price level.

In order to compare real GDPs in our present example, we would want to value the output produced in 1980 at 1970 prices (or the output of 1970 at 1980 prices). Of course, our economy is much too large to permit us to multiply all the products produced in 1980 by 1970 prices. But we can do something that accomplishes essentially the same thing: We can use the Implicit Price Deflator, introduced earlier in this chapter. Suppose that we want to compare the 1970 and 1980 GDPs, using 1970 as the base year. The price index for 1970 would be 100—the starting point for the comparison. What happened to prices between 1970 and 1980? According to the Implicit Price Deflator, they went up about 90 percent, which means that the price index for 1980 should read 190. (Remember, we start with a base of 100, so an index of 190 means that prices have increased by 90 percent, not 190 percent.) Once we have that price index, we can convert the 1980 money GDP to real GDP. All we have to do is divide by the 1980 price index (expressed as a decimal). The result is real GDP for 1980:

$$\text{Real GDP for year } Y = \frac{\text{GDP in year } Y}{\text{Price index for year } Y}$$

$$\text{Real GDP for 1980} = \frac{\$2,632 \text{ billion}}{1.90}$$

$$= \$1,385 \text{ billion}.$$

As you can see, the increase in the real GDP was much smaller than the increase in money GDP. Although money GDP increased from $993 billion to $2,632 billion (an increase of 165 percent), real GDP increased from $993 billion to $1,385 billion (an increase of only 39 percent). In other words, much of the increase in GDP was due to inflation. Therefore, when we compare GDPs, we always want to compare real GDPs. This gives us a much better picture of what's actually happening to the economy's output and the nation's standard of living.

What GDP Does Not Measure. Even real GDP figures should be interpreted with caution. They don't measure all of our society's production, and they certainly don't provide a perfect measure of welfare or happiness. Some of the things that GDP does not consider are as follows:

1. *Excluded production.* GDP does not measure all production or output but rather only production that is intended to be sold. This means that GDP excludes the production of homemakers and do-it-yourselfers, as well as all barter transactions—transactions in which one person directly exchanges goods or services with another.

2. *Population.* GDP statistics tell us nothing about the size of the population that must share a given output. A GDP of $500 billion means one thing in an economy of 100 million people and something completely different in an economy of 500 million people. (It's like the difference between an income of $20,000 for a single person and an income of $20,000 for a family of five.) Economists generally attempt to adjust for this problem by talking about GDP per capita, or per person—that is, GDP divided by the population of the country.

3. *Leisure.* GDP does not measure increases in leisure, but such increases clearly have an impact on our well-being. Even if real gross domestic product didn't increase, if we could produce a constant real GDP with shorter and shorter workweeks, most of us would agree that our welfare had improved.

4. *Externalities.* We have a very sophisticated accounting system to keep track of all the goods and services we produce, but we have no established method of subtracting from GDP when the production process yields negative externalities—air and water pollution, for example. (See Chapter 8 for a review of this concept.)

In response to concerns about our environment, in May 1994 the Commerce Department began publishing supplementary, or "satellite," GDP accounts to record changes in our stocks of natural resources. These satellite accounts are still in the experimental stage and will not replace the regular

GDP reports. The addition of these accounts should help to address the concern about ignoring externalities in our GDP reporting. But the other limitations remain. For now, we'll have to be satisfied with imperfect GDP statistics and an understanding of their limitations.

Summary

To keep track of the economy's performance, people watch *economic indicators*—signals or measures that tell us how well the economy is performing. Three major economic indicators are the unemployment rate, price indexes (the Consumer Price Index, the Producer Price Index, and the Implicit Price Deflator), and the gross domestic product. Each of these indicators looks at a different dimension of the economy's performance.

The *civilian unemployment rate* is the percentage of the civilian labor force that is unemployed. (The civilian labor force is made up of all persons over the age of sixteen who are not in the armed forces and who are either employed or actively seeking employment.) Each month, the Bureau of Labor Statistics surveys some 60,000 households to determine the employment status of the residents. It then uses the results from this sample to estimate the size of the labor force and the rate of unemployment.

We attempt to measure inflation with something called a *price index*. A price index is a ratio of two prices: a price in some base period that serves as a reference point, divided into the price in whatever period we wish to compare to the base period. For example, if tennis shoes sold for $50 in 1990 and $80 in 1995, the price index for tennis shoes would be 160 if 1990 were used as the base year:

$$\text{Price index} = \frac{\text{Price in a given period}}{\text{Price in the base period}}$$

$$= \frac{\$80.00}{\$50.00}$$

$$= 1.60 \text{ or } 160 \text{ percent.}$$

Since the price index in the base period is always 100, an index of 160 means that price has increased by 60 percent since the base period. By the same logic, an index of 75 would indicate that price has decreased by 25 percent since the base period.

The other major indicator, the *gross domestic product* (or GDP), is the total monetary value of all final goods and services produced in one year. In other words, it is a measure of the economy's annual production or output. GDP can be estimated by the expenditures approach or by the income approach. The expenditures approach sums the categories of expenditures made for final goods and services. The income approach looks at the forms of income that are created when final goods are produced and adds to those income figures certain nonincome payments.

Since GDP is measured in monetary units (dollars), it is possible to add apples and oranges (that is, to sum the economy's output of eggs, stereos, houses, tractors, and so on) and arrive at a meaningful measure of the economy's total output. GDP figures must be interpreted with caution, however. When we compare the GDPs for two different years, we must be sure to correct for the impact of changing prices—to compare real GDPs, not money GDPs. We must also recognize that GDP is not a complete measure of our economy's production, because it excludes the work of homemakers and do-it-yourselfers as well as other nonmarket transactions. Nor is it a complete measure of welfare or happiness; it doesn't take into account the value of leisure, for example, or the negative externalities associated with the production of some goods and services.

Glossary

Annual inflation rate. The percent change in a price index from one year to the next.

Civilian labor force. All persons over the age of sixteen who are not in the armed forces and who are either employed or actively seeking employment.

Civilian unemployment rate. The percentage of the civilian labor force that is unemployed.

Cyclical unemployment. Joblessness caused by a reduction in the economy's total demand for goods and services.

Economic indicators. Signals or measures that tell us how well the economy is performing.

Frictional unemployment. People who are out of work because they are in the process of changing jobs or are searching for their first job.

Full employment. When the actual rate of unemployment is equal to the natural rate of unemployment.

Gross domestic product. The total monetary value of all final goods and services produced within a nation in one year.

Gross national product. The total monetary value of all final goods and services produced by domestically owned factors of production within a nation in one year.

Inflation. A rise in the general level of prices.

Macroeconomics. The study of the economy as a whole and the factors that influence the economy's overall performance.

Natural rate of unemployment. The minimum level of unemployment that an economy can achieve in normal times. The rate of unemployment that would exist in the absence of cyclical unemployment.

Price index. A measure of changes in the general level of prices. Three basic price indexes are used in the United States: the Consumer Price Index, the Producer Price Index, and the Implicit Price Deflator.

Real gross domestic product. Gross domestic product that has been adjusted to eliminate the impact of changes in the price level.

Real income. The purchasing power of your income; the amount of goods and services it will buy.

Structural unemployment. Unemployment caused by changes in the makeup, or structure, of the economy, whereby some skills become obsolete or in less demand.

Unemployment rate. See *Civilian unemployment rate.*

Study Questions

Fill in the Blanks

1. The study of the economy's overall performance and the factors that influence that performance is called _____.

2. Clauses that provide for automatic wage and salary adjustments to compensate for inflation are called _____ clauses.

3. _____ are signals or measures that tell us how well the economy is performing.

4. The price index that is used to adjust union wage contracts and Social Security payments for inflation is the _____.

5. Unemployment caused by a reduction in the economy's total demand for goods and services is called _____ unemployment.

6. A common estimate for the natural rate of unemployment is between _____ and _____ percent.

7. People who stop looking for jobs because they are convinced that none are available are called _____.

8. The two approaches to measuring GDP are the _____ approach and the _____ approach.

9. GDP that has been adjusted to eliminate the impact of changes in the price level is called _____ GDP.

10. The largest component of spending in GDP is _____ spending.

Multiple Choice

1. The civilian labor force is made up of
   a) all persons over the age of sixteen.
   b) all persons over the age of eighteen who are not in the armed forces.
   c) all persons over the age of sixteen who are not in the armed forces and who are either employed or actively seeking employment.
   d) all persons over the age of eighteen who are not in the armed forces and who are either employed or actively seeking employment.

2. If you are out of work because you are in the process of looking for a better job, economists would say that you are
   a) frictionally unemployed.
   b) cyclically unemployed.
   c) structurally unemployed.
   d) None of the above

   — *need to understand study examples*

3. People who are unemployed because they have no marketable skills are said to be
   a) frictionally unemployed.
   b) cyclically unemployed.
   c) structurally unemployed.
   d) None of the above

4. The unemployment rate for blacks is about
   a) three times the rate for whites.
   b) twice the rate for whites.
   c) 2 percent higher than the rate for whites.
   d) the same as the rate for whites.

5. Which of the following is *not* a true statement?
   a) Inflation tends to redistribute income.
   b) Inflation is particularly hard on people with fixed incomes.
   c) No one benefits from inflation.
   d) COLA clauses help protect workers from inflation. ✓

6. If the Consumer Price Index is 250, that means
   a) the average price of a product is $2.50.
   b) prices are 2 times as high as they were in the base year.
   c) prices have risen 150 percent since the base year.
   d) b and c are correct.

7. The price index used to adjust GDP to eliminate inflation is called the
   a) Consumer Price Index.
   b) Wholesale Price Index.
   c) Implicit Price Deflator.
   d) Producer Price Index.

8. Which of the following items would be counted in GDP?
   a) The work of a homemaker
   b) The sale of a used car
   c) A soda you buy at your local drive-in
   d) The firewood you cut for your home last winter

9. If the GDP in 1980 was $2,000 billion and the price index was 150, real GDP
   (1980 GDP in base-year prices) would be
   a) $1,333 billion.
   b) $3,000 billion.
   c) $1,500 billion.
   d) $2,150 billion.

10. If both output and prices are higher in year 2 than they were in year 1, which
    of the following is true?
    a) Real GDP declined from year 1 to year 2.
    b) GDP declined from year 1 to year 2.
    c) GDP increased from year 1 to year 2, but real GDP declined.
    d) Both GDP and real GDP increased from year 1 to year 2.

11. The Consumer Price Index was 130.7 in 1990 and 136.2 in 1991. Therefore the
    rate of inflation between 1990 and 1991 was
    a) 30.7 percent.
    b) 5.5 percent.
    c) 4.2 percent.
    d) about 136 percent.

12. In comparison with other major industrialized nations,
    a) the U.S. unemployment rate is higher than average.
    b) the U.S. inflation rate is lower than average.
    c) the U.S. inflation rate has been about average over the past decade.
    d) the U.S. unemployment rate has been about average over the past decade.

Problems and Questions for Discussion

1. What is the purpose of economic indicators? Can they be of any value to you?
   Explain.

2. A student could be counted as employed, unemployed, or "not participating" in the labor market. Explain.

3. An increase in the unemployment rate is not always a sign of growing weakness in the economy. Explain.

4. Some frictional and structural unemployment are probably signs of a healthy economy. Why is that true?

5. How does inflation redistribute income?

6. How can savers be hurt by inflation?

7. Why is it true that "the people who are most hurt by inflation are those who have the least bargaining power in the marketplace?"

8. Use the following information to compute the change in real GDP from 1950 to 1960.

YEAR	MONEY GDP	PRICE INDEX
1950	$500	100
1960	700	120

9. Use the following information to compute GDP by the expenditures approach. (Some figures are not required in solving the problem.) *Net Expo = Total Exports - Total Imports*

Personal consumption	$500 ✓	Exports	$ 10
Gross investment	200 ✓	Imports	12
Proprietors' income	450 *× Inc*	Government purchases	250 ✓
Corporate profits	50 *Inc*		

10. Why must total income always equal total output?

Answer Key

Fill in the Blanks

1. macroeconomics
2. cost-of-living adjustment (COLA)
3. Economic indicators
4. Consumer Price Index
5. cyclical
6. $5\frac{1}{2}$, 6
7. discouraged workers
8. expenditures, income
9. real
10. consumption

Multiple Choice

1. c
2. a
3. c
4. b
5. c
6. c
7. c
8. c
9. a
10. d
11. c
12. c

An Introduction to Aggregate Demand, Aggregate Supply, and the Debate on Policy Activism

1. Define aggregate demand and aggregate supply.
2. Illustrate how an economy's equilibrium GDP and price level are determined and how they can change.
3. Define potential GDP and identify some of the factors that determine an economy's potential GDP.
4. Use aggregate demand and supply curves to illustrate the possibility of unemployment or inflation.
5. Explain the difference between activist and nonactivist economists.
6. Discuss why the classical economists believed that a market economy would automatically tend toward full employment.
7. Explain why Keynes rejected the views of the classical economists.
8. Compare the views of Keynes and the classical economists with regard to the proper role of government.

Chapter 9 identified some important dimensions of the economy's overall performance and examined techniques used to measure performance in those areas. Now, in Chapter 10, we will begin to explore why the aggregate economy behaves as it does and how its performance changes. We will also examine the origin of an ongoing debate in macroeconomics—the debate about the appropriateness of government attempts to influence or manage the performance of our overall economy.

First, we introduce the concepts of aggregate demand and aggregate supply. Just as demand and supply are important tools in microeconomics, aggregate demand and aggregate supply are important in macroeconomics. We examine how aggregate demand and aggregate supply interact to determine the levels of output, employment, and prices, and how unemployment and inflation arise.

As you discovered in Chapter 9, unemployment and inflation impose costs on our society. Today many Americans assume that it is the federal government's responsibility to reduce those costs by combating unemployment and inflation when they occur. But the issue of government intervention to combat macroeconomic problems provokes sharp disagreement among economists. Economists known as "activists" support a significant role for government. "Nonactivists" are economists who believe that government intervention should be avoided.

We will use the framework of aggregate demand–aggregate supply to explore the origin of the activist-nonactivist controversy. This controversy originated more than 50 years ago with a debate between John Maynard Keynes and the then-dominant classical economists. Our examination of this debate sets the stage for the more detailed discussion of the Keynesian model contained in the next chapter. Examining the classical model offers an additional benefit: Some of the views of the classical economists have resurfaced in modern debates about economic theory and policy. The historical debate will provide an important backdrop for understanding the modern controversy about policy activism.

An Introduction to Aggregate Demand and Aggregate Supply

Chapter 3 showed how demand and supply interact to determine the prices and quantities of products in particular markets. In macroeconomics aggregate demand and aggregate supply determine the general price level and the level of domestic output, or real GDP. This section presents an overview of the aggregate demand–aggregate supply framework. Chapter 14 will consider these concepts in more detail.

Aggregate Demand

One of the forces that determines the economy's level of output, employment, and prices is aggregate demand. **Aggregate demand** is the total quantity of output demanded by all sectors in the economy together at various price levels in a given time period. As we saw in Chapter 9, four sectors purchase our economy's output: households, businesses, governments, and foreigners. Thus aggregate demand is the sum of consumption spending by households, investment spending by businesses, government spending for goods and services, and net purchases by foreigners (exports minus imports).

Because the quantity of output demanded by these sectors depends in part on the price level, the *AD* curve slopes downward and to the right, like the demand curve for a single product (see Exh. 10.1). But the demand curve and the aggregate demand curve are very different concepts. The demand curve shows the relationship between the price of a particular product and the quantity of that product demanded. The aggregate demand curve relates the overall price level in the economy (as measured by a price index, such as the CPI) to the total quantity of real output that consumers, businesses, governments, and foreigners want to buy.

The demand curve and the aggregate demand curve slope downward for different reasons. When we are considering the demand curve for a single product, we assume that the prices of all other products remain constant as we reduce the price of the product in question. Consumers, of course, respond by buying (substituting) more of this relatively cheaper product. This *substitution effect* cannot, however, explain the downward slope of the aggregate demand curve. The aggregate demand curve is constructed with the price level for the *entire economy* measured on the vertical axis. A reduction in the overall price level means that the average price of *all* goods and services has fallen.

EXHIBIT 10.1

Aggregate Demand and Supply Curves

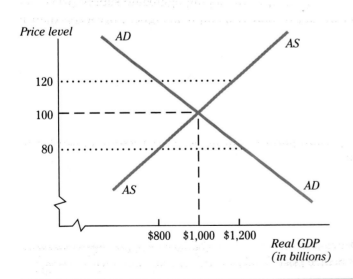

The aggregate demand curve shows the quantity of real output demanded at each price level. The aggregate supply curve shows the amount of real output supplied at each price level.

The intersection of the aggregate demand and supply curves determines the equilibrium level of real GDP and the equilibrium price level in the economy.

Since all prices are falling, the substitution effect cannot explain the increase in the quantity of real GDP demanded.

The downward slope of the aggregate demand curve is due in part to the **real balance effect** (additional reasons will be introduced in Chapter 14). According to the real balance effect, a reduction in the overall price level will increase the quantity of real output demanded because the lower overall price level will enable people to buy more with their cash and other financial assets. If the prices of goods and services fall, the real value or purchasing power of your financial assets—the cash in your wallet, the balance in your savings account, the wealth you have accumulated in government bonds—will increase. In other words, the same amount of money will stretch farther than before— will buy more than before. As a result, a reduction in the price level will cause people to purchase more goods and services. Of course, an increase in the price level will have the opposite effect; it will reduce spending on goods and services.

Aggregate Supply

The second force determining the economy's overall output and the general price level is aggregate supply. **Aggregate supply** is the total quantity of output supplied by all producers in the economy together at various price levels in a given time period.

Economists have suggested several possible shapes for the aggregate supply curve. For now, we'll assume that it is upward sloping, like the supply curve for a single product. An upward-sloping aggregate supply curve implies that producers will supply more real output at higher price levels than at lower price levels. Why might producers respond to higher prices by expanding output? One reason is that certain input costs—wage rates, for instance— tend to be fixed by contracts in the short run. As a consequence, when prices rise, producers can profit by expanding output and pocketing the difference between the higher product prices they receive and the fixed input prices they must pay. We'll have more to say about the shape of the AS curve later in the text. For now the important point is that higher prices induce producers to supply more output. The aggregate supply curve labeled AS in Exh. 10.1 depicts this relationship.

The Equilibrium Price Level and Real GDP

The interaction of aggregate demand and aggregate supply simultaneously determines the equilibrium price level and the equilibrium level of real GDP. This process is illustrated in Exh. 10.1, which shows the intersection of AS and

AD resulting in an equilibrium price level of 100 and an equilibrium real GDP of $1,000 billion. The level of employment in the economy is directly related to the level of output; the greater the economy's real GDP, the more workers that are needed (ceteris paribus) and the higher the level of employment. Thus we can say that the interaction of aggregate demand and aggregate supply determines the level of prices, output, and employment in the economy.

Whenever the economy is not in equilibrium, it will tend to move toward it. For instance, if the price level is too high for equilibrium (say, 120 in our example), there will be a surplus of goods and services, causing prices and output to fall. If the price level is too low to provide equilibrium (80, for example), there will be a shortage, and prices and output will tend to rise. The equilibrium combination of the price level and real GDP is the only combination that can be maintained; other combinations will be unsustainable.

Full Employment and Potential GDP

An important question in macroeconomics is whether the economy will achieve full employment. In other words, will the aggregate demand and supply curves intersect at a level of GDP sufficient to provide full employment? You will recall that full employment does not mean zero unemployment. As we saw in Chapter 9, some frictional and structural unemployment are unavoidable, perhaps even desirable. Today, an unemployment rate in the vicinity of $5\frac{1}{2}$ to 6 percent is regarded as the natural rate of unemployment because that is the best we can hope to attain in normal times. When the actual unemployment rate in the economy is equal to the natural rate, the economy has achieved full employment.

The level of output the economy produces when it operates at full employment, at the natural rate of unemployment, is called potential GDP. **Potential GDP** represents the economy's maximum sustainable level of production; output can expand beyond potential, but it cannot be sustained.

A variety of factors influence the size of the economy's potential GDP. One of the most important is the size of the labor force; the more people who are willing and able to work, the more output the economy can produce. Another important factor is the size of the economy's capital stock—its supply of factories, machinery, tools, and other aids to production. The more capital equipment the labor force has to work with, the more output it is capable of producing.

Of course, labor and machinery won't produce very much output unless businesses also have raw materials. That's the third determinant of the economy's potential GDP—the economy's stock of raw materials. The more timber, iron, coal, and other natural resources the economy possesses, the greater its ability to produce output.

The final determinant of the economy's production capability is technology—the state of knowledge about how to produce products. At any given time, the machinery that businesses use and the production techniques they employ reflect the current technology. The more advanced the technology, the more output businesses can obtain from a given amount of inputs.

In summary, the economy's potential GDP is determined by the size of the labor force, the capital stock, the stock of raw materials, and technology. Whenever the economy is operating at its potential GDP, it is also enjoying full employment.

The Possibility of Unemployment

Exhibit 10.2 represents a hypothetical economy that is initially in equilibrium at full employment. As you can see, AD_1 and AS_1 intersect at a real GDP of $1,000 billion (the economy's potential GDP) and a price level of 100. Given this starting point, how would the economy react to a reduction in aggregate demand? Suppose, for example, that business executives become pessimistic about the future and reduce their spending for buildings and equipment. Ceteris paribus, this will cause the aggregate demand curve to shift to the left, since there will now be less output than before demanded at any given price level. This is represented in Exh. 10.2 by the movement from AD_1 to AD_2. The

EXHIBIT 10.2

The Impact of a Reduction in Aggregate Demand

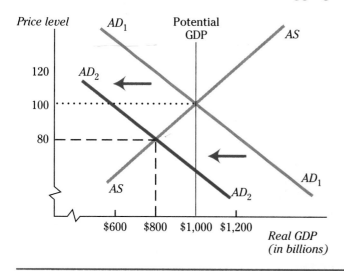

When aggregate demand declines from AD_1 to AD_2, the equilibrium real GDP and the overall price level also decline. This causes real GDP to fall below potential and results in unemployment.

reduction in aggregate demand causes the equilibrium price level to fall from 100 to 80 and reduces real GDP from $1,000 billion to $800 billion. Note that the economy's equilibrium real GDP is now below potential, so the society is no longer enjoying full employment; the reduction in aggregate demand has led to unemployment.

Unemployment can also result from a reduction in aggregate supply. Suppose, for instance, that the economy experienced a supply shock, such as the runup in oil prices caused by OPEC in the 1970s or the conflict with Iraq in 1990. The increase in oil prices would mean higher production costs for a wide range of products. As a consequence, producers would require higher prices to supply a given level of output. This is represented graphically by the movement from AS_1 to AS_2 in Exh. 10.3. Again the economy's real GDP is reduced below potential. However, in this instance the overall price level is increased, not reduced as it was in Exh. 10.2. Because supply shocks tend to raise prices while lowering the overall level of output and employment, they are particularly troublesome. We'll have much more to say about supply shocks in later chapters.

EXHIBIT 10.3

The Impact of a Reduction in Aggregate Supply

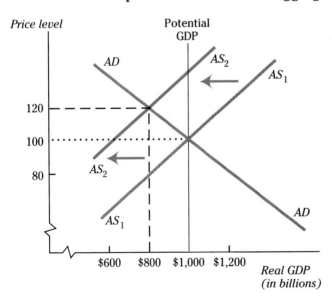

When aggregate supply declines from AS_1 to AS_2, the equilibrium real GDP falls from $1,000 billion to $800 billion, and the overall price level is increased from 100 to 120. The economy experiences unemployment with inflation.

The Possibility of Inflation

Our examples were intended to show that the interaction of the forces of aggregate demand and aggregate supply can result in an equilibrium level of output that is less than the economy's potential, or full-employment, GDP. It is also possible for the equilibrium level of GDP to *exceed* potential GDP. To see how, suppose that the federal government decides to spend several billion additional dollars rebuilding the nation's roads and bridges. This added government spending will shift the aggregate demand curve to the right, from AD_1 to AD_2 in Exh. 10.4.

As you can see from the exhibit, this increase in aggregate demand causes the equilibrium level of real GDP to rise from $1,000 billion to $1,200 billion—more than the economy's potential. Unfortunately the price level in the economy has also risen, from 100 to 120 in this example. In short, the increase in aggregate demand has propelled the economy to a higher level of real GDP, but it has also resulted in inflation.

How will the economy respond to these situations—to equilibrium outputs that are greater or less than potential GDP? How can the economy oper-

EXHIBIT 10.4

The Impact of an Increase in Aggregate Demand

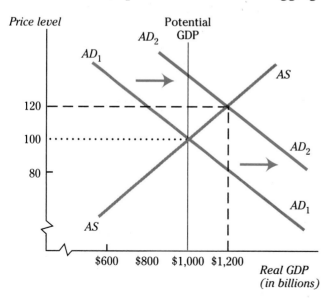

When aggregate demand increases from AD_1 to AD_2, the equilibrium real GDP rises from $1,000 billion to $1,200 billion while the overall price level is increased from 100 to 120.

ate beyond its potential, and how long can it maintain such production? If the economy is experiencing unemployment, will it ever return to the full-employment (potential) GDP? If the economy is experiencing unemployment or inflation, should government attempt to improve the economy's performance by influencing aggregate demand or supply? These important questions of theory and policy are the subject matter of subsequent chapters. Many of these questions first emerged in the debate between the classical economists and John Maynard Keynes. The remainder of this chapter is devoted to that debate.

The Classical Model: The Case for Laissez-Faire

We will begin our exploration of the activist-nonactivist debate by considering the views of the classical economists. The term **classical economist** describes the mainstream economists who wrote from about 1776 through the early 1930s. For our purposes the most important element of classical economic thought was the belief that a market economy would automatically tend toward full employment. Virtually all of the major classical economists held that belief, and apparently people were satisfied with this description of the real world until the Great Depression caused them to question its validity.

Say's Law

The classical economists based their predictions about full employment on a principle known as **Say's Law,** the creation of French economist J. B. Say (1776–1832). Like the laws of demand and supply, Say's Law is nothing more than a theory—one that attempts to explain why a market economy will always tend toward full employment. According to Say's Law, "Supply creates its own demand." In other words, in the process of producing output, businesses also create enough income to ensure that all the output will be sold. Because this theory occupies such an important place in classical economics, we will examine it in more detail, beginning with a simple circular-flow diagram, Exh. 10.5.

Exhibit 10.5 shows that when businesses produce output, they create *income,* payments that must be made to the providers of the various economic resources. Assume, for example, that businesses want to produce $100 worth of output to sell to households. To do that, businesses must first acquire the economic resources necessary to produce those goods and services. The owners of the economic resources are households, and they expect to be paid—in

EXHIBIT 10.5

Say's Law: Supply Creates Its Own Demand

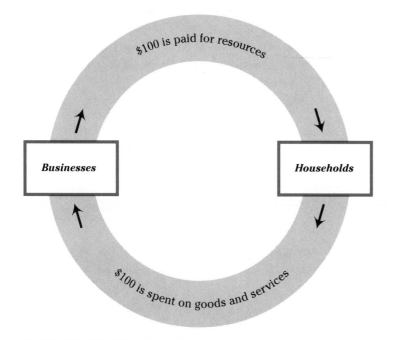

If all the income created in the act of producing output is spent by households, supply will have created its own demand, and all the output will be sold.

wages, rent, interest, and profits (remember, profits are the *payment* for entrepreneurship). Therefore $100 in income payments flows to the household sector. If households spend all the income they receive, everything that was produced will be sold. Supply will have created its own demand.

Because the classical economists accepted Say's Law, they believed that there was nothing to prevent the economy from expanding to full employment. As long as job seekers were willing to work for a wage that was no more than their productivity (their contribution to the output of the firm), profit-seeking businesses would desire to hire everyone who wanted a job. There would always be adequate demand for the output of these additional workers, because "supply creates its own demand."

Many students will immediately recognize that saving could disrupt that simple process. If households decided to save a portion of their earnings, not all of the income created by businesses would return in the form of spending. Thus the demand for goods and services would be too small for the supply, and some output would remain unsold. Businesses would then react by cutting back on production and laying off workers, thus causing unemployment.

But the classical economists did not see saving as a problem. Saving would *not* cause a reduction in spending, because businesses would borrow all the saved money for investment—the purchase of capital goods, such as factories and machinery. Why were the classical economists so sure that the amount households wished to save would equal the amount businesses wanted to invest? Because of interest rates. In the classical model the interest rate is determined by the demand and supply of **loanable funds,** money available to be borrowed. If households desired to save more than investors wanted to borrow, the surplus of funds would drive down the interest rate. Because the interest rate is both the reward households receive for saving *and* the price businesses pay to finance investment, a declining interest rate would both discourage saving and encourage investment. The interest rate would continue to fall until the amount that households wanted to save once again equaled the amount businesses desired to invest. At this equilibrium interest rate there would be no uninvested savings. Businesses would be able to sell all their output either to consumers or to investors, and full employment would prevail.

The Role of Flexible Wages and Prices

The classical economists believed that Say's Law and the flexibility of interest rates would ensure that spending would be adequate to maintain full employment. But some critics were unconvinced. Suppose that households chose to "hoard" some of their income. (Hoarding money is the act of hiding it or storing it.) When people are concerned about the future, they may choose to hide money in a mattress or in a cookie jar so that they will have something to tide them over during hard times. (Households may prefer this form of saving if they lack confidence in the banking system—a situation that existed in the 1920s, when there were numerous bank failures.) This method of saving creates problems for Say's Law because it removes money from circulation. If households choose to hoard money in cookie jars, that money can't be borrowed by businesses and invested. As a consequence, spending may decline and unemployment may appear.

Although the classical economists admitted that hoarding could cause spending to decline, they did not believe that it would lead to unemployment. Full employment would be maintained because wage and price adjustments would compensate for any deficiency in total spending.

The existence of flexible wages and prices implies an *AS* curve that is vertical, not upward sloping as in the initial section of this chapter. Recall that the upward slope of the earlier *AS* curve resulted from the assumption that wage rates and some other input prices remain fixed in the short run. Given these rigidities, an increase in the price level would allow businesses to profit by expanding output, thus producing the upward-sloping *AS* curve. But the classical economists believed that *all* prices—including wage rates (the price of labor) and other input prices—were highly flexible. An increase in product prices would therefore be quickly matched by higher costs, which would eliminate any incentive to expand output.

Thus the existence of highly flexible wages and prices implies an *AS* curve that is vertical at the full-employment level of output (potential GDP), as represented in Exh. 10.6.

To illustrate how flexible wages and prices guarantee full employment, let us assume that the economy is operating at a price level of 100 and a real GDP of $1,000 billion, the intersection of *AS* and *AD₁*. Now suppose that consumers become pessimistic about the future and hide some of their income in cookie jars rather than spend it. What will happen? Aggregate demand will fall—the *AD* curve will shift from *AD₁* to *AD₂*—because households are spending less and thus demanding less real output at any given price level. Reasoning from the assumptions of the classical economists, a reduction in aggregate demand leads quickly to falling prices. In our example the price level will not be maintained at 100; it will fall to 80. If that occurs, businesses will be able to sell the same amount of real output as before but at lower

EXHIBIT 10.6

The Classical Aggregate Supply Curve

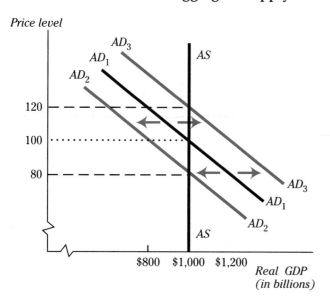

In the classical model a reduction in aggregate demand would immediately lead to falling prices and wages, so that real GDP would be maintained and employment would not fall. Higher aggregate demand would lead to inflation, with no change in output.

prices. Wages will also decline, because reductions in the demand for goods and services will be accompanied by falling demand for labor, which will lead to labor surpluses and wage reductions. Thus employers will still be able to make a profit at the lower price level.

If *AD* were to increase (due to dishoarding—spending the money that had been hoarded—for example), this entire process would work in reverse. An increase in aggregate demand from AD_1 to AD_3 would quickly push up product prices. On the surface this would seem to make it attractive for businesses to increase output; if product prices rise while input prices remain stable, producers can make a profit by expanding output to satisfy the higher level of demand. But in the classical model wage rates and other input prices are also highly flexible, and they would tend to rise, because increases in the demand for goods and services would be accompanied by rising demand for labor and other inputs. Thus businesses would have no incentive to expand output. The higher level of aggregate demand would lead to inflation, leaving output and employment unchanged.

In summary, the classical economists did not believe that changes in aggregate demand would have any impact on real GDP or employment; they maintained that only the price level would be affected.

Full Employment and Laissez-Faire

As a consequence of their faith in Say's Law and the flexibility of wages and prices, the classical economists viewed full employment as the normal situation. They held this belief in spite of recurring periods of observed unemployment. By the mid-1800s economists recognized that capitalist economies tend to expand over time but not at a steady rate. Instead, output and employment fluctuate up and down, growing rapidly in some periods and more slowly, or even declining, in others. Today we call these recurring ups and downs in the level of economic activity the **business cycle.** A period of rising output and employment is called an *expansion*; a period of declining output and employment is called a *recession*.

The occasional bouts of unemployment that accompanied the recession stage of the business cycle were not, however, viewed with alarm or seen as contradicting the classical model. Instead, such unemployment was attributed to external shocks (wars and natural disasters, for example) or to changes in consumer preferences.[1] Because the economy required time to ad-

---

[1] Because the classical economists believed that supply created its own demand, they did not believe that it was possible to have a *general* surplus of goods and services throughout the economy. They recognized, however, that there could be an oversupply of individual products. For example, automobile manufacturers might miscalculate and produce too many automobiles for the prevailing market. In the short run this would result in unsold inventories and unemployment:

just to these events, there might be some unemployment in the interim. But such unemployment would be very short term; it could not persist. Prolonged unemployment would result only if workers' unreasonable wage demands made it unprofitable for firms to hire them. Such unemployment was considered "voluntary"; that is, at the prevailing wage, the people preferred leisure to work. Because prolonged unemployment was regarded as an impossibility and short-term unemployment not deemed a significant social problem, the classical economists focused their energies elsewhere, on studying microeconomic issues and attempting to understand the forces underlying an economy's long-term rate of economic growth (the growth rate of potential GDP).

The classical theorists' belief in the economy's ability to maintain full employment through its own internal mechanisms caused them to favor a policy of laissez-faire, or government by nonintervention. Society was advised to rely on the market mechanism to take care of the economy and to limit the role of government to the areas where it could make a positive contribution—maintaining law and order and providing for the national defense, for example.

The Keynesian Revolution: The Case for Policy Activism

The classical doctrine and its laissez-faire policy prescriptions were almost universally accepted by economists and policymakers until the time of the Great Depression. Then the massive and prolonged unemployment that characterized the industrialized world challenged the predictions of the classical model.

The term "depression" was coined to describe a severe recession. The Great Depression lived up to its name. In 1929, when it began, unemployment stood at 3.2 percent. By 1933, when the economy hit bottom, the unemployment rate had risen to almost 25 percent. During the same period, the economy's output of goods and services (real GDP) fell by more than 25 percent. Moreover, in 1939, ten years after the depression began, unemployment still exceeded 17 percent, and GDP had barely edged back to the levels achieved a decade earlier. Clearly the classical belief that any unemployment would be moderate and short-lived seemed in direct conflict with reality.

The current number of workers could no longer be profitably employed by the automobile industry. In the long run, however, both problems would be eliminated. The surplus of automobiles would cause their prices to fall, which would shift labor and other economic resources out of the automobile industry and into some other industry, one characterized by shortages and rising prices.

The most forceful critic of the classical model was John Maynard Keynes, a British economist. His major work, entitled *The General Theory of Employment, Interest, and Money,* was first published in 1936. In a sense Keynes stood classical economics on its head. Whereas the classical economists believed that supply created its own demand, Keynes argued that causation ran the other way—from demand to supply. In Keynes's view businesses base their production decisions on the level of expected demand, or expected total spending. The more that consumers, investors, and others plan to spend, the more output businesses will expect to sell and the more they will produce. In other words, supply (or output) responds to demand—not the converse, as the classical economists suggested. Most important, Keynes argued that the level of total spending in the economy could be inadequate to provide full employment, that the classical economists were wrong in believing that interest rate adjustments and wage/price flexibility would prevent unemployment. According to Keynes, full employment is possible only when the level of total spending is adequate. If spending is inadequate, unemployment will result.

In summary, Keynes rejected the classical contention that market economies automatically tend toward full employment and focused attention on the level of demand or total spending as the critical determinant of an economy's health. We now turn to a more detailed look at his model and the errors he detected in the classical theory.

John Maynard Keynes (shown here with his wife, Lydia) contended that the classical economists were wrong in their belief that a market economy automatically tends toward full employment.

The Meaning of Equilibrium Output

To understand the Keynesian model, you need to become more familiar with the concept of **equilibrium output.** As you know, equilibrium means stability: a state of balance or rest. In microeconomics an equilibrium price is a stable price, one that won't change unless there are changes in the underlying supply and demand conditions. In macroeconomics an equilibrium output is a stable output, one that is neither expanding nor contracting.

We can illustrate the concept of equilibrium output with the circular-flow diagram in Exh. 10.7. This diagram depicts a very simplified economy; there

EXHIBIT 10.7

Equilibrium Output with Saving and Investment

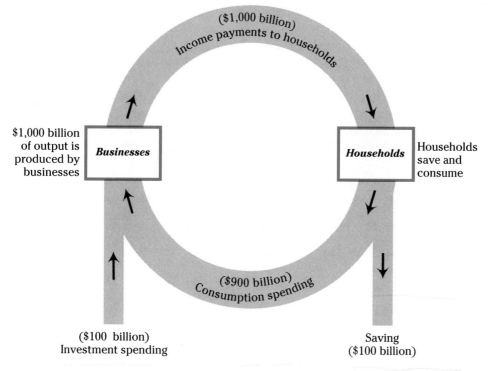

In a simple private economy we can identify the equilibrium output in either of two ways: (1) total spending equals total output, or (2) investment equals saving. In our example, when $1,000 billion worth of output is produced, it creates $1,000 billion worth of spending (consumption of $900 billion plus investment of $100 billion). At the same time, the amount that households desire to save is equal to the amount that businesses want to invest. Hence $1,000 billion is equilibrium output.

is no government sector (hence there will be no government spending and no taxation) and no foreign sector (so there will be no imports and exports). These simplifications will make it easier for us to grasp the concept of equilibrium. A more complex economy will be introduced in later chapters.

We assume here that businesses expect to sell $1,000 billion worth of output, so they produce that amount. Of course, that sends to households $1,000 billion in income, which they can either spend or save. In this example we imagine that they choose to save $100 billion. Economists refer to saving as a **leakage,** a subtraction from the flow of spending. Leakages mean that less money returns to businesses, unless the economy can somehow compensate for the loss. In our example the $100 billion leakage means that only $900 billion will be spent on consumption goods. That $900 billion is what we called *personal consumption expenditures* when we showed you how to calculate gross domestic product in Chapter 9.

Consumption spending is not the only form of spending for goods and services, even in the simple private economy we are analyzing. Business investors also purchase a substantial amount of our economy's output (GDP). To keep it simple, let's assume that businesses coincidentally desire to purchase $100 billion worth of output. That investment spending is described as an **injection,** since it adds to the basic flow of consumption spending. Total spending for goods and services (consumption spending plus investment spending) amounts to $1,000 billion. As you can see from Exh. 10.7, that is just enough to purchase everything that was produced—the entire $1,000 billion. That means the producers' expectations have been fulfilled; they expected to sell $1,000 billion of output, and they have sold precisely that amount. Because producers are usually guided by their successes and failures, this would be an important finding. It would be a signal to produce the same amount next year, a response that would mean that the economy was in equilibrium.

As you can see from this example, the economy will be in equilibrium whenever the amount of total spending is exactly sufficient to purchase the economy's entire output (when total spending = total output). When that happens, producers can sell exactly what they've produced, and they have no incentive to alter the level of production.

Note that when the economy is in equilibrium, the amount that households want to save is equal to the amount that businesses desire to invest. The reason for that may be apparent to you. When the amount that is being injected into the spending flow in the form of investment is equal to the amount that is leaking out in the form of saving, the size of the flow is unchanged. The amount returning to businesses will be equal to the amount they paid out; therefore they will be able to sell exactly what they produced, and the economy will be in equilibrium.

The Problem of an Unemployment Equilibrium

Keynes and the classical economists agreed that the economy would always tend toward equilibrium. We'll save the discussion of the forces that will tend to move the economy toward equilibrium until the next chapter. For now the important point is that Keynes and the classical economists disagreed about whether the level of output at which the economy stabilized would permit full employment. In the classical model the economy tends to stabilize at a full-employment equilibrium (at potential GDP). In the Keynesian model the economy tends toward equilibrium but not necessarily at full employment. When the economy is in equilibrium at less than full employment, an **unemployment equilibrium** exists.

We can illustrate why Keynes and the classical economists reached different conclusions about the likelihood of full employment by returning to the circular-flow diagram in Exh. 10.7. Recall that in this example households are saving $100 billion, businesses are investing $100 billion, and $1,000 billion is the economy's equilibrium output. To facilitate our comparison between the classical and Keynesian models, let's assume that $1,000 billion is the economy's potential GDP, so the economy is operating at full employment.

Now suppose that households decide to increase their saving from $100 billion to $200 billion. What will happen? Obviously, more money is leaking out of the circular flow, in the form of saving. But as we noted earlier, the classical economists did not believe saving would invalidate Say's Law. According to the classical model, this increased saving would simply increase the supply of loanable funds, which would drive down the interest rate and stimulate investment spending. Investment spending would rise from $100 billion to $200 billion, thus maintaining the equilibrium output at $1,000 billion—full employment.

Keynes found fault with this optimistic scenario. According to Keynes, interest rate adjustments cannot be relied on to make saving equal to investment, because the interest rate is not the major motivating force in either the saving or the investment decision. In his view the level of *income* is the primary factor influencing the amount that households plan to save; the higher the income, the greater the level of saving. Changes in interest rates have a relatively minor impact on saving decisions. Investment decisions, said Keynes, are governed by profit expectations. The interest rate is only one factor influencing the profitability of an investment, and not the most important factor. If sales are poor and the future looks bleak, businesses are unlikely to undertake new investment, even if the prevailing interest rate is low. Since the interest rate is not the major force guiding saving and investment decisions, it cannot "match up" the plans of savers and investors. As a consequence, when households want to save more than businesses desire to invest, the level of output and employment in the economy will tend to fall. In short, increased saving (reduced spending) can lead to unemployment.

Rejecting the Wage Flexibility Argument

By itself, Keynes's discrediting of the link between saving and investment was not sufficient to refute the classical claim of a full-employment equilibrium. Remember, the classical economists described *two* forces that ensure full employment in a market economy: interest rate adjustments and wage/price flexibility. If interest rate adjustments fail to synchronize the plans of savers and investors and if this results in too little spending, wage and price flexibility can still ensure full employment. In competitive labor and product markets inadequate demand would lead to falling wages and prices, which in turn would guarantee that all output was sold and thus prevent involuntary unemployment.

Again Keynes disagreed. He argued that the classical assumption of highly flexible wages and prices was not consistent with the real world. According to Keynes, a variety of forces prevent prices and wages from adjusting quickly, particularly in a downward direction. First, markets are less competitive than the classical theory assumed. Keynes saw that many product markets were monopolistic or oligopolistic. When sellers in these markets noted that demand was declining, they often chose to reduce output rather than lower prices. And in labor markets, particularly those dominated by strong labor unions, workers tended to resist wage cuts. As a consequence, wages and prices did not adjust quickly; they tended to be rigid or "sticky."

The consequences of rigid prices can be seen in Exh. 10.8, which uses the aggregate demand–aggregate supply framework. Let's consider the same scenario outlined in our discussion of the classical model. Assume that consumers become pessimistic about the future and decide to hoard some of their income. Aggregate demand will fall—the AD curve will shift from AD_1 to AD_2—because households demand fewer goods and services at any given price level. This time we will make the assumption that the price level remains stuck at 100 because labor and other contracts prohibit reductions in input costs, which means that firms cannot afford to reduce prices. The assumption of rigid prices and wages implies a flat, or horizontal, AS curve since any reduction in aggregate demand leads to a reduced level of real GDP but no change in the price level. In this example the level of equilibrium GDP would decline from $1,000 billion to $800 billion. Businesses still want to produce $1,000 billion of output, but since they can sell only $800 billion, they must cut production back to that level. Of course, employment would also decline; if employers produce less real output, they require fewer workers. This

EXHIBIT 10.8

The Keynesian Aggregate Supply Curve

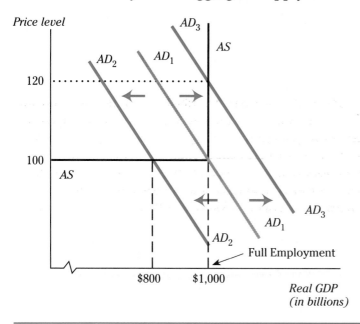

According to Keynes, prices and wages tend to be rigid in the face of falling demand. Thus a reduction in aggregate demand is quickly translated into lower real GDP and reduced employment (greater unemployment). Attempts to purchase more than the full employment output will lead to inflation without increasing real GDP.

is essentially the manner in which Keynes explained the Great Depression—as a prolem caused by too little aggregate demand, combined with wage and price rigidity.

Although Keynes was concerned primarily with the problem of unemployment, he agreed with the classical economists that inflation would result if consumers, investors, and others attempted to purchase more than the economy was capable of producing.[2] As you can see, the Keynesian AS curve becomes vertical at full employment. If aggregate demand were increased from AD_1 to AD_3, the price level would be pushed up, without any increase in real output or employment.

The Case for Government Intervention

Because Keynes did not believe that a market economy could be relied on to automatically preserve full employment and avoid inflation, he argued that the central government must manage the level of aggregate demand to

---

[2] Keynes viewed the economy's full employment, or potential GDP, as the maximum output the economy was capable of producing rather than as the maximum *sustainable* level of production.

achieve those objectives. How could this be accomplished? One approach was through **fiscal policy**—the manipulation of government spending and taxation in order to guide the economy's performance. When unemployment exists, the federal government should increase its spending on goods and services (without increasing taxes). This will shift the aggregate demand curve to the right and increase the equilibrium level of real GDP and employment. A reduction in income taxes (without a reduction in government spending) will accomplish the same thing, because it will cause households to spend more at any given price level. When inflation exists, government spending should be reduced or taxes increased. These policies will reduce aggregate demand and thus reduce inflationary pressures.

Another approach would be to use **monetary policy:** policy intended to alter the supply of money in order to influence the level of economic activity. When unemployment exists, the Federal Reserve—the governmental agency that regulates the money supply—should increase the amount of money in circulation so that households and businesses will find it easier to borrow funds. This will tend to increase spending for goods and services, which will shift the *AD* curve to the right and raise the level of equilibrium output and employment. Inflation calls for a reduction in the money supply. By making it more difficult to borrow funds, the Federal Reserve can reduce spending and thereby combat inflation. We'll have more to say about fiscal and monetary policy later in the text.

The 1990s: The Debate Continues

Keynesian theory held sway through the 1960s, and many economists remain Keynesians today. But Keynesian thinking began to lose influence in the 1970s, when the Keynesian model seemed unable to explain the stagflation—simultaneous unemployment and inflation—that characterized that period. Since then, Keynesians have been rethinking and modifying their views, and new schools of thought have emerged to challenge their position.

Interestingly, some of these challengers—monetarists and rational expectations theorists—bear a striking resemblance to the classical economists of old. In particular they generally argue that the economy tends toward full employment and that government intervention is unnecessary and even counterproductive. Thus the debate about economic policy has come full circle; economists are once again arguing about the proper role of government in economic policy: Should government actively attempt to stabilize the economy to prevent unemployment or inflation, or should it keep "hands off"? We will return to the aggregate demand–aggregate supply framework and our discussion of the activist-nonactivist debate after taking a closer look at the Keynesian model, in Chapter 11, and examining Keynesian fiscal and monetary policies in more detail, in Chapters 12 and 13, respectively.

Summary

In market economies the interaction of aggregate demand and aggregate supply determines the equilibrium level of real GDP and the overall price level. *Aggregate demand* is the total quantity of output demanded by all sectors in the economy at various price levels in a given period of time. The aggregate demand curve slopes downward, reflecting the fact that more aggregate output is demanded at lower price levels than at higher price levels. *Aggregate supply* is the total quantity of output supplied by all producers in the economy together at various price levels in a given period of time. The aggregate supply curve may be horizontal, vertical, or upward sloping; its shape depends on the behavior of wages and prices.

The level of output the economy produces when it operates at full employment is called *potential GDP*. An economy's potential GDP is determined by the size of the labor force, the capital stock, the stock of raw materials, and technology.

The interaction of aggregate demand and supply may give rise to an equilibrium output that is less than potential GDP. When this occurs, unemployment will exist. Economists are in disagreement about the desirability of government efforts to combat macroeconomic problems, such as unemployment. Some economists are "activists," supporting a significant role for government; others are "nonactivists," believing that government intervention should be avoided.

The activist-nonactivist controversy originated more than 50 years ago with a debate between John Maynard Keynes and the classical economists, who dominated that period. The classical economists felt that a market economy allowed to function without artificial restrictions would provide members of a society with the goods and services they desired while simultaneously maintaining full employment.

The foundation of the classical theory of employment was Say's Law: Supply creates its own demand. More precisely, the act of producing output creates the income that will take that output off the market. Because everything that businesses produce will be sold, there should be nothing to prevent the economy from expanding to full employment.

Even an increase in saving was not considered a problem. The increased availability of loanable funds would cause the interest rate to fall, thereby encouraging businesses to borrow those funds and invest them. If the interest rate somehow failed to equate the plans of savers and investors, wage and price adjustments would compensate for any deficiency in spending. Prolonged unemployment would result only if workers made unreasonable wage demands.

The massive and prolonged unemployment that accompanied the Great Depression cast doubt on the predictions of the classical economists and subjected their model to criticism. The most devastating attack came from John Maynard Keynes. Keynes argued that a market economy does not contain any internal mechanism to ensure full employment. In his view the primary determinant of an economy's health is the level of total spending, or total demand for goods and services. If spending is inadequate, unemployment will result; if it is excessive, inflation will occur.

Keynes believed that it was the responsibility of the federal government to combat unemployment or inflation. This could be accomplished through *fiscal policy*—the manipulation of government spending and taxation in order to guide the economy's performance—or through *monetary policy*—policy intended to alter the money supply as a method of influencing total spending and the economy's performance.

Glossary

Aggregate demand. The total quantity of output demanded by all sectors in the economy together at various price levels in a given time period.

Aggregate supply. The total quantity of output supplied by all producers in the economy together at various price levels in a given time period.

Business cycle. The recurring ups and downs in the level of economic activity.

Classical economists. The mainstream economists who wrote from 1776 through the early 1930s. They believed that a market economy would automatically tend to maintain full employment.

Equilibrium output. A stable output, one that is neither expanding nor contracting.

Fiscal policy. The manipulation of government spending and taxation in order to guide the economy's performance.

Injection. An addition to the circular flow of spending; e.g., investment spending.

Leakage. A subtraction from the circular flow of spending; e.g., saving.

Loanable funds. Money available to be borrowed.

Monetary policy. Policy intended to alter the money supply in order to influence the level of economic activity.

Potential GDP. The level of output produced when the economy is operating at full employment; the maximum sustainable level of production.

Real balance effect. The increase in the amount of aggregate output demanded that results from an increase in the real value of the public's financial assets.

> ***Say's Law.*** The theory that supply creates its own demand. In the process of producing output, businesses create enough income to ensure that all the output will be sold.
>
> ***Unemployment equilibrium.*** A stable level of output that is not large enough to permit full employment.

Study Questions

Fill in the Blanks

1. The level of output the economy produces when it operates at full employment is called _____.

2. Economists who support a significant role for government in combating macroeconomic problems are called _____; those who believe that government intervention should be avoided are called _____.

3. The theory that supply creates its own demand is called _____ _____.

4. According to Keynes, the primary cause of unemployment is _____ _____.

5. The classical economists did not believe that saving would lead to too little spending, because they felt that all saving would be _____.

6. In the classical model any long-term unemployment must be _____ _____.

7. In terms of the circular-flow diagram, saving is often described as a _____ _____, whereas investment is an _____.

8. According to Keynes, the level of output and employment is determined primarily by the level of _____.

9. In the classical model the flexibility of interest rates was not the only factor ensuring full employment; flexible _____ and _____ provided an additional safeguard.

10. The classical economists argued that the proper role for government in the economy was a very _____ one.

11. According to Keynes, one way to combat unemployment is for the federal government to increase its spending or reduce _____.

12. If there is no tendency for the level of output to expand or contract, the economy must be producing the _____ level of output.

13. Manipulating the level of government spending in order to guide the economy's performance is one form of _____ policy.

14. Keynes believed that a reduction in aggregate demand would lead to lower output and employment rather than to lower _____, as the classical economists suggested.

15. Altering the money supply in an attempt to influence the economy's performance is termed _____ policy.

Multiple Choice

1. The aggregate demand curve is downward sloping because
   a) when the price of a product falls, consumers tend to substitute that product for other things.
   b) certain input prices tend to be fixed by contracts in the short run.
   c) as the price level falls, the real value of financial assets increases.
   d) as the price level increases, the purchasing power of consumers' paychecks rises, and they tend to buy more.

2. The aggregate supply curve will be upward sloping if
   a) all product and input prices (including wage rates) are highly flexible.
   b) higher prices lead to more spending for goods and services.
   c) certain input prices tend to be fixed in the short run.
   d) all product and input prices are inflexible due to long-term contracts.

3. Given an upward-sloping aggregate supply curve, a reduction in aggregate demand would tend to
   a) increase the level of equilibrium real GDP and the overall price level.
   b) decrease the level of equilibrium real GDP and the overall price level.
   c) increase the level of equilibrium real GDP and decrease the overall price level.
   d) decrease the level of equilibrium real GDP and increase the overall price level.

4. Given an upward-sloping aggregate supply curve, an increase in aggregate demand, coupled with a decrease in aggregate supply, would tend to
  a) increase the economy's equilibrium real GDP and the overall price level.
  b) decrease the economy's equilibrium real GDP but raise the overall price level.
  c) increase the economy's overall price level, but the impact on equilibrium real GDP is indeterminate (depends on the relative magnitude of the two shifts).
  d) increase the economy's equilibrium real GDP, but the impact on the overall price level is indeterminate (depends on the relative magnitude of the two shifts).

5. According to the classical economists,
  a) unemployment is caused by too little spending.
  b) the interest rate will ensure that the amount households plan to save will equal the amount businesses desire to invest.
  c) increasing government spending is the most reliable method of restoring full employment.
  d) the amount households plan to save is determined primarily by their income.

6. Keynes would suggest that during a period of unemployment, government
  a) do nothing.
  b) reduce its spending to stimulate the economy.
  c) increase its spending to stimulate the economy.
  d) take legal action against unions in order to make wages more flexible.

7. The aggregate supply curve implied by the classical model is _____ _____ so a reduction in aggregate demand will mean a lower overall level of _____.
  a) vertical, prices
  b) vertical, output
  c) horizontal, prices
  d) horizontal, output

8. In the Keynesian model, if leakages exceed injections,
  a) the economy is producing the equilibrium output.
  b) the level of output will tend to fall.
  c) the level of output will tend to rise.
  d) the economy must be at full employment.

9. According to the classical model, even when all saving is not invested, full employment will be maintained because
  a) the government will step in and stimulate spending.
  b) the equilibrium wage rate will rise to stimulate spending.
  c) wages and prices will fall to permit businesses to continue hiring everyone who wants to work.
  d) the government will establish special work programs.

10. According to Keynes, the amount that households desire to save is determined primarily by
    a) the rate of interest.
    b) the investment plans of businesses.
    c) the incomes of the households.
    d) None of the above

11. In the Keynesian model the economy is producing the equilibrium output when
    a) total spending equals total output.
    b) total income equals total output.
    c) total saving exceeds total investment.
    d) surplus inventories are maximized.

12. Perhaps the most important implication of Keynesian economics is that
    a) the economy automatically tends toward full employment.
    b) government should not interfere in the operation of the economy.
    c) the economy always tends toward the equilibrium output.
    d) the economy can come to rest at an unemployment equilibrium.

13. According to the classical economists, prolonged unemployment could be caused only by
    a) too little spending.
    b) workers making unreasonable wage demands.
    c) external shocks.
    d) changes in consumer preferences.

14. In the Keynesian model of a private economy the equilibrium output exists when
    a) total spending equals total demand.
    b) consumption plus investment equals total spending.
    c) the amount that households want to save equals the amount that businesses want to invest.
    d) All of the above

15. Which of the following is an example of the fiscal policy Keynes would find appropriate for a period of unemployment?
    a) Decrease government spending
    b) Increase the money supply
    c) Reduce personal income taxes
    d) Reduce the money supply

Problems and Questions for Discussion

1. What are the determinants of the economy's potential GDP?

2. Why did the classical economists believe that any long-term unemployment had to be voluntary?

3. What flaws did Keynes find in the classical theory's wage-flexibility argument?

4. In what sense did Keynes "stand classical economics on its head"?

5. Explain the concept of equilibrium output and describe how to identify equilibrium in the Keynesian model.

6. In the Keynesian model, why is a private economy in equilibrium when the amount that households plan to save is equal to the amount that businesses plan to invest?

7. Why did Keynes believe that the proper response to a period of unemployment was for government to increase its spending? How could this policy help to combat unemployment?

8. How did the classical economists explain the existence of short-term unemployment?

9. Explain the role of interest rates in the classical model.

10. Many economists argue that the Great Depression was brought to an end by World War II. In Keynesian terms how could a war contribute to combating unemployment?

Answer Key

Fill in the Blanks

1. potential GDP	6. voluntary	11. taxes
2. activists, nonactivists	7. leakage, injection	12. equilibrium
3. Say's Law	8. total spending	13. fiscal
4. too little spending	9. wages, prices	14. prices
5. invested	10. limited	15. monetary

Multiple Choice

1. c	4. c	7. a	10. c	13. b
2. c	5. b	8. b	11. a	14. c
3. b	6. c	9. c	12. d	15. c

The Basic Keynesian Model: Determining the Levels of Income, Output, and Employment

What determines how much output our economy will produce and how many people will be employed? For Keynesians, the answer is *total spending—total demand for goods and services.* When total spending increases, businesses produce more output and hire more people. As you learned in Chapter 10, that's the central idea in Keynesian macroeconomic theory: *Total spending is the critical determinant of the overall level of economic activity.*

Now we will explore the factors that influence the level of total spending. Why does total spending fluctuate? How can it be too low at some times and too high at others? We take up these questions in the next two chapters as we examine a hypothetical economy. In Chapter 11 we confine our analysis to a two-sector economy—households and businesses. We assume that there is no government and no foreign trade. (The appendix to this chapter expands the model to include trade.) We also assume that all saving is done by households and all investment by businesses. Further, we assume that the price level remains constant until full employment is reached. (Remember, Keynes believed that prices and wages tend to be rigid, not flexible as the classical economists assumed.)

We first explore the determinants of consumption and investment spending. Then we consider the way in which consumption, investment, and saving interact to determine the level of equilibrium income and output. We then investigate the possibility of an unemployment or an inflationary equilibrium.

Consumption Spending

The largest component of total spending is consumption spending—spending by households for food, clothing, automobiles, education, and all the other goods and services that consumers buy. The most important factor influencing the amount of consumer spending is the level of disposable income. **Disposable income** is your take-home pay, the amount you have left after taxes have been deducted. Because there is no government sector in this chapter's hypothetical economy, no taxes are collected, which means that disposable income will equal total income, or GDP. For both individual households and society as a whole, a positive relationship exists between the amount of disposable income and the amount of consumption spending: The more people earn, the more they spend.

The Consumption Function

The relationship between disposable income and consumption spending is called the **consumption function.** A consumption function shows the amounts that households plan to spend at different levels of disposable income. Exhibit 11.1 shows a hypothetical consumption function that is consistent with Keynesian theory. Note that the amount households plan to spend increases with income, but by a smaller amount than the increase in income. In other words, households will spend part of any increase in income and save the rest. Whatever disposable income is not spent by households is

EXHIBIT 11.1

A Hypothetical Consumption Function (in billions)

TOTAL INCOME* AND OUTPUT (GDP)	PLANNED CONSUMPTION EXPENDITURES	PLANNED SAVING
$300	$325	$−25
400	400	0
500	475	25
600	550	50
700	625	75
800	700	100

*In our simplified economy total income = total disposable income = GDP.

saved. **Saving** is the act of not spending; putting money in a savings account, buying stocks and bonds, and stashing cash in a cookie jar are all acts of saving.

According to Exh. 11.1, when income is $300 billion, households desire to spend $325 billion. At that income, they are **dissaving** $25 billion; that is, they are dipping into their savings accounts or borrowing to help finance some minimum standard of living. Higher levels of income involve more consumption spending and more saving, or less dissaving. In our example $400 billion represents the income level at which every dollar earned is spent; there is neither saving nor dissaving. At higher incomes, households wish to save a portion of their income. For instance, at an income of $500 billion, households plan to save $25 billion; at an income of $600 billion, they desire to save $50 billion.

Exhibit 11.2 plots the consumption function depicted in Exh. 11.1. The consumption function slopes upward and to the right, because consumption spending increases with income. We determine the income level where every dollar is spent by using the 45-degree line drawn in the diagram. Because the vertical and horizontal axes meet at a 90-degree angle, the 45-degree line represents a series of points that are equidistant from the horizontal axis (income) and the vertical axis (consumption). Therefore at every point along the 45-degree line, consumption expenditures equal income. Where the consumption function crosses the 45-degree line, consumers plan to spend everything they earn and save nothing. In our example that happens at an income of $400 billion.

At incomes less than $400 billion, there is dissaving, or negative saving. You can see that when income is $300 billion consumers plan to dissave $25

EXHIBIT 11.2

Graphing a Consumption Function

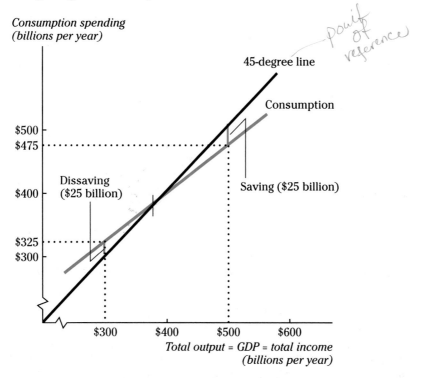

A consumption function shows the amounts that households desire to spend at different income levels. According to this hypothetical function, households would spend $325 billion per year if the total income in the economy were $300 billion. Thus they would be dissaving—dipping into their savings accounts or borrowing—$25 billion at that income level.

Note that the amount of consumption spending rises with the level of income. At an income of $400 billion, households desire to spend exactly what they earn. There would be no saving and no dissaving. At an income of $500 billion, households would spend $475 billion each year and save $25 billion.

billion. The vertical distance between the 45-degree line and the consumption function represents the amount of dissaving at that income. At incomes in excess of $400 billion, there is positive saving. When income is $500 billion, saving is equal to $25 billion. The distance between the 45-degree line and the consumption function gets wider as income increases, because the amount of saving increases with income.

The Marginal Propensity to Consume

The way that households react to changes in income depends on their **marginal propensity to consume (MPC)**. The *MPC* is the fraction of each additional earned dollar that households spend on consumption, or the change in consumption spending divided by the change in income:

$$\text{Marginal propensity to consume } (MPC) = \frac{\text{Change in consumption spending}}{\text{Change in income}}.$$

If you receive a $1,000 raise and you plan to spend $900 of that increase, your *MPC* is 9/10, or 0.90. In other words, you'll spend 90 percent of any additional income you receive. In our hypothetical economy the marginal propensity to consume is 3/4, or 0.75. Note that in Exhs. 11.1 and 11.2, for every $100 billion increase in GDP (income), consumption spending increases by $75 billion:

$$MPC = \frac{\$\,75\,\text{billion}}{\$100\,\text{billion}} = \frac{3}{4} = 0.75.$$

You can relate the marginal propensity to consume to the consumption function easily if you know that the slope of any line is, by definition, the vertical change divided by the horizontal change. The slope of the consumption function is the change in consumption spending divided by the change in income, which is precisely how we define the marginal propensity to consume. In other words, the slope of the consumption function is equal to the economy's *MPC*. If the *MPC* in our example were higher (0.90 instead of 0.75, for example), the slope of the consumption function would be steeper; if the *MPC* were lower (perhaps 0.50), the consumption function would be flatter.

According to our consumption function, only part of an increase in income is spent; the rest is saved. The **marginal propensity to save (MPS)** is the fraction of each additional earned dollar that is saved, or the change in saving divided by the change in income:

$$\text{Marginal propensity to save } (MPS) = \frac{\text{Change in saving}}{\text{Change in income}}.$$

Calculating *MPS* is no problem once you know *MPC*. The marginal propensity to consume and the marginal propensity to save have to add up to 1.00, or 100 percent: If *MPC* is 0.75, you know that *MPS* must be 0.25. That is, 75 cents from each additional dollar is spent, and 25 cents is saved.

As you study Exhs. 11.1 and 11.2, keep in mind that the consumption function indicates the desired—or planned—levels of consumption, not necessarily the actual levels. Just as the demand curves we encountered in Chapter 3 showed the amount of a product consumers are "willing and able to buy at various prices," the consumption function shows the amounts that households *desire* to consume at various income levels. How much of a product people actually buy depends on the prices that actually prevail. Similarly, the actual level of consumption depends on the actual level of income in the economy.

The Nonincome Determinants of Consumption Spending

Although consumption spending is determined primarily by the level of disposable income, nonincome factors also play a role. These nonincome factors include (1) people's expectations about what will happen to prices and to their incomes, (2) the cost and availability of consumer credit, and (3) the overall wealth of households.

It is easy to see why consumer expectations can have an impact on spending behavior. If people expect prices to be higher next month or next year, they tend to buy now. Why wait to pay $14,000 for a car next year if you can buy it for $13,000 today? Buying now to avoid higher prices later creates a greater amount of current consumption spending than would normally be expected at each level of income. Similarly, if people expect an increase in income, they will probably spend more from their current income. If you're convinced that you're going to be earning more next year, you'll probably be a little bit freer in your spending habits this year.

The cost and availability of consumer credit also influence the level of consumption spending. Most of us don't limit our spending to our current income. If we really want something, we borrow the money to buy it. But the cost of borrowing money and the ability to get consumer credit can change with the state of the economy. In general, the higher the interest rate and the more difficult it is to get consumer loans, the less consumption spending there will be at any level of total income (GDP).

The third nonincome determinant of consumption spending is the overall wealth of households. A household's wealth includes cash, bank accounts, stocks and bonds, real estate, and other physical assets. Since households can finance consumption spending by depleting bank accounts or selling other forms of wealth, an increase in wealth will permit households to spend more at any given income level. For this reason, an increase in wealth will tend to shift the consumption function upward; a decrease will have the opposite effect.

The consumption function assumes that these nonincome determinants of consumption spending remain unchanged. If that assumption is violated, the entire consumption function shifts. Exhibit 11.3 shows how changing expectations about prices result in different levels of planned consumption spending at each level of income. (Imagine that you're rich, with major holdings of

EXHIBIT 11.3

Changes in the Nonincome Determinants of Consumption

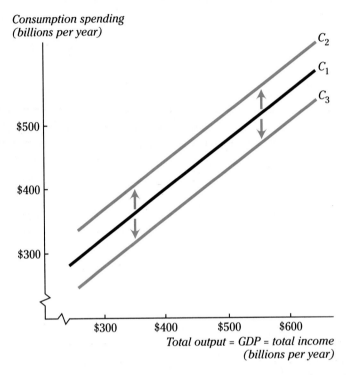

The consumption function assumes that the nonincome determinants of consumption spending remain unchanged. If that assumption is violated, the consumption function will shift to a new position. For example, if consumers expect prices to be higher next year, they will probably choose to purchase more consumer goods this year. The consumption function will shift upward (from C_1 to C_2). If consumers lower their expectations regarding future prices, they will probably choose to purchase fewer consumer goods this year. The consumption function will shift downward (from C_1 to C_3).

stocks and bonds, and that you woke up one morning and discovered that the value of those assets had plummeted. How would you react? Read "Feeling Poorer and Spending Less," on page 334, to learn about the "wealth effect" of such an event.) Read "Feeling Poorer and Spending Less," on page 334

Except under extreme conditions, such as those that prevailed during the Great Depression or World War II, the consumption function has been relatively stable; it hasn't shifted up or down very much. Knowing that planned consumption has been stable, how do we explain the fluctuations in total spending that occur in our economy? According to Keynes, the major cause of fluctuations in total spending is the ever-changing rate of investment spending.

Investment Spending

The term *investment*, as you saw in Chapter 9, refers to spending by businesses on capital goods—factories, machinery, and other aids to production. Investment spending has a dual influence on the level of economic activity. First, as a major component of total spending, investment spending helps determine the economy's level of total output and total employment. Second, investment is a critical determinant of the economy's rate of growth. We define economic growth as an increase in the economy's productive capacity or potential GDP. Investment spending contributes to economic growth because it enlarges the economy's stock of capital goods and thereby helps increase the economy's capacity to produce goods and services.

The Determinants of Investment

As you discovered in Chapter 10, profit expectations are the overriding motivation of all investment-spending plans in a market economy. Those expectations are based on a comparison of costs and revenues.

Suppose you are considering investing in a soft-drink machine for the lobby of the student union. How do you decide whether to make the investment? Like any other businessperson, you compare costs and revenues. On the cost side, you consider the price of the machine and the interest charges on the money you would have to borrow to buy it. If you would be using your own money, you consider the opportunity cost of those funds—the amount of interest you will sacrifice if you withdraw that money from your savings to purchase the machine. On the revenue side, you would include the expected income from selling the soft drinks minus the cost of the drinks. If you expect the machine to generate revenues exceeding all your anticipated costs, you have incentive to make the investment. If not, the investment should not be made. All investment decisions involve a similar comparison.

Interest Rates: The Cost of Money. The rate of interest can be an important factor in determining whether an investment will be profitable. A project that does not appear profitable when the interest rate is 20 percent, for ex-

Feeling Poorer and Spending Less

WASHINGTON April 8—The American economy will grow somewhat less rapidly this year and next if stock and bond prices do not recover from their recent plunge, Administration officials and some private economists said today.

They cite higher interest rates, which discourage companies and individuals from borrowing and spending money. Moreover, they cite the so-called wealth effect: many American consumers will likely spend less money if they feel poorer because of the shrinkage of their portfolios.

After running various computer simulations of the economy, President Clinton's Council of Economic Advisers has concluded that if the stock market falls 10 percent below its peak in early February and stays down, this will gradually knock four-tenths of a percentage point off the nation's expected annual economic output, reducing it by about $26 billion. Growth is now running a little over 3 percent. The stock market is currently trading about 7 percent below its peak.

"There is a wealth effect; it's a relatively small effect but it does require a sustained, that is, long-term

reduction in the value of stocks," said Laura D'Andrea Tyson, the head of the Council of Economic Advisers. But the braking effect of a falling stock market and rising interest rates on the economy may be hard to notice, if, as may well be the case, it is offset by the economy's generally growing strength. A survey this week of prominent economists by Blue Chip Economic Indicators found that their consensus forecast of economic growth this year had actually risen, to 3.7 percent from a 3.6 percent forecast in early March.

Lehman Brothers, the New York investment firm, estimated that the wealth effect from the stock market's recent retreat would reduce economic growth by only two-tenths of a percentage point if the stock market stayed 10 percent below its peak. But when bond market losses and the economy-slowing effects of higher interest rates are included in the calculation, the harm to American economic output grows to five-tenths of a percentage point this year and seven-tenths to eight-tenths of a percentage point next year, said Allen Sinai, Lehman's chief economist.

The key question, Ms. Tyson and other economists

said, is not how deeply the stock market has fallen but how long it will stay down. The reason is that consumers appear to be very slow in revising their spending plans in response to financial losses.

Nobody knows how long the stock market will take to recover from last month's selloff. Mr. Sinai said that he expected the market to recover soon because the overall economy remained strong.

But Mr. Sinai added that he expected interest rates to stay up. As a result, Lehman Brothers has just revised downward its projections of economic growth, but not drastically, he said. Mr. Sinai revised his forecast down to 3.4 or 3.5 percent growth this year from a 3.7 percent forecast a month ago, and revised his forecast for next year down to 3 percent from 3.4 percent.

When the stock market crashed in 1987, many doomsayers predicted that the economy would be severely damaged. They were proved wrong, since the economy grew 3.9 percent in 1988, a rate not equaled for any year since then.

That striking miscalculation set off strong criticisms of the wealth effect theory at universities. The effect now is "something that's not emphasized by academic economists but is emphasized by economic forecasters," said Laurence M. Ball, an economics professor at Johns Hopkins University.

Forecasters are quick to defend their continued reliance on the wealth effect, saying that it plays a limited role in their computer simulations and helps improve the accuracy of their predictions. They contend that when the Fed lowered interest rates after the 1987 crash, the resulting stimulus to the economy outweighed consumers' losses on stocks.

Yet the wealth effect also plays a dwindling role in forecasters' calculations. Mr. Sinai, who specializes in the effects of financial markets on the real economy, said his model now assumed that consumer spending would drop by only 3 cents for every dollar of decline in the value of financial assets.

Before 1987, the model assumed that for each dollar of losses, consumer spending declined by a nickel. The Council of Economic Advisers' model still assumes that the effect is a nickel for each dollar. . . .

—*Keith Bradsher*

SOURCE: Keith Bradsher, "Feeling Poorer and Spending Less," April 1, 1994. Copyright © 1994 by The New York Times Company. Reprinted with permission.

Use Your Economic Reasoning

1. Consumers tend to spend less when there is a decline in the value of their portfolios, the stocks and bonds they own. Explain this behavior.

2. According to Alan Sinai's economic model, each $1.00 drop in the value of financial assets will reduce consumption spending by about $0.03. How would this affect the consumption function?

3. The article suggests that higher interest rates have also helped to discourage consumption (and investment) spending. Why do higher rates have this impact?

4. Think back to Chapter 10. What concerns would Keynes have if he learned that consumers were spending less? Are similar concerns being expressed in this article?

ample, may be attractive if the interest rate drops to 15 percent or 12 percent. To illustrate, suppose that you can purchase a soft-drink vending machine (which has a useful life of one year) for $1,000 and can borrow the money at 20 percent interest. Assume also that you expect to sell 5,000 cans of soft drink a year at $0.60 a can and plan to pay 0.36\frac{1}{2}$ for each can you buy. Would your investment be profitable? A few calculations show that it wouldn't be.

Anticipated revenue (5,000 cans sold at $0.60 per can)		$3,000
Anticipated costs		
Cost of the vending machine	$1,000	
Cost of the soft drinks (5,000 cans at 0.36\frac{1}{2}$)	$1,825	
Cost of borrowed funds ($1,000 at 20 percent)	$ 200	
Total cost		$3,025
Anticipated loss		$ 25

According to these calculations, you could expect to lose $25 on your investment if you had to pay 20 percent interest to borrow the money. So of course you wouldn't make the investment under those conditions. But if the interest rate declined to 15 percent, the cost of borrowing $1,000 for a year would drop to $150, and the investment would earn a profit of $25. If the interest rate declined further, the profit would be even greater. The point we are making is that lower interest rates encourage businesses to undertake investments that would be unattractive at higher rates. Thus we have a negative, or inverse, relationship between the rate of interest and the level of investment spending; the lower the interest rate, the higher the level of investment spending. This relationship is illustrated in Exh. 11.4.

Expectations about Revenues and Costs. Although the interest rate influences investment spending plans, it should be clear from our example that it is not the only factor to take into consideration. Businesses will continue to borrow and invest in spite of high interest rates if they are optimistic about future revenues (and costs) and the likelihood of earning a profit. For example, even a 20 or 25 percent interest rate would not discourage you from investing in the vending machine if you were convinced that you could sell 6,000 cans of the soft drink a year. On the other hand, an interest rate as low as 6 percent would be prohibitive if you were forecasting sales of only 4,500 cans. (Take the time to make some calculations and convince yourself of these conclusions.) In short, it is not interest rates themselves that determine the attractiveness of investment projects and the level of investment spending in the economy but rather the interaction of interest rates and expectations about future revenues and costs.

EXHIBIT 11.4

Investment and the Rate of Interest

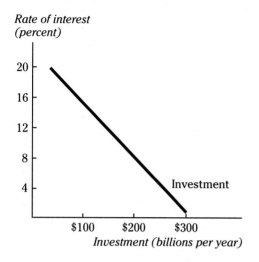

The rate of interest and the level of investment spending are negatively, or inversely, related; the lower the interest rate, the higher the level of investment spending.

The Instability of Investment

The preceding discussion shows why investment spending is much less stable than consumption spending. There are several reasons. First, the interest rate tends to change over time, and these changes cause businesses to alter their investment plans.

Second, businesses' expectations are quite volatile, or changeable. They are influenced by everything from current economic conditions to headlines in the newspaper. If a wave of optimism hits the country, planned investment may skyrocket. When pessimism strikes, investment plunges.

A third source of instability is the simple fact that plans to invest can be postponed. A business may want to build a more modern production plant to improve its competitive position. But if economic conditions suggest that this may not be the best time to build, the business can decide to make the old plant last a little longer.

Finally, investment opportunities occur irregularly, in spurts. New products and new production processes provide businesses with investment opportunities, but these developments do not occur in predictable patterns. A business may encounter several profitable investment opportunities one year and none the next.

Changing interest rates, the volatility of expectations, the ability to postpone investment spending, and the ups and downs of investment opportunities all lead to fluctuations and instability in the level of investment spending. Because investment spending accounts for more than 15 percent of the GDP, these changes can have a major impact on total output and employment in the economy. We'll have more to say about that impact later in this chapter.

The Equilibrium Level of Output

Now that we have analyzed the individual components of spending in our hypothetical economy, we are ready to combine them to see how total spending determines the level of output and employment. Remember: According to Keynesian theory, the level of demand—that is, total spending—determines the amount of output that will be produced and the number of jobs that will be made available. To see how the spending plans of consumers and investors determine the level of output and employment, we turn to Exh. 11.5.

Column 1 in Exh. 11.5 shows several possible levels of output (GDP) that our hypothetical economy could produce. Which level will be chosen by businesses depends on how much they expect to sell. Let's assume that businesses believe they can sell $600 billion worth of output. To produce this output, they hire economic resources: land, labor, capital, and entrepreneurship. This transaction provides households with $600 billion of income, an amount exactly equal to the value of total output. Recall that total income

EXHIBIT 11.5

Determination of Equilibrium Income and Output (data in billions)

(1) TOTAL OUTPUT AND INCOME* (GDP)	(2) PLANNED CONSUMPTION EXPENDITURES	(3) PLANNED SAVING (1–2)	(4) PLANNED INVESTMENT EXPENDITURES	(5) TOTAL PLANNED EXPENDITURES (2 + 4)	(6) TENDENCY OF OUTPUT
$300	$325	$−25	$50	$375	Increase
400	400	0	50	450	Increase
500	475	25	50	525	Increase
600	550	50	50	600	Equilibrium
700	625	75	50	675	Decrease
800	700	100	50	750	Decrease

*In our simplified economy total income = total disposable income = GDP.

must equal total output, because all the money received by businesses must be paid to someone.

Column 2 shows the amount that households plan to consume for each level of income (GDP) given in column 1. If the tabular data in column 2 were plotted on a graph, you would recognize the consumption function (Exh. 11.1). You can see that when GDP is $600 billion, households desire to consume $550 billion. Moving to column 3, you see that households want to save $50 billion when GDP is $600 billion.

The next category of spending is investment spending (column 4). Our example assumes that investment spending is autonomous, or independent of the level of current output. Unlike consumption spending, investment spending is determined by the factors described earlier: the rate of interest and expectations regarding future revenues and costs. The level of investment spending changes only if those determinants change. Here we've set the level of investment spending at $50 billion. (Later we'll allow the level of investment to change so that we can trace the impact of that change on the level of output and employment.)

In our simplified economy total spending (column 5) is the sum of consumption spending and investment spending. Note that the amount of total spending rises with the economy's GDP; higher levels of GDP signal higher levels of total spending, because consumption spending increases with income. If the business sector produces $600 billion of output, the result will be the creation of $550 billion of consumption spending and $50 billion of investment spending, or a total of $600 billion. This amount will be precisely enough to clear the market of that period's production. Most important, because businesses can sell exactly what they have produced, they will have no incentive to increase or decrease their rate of output. As you learned in Chapter 10, this means that the economy has arrived at its equilibrium output, the output that it will tend to maintain. Businesses can be expected to produce the same amount every year until they have reason to believe that the spending plans of consumers or investors have changed.

Inventory Adjustments and Equilibrium Output

The preceding example demonstrates that the economy will be in equilibrium only when *total spending is exactly equal to total output*.[1] In other words, an economy has arrived at its equilibrium output when the production of that

---

[1] You may remember from Chapter 10 that there is another way to identify the equilibrium output—by finding the output at which planned saving is equal to planned investment. You can see in Exh. 11.5 that planned saving is equal to planned investment at an output of $600 billion, the output already identified as equilibrium.

output level gives rise to precisely enough spending, or demand, to purchase everything that was produced. In our example $600 billion is the only output that satisfies this requirement. At any other output level, there will be either too much or too little demand, and producers will have incentive to alter their level of production.

Consider, for example, an output of $700 billion. As you have seen, producing $700 billion of output means creating $700 billion of income. Note, however, that not all this income will find its way back to businesses in the form of spending. Column 5 in Exh. 11.5 shows that only $675 billion of spending will be created—too little to absorb the period's production. Inventories of unsold merchandise will grow, signaling businesses to reduce the rate of output; this move will take the economy closer to equilibrium.

If spending initially exceeded output, the reaction of businesses would be exactly the opposite. For example, if $500 billion of output were produced, it would generate $525 billion of total spending. Because the amount that consumers and investors desire to spend exceeds the level of output, businesses can meet demand only if they supplement their current production with merchandise from their inventories. This unintended reduction in inventories is a signal to increase the rate of output, which in turn will push the economy closer to the equilibrium GDP.

As you can see, whenever spending is greater or less than output, producers have incentive to alter production levels; there is a natural tendency to move toward equilibrium. The only output that can be maintained is the output at which total spending is exactly equal to total output; this is the equilibrium output.

Equilibrium Output: A Graphic Presentation

The data in Exh. 11.5 are graphed in Exh. 11.6. The line labeled "C + I" (consumption plus investment) is the total-expenditure (or total-spending) function. This function is simply a graphic representation of column 5 from Exh. 11.5, showing the total amount of planned spending at each level of GDP. It is easy to understand why the total-expenditure function looks so much like the consumption function. Because we have assumed investment spending to be an autonomous constant—$50 billion per year—the total-spending function can be constructed simply by drawing a line parallel to line C (consumption) and exactly $50 billion above it. The other element of the output-expenditure diagram is the 45-degree line. At every point on this line, total-spending equals total output. We locate the equilibrium output where the total-spending function intersects the 45-degree line ($600 billion).

EXHIBIT 11.6

Determination of Equilibrium Income and Output

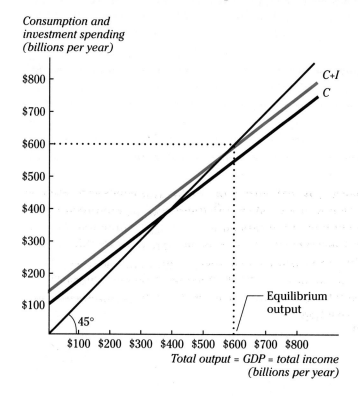

We can identify the equilibrium output by locating the output at which the total-expenditures function crosses the 45-degree line.

Changes in Spending and the Multiplier Effect

Changes in the spending plans of either consumers or investors will alter the equilibrium level of income and output in our hypothetical economy. At any given level of income (GDP), consumers may decide to spend more if they believe that prices are going to rise in the near future or if they expect wage and salary increases. Such a change in consumer expectations would be represented graphically by an upward shift of the consumption function. Similarly, investors may increase their rate of investment spending if they become more optimistic about the future or if interest rates decline. This change in the level of planned investment would be depicted by an upward shift of the investment function.

Because the economy's total-expenditure function is nothing more than the sum of the consumption and investment functions, an upward shift of either one would cause an upward shift of the total-expenditure function, which in turn would increase the equilibrium level of output. Any change resulting in a downward shift of the consumption or investment functions would reduce the equilibrium output.

To illustrate the impact of a change in the level of planned expenditures, let's assume that the rate of autonomous investment increases by $50 billion per year. This change is represented in Exh. 11.7 by a shift of the total expenditure function from $C + I_1$ to $C + I_2$. The most important thing to notice about this example is the relationship between the initial change in investment spending and the resulting change in total output. When investment spending increases by

EXHIBIT 11.7

The Multiplier Effect

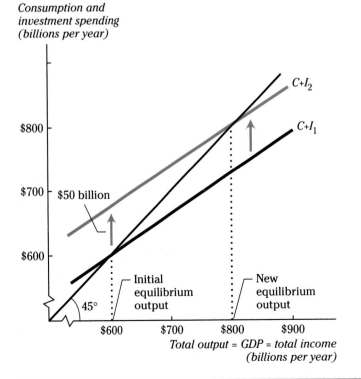

Because of the multiplier effect, an initial $50 billion increase in spending leads to a $200 billion increase in GDP.

$50 billion, total output increases by much more than that—by $200 billion, to be exact. This phenomenon—the fact that small changes in spending are magnified into larger changes in income and output—is called the **multiplier effect.**

The Multiplier Effect

In order to understand how the multiplier effect operates, let's trace the impact of this increase in investment spending as it works its way through the economy. Exhibit 11.8 illustrates the process. Period one shows the original equilibrium situation from Exh. 11.7 (note that total output equals total spending at $600 billion). In period two output and consumption spending remain unchanged, but investment spending increases from $50 billion to $100 billion. That pushes total spending up to $650 billion and disturbs the economy's equilibrium. Since the level of total spending in period two exceeds the economy's output, the demand can be met only by drawing inventories below their desired levels.

In period three producers increase their output to $650 billion in an attempt to catch up with demand. But when producers expand their output by $50 billion, they create an additional $50 billion of new income—the money that is paid to the owners of economic resources. Recall that our hypothetical economy was constructed with an *MPC* of 0.75. Therefore this $50 billion in-

---

EXHIBIT 11.8

Tracing the Impact of a Spending Increase (hypothetical data in billions)

PERIOD	TOTAL OUTPUT AND INCOME (GDP)	PLANNED CONSUMPTION EXPENDITURES	PLANNED INVESTMENT EXPENDITURES	TOTAL PLANNED EXPENDITURES
One	**$600.00**	$550.00	$ 50.00	**$600.00**
Two	600.00	550.00	100.00	650.00
Three	650.00	587.50	100.00	687.50
Four	687.50	615.63	100.00	715.63
Five	715.63	636.73	100.00	736.73
Six	736.73	652.56	100.00	752.56
—	—	—	—	—
—	—	—	—	—
Ultimately	**800.00**	700.00	100.00	**800.00**

crease in income leads to an additional $37.5 billion of consumption spending (75 percent of $50 billion). As a result, total spending rises by an additional $37.5 billion in period three, and output again fails to keep pace with demand.

In period four businesses expand their production to $687.5 billion, the level of demand in period three. This $37.5 billion increase in income (output) causes consumption spending to increase by $28.13 billion (75 percent of $37.5 billion). As a consequence, total spending in period four will rise by $28.13 billion, and since total spending continues to exceed total output, inventories again will fall.

As you can see, once equilibrium is disrupted, income and consumption spending continue to feed each other. Any change in income causes consumption spending to expand, which in turn causes income and output to expand still further. In theory the new equilibrium would be reached only after an infinite number of time periods. However, the increases in income and consumption become smaller as equilibrium is approached, so most of the expansionary effect is felt after the first half-dozen or so periods. In our example equilibrium is finally attained when output is equal to total spending at $800 billion. (Note that this is the output level at which the total-expenditure function crosses the 45-degree line in Exh. 11.7.)

Calculating the Multiplier

In the preceding example a $50 billion increase in investment spending led to a $200 billion increase in income and output. Thus the *multiplier* is 4. The **multiplier (M)** is the number by which any initial change in spending is multiplied to find the ultimate change in income and output.

If we know the marginal propensity to consume in our economy, we can estimate the size of the multiplier before the change in spending has run its course. Either of two simple formulas can be used:

$$M = \frac{1}{1 - MPC}$$

or, since $1 - MPC = MPS$,

$$M = \frac{1}{MPS}.$$

Applying the formula to our hypothetical economy (with an *MPC* of 0.75), we can verify that the multiplier is indeed 4:

$$M = \frac{1}{1 - MPC}$$

$$M = \frac{1}{1 - 0.75}$$

$$M = 4.$$

As we've already seen, a multiplier of 4 tells us that any increase in spending will generate an increase in equilibrium output that is four times as large. (The multiplier also works in reverse; if spending drops, we can expect equilibrium output to decline by four times as much.) Of course, the multiplier can take on different values, depending on the economy's *MPC*. If the *MPC* is 0.5, the multiplier will be 2; if the *MPC* is 0.8, the multiplier will be 5. As you can see, the size of the multiplier is related directly to the size of the economy's marginal propensity to consume: The larger the *MPC*, the larger the multiplier. This relationship exists because when the *MPC* is larger, a greater fraction of any increase in income is spent—meaning that more income is passed on to the next round of consumers, and the ultimate increase in GDP is larger. Studies of the U.S. economy show that the actual U.S. value of the multiplier in this country is about 2. (The U.S. economy's multiplier is significantly smaller than our hypothetical multiplier because taxes and spending for imports reduce the amount of income remaining to be passed on to the next household. When households pay taxes, they have less money to spend for products. Similarly, the money that goes to purchase Japanese autos and French wines leaves the country and is not available to be passed on to other U.S. consumers. The impact of taxation is discussed in the next chapter. To understand more about the effect of foreign trade on the economy's equilibrium GDP and multiplier, see the appendix at the end of this chapter.)

Equilibrium with Unemployment or Inflation

Now that we know how the equilibrium output is determined, we want to consider the desirability—from the standpoint of full employment and price stability—of a particular equilibrium GDP. We want to know whether a particular equilibrium is consistent with full employment, unemployment, or inflation.

The Recessionary Gap

Chapter 10 explained that a major conclusion of the Keynesian revolution is that a capitalist economy can be in equilibrium at less than full employment. Consider the economy represented in Exh. 11.9. Let's assume that $(C + I)_1$ represents the economy's total-expenditure function and that the existing level of equilibrium GDP is $600 billion. Let's make the additional assumption that $700 billion is the full-employment output—the level of output that allows us to achieve our target rate of unemployment. (Recall that our target rate of unemployment is higher than zero because a certain amount of frictional and

EXHIBIT 11.9

The Recessionary Gap

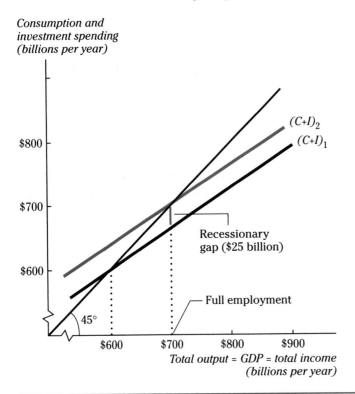

The recessionary gap is the amount by which spending falls short of what is needed to produce full employment.

structural unemployment is unavoidable, even in the best of times.) Given these assumptions, it is obvious that our hypothetical economy is in equilibrium at less than full employment. The problem, in Keynesian terms, is *too little spending.* If full employment is to be achieved, the level of planned spending must be increased so that the total-expenditure function intersects the 45-degree line at $700 billion.

You can see that a function such as $(C + I)_2$ would give such an intersection. The vertical distance between $(C + I)_1$ and $(C + I)_2$ is the **recessionary gap**—the amount by which total spending falls short of what is needed for full employment. It is called a recessionary gap because a deficiency of spending tends to produce a period of recession, or unemployment.[2] In our example

---

[2] Technically, a recession is a period during which the economy's real output declines. Of course, if less output is being produced, fewer employees are needed, so unemployment tends to rise.

the recessionary gap equals $25 billion. With a multiplier of 4, a $25 billion increase in planned expenditure would increase the equilibrium output by $100 billion and bring about full employment.

The Inflationary Gap

Although Keynes devoted most of his efforts to studying unemployment, the Keynesian framework can also be used to explain inflation. Referring to Exh. 11.10, let's assume that $(C + I)_1$ is the existing planned-expenditure function and that the prevailing level of equilibrium GDP is $800 billion. Recalling that the full-employment output is $700 billion, you will recognize that our hypothetical economy now faces a different problem: inflation.

If $700 billion is the full-employment output, the economy cannot provide more than $700 billion worth of goods and services. In the Keynesian model full employment implies that the economy is operating at full capacity, that it is not capable of producing any more output. If consumers and investors at-

---

EXHIBIT 11.10

The Inflationary Gap

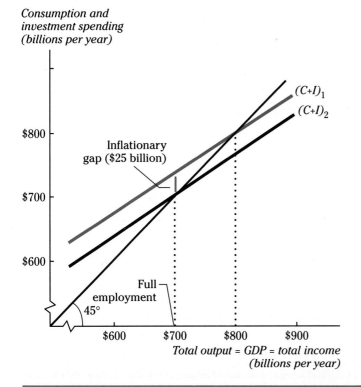

The inflationary gap is the amount by which total spending exceeds what is needed to produce full employment.

tempt to purchase more output than the economy is capable of producing, higher prices result as prospective buyers bid against one another. Real GDP, however, will not increase.

In this simple model prices are assumed to be constant until full employment is reached. So long as there are unemployed resources, any increase in spending is translated into an increase in output and employment. Once full employment is reached, however, further output increases become impossible. From this point on, increases in spending cannot increase real GDP; they can increase only money GDP. The difference between a GDP of $700 billion and a GDP of $800 billion is not that the larger figure represents more output, but simply that higher prices are being paid for the full-employment output.[3]

If inflation is to be eliminated without sacrificing full employment, the level of planned spending must be reduced so that the total-expenditure function intersects the 45-degree line at $700 billion. The expenditure function $(C + I)_2$ would give such an intersection. The vertical distance between $(C + I)_1$ and $(C + I)_2$ is the **inflationary gap**—the amount by which total spending exceeds what is needed to achieve full employment.

In this example the inflationary gap is $25 billion. With a multiplier of 4 in our hypothetical economy, a $25 billion decrease in planned expenditures would reduce equilibrium GDP by $100 billion while still maintaining full employment.

As you can see, the Keynesian model suggests that a market economy does not always come to rest at a full-employment equilibrium. Instead, the equilibrium output may be consistent with unemployment or inflation. In the next chapter we will examine how government spending and taxation policy can be used to combat these problems. We will also discuss some of the difficulties associated with attempting to guide the economy's performance.

Summary

According to Keynesian theory, the primary determinant of the level of total output and total employment is the level of total spending. The greater the level of total spending, the more output businesses will want to produce and the more employees they will hire. In a simplified economy with no government sector and no foreign trade, the level of output and employment would be determined by the level of consumption and investment spending.

The most important factor influencing the amount of consumption spending is the level of *disposable income,* or income after taxes. The relationship

---

[3] In reality, increases in total expenditures or aggregate demand can lead to increased output *and* higher prices even before full employment is reached. This possibility was previewed in Chapter 10 and will be considered in more detail in Chapter 14.

between disposable income and consumption spending is called the *consumption function*. In Keynesian theory a positive relationship exists between disposable income and consumption spending; the more people earn, the more they spend.

The way that households react to changes in income depends on their *marginal propensity to consume (MPC)*. The *MPC* is the fraction of each additional earned dollar that households spend on consumption. The *marginal propensity to save (MPS)* is the fraction of each additional earned dollar that is saved. The *MPC* and *MPS* must add to 1.00, or 100 percent: If *MPC* is 0.80, *MPS* is 0.20.

Profit expectations are the overriding motivation in all investment-spending plans. These expectations are based on a comparison of costs (including the cost of the capital equipment and the cost of borrowing the money to buy that equipment) and revenues (the revenues the investment project is expected to generate). If the investment is expected to generate revenues that exceed all anticipated costs, the investment should be made; if not, the investment should not be made.

In deciding how much output to produce, businesses attempt to estimate the spending plans of consumers and investors. If they estimate demand correctly, they will be able to sell exactly what they produced; hence they will tend to produce the same amount in the next period. If not, they will alter their production plans in order to match demand more closely.

The level of output at which the economy stabilizes is the equilibrium output. The equilibrium output is one that is neither expanding nor contracting and that tends to be maintained. It can be identified by finding the level of output at which total spending (consumption plus investment) is equal to total output. The equilibrium output can be determined graphically by finding the output at which the total-expenditures function ($C + I$) intersects the 45-degree line.

Once the equilibrium output has been established, it will be maintained until there is some change in the spending plans of consumers or investors. To determine the ultimate impact on equilibrium of any change in spending, it is necessary to know the value of the *multiplier (M)*, the number by which any initial change in spending is multiplied to get the ultimate change in equilibrium income and output. The multiplier can be calculated by using either of the following formulas:

$$M = \frac{1}{1-MPC}$$

or, since $1 - MPC = MPS$,

$$M = \frac{1}{MPS}.$$

Perhaps the most important contribution Keynes made was to demonstrate that a market economy can be in equilibrium at less than full employment. He attributed this occurrence to too little spending. The amount by which total spending falls short of what is needed to provide full employment is called the *recessionary gap*. When inflation exists, the problem is too much spending. The *inflationary gap* is the amount by which total spending exceeds what is needed to achieve full employment.

Glossary

Consumption function. The relationship between disposable income and consumption spending. A consumption function shows the amount that households plan to spend at different levels of income.

Disposable income. Income after taxes. Disposable income is sometimes described as your take-home pay.

Dissaving. Taking money out of savings accounts or borrowing in order to finance consumption spending.

Inflationary gap. The amount by which total spending exceeds what is needed to achieve full employment.

Marginal propensity to consume (MPC). The fraction of any increase in income that is spent on consumption. The formula for the marginal propensity to consume (*MPC*) is

$$MPC = \frac{\text{Change in consumption spending}}{\text{Change in income}}.$$

Marginal propensity to save (MPS). The fraction of any increase in income that households plan to save. The formula for the marginal propensity to save (*MPS*) is

$$MPS = \frac{\text{Change in saving}}{\text{Change in income}}.$$

Multiplier (M). The number by which any initial change in spending is multiplied to get the ultimate change in equilibrium income and output. The formula for the multiplier (*M*) is

$$M = \frac{1}{1 - MPC} \text{ or } M = \frac{1}{MPS}.$$

Multiplier effect. The magnified impact on GDP of any initial change in spending.

Recessionary gap. The amount by which total spending falls short of what is needed to produce full employment.

> *Saving.* The act of not spending. Also, the part of income not spent on goods and services.

Study Questions

Fill in the Blanks

1. According to Keynes, the primary determinant of the level of total output and total employment is the level of _____.

2. The _____ is the fraction of any increase in income that households plan to save.

3. Keynes believed the primary determinant of the level of consumption spending to be the level of _____.

4. In the Keynesian model, if the economy is suffering from unemployment, the problem is caused by _____ ; if the economy is suffering from inflation, the problem is caused by _____.

5. The _____ shows the precise relationship between income and consumption spending.

6. The level of output that tends to be maintained is called the _____ output.

7. If total spending exceeds the amount necessary to achieve full employment, the economy must be suffering from _____.

8. We can determine the equilibrium output by finding the output at which total spending equals _____.

9. Graphically, equilibrium exists where the total-expenditures function ($C + I$) crosses the _____.

10. The amount by which total spending falls short of what is needed to provide full employment is called the _____.

Multiple Choice

1. When Jim's income increased by $1,000, he decided to spend $600 and save the rest. That means his marginal propensity
   a) to save is 0.6.
   b) to consume is $600.
   c) to consume is 0.6.
   d) to consume is 0.4.

2. If the economy's *MPS* is 0.2, the multiplier would be
   a) 0.8.
   b) 20.
   c) 5.
   d) 4.

Use the following information to answer questions 3–6.

INCOME	CONSUMPTION
$100 billion	$160 billion
200	240
300	320
400	400
500	480
600	560

3. What is the marginal propensity to consume in this hypothetical economy?
   a) 0.8
   b) 0.5
   c) 0.75
   d) $80

4. At what income level would the consumption function cross the 45-degree line in this hypothetical economy?
   a) $200 billion
   b) $300 billion
   c) $400 billion
   d) $500 billion
   e) None of the above

5. If businesses plan to invest $20 billion, what would be the equilibrium level of output in this economy? (*Hint:* Remember what makes up total expenditures.)
   a) $200 billion
   b) $300 billion
   c) $400 billion
   d) $500 billion
   e) None of the above

6. At an income of $700 billion, how much would households desire to consume? (It's not on the schedule, but you can use your previous answers to figure it out.)
   a) $560 billion
   b) $580 billion
   c) $620 billion
   d) $640 billion
   e) $700 billion

7. Assuming that the economy's *MPC* is 0.8, if autonomous investment spending increases by $15 billion, how much will equilibrium GDP increase?
   a) $15 billion
   b) $30 billion

   c) $45 billion
   d) $60 billion
   e) $75 billion

8. If people expected prices to be higher in the future, this would probably cause
   a) their current consumption function to shift down.
   b) their current saving function to shift up.
   c) their current consumption function to shift up.
   d) the investment function to shift down.

9. Keynes focused particular attention on investment spending because
   a) investment spending is the largest component of total spending.
   b) only investment spending is subject to a multiplier effect.
   c) investment spending is very volatile, or changeable.
   d) investment spending is the most reliable, or predictable, component of total spending.

10. If the economy produces a level of output that is too small for equilibrium,
    a) there will be an unintended, or unplanned, increase in inventories.
    b) businesses will not be able to sell everything that they've produced.
    c) there will be an unintended, or unplanned, decrease in inventories.
    d) there will be a tendency for output to fall (decline) in the next period.

Problems and Questions for Discussion

1. In the hypothetical economy we explored in this chapter, total income equals disposable income. What assumption makes that true?

2. If the consumption function were a 45-degree line, what would that mean?

3. How do businesses decide which investment projects to pursue and which to reject?

4. Discuss the reasons why the rate of investment spending is less stable than the rate of consumption spending.

5. How can a change in the level of investment spending indirectly cause a change in the level of consumption spending?

6. Referring to Exh. 11.5, assume that the level of autonomous investment is $25 billion instead of $50 billion. What would be the equilibrium level of output?

7. What might cause the level of investment spending to decline, as hypothesized in the preceding question?

8. What is the difference between the equilibrium output and a full-employment equilibrium?

9. What are the recessionary and inflationary gaps? Represent them graphically.

10. What assumption is made about the behavior of prices in the simple model used in this chapter?

Answer Key

Fill in the Blanks

1. total spending
2. marginal propensity to save
3. disposable income
4. too little spending; too much spending
5. consumption function
6. equilibrium
7. inflation
8. total output
9. 45-degree line
10. recessionary gap

Multiple Choice

1. c	3. a	5. d	7. e	9. c
2. c	4. c	6. d	8. c	10. c

APPENDIX: Incorporating Foreign Trade into the Keynesian Model

For simplicity, we've ignored foreign trade as we've discussed the Keynesian model. But we can consider the more important aspects without making the analysis too complex.

Imports are goods and services purchased from foreign producers. Americans' purchases of Sony TVs and BMW automobiles and Reebok tennis shoes are imports. Import spending represents a leakage (like saving), since it reduces the amount of income spent on the consumption of domestic goods and services. (To refresh your memory regarding leakages and injections, review the discussion of equilibrium output in Chapter 10.) Column 3 in Exh. A.1 shows our hypothetical imports of foreign products. As you can see, import spending increases with income, just as consumption spending does. If we deduct imports from our total consumption spending, we arrive at our *domestic consumption spending*—the amount that households spend on products made in the United States. Of course, only domestic consumption spending helps to employ Americans; import spending employs workers in other countries.

Imports are only half of the foreign-trade component; the other half is *exports*—goods and services produced domestically and sold to customers in other countries. When consumers in Japan and Great Britain buy Ford Mustangs and Apple computers, U.S. exports increase. Like investment spending, exports are an injection, an addition to the basic flow of consumption spending. Spending for exports increases total spending for domestic products and thereby stimulates total output and employment. Column 6 shows exports as an autonomous constant equal to $100 billion.

EXHIBIT A.1

Imports, Exports, and Equilibrium Output (in billions)

(1) TOTAL INCOME	(2) TOTAL CON-SUMPTION	(3) IMPORTS	(4) DOMESTIC CON-SUMPTION	(5) INVEST-MENT	(6) EXPORTS	(7) TOTAL SPEND-ING	(8) TENDENCY OF OUTPUT
$400	$400	$ 50	$350	$ 50	$100	$500	Increase
500	475	75	400	50	100	550	Increase
600	550	100	450	50	100	600	Equilibrium
700	625	125	500	50	100	650	Decrease

When imports equal exports, the amount that the foreign sector is subtracting from the spending flow is exactly equal to the amount that is being added, and the economy's equilibrium output is unaffected by foreign trade. In other words, the level of equilibrium GDP will be the same with trade as without. In our example imports equal exports at $600 billion, so the level of equilibrium GDP is unaltered from that presented in Exh. 11.5.

Now suppose that Americans decide to start buying more Japanese Toyotas and Hondas instead of U.S. Fords and Chevrolets and that they switch from U.S. wines to those from France and Italy. What will these changes do to the level of equilibrium GDP in our economy? To find out, let's assume that Americans decide to spend $50 billion more on imports at every income level (Exh. A.2). Since spending on imports (column 3) has increased, more is being subtracted from total consumption (column 2), and domestic consumption (column 4) will fall. Of course, this will reduce total spending for domestic products and cause the economy's equilibrium GDP to fall.

How far will the equilibrium level of GDP decline? As you already know, we can predict the change in equilibrium GDP by multiplying the initial change in spending times the multiplier. In this instance the initial change in spending is $50 (the increase in imports), but what is the multiplier? As before, the multiplier is equal to $1/1 - $ MPC. But when imports exist, we must consider the marginal propensity to consume *domestic products*. As you can see from column 4, each $100 billion increase in income causes domestic consumption to rise by $50 billion; the marginal propensity to consume domestic products is 0.50, or $\frac{1}{2}$. That means that the multiplier is 2 (1/0.5 = 2). If you multiply the change in imports ($50 billion) times the multiplier (2), you see that equilibrium GDP falls by $100 billion. Exhibit A.2 confirms that answer; equilibrium GDP falls from $600 billion to $500 billion.

EXHIBIT A.2

The Impact of a Change in Imports (in billions)

(1) TOTAL INCOME	(2) TOTAL CONSUMPTION	(3) IMPORTS	(4) DOMESTIC CONSUMPTION	(5) INVESTMENT	(6) EXPORTS	(7) TOTAL SPENDING	(8) TENDENCY OF OUTPUT
$400	$400	$100	$300	$ 50	$100	$450	Increase
500	475	125	350	50	100	500	Equilibrium
600	550	150	400	50	100	550	Decrease
700	625	175	450	50	100	600	Decrease

Of course, falling imports (or rising exports) would have the opposite effect; it would raise equilibrium GDP. If more Americans decide that they prefer domestic cars to those made by the Japanese (or more Japanese decide that they prefer those made in the United States), total spending for domestic products will increase, and so will equilibrium GDP.

In summary, anything that causes Americans to buy more imports or foreigners to buy fewer U.S. exports will shift the total expenditure curve downward and lower the equilibrium GDP. Anything that causes Americans to buy fewer imports or foreigners to buy more of our exports will shift the total expenditure curve upward and expand equilibrium GDP. To test your understanding of the impact of foreign trade on equilibrium GDP, answer the following questions:

1. In 1994 the prices of many imported products were rising more rapidly than the prices of domestically produced goods and services. What impact would you expect this trend to have on U.S. imports, exports, and GDP?

2. Recessions elsewhere in the world can sometimes spill over and reduce equilibrium GDP (or at least slow the rate of economic growth) in the United States. Explain how this can occur.

3. Items such as Levis blue jeans and Ford Mustangs have become increasingly popular in Japan and other foreign countries. How would this increased popularity affect U.S. gross domestic product, and why would it have this impact?

4. The *exchange rate* is the price of one country's currency stated in terms of some other country's currency. For example, at present $1 costs, or exchanges for, approximately 100 Japanese yen. Thus a U.S. product selling for $100 would cost the Japanese 10,000 yen.

   Suppose that the exchange value of the dollar declined (the technical term is "depreciated") so that $1 would buy only 50 yen. Would you expect U.S. imports to rise or to fall? What would happen to U.S. exports? What impact would these changes have on equilibrium GDP?

5. When we introduce imports into an economy, the size of the economy's multiplier gets smaller. Why does the introduction of imports reduce the size of an economy's multiplier. (*Hint:* Why does the multiplier get smaller when the marginal propensity to save increases?)

Fiscal Policy

When politicians speak of "stimulating the economy through a tax cut" or "imposing austerity measures to combat inflation" or "creating jobs through government spending," they are talking about **discretionary fiscal policy**—the deliberate changing of the level of government spending or taxation in order to guide the economy's performance.[1]

In the Keynesian model, as you have learned, spending is the key to the economy's aggregate performance. More total spending means more output and more jobs. If there is unemployment, the source of the problem is too little spending—too little demand for goods and services. Keynes pointed out that

---

[1] In addition to discretionary fiscal policy, the economy is also influenced by automatic fiscal policy, or built-in stabilizers that reduce the magnitude of fluctuations in total spending without any discretionary action by decision makers. These built-in stabilizers are discussed later in the chapter.

the federal government can combat unemployment by increasing government spending, reducing taxes, or doing both. These policies will increase the amount of total spending in the economy, which in turn will increase the level of output and employment.

If inflation occurs, a different set of policies is called for. According to the Keynesian model, inflation is caused by too much spending, by people trying to buy more goods and services than the economy can produce. The proper fiscal response to inflation is a reduction in government spending, an increase in taxes, or both.

In this chapter we take a detailed look at how Keynesians believe fiscal policy can be used to combat unemployment or inflation. In addition, we consider the limitations of fiscal policy and examine the impact of specific policy measures on the federal budget and the federal debt.

Fiscal Policy and the *AD-AS* Model

We can use the aggregate demand–aggregate supply framework introduced in Chapter 10 to illustrate how fiscal policy can be used to combat unemployment or inflation.

Recall that in the Keynesian model, the price level is assumed to be constant until full employment is reached. This gives us an aggregate supply curve that is horizontal until full employment is reached. Once full employment is reached, the aggregate supply curve becomes vertical because attempts to purchase more than the full employment output cause the price level to rise with no change in output. The aggregate supply curve represented in Exhibit 12.1 is consistent with these assumptions.

Suppose that the economy is in equilibrium at point A with an output of $800 billion and a price level of 100 billion. As you can see from the exhibit, the economy is well below the full employment output of 100 billion, so it is experiencing substantial unemployment. The Keynesian remedy for this problem is to increase government spending or reduce taxes. Because each aggregate demand curve assumes a constant level of government spending and taxation, altering either of these variables will shift the curve. For example, increasing government spending will cause more total output to be demanded at each and every price level, shifting the *AD* curve to the right. A tax reduction could have the same effect, since reducing taxes would allow consumers to increase their spending. By using either of these policies the federal government could shift the aggregate demand curve from AD_1 to AD_2 and restore the full employment equilibrium of 1,000 billion.

Fiscal policy can also be used to combat inflation. Suppose, for the example, that the economy is in equilibrium at point B; it is experiencing full em-

EXHIBIT 12.1

Using Fiscal Policy to Combat Unemployment or Inflation

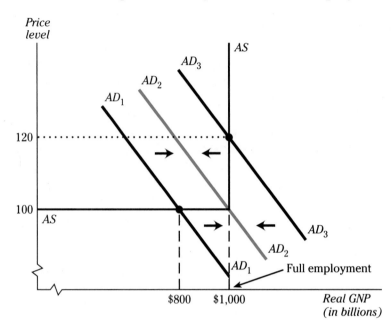

If the economy is in equilibrium at point A, increasing government spending or reducing taxes can shift aggregate demand from AD_1 to AD_2 and restore full employment. If the economy is operating at point B, the price level can be reduced by increasing taxes or lowering government spending to shift the aggregate demand curve from AD_3 to AD_2.

ployment but the price level has been pushed up to 120. Policymakers can attack the inflation problem by reducing government spending and/or increasing taxes. Either of these policies will cause less total output to be demanded at each price level, and will thereby shift the AD curve to the left. By shifting the AD curve from AD_3 to AD_2, the economy can reduce total spending in the economy and thereby reduce inflationary pressures.

Now that you have a general understanding of how fiscal policy works, we turn to a more detailed analysis using the Keynesian aggregate expenditures model studied in Chapter 11. Readers wishing to omit this coverage can turn to page 367 and resume reading with the section entitled "Automatic Fiscal Policy: The Built-In Stabilizers."

Government Spending and Equilibrium Output

The Keynesian aggregate expenditures model explored in Chapter 11 contained only two sectors, households and businesses. So before we can use this model to discuss fiscal policy, we must incorporate government spending and taxation into the model. To keep the presentation as clear as possible, we will introduce government spending first, note the impact on equilibrium output, and then introduce taxation.[2]

For the sake of our analysis, we assume that the level of government spending is determined by political considerations and is independent of the level of output in the economy. These assumptions allow us to add government spending to the model as an autonomous constant. Recall from Chapter 11 that investment spending was introduced in the same way, as a component of spending that did not vary with GDP.

Exhibit 12.2 shows how the inclusion of government spending alters the process of determining equilibrium. Let's assume that the government plans to spend $40 billion per year and that it intends to finance its spending by borrowing rather than by imposing taxes. To incorporate this decision into our analysis, we need only add the amount of government spending for goods and services (G) to the total-expenditure function ($C + I$) we constructed in Chapter 11. (You may find it helpful to review Exhs. 11.5 and 11.6.) In our two-sector economy total spending was represented as consumption spending (C) plus investment spending (I). In Exh. 12.2, total spending is labeled $C + I + G$. Adding government spending raises total spending by $40 billion at every level of output.

The equilibrium output is determined by the intersection of the total expenditure function (now $C + I + G$) and the 45-degree line. You can see that the addition of $40 billion of government spending increases the equilibrium output by $160 billion—that is, from $600 billion to $760 billion. Here we see the multiplier effect in operation. Recall from Chapter 11 that in our hypothetical economy the marginal propensity to consume is 0.75. The multiplier [$M = 1/(1 - MPC)$], therefore, is 4. This tells us that any change in spending will produce a change in income and output that is four times larger than the initial spending change.

In practical terms what happens here is identical to what happened when there was a change in the level of investment spending. The immediate impact of the addition of $40 billion of government spending is to increase the economy's income by $40 billion. With an MPC of 0.75, this will cause a $30 billion increase in consumption spending and a $10 billion increase in saving. When the $30 billion is spent, it will provide new income to yet another group, which will spend part of what it receives (75 percent of $30 billion) and

---

[2] We use the term *government spending* to mean purchases of goods and services. Economists always distinguish between expenditures for goods and services and transfer payments. *Government transfer payments* are expenditures made by the government for which it receives no goods or services in return (welfare payments, unemployment compensation, and Social Security benefits, for example). To avoid unnecessary complexity, our model will ignore transfer payments. Later in the chapter, however, we will discuss the role of transfer payments as "built-in stabilizers" of the economy.

EXHIBIT 12.2

Adding Government Expenditures

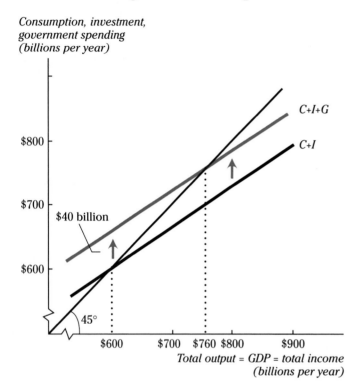

Consumption, investment, government spending (billions per year)

$800

$700

$40 billion

$600

45°

$600 $700 $760 $800 $900

Total output = GDP = total income (billions per year)

$C+I+G$

$C+I$

With a multiplier of 4, the addition of $40 billion worth of government spending raises the equilibrium GDP by $160 billion.

save the rest. This expansion in spending and output will continue until eventually total spending equals total output (where the $C + I + G$ function crosses the 45-degree line) so that the economy is again in equilibrium. In our example this occurs at a GDP of $760 billion.

Taxation and Equilibrium Output

Now that we've incorporated government spending into our model, we can introduce taxation and note its impact on the equilibrium level of output. To simplify our analysis, we will assume that personal income taxes are the only form of taxation in our hypothetical economy.

Suppose the government decides to collect $40 billion in personal income taxes in order to finance its spending plans. How does this affect the equilibrium level of GDP? The initial impact of this action is to reduce disposable in-come—income after taxes, or take-home pay—by $40 billion. So long as we ig-nored taxes, total income (GDP) equaled disposable income (*DI*). But now that we are introducing taxes, this equality no longer holds. The imposition of taxes reduces the amount of disposable income that households have avail-able at any given level of GDP. We have seen that the level of disposable in-come determines the level of consumption spending. If disposable income declines, consumption spending will decline. Thus the ultimate impact of tax-ation is a reduction in the amount of consumption spending at any given level of GDP. This can be represented by a downward shift of the consumption function, which in turn will cause a downward shift of $C + I + G$ (the total ex-penditure function).

Exhibit 12.3 shows that the total-expenditure function shifts downward by $30 billion when the government imposes taxes of $40 billion. Why doesn't

---

EXHIBIT 12.3

The Effect of Taxation

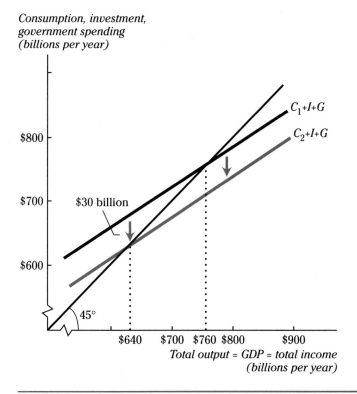

Consumption, investment, government spending (billions per year)

Total output = GDP = total income (billions per year)

When the government imposes taxes of $40 billion, the total-expenditure function shifts down by $30 billion. Because the *MPC* is 0.75, a reduction in disposable income of $40 billion (the amount of the taxes) will reduce consumption spending by 3/4 of that amount, or $30 billion. This $30 billion is then subject to the multiplier of 4, so the ultimate impact of the taxation is to reduce the equilibrium GDP by $120 billion.

the total expenditure function shift downward by *$40* billion? The answer is that households react to reductions in disposable income by reducing both their consumption and their saving. If the marginal propensity to consume is 0.75, 75 percent of the reduction in disposable income will come from planned consumption spending, and 25 percent will come from planned saving. Thus the consumption function—and consequently the total-expenditure function—will shift downward by 75 percent of $40 billion, or $30 billion.

Note that in this case the equilibrium level of GDP falls from $760 billion to $640 billion, a reduction of $120 billion. Once again, this represents the impact of the multiplier. The $30 billion reduction in consumption spending is magnified by the multiplier of 4 and thus produces a $120 billion reduction in GDP.

Given the fact that government spending and taxation affect total spending and equilibrium output, let's see how changes in government spending and taxation can be used as economic policy tools to combat the problems of unemployment or inflation.

Fiscal Policy to Achieve Full Employment

Suppose our economy's full-employment output is $700 billion. With our present equilibrium of $640, some unemployment will result. According to the Keynesian model, the source of the problem is too little spending; in other words, a recessionary gap exists.

One corrective approach is the use of discretionary fiscal policy. According to Keynesian theory, if the problem is unemployment, the appropriate policy response is to increase government spending or reduce taxes (or effect some combination of the two). Let's consider these alternatives.

If government spending is increased while taxes remain unchanged, the amount of total spending in the economy will increase. More spending for goods and services means that businesses will be justified in increasing their production, which will create more jobs.

We must use our knowledge of the multiplier to determine how much more government spending will be necessary. The multiplier in our hypothetical economy is 4; therefore every additional dollar that the government spends will ultimately produce a four-dollar increase in total spending and equilibrium output. If we wish to increase GDP by $60 billion, government spending must be increased by $15 billion ($60 billion ÷ 4 = $15 billion). Exhibit 12.4 shows that a $15 billion increase, when expanded by a multiplier of 4, will produce the needed $60 billion increase in GDP and permit our hypothetical economy to achieve full employment. In an economy with a multiplier of 2, the government would have to increase spending by $30 billion to

EXHIBIT 12.4

Expansionary Fiscal Policy

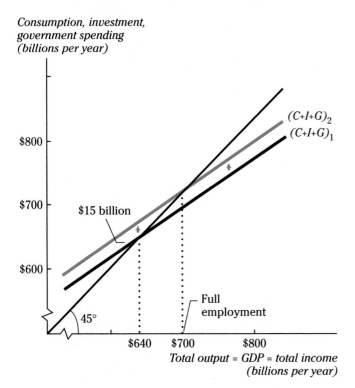

*Consumption, investment,
government spending
(billions per year)*

$(C+I+G)_2$

$(C+I+G)_1$

$800

$700

$15 billion

$600

45°

Full
employment

$640 $700 $800

*Total output = GDP = total income
(billions per year)*

In order to increase the equilibrium output by $60 billion (and achieve full employment), we must either increase government spending by $15 billion or reduce taxes by $20 billion. Either policy will shift the total-expenditure function upward by $15 billion. This amount, when expanded by the multiplier of 4, will result in an increase in GDP of $60 billion, the amount needed to reach full employment.

achieve the same $60 billion increase in GDP. (Recall from Chapter 11 that studies show the value of the multiplier in the U.S. economy to be approximately 2.)

The goal of full employment can also be pursued by cutting taxes and leaving government spending unchanged. If taxes are reduced, consumers are left with more disposable income, which enables them to increase their consumption spending. This increase in the demand for consumer goods stimulates producers to increase their output and creates additional jobs. Determining the precise amount of a tax reduction to combat unemployment is more complicated than determining the right amount to increase government spending. When taxes are reduced, consumers will not spend all of the additional disposable income the reduction provides; they will save some portion of their increased income.

We saw that $15 billion in increased spending is needed to close the recessionary gap. By what amount must we reduce income taxes to prompt consumers to spend an additional $15 billion? If the *MPC* is 0.75, taxes must be reduced by $20 billion (0.75 × $20 billion = $15 billion).[3] Because consumers will spend 75 percent of any increase in disposable income, a tax reduction of $20 billion will lead to a $15 billion increase in consumption spending and, through the multiplier, a $60 billion increase in equilibrium GDP. Because not all of it will be spent, a tax reduction used to stimulate spending and promote full employment must be somewhat larger than the increase in government spending that would accomplish the same objective.

Fiscal Policy to Combat Inflation

When Keynes developed his landmark economic theory in the mid-1930s, his main concern was unemployment. The remedy he prescribed was an expansionary fiscal policy that would increase government spending or reduce taxes to get the economy moving. But Keynes realized that fiscal policy could also serve to combat inflation. If society attempts to purchase more goods and services than the economy is capable of producing, a reduction in government spending or an increase in taxes will help reduce inflationary pressures.

If the government spends less, one component of total spending (*G*) is reduced directly, and consumption spending (*C*) is reduced indirectly through the multiplier effect. A tax increase has a different impact. Consumers who pay higher taxes find themselves with less disposable income; this forces them to reduce their consumption spending. Either way, total spending is reduced.

As you might expect, the fiscal policy used to fight inflation is considerably less popular than the policy used to combat unemployment. The prescriptions for dealing with unemployment—reducing taxes and increasing government spending—are generally applauded. Inflation-fighting measures usually meet with less widespread approval.

In 1966, when increased defense spending began to push an already strong economy closer to its productive capacity, many economists were calling for a tax increase to slow the growth of spending and prevent inflation.[4] President Johnson decided not to request such an increase at that time, believing that it would increase opposition to the Vietnam War. When the tax in-

---

[3] To determine the proper amount to increase or decrease taxes, you must divide the needed change in spending by the *MPC* (needed change in spending ÷ *MPC* = amount of tax change). In this example the needed spending change is $15 billion and the *MPC* is 0.75, so taxes ought to be altered by $15 billion ÷ 0.75 = $20 billion. Remember that to increase spending, taxes must be *reduced*, so it is a $20 billion tax reduction. TAXES increase   Spending decrease
[4] Concern about a weak economy had prompted a tax *cut* only two years earlier. That 1964 tax cut is discussed later in the chapter.

crease was finally requested in 1967, Congress delayed action until 1968. By that time inflation was well under way and proved very difficult to combat. The reluctance of politicians to employ restrictive policies—to increase taxes or reduce government spending—adds a dimension of uncertainty to the logic of economics where inflation is concerned. (U.S. policymakers have used Keynesian fiscal policy to influence our economy's performance. But what about other nations? Read "Hosokawa Produces Stimulus Package," on page 368, to learn how the Japanese attempt to guide their economy.)

Automatic Fiscal Policy: The Built-In Stabilizers

One of the major limitations of discretionary fiscal policy is the fact that a significant time can elapse between the appearance of unemployment or inflation and the response of policymakers. Policymakers may respond more promptly to unemployment than to inflation (since the policies for combating unemployment are more palatable politically), but even here some lag exists. It takes time for policymakers to get a clear signal that a problem exists and to gain subsequent legislative approval for a tax or spending bill. Meanwhile the problem may worsen and become more difficult to combat. Fortunately the fiscal system of the U.S. economy contains a number of **built-in stabilizers:** automatic changes that reduce the magnitude of fluctuations in total spending and thereby help prevent wide swings in the level of output and employment.[5]

The federal income tax is one such powerful built-in stabilizer. As you know, your income taxes increase as your income increases. (Taxes in the real world are not as independent of income as they are in our hypothetical economy.) Whenever taxes depend on income, any increase in salaries and wages means higher taxes as well. Thus when incomes rise, consumption spending does not rise as much as it would without taxes. Because this limits the rapid growth of spending during a period of economic expansion, it helps to prevent or slow inflation. As the economy weakens, the tax system operates in reverse. Declines in income mean lower taxes; consumers are left with more income to spend than they would have if taxes remained constant. Thus the income tax helps stabilize spending and retard the weakening of the economy.

Unemployment compensation and welfare benefits also operate as built-in stabilizers. When the level of economic activity declines and the jobless rate begins to rise, the total amount paid out by the government in the form of un-

---

[5] Built-in stabilizers are sometimes referred to as automatic, or nondiscretionary, fiscal policy.

Hosokawa Produces Stimulus Package

Analysts Expect the Impact on Japan's Economy to be Slight, Temporary

TOKYO

Prime Minister Morihiro Hosokawa hammered out a $140 billion stimulus package that may not get Japan's economy racing but should keep it from reversing again.

The package, which includes a one-year cut in income taxes totaling 5.47 trillion yen ($50.3 billion) and much-needed aid for the nation's struggling banks, ought to add between one and two percentage points of growth to the economy, analysts say. But they warn that the steps won't end Japan's downturn, and worry that the temporary nature of the tax cut might blunt its stimulative effect.

"It's not the best outcome possible, but it's better than waiting further," said Mitsubishi Bank Ltd. economist Donald Kimball. "At best, it might just shore up the economy in the medium term." . . .

Meeting in Washington

Mr. Hosokawa rushed out the measures in order to have something to show President Clinton when the two leaders meet in Washington on Friday. The U.S. has been pressing Japan to boost its economy so that it will import more. But economists say the package probably won't fully satisfy Mr. Clinton.

In Washington—where U.S. officials have argued that only Japan has the wherewithal to cut taxes and spur world economic growth—Treasury Secretary Lloyd Bentsen responded cautiously. "This is a modest step. Every little bit helps," he said. "It remains to be seen whether this package will be adequate to spur strong demand.". . .

U.S. officials say it's hard to tell how much stimulus will result from a Japanese government spending package without knowing how much of the money would have been spent otherwise or where offsetting spending cuts are being proposed. As U.S. experience illustrates, a tax cut billed as temporary is less potent than a permanent cut because consumers are more likely to save the windfall than spend it. . . .

Fourth Try

The stimulus plan announced Tuesday represents Japan's fourth attempt in 18 months to rev up the economy. The centerpiece is 5.85 trillion yen in tax cuts, including 5.47 trillion yen in national and local income-tax reductions. Other tax breaks include reducing new-car sales tax to 3% from 4.5%, a move that could boost sales by 50,000 vehicles a year.

In addition, the package calls for 7.2 trillion yen in spending and investment for items such as home financing and new medical and research facilities. The steps also include cheap loans and other help for small businesses. . . .

Small Impact

Economists expect these measures to provide enough of a jolt to business activity to keep the economy afloat this year. But the effect might not be felt until June or later, and even then no one expects the package to kill off Japan's slump, which began nearly three years ago. The consensus: Even with the package,

Japan's economy will grow less than 1% in 1994.

What's more, business leaders and economists worry that the last-minute compromise on the income-tax reduction may hinder its impact on consumer spending. A TV news program estimated that a typical family of four, earning $46,000 a year, will pocket just $375 in tax savings.

Last week, Mr. Hosokawa unveiled a plan to cut taxes by six trillion yen a year, to be offset three years later by more than doubling the nation's sales tax. Mr. Hosokawa's Socialist allies threatened to bolt from his government if levies were raised, while the conservative Finance Ministry resisted raising taxes without some guarantee of higher levies later.

The final solution split the difference: The national income-tax cut, retroactive to Jan. 1, will be effective for just this year. Later this year, leaders promised to decide whether to extend the reduction and how to pay for it. The tax reductions will be returned to consumers in two chunks, one in June and one in December. The government will issue roughly six trillion yen in bonds to bridge the revenue shortfall.
—*Michael Williams*

SOURCE: Michael Williams, "Hosokawa Produces Stimulus Package," February 9, 1994. Reprinted by permission of *The Wall Street Journal*, © 1994 Dow Jones & Co., Inc. All Rights Reserved Worldwide.

Use Your Economic Reasoning

1. What is Japan doing to try to stimulate its slow-growing economy? Are these the kinds of measures a Keynesian would call for?

2. According to the article, a "tax cut billed as temporary will be less potent than a permanent cut." Why? What concerns may have prompted the Japanese to make it temporary?

3. Why is the United States interested in having the Japanese economy grow more rapidly; how will it benefit?

4. U.S. Treasury Secretary Lloyd Bentsen said, "Only Japan has the wherewithal to cut taxes and spur world economic growth." Why can't the United States assume that role? (If you can't answer this question now, try again after finishing the chapter.)

employment compensation and welfare benefits increases automatically. These expenditures for which the government receives no goods or services in exchange are known as **transfer payments.** Government transfer payments compensate somewhat for the declining incomes of the unemployed, and in so doing they prevent a steeper drop in consumption expenditures. This action retards the downward spiral of spending and slows the deterioration of the economy.

When the economy begins to recover and the unemployment rate drops, these transfer payments automatically decrease, which helps prevent inflation by slowing the growth of spending.

Although built-in stabilizers do reduce the magnitude of fluctuations in economic activity, they do not ensure full employment and stable prices. They cannot stop severe inflation once it is under way, and they cannot pull the economy out of a deep recession. In fact the same fiscal features that tend to stabilize the economy can also retard the economy's recovery from a recession. As the recovery begins, personal income starts to rise, but higher taxes reduce the growth of spending and therefore slow the recovery. For these reasons many economists believe that built-in stabilizers must be supplemented by the kinds of discretionary (deliberate) fiscal policies we have just examined.

Fiscal Policy and the Federal Budget

When we resort to fiscal policy to combat unemployment or inflation, we are deliberately tampering with the federal budget. That's what fiscal policy really is—budget policy.

The **federal budget** is a statement of the federal government's planned expenditures and anticipated receipts for the upcoming year. Using the Keynesian model, our analysis of macroeconomic problems suggests that whenever unemployment exists, the federal government should plan a **deficit budget**; that is, it should plan to spend more than it expects to collect in taxes. By taking this action, the government will inject the economy with additional spending that should help drive it toward full employment. Inflationary times call for the opposite approach, a **surplus budget,** wherein the government plans to spend less than it expects to collect in taxes. A surplus budget will help reduce the amount of total spending in the economy and thereby moderate the pressures of inflation. According to our model, a **balanced budget**—a plan to match government expenditures and tax revenues—is appropriate only when the economy is operating at full employment, when it has achieved a satisfactory equilibrium and needs neither stimulus nor restraint.

Although the Keynesian model indicates that budget deficits sometimes make economic sense, that's not the view held by many (perhaps a majority of) Americans. In their opinion deficit spending is always unwise. A government that cannot balance its budget, they contend, is like a spendthrift who lives continually beyond his or her means; eventually both will suffer financial ruin. But those who voice this blanket condemnation fail to recognize that government deficits arise for a variety of reasons, some of which are legitimate and defensible.

Planned and Unplanned Deficits and Surpluses

In examining government deficits, we find it useful to distinguish between deficits that are deliberate, or planned, and those that are unintentional, or unplanned. No one preparing the federal budget expects the actual level of government expenditures and tax receipts to agree exactly with the estimates. Changes in the level of national income and employment will mean automatic changes in tax revenues and government expenditures, because those income and employment changes trigger the built-in stabilizers. The same built-in stabilizers that help reduce the magnitude of economic swings lead to deficits when the economy experiences a downturn and to surpluses during periods of expansion.

Even the most carefully planned budget will be inaccurate if the economy performs in unexpected ways. Consider an experience of the Reagan administration. Early in 1981 President Reagan recommended to Congress a budget with a projected deficit of $45 billion for the 1982 fiscal year. This budget assumed that the economy's real gross domestic product would grow at a rate of 4.2 percent in 1982 and that the unemployment rate would average 7.2 percent for that year. Both assumptions turned out to be incorrect. Real GDP actually *declined* by 2.1 percent in 1982, and the unemployment rate averaged 9.5 percent. As a result of this unexpectedly weak performance, the federal government's outlay for unemployment compensation and welfare was higher than anticipated, and tax revenues were lower. This produced a budget deficit of approximately $110 billion, a far cry from the administration's $45 billion projection.

Sometimes the economy outperforms the projections of planners. When that happens, the built-in stabilizers have the opposite effect on the government's receipts and expenditures. As the economy expands, tax revenues rise, and expenditures for unemployment compensation and welfare decline. Thus the built-in stabilizers tend to increase the size of the surplus or decrease the size of the deficit.

Unemployment and the Federal Budget

Efforts to balance the budget in the face of a recession can have undesired effects on the economy. Suppose that the economy is initially operating at full employment and that the federal government projects a balanced budget.

What will happen to the budget if the economy suddenly weakens and unemployment begins to rise? As you know, the fiscal system's built-in stabilizers will work automatically to retard the downturn. But what will this do to the balanced federal budget? It will push it into a deficit.

Suppose that Congress insists on restoring a balanced budget. What should be done? The logical response would be to increase taxes and reduce government spending. But wait; this response is clearly inconsistent with Keynesian remedies for unemployment. The reduced level of government spending and concomitant higher taxes will mean less total spending for goods and services, which will cause the downturn to deepen and unemployment to worsen. Moreover, because this effort to balance the budget prolongs the recession, it may result in a larger cumulative deficit.

According to our model, whenever the economy is in a recession, the preferred route to a balanced budget entails a deliberate increase in government spending or a reduction in taxes. Obviously either measure would increase the short-term deficit, but by stimulating output and employment, either action could help pull the economy out of its depressed state. When the economy improves, tax revenues will rise automatically, and government spending for transfer payments will decline automatically. Thus expansionary fiscal policy may create a larger deficit in the short run. But by restoring the health of the economy, it can lead to a balanced budget.

We can see how this process works if we look at the tax cut instituted by President Johnson in the mid-1960s. In 1964 the federal budget was already in deficit when Congress finally approved an $11 billion tax reduction (originally requested by President Kennedy in 1963) designed to push the economy closer to full employment. The stimulus provided by this tax cut helped increase GDP by some $36 billion and lower the unemployment rate from about 6 percent to 4.7 percent. According to Arthur Okun, Chairman of the Council of Economic Advisors under President Johnson, the higher tax revenues that resulted from the improved economy brought the federal budget into surplus in the first half of 1965.[6]

The Public Debt

Whenever the federal government incurs a deficit—be it planned or unplanned—it must finance that deficit by borrowing. This is accomplished by instructing the U.S. Treasury to sell government bonds to individuals, busi-

---

[6] Arthur M. Okun, *The Political Economy of Prosperity* (New York: W. W. Norton, 1967), pp. 47–48.

nesses, financial institutions, and government agencies. Each of these transactions increases the **public debt**—the accumulated borrowings of the federal government. The public debt is often referred to as the national debt. At the end of 1994, the U.S. national debt stood at $4.6 trillion, a figure so large that it is virtually beyond the comprehension of most of us. That amount represents all the borrowing it took to finance several wars, numerous economic downturns, and a variety of government projects and programs.

Concerns about the Public Debt

The size and growth of the public debt trouble many Americans. Some of their concerns are justified and some are not. In this section we want to lay to rest some myths and examine the real burden of the debt.

Can We Ever Pay Off the Debt?

Can We Ever Pay Off the Debt? A common misconception about the public debt is that it must be paid off at some time in the future. In reality there is no requirement that the federal government ever pay off the debt. The government simply refinances the debt year after year with new borrowing. As government bonds become due, the Treasury sells new bonds to take their place. So long as there is a market for government bonds, the government will keep issuing them. And because U.S. Government Bonds are probably the most secure investment in the world, there is really no likelihood that this market will ever disappear.

Does the Public Debt Impose a Burden on Future Generations?

Does the Public Debt Impose a Burden on Future Generations? Some critics of the public debt suggest that it imposes an unfair burden on future generations. What this logic overlooks is that one person's debt is another's asset. Future generations will inherit not only the public debt but also the bonds and other securities that make up the debt. When a future generation pays taxes to service the debt, its members will also be the recipients of the interest payments made by the government.

Some of our public debt is owed to foreigners, however, and this portion does threaten to burden future generations. You and your children will pay taxes in order to provide interest payments to foreign investors, whose dollars thus acquired will permit them to claim a share of the goods and services that might otherwise go to Americans. Consequently our standard of living may be lowered somewhat. At the end of 1994, 13.7 percent of our public debt was owed to foreigners, about the same percentage as in 1980. Between 1980 and 1992, interest payments to foreign investors increased, both as a percentage of the federal budget and in relation to our gross domestic product. Since 1992, however, these trends have reversed. The next section will clarify the significance of these changes.

Can Americans Afford the Interest Payments on the Growing Public Debt? Even if the federal government never has to pay off the national debt, it must continue to make interest payments on what it owes. After all, that's why people buy government securities—to earn interest.

We've already discussed the burden of interest payments to foreign investors. Payments to domestic bond owners, too, carry certain negative effects. Because the United States must continue to make interest payments on the debt, either our taxes are higher than they would otherwise be or we must sacrifice some government programs. If we all owned equal shares of the public debt, paying higher taxes would be offset by receiving interest payments on our shares. But whereas all people pay taxes, only some hold bonds and receive interest on the national debt. To the extent that bondholders commonly have higher incomes to begin with, this process tends to produce greater inequality. This effect is at least partially modified by our progressive income tax system.[7] Those with higher incomes may receive more in interest payments, but they also pay more in taxes.

The higher tax rates needed to service the debt (that is, to make the interest payments on it) may also have a negative effect on the incentive to work and earn taxable income. If individuals are allowed to keep less of what they earn, some may choose to work less. Others may attempt to avoid taxation by performing work that is not reported to taxing authorities—work for friends and barter transactions, for example.

Until about 1975, the burden imposed on taxpayers by the interest charges on the public debt was relatively stable. Exhibit 12.5 shows that although annual interest payments were growing, so was our GDP—our measure of the economy's income and output. Thus our ability to make those interest payments was growing also. The last column in Exh. 12.4 shows that from World War II until 1975, interest payments on the debt represented a relatively constant percentage of GDP—between 1.7 and 2.2 percent. Then in the late 1970s and early 1980s, the interest cost of the debt began to grow much more rapidly than GDP, due primarily to the record budget deficits that characterized this period (note that interest payments on the debt climbed to 2.8 percent of GDP in 1980 and to 4.8 percent of GDP in 1990). This trend has been a major concern for economists and politicians. Fortunately in 1992 interest payments began to decline as a percent of GDP. It remains to be seen whether this new trend will continue.

---

[7] Existing tax law is somewhat progressive; that is, people with higher incomes pay a higher fraction of those incomes in the form of taxes. Prior to the Tax Reform Act of 1986, taxation was more progressive than it is today.

EXHIBIT 12.5

The Public Debt and Interest Payments in Relation to Gross Domestic Product

YEAR	PUBLIC DEBT (billions)	INTEREST PAYMENT ON DEBT (billions)	GROSS DOMESTIC PRODUCT (billions)	INTEREST AS A PERCENTAGE OF GDP
1930	$ 16.2	$ 0.7	$ 90.7	0.8%
1935	28.7	0.8	68.7	1.2
1940	43.0	1.0	95.4	1.0
1945	258.7	3.6	212.0	1.7
1950	256.1	5.7	265.8	2.1
1955	272.8	6.4	384.7	1.7
1960	284.1	9.2	504.6	1.8
1965	313.8	11.3	671.0	1.7
1970	370.1	19.3	985.4	2.0
1975	533.2	32.7	1,509.8	2.2
1980	907.7	74.9	2,644.1	2.8
1985	1,821.0	178.9	3,967.7	4.5
1990	3,206.3	264.9	5,481.5	4.8
1994	4,643.7	296.3	6,738.4	4.4

SOURCE: Office of Management and Budget, *Budget of the United States Government, Fiscal Year 1996.*

Will Government Borrowing Crowd Out Private Investment? When the federal government borrows money to finance additional public debt caused by budget deficits, it must compete with private borrowers for funds. Under certain circumstances this increased demand for loanable funds will drive up interest rates, which will discourage private businesses from borrowing for investment purposes. This phenomenon is known as **crowding out:** Government borrowing pushes aside, or crowds out, private borrowing. Since investment spending plays a major role in expanding the economy's productive capacity, this reduction in the rate of investment spending will tend to reduce economic growth.

According to the Keynesian model, crowding out should be a problem only when the economy is operating at or near full employment. If there are unemployed resources, deficit spending should stimulate the economy, raise incomes, and increase the level of saving. With more savings available to be borrowed and with more total spending in the economy, business investment may actually increase rather than decrease as a result of the deficit. But when the economy has reached full employment, there can be no further increase in real income or saving; then government borrowing tends to crowd out private borrowing.[8]

The Public Debt: A Look at the Future

According to Clinton administration estimates, the federal government will continue to incur significant but declining budget deficits through the end of the century. The Office of Management and Budget predicts a deficit of $165 billion for 1995, down from a high of $290 billion in 1992. Deficits of similar size are predicted for the remainder of the decade. Although these deficits imply substantial growth of the public debt—to more than $6 trillion by the end of 1999—a downward trend in the size of the deficit would be significant. Smaller deficits imply less government borrowing and consequently less upward pressure on interest rates. In addition, slower growth of the public debt (caused by smaller deficits) would help to ensure that interest payments on the public debt continue to decline as a percentage of GDP. Predicting deficits is a difficult task, however, because projections must be based on assumptions regarding the economy's performance. If the economy grows more slowly than assumed, the budget deficits will be larger than projected, and the interest burden of the public debt may resume its upward climb.

The Limits to Fiscal Policy

Keynesian theory calls for budget deficits during periods of high unemployment and surpluses during periods of inflation. But the recent budget history is one of continuing deficits, even during periods of low unemployment. In short, Congress has been unable or unwilling to reduce spending (or increase

---

[8] Most studies indicate that borrowing to finance federal deficits did not crowd out much investment in the 1980s. Instead, high interest rates—resulting in part from government borrowing—attracted foreign funds to help us finance our deficit. Unfortunately the inflow of capital funds increased the value of the dollar in foreign exchange markets, and this harmed U.S. exporters, whose products became more expensive for foreigners. Chapter 17 will consider these issues in some detail.

taxes) even when Keynesian theory suggests that such changes are appropriate. We conclude our discussion by briefly examining this "expansionary bias" and two other problems that may complicate efforts to use discretionary fiscal policy to guide the economy's performance. (The article "The Coming Tax Cuts," on page 378, illustrates how political considerations influence the formulation of fiscal policy.)

The Expansionary Bias

As you know, the Keynesian model calls for an expansionary fiscal policy to combat unemployment and a contractionary policy to combat inflation. But expansionary policies are more attractive politically than contractionary policies. Incumbent officials don't want to sacrifice votes, and voters want neither to pay higher taxes nor to lose the government programs that benefit them. The result is a bias in favor of expansionary fiscal policies. It may be relatively easy for Congress to pass measures to stimulate the economy, but it's quite difficult to muster the votes necessary to trim government spending or increase taxes.

Time Lags

Often a substantial interlude passes between the time when a policy change is needed and the economic impact of any change that is actually made. This lag may reduce the effectiveness of the remedial fiscal policy; in some instances it may even make the change counterproductive.

There are several reasons for this time lag. First, the economy does not always provide clear signals as to what the future will bring. This means that some lag may occur before the need for policy change is recognized. Second, even after the need is acknowledged, action is historically slow to transpire. It takes a certain amount of time to draft legislation and get it through Congress, even if lawmakers are in general agreement that action is needed. Third, when the bill is finally passed, more time is required for implementation, and still more time is needed for the economy to begin to respond. Some measures take less time than others. Implementing a tax cut is a speedier process than implementing an increase in government spending on highways and parks, for example, but in both situations some lag exists.

These lags mean that by the time the policy effects are felt, they may well be the wrong policies for the state of the economy. For example, it makes no sense to implement a long-awaited tax cut just as the economy has begun to recover on its own from a recession. Extra disposable income at this time could be the stimulus that leads to inflation.

The Coming Tax Cuts

America, there is a tax bill in your future, and not just the one that's due on April 15. The new Republican majority in Congress has promised angry middle-class voters that it will cut their taxes, and the panicked Democrat in the White House wants to extend his lease beyond 1996. These warring factions may not agree on much, but they both want to hand out fistfuls of dollars by cutting your taxes.

A host of tax goodies may be in store in 1995. A long-debated cut in capital-gains taxes, strongly backed by both GOP legislators and centrist Democrats, appears to be a shoo-in. Bill Clinton's White House may have little choice but to go along—and try to explain why it has changed its mind about enacting tax cuts that mostly benefit the rich. Meanwhile, making good at last on a 1992 campaign promise, the administration is struggling to find the money for a modest middle-class tax cut. And Republican House members have pledged a mammoth tax cut worth $107 billion over the next five years in the form of a $500-per-child annual tax credit for virtually all American families.

The House Republicans also want to reduce the so-called marriage penalty so married couples don't pay dramatically higher taxes than they would if still single. Both Republicans and Democrats propose to expand tax-favored individual retirement accounts so more Americans can salt away money for retirement or a rainy day. House Republicans also have pitched a massive cut in taxes for both small and large businesses to spur investments in factories and equipment. . . .

Although recent polls show that more than 80 percent of Americans favor a cut in taxes for most Americans, the key question is whether America can afford all this government largess. Already there are signs that a tax cut bidding war could break out as each political party tries to outdo the other. Top Clinton administration officials are so worried about such an "open auction" that they have laid down a stern marker: Any proposed tax cut must be paid for, either with other tax hikes or with spending cuts, so it does not drive up the federal budget deficit. "My standard [for a tax cut] will be, Will it help increase incomes for the middle class,

will it promote jobs and growth, and can we pay for it?" Clinton said before meeting with GOP leaders last week.

Time bombs

House Republicans have also vowed fiscal austerity, promising to find spending cuts to more than offset $205 billion in tax cuts over the next five years. But the history of the 1980s shows that legislators and presidents alike are often more willing to make popular tax cuts than to make unpopular spending cuts. Moreover, several of the tax cuts the Republicans have proposed— notably the House GOP proposal to cut capital-gains taxes—are fiscal time bombs that could explode into hundreds of billions of dollars in lost tax revenue in future years. Their backers may be able to push through such cuts only if they play with economic assumptions and project more economic and revenue growth from tax cuts than history suggests is warranted.

Another major concern is who will reap the tax cut windfall, especially at a time when the gap between America's rich and poor continues to widen. At least half the direct benefits of a cut in capital-gains taxes is likely to go to the top 2 percent of taxpayers—one reason columnist Mark Shields calls slicing capital-gains taxes "Head Start for the rich." And if such a cut were enacted, would it leave any room to reduce taxes for folks in the middle?

Moreover, with the economy steamrolling ahead at nearly full employment, many economists think this is not an auspicious time for a growth-stimulating tax cut, especially one that risks bumping up the budget deficit. If Congress does not offset its tax cuts by further reducing spending, the Federal Reserve is likely to do so by continuing to raise interest rates—a recipe for choking the economic expansion the Republicans say they want to promote. . . .
—*Susan Dentzer with Kenneth T. Walsh, David Bowermaster, and David Fischer*

SOURCE: Susan Dentzer, "The Coming Tax Cuts," December 12, 1994. Copyright © U.S. News & World Report. Reprinted with permission.

Use Your Economic Reasoning

For your information, capital gains taxes are paid on the difference between the purchase price of assets, such as stocks, bonds, and real estate, and the price at which they are later sold.

1. The article talks about a "tax cut bidding war" between the two parties. What is the motivation for this competition?

2. Tax cuts are always more likely to be approved by Congress than cuts in government spending. Why?

3. Why do many economists believe that this is not a good time for tax cuts?

4. Suppose that Congress approved tax and government spending cuts of the same amount, say, $100 billion. Pick any *MPC* and calculate the impact on equilibrium GDP.

Crowding Out, Again

As you already know, when the federal government borrows money to finance its deficit spending, such borrowing may drive up interest rates. This in turn may reduce private investment. If that happens, the net effect of the increased government spending will not be as beneficial as it would if private investment had not been reduced. In addition, the reduced rate of investment spending will mean a slower rate of economic growth.

By now you can see that discretionary fiscal policy is not without its limitations. The significance of these limitations is open to debate. In general, Keynesians believe that fiscal policy can be useful when employed correctly and selectively. But other economists disagree. *Monetarists* are economists who believe that the problem of crowding out makes fiscal policy essentially useless. *New classical economists* argue that fiscal policy is ineffective, because individuals anticipate its impact and take actions that neutralize the government's efforts. These economists believe that an expansionary fiscal policy does nothing but cause inflation. This isn't the place to take a detailed look at the monetarists and the new classical economists; their views will be examined in Chapter 15. For now, the important point is that economists disagree about the advisability of using discretionary fiscal policy to guide the economy's performance.

Summary

Fiscal policy is the manipulation of government spending and taxation in order to guide the economy's performance. There are two forms of fiscal policy: discretionary and automatic. *Discretionary fiscal policy* requires a conscious decision by policymakers to alter the level of government spending or taxation. Automatic fiscal policy is a system of *built-in stabilizers* that automatically reduce the magnitude of fluctuations in total spending and thereby help prevent wide swings in the level of output and employment.

According to the Keynesian model, the proper discretionary fiscal policy when unemployment exists is to increase government spending, reduce taxes, or do both. These actions increase the amount of total spending, which in turn increases the level of output and employment. If inflation is the problem, the opposite course of action is recommended. Government spending should be reduced, taxes should be raised, or both actions should be taken simultaneously.

When we resort to fiscal policy to combat unemployment or inflation, we are deliberately tampering with the *federal budget*. When unemployment exists, the Keynesian model suggests that the government should plan a *deficit budget* in order to stimulate the economy. When inflation is the problem, a *surplus budget* is called for. Only when the economy is operating at full employment is a *balanced budget* appropriate.

When the federal government incurs a deficit, it finances that deficit by borrowing. This is accomplished by instructing the U.S. Treasury to sell government bonds to individuals, businesses, financial institutions, and government agencies. These transactions result in an increase in the *public debt*—the accumulated borrowings of the federal government.

The public debt is a source of concern to many Americans and does impose some burdens on our society. The fact that the government must make interest payments on the debt means that taxes will be higher than would be necessary otherwise. Since not all taxpayers are bondholders, this results in some income redistribution from taxpayers in general to bondholders in particular. In addition, the dollars that foreign investors acquire as interest payments permit them to claim a share of the goods and services produced in our economy.

The government borrowing necessary to finance additions to the debt (caused by deficit spending) may also drive up interest rates and *crowd out* private borrowing for investment purposes. Because investment spending plays a major role in expanding the economy's productive capacity, this reduction in the rate of investment spending will tend to reduce economic growth.

Discretionary fiscal policy is subject to several limitations and shortcomings: There are often substantial time lags between the appearance of a problem and the economic impact of a remedial policy. Expansionary fiscal policy is more attractive politically than contractionary policy. Elected officials may be unwilling to support the restrictive policies that combat inflation, fearing such support will cost them votes. Finally, when increases in government spending are deficit financed, some investment spending may be crowded out, so the expansionary effect is reduced.

Glossary

Balanced budget. A plan to match government expenditures and tax revenues.

Built-in stabilizers. Automatic changes in taxes and government spending that help reduce the magnitude of fluctuations in the level of economic activity; sometimes called automatic, or nondiscretionary, fiscal policy.

Crowding out. The phenomenon that occurs when increased government borrowing drives up interest rates and thereby reduces the rate of investment spending.

Deficit budget. A plan to spend more than will be collected in tax receipts.

Discretionary fiscal policy. The deliberate changing of the level of government spending or taxation in order to guide the economy's performance.

Federal budget. A statement of the federal government's planned expenditures and anticipated receipts for the upcoming year.

Public debt. The accumulated borrowings of the federal government; also known as the *national debt*.

Surplus budget. A plan to collect more in taxes than will be spent.

Transfer payments. Expenditures for which no goods or services are received in exchange.

Study Questions

Fill in the Blanks

1. According to the Keynesian model, if an economy is experiencing unemployment, the federal government should _____ or _____ _____ or do both.

2. If the federal government spends more than it takes in from tax revenues, we say that it is incurring a _____; if it takes in more in taxes than it spends, it has a _____.

3. The deliberate changing of government spending or taxation in order to guide the economy's performance is _____.

4. The magnitude of fluctuations in total spending is automatically reduced by _____.

5. According to the Keynesian model, the appropriate fiscal policy to combat inflation would be to _____ or _____ or do both.

6. If the economy is experiencing full employment, deficit spending may lead to _____.

7. According to our model, a _____ budget would be appropriate if the economy were operating at full employment.

8. The accumulated borrowings of the federal government are called the _____ _____ .

9. Our economy's built-in stabilizers include unemployment compensation, welfare benefits, and the _____ .

10. Political considerations may make it particularly difficult to use fiscal policy in combating _____ .

Multiple Choice

1. Let's assume that the economy is in a significant recession, operating $100 billion below the full-employment output. If the marginal propensity to consume is 0.8, in what direction and by what amount should the level of government spending be changed?
   a) Decrease government spending by $100 billion.
   b) Increase government spending by $100 billion.
   c) Decrease government spending by $20 billion.
   d) Increase government spending by $20 billion.
   e) Increase government spending by $80 billion.

2. Select the best evaluation of the following statement: *Increasing government spending by $10 billion will have a greater impact on the level of equilibrium output than decreasing taxes by the same amount ($10 billion).*
   a) False; both changes will have the same impact on GDP.
   b) False; a $10 billion decrease in taxes will have a greater impact than a $10 billion increase in spending.
   c) True; since only part of the tax reduction will be spent, the remainder will be saved and will not stimulate the economy.
   d) True; a tax reduction will always create twice as much stimulus as a spending increase of equal size.

3. If the marginal propensity to consume is 0.75, a $20 billion increase in personal income taxes will initially reduce consumption spending by
   a) $20 billion.
   b) $80 billion.
   c) $15 billion.
   d) $40 billion.

4. The ultimate impact of the tax increase noted in question 3 would be to
   a) reduce the equilibrium GDP by $20 billion.
   b) reduce the equilibrium GDP by $80 billion.
   c) reduce the equilibrium GDP by $60 billion.
   d) increase the equilibrium GDP by $20 billion.

5. Which of the following is *not* an advantage of built-in stabilizers?
   a) They do not involve the political hassle associated with discretionary fiscal policy.
   b) They help speed recovery from a recession.
   c) They go to work automatically, so lags are minimal.
   d) They help prevent a minor downturn from becoming a major recession.

6. Because of built-in stabilizers, the budget will
   a) tend toward surplus during a recession.
   b) tend toward deficit during an economic expansion.
   c) tend toward deficit during a recession.
   d) always remain in balance.

7. According to the Keynesian model, when the economy is in a recession, the shortest route to a balanced budget may entail
   a) higher taxes.
   b) less government spending.
   c) lower taxes and more government spending.
   d) both a and b.

8. Which of the following statements is false?
   a) If the economy is operating at full unemployment, a reduction in taxes may lead to inflation.
   b) If the economy is experiencing unemployment, increased government spending may help combat the problem.
   c) Deficit spending is desirable only when the economy is experiencing inflation.
   d) If we attempt to balance the budget during a period of unemployment, we may aggravate the unemployment problem.

9. A legitimate concern regarding the national debt relates to
   a) the higher taxes that are necessary to make the interest payments on the debt.
   b) our inability to pay off such a large sum.
   c) the fraction of the debt owed to foreign factions.
   d) both a and c.

10. "Crowding out" occurs when
    a) U.S. producers lose sales due to foreign competition.
    b) an increase in taxes results in a lower level of consumption spending.
    c) foreign interests buy government securities.
    d) government borrowing forces up interest rates and reduces the level of private investment spending.

Problems and Questions for Discussion

1. When the government increases spending to combat unemployment, why shouldn't it increase taxes to pay for the increased spending? Why run a deficit instead?

2. Assuming that the economy's *MPC* is 0.666 and that government spending increases by $20 billion, what would be the impact on the equilibrium level of GDP?

3. What is the burden of the national, or public, debt?

4. If Keynes was correct that consumption spending depends primarily on the level of disposable income, how is it possible for an increase in government spending to lead to an increase in consumption spending?

5. If the prevailing level of output is $800 billion and the full-employment output is $600 billion, we know that the economy is enduring inflation. If the economy's *MPC* is 0.5, how much should government spending be reduced in order to eliminate the inflation without generating unemployment? If taxes were increased instead, how much would the increase have to be?

6. What advantages can you see to using tax reductions rather than government spending increases to combat unemployment? Can your personal values influence which of these approaches you prefer? Explain.

7. George Humphrey, Secretary of the Treasury during the Eisenhower administration, once declared: "We cannot spend ourselves rich." What do you suppose he meant? Would Keynes agree? Why or why not?

8. List the various types of lags associated with fiscal policy. Why is the existence of lags a serious limitation of such policies?

9. Suppose the federal government decided to pay off the public debt. How would it go about doing it? What do you suppose would be the impact on the economy?

10. Concern over continuing federal deficits has spawned a movement to amend the Constitution of the United States to require the federal government to balance its budget each year. Can you think of any reasons to argue against a balanced-budget amendment? Why would it be difficult to carry out such a rule during a recession?

Answer Key

Fill in the Blanks

1. increase government spending, decrease taxes
2. deficit; surplus
3. discretionary fiscal policy
4. built-in stabilizers
5. reduce government spending, increase taxes
6. inflation
7. balanced
8. public debt, or national debt
9. income tax
10. inflation

Multiple Choice

1. d
2. c
3. c
4. c
5. b
6. c
7. c
8. c
9. d
10. d

CHAPTER 13

Money, Banking, and Monetary Policy

1. State the three basic functions of money and explain each.
2. Distinguish between money and near money.
3. Distinguish between the M-1 and M-2 money supply definitions.
4. Explain how depository institutions create money.
5. Calculate the deposit multiplier and explain its purpose.
6. Discuss the functions of the Federal Reserve.
7. Define monetary policy.
8. Describe the three major policy tools the Fed uses to control the money supply.
9. Explain how Keynesians believe that changes in the money lead to changes in output, employment, and prices.
10. Discuss the factors that limit the effectiveness of monetary policy.

In Chapter 10 we introduced the views of John Maynard Keynes and examined the origin of the debate on policy activism. Chapter 11 provided additional detail on the Keynesian model, and Chapter 12 explored Keynesian fiscal policy.

In Chapter 13 we consider the role of money in an economy and complete our expansion of the Keynesian model by exploring Keynesian monetary policy. Most of us take the use of money for granted. We pay our bills in money and expect to be paid in money. We compare prices, incomes, and even our gross domestic product in terms of money. But exactly what *is* money, and what functions does it perform in our economy? How do banks "create" money, and why can't individuals do the same? These are some of the questions addressed in this chapter. Perhaps most important, you'll learn about the Federal Reserve—the independent government agency responsible for regulating the money supply and performing other duties related to the banking system. And you'll find out how Keynesians believe that the money supply can be used as a tool for guiding the performance of the economy. We begin by examining what is meant by "money."

What Is Money?

Economists define money in terms of the functions it performs; anything that performs the functions of money *is* money. Money performs three basic functions. First, money serves as a **medium of exchange:** the generally accepted means of payment for goods and services. A medium of exchange enables members of a society to transact their business without resorting to barter. In a barter economy goods are exchanged for goods. A shoemaker who wants to buy a painting must locate an artist in need of shoes. As you can imagine, this requirement makes trading slow and burdensome. Money facilitates trade by permitting the shoemaker to exchange shoes for money and then use the money to purchase a painting or other goods and services.

The second function of money is to provide a **standard of value,** a unit for expressing the prices of goods and services. In a barter economy we would need an almost endless list of prices, one for each possible exchange. For example, we might find that one painting equals (exchanges for) one pair of shoes and that one pair of shoes equals four bushels of apples and that four bushels of apples equals two shirts. Which is more expensive: a shirt or a pair of shoes? It may take you a moment to figure out the answer, because the absence of a standard of value makes the communication and comparison of prices very difficult. The use of money simplifies this process by enabling us to state all prices in terms of a particular standard of value, such as the dollar. Using the dollar as a standard of value, we can easily determine that if a pair of shoes sells for $20 and a shirt sells for $10, the shoes are twice as expensive as the shirt.

Finally, money is a **store of value,** a vehicle for accumulating or storing wealth to be used at some future date. A tomato farmer would find it difficult to accumulate wealth in the form of tomatoes. They don't keep very well! Money is not a perfect store of value, especially in inflationary times, but clearly it is better than a bushel of perishable tomatoes. By exchanging the tomato crop for money, the farmer can begin to build a nest egg for retirement or to save for some major purchase—a tractor or a new barn, for example. In a sense the availability of a store of value widens the range of spending choices available to individuals and businesses. Their options are no longer limited to what they can afford to buy (trade for) with a single period's income.

Money and Near Money

What qualifies as money in the U.S. economy? We all know that coins and paper currency are money, and a check is usually as good as cash. Non-interest-bearing checking deposits at commercial banks[1] are known as **demand deposits,** since the bank promises to pay at once, or "on demand," the amount specified by the owner of the account. Checks drawn on demand-deposit accounts are an accepted medium of exchange; they are measured in dollars, the standard of value in the United States, and it is certainly possible to accumulate wealth in your checking account. But although it is relatively easy to agree that currency—coins and paper money—and demand deposits are money, some other assets are more difficult to categorize. An **asset** is anything of value owned by an **entity**—that is, by an individual or an organization, such as a business. Many assets perform some, but not all, of the functions of money. Others perform all the functions of money but do so incompletely.

Near money

One debate among economists concerns the proper classification of **savings deposits**—interest-bearing deposits at banks and savings institutions. The traditional passbook savings account cannot be used directly to purchase goods and services; hence such deposits do not qualify as a medium of exchange. As a consequence, economists have generally classified savings deposits as **near money**—assets that are not money but that can be converted quickly into money. Not everyone has supported this position, however. Some economists argue that savings deposits should be considered money because they can be converted easily into cash or demand deposits and therefore have essentially the same impact on spending as do other financial assets.

Innovations in banking, moreover, have blurred the distinction between savings deposits and demand deposits. Consider, for example, the negotiable order of withdrawal (NOW) account commonly offered by banks and other financial institutions. The **NOW account** is essentially a savings account on which the depositor is permitted to write checks. Here we seem to have the best of both worlds: the convenience of a checking account plus the earning power of a savings account. Banks have also developed automatic transfer service (ATS) accounts, in which funds from savings can be transferred automatically to a checking account. These types of deposits probably should be considered along with demand deposits as a form of money. But we still face the task of categorizing financial assets that do not function as media of ex-

---

[1] Commercial banks are so named because in their early days, they specialized in loans to businesses. Today commercial banks engage in a much wider range of lending, including home-mortgage loans, automobile loans, and other consumer loans.

change. These include passbook savings accounts, U.S. Government savings bonds, and shares in money-market mutual funds.[2] Are such assets money or not? The answer is not clear, even to the Federal Reserve.

Definitions of the Money Supply

As we noted earlier, the Federal Reserve is responsible for controlling the money supply—the total amount of money in the economy. Before the Fed (as the Federal Reserve is often called) can attempt to control the money supply, it must, of course, decide what money is.

Rather than settling on a single definition, the Fed has developed several. The narrowest, **M-1,** is composed of currency in the hands of the public *plus* checkable deposits. **Checkable deposits** are all types of deposits on which customers can write checks: demand deposits at commercial banks; NOW accounts; credit union share draft accounts, which are essentially the same as NOW accounts but are provided by credit unions; and ATS accounts. The primary characteristic of all M-1 money is that it can function easily as a medium of exchange. As you can see from Exh. 13.1, only about 31 percent of this readily spendable money is in the form of currency. Demand deposits account for another 33 percent of the M-1 money supply. The remaining 36 percent—the largest share—is in other checkable deposits.

The Federal Reserve also classifies the money supply according to two broader definitions: M-2 and M-3. The **M-2** portion of the money supply includes everything in M-1 *plus* money-market mutual-fund balances, money-market deposits at savings institutions, and certain other financial assets that do not function as a medium of exchange but that can be converted easily into currency or checkable deposits—small savings deposits (less than $100,000) at banks and savings institutions, for example.

An even broader measure of the money supply is **M-3**. It includes everything in M-2 *plus* large savings deposits (over $100,000) and other financial assets that are designed essentially to be used as business savings accounts.

Throughout this chapter and the remainder of the text, we will use the M-1 definition of money: We assume that money consists of currency plus checkable deposits. These assets function easily as a medium of exchange, the function that many economists regard as the most important characteristic of money.

---

[2] A mutual fund is an organization that pools people's money and invests it in stocks or bonds or other financial assets. A money-market mutual fund invests in short-term securities, such as U.S. Treasury bills. If you own shares in a money-market mutual fund, you can write checks against your account, but generally they must exceed some minimum amount (commonly $500). This makes money-market funds less useful for everyday transactions involving smaller amounts of money.

EXHIBIT 13.1

M-1, M-2, and M-3 as of January 1995 (billions of dollars)

M-1

Currency (coins and paper money)	$357.7
Demand deposits	383.5
Other checkable deposits	407.7
Total M-1	$1,148.9

M-2

M-1 plus small savings accounts and money-market mutual fund balances	$3,625.9

M-3

M-2 plus large savings deposits and other financial assets that provide an outlet for business saving	$4,325.1

Source: *Federal Reserve Bulletin*, April 1995.

How Depository Institutions Create Money

Where does M-1 money come from? The currency component is easy to explain. It comes from the Federal Reserve, which supplies banks with enough coins and paper money to meet the needs of their customers. (Here and throughout the chapter, we use the term "bank" in a general way, to refer to all types of depository institutions—commercial banks and savings, or thrift institutions.[3]) But the checkable-deposits element of M-1 is more of a mystery. Checkable deposits are actually created by the numerous banks that offer such accounts.

A Bank's Balance Sheet

To demonstrate how banks create checkable deposit money, we can use a simple accounting concept known as a balance sheet. A **balance sheet** is a statement of a business's assets and liabilities. The assets of a business are, as we saw earlier, the things of value that it owns. **Liabilities** are the debts of the business, what it owes. The difference between the business's assets and lia-

---

[3] There are three major types of thrift institutions: savings and loan associations, mutual savings banks, and credit unions.

bilities is the **owner equity,** which represents the interest of the owner or owners of a business in its assets. These accounting statements "balance"; whatever value of the business is not owed to creditors must belong to the owners: assets = liabilities + owner equity.

We turn now to Exh. 13.2 to examine the balance sheet of a hypothetical bank, the Gainsville National Bank. The left-hand side of the balance sheet lists the bank's assets. The first entry, reserves, includes cash in the bank's vault plus funds on deposit with the Federal Reserve. Banks are required by law to hold a certain amount of their assets as required reserves. The **reserve requirement** is stated as a percentage of the bank's checkable deposits and can be met only by cash in its vault and deposits with the Fed. Because reserves earn no interest income, banks understandably try to maintain only the minimum legal requirement. Reserves greater than the minimum requirement are called **excess reserves,** and they play an important role in a bank's ability to create checkable deposit money.

The next two entries on the left-hand side, Securities and Loans, are the interest-earning assets of the bank. Banks usually have substantial holdings of U.S. Treasury bills and other securities that are both safe and highly liquid—that is, easily converted into cash. Loans offer less liquidity but generally have the advantage of earning a higher rate of interest.

The final entry on the left-hand side of the balance sheet is *Property*, the physical assets of the bank: the bank building, its office equipment, and any other nonfinancial holdings of the organization.

The right-hand side of the balance sheet lists liabilities and owner equity. In our example the only liabilities entered are *Checkable deposits* and *Savings*

EXHIBIT 13.2

A Hypothetical Balance Sheet: Gainsville National Bank

ASSETS		LIABILITIES AND OWNER EQUITY	
Reserves (vault cash plus deposits with the Federal Reserve)	$ 200,000	Checkable deposits	$1,000,000
		Savings deposits	360,000
		Owner equity	240,000
Securities	450,000		
Loans	800,000		
Property	150,000	Total liabilities	
Total assets	$1,600,000	+ owner equity	$1,600,000

deposits. Although both items are assets for customers, they are debts to the bank. If we write a check on our checking account or ask to withdraw money from our savings account, the bank has to pay. That makes each of those accounts a liability to the bank.

The only remaining entry on the right-hand side of Exh. 13.2 is *owner equity,* the owners' claims on the assets of the business. As you know, the two sides of the statement have to balance, because whatever value of the business is not owed to creditors (the bank's liabilities) must belong to the owners (owner equity).

The Creation of Checkable Deposits

Earlier we noted that all banks must meet a reserve requirement established by the Federal Reserve. Let's assume that the reserve requirement for our hypothetical bank is 20 percent. Our bank has $1,000,000 in checkable deposits; therefore it is required by law to maintain $200,000 in reserves ($1,000,000 $\times$ 0.20 = $200,000). As you can see from the bank's balance sheet, it has precisely $200,000 in reserves.

Even in the absence of regulation, banks would need to maintain some reserves against their deposits. The bank must have the currency to pay a depositor who walks into the Gainsville Bank and writes a check for "cash." However, the bank does not have to maintain $1 in reserve for every $1 of checkable deposits it accepts, because it is unlikely that all depositors will request their money simultaneously. In fact, while some depositors are writing checks and drawing down their accounts, others are making deposits and thereby increasing their balances.

The key to a bank's ability to create money is this **fractional reserve principle,** the principle that a bank need maintain only a fraction of a dollar in reserve for each dollar of its checkable deposits. Once a bank discovers this principle, it can loan out the idle funds and earn interest. That's the name of the game in banking—earning interest by lending money. In the process of making loans, banks create money: specifically, checkable deposits. We can see how this is true by working through the balance sheet entries of the lending bank. In order to simplify things somewhat, we will show only the changes in assets and liabilities for each entry, not the entire balance sheet.

Step One: Accepting Deposits.
Let's assume that one of the bank's depositors, Adam Swift, deposits $1,000 in cash in his checking account. We would reflect this change by increasing the bank's checkable deposits by $1,000 and increasing its reserves by the same amount.

The bank now has an additional $1,000 in cash reserves (clearly an asset) and the liability of paying out that same amount should Mr. Swift write checks totaling $1,000. Because the bank's deposits have increased by $1,000, it must now maintain an additional $200 in required reserves (20 percent of $1,000). The Gainsville Bank now finds itself with excess reserves of $800.

GAINSVILLE NATIONAL BANK

ASSETS		LIABILITIES	
Reserves	+$1,000	Checkable deposits	+$1,000
required +$200			
excess +$800			
	+$1,000		+$1,000

What will the Gainsville Bank do with those excess reserves? If it simply let them sit in the vault, it would be sacrificing the interest that could be earned on $800. Because the bank wants to show a profit, it will probably use those excess reserves to make loans.

Step Two: Making a Loan. Let's assume that another resident of Gainsville, June Malthus, walks in and asks to borrow $800. How will we record this transaction? On the asset side, we will record a loan for $800. The bank receives this asset in the form of a note, or IOU, agreeing to repay the $800 plus interest. On the liability side of the balance sheet, we increase checkable deposits by $800 (from $1,000 to $1,800).

GAINSVILLE NATIONAL BANK

ASSETS		LIABILITIES	
Reserves	$1,000	Checkable deposits	$1,800
Loans	+$ 800	Adam Swift $1,000	
		June Malthus $ 800	
	$1,800		$1,800

This last entry may seem puzzling to you if you have not yet borrowed money. The way you generally receive money borrowed from a bank is in the form of a checking account with your name on it. This is the money-creating transaction of the bank. Ms. Malthus has exchanged a piece of paper (an IOU) that is *not* money for something that *is* money, checkable deposits. If you think about this process, you'll see the logic of it: The Gainsville Bank is now using $1,000 in reserves to support $1,800 of checkable deposits. And because of the fractional reserve principle, bank officials can be confident that this support is adequate; they know that not all the original depositors will withdraw their money simultaneously.

Not everyone can create money through lending. When you lend money to a friend, your friend ends up with more money, but you have less. The total money supply has not increased. However, when you borrow money from a bank, you end up with more money, but no one has any less. And the money supply actually increases.

How do we explain the difference? Your IOU does not circulate as money, whereas the IOU of a bank does. What happens when you deposit cash in your checking account? You do not reduce your personal money supply as you would if you had made a loan to your friend. Instead, you merely exchange cash (a form of money) for an IOU known as a checkable deposit (a different form of money). Your currency then serves as reserves for supporting loans that result in the creation of additional deposits. Someone else ends up with more money, but you don't have any less. Once you understand this process, you can see that the bank has really "created" money.

Step Three: Using the Loan. Now that we have seen how banks create money, we can ask what happens to that money when it is used to buy something. Let's assume that Ms. Malthus uses her newly acquired checking account to buy furniture in the nearby town of Sellmore—at the Sellmore Furniture Store. Let's also assume that she spends the entire amount of her loan. She will write a check on the Gainsville Bank and give it to the owner of the Sellmore Furniture Store, who will deposit it in the firm's account at the First National Bank of Sellmore. The Sellmore Bank will then send the check to the district Federal Reserve Bank for collection. (One function of the Federal Reserve is to provide a check collection and clearing service. We'll discuss this and other functions of the Fed later in the chapter.) After the Federal Reserve Bank receives the check, it will reduce the reserve account of the Gainsville Bank by $800 and increase the reserve account of the Sellmore Bank by $800. It will then forward the check to the Gainsville Bank, where changes in assets and liabilities will be recorded. Ms. Malthus has spent the $800 in her checking account, so checkable deposits will be reduced by that amount (from $1,800 to $1,000). The bank's reserves have also fallen by $800 (from $1,000 to $200), the amount of reserves lost to the Sellmore Bank.

GAINSVILLE NATIONAL BANK

ASSETS		LIABILITIES	
Reserves ($1,000 − $800)	$ 200	Checkable deposits ($1,800 − $800)	$1,000
required $200		Adam Swift $1,000	
excess 0		June Malthus 0	
Loans	+$ 800		
	$1,000		$1,000

Note that the Gainsville Bank no longer has any excess reserves. It has reserves of $200, the exact amount required. If the bank had loaned Ms. Malthus more than $800 (the initial amount of its excess reserves), it would now be in violation of the reserve requirement. But each bank realizes that when it makes a loan, it will probably lose reserves to other banks as the borrower spends the loan. For that reason, *individual banks must limit their loans to the amount of their excess reserves.* That's one of the most important principles in this chapter, so be sure you understand it before reading any further.

The Multiple Expansion of Loans and Deposits

Recall that the money lent in the form of checkable deposits circulates. Thus the money created when the Gainsville Bank made a loan to Ms. Malthus is not destroyed when she uses the loan but rather is simply transferred from one bank to another. The checkable deposits and reserves originally represented on the balance sheet of the Gainsville Bank may now be found on the balance sheet of the Sellmore Bank. This means that the Sellmore Bank will now be able to expand its loans.

We know that each bank can expand its loans to create checkable deposits equal to the amount of its excess reserves. Assuming that the Sellmore Bank also faces a reserve requirement of 20 percent and that it had no excess reserves to begin with, it will now have excess reserves of $640. How did we arrive at that amount? The Sellmore Bank increased its checkable deposits, and thus its reserves, by $800, the amount deposited by the owner of the Sellmore Furniture Store. With a 20 percent reserve requirement, the increase in required reserves is $160 ($800 × 0.20 = $160). That leaves $640 in excess reserves, which can be used to support new loans and create additional checking deposits.

This expansion of loans and deposits continues as the money created by one bank is deposited in another bank, where it is used to support even more loans. In Exh. 13.3, we see that the banking system as a whole can eventually create $4,000 in new loans and new money (checkable deposits) from the initial $800 increase in excess reserves received by the Gainsville Bank. We also see the difference between the ability of a single bank and the banking system as a whole to create money. Whereas an individual bank must restrict its loans—and consequently its ability to create money—to the amount of its excess reserves, the banking system as a whole can create loans and deposits equal to some multiple of the excess reserves received by the system. In our example that multiple is 5; the banking system was able to create loans and deposits five times greater than the initial increase in excess reserves ($800 × 5 = $4,000).

EXHIBIT 13.3

The Creation of Money by the Banking System

BANK	NEWLY ACQUIRED DEPOSITS AND RESERVES	REQUIRED RESERVES (20 percent of checkable deposits)	POTENTIAL FOR NEW LOANS (creating money)
Gainsville	$1,000.00	$200.00	$ 800.00
Sellmore	800.00	160.00	640.00
Third Bank	640.00	128.00	512.00
Fourth Bank	512.00	102.40	409.60
Fifth Bank	409.60	81.92	327.68
Sixth Bank	327.68	65.54	262.14
Seventh Bank	262.14	52.43	209.71
All others	1,048.58	209.71	838.87
Total amount of money created by the banking system			$4,000.00*

*This figure represents the *maximum* amount of money that the banking system could create from an initial $800 increase in excess reserves. The example assumes that all banks face a 20 percent reserve requirement and that they are all "loaned up" (have no excess reserves) initially.

The Deposit Multiplier

Fortunately we need not work through all the individual transactions to predict the maximum amount of money that the banking system will be able to create. As a general rule the banking system can alter the money supply by an amount equal to the initial change in excess reserves times the reciprocal of the reserve requirement:

$$\text{Change in excess reserves} \times \frac{1}{\text{Reserve requirement (written as a decimal)}} = \text{Maximum possible increase in checkable deposits by the banking system as a whole.}$$

The reciprocal of the reserve requirement, 1 divided by the reserve requirement, yields a number called the deposit multiplier. The **deposit multiplier** is the multiple by which checkable deposits (in the entire banking system) increase or decrease in response to an initial change in excess reserves. Be careful to distinguish between the deposit multiplier we speak of here and the spending multiplier introduced in Chapter 11. Both multipliers show how an initial change is magnified into a larger amount, but the similarity ends there. The spending multiplier told us the eventual change in income and output (GDP) that would result from any initial change in spending. The deposit multiplier allows us to compute the eventual change in checkable deposits resulting from any initial change in excess reserves.

The reserve ratio in our hypothetical example is 0.20, so the deposit multiplier must be 1/0.20, or 5. Therefore an $800 increase in excess reserves will permit the banking system to create up to $4,000 of new demand deposits. This $4,000 figure is really the _maximum_ possible expansion in checkable deposits, given the stated change in excess reserves and the existing reserve requirement. The actual amount may, for a variety of reasons, be less than the maximum predicted.

An illustration will help: Suppose that the recipient of Ms. Malthus's check decides not to redeposit the entire amount in a checking account. This event will reduce the amount of money being passed on to the remaining banks in the system and thus reduce the amount the system can create through lending. The expansion in checkable deposits will also be less than the maximum if bankers maintain some excess reserves. For instance, perhaps some bankers anticipate deposit withdrawals and prepare for them by holding, rather than lending, excess reserves. Or banks may be forced to hold excess reserves simply because they cannot find enough loan customers. For all of these reasons, the expansion in the checkable-deposit component of the money supply may be substantially less than the maximum predicted by the deposit multiplier.

The Destruction of Checkable Deposits

The deposit multiplier can also work in reverse. Suppose that Adam Swift, our original depositor, withdrew $1,000 in cash from his account at the Gainsville Bank and kept it in his wallet. What would this transaction do to the money supply? The initial transaction merely changes its composition: Mr. Swift is giving up his claim to $1,000 in checkable deposits (a form of money) and is receiving in return $1,000 in cash (another form of money). The size of the money supply remains the same even though more cash and fewer checkable deposits are in circulation.

What happens next? When Mr. Swift withdraws $1,000 from his checking account, the Gainsville Bank loses $1,000 in deposits and reserves.

GAINSVILLE NATIONAL BANK

ASSETS		LIABILITIES	
Reserves	−$1,000	Checkable deposits	−$1,000

Assuming that the bank had no excess reserves to begin with, it now finds itself with a reserve deficiency; that is, it doesn't have sufficient reserves to meet the 20 percent reserve requirement. What is the amount of the deficiency? It is $800—the difference between the amount that Mr. Swift has withdrawn from his checking account ($1,000) and the reserve that the bank was required to maintain on that deposit ($200). In order to correct this deficiency, the bank has two choices. One is to sell $800 worth of securities (remember, banks hold securities, particularly government securities, because they earn interest and can be converted easily into cash); another is to allow $800 worth of loans to be repaid without making new loans. In either case, the next bank in the sequence is going to lose $800 worth of deposits and reserves as its depositors buy those securities or repay those loans. That bank will then be faced with a reserve deficiency; it too may need to sell securities or reduce the amount of its loans to build up reserves.

As you may suspect, this contractionary process can spread to other banks in the system and result in a multiple contraction of loans and deposits that is similar to the multiple expansion we observed earlier. Once again, the limit to this process is set by the reserve requirement and the deposit multiplier derived from that requirement. To predict the maximum contraction in checkable deposits, we multiply the initial reserve deficiency times the deposit multiplier. In our example that would mean a reduction of $4,000 ($800 × 5 = $4,000).

The Federal Reserve System

Now we are ready to examine the role of the Federal Reserve. As a central bank, the Federal Reserve influences the process of expanding or contracting the entire U.S. money supply. Virtually every industrialized nation in the world has a **central bank**—a government agency responsible for controlling the national money supply. In the United Kingdom, for example, the central bank is the Bank of England; in Germany, it's the Bundesbank; in the United States, it is the Federal Reserve System.

Unlike central banks in other nations, the Federal Reserve is an independent organization that is not required to take orders from any other agency or branch of government. This gives the Fed somewhat greater independence than other central banks.

The Origin of the Federal Reserve

The Federal Reserve System was established in 1913 to provide some stability to the banking system. In 1873, 1884, 1893, and 1907 the United States experienced major financial panics in which people feared for the safety of their deposits. Without a central bank to provide loans to member banks, a shortage of cash reserves meant that banks lacking the funds necessary to satisfy their customers would have to close their doors. Once the banks began to close, the panic would become widespread, resulting in even more bank closings.

Shortly after the financial panic of 1907, a National Monetary Commission was set up to study the problem and make a recommendation. That recommendation led eventually to the passage of the Federal Reserve Act (1913), which created the Federal Reserve System. The original purpose of the Federal Reserve was to act as a "lender of last resort," to make loans to banks only when all other sources had dried up. It was thought that the Federal Reserve, by acting as lender of last resort, would stop any financial panic before it got under way and would thus prevent the bank closings and business failures of previous panics. The Federal Reserve was also authorized to provide an efficient mechanism for collecting and clearing checks throughout the United States and to help supervise banks to ensure the prudence of their investment and lending practices.

Today the primary responsibility of the Fed is to help stabilize the economy by controlling the money supply. We expect the Federal Reserve to manipulate the money supply in an effort to prevent (or combat) unemployment or inflation, a responsibility much broader than the one envisioned by Congress in 1913. Because the responsibility for controlling the money supply grew as the federal government assumed a greater role in managing the economy, the modern Federal Reserve organization is far more powerful than Congress intended it to be. Some contemporary economists believe that the Fed's powers to influence the economy should be sharply curtailed; others argue that a strong Federal Reserve is necessary to combat unemployment and inflation. (We'll look further at this debate in Chapter 15.)

The Organization of the Federal Reserve System

The Federal Reserve System is composed of a Board of Governors, twelve Federal Reserve Banks, and several thousand member banks. The Board of Governors is the policymaking body of the Federal Reserve. It consists of a chairperson (currently Alan Greenspan) and six members, all appointed by the President of the United States to serve fourteen-year terms. These terms are structured so that only one expires every two years, which helps to provide continuity and to insulate board members somewhat from political pressure. The primary function of the board is to make the major policy decisions that determine how rapidly or slowly the nation's money supply will grow.

To implement these decisions, twelve Federal Reserve Banks (plus twenty-four branches) are located strategically throughout the country. Their primary function is to oversee the actions of the member banks and other de-

Alan Greenspan, Chairman of the Federal Reserve, has been described as the second most powerful person in the world.

pository institutions within their districts. Member banks include all nationally chartered commercial banks, which are required to join the Federal Reserve System, as well as any state-chartered banks that have chosen membership.

The Monetary Control Act of 1980

Prior to 1980, the distinction between member and nonmember banks was significant: Only member banks were subject to the direct regulation of the Fed. Nonmember banks were subject only to regulations imposed by the states that chartered them. Because the Fed's reserve requirements were generally higher than those imposed by the states, member banks were forced to sacrifice more interest income. (Remember, reserve dollars don't earn interest.)

In the days of relatively low interest rates (4–5 percent) many banks were willing to forgo this interest income in order to obtain the check-collection services and borrowing privileges provided by the Fed. But as interest rates rose, the opportunity cost of those idle reserves increased, and Federal Reserve membership grew less and less attractive. As a consequence, more than 300 banks withdrew from the Federal Reserve between 1973 and 1979; 25 of those were relatively large banks with assets of $100 million or more. Faced with declining membership, the Federal Reserve began to search for some way either to stem the loss of member banks or to establish more effective control over the money-creating activities of nonmember banks.

During this time, the Federal Reserve was concerned also about NOW accounts, which enabled savings and loan associations, mutual savings banks, and credit unions (institutions beyond the Fed's control) to create money. The emergence of NOW accounts further threatened the Fed's ability to monitor and control the money supply. To counter this, the Fed pressed for substantial regulatory changes, and Congress responded with the Depository Institutions Deregulation and Monetary Control Act of 1980.

The Monetary Control Act virtually eliminated the distinction between member and nonmember commercial banks and significantly reduced the distinction between commercial banks and other financial institutions. The act required that all depository institutions—member commercial banks, nonmember commercial banks, savings and loan associations, mutual savings banks, and credit unions—meet the same standards with regard to reserve requirements. It lifted many of the regulations that historically had limited competition among various types of financial institutions, and it opened to all such institutions the option to purchase any of the services offered by the Federal Reserve. These changes improved the Fed's ability to monitor and control the money supply and intensified competition among the various types of depository institutions for depositors and loan customers alike.

Deregulation, Bank Failures, and Changing Financial Markets

Not all of the consequences of the Monetary Control Act and subsequent banking reforms were positive. Many analysts argue that the relaxed regulatory environment contributed to an enormous number of bank and savings and loan failures in the 1980s. With fewer restrictions and more competitive pressure, financial institutions ventured into new lending areas. For instance, many savings institutions began making commercial real estate loans, a type of loan not previously permitted. When real estate markets collapsed, many of these loans became uncollectable, leading to massive losses and the failure of lending institutions. Deregulation was not the only cause of these failures; economic factors, such as low oil prices and depressed agricultural markets, also played an important role. Poor management and in some instances fraud were also to blame. But reduced regulation and lax supervision clearly were contributing factors. Unfortunately many financial institutions remain in weakened condition, and billions of dollars will be required to close these institutions or merge them with stronger ones.

The bank failures of the 1980s led to closer regulatory supervision in the 1990s. But increased supervision brings with it higher costs for the supervised institutions, and that can have unintended consequences. Because today's financial markets are increasingly international, countries that impose costly regulations risk driving businesses to other, less regulated countries. (This concern has resulted in growing international coordination of banking regulations.) Another consequence is the diversion of money from depository institutions, such as banks and savings and loans, to nondepository institutions, such as mutual funds and insurance companies. Nondepository institutions have been growing very rapidly, in part because they can afford to pay higher interest rates than the more highly regulated depository institutions with which they compete. But since these nondepository institutions are largely beyond the control of the Fed, its policymakers are concerned that this trend is undermining their ability to control the money supply. It remains to be seen how the Fed will address this challenge.

The Functions of the Federal Reserve

The foregoing discussion highlights the dynamic nature of our financial institutions and the difficulty of determining the proper level of supervision. Supervising financial institutions is one of the functions of the Fed, a responsibility it shares with the Federal Deposit Insurance Corporation (FDIC), the primary agency insuring deposits at financial institutions.

The Fed also performs a number of other functions. First, the twelve Federal Reserve Banks hold the reserves (other than vault cash) of all the depository institutions in their districts. Second, as lenders of last resort, the Federal Reserve banks stand ready to make loans to depository institutions in temporary need of funds. Third, the Federal Reserve supplies the economy with coins and paper money. Fourth, as we have seen, the Fed provides a system for collecting and clearing checks throughout the United States, making it possible for checks drawn on out-of-town banks to be returned to the home institution for collection. But all of these functions are secondary to the Fed's primary responsibility: the control of the nation's money supply. That is the topic we will examine next.

Monetary Policy and the Federal Reserve

Monetary policy is designed to control the supply of money. More precisely, monetary policy is any action intended to alter the supply of money in order to influence the level of total spending and thereby combat unemployment or inflation.

Although the objective of monetary policy is the same as that of fiscal policy (to prevent or combat unemployment and inflation), its methodology is somewhat different. In Chapter 12 you saw how fiscal policymakers use the government's spending and taxation powers to alter total spending and thereby stimulate employment or reduce inflationary pressures. Likewise, monetary policy works to influence spending but through a different mechanism: by increasing or decreasing the money supply.

The Fed does not manipulate the amount of money by printing more currency or by removing existing paper money from circulation. Remember, most of our nation's money supply is composed of balances in checking accounts—demand-deposit accounts, NOW accounts, and other forms of checkable deposits. It is this element of the money supply that the Fed's actions are designed to influence. You have seen how depository institutions create checkable deposits when they make loans. Now you will discover how the Federal Reserve can influence the lending ability of depository institutions and thereby alter not only the supply of money but also the amount of total spending in the economy.

The Federal Reserve uses three major policy tools to control the money supply: (1) the buying and selling of government securities, a process known as **open-market operations;** (2) its ability to alter the reserve requirement of depository institutions; and (3) its control over the **discount rate**—the interest rate at which banking institutions can borrow from the Federal Reserve. All three policy tools affect the reserve positions of depository institutions. As you have learned, the more excess reserves a bank has, the more loans it can make and the more money (checkable deposits) it can create. By altering the volume of excess reserves, the Fed is able to influence the banking system's ability to make loans. Because making loans means creating more money, the Fed's actions influence the money supply.

Open-Market Operations

The Federal Reserve controls the money supply primarily through its open-market operations: buying and selling government securities on the open market. Whenever the U.S. government runs a deficit, the Treasury finances that deficit by selling government securities to individuals, businesses, financial institutions, and government agencies. Most are marketable, or *negotiable,* meaning that they can be held until maturity or resold to someone else.[4] Banks find such securities an attractive investment. They not only earn interest but also convert easily into cash in the event that additional reserves are

---

[4] There are different types of marketable government securities. *Treasury bills* are short-term securities with maturities of 91 days to one year. *Government notes* are intermediate-term securities maturing in one to five years. Finally, *government bonds* are long-term securities with maturities of more than five years.

needed. The Federal Reserve uses the market for negotiable securities as a vehicle for controlling the money supply. Let us see how open-market operations work.

If the Fed wants to increase the money supply by expanding loans, it can offer to buy government securities at attractive prices in the open market. The Fed pays for securities purchased from a commercial bank, for example, by increasing the bank's reserve account at the district Federal Reserve Bank. Because this transaction does not increase the bank's deposit liabilities, the additional reserves are all excess and can be used to expand loans and deposits—up to the maximum predicted by the deposit multiplier. As you know, any change in the excess reserves of one bank will lead eventually to a much larger change in the total system's loans and checkable deposits. As commercial banks and other depository institutions make more loans and create more checkable deposits, the money supply will expand.

If the Fed wishes to reduce the money supply, it can shift its open-market operations into reverse and cut the lending ability of banks by selling them government securities. The purchasing banks will experience a reduction in their reserve accounts at district Federal Reserve banks. As their reserves decline, these institutions will have to contract loans or at least limit their expansion. This will cause the money supply to decline or expand at a slower rate.

Changing the Reserve Requirement

The Fed can also influence the reserve position of banks by changing the reserve requirement. Under existing law, the Federal Reserve has the power to specify reserve requirements between 8 and 14 percent for depository institutions above a specified size. This flexibility provides the Federal Reserve with a tool for influencing the money supply by changing the lending ability of depository institutions.

Lowering the reserve requirement would convert some required reserves into excess reserves and thereby expand the lending ability of depository institutions. When these institutions increase their loans, they create checkable deposits, and the money supply expands. Increasing the reserve requirement has the opposite effect. As excess reserves are converted into required reserves, lending contracts and the money supply shrinks.

Modifying the reserve requirement is effective but somewhat dangerous. Even changes as small as one half of one percent can alter by several billion dollars the banking system's ability to make loans. Changes of this magnitude, particularly when they are sudden, can jolt the economy severely. Therefore the Federal Reserve uses this tool sparingly, adjusting the reserve requirement only infrequently and relying mainly on other tools to control the money supply.

Changing the Discount Rate

Since the passage of the Monetary Control Act of 1980, any depository institution may ask to borrow reserves from its district Federal Reserve Bank to avoid reducing the number of loans it can grant or to increase its volume of loans and thereby earn additional interest income.[5]

Recall that the rate of interest charged by the Federal Reserve on loans to depository institutions is called the *discount rate.* In theory increasing the discount rate should discourage borrowing from the Federal Reserve and thus force banks to limit or even contract the number of loans they grant. We know that if banks contract their loans, the money supply will fall.

Lowering the discount rate should have the opposite effect. By encouraging depository institutions to borrow from the Fed and create additional loans and deposits, the lowered rate should lead to an increase in the money supply.

Note the use of the terms "in theory" and "should." In practice, changes in the discount rate have proved to be a very weak policy tool. Bankers tend to equate loans from the Federal Reserve with money borrowed from in-laws; it's something you avoid unless you have no other options. This attitude is not surprising when one considers the Fed's corresponding view that borrowing is a privilege and not a right: If Federal Reserve authorities believe that a bank has overextended itself through poor planning or has borrowed too often or for the wrong purposes, they can refuse to lend the needed reserves. This disciplinary action will force the wayward bank to contract loans, sell securities, or look elsewhere for reserves. Because bankers don't like such restrictions, they prefer to borrow through the **federal funds market,** a market that brings together banks that need reserves and banks that temporarily have excess reserves. The rate charged on such loans is called the **federal funds rate** and usually applies to reserves borrowed on a very short-term basis— often overnight to meet temporary reserve deficiencies.

Because banks borrow from the Federal Reserve only infrequently, changes in the discount rate have little impact on the banking system's lending ability and thus register little effect on the money supply. In fact many economists tend to view a change in the discount rate more as an indication of the Fed's intentions than as an effective policy move. Increases in the discount rate are thought to indicate the Fed's intention to contract the money supply or slow its rate of growth; decreases signal a desire to expand the money supply or increase its rate of growth.

---

[5] When depository institutions repay these loans to the Fed, their reserves will decline, and they will be forced to contract loans or find other sources of reserves.

Money, Interest Rates, and the Level of Economic Activity

Now that we've seen how the Federal Reserve can expand or contract the money supply, let's explore how changes in the money supply affect the economy. According to the Keynesian model, changes in the money supply affect output and employment primarily by altering interest rates and thereby influencing the level of total spending. Because a significant amount of consumption and investment spending is financed by borrowing, changes in the interest rate can affect the amount of spending in the economy. For example, a lower interest rate may encourage more people to buy new cars and new homes and may encourage businesses to invest in new factories and machinery.

Why would changes in the money supply tend to alter the rate of interest? To answer that question, we need to think back to Chapter 3, where we discussed price determination in competitive markets. Like the price of wheat or the price of cattle, the interest rate—the price of money—is determined by the

Federal Reserve policies are not always popular. Here, demonstrators protest policies which raised interest rates to slow the economy and prevent inflation.

forces of demand and supply. As a consequence, any change in either the demand for money or its supply will affect the rate of interest.[6] If the supply of money increases relative to demand, the interest rate will tend to decline; if the supply of money declines in relation to demand, the rate of interest will tend to increase. (In November 1994 Fed policymakers raised interest rates by the largest amount in more than a dozen years. Read the article on page 410 to find out why they took this action.)

Interest Rate Determination

Individuals and businesses demand money for a variety of reasons. Individuals need money to pay rent, buy groceries, and cover the other expenses that they incur from one payday to the next. Businesses must keep enough money on hand to compensate their suppliers and their employees and pay the other daily expenses associated with running a business.

According to Keynes, the quantity of money demanded by individuals and businesses is inversely related to the interest rate: The higher the rate of interest, the less money demanded. To understand that relationship, remember that the money you hold (cash in your wallet or money in your checking account) generally pays little or no interest. But other assets you could hold instead of money—bonds, for instance, or bank certificates of deposit—do pay interest. The higher the prevailing interest rate, the more attractive it becomes to hold these assets instead of money. As a consequence, less money will be demanded when interest rates are *high* than when they are *low*. The demand curve in Exh. 13.4 shows that $100 billion dollars would be demanded at an interest rate of 10 percent, whereas $300 billion would be demanded at an interest rate of 6 percent.

The supply of money is depicted as a vertical line in Exh. 13.4 to illustrate that the quantity of money supplied does not respond automatically to changes in the interest rate; instead, it remains constant at the level determined by the Federal Reserve. The intersection of the demand curve and the vertical supply curve determines the equilibrium interest rate: the interest rate at which the amount of money that people want to hold is exactly equal to the amount available. In our hypothetical example the equilibrium interest rate is 8 percent. At that interest rate individuals and businesses are willing to hold $200 billion, exactly the amount being supplied by the Federal Reserve.

---

[6] To simplify matters, we will assume a single rate of interest, but in fact there are several. For example, short-term borrowers generally pay a lower interest rate than those who require the money for a longer period. In addition, borrowers with good credit ratings usually pay lower rates than those with poor ratings.

EXHIBIT 13.4

The Equilibrium Interest Rate

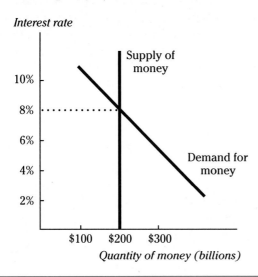

Interest rate

Supply of money

Demand for money

$100 $200 $300

Quantity of money (billions)

The intersection of the demand curve for money and the supply curve of money determines the equilibrium interest rate—the interest rate at which the amount of money that individuals and businesses want to hold is exactly equal to the amount available. In this example the equilibrium interest rate is 8 percent.

Monetary Policy and the Level of Economic Activity

In the Keynesian model monetary policy works primarily through altering the equilibrium interest rate. By adjusting the money supply, the Federal Reserve is able to push the equilibrium interest rate up or down, which influences the level of total spending in the economy and thereby affects unemployment or inflation. This transmission process can be summarized as follows:

$$\text{Money supply} \rightarrow \text{Interest rate} \rightarrow \text{Spending} \rightarrow \begin{array}{c}\text{Output,} \\ \text{employment,} \\ \text{and prices.}\end{array}$$

To illustrate the way monetary policy works, let's assume that the economy is suffering from unemployment. You already know that according to the Keynesian model, unemployment is caused by too little spending. The Federal Reserve can stimulate spending by increasing the money supply. For example, suppose the Fed reduces the reserve requirement, buys government securities, or lowers the discount rate and thereby shifts the money supply curve in Exh. 13.5 from S_1 to S_2, denoting an increase in the money supply from $200 billion to $300 billion. Since the demand for money is unchanged, the equilibrium interest rate will fall from 8 percent to 6 percent. At this lower

Federal Reserve Increases Interest Rates by ¾ Point; Jump Is Largest Since 1981

Aim Is Slower Economic Growth, to Avert Any Surge of Inflation

WASHINGTON

Nov. 15—Determined to prevent strong economic growth from feeding inflation, the Federal Reserve raised short-term interest rates today by the largest amount since 1981 and left open the possibility of further increases. Banks followed by raising the rates they charge for loans.

The increases are likely to show up immediately in the rates charged millions of Americans on everything from home equity loans to credit cards to small-business loans. . . .

While rising rates are intended to slow economic growth, the Federal Reserve's five previous increases, which began in February, have had mixed results. Some industries, like auto making, that depend on customers who need loans have had robust sales, while others, like home building, have begun to slow. Critics of the Federal Reserve say that in-

terest rate changes take up to 18 months to show results and that the previous increases may yet do so. . . .

The decision by the Federal Reserve came five hours after it reported that American factories operated at 84.9 percent of capacity in October, the highest level in nearly 15 years. When factories work at top speed, production bottlenecks often occur and can lead to inflation as companies bid up the prices of scarce materials and skilled workers.

"These measures were taken against the background of evidence of persistent strength in economic activity and high and rising levels of resource utilization," the Federal Reserve said in a statement.". . .

Even before the rate decision was made today, more than 100 people from labor unions and community groups protested the anticipated increase outside the Federal Reserve headquarters, the first such rally

against rising interest rates since the early 1980's.

A series of speakers pointed out that while the nation's unemployment rate may be relatively low now at 5.8 percent, 7.6 million Americans remain unemployed, while millions more are stuck in low-wage jobs.

The National Association of Manufacturers also criticized the move, contending that the nation's factories may have more capacity than Federal Reserve statisticians realize, given heavy corporate investment this year.

Alice M. Rivlin, President Clinton's budget director, warned today that more inflation might result if Congressional Republicans stimulated the economy by enacting tax cuts without matching spending cuts. That might push the Federal Reserve to raise interest rates higher. "It would certainly put enormous upward pressure on interest rates and the Fed would have to continue to raise rates," she said. . . .

While the Federal Reserve has raised rates by a full percentage point in the past, most recently on May 5, 1981, Fed officials were unable to find any prior case today of a move of three quarters of a point.

The action appeared to represent a compromise between those officials most worried by inflation, led by J. Alfred Broaddus Jr., the president of the Federal Reserve Bank of Richmond, and officials more inclined to wait and see whether the strong economic growth actually produced inflation.

Officials worried about inflation have pushed for big increases in short-term rates that would shock bond traders into believing that inflation is under control, thereby halting the upward creep in long-term interest rates. . . .

Alan Greenspan, the Federal Reserve's chairman, has said that the central bank should err, if at all, on the side of raising rates too much. It is easier to reverse an unexpected drop in economic output by lowering interest rates than it is to stop an inflationary spiral with higher rates, he testified last summer. . . .

One of the Federal Reserve's biggest worries is that prices for commodities and some industrial materials, like plywood and ball bearings, have been increasing steadily this year. Consumer prices have not yet reflected these increases, mostly because labor accounts for two-thirds of the cost of consumer goods and wages have been rising fairly slowly this year.

But the Labor Department reported on Nov. 4 that average hourly wages had spurted up 8 cents in October, to $11.24. As a result, Fed officials worry about whether inflation will stay limited to commodity prices.

"I don't think that can last very long; it's going to have to show through or recede," Edward W. Kelley Jr., a Federal Reserve Board governor, said on Nov. 4.

—*Keith Bradsher*

SOURCE: Keith Bradsher, "Federal Reserve Increases Interest Rates by 3/4 Point; Jump Is Largest Since 1981," November 16, 1994. Copyright ©1994 by The New York Times Company. Reprinted with permission.

Use Your Economic Reasoning

1. The Fed raised interest rates to prevent inflation. What factors led Fed policymakers to believe that inflationary pressures were building?

2. If the Fed wanted to raise interest rates, would it buy or sell government securities in the open market?

3. According to the Keynesian model, what impact would higher interest rates have on the overall economy? How would you show this result graphically?

4. Some critics believe that the Fed acted prematurely. What would be the opportunity cost of premature action by the Fed?

EXHIBIT 13.5

The Effect of Changes in the Money Supply on the Equilibrium Interest Rate

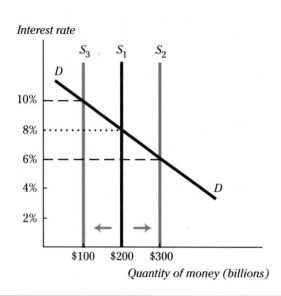

By adjusting the money supply, the Federal Reserve may be able to alter the interest rate. For example, if the money supply is increased from S_1 to S_2 (from $200 billion to $300 billion), the equilibrium interest would tend to fall from 8 percent to 6 percent. On the other hand, if the money supply is decreased from S_1 to S_3 (from $200 billion to $100 billion), the interest rate would tend to rise from 8 percent to 10 percent.

interest rate, businesses will find it profitable to borrow additional money to invest in plants and equipment; households will be inclined to borrow and spend more on new homes, automobiles, and other consumer goods. An increase in the money supply thus lowers the interest rate and leads to increased total spending, which in turn boosts the level of total output and employment.

To attack inflation, the Federal Reserve must reduce the level of total spending by contracting the money supply. This can be accomplished by increasing the reserve requirement, selling government securities, or increasing the discount rate. You can see in Exh. 13.5 that reducing the money supply from S_1 to S_3, a decrease from $200 billion to $100 billion, pushes the interest rate from 8 percent to 10 percent. What is the effect of the higher rate of interest? Businesses will tend to reduce investment spending, and households will be likely to spend less on new homes, boats, camping trailers, and other items that they buy on credit or through borrowing. Reducing the money supply thus raises the interest rate and leads to a reduction in the level of total spending in the economy, which in turn helps reduce inflationary pressures.

Thus you can see how monetary policy works in the Keynesian model through its impact on the interest rate. By adjusting the cost of money, the Fed is able to influence the level of total spending in the economy and thereby combat unemployment or inflation.

The Limits to Monetary Policy

The Federal Reserve's independent status gives monetary policy some distinct advantages over fiscal policy. When the Fed's Board of Governors decides that action should be taken to combat unemployment or inflation, it does not need to wait for Congress to agree. The board can approve the needed policy changes and have them implemented in a very short time. Board members' fourteen-year terms also serve to insulate them from political pressures, although the insulation is not complete in view of the periodic threats to bring the Fed under the direct control of Congress.

But monetary policy has limitations as well. (Recall the limitations of fiscal policy that we examined in Chapter 12.) Here we will look at two problems that may be encountered when monetary policy is used in an attempt to guide the economy's performance.

Time Lags

Like fiscal policy, monetary policy is subject to some time lags. Although Federal Reserve authorities don't need the approval of Congress to implement policy changes, they do need time to recognize that a problem exists and to agree on the needed action. As we learned earlier, our economic indicators sometimes send mixed or unclear messages, so some time may elapse before members of the Board of Governors identify a problem and prescribe a remedy. Once they take action, additional time passes before their policy change exerts its impact on the economy. If the board members decide to stimulate the economy, for example, it will take time for an increase in lending to trigger the associated increases in spending, output, and employment. If this time lag is too long, the added stimulus may hit the economy when it is already on the road to spontaneous recovery. In that event the Fed's actions may contribute to inflation rather than help reduce unemployment.

Uneven Effectiveness

Monetary policy may be less effective in combating unemployment than in combating inflation. When the Fed reduces banks' reserves to combat inflation, banks are forced to restrict (or even contract) lending. However, when it implements an easy-money policy to combat unemployment and makes more reserves available to depository institutions, bankers need not use those reserves to support loans. If bankers doubt the ability of customers to repay loans, they refuse to lend; if households and businesses are pessimistic about the future, they may decide not to borrow. Without greater lending and borrowing, spending will not increase; thus the economy will not receive the stimulus needed to pull it from its depressed state.

How significant are the monetary policy limitations noted here? As with fiscal policy, the issue is open to debate. But the performance of the Federal Reserve in the 1980s seems to provide evidence that discretionary policy can be successful in guiding the economy's performance. After halting inflation early in the decade, the Fed manipulated interest rates to achieve a seven-year expansion without significant inflation. Many economists argue that this experience demonstrates the wisdom of an activist monetary policy.

But all do not agree with this assessment. Monetarists believe that the lags in monetary policy are long and unpredictable. Consequently, they contend, attempts to use monetary policy to guide the economy's performance can result in worse rather than better economic performance. New classical economists also argue against discretionary monetary policy, believing that, as with fiscal policy, the actions of policymakers will be anticipated and neutralized. They argue that an expansionary monetary policy will have no beneficial impact on the economy; it will only lead to inflation. The views of the monetarists and the new classical economists will be considered in detail in Chapter 15.

Summary

Economists define *money* as anything that serves as a *medium of exchange,* a *standard of value,* and a *store of value.* Currency (coins and paper money) and *checkable deposits* (checking accounts at banks and savings institutions) clearly perform all the functions of money. Other *assets*—passbook savings accounts, for example—perform some, but not all, of the functions of money or perform those functions incompletely. Assets that are not money but that can be quickly converted into money are termed *near money.*

In its role as controller of the U.S. money supply, the Federal Reserve defines that supply according to three classifications. The narrowest is *M-1,* composed of currency in the hands of the public plus all checkable deposits. A somewhat broader definition of the nation's money supply, *M-2* includes everything in M-1 plus money-market mutual fund balances, money-market deposits at savings or thrift institutions, and small savings deposits. The broadest definition of the money supply, *M-3,* includes everything in M-2 plus savings deposits in excess of $100,000.

Approximately 70 percent of the M-1 money supply is in the form of checkable deposits; the remainder is currency. The Federal Reserve provides depository institutions (commercial banks and thrift institutions) with the coins and paper currency they need in order to serve their customers. Checkable deposits, on the other hand, are actually created by the depository institutions themselves when they make loans.

According to the *fractional reserve principle,* a bank need maintain only a given fraction of a dollar in *required reserves* for each dollar in checkable deposits; the balance of those funds can be loaned out to earn interest. In the process of making these loans, banks create checkable deposit money. For example, when a person borrows money from a bank, he or she exchanges something that is not money (an IOU) for something that is money (a checking account balance). This increases the money supply by the amount of the loan.

Each depository institution must limit its loans to the amount of its *excess reserves*—reserves in excess of the sum it is legally required to maintain in the form of vault cash and deposits with the Federal Reserve. This limitation is necessary because as loans are spent, reserves are likely to be lost to other depository institutions. Thus each institution can expand the money supply by an amount equal to its excess reserves but no more than that.

The banking system (including all depository institutions) does not have to worry about losing reserves. Reserves lost by one depository institution must be deposited in some other bank in the system. The banking system as a whole, then, can create loans and deposits equal to some multiple of its excess reserves. To be precise, it can expand loans and deposits by an amount equal to the initial change in excess reserves times the reciprocal of the reserve requirement (the *deposit multiplier*).

The Federal Reserve, our nation's *central bank,* influences the ability of depository institutions to expand or contract deposits and thereby regulates the size of the nation's money supply. The Fed's Board of Governors makes all major policy decisions and communicates them to the twelve Federal Reserve banks, which oversee the actions of all depository institutions in their districts.

The Federal Reserve has three major tools with which to control the money supply: (1) the buying and selling of government securities, a process known as *open-market operations;* (2) the ability to alter the reserve requirement; and (3) control over the *discount rate*—the interest rate at which commercial banks and other depository institutions can borrow from the Federal Reserve.

All these policy tools affect the reserve position of banks. By influencing the volume of excess reserves, the Fed is able to affect the banking system's ability to make loans and is thereby able to influence the money supply. This control over the money supply enables the Federal Reserve to alter the interest rate, which in turn influences the level of total spending in the economy.

Monetary policy has some distinct advantages over fiscal policy. The lags in monetary policy tend to be shorter than those in fiscal policy, and because the Fed tends to be somewhat insulated from political pressures, it may have more freedom to pursue long-run goals than does Congress.

Monetary policy is also subject to limitations: (1) Although the lags in monetary policy are generally shorter than those in fiscal policy, they do exist and have the potential to make monetary policy counterproductive. (2) Monetary policy may be more effective in combating inflation than in dealing with unemployment.

Glossary

Asset. Anything of value owned by an entity.

Balance sheet. A statement of a business's assets and liabilities.

Central bank. A government agency responsible for controlling a nation's money supply.

Checkable deposits. All types of deposits on which customers can write checks.

Demand deposits. Non-interest-bearing checking accounts at commercial banks.

Deposit multiplier. The multiple by which checkable deposits (in the entire banking system) increase or decrease in response to an initial change in excess reserves.

Discount rate. The rate of interest charged by the Federal Reserve on loans to depository institutions.

Excess reserves. Bank reserves in excess of the amount required by law.

Federal funds market. A market that brings together banks in need of reserves and banks that temporarily have excess reserves.

Federal funds rate. The rate of interest charged by banks for lending reserves to other banks.

Fractional reserve principle. The principle that a bank need maintain only a fraction of a dollar in reserve for each dollar of its demand deposits.

Liabilities. The debts of an entity, or what it owes.

M-1. Federal Reserve definition of the money supply that includes currency in the hands of the public plus all checkable deposits; the narrowest definition of the money supply.

M-2. Federal Reserve definition of the money supply that includes all of M-1 plus money-market mutual fund balances, money-market deposits at savings institutions, and small savings deposits.

M-3. Federal Reserve definition of the money supply that includes all of M-2 plus large savings deposits.

Medium of exchange. A generally accepted means of payment for goods and services; one of the three basic functions of money.

Monetary policy. Any action intended to alter the supply of money in order to influence the level of total spending and thereby combat unemployment or inflation.

Near money. Assets that are not money but that can be converted quickly to money.

NOW account. A savings account on which the depositor can write checks; NOW stands for negotiable order of withdrawal.

Open-market operations. The buying and selling of government securities by the Federal Reserve as a means of influencing the money supply.

Owner equity. The interest of the owner or owners of a business in its assets.

Required reserves. The amount of reserves a depository institution is required by law to maintain. These reserves must be in the form of vault cash or deposits with the Federal Reserve.

Reserve requirement. The fraction of a bank's checkable deposits that must be held as required reserves.

Savings deposits. Interest-bearing deposits at commercial banks and savings institutions.

Standard of value. A unit in which the prices of goods and services can be expressed; one of the three basic functions of money.

Store of value. A vehicle for accumulating or storing wealth to be used at a future date; one of the three basic functions of money.

Study Questions

Fill in the Blanks

1. Money functions as a _____, a _____ _____, and a _____.

2. Demand deposits, NOW accounts, and ATS accounts are all examples of _____ _____.

3. The primary characteristic of all M-1 money is that it can easily function as a _____.

4. A bank must maintain reserves equal to a specified fraction of its _____ _____.

5. Banks create money when they _____; the amount of money that a bank can create is equal to its _____.

6. Today the primary purpose of the Federal Reserve is to regulate or control the _____ in order to combat unemployment and inflation.

7. According to the Keynesian model, an increase in the money supply would tend to (increase/decrease) _____ the interest rate, which would tend to (increase/decrease) _____ investment spending, which in turn would (increase/decrease) _____ GDP.

8. The Federal Reserve controls the money supply primarily through (which policy tool?) _____.

9. The rate charged by the Federal Reserve on loans to depository institutions is called the _____.

10. Monetary policy may be less effective in combating _____ than _____.

Multiple Choice

1. Which of the following is the largest component of the M-1 money supply?
   a) Currency
   b) Passbook savings accounts M2
   c) Checkable deposits
   d) Money-market accounts M2

2. Which of the following is *not* an example of near money?
   a) A savings account M1
   b) A government bond

   c) A piece of prime real estate

   d) An account with a money-market fund

3. Which of the following does *not* appear as an asset on the balance sheet of a bank?

   a) Demand deposits

   b) Reserves

   c) Securities

   d) Loans

4. Assuming that the reserve requirement is 30 percent, how much additional money can the bank represented below create? (All figures are in millions of dollars.)

ASSETS		LIABILITIES	
Reserves	$23	Checkable deposits	$50
Securities	25	Owner equity	40
Loans	17		
Property	25		

   a) $ 8 million

   b) $12 million

   c) $15 million

   d) $25 million

5. Assuming a reserve requirement of 25 percent, how much additional money can the bank represented below create? (All figures are in millions.)

ASSETS		LIABILITIES	
Reserves	$35	Checkable deposits	$80
Securities	30	Owner equity	20
Loans	25		
Property	10		

   a) $20 million

   b) $15 million

   c) $10 million

   d) $ 5 million

6. If the reserve requirement is 25 percent, the deposit multiplier would be equal to

   a) 4.

   b) 5.

   c) 1/4.

   d) 10.

7. If the balance sheet represented in question 5 were for the banking *system* rather than for a single bank, the system could expand the money supply by an additional

   a) $15 billion.
   b) $30 billion.
   c) $60 billion.
   d) $80 billion.

8. Which of the following was *not* accomplished by the Monetary Control Act of 1980?

   a) It virtually eliminated the distinction between member and nonmember commercial banks.
   b) It enhanced competition between the various types of financial institutions.
   c) It established uniform reserve requirements for all depository institutions.
   d) It eliminated the "lender of last resort" function of the Federal Reserve.

9. If banks hold checkable deposits of $200 million and reserves of $50 million and if the reserve requirement is 20 percent, how much additional money can the banking *system* create?

   a) $20 million
   b) $50 million
   c) $100 million
   d) $200 million

10. Which of the following is *not* a function of the Federal Reserve?

    a) To control the money supply
    b) To make loans to depository institutions
    c) To insure the deposits of customers
    d) To provide a check-collection service

11. If the Federal Reserve wants to reduce the equilibrium interest rate, it should

    a) increase the reserve requirement in order to expand the money supply.
    b) sell securities on the open market in order to expand the money supply.
    c) buy government securities in order to expand the money supply.
    d) increase the discount rate in order to expand the money supply.

12. When the Federal Reserve sells government securities on the open market, the lending ability of banks

    a) tends to decline; the money supply shrinks, and the interest rate tends to decline.
    b) tends to decline; the money supply expands, and the interest rate tends to rise.
    c) increases; the money supply expands, and the interest rate tends to fall.
    d) tends to decline; the money supply shrinks, and the interest rate tends to rise.

13. Let's assume that all banks in the system are loaned up (have no excess reserves) and that they all face a reserve ratio of 20 percent. If the Federal Reserve buys a $100,000 security from Bank A, how much new money can the banking *system* create? (*Hint:* Remember that the Fed will pay for the security by increasing the reserve account of Bank A.)

    a) $100,000
    b) $1,000,000
    c) $400,000
    d) $500,000

14. If the Federal Reserve wanted to reduce inflationary pressures, what would be the proper combination of policies?

    a) Increase the reserve ratio, decrease the discount rate, and sell securities.
    b) Increase the reserve ratio, increase the discount rate, and sell securities.
    c) Increase the reserve ratio, increase the discount rate, and buy securities.
    d) Decrease the reserve ratio, decrease the discount rate, and buy securities.

15. To combat unemployment, the Federal Reserve should

    a) reduce the money supply by selling government securities.
    b) reduce the money supply by lowering the reserve requirement.
    c) increase the money supply by raising the discount rate.
    d) increase the money supply by buying government securities.

Problems and Questions for Discussion

1. Explain each of the functions of money. Which of these functions does a traditional savings account perform? A NOW account?

2. Explain what is meant by the fractional reserve principle. How is it related to a bank's ability to create money?

3. Why must individual banks limit their loans to the amount of their excess reserves?

4. If a bank can create money, why can't you?

5. What is the money multiplier, and how is it calculated?

6. If you asked for your loan in cash rather than accepting a checking account, what impact would this action have on the money-creating ability of your bank? What about the banking system as a whole?

7. Suppose that you have a credit card with a $1,000 limit (you cannot charge more than $1,000). Should that $1,000 be considered part of the money supply? Why or why not?

8. Why might monetary policy be less effective in combating unemployment than in combating inflation?

9. Discuss the reasons for the passage of the Monetary Control Act of 1980.

10. According to Keynesians, monetary policy works through the rate of interest. Explain.

11. Suppose that the Federal Reserve were to increase the reserve requirement. Explain the step-by-step impact of that change on the economy.

12. Why is the discount rate often described as a weak policy tool?

13. What are the advantages of open-market operations over changes in the reserve requirement?

14. Suppose that the housing industry is depressed. What monetary policy actions would you recommend to help the housing industry? Why do you think they would help?

15. If the Fed buys a government security from a private individual, the money supply will immediately be increased. If the Fed buys a government security from a bank, this action will not affect the money supply until a loan is made. Explain the difference. That is, why does one transaction have an immediate impact and the other does not?

Answer Key

Fill in the Blanks

1. medium of exchange, standard of value, store of value
2. checkable deposits
3. medium of exchange
4. checkable deposits
5. make loans; excess reserves
6. money supply
7. decrease, increase, increase
8. open-market operations
9. discount rate
10. unemployment, inflation

Multiple Choice

1. c	4. a	7. c	10. c	13. d
2. c	5. b	8. d	11. c	14. b
3. a	6. a	9. b	12. d	15. d

CHAPTER 14

Aggregate Demand and Supply: The Model of the Self-Correcting Economy

1. Define aggregate demand and explain why the aggregate demand curve is downward sloping.
2. Discuss the factors that will shift the aggregate demand curve to a new position.
3. Define aggregate supply and explain why the aggregate supply curve is upward sloping.
4. Discuss the factors that will shift the aggregate supply curve to a new position.
5. Explain how the economy's equilibrium output and price level are determined, and represent this process graphically.
6. Predict the impact of changes in aggregate demand or supply on the economy's equilibrium output and price level.
7. Explain how changes in aggregate demand or supply can lead to unemployment, inflation, or stagflation.
8. Explain how the economy will tend to automatically eliminate unemployment in the long run.

Throughout the last three chapters we have expanded on the Keynesian model that was introduced in Chapter 10. We've examined the forces that determine output and employment in the Keynesian model and considered its policies for combating unemployment and inflation.

The Keynesian model is useful because it calls attention to the level of demand as an important determinant of the economy's performance. But the model is subject to some significant limitations. First, it does not bring the price level explicitly into the analysis. Recall that the Keynesian model assumes that prices remain stable until full employment is reached. As a consequence, the model cannot depict a situation in which both real output and prices rise simultaneously, a situation that is commonplace in the real world.

Second, the Keynesian model considers only the demand side of the economy: Unemployment results from too little demand for goods and services; inflation results from too much demand. Although these observations are valid and important, they don't tell the whole story, because they fail to consider the supply side of the overall economy. In short, there are sources of unemployment and inflation that are ignored by the basic Keynesian model.

Finally, the Keynesian model totally dismisses the classical contention that the economy is self-correcting. Because prices and wages refuse to fall, reductions in spending lead to unemployment, which must be attacked by government policy. But modern economists (including modern Keynesians) generally agree that prices and wages will eventually decline in the face of falling demand. This possibility implies that the economy may be self-correcting and calls into question the desirability of discretionary monetary and fiscal policies.

This chapter addresses the shortcomings of the basic Keynesian model by expanding the aggregate-demand/aggregate-supply framework that was briefly introduced in Chapter 10. By bringing the supply side of the economy into the analysis, we can obtain a more complete picture of how our economy operates. We will see how the overall price level can change and how changes in aggregate supply can result in simultaneous unemployment and inflation. Finally, the aggregate-demand/aggregate-supply framework will allow us to examine the possibility that the economy is self-correcting.

An Overview of the Model

Understanding the determinants of demand or total spending—the thrust of Keynesian macroeconomics—is only the first step in explaining the economy's overall performance. Modern macroeconomics sees the economy's performance as resulting from the interaction of aggregate demand and aggregate supply. As we discovered in Chapter 10, the intersection of the aggregate demand and aggregate supply curves determines the economy's equilibrium level of real GDP and the overall price level. This is represented in Exh. 14.1, which shows the intersection of *AD* and *AS* determining an overall price level of 100 and an equilibrium real GDP of $1,000 billion.

Chapter 10 provided a brief introduction to aggregate demand and aggregate supply. Our first task in this chapter is to examine these concepts in greater detail. Then we review the process by which the equilibrium output and price level are determined and consider the economy's response to changes in aggregate demand and supply. We begin by reviewing and extending our analysis of aggregate demand.

EXHIBIT 14.1

An Overview of Aggregate Demand and Supply

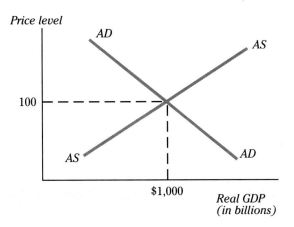

The intersection of the aggregate demand and supply curves determines the equilibrium level of real GDP and the equilibrium price level in the econony.

Aggregate Demand

Aggregate demand is the total quantity of output demanded by all sectors in the economy together (households, businesses, governments, and foreigners) at various price levels in a given time period. Like the demand curve for a single product, the *aggregate demand curve* slopes downward and to the right, indicating that more real output will be demanded at a lower price level than at a higher price level. But the aggregate demand curve slopes downward for different reasons. When we are considering the demand for a single product—steak, for example—we assume that the prices of all similar products—chicken, fish, and pork, for instance—remain constant as we reduce its price. As steak becomes relatively cheaper than before, consumers tend to substitute it for other products, thus increasing the quantity of steak demanded. When we examine the aggregate demand curve, it is not the price of a single product that falls, but rather the price level: the average price of all goods and services. Therefore there must be a different reason for the aggregate demand curve's downward slope. In fact, there are three reasons: the real balance effect, the interest rate effect, and the international trade effect.

The Real Balance Effect

When the price level falls, the real value, or purchasing power, of the public's financial assets—savings accounts, retirement funds, and other financial assets with fixed money values—tends to increase. This makes people feel wealthier, and they tend to demand more goods and services—more real output. The **real balance effect** is the increase in the amount of aggregate output demanded that results from the increased real value of the public's financial assets.

As an example, suppose that you work each summer to help pay for college. This summer you managed to save $2,000, your share of the year's anticipated expenses. Now assume that the overall price level falls to half of what it was when you established your $2,000 objective. In essence, that means that all prices have been cut in half, so your $2,000 will now stretch twice as far as before. How will you react? You will probably start buying things you don't normally purchase, because you have $1,000 in your savings account that won't be needed for anticipated college expenses. That's the real balance effect in action; the real value, or purchasing power, of the money balance in your savings account has increased, and this increase in wealth is spurring you to purchase more goods and services. Of course, if the price level increased, everything would work in reverse; your savings would be worth less, so you would feel less wealthy and would demand fewer goods and services than before. Either way we describe it, the price level and spending on real output are moving in opposite directions, so the aggregate demand curve must slope downward. Exhibit 14.2 depicts the aggregate demand curve for a hypothetical economy.

EXHIBIT 14.2

The Aggregate Demand Curve

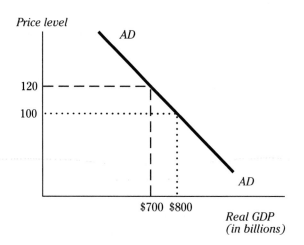

The aggregate demand curve shows an inverse relationship between the overall price level and the quantity of real output demanded. For instance, when the price level decreases from 120 to 110, the quantity of real GDP demanded increases from $700 billion to $800 billion.

The Interest Rate Effect

In addition to its impact on real balances, a change in the price level also has an effect on the prevailing interest rate. The interest rate is determined by the demand and supply of money. When the price level falls, consumers and businesses will require less money for their day-to-day transactions, because a given amount of money will buy more goods and services than before. In other words, a reduction in the price level will reduce the demand for money. Since each aggregate demand curve assumes a fixed supply of money in the economy, a reduction in the demand for money will tend to reduce the price of money—the interest rate. When the interest rate falls, the lower cost of borrowing money tends to stimulate investment spending and some types of consumer spending. The **interest rate effect** is the increase in the amount of aggregate output demanded that results when a reduction in the overall price level causes interest rates to fall.[1]

To illustrate, let's suppose that the price level—the average price of goods and services—fell to half of what it is today. Homes that had been selling for $200,000 would cost $100,000; automobiles that had been priced at $20,000 would be available for $10,000. As a consequence, consumers would need to borrow only half as much money as before to finance their new homes and automobiles and other credit purchases. This reduced demand for money would tend to lower interest rates and stimulate spending. Thus more real output would be demanded at the lower price level. Of course, if the price level increased (which may seem a more realistic possibility), the demand for money would tend to increase, pushing up interest rates and depressing spending on real GDP.

The International Trade Effect

The third way in which price-level changes can affect the amount of aggregate output demanded is through international trade. The two basic transactions in international trade are the importing and exporting of products. **Imports** are goods and services that are purchased from foreign producers. Americans' purchases of German automobiles, French wines, and Japanese electronics are

---

[1] The interest rate effect actually has to do with the impact of a price level change on the "real" interest rate—the interest rate after adjustment for inflation. If the nominal interest rate (the interest rate before adjustment) is 15 percent a year and the expected rate of inflation is 5 percent, the real interest rate is 10 percent.

   Business investment decisions are influenced by real interest rates not nominal rates. A higher nominal interest rate (resulting from a higher expected rate of inflation) would not necessarily discourage businesses from borrowing, since they would also anticipate receiving higher prices for their products (and thus a higher nominal rate of return). The proof that a higher price level causes a higher real interest rate is beyond the scope of this text.

examples of imports. **Exports** are goods and services that are produced do-mestically and sold to customers in other countries. The Ford automobiles, California wines, and Apple computers that are sold to customers in Germany, France, and elsewhere are examples of exports.

How would U.S. imports and exports be affected if the overall price level in the United States fell by, say, 10 percent and everything else (including prices in other countries)[2] remained constant? Since U.S. products would become more attractive in price, we'd expect fewer Americans to buy imported products (because they'd buy domestic products instead) and more foreigners to buy U.S. exports. To illustrate, suppose that the prices of U.S. automobiles fell by 10 percent and the prices of comparable foreign cars remained unchanged. Under these conditions, we'd expect to see more Americans buying cars made in the United States (and fewer buying imports) and increased auto exports as well. In short, at the lower U.S. price level a larger quantity of U.S. automobiles would be demanded. The **international trade effect** is the increase in the amount of aggregate output demanded that results when a reduction in the price level makes domestic products less expensive relative to foreign products. It provides us with a third reason for the downward slope of the aggregate demand curve.

Changes in Aggregate Demand

As with the demand curve for a single product, we need to distinguish between *movement along* an *AD* curve and a *shift* of the *AD* curve. We've seen that changes in the price level will cause movement up or down along a stationary curve. Any change in the spending plans of households, businesses, governments, or foreigners that results from something other than a change in the price level will shift the *AD* curve. Factors that will shift the aggregate demand curve include changes in the expectations of households and businesses, changes in aggregate wealth, changes in government policies, and changes in foreign income and price levels.

Household and Business Expectations

Suppose that households and businesses become less optimistic about the future (perhaps because they anticipate a recession). What impact would that have on aggregate demand? Households might be expected to save more (and thus consume less), whereas businesses would probably reduce their spending for factories and machinery. Because total spending at any price level

---

[2] Another factor that is assumed constant is the foreign exchange rate, the rate at which one country's currency exchanges for that of another.

would be less than before, the *AD* curve would shift to the left (from AD_1 to AD_3 in Exh. 14.3), a reduction in aggregate demand. More optimistic expectations would have the opposite effect: The *AD* curve would shift to the right.

Aggregate Wealth

An increase in the overall wealth of the society would also tend to shift the aggregate demand curve to the right. Consider, for example, the impact of a stock market boom that increased the value of households' stock holdings. Since consumers can finance spending by selling shares of stock and other forms of wealth, this increase in stock values would tend to spur spending; households might be expected to demand more real output than before at any price level. A reduction in wealth—due, perhaps, to a decline in the stock market—would shift the *AD* curve to the left.

Government Policy

Government can also influence aggregate demand through its policies. For instance, a reduction in government spending for goods and services would cause the *AD* curve to shift to the left, as would an increase in personal income taxes (since consumers would have less to spend at each price level). A reduction in the money supply would also cause aggregate demand to fall. The size of the economy's money supply is determined by the Federal Reserve, or Fed. If the Fed decreases the money supply, the interest rate that businesses and others have to pay to borrow money will tend to increase. This

---

EXHIBIT 14.3

Shifts of the Aggregate Demand Curve

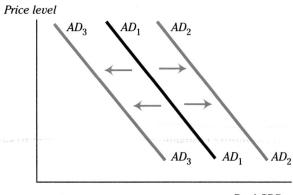

Any change in the spending plans of households, businesses, or government that results from something other than a change in the price level will shift the *AD* curve. A shift to the right is an increase in aggregate demand; a shift to the left is a decrease.

in turn will tend to depress investment spending by businesses and some forms of consumption spending by households, shifting the aggregate demand curve to the left.

Consider an increase in military spending by the federal government. What impact would that have on aggregate demand? It would increase the amount of real GDP demanded at any price level, so it would shift the *AD* curve to the right (from AD_1 to AD_2 in Exh. 14.3). A tax reduction or an increase in the money supply would also tend to increase aggregate demand.

Foreign Incomes and Prices

When foreign incomes grow, foreign households increase their consumption spending. Some of this increased spending will be for U.S. products, causing U.S. exports to increase and shifting the aggregate demand curve to the right. Increased foreign prices would also stimulate spending for U.S. products. An increase in foreign price levels would, ceteris paribus, cause U.S. products to appear more attractive and cause foreign consumers to substitute them for those produced domestically. At the same time, Americans would find foreign products less attractive in price, decreasing our imports. Thus an increase in foreign incomes or price levels would stimulate the demand for U.S. products and shift the *AD* curve to the right.[3] Reductions in foreign incomes or price levels would shift the aggregate demand curve for U.S. products to the left.

In summary, the aggregate demand curve will shift due to changes in the expectations of households or businesses, wealth, government policy, foreign incomes, or foreign price levels. These are the major causes of shifts in aggregate demand, but the list is not exhaustive; other changes could have a similar impact. The important point is that any change in spending plans that stems from something other than a change in the price level will shift the *AD* curve; changes in the price level will cause movement *along* a stationary curve. The article "Repricing of Variable-Rate Debt to Curb Consumer Spending . . . ," on page 432, examines the impact on the economy of rising interest rates. Take a moment to read the article and test what you've learned.

Aggregate Supply

Aggregate demand is only half of the model; the other half is aggregate supply. **Aggregate supply** refers to the total quantity of output supplied by all producers in the economy together at various price levels in a given time period.

---

[3] This assumes that the foreign exchange rate does not change. Chapter 17 will discuss exchange rates in some detail.

As we saw in Chapter 10, the shape we assign to the *aggregate supply curve* depends on the assumptions we make about the behavior of wages and prices. If we believe that wages and prices are highly flexible, the *AS* curve will be vertical. If we assume that wages and prices are rigid, the *AS* curve will be horizontal. Most modern economists take a position in the middle; they argue that all wages and prices are flexible in the long run, but that at least some wages and input prices are rigid in the short run. This belief results in an *AS* curve that is upward sloping in the short run.

An upward-sloping aggregate supply curve indicates that businesses tend to supply more aggregate output at higher price levels than at lower price levels. Businesses behave in this manner because the wage and input price rigidities we have described cause certain costs to be fixed in the short run. This makes it profitable for businesses to expand output if aggregate demand increases and pushes up the prices they can charge for their products.

The major reason for the rigidity of costs is long-term contracts. Contracts with labor unions, for example, are commonly renegotiated every three years. During the term of the agreement, wage rates are at least partially fixed. The prices paid for raw materials and manufactured inputs may also be governed by long-term contracts. Because wage rates and other input prices are commonly fixed in the short run, businesses find it profitable to expand output when the selling prices of their products rise. This positive relationship between the overall price level and the economy's real GDP is reflected in the upsloping *AS* curve depicted in Exh. 14.4.

EXHIBIT 14.4

The Aggregate Supply Curve

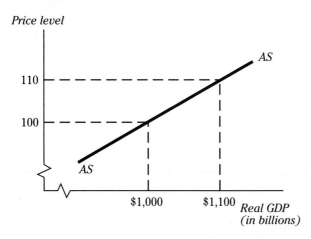

The aggregate supply curve is upward sloping because businesses tend to supply more real output at higher price levels than at lower price levels.

Repricing of Variable-Rate Debt to Curb Consumer Spending, Economic Growth

It's payback time on variable-rate loans.

As more and more variable-rate mortgages and credit cards are repriced in coming months, the long-awaited economic slowdown will gradually begin to take hold, economists say.

Call it "the reverse of the refi boom," says Susan Sterne of Economic Analysis Associates of Greenwich, Conn., referring to the billions of dollars freed up when consumers refinanced their mortgages at lower rates in 1992 and 1993. That extra cash in consumers' pockets triggered a spending spree and was a major force behind the economy's current strength. But as consumers spend more to service debt, there will be less money "left over for consumption and savings," Ms. Sterne says.

Recent economic indicators show few, if any, signs of a slowdown. The latest employment report, for example, suggested that the economy is booming, with employers adding 350,000 new jobs last month. Other indicators also have suggested that the economy has considerable momentum, despite the Federal Reserve's efforts to slow it down by raising short-term interest rates.

But with $900 billion of adjustable-rate home loans due to be reset at higher interest rates and $200 billion of credit-card debt tied to the prime rate—which has risen to 8.5% from 6% at the start of the year—economists say it's hard to imagine that the current pace of economic activity can continue.

The loss of spending because of higher rates on those loans will take at least half a point off the growth rate in 1995 while slowing inflation, says David Wyss of DRI/McGraw Hill. With most of the slowdown occurring in the second half, gross domestic product may grow about 2.6%, he says. That's a marked slowdown from the 4% GDP growth he expects this year.

A slowdown to that level would give the economy a "soft landing" similar to 1986. Then, about nine months after interest rates began rising in mid-1985, the growth of GDP in the succeeding four quarters slowed to a 1.8% rate from 4% in the prior year. It was almost a year before rates that began rising in the second quarter of 1988 slowed housing and other consumer expenditures. That slowdown rolled into a recession.

Economists aren't expecting a recession anytime soon because they see a pickup in exports as world economies strengthen. But that won't be enough, they add, to entirely offset the slowdown in consumer spending as variable mortgage and adjustable credit-card rates rise. . . .

If short-term interest rates rise at least another full percentage point next year, as many economists expect, homeowners will pay an added $5 billion in interest costs. That would bring the total additional cost of higher rates on roughly $900 billion of variable-rate mortgages to as much as $15 billion in 1995, the experts say.

Of course, many mortgage holders whose payments are rising are still ahead of the game if they refinanced mortgages that had even higher rates. But refinancing is dormant now, and most new mortgages increasingly are made at variable, rather than fixed, rates. That means a year from now, when low introductory rates expire, today's new mortgage holders will be making increased payments, even if rates hold at current levels.

Marlene Brown, a freelance food consultant in Los Angeles, has just begun giving back about $150 of the $450 a month she saved a year ago when she turned a 9.5% fixed-rate mortgage into an adjustable one starting at 4.5%. Still, she says, when her current mortgage rate rose by the yearly maximum two percentage points to 6.5%, "it felt like I was throwing money out the window.". . .
—*Fred R. Bleakley*

SOURCE: Fred R. Bleakley, "Repricing of Variable-Rate Debt to Curb Consumer Spending, Economic Growth," December 6, 1994. Reprinted by permission of *The Wall Street Journal*, © 1994 Dow Jones & Co., Inc. All Rights Reserved Worldwide.

Use Your Economic Reasoning

The interest rate charged on variable-rate loans is commonly lower than that on fixed-rate loans, but the drawback is that the interest rate (and thus the monthly payment) on variable loans can change. The following questions examine the impact of those changes.

1. What types of spending would be most affected by the rise in interest rates described in the article?

2. How will the rise in interest rates affect aggregate demand? Will it shift the aggregate demand curve or cause movement along the curve?

3. Increases in U.S. exports are expected to partially offset the effect of higher interest rates. Use a graph to show the impact of increased demand for U.S. exports.

The Aggregate Supply Curve: A Closer Look

An example from microeconomics may help to illustrate why the *AS* curve is upward sloping. Consider the behavior of the competitive firm. Recall that in the model of pure competition the individual firm is a price taker; it must charge the price dictated by the market. But the firm can sell as much output as it chooses at that price. The firm will continue to expand output so long as the additional (marginal) revenue it will receive from selling an additional unit of output is greater than the additional (marginal) cost of producing that unit. When marginal cost is exactly equal to marginal revenue, the firm will be maximizing its profit (or minimizing its loss). This situation is represented in Exh. 14.5, which shows a firm that is initially maximizing its profit by producing an output of 1,000 units, the output dictated by the intersection of MR_1 and MC_1.

Now suppose that the market price of the firm's product increases from $10 to $14. This would be represented by shifting the demand curve upward from D_1 to D_2. Note what happens to the firm's profit-maximizing output: It increases from 1,000 units to 1,200 units! The higher price provides incentive for the firm to expand output, because the firm can earn a marginal profit on the additional units.

Note that it is not profitable for the firm to expand output indefinitely. Because the marginal cost curve is upward sloping, marginal cost will eventu-

---

EXHIBIT 14.5

Price Level Adjustments and the Individual Firm

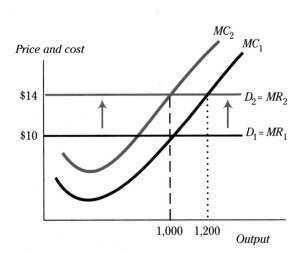

When the price of its product rises and input prices remain unchanged, the competitive firm responds by expanding output. Here output is increased from 1,000 to 1,200 units when selling price rises from $10 to $14. However, if input prices rise by the same percent as the product price, *MC* will shift up from MC_1 to MC_2, and the profit-maximizing output will be unchanged.

ally increase enough to match the new price. Of course, production beyond that point will not be profitable. Why does MC increase as the firm expands its output? Why is the MC curve upward sloping? Think back to Chapter 5. In the short run, if the firm wants to produce more output, it has to squeeze that production from its fixed factory. It does this by hiring more labor and using its factory and equipment more intensively. But this leads to more and more crowding of the fixed facility. Workers have to wait to use equipment; machines are subject to more frequent breakdowns; workers begin to get in one another's way, and so on. As a consequence, successive units of output become more costly to produce; that is, marginal cost rises. Eventually the cost of producing another unit will have increased enough to match the new product price. At that point the output expansion will cease; the firm will have achieved its new profit-maximizing level of production.

It is essential to note that the firm would not have expanded output if wage rates and other input prices had increased along with the price of the firm's product. Proportionally higher wages and other input prices would have shifted the marginal cost curve up from MC_1 to MC_2. Note that MC_2 intersects MR_2 (the new, higher product price) at 1,000 units of output, the original profit-maximizing output. The higher input prices have completely offset the higher product price, eliminating any incentive to expand output. In the long run this is precisely what we expect to happen, since contracts eventually expire, and wage rates and other input prices are able to adjust upward. But in the short run wage contracts and other rigidities provide a gap between product prices and production costs that makes it profitable for firms to expand output.

Changes in Aggregate Supply

The aggregate supply curve is upward sloping because there is a positive relationship between the general price level and the quantity of aggregate output supplied. This relationship assumes that the other factors that influence the amount of real GDP supplied are held constant. Changes in these other factors will cause a change in aggregate supply; the entire AS curve will shift to a new position. The factors that will shift the AS curve include changes in wage rates, the prices of nonlabor inputs, labor productivity, labor supplies, and the capital stock.

The Wage Rate

Suppose that the average wage rate paid by firms in the economy increases. What will that do to the AS curve? If it costs more to produce a given level of output, firms will require higher prices in order to produce that output;

thus the *AS* curve must shift upward (leftward). This is represented in Exh. 14.6 by the movement of the aggregate supply curve from AS_1 to AS_2. Lower wages would have the opposite effect; they would tend to shift the *AS* curve downward (rightward), from AS_1 to AS_3. Remember that wage rates tend to be fixed by contract in the short term. But when these labor contracts expire, wage rates may be renegotiated up or down, causing the *AS* curve to shift.

The Prices of Nonlabor Inputs

Labor is only one of the resources required to produce output. Businesses also need capital equipment, raw materials, manufactured inputs, and managerial talent. Changes in the price of any of these inputs will tend to shift the position of the *AS* curve; increases will shift it upward, and decreases will shift it downward.

Consider, for instance, the impact of the increase in the price of petroleum products resulting from Iraq's invasion of Kuwait in 1990. When crude oil prices increased, the cost of producing a given level of output rose; thus the *AS* curve shifted upward. Bad weather that reduced agricultural output could have a similar impact, since it would tend to increase the price of wheat, corn,

---

EXHIBIT 14.6

Shifts of the Aggregate Supply Curve

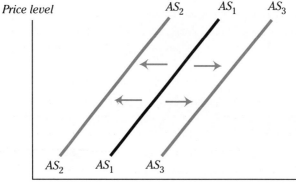

The *AS* curve will shift upward (leftward) if there is a hike in wage rates, an increase in the prices of nonlabor inputs, or a reduction in labor productivity. It will shift downward (rightward) if wages or other input prices fall or if labor productivity rises.

and other agricultural products that are inputs in the production of breakfast cereals and other food items.

The Productivity of Labor

The cost of producing output is influenced not only by wage rates and other input prices but also by the productivity of labor—by how efficient labor is at transforming inputs into finished products. If the productivity of labor increases, the cost of producing the finished product tends to fall. Suppose that labor is paid $8 per hour and that the average worker is able to produce ten units of output per hour. The average labor cost of producing each unit of output is $.80 ($8.00 per hour divided by ten units per hour). Now suppose that due to improved training or new technology the average worker could produce twenty units of output per hour. The labor cost per unit of output would fall to $.40 ($8.00 per hour divided by twenty units of output per hour). As you can see, an increase in labor productivity reduces the cost of producing a given level of output.

A variety of factors can influence the productivity of labor. For example, if the labor force became more highly educated, we would expect its productivity to rise. A technological change that improved the quality of the capital equipment used by labor could also raise productivity. For instance, a faster computer would allow more work to be done per hour.

Supplies of Labor and Capital

Finally, the position of the economy's aggregate supply curve is influenced by the economy's supplies of labor and capital. The larger the labor supply and the stock of capital equipment, the more output the economy is capable of supplying at any price level. Increases in either the labor force or the capital stock will cause the aggregate supply curve to shift right. Decreases would have the opposite effect.

Before continuing, let's review. We've seen that the aggregate demand curve shows the quantity of real GDP that will be demanded at each price level, whereas the aggregate supply curve shows the quantity of real GDP that will be supplied at each price level. The aggregate demand curve will shift to a new position if there is a change in the expectations of households or businesses, the level of aggregate wealth, government policy, foreign incomes, or foreign price levels. The aggregate supply curve will shift in response to a change in the wage rate, the prices of nonlabor inputs, labor productivity, or the supplies of labor or capital.

The Equilibrium Output and Price Level

The interaction of aggregate demand and aggregate supply simultaneously determines the equilibrium price level and real GDP in the economy. This process is illustrated in Exh. 14.7, which shows the intersection of *AS* and *AD* resulting in an equilibrium price level of 100 and an equilibrium real GDP of $1,000 billion.

As you can see in the graph, if the price level was initially above equilibrium (120, for example), the amount of real GDP supplied would exceed the amount of real GDP demanded. This would mean unsold merchandise and pressure to cut prices. The price level would decline until the amount of aggregate output demanded was equal to the amount supplied. If the price level was initially below equilibrium (80, for instance) the result would be a shortage that would put upward pressure on prices until the equilibrium price level was achieved and the shortage was eliminated.

In summary, only at the equilibrium price level is the amount of real GDP demanded equal to the amount supplied. At any other price level, there will be an overall surplus or shortage, which will tend to alter the prevailing price level.

EXHIBIT 14.7

Equilibrium GDP and Price Level

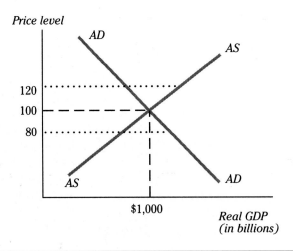

The intersection of the aggregate demand and supply curves determines the price level and the level of output in the economy. Here the equilibrium real GDP is $1,000 billion, and the equilibrium price level is 100.

The Impact of Changes in Aggregate Demand or Supply

In a dynamic economy aggregate demand and supply change frequently. As these changes occur, the equilibrium price and output levels are disturbed and new levels are established. Suppose, for example, that less optimistic expectations caused businesses to cut back on investment spending. Since this would result in less output being demanded at any given price level, the aggregate demand curve would shift to the left. What impact would this have on the economy? As you can see in Exh. 14.8, when aggregate demand declines from AD_1 to AD_2, the level of real GDP in the economy contracts from $1,000 billion to $850 billion, and the overall price level falls from 100 to 90. Since the economy's ability to provide jobs is tied to the level of production, employment in the economy will also tend to fall (which means that, ceteris paribus, unemployment will rise).

EXHIBIT 14.8

The Effects of Changes in Aggregate Demand on Real Output and Prices

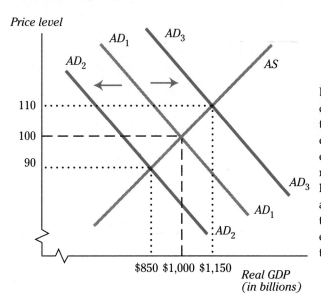

Decreases in aggregate demand will tend to lower the levels of output and employment in the economy while also reducing the overall price level. Increases in aggregate demand will tend to raise output and employment while raising the level of prices.

If aggregate demand increased due to increased government spending, a tax cut, or some other spur to aggregate demand, the *AD* curve would shift to the right, from AD_1 to AD_3. This would result in higher output and employment but would also push the price level upward.

Note that the impact of a change in aggregate demand when the *AS* curve is upward sloping is somewhat different from that predicted by the basic Keynesian model we analyzed in preceding chapters. The simple Keynesian model implies an *AS* curve that is flat, because prices are assumed to be rigid until full employment is reached. This means that so long as excess capacity exists, any change in aggregate demand will alter output and employment without changing the price level. The modern aggregate-demand/aggregate-supply framework provides for price flexibility, so it predicts a different outcome. A reduction in aggregate demand reduces real GDP while putting downward pressure on prices; increased aggregate demand raises output and employment but also generates demand-side, or **demand-pull inflation.**

The differences between the predictions of the simple Keynesian model and the *AD/AS* model are important. They indicate that policies designed to combat unemployment or inflation do not have entirely beneficial results. Policies to combat unemployment cause inflation; policies to combat inflation cause unemployment.

The economy's equilibrium can also be disturbed by changes in aggregate supply. Suppose that aggregate supply decreased due to a supply shock, such as an increase in the price of imported oil or a drought that raised grain prices. Exhibit 14.9 shows that when aggregate supply falls from AS_1 to AS_2, the overall price level is driven up, and the equilibrium level of real GDP is reduced.

In this instance the economy is experiencing supply-side, or **cost-push inflation**; higher production costs are pushing up prices. Although both demand-pull and cost-push inflation mean higher prices for consumers, cost-push inflation is doubly destructive because it is associated with falling real output. As you can see from Exh. 14.9, when the aggregate supply curve shifts to the left, the level of equilibrium real GDP falls from $1,000 billion to $850 billion. In short, cost-push inflation raises prices while lowering output and employment. This provides us with one possible explanation for the problem of **stagflation,** high unemployment combined with high inflation.

If reductions in aggregate supply are particularly harmful, increases in aggregate supply appear most beneficial. Suppose that aggregate supply expands due to an increase in labor productivity. As the *AS* curve shifts to the right (from AS_1 to AS_3 in Exh. 14.9), the price level is driven down *and* output and employment are expanded. It is these obviously desirable outcomes that led to a surge of interest in supply-side economics in the 1980s. Supply-siders promoted a variety of policies designed to enhance labor productivity and

EXHIBIT 14.9

**The Effects of Changes in Aggregate Supply
on Real Output and Prices**

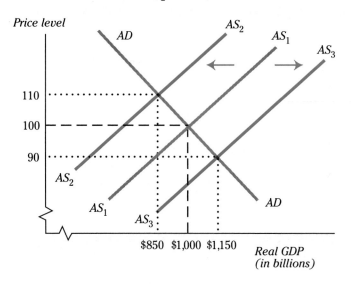

Decreases in aggregate supply will tend to lower the levels of output and employment in the economy while raising the overall price level. Increases in aggregate supply will tend to raise output and employment while lowering the level of prices.

otherwise lower production costs in an attempt to increase aggregate supply. Chapter 15 will take a closer look at supply-side problems and remedies.

As the preceding discussion indicates, changes in aggregate demand or supply can lead to unemployment, inflation, or even stagflation. The next section examines the economy's response to these problems and considers the possibility that the economy contains a self-correcting mechanism. (Before proceeding, take a moment to read "Why Policy Makers . . . Want Economic Growth to Slow Down," on page 442. It will test your understanding of the *AD-AS* framework.)

The Model of the Self-Correcting Economy

As you will recall from Chapter 10, the classical economists believed in a self-correcting economy that always tended to operate at full employment. According to the classical model, Say's Law and interest rate flexibility would ensure that aggregate demand was always sufficient to maintain full employment. If these defenses somehow failed, reductions in aggregate demand

Why Policy Makers at the Fed Want Strong Economic Growth to Slow Down

WASHINGTON

Federal Reserve policy makers are expected to raise short-term interest rates at their meeting tomorrow by at least one-half percentage point, trying to slow the surprisingly strong economy so as to avoid an acceleration of inflation. . . .

Here's a primer on what Fed officials are thinking as they go into tomorrow's meeting.

What's so bad about growth that exceeds 2.5%?

The Federal Reserve and many economists say a sustained growth rate greater than about 2.5% to 2.8% will bring capacity and labor shortages, and thus higher prices. They fix that range by adding the annual growth of the labor force—1.5%—to the average yearly increase of worker productivity—1%. Productivity equals output for each hour worked. "If we start growing consistently faster than productivity and the growth in the number of people available to do the work, the system gets overheated," said Alan Gayle, head of short-term invest-

ments for Capitoline Investment Services Inc. in Richmond, Va. . . .

Isn't the U.S. rate of productivity increasing?

Yes. Productivity has been above-trend for the last two years—1.4% in 1993 and 3% in 1992. The annual rate through this year's first nine months is 1.2%.

Doesn't that mean the U.S. can then grow faster without risking inflation?

Not necessarily. Productivity usually increases by large amounts during and immediately after a recession as companies work hard to cut costs and produce more goods with fewer workers. If that's what is happening now, faster growth would still lead to inflation eventually.

However, some economists feel productivity gains in recent years are a part of a structural shift toward higher productivity over the long term. Stephen Roach, senior economist for Morgan Stanley & Co., said companies will continue to invest in capital equipment to improve efficiency. If that brings

sustained productivity gains, then faster economic growth may be possible without the usual rise of inflation.

But it's too soon for the Fed or anyone else to be sure whether increases are structural or just another cyclical pop. But if productivity improves over the long term, the Fed may use that information in setting future interest-rate policy.

Why is the Fed trying to slow the economy when there are still 7.6 million Americans unemployed?

"There is no way the economy can be made to grow fast enough to absorb all the people in the labor force. Some people may want a job, but may not have the skills," Mr. Brimmer said. And although this is something the Fed seldom discusses, it believes the unemployment rate can fall too low, causing severe wage pressures as companies vie for a limited number of available workers.

Economists differ, though, on just how low the unemployment rate can be before wage pressures mount. Most assume the rate is somewhere between 5.75% and 6.3%. In October, unemployment fell to 5.8%. . . .

Is there any evidence that prices are heating up now?

Consumer prices are still well-behaved. The consumer price index in September was up 3% year-on-year. But the Fed is more concerned with the inflation picture tomorrow than the inflation picture today. By the time the government's index reveals big price increases, the Fed may be too late to fight it off.

That said, there are signs that price pressures are on the increase. Commodity prices are rising at a fast clip and a national survey of purchasing managers shows increasing prices for what factories pay their suppliers. Also, the Fed's own survey of its 12 district banks found wage pressures in some regions, though national figures on wage costs remain roughly in line with inflation.

Is there a case to be made against raising interest rates?

Yes. A diverse group of economists and business leaders—from the former chief executive of American Express Co. to the AFL-CIO's chief economist—made just that case at a news conference Friday. "The notion that American companies can really raise their prices because there has been some revival of demand is simply not realistic," said Preston Martin, a former Fed vice chairman. Because the economy has changed so much in the past few years," said Jerry Jasinowski, president of the National Association of Manufacturers, "we can now produce more with less inflation than in the past."

In short, the group said, corporate restructuring, intensifying global competition and the reluctance and inability of most workers to seek wage increases all minimize the likelihood that a strong economy will yield significantly higher inflation rates. Moreover, Harvard economist James Medoff said, the Fed fails to see how much less important manufacturing is to the U.S. economy and how much room there is for noninflationary growth outside manufacturing. Gauging the demand for labor by the volume of help-wanted ads, he also concludes the risk of upward pressure on wages is far lower than the 5.8% unemployment rate suggests. . . .

—*Lucinda Harper*

SOURCE: Lucinda Harper, "Why Policy Makers at the Fed Want Strong Economic Growth to Slow Down," November 14, 1994. Reprinted by permission of *The Wall Street Journal*, © 1994 Dow Jones & Co., Inc. All Rights Reserved Worldwide.

Use Your Economic Reasoning

1. If the economy's labor force is increasing and also becoming more productive, what will happen to the aggregate supply curve?

2. Suppose that the aggregate supply curve is shifting to the right by 2.5 percent a year. If aggregate demand is also increasing at 2.5 percent a year, what will happen to the overall price level?

3. If aggregate supply is increasing at 2.5 percent a year and aggregate demand is expanding at 4 percent a year, what will happen to the overall price level? What action would you anticipate from the Federal Reserve?

would be quickly met by falling prices and wages, which would keep the economy operating at potential GDP.

When the Great Depression called the classical model into question, Keynes provided an alternative model to explain the widespread unemployment. According to Keynes, interest rate adjustments cannot be relied on to match up saving and investment plans and ensure adequate aggregate demand. Perhaps most important, Keynes did not believe that reductions in aggregate demand would lead to falling prices and wages. Instead, the rigidity of prices and wages would transform these downturns in aggregate demand into lower real GDP and unemployment.

Many economists argue that the crucial distinction between the classical and Keynesian models is their different assumptions about the behavior of prices and wages. Price-wage flexibility is the final line of defense in the classical model; without that assumption, hoarding can result in unemployment. The assumption of rigid prices and wages is equally important to Keynes; if prices and wages are highly flexible, falling demand does not pose a threat to the economy.

Given the importance of these assumptions, it is interesting to note that most modern economists see some validity in *both* the classical and Keynesian positions. In the short run, at least some prices and wages are inflexible, as Keynes suggested, so reductions in aggregate demand can cause unemployment. But in the long run, all prices and wages become flexible. Thus reductions in aggregate demand must ultimately result in falling prices and wages, which return the economy to potential GDP and full employment.

The important conclusion of the foregoing discussion is that the economy does contain a self-correcting mechanism. To illustrate that mechanism, let's consider an economy that is presently operating at potential GDP and examine its short-run and long-run reactions to a change in aggregate demand. We will begin with an increase in aggregate demand and then consider a decrease.

Adjustments to an Increase in Aggregate Demand

Suppose that aggregate demand expands because the federal government reduces personal income taxes. Households now have more to spend, so they tend to demand more goods and services at each price level—the aggregate demand curve shifts to the right, from AD_1 to AD_2 in Exh. 14.10.

When aggregate demand increases, the resulting higher price level creates incentive for businesses to expand output. This incentive is provided by the fact that many of a business's costs—particularly wage rates—are fixed by long-term contracts. When product prices rise, these costs do not; thus firms stand to profit by expanding output. In our example, output will be increased up to the point where AS_1 is intersected by AD_2 (point B in Exh. 14.10), well beyond potential GDP.

EXHIBIT 14.10

Adjusting to Higher Aggregate Demand

✗ add to notes

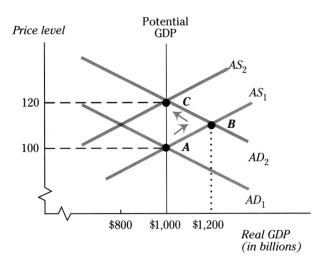

When aggregate demand increases, businesses initially find it profitable to expand output, because wage rates and certain other costs are fixed by long-term contracts. Thus equilibrium real GDP expands beyond potential. But when these contracts expire and costs rise, the *AS* curve shifts upward and eventually reduces equilibrium output to the level of potential GDP.

It may seem contradictory to suggest that the economy can operate beyond its potential. The term "potential" is commonly interpreted to mean "maximum." But the meaning of potential is somewhat different in this context. Potential GDP is not the maximum output the economy is capable of producing but rather the maximum *sustainable* level of production. Businesses can run factories beyond their designed or intended capacities for some period of time, and workers may be willing to work overtime. However, neither of these practices is sustainable; ultimately equipment breaks down and employees become disgruntled and unproductive. But in the short run, these actions permit the economy to operate beyond its potential; that is, they allow actual GDP to exceed potential GDP.

As we've seen, businesses expand output beyond potential GDP because higher prices make it profitable for them to do so. But the higher prices that are attractive to businesses are bad news for employees. Workers find that they must pay more for the goods and services they buy, even though their wage rates are unchanged; thus their *real* wages—the purchasing power of their money wages—have declined.

Eventually firms will have to renegotiate their labor contracts. When that happens, workers will demand higher wages. Other input suppliers, also pressed by higher prices, will demand more for their resources. The result of the higher renegotiated input prices will be an upward shift of the aggregate supply curve. (Remember that a change in input prices will shift the AS curve.) Tight markets for labor and other inputs will put continuing upward pressure on wages and other input prices. The AS curve will continue to shift upward until workers and other input suppliers have regained their original purchasing power. This is represented in Exh. 14.10 by the shift from AS_1 to AS_2. Note that when contracts have been renegotiated, the incentive that originally motivated businesses to expand real output to $1,200 billion will have evaporated. Equilibrium real GDP will return to $1,000 billion (point C in the exhibit), the level of GDP consistent with the economy's potential output. The self-correcting forces have returned the economy to its potential GDP. As you can see, the long-run impact of the increase in aggregate demand is simply a higher price level, since the increase in production cannot be sustained.

Adjustments to a Decrease in Aggregate Demand

The economy's response to a reduction in aggregate demand is similar to its adjustments to an increase, but in the opposite direction. To illustrate, let's again assume that the economy is operating at its potential GDP (at point A in Exh. 14.11). If aggregate demand fell from AD_1 to AD_2, firms would initially find their prices falling while some of their costs were fixed by long-term contracts. This would cause them to cut back on output (since output levels that had been profitable at a higher price level are no longer profitable) and reduce equilibrium GDP below potential. This is represented in Exh. 14.11 by the movement along AS_1 from A to B. Of course, when actual GDP falls below potential, the rate of unemployment rises above the full employment level.

Eventually labor and other contracts will be renegotiated. At that point, the high unemployment rates and unused productive capacity of input suppliers will cause wages and other resource prices to fall. As that occurs, the AS curve will begin shifting to the right, eventually shifting from AS_1 to AS_2 (from B to C) and returning the economy to potential GDP and full employment. The long-run impact of the reduction in aggregate demand is a lower price level; output and employment have returned to their initial levels.

The preceding examples suggest that although the economy can deviate from potential GDP in the short run, these deviations are ultimately corrected, so that in the long run, the economy tends to operate at potential GDP and full employment.[4] If the economy always returns to full employment, is there any justification for government intervention to alter the economy's performance?

---

[4] This implies that in the long run the economy's aggregate supply curve is a vertical line at potential GDP. Although a change in aggregate demand can alter output in the short run, in the long run only the price level is affected.

EXHIBIT 14.11

Adjusting to Lower Aggregate Demand

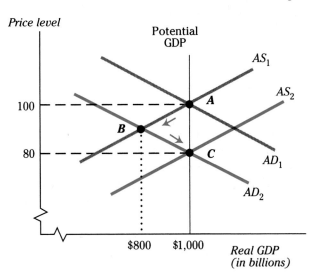

When aggregate demand declines, businesses initially find it necessary to reduce output because wage rates and certain other costs are fixed by long-term contracts. Thus equilibrium real GDP drops below potential. But when these contracts expire and costs fall, the AS curve shifts downward and eventually increases equilibrium output to the level of potential GDP.

Chapter 15 will address this issue as it considers the modern activist-nonactivist debate.

Summary

Economists use the concepts of aggregate demand and aggregate supply to represent the forces that determine the economy's equilibrium GDP and price level. *Aggregate demand (AD)* is the total quantity of output demanded by all sectors in the economy together at various price levels in a given period of time. The *aggregate demand curve* slopes downward and to the right, indicating that more real output will be demanded at a lower price level than at a higher price level. There are three reasons for the downward slope of the aggregate demand curve: the real balance effect, the interest rate effect, and the international trade effect. The factors that will shift the aggregate demand curve include changes in the expectations of households and businesses, aggregate wealth, government policy, foreign incomes, and foreign price levels.

Aggregate supply (AS) refers to the quantity of output supplied by all producers in the economy together at various price levels in a given period of time. The *aggregate supply curve* is upward sloping because higher price levels stimulate businesses to expand output. Since wage rates and some other input prices are commonly fixed by contracts, an increase in the price level provides incentive for firms to increase output. A given aggregate supply curve assumes the prevailing wage rates and prices of nonlabor inputs, the current level of productivity, and the existing supplies of labor and capital. If any of these factors changes, the *AS* curve will shift to a new position.

The intersection of the aggregate demand and supply curves simultaneously determines the level of equilibrium real GDP and the equilibrium price level in the economy. Shifts in aggregate demand or supply will tend to alter these equilibrium values. If aggregate demand increases, both real GDP and the price level will tend to increase. The economy enjoys higher levels of output and employment, but it experiences *demand-pull inflation*. If aggregate demand declines, the levels of output, employment, and prices decline.

Changes in equilibrium can also be caused by changes in aggregate supply. A supply shock, such as an increase in the price of imported oil, will tend to reduce aggregate supply. This will cause *cost-push inflation*, since the higher cost of oil pushes up prices. When aggregate supply is reduced, the levels of output and employment in the economy also decline. Supply shocks provide one possible explanation for *stagflation*, high unemployment combined with high inflation. If aggregate supply increased, the results would be doubly beneficial; the levels of output and employment in the economy would tend to increase, whereas the overall price level would decline.

Most modern economists agree that to some extent the economy contains a self-correcting mechanism. In the short run, the economy can deviate from potential GDP because certain wages and prices are rigid. In the long run, however, all wages and prices become flexible. As a consequence, reductions in aggregate demand are ultimately met by falling wages and input prices that cause aggregate supply to expand and return the economy to potential GDP. Increases in aggregate demand eventually lead to higher wages and input prices, which cause aggregate supply to contract and output and employment to fall. Thus wage and price adjustments ultimately return the economy to potential GDP and full employment.

Glossary

Aggregate demand. The total quantity of output demanded by all sectors in the economy together at various price levels in a given time period.

Aggregate supply. The total quantity of output supplied by all producers in the economy together at various price levels in a given time period.

Cost-push inflation. Inflation caused by rising costs of production.

Demand-pull inflation. Inflation caused by increases in aggregate demand.

Exports. Goods and services that are produced domestically and sold to customers in other countries.

Imports. Goods and services that are purchased from foreign producers.

Interest rate effect. The increase in the amount of aggregate output demanded that results from the lower interest rates that accompany a reduction in the overall price level.

International trade effect. The increase in the amount of aggregate output demanded that results when a reduction in the price level makes domestic products less expensive in relation to foreign products.

Real balance effect. The increase in the amount of aggregate output demanded that results from an increase in the real value of the public's financial assets.

Stagflation. High unemployment combined with high inflation.

Study Questions

Fill in the Blanks

1. The _____ curve shows the amount of real output that will be demanded at various price levels.

2. According to the _____ effect, an increase in the price level will reduce the purchasing power of financial assets and cause society to demand less real output.

3. Any change in the spending plans of consumers, businesses, or government that results from something other than a change in the _____ will shift the aggregate demand curve.

4. A broad-based technological advance will tend to shift the aggregate _____ _____ curve to the _____.

5. According to the interest rate effect, a reduction in the price level will tend to (increase/decrease) _____ the demand for money, which in turn will (increase/decrease) _____ the rate of interest and lead to (an increase/a reduction) _____ in the quantity of real output demanded.

6. Increases in the price level cause businesses to expand output because _____ _____ and other _____ prices are commonly fixed in the short run.

7. An increase in government spending will tend to shift the aggregate _____ _____ curve to the _____.

8. Cost-push inflation is caused by the aggregate _____ curve shifting to the (right/left) _____.

9. The term _____ is used to describe high inflation combined with high unemployment.

10. If the aggregate supply curve remains stationary, policymakers can reduce inflation if they are willing to accept higher _____.

Multiple Choice

1. The type of inflation caused by increased spending for goods and services is
   a) demand-pull inflation.
   b) cost-push inflation.
   c) structural inflation.
   d) expenditure inflation.

2. If a reduction in the price level causes more real output to be demanded,
   a) the aggregate demand curve will shift to the right.
   b) the aggregate demand curve is downward sloping.
   c) the aggregate supply curve will shift to the right.
   d) the aggregate supply curve is downward sloping.

3. Which of the following will shift the aggregate demand curve to the left? upward
   a) An increase in government spending
   b) A reduction in labor productivity
   c) An increase in personal income taxes
   d) An increase in society's aggregate wealth

4. Which of the following will increase both the price level and real GDP?
   a) A nationwide drought that drives up the prices of agricultural products
   b) A reduction in government spending for goods and services
   c) A reduction in the money supply
   d) Greater optimism among business executives

5. In 1974 disease killed many anchovies and raised anchovy prices. Anchovies are used in cattle feed as a source of protein. The likely impact of this event would be to
   a) raise both the price level and real GDP.
   b) lower both the price level and real GDP.
   c) raise the price level but lower real GDP.
   d) lower the price level but raise real GDP.

6. According to the real balance effect,
   a) a reduction in the price level stimulates spending by lowering interest rates.
   b) an increase in the money supply will shift the aggregate demand curve to the right.
   c) an increase in the price level reduces spending by lowering the real value of society's financial assets.
   d) an increase in society's aggregate wealth will shift the aggregate demand curve to the right.

7. An increase in the productivity of the labor force would be likely to shift
   a) the aggregate supply curve to the right.
   b) the aggregate supply curve to the left.
   c) the aggregate demand curve to the right.
   d) the aggregate demand curve to the left.

8. A decrease in foreign income levels would, ceteris paribus, tend to shift the aggregate _____ curve for U.S. products to the _____ _____.
   a) demand, right
   b) demand, left
   c) supply, right
   d) supply, left

9. The international trade effect provides a rationale for
   a) shifts in the aggregate demand curve.
   b) shifts in the aggregate supply curve.
   c) the slope of the aggregate demand curve.
   d) the slope of the aggregate supply curve.

10. In the short run, an increase in the money supply will
    a) reduce both real GDP and the price level.
    b) reduce real GDP and increase the price level.
    c) increase both real GDP and the price level.
    d) increase real GDP and reduce the price level.

11. If the prevailing price level was initially below equilibrium,
    a) there would be a surplus of output.
    b) the price level would tend to fall.
    c) the amount of real GDP supplied would exceed the amount demanded.
    d) there would be a shortage of output.

12. Suppose that Congress increased government spending at the same time that the price of imported oil (which is used to manufacture gasoline and heating oil) increased. In the short run, this would clearly
    a) increase both the price level and real GDP.
    b) reduce both the price level and real GDP.
    c) increase the price level, but the impact on real GDP is uncertain.
    d) increase real GDP, but the impact on the price level is uncertain.

13. The aggregate supply curve is upward sloping
    a) due to the real balance effect and the interest rate effect.
    b) if all wages and input prices are flexible in the short run.
    c) because increases in the overall price level result in enhanced labor productivity and higher real output.
    d) because input price rigidities make it profitable for firms to expand output when product prices rise.

14. Suppose that the economy is operating below potential GDP. According to the self-correcting model, the economy will ultimately return to potential because
    a) the Fed will expand the money supply.
    b) wages and resource prices will fall as contracts expire and are renegotiated.
    c) workers will eventually demand higher wages, and resource suppliers will demand higher input prices.
    d) aggregate demand will automatically increase enough to push the economy back to potential GDP.

15. When the overall price level rises,
    a) businesses tend to reduce output because production becomes less profitable.
    b) wage rates and other input prices tend to increase immediately, forcing businesses to cut back on production.
    c) businesses have incentive to expand output because many costs are fixed by long-term contracts.
    d) businesses may either increase or decrease output, depending on the magnitude of the hike in the price level.

16. According to the self-correcting model, if the economy is producing a level of output in excess of potential GDP,
    a) potential GDP will automatically expand to match the actual level of production.
    b) workers and input suppliers will eventually negotiate higher wages and prices, which will return the economy to potential GDP.
    c) wages and input prices will ultimately fall, which will return the economy to potential GDP.
    c) None of the above are correct; the economy cannot operate beyond potential GDP.

17. According to the self-correcting model,
   a) unemployment can exist indefinitely.
   b) the economy can never operate beyond potential GDP.
   c) unemployment is eventually eliminated by falling wages and prices.
   d) the economy always operates at potential GDP.

Problems and Questions for Discussion

1. Explain in detail why the aggregate demand curve is downward sloping.

2. Given a stationary aggregate supply curve, policymakers should be able to reduce unemployment if they are willing to accept higher inflation. Explain and supplement your explanation with a graph.

3. What role do contracts play in explaining the upward slope of the aggregate supply curve?

4. Suppose that, on average, wage rates increase less than the increase in labor productivity. What will happen to the overall price level and real GDP? Explain how you arrived at your conclusion.

5. When we use the aggregate-demand/aggregate-supply framework to predict the impact of an increase in government spending, we reach somewhat different conclusions from those obtained when we use the total expenditures model (the basic Keynesian model employed in Chapters 11 and 12). Why are the conclusions different? Would policymakers find these differences important?

6. Explain the difference between demand-pull and cost-push inflation. Use aggregate demand and supply curves to show how each problem would be represented graphically.

7. Suppose that the economy is in equilibrium at potential GDP and that policymakers increase aggregate demand (perhaps because they do not recognize that the economy is operating at potential). Discuss the short-run and long-run impact of this change. Supplement your answer with graphs.

8. Consider the short-run impact of the changes listed below. Which changes would cause the economy's price level and real GDP to move in the same direction (both increase, both decrease), and which would cause the price level and real GDP to move in opposite directions (increasing the price level but reducing real output, for example)? After you have worked through the list, see if you can draw any general conclusions.
   a) An increase in government spending
   b) A severe frost that destroys crops
   c) A large decline in the stock market
   d) An increase in labor productivity
   e) An increase in consumer optimism
   f) Higher prices for imported raw materials

9. Suppose that government spending in support of education were increased. Would this action shift the aggregate demand curve, the aggregate supply curve, or both curves? What would happen to the price level and real GDP?

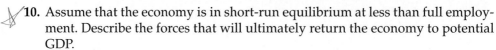 10. Assume that the economy is in short-run equilibrium at less than full employment. Describe the forces that will ultimately return the economy to potential GDP.

Answer Key

Fill in the Blanks

1. aggregate demand
2. real balance
3. price level
4. supply, right

5. decrease, decrease, an increase
6. wage rates, input

7. demand, right
8. supply, left
9. stagflation
10. unemployment

Multiple Choice

1. a
2. b
3. c
4. d

5. c
6. c
7. a
8. b

9. c
10. c
11. d

12. c
13. d
14. b

15. c
16. b
17. c

The Activist-Nonactivist Debate

What are the policy implications of the self-correcting model? If the economy tends to operate at potential GDP and full employment, is there any reason for government intervention to guide the economy's performance? Can demand-management policies (the fiscal and monetary policies discussed in Chapters 11 and 12) be used to speed the adjustment to full employment, or do such policies have a destabilizing effect on the economy? These are the issues that concern us in this chapter.

As you can see, we have returned to the activist-nonactivist debate that we first encountered in Chapter 10. Just as Keynes and the classical economists disagreed about the advisability of government intervention to guide our economy, today's neo-Keynesians disagree with monetarists and new classical economists (also known as rational-expectations theorists). This chapter introduces you to the views of these competing schools of thought and examines the modern debate about demand-management policies. It also takes a brief look at supply-side economics. We turn first to a short review of the Keynesian, or activist, position.

The Activist Position: Keynes Revisited

As you learned in Chapters 10 and 11, Keynes did not believe that capitalist economies necessarily tend to full employment. Rather, he argued that because of the volatility of spending, particularly investment spending, they could be in equilibrium at a level of output either less or greater than potential GDP. If business executives were pessimistic, they might choose to cut back on investment spending, sending the economy into a tailspin and causing unemployment. If they were optimistic about the future, they might choose to expand investment spending, pushing GDP above potential and causing inflation.

Keynes was an activist economist in the sense that he advocated government action to prevent outbreaks of unemployment or inflation and to combat these problems should they occur. According to Keynes, the central government should use fiscal and monetary policies to ensure sufficient aggregate demand to achieve full employment without inflation.

Fiscal policy, you will recall, is the manipulation of government spending or taxation in order to guide the economy's performance. The appropriate Keynesian fiscal policy for a period of unemployment would be to increase government spending for goods and services or to reduce taxes. These policies would expand aggregate demand, raise the equilibrium GDP, and lower unemployment. Inflation calls for reductions in government spending or higher taxes. By reducing aggregate demand, these policies will reduce inflationary pressures.

Monetary policy—deliberately changing the money supply to influence the level of economic activity—can also be used to combat unemployment or inflation. If unemployment exists, the Federal Reserve (the government agency that regulates the money supply) can increase the money supply in order to drive down the market rate of interest. The lower interest rate will tend to stimulate investment spending and certain forms of consumption spending. By stimulating aggregate demand in this manner, monetary policy can raise equilibrium GDP and lower unemployment. Inflation can be attacked by reducing the money supply and thereby raising the prevailing rate of interest. A higher interest rate will cause businesses and consumers to cut back on their borrowing (and spending) and reduce inflationary pressures.

Even if fiscal and monetary policies work in the manner Keynesians suggest, why would anyone consider using them? If the economy is self-correcting in the long run, why not let it take care of itself? In describing the problems posed by an unemployment equilibrium, the neo-Keynesian response echoes that of Keynes himself more than fifty years ago: "In the long run, we are all dead!" The adjustment process described in Chapter 14 takes time, perhaps a substantial period of time. In the interim society loses output that will never be regained, individuals suffer the humiliation of being without work, and families deplete their savings or go on welfare. In short, unemployment is costly, and the losses incurred as we wait for self-correction may be unacceptable.

Production above potential also imposes costs on society. As we saw in Chapter 14, when equilibrium GDP exceeds potential, the price level is pushed up, generating inflation. Although society benefits from the additional output and employment, unanticipated inflation tends to redistribute income in an arbitrary way. Moreover, the long-run adjustment process will ultimately eliminate the short-term gain in output and leave the economy with a still higher price level.

In summary, neo-Keynesians believe that capitalist economies are inherently unstable so they are always in danger of operating either above or below potential GDP. Although the economy will ultimately return to potential GDP, waiting for this long-run adjustment to occur is needlessly costly to society. Instead, fiscal and monetary policies should be used to prevent deviations from potential GDP or to minimize their duration should they occur.

The Nonactivist Position: The Monetarists

Not all economists agree with the activist, or neo-Keynesian, position. The two major groups, or schools, of nonactivist economists are the monetarists and the new classical economists (rational-expectations theorists). We will begin by examining the monetarist position.

Monetarism is the belief that changes in the money supply play the primary role in determining the level of aggregate output and prices in the economy. Economists who hold this belief are called *monetarists*.

According to monetarists, an increase in the money supply will tend to stimulate consumption and investment spending, raising equilibrium output and the price level; a reduction in the money supply will have the opposite effect. Neo-Keynesians agree that changes in the money supply can alter output and prices, but they emphasize that other factors—changes in autonomous investment or government spending, for instance—can also influence the economy. Monetarists tend to see these other factors as decidedly secondary; changes in the money supply are what really matter.

Fiscal Policy and Crowding Out

The paramount importance that monetarists attach to the money supply is illustrated by their criticism of Keynesian fiscal policy. According to monetarists, fiscal policy is ineffective unless it is accompanied by monetary policy. To illustrate this view, let's suppose that the economy is suffering from unemployment and that Congress decides to increase government spending to combat the problem. What will happen? The monetarists believe that if the money supply is not increased, government borrowing to finance the larger deficit will drive up the interest rate and discourage, or crowd out, investment spending. In an economy with more government spending but less investment spending, the net effect will be no stimulus to the economy. However, if the Federal Reserve were to allow the money supply to expand while the government borrowed, it *would* be possible to provide some net stimulus to the economy. The interest rate would not be bid up, so investment spending would not be discouraged; thus total spending would actually expand. Monetarists are quick to point out that the stimulus in this situation results from the increase in the money supply, not from the added government spending.

Monetary Policy and the Monetary Rule

Because monetarism focuses attention on the money supply, eager students sometimes conclude that monetarists must favor the use of discretionary monetary policy to guide the economy's performance. But that's not the case. Monetarists believe that changes in the money supply are too important to be left to the discretion of policymakers. Instead, they support a **monetary rule** that would require the Federal Reserve to expand the money supply at a constant rate, something like 3 percent a year.[1]

If the Fed were required to increase the money supply at a constant annual rate, it would no longer be free to use changes in the money supply as a policy tool; it could not increase the money supply more rapidly to combat unemployment or slow the growth of the money supply to combat inflation. In other words, a monetary rule would eliminate the possibility of the Keynesian monetary policies described in Chapter 14. In a sense the Fed would be

---

[1] Monetarists believe that the money supply should be expanded at 3 percent a year because they think that potential GDP expands at about that rate. If sustainable output is growing at 3 percent a year, a 3 percent larger money supply is needed in order to facilitate this greater volume of transactions. But whether we choose to increase the money supply at 3 percent or 4 percent or 6 percent is not too important, so long as we pick *some* rate and stick with it. If the money supply is growing more rapidly than the economy's ability to produce output, inflation will result. But it will be a reasonably constant rate of inflation, so we will know what to expect and will be able to build it into our wage agreements and other contracts. Thus it will not tend to redistribute income the way that unanticipated inflation does.

Milton Friedman, shown here accepting his Nobel Prize in economics, would like to see the Federal Reserve adhere to a monetary rule.

put on autopilot. Monetarists favor this approach because they are convinced that the Fed's attempts to combat unemployment or inflation have often made things worse rather than better.

Policy Lags and the Self-Correcting Economy

According to the monetarists, it is time lags that tend to make Keynesian monetary policies counterproductive. Obviously, Fed policymakers cannot take action until they recognize that a problem exists. Unfortunately, the economy commonly sends mixed signals about its performance. For this reason there is a **recognition lag** before agreement is reached that a problem exists. Even after the problem is recognized and policymakers take action, there will be an **impact lag** before the effect on spending is felt in the economy. Moreover, once the policy does begin to influence spending, the effect will continue for some time. (See "Fed Rate Rises Take Longer to Have Effect . . . ," on page 460, for a discussion of factors that may be lengthening one of these lags.)

The existence of lags would not be a major argument against discretionary monetary policy if the economy tended to remain in an unemployment or inflationary equilibrium indefinitely. But that's not what happens. As our discussion of the self-correcting mechanism indicates, the economy ultimately begins to solve its own problems. When we recognize this self-correcting tendency, lags can mean trouble for policymakers. To illustrate, suppose that the economy gradually weakens and begins to experience a recession. Fed policymakers eventually recognize the problem and take action to expand the money supply. But if the recognition and impact lags are long

Fed Rate Rises Take Longer to Have Effect on Economy

WASHINGTON

Dec. 4—As growth continues unabated 10 months after the Federal Reserve began trying to slow it, more and more economists are concluding that the Fed's all-purpose tool, raising or lowering interest rates, is not as effective as it used to be. . . .

No one questions the tremendous power the Fed can wield if it raises rates sharply or keeps them high for a long time. But changes in the country's financial system, notably the declining role of banks as providers of money for companies and consumers, may make it necessary for the Fed to make bigger increases or to wait longer to get the same effect, they say.

Last month, for instance, the Fed abandoned the pattern of quarter-point or half-point increases it had followed since February, instead pushing up the rates that banks pay for short-term borrowing by three-quarters of a percentage point, its biggest increase in 13 years.

The danger, debated among current and former Fed officials, is that in switching to a heavier hammer, it becomes easier to miss the nail.

Preston Martin, who was vice chairman of the Federal Reserve from 1982 to 1986, said that "the Fed just doesn't have the leverage that it had when I was on the board." He sees a serious risk of a recession in 1996 from the bigger increases, which he thinks may have been prompted by growing impatience for results.

Andrew F. Brimmer, a former Federal Reserve governor, said that the six rounds of interest rate increases this year are "having some effects, but they're more modest and it's taking longer."

Current officials of the central bank dispute this. . . .

Alan S. Blinder, the Fed's vice chairman, said in an interview Friday that he saw no persuasive evidence of change in the economy's overall responsiveness to interest rate moves. While some effects of monetary policy may be less powerful, others have become more so and the balance has shifted little, if at all, he said. . . .

To be sure, monetary policy has never been a precise tool, and has always been subject to long and variable lags between action and ef-

fect. Corporate decisions—whether to build a factory or to stock more goods for sale—are based on current interest rate costs, but take a year or more to affect the economy. So last year's low rates may still be driving growth, Mr. Blinder said.

The Fed's position is like that of a supertanker captain steering down a narrow channel. Quick changes of course are not possible, and trying too hard to avoid one set of problems only makes other problems worse. If interest rate changes take longer to take effect, then the Fed has an even looser rudder as it guides the economy.

Many Congressional Democrats and others who have opposed the Fed's rate increases would, of course, welcome any weakening of its influence.

And even some Fed supporters see benefits along with potential dangers. Treasury Secretary Lloyd Bentsen said he thought that the Fed's moves seemed to have a slower effect than usual on the economy this year, because of the rise in initially cheaper adjustable-rate mortgages. Home buyers "are not feeling the pain to the degree they normally would," he said.

"It may actually make it a smoother influence on the economy," Mr. Bentsen added.

But a slower impact by the Fed also holds risks, he said, "The problem now is judging how much and when the impact will hit with things already in the pipeline," he said. . . .

Economists who think the Fed now takes longer to affect the economy note that the central bank most directly controls the Federal Funds rate, the overnight interest rate at which banks borrow money from each other. But banks play a dwindling role in financing the nation's growth and are becoming less dependent on overnight borrowing. More corporations are borrowing money by selling notes and bonds while more consumers are turning to mortgage brokers and car makers for loans to buy houses and vehicles.

The Detroit auto makers are still flourishing partly because the interest rates on car loans have not risen all that much this year and increasingly, cars are being leased rather than sold.

The average interest rate on a new-car loan from a bank has risen only 1.37 percentage points this year while the Federal funds rate has climbed nearly twice as much. Car makers and finance companies, which raise money by selling bonds, are providing more competition for the banks and holding down costs for consumers, Mr. Lindsey said.

Interest rates controlled by the Fed only indirectly influence the rates that the auto makers and finance companies pay on the bonds they issue. These bond rates have typically not gone up as much as the overnight rate that the Fed controls.

Home building is another industry that has traditionally suffered when the Fed raised rates. Yet the sharp rise in adjustable-rate mortgages this year, with first-year rates of 6.5 percent still available in some places, has allowed Americans to go on buying new houses even though they no longer qualify for fixed-rate mortgages at 9.25 percent. . . .

Combined with the elimination a decade ago of regulations that used to limit the interest rates that banks could pay to attract deposits, the changes in housing finance have weakened the Fed, said Martin Mayer, an analyst at the Brookings Institution. "Whereas Bill Martin could put the foot lightly on the brake and everything shuddered, now you have to put the foot all the way down," said Mr. Mayer, referring to William McChesney Martin, who was chairman of the Federal Reserve from 1951 to 1970. . . .

—*Keith Bradsher*

SOURCE: Keith Bradsher, "Fed Rate Rises Take Longer to Have Effect on Economy," December 5, 1994. Copyright © 1994 by The New York Times Company. Reprinted with permission.

Use Your Economic Reasoning

1. What changes in the nation's financial system may be diluting the power of the Federal Reserve?

2. The article suggests that the Fed must now "wait longer to get the same effect" from its policies. Does this suggest a lengthening of the recognition lag or the impact lag? Why should Fed officials be concerned about this development?

3. If the changes described in this article are in fact occurring, do they strengthen or weaken the monetarists' case for a monetary rule? Defend your conclusion.

enough, the economy may begin to recover on its own before these policies start to take effect. Thus monetary policy may begin to stimulate spending when such stimulus is no longer welcome. Of course, too much spending can lead to inflation, which is precisely what monetarists believe has happened on several occasions.

In summary, monetarists shun discretionary monetary policy because they believe that it often has a destabilizing effect on the economy—creates additional problems—rather than the stabilizing effect that neo-Keynesians predict. In fact, monetarists believe that government tinkering with the money supply may be the major destabilizing force in the economy. For example, Milton Friedman—who is sometimes referred to as the father of monetarist economics—argues that it was inept monetary policy that caused the Great Depression. According to Friedman, the Fed turned what could have been a serious downturn into a major catastrophe by allowing the money supply to fall substantially in the early 1930s. He contends that a policy of stable money growth would have been vastly superior.[2]

Monetarism: Concluding Points

Perhaps the major source of disagreement between neo-Keynesians and monetarists is about the nature of economy. Like Keynes, neo-Keynesians tend to see the economy as inherently unstable and relatively slow to recover from demand and supply shocks. Monetarists, on the other hand, believe that the economy is fundamentally stable and returns fairly rapidly to potential GDP whenever deviations occur. If it persists in deviating from potential GDP, it is due to government tinkering, not to the nature of the economy.

Monetarists emphasize that eliminating the Fed's ability to tinker with the money supply would not completely eliminate unemployment or inflation. Fluctuations in spending would still occur, and some unemployment or inflation would result. But the adoption of a monetary rule would eliminate the major source of fluctuations in spending—fluctuations in the growth of the money supply—and would therefore tend to minimize any unemployment or inflation.

Criticisms of Monetarism

Neo-Keynesian economists disagree with monetarists on several basic points. First, they believe that monetarists attach too much importance to the money supply. Neo-Keynesians agree that changes in the money supply can alter

---

[2] Milton Friedman, "The Case for a Monetary Rule," *Newsweek*, February 7, 1972. Reprinted in M. Friedman, *Bright Promises, Dismal Performance: An Economist's Protest*, published by Thomas Horton and Daughters, 1983.

GDP, but they argue that other factors are also important—perhaps even more important. These factors include changes in the level of planned investment or government spending. Neo-Keynesians believe that such autonomous changes can lead to inflation or unemployment even if the money supply expands at a constant rate. For instance, Neo-Keynesians argue that pessimism about the future might cause businesses to cut back on investment, and this might lead to unemployment even if the money supply continues to expand at a steady rate.

Second, although virtually all neo-Keynesians agree with monetarists that crowding out reduces the effectiveness of fiscal policy, neo-Keynesians believe that only a small amount of investment spending will normally be crowded out, so expansionary fiscal policy can still have a significant impact on equilibrium GDP.

But many modern Keynesians are quite critical of the long lags involved in implementing changes in taxation and government spending. Since the lags in implementing monetary policy are generally shorter than the lags in implementing fiscal policy (though prorule monetarists argue that they are still too long), monetary policy is seen as the primary technique for stabilizing the economy.

Third, neo-Keynesians are critical of the monetary rule because they believe that it could contribute to greater, rather than less, unemployment and inflation. Because neo-Keynesians believe that the economy is *inherently* unstable (due to the volatility of investment spending), they argue that Fed policymakers need discretion to be able to offset fluctuations in spending and thereby maintain full employment without inflation.

The Nonactivist Position: The New Classical Economists

As you probably noted, monetarists have much in common with the classical economists we discussed in Chapter 10. Both groups see the economy as fundamentally stable and believe in laissez-faire policies. But another school of modern economists has even more in common with the original classical theorists, so much so that this school has been dubbed the "new" classical school of economics.

The new classical economics is based on two fundamental beliefs: (1) wages and prices are highly flexible, and (2) expectations about the future are formed "rationally." The remainder of this section investigates the implications of those beliefs.

Wage/Price Flexibility and Full Employment

Like the classical theorists of old, the economists of the new classical school (of which the most prominent members are Robert Lucas of Chicago, Thomas Sargent of Stanford, and Robert Barro of Harvard) believe that wages and prices are highly flexible. This flexibility permits markets to adjust quickly to changes in supply or demand, so shortages or surpluses are prevented. In short, highly flexible prices ensure that the quantity of the good or service demanded will equal the quantity supplied; markets will "clear."

New classical economists believe that the market-clearing principle applies not only to individual markets—the markets for shoes or cars or accountants, for instance—but also to the aggregate economy. Its implications for the overall labor market are particularly important. To illustrate, let's suppose that the economy experiences a decline in aggregate demand. Of course, when the overall demand for products declines, the demand for labor must also fall. But the new classical economists do not believe that this reduction in labor demand will result in unemployment. Because wages are highly flexible, the reduced level of labor demand will cause wages to drop. Lower wage rates will both encourage employers to hire more workers and reduce the amount of labor supplied (at the lower wage, some workers will prefer leisure to work). The reduction in wages will thus restore equilibrium in the labor market; everyone who is willing to work at the new, lower wage will find employment, and every employer who is willing to pay that wage will find workers.[3] Any unemployment must be voluntary.

The Importance of Expectations

The belief in highly flexible wages and prices and the voluntary nature of unemployment is not new; this view was held by the original classical economists. But the new classical economists are not clones of the originals; they have made their own distinctive contribution to economic thinking. The distinctive feature of the new classical economics is its focus on expectations and the way that expectations influence people's behavior.

These economists remind us that different expectations about the future can lead to different decisions today. For instance, if consumers expect new-car prices to be lower in a few months, they will probably wait to buy; if they expect prices to be higher, they will buy now. These are commonsense observations that few of us would challenge. But the new classical economists go

---

[3] The new classical economists do not believe that labor contracts make wages so inflexible as to prevent these adjustments.

well beyond these observations. They are interested in how expectations are formed; in other words, they want to know how individuals come to expect whatever they expect—higher car prices, lower interest rates, or more rapid inflation, for instance.

Neo-Keynesians and monetarists disagree about many things, but both groups have assumed that individuals base their expectations only on experience—by looking backward at past events. The new classical economists argue that this assumption implies that individuals are irrational, because it presumes that they ignore current events they know will influence the future. As an alternative, the new classical economists have proposed the theory of rational expectations.

The **theory of rational expectations** suggests that people use all available information to develop realistic (rational) expectations about the future. According to this theory, the public is quite perceptive in forming its expectations. Households and businesses do not merely project past trends into the future; they also take current economic developments quickly into account.

For instance, when forecasting inflation, people will consider the inflation of recent years, but they will also consider the potential impact of upcoming labor negotiations, the rate of productivity growth, the anticipated quality of agricultural harvests (and their impact on food prices), developments in the Middle East (and their impact on oil prices), and—perhaps most important of all—the expected government response to inflation.

Rational Expectations and Discretionary Policy

The belief that wages and prices are highly flexible and that expectations are formed "rationally" leads the members of the new classical school to some interesting policy conclusions. According to the new classical economists, *systematic* monetary and fiscal policies cannot alter the level of output or employment in the economy; they can only change the price level. This belief is known as the **policy ineffectiveness theorem.** The implications of the policy ineffectiveness theorem are clear: Government attempts to reduce unemployment are doomed to failure; they will result only in inflation.

The problem, according to the new classical theorists, is that systematic policies whereby the government always responds to a particular set of economic conditions in a given way are *predictable.* But if discretionary policies are predictable, individuals will anticipate those policies and alter their behavior in ways that make the policies ineffective. Thus individuals, *acting on rational expectations,* make government stabilization policies ineffective.

To illustrate, let's suppose that historically the Fed has expanded the money supply whenever the measured unemployment rate reached 8 percent.[4] Now let's assume that the unemployment rate reaches that magic number and the Fed feels compelled to take action. Of course, when the money supply is expanded, the aggregate demand curve will shift to the right, as depicted in Exh. 15.1 by the movement from AD_1 to AD_2. This increase in aggregate demand would, ceteris paribus, tend to raise the level of output in the economy. In our example output would be expanded from the original equilibrium of $900 billion to $1,000 billion (the intersection of AS_1 and AD_2). Because increased output normally means additional jobs, employment would also tend to expand.

But supporters of the theory of rational expectations believe that the assumption of ceteris paribus is unreasonable in this situation. They argue that workers and businesses have learned to anticipate the Fed's policy response to unemployment. Moreover, they have discovered that when the money supply is increased, inflation inevitably follows. (Note that the increase in aggregate demand pushes up the price level along with the level of output.) So when the public perceives that the Fed is likely to increase the money supply, it takes actions to protect itself from the anticipated inflation. Workers ask for higher wages, suppliers raise their input prices, and businesses push up product prices. Because prices and wages are assumed to be highly flexible, these adjustments occur immediately, the moment the public anticipates higher prices. Of course, if wage rates and other costs rise, the aggregate supply curve will tend to shift upward (from AS_1 to AS_2 in Exh. 15.1), so less real output will be supplied at any given price level. Since the government-mandated increase in aggregate demand has been immediately offset by a *reduction* in aggregate supply, the net effect is to leave output and employment unchanged. The only impact of the expansionary monetary policy has been an increase in the price level from 100 to 110.

The preceding example focused on efforts to combat unemployment, but the theory of rational expectations has equally interesting implications for the the battle against inflation. To illustrate, let's suppose that the inflation rate rises to some level that Fed policymakers have openly designated as unacceptable. According to the theory of rational expectations, if the public is con-

---

[4] How can the unemployment rate reach 8 percent if wages and prices are highly flexible? According to the new classical economists, this can occur as a result of *unexpected* shocks in aggregate demand or supply—reductions in planned investment, the outbreak of war, or significant crop failures, for instance. Because these events are unexpected, they may be misperceived by workers. For instance, if the economy experiences a reduction in aggregate demand, some workers may mistakenly assume that the downturn has affected only their industry. Equally important, they may fail to recognize that the overall price level has also fallen, so the real wage—the purchasing power of their money wage—is unchanged. Suffering from these misperceptions, they are unhappy with their lower money wage. Thus workers quit their jobs and set out in search of positions that pay as much as they are accustomed to earning. In this way an unexpected shock may lead to unemployment.

EXHIBIT 15.1

Rational Expectations and Economic Policy

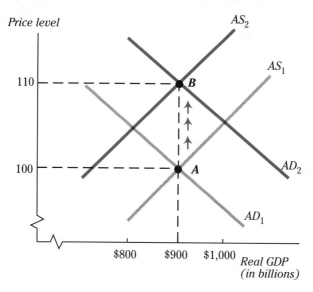

According to the theory of rational expectations, anticipated changes in monetary or fiscal policies cannot alter the level of output or employment; they can only change prices. In this example the expansionary monetary policy that shifts the aggregate demand curve from AD_1 to AD_2 is anticipated, causing workers to ask for higher wages and suppliers to ask for higher input prices. These changes cause the AS curve to shift upward from AS_1 to AS_2, neutralizing the output effect of the monetary expansion and raising the overall price level.

vinced of the Fed's commitment to reducing inflation, it will expect lower inflation; workers will therefore immediately accept wage cuts, and input suppliers will accept lower prices. As a consequence, the AS curve will quickly shift downward, lowering the price level but preserving the same level of output and employment. Once again, discretionary policy alters only the price level; it has no impact on real output or the level of employment. (Note that this result is quite different from the effect predicted by neo-Keynesians. Neo-Keynesians would argue that because *some* wages and prices are rigid due to contracts, a reduction in aggregate demand would lower both the *overall* price level and the levels of output and employment. In fact, a major concern of neo-Keynesians has been the unemployment "cost" of combating inflation.) Although these examples have dealt with monetary policy, the same conclusions would hold for systematic applications of fiscal policy.

The Need for Policy Rules

What conclusions can we reach from the preceding examples? The primary conclusion is that systematic monetary and fiscal policies affect only the price level; they do not alter either the level of output or employment. Of course, in order for discretionary policies to have the effect intended by neo-Keynesians, they must be systematic; it wouldn't make sense to expand the money supply or to cut taxes at random time intervals. So in effect the new classical economists are arguing that discretionary monetary and fiscal policies cannot be used to reduce unemployment.

Because the new classical economists are convinced that government policies cannot be used to alter employment, they believe that policymakers should concentrate on achieving and maintaining a low rate of inflation. This, they suggest, can be best accomplished by permitting a slow, steady growth of the money supply and avoiding large budget deficits. Thus the new classical economists favor rules much like the monetarists': Increase the money supply at a constant rate, and balance the federal budget over some agreed-on period (not necessarily on an annual basis but over some predictable time frame). These rules will prevent government policymakers from aggravating inflation in their well-intentioned but futile attempts to lower unemployment. (If a balanced-budget amendment is approved, Congress will have a new rule governing its fiscal policy. What do economists think of this proposed rule? Read "Balanced-Budget Proposal Challenged . . . ," on page 470, to find out.)

Criticisms of the New Classical Economics

The new classical economics is quite controversial. Both the assumption of wage/price flexibility and the assumption of rational expectations have been criticized. Few economists seem willing to accept the assertion that wages are sufficiently flexible to ensure that labor markets are continually in equilibrium. These economists point to the prolonged unemployment of the Great Depression and periods in the 1970s and 1980s as evidence that wages adjust slowly, not rapidly as the new classical model implies.

The belief that expectations are formed rationally has also been met with skepticism, both by neo-Keynesians and by many monetarists. Critics argue that the public does not gather and analyze information as intelligently as the theory suggests; nor does it always make fully rational decisions based on that information. Studies of the theory of rational expectations have produced mixed results. Although some early evidence supported the theory, its performance on more recent tests has not upheld its initial promise.

If either of the basic assumptions is incorrect, the policy ineffectiveness theorem of the new classical economists is invalidated. In other words, monetary and fiscal policies would be capable of generating short-run changes in the levels of output and employment. This seems to be the view held by most economists. Of course, whether or not such policies should be used to change output and employment still depends on the length of the lags involved in policy implementation—the issue raised by the monetarists.

A New Form of Activism: Managing Aggregate Supply

The debate about the desirability of government efforts to manage aggregate demand has been with us for a long time. And given that it is very difficult to prove statistically which of the schools of thought has the most accurate model of the economy, the debate is likely to continue. We'll indicate a few areas of consensus among macroeconomists after we take a brief look at supply-side economics.

Even if monetary and fiscal policies work as Keynesians suggest (which is certainly not the conclusion of the monetarists or the new classical economists), they produce mixed results. As we saw in Chapter 14, efforts to reduce unemployment tend to aggravate inflation, whereas policies to reduce inflation lead to greater unemployment. In addition, demand-management policies are incapable of offsetting supply shocks—unexpected reductions in aggregate supply. Since supply shocks lead to stagflation, they put pressure on policymakers to combat the two problems instead of one. But once again policymakers are confronted by trade-offs. If they choose to combat inflation, they make the unemployment problem even worse; if they decide to attack unemployment, the inflation rate escalates. In the late 1970s these limitations led to an intense interest in supply-side remedies.

Supply-Side Economics

Supply-side remedies are policies designed to shift the aggregate supply curve to the right (downward). Remember, a shift of the aggregate supply curve to the right means an increase in aggregate supply: More is being supplied than before at each price level.

Unlike monetary and fiscal policies, supply-side remedies have the very desirable feature of being able to combat unemployment and inflation at the same time. As you consider Exh. 15.2, suppose that the economy is operating at point A, the intersection of AD and AS_1. If policymakers can increase aggregate supply from AS_1 to AS_2, they can move the economy to point B; they will have increased equilibrium output (and employment) in the economy while reducing the overall price level. Policymakers will have succeeded in simultaneously reducing unemployment and inflation.

Balanced-Budget Proposal Challenged by Many Economists on Eve of Meeting

WASHINGTON

A balanced-budget amendment may be good politics, but it won't pass Economics 101.

That's the view of many of the thousands of economists flocking to this city for their big annual meeting that begins today. From liberal Democratic economic pundits like Robert Eisner to former Nixon and Reagan White House economists Herbert Stein and Murray Weidenbaum, a wide range of economists say that forcing the budget into balance, as the Republicans have promised to achieve with a constitutional amendment, violates principles they've long written about, studied and taught.

"Locking yourself into a balanced budget rigidly is bad economics," maintains Paul Krugman, an economics professor at Stanford University, "What you are supposed to do according to the textbooks is run deficits during the bad years and surpluses during the good years.". . .

As proposed, the amendment before Congress would require that the federal bud-

get be balanced by the year 2002 or sooner. That would mean cutting spending or raising revenue by nearly $1 trillion over the next seven years. If the Republicans pass their proposed tax cuts this year, it would add $380 billion to that total, according to the Treasury Department.

In remarks prepared for a hearing before the Senate Judiciary Committee yesterday, Dr. Stein, a senior fellow at the American Enterprise Institute and head of the Council of Economic Advisers under presidents Nixon and Ford, cited a host of what he calls "technical difficulties."

"It is practically inoperable," said Dr. Stein in his prepared remarks. "How is the budget to be defined? Does it include the Social Security Trust Account? Is a private obligation insured by the federal government part of the federal debt? How do we deal with cyclical fluctuations in the economy?"

From the other end of the political spectrum, Robert Eisner agrees. "It would be a disaster if it were forced. I think it would be [a lot] like

the prohibition amendment," says the Northwestern University economics professor, who calls himself a liberal Democrat. "I could make a fortune showing ways to evade it."

Of course, not everyone agrees that such an amendment would be unworkable. James Buchanan, a professor at George Mason University and Nobel Prize winner in economics in 1986, has long favored a constitutional balanced-budget provision as a counterbalance to politicians' tendencies to spend to satisfy constituencies. Prof. Buchanan also submitted his written views yesterday before the Senate Judiciary Committee.

Others who favor it do so only on condition that Congress can get around it. The amendment allows for deficit spending if a three-fifths majority of Congress approves it. "The three-fifths override means that you don't run the risk of being forced to raise taxes during a recession," says Martin Feldstein, a professor of economics at Harvard University and a former head of the Council of Economic Advisers under President Reagan.

Opponents say that's not enough flexibility. Tax revenue and the need to spend government money both wax and wane with economic conditions. "When the economy slumps you want a deficit. You want to have a cushion," Prof. Eisner argues. "You don't want to start taxing people more when their purchasing power is down, and you don't want to stop outlays at that time either. That would force government to follow perverse policy.". . . .

Still, being opposed to a balanced-budget amendment doesn't mean being in favor of deficits. Even some economists who aren't troubled by the current $200 billion deficit level see problems ahead. Victor Fuchs, a professor of economics at Stanford and the incoming president of the American Economic Association, feels budget deficits can be appropriate if the money the government is borrowing goes for productive uses, such as education. Still, he sees large deficits in the future as a result of increased spending on health care, and because of demographic changes. "The country as a whole is not really thinking a lot about the future," he says.

Murray Weidenbaum, director of the Center for Study of American Business at Washington University in St. Louis and head of the Council of Economic Advisers un-

der President Reagan, opposes budget deficits in general. "A budget deficit pulls out badly needed investment capital from the public sector," he says. Still, even he opposes a balanced-budget amendment—because he thinks it won't work.

"For many people, it's an excuse not to move ahead right now to reduce the deficit," he says.

—Amanda Bennett and Christopher Georges

SOURCE: Amanda Bennett and Christopher Georges, "Balanced-Budget Proposal Challenged by Many Economists on Eve of Meeting," January 6, 1995. Reprinted by permission of *The Wall Street Journal*, © 1995 Dow Jones & Co., Inc. All Rights Reserved Worldwide.

Use Your Economic Reasoning

1. Economists of all persuasions recognize that when the economy unexpectedly slips into a recession, a budget deficit results. Why do recessions lead to deficits? If the federal government was required to balance its budget, what actions would it need to take to respond to the deficit?

2. Robert Eisner describes raising taxes during a recession as "perverse" fiscal policy. What is perverse (improper) about this policy?

3. According to Paul Krugman, "locking yourself into a balanced budget rigidly is bad economics." Martin Feldstein says, "you don't [want to be forced] to raise taxes." Are these economists in favor

of permitting the federal government some discretion in fiscal policy, or do they favor rules? Does that make them activists or nonactivists?

4. Murray Weidenbaum, although not favoring the amendment, opposes budget deficits in general because he believes that they lead to offsetting reductions in investment spending. How can budget deficits lead to reductions in investment spending? Does Weidenbaum sound like a Keynesian or a monetarist?

5. Would a new classical economist be likely to favor or oppose a rule forcing the federal government to balance its budget?

EXHIBIT 15.2

The Impact of Supply-Side Remedies

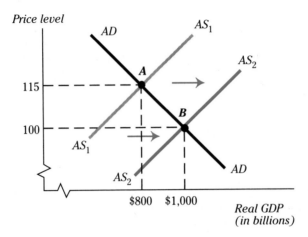

The purpose of supply-side remedies is to shift the aggregate supply curve to the right, thereby reducing the overall price level while increasing output and employment.

What policies do supply-side economists advocate? The complete list is too long to present here, but the following are illustrative.

1. *Encourage saving and investment through tax policies.* By encouraging saving through a reduction in taxes on interest income, for example, the government can make more funds available for investment purposes. Various techniques can then be used to encourage businesses to borrow this money and invest it. *Investment tax credits* would allow firms to deduct a certain percentage of their investment outlays from their tax liabilities. To the extent that such policies encourage business to borrow and invest in new factories and equipment, they help to increase the economy's productive capacity so that more output is supplied at any given price level. Of course, if more output is produced at each price level, the aggregate supply curve shifts to the right as depicted in Exh. 15.2.

2. *Reduce government regulations that drive up the cost of doing business.* We all recognize that government regulations are necessary to protect consumers, the environment, and the health and safety of workers. In some instances, however, regulations may add substantially to the cost of producing goods and services yet provide little real benefit for the society. For example, the Food and Drug Administration has been accused of driving up the cost of developing new drugs by needlessly prolonging the testing that is required to gain FDA approval. Reducing such costs should free resources to pro-

duce other goods and services; thus more output can be supplied at each price level.

3. *Encourage individuals to work harder and longer by reducing marginal tax rates.* Marginal tax rates are the tax rates paid on the last increment of income. For example, under a progressive income tax system, an individual earning $15,000 might be required to pay a tax of 15 percent on the first $10,000 and 20 percent on the remaining $5,000. Supply-siders insist that high marginal tax rates discourage work. The way to get people to work more (and thereby increase aggregate supply) is to reduce marginal tax rates and let them keep more of what they earn.

The Reagan Supply-Side Experiment

When President Reagan took office, he presented several supply-side features in his Program for Economic Recovery (announced in February 1981). The cornerstone of Reagan's program was the Economic Recovery Tax Act (ERTA) of 1981. Patterned after legislation proposed by two supply-siders, Representative Jack Kemp of New York and Senator William Roth of Delaware, ERTA called for a 5 percent reduction in tax rates in 1981 and a 10 percent reduction in 1982 and 1983. ERTA also contained provisions to encourage saving and to stimulate business investment. According to its supporters, the reduction in tax rates would cause the economy to grow rapidly as the lower tax rates stimulated saving and investment and convinced Americans to work harder. In fact, some supply-siders argued that the economy's growth would be sufficiently rapid that the additional tax revenue generated by the new jobs and expanded hours would more than offset the tax revenue lost through the initial tax cuts. In short, government would take in more revenue at the lower tax rates than it had at the higher rates.[5]

What actually happened? Initially, the effects of the Reagan administration's tax cuts were more than offset by a restrictive monetary policy engineered by the Federal Reserve to combat inflation (which was running at more than 12 percent a year in 1980). While these policies helped to quell inflation, they also pushed the economy into the deepest recession since the Great Depression.

The recession ended in December 1982 and output and employment expanded rapidly through 1984. However, for the remainder of the 1980s economic growth was unspectacular (President Reagan's term ended in 1988). Overall, the rate of economic growth experienced in the decade of the 1980s

---

[5] This possibility was originally suggested by Arthur Laffer, professor of economics at Pepperdine University and one of the early proponents of supply-side measures.

President Reagan's Program for Economic Recovery contained several supply-side features.

was identical to the experience of the previous decade; in both decades the average annual growth rate of real GDP was 2.7 percent. Clearly the supply-side measures did not lead to the spectacular economic growth that some supporters expected. In addition, empirical evidence suggests that the supply-side tax cuts did little to encourage work or saving (the personal savings rate actually declined throughout the 1980s). Instead, these tax cuts combined with increases in government spending to result in huge government deficits which tripled the public debt during Reagan's term in office.

Judged by what some supply-siders initially promised—an explosion in work effort, investment, and saving—the Economic Recovery Tax Act was clearly a failure. Moreover, neo-Keynesian economists attributed most of the economic expansion of the Reagan years not to the supply-side policies but to the demand-side stimulus provided by the substantial budget deficits.

These economists argue that tax cuts shift both the aggregate demand curve (the traditional Keynesian impact) and the aggregate supply curve (the supply-side impact). However, they believe that in the short run, the supply-side impact tends to be minor in comparison with the demand-side effect. Most statistical studies support this view.

In 1995 many of the supply-side arguments we have discussed reemerged as Republicans and Democrats attempted to appease voters by proposing a "middle-class tax cut." Once again there were claims that supply-side tax cuts could be relied on to increase growth substantially and to pay for themselves. And once again neo-Keynesians were disputing those claims and forecasting budget deficits.[6]

The Long-Run Importance of Supply-Side Measures

Even if neo-Keynesians are correct about the short-run impact of supply-side policies, we should not conclude that measures to enhance aggregate supply should be ignored. On the contrary, virtually all economists agree that policies designed to expand aggregate supply are crucial to the long-run well-being of Americans. The same policies that cause the aggregate supply curve to shift to the right also cause potential GDP to increase. The ability to increase potential GDP is probably the most important impact of supply-side policies. Although studies suggest that supply-side measures contribute little to the short-run battle against inflation and unemployment, the long-run impact of such policies can be quite important.

To understand why supply-side policies may play an important role in the long run, think about the objective of increasing the living standard of Americans. One measure of a society's standard of living is GDP per person (total GDP divided by population). The first step in ensuring a high standard of living is making the most of our potential, ensuring that the economy operates at full employment. That's the objective of monetary and fiscal policies: to push the economy up to its potential. (As we've already seen, monetarists and new classical economists would argue that these efforts to manage aggregate demand are ill-advised.) But another objective is to keep potential GDP expanding so that it grows more rapidly than the society's population. That objective might be thought of as the domain of supply-side economics.

How do we keep potential GDP increasing more rapidly than population? Consensus holds that the key is in improving labor productivity—output per worker. This means providing workers with more and better capital equipment. (Recall that one of the objectives of supply-siders was to stimulate investment spending and spending on research and development.) It also means developing a better-educated and more highly motivated work force. Unfortunately, these changes do not occur automatically. The growth of labor productivity in the United States slowed significantly in the early 1970s and has

---

[6] Both Republicans and Democrats promised to reduce government spending by enough to offset the tax cut and to prevent the deficit from growing. But some Republicans argued that the economic growth resulting from the tax cut would substantially trim the size of the needed spending cuts.

remained sluggish. Economists have been unable to provide a convincing explanation for the slowdown or a palatable plan for remedying the problem. Two things are clear. First, it is more difficult to stimulate labor productivity than the original supply-siders suggested. Second, these efforts generally require society to sacrifice *today* in order to have a higher standard of living in the future. For instance, improving education requires higher taxes, which in turn means less disposable income for households. One reason for the productivity slowdown may be a lessening of our willingness to make these sacrifices.

Summing Up: The Current State of Macro Thinking

Economists obviously disagree about the role of government in attempting to maintain full employment and about the possible benefits of supply-side remedies. This section is the author's interpretation of current thinking.

1. Virtually all economists agree that the economy contains, to one degree or another, a self-correcting mechanism. The economy tends to return to potential GDP and full employment in the long run. Economists disagree about how long this adjustment process takes.

2. Economists disagree about the ability of demand-management policies to speed up the adjustment to potential GDP and full employment. Neo-Keynesians support such measures; monetarists and new classical economists do not.

   The differences between activists and nonactivists may not, however, be quite as great as they first appear. Even neo-Keynesians recognize that discretionary policies are subject to lags. Thus modern Keynesians believe that it is undesirable to attempt to fine tune the economy—to try to correct every minor increase in unemployment or in the overall price level. Instead, policymakers should confine their efforts to combating major downturns or inflationary threats.

3. The new classical economics has clearly shaken up macroeconomic thinking but hasn't gained very many converts thus far. Most economists do not appear to believe that expectations are formed in a totally "rational" manner. Even fewer economists are willing to accept the classical contention that wages are highly flexible and that markets are continuously in equilibrium. If economists reject these arguments, they must reject the policy ineffectiveness theorem that grows from them.

   Although few economists seem willing to embrace the entire new classical model, most tend to agree that the theory of rational expectations is an improvement on the expectations models previously applied by Keynesians and monetarists. Moreover, there appears to be growing support for a weaker version of the policy ineffectiveness theory: Fully anticipated policy changes have *smaller* effects than unanticipated changes.

4. Virtually all economists support measures to stimulate aggregate supply. But evidence suggests that supply-side measures do little in the short run to stimulate GDP or to lower the price level. The major impact of supply-side policies comes in the long run, when their benefits can be substantial.

Summary

Although economists generally agree about the existence of a self-correcting mechanism, they disagree about the speed with which this adjustment process occurs and about the desirability of government efforts to enhance these naturally occurring forces.

Neo-Keynesians believe that the economy's self-correcting mechanism works quite slowly. Thus they support an active role for government in speeding the adjustment process through discretionary monetary and fiscal policies.

Monetarists believe that the economy's self-adjustment mechanism works reasonably quickly and that government efforts to aid this process are either ineffective or counterproductive.

According to monetarists, changes in the money supply play the primary role in determining the level of aggregate output and prices in the economy. Government efforts to stimulate the economy through fiscal policy are futile because they lead to the crowding out of investment spending.

The monetarists also argue against the use of discretionary monetary policy. Because of the *recognition lag* and the *impact lag*, the effect of a monetary policy change may be felt when it is no longer appropriate. Thus discretionary monetary policy has a destabilizing effect on the economy: It contributes to greater unemployment and inflation.

Because monetarists believe that discretionary monetary policy tends to intensify the economy's problems rather than lessen them, they support a *monetary rule* that would require the Fed to expand the money supply at a constant annual rate.

Monetarists are not alone in opposing the use of discretionary policies to guide the economy's performance; *new classical economists* also argue against such intervention. The new classical economics is founded on two basic tenets: (1) wages and prices are highly flexible, and (2) expectations about the future are formed rationally.

Because new classical economists believe that wages and prices are highly flexible, they believe that the economy quickly tends toward full employment. Reductions in aggregate demand are met by falling wages and prices, which quickly restore equilibrium. Any unemployment is voluntary.

New classical economists emphasize the impact of expectations on behavior; different expectations about the future can lead to different decisions today. The *theory of rational expectations* suggests that people use all available information to develop realistic expectations about the future.

The new classical economists' belief in highly flexible wages and prices and rational expectations led to the *policy ineffectiveness theorem.* According to this theorem, systematic monetary and fiscal policies cannot alter the level of output or employment in the economy; they can change only the price level.

Because the new classical economists are convinced that government policies cannot be used to alter output or employment, they believe that policymakers should concentrate on achieving and maintaining a low rate of inflation. The new classical economists, like the monetarists, favor rules to achieve this objective.

The activist-nonactivist debate has focused on the desirability of demand-management policies. But in the late 1970s supply-side remedies—policies to increase aggregate supply—attracted a great deal of attention. The desirable feature of such policies is that they can reduce unemployment and inflation at the same time. Available evidence suggests that supply-side measures have a relatively modest impact on aggregate supply in the short run; most of the impact comes in the long run.

Glossary

Impact lag. The time that elapses between the implementation of a policy change and its initial effect on the economy.

Monetarism. The belief that changes in the money supply play the primary role in determining the level of aggregate output and prices in the economy.

Monetary rule. A rule that would require the Federal Reserve to increase the money supply at a constant rate.

Policy ineffectiveness theorem. The theory that systematic monetary and fiscal policies cannot alter the level of output or employment in the economy; they can change only the price level.

Recognition lag. The delay in implementing policy that results from the mixed signals sent by the economy.

Theory of rational expectations. The theory that people use all available information to develop realistic expectations about the future.

Study Questions

Fill in the Blanks

1. Neo-Keynesian economists who advocate government intervention to guide the economy's performance are also known as _____.

2. The two modern schools of thought that oppose the use of demand-management techniques are the _____ and the _____

   _____.

3. The two types of lags associated with discretionary monetary policy are the _____ lag and the _____ lag.

4. According to the _____ and the _____, the Fed should be required to expand the money supply at a constant rate.

5. _____ is often called the father of monetarism.

6. According to the _____, expectations are formed rationally.

7. The belief that systematic monetary and fiscal policies cannot alter the level of output or employment is known as the _____ theorem.

8. The requirement that the Fed expand the money supply at a constant rate is known as the _____.

9. The use of monetary or fiscal policy in an attempt to eliminate even minor increases in unemployment or inflation is known as _____ the economy and is opposed by virtually all modern economists.

10. Unlike monetary and fiscal policies, _____ remedies can be used to reduce unemployment and inflation at the same time.

Multiple Choice

1. Which of the following schools of economists would be described as "activists"?
   a) Classical economists
   b) Neo-Keynesian economists
   c) Monetarist economists
   d) New classical economists

2. Which of the following statements about the activist-nonactivist debate is true?
   a) Monetarists advocate the use of discretionary monetary policy to manage aggregate demand and to ensure full employment.
   b) New classical economists support the use of fiscal policy to guide the economy but believe that monetary policy is ineffective
   c) Neo-Keynesians advocate government intervention because they believe that the self-correcting mechanism works too slowly.
   d) All of the above

3. According to the monetarists,
   a) fiscal policy is ineffective because of crowding out.
   b) fiscal policy is more effective than monetary policy.
   c) increases in government spending tend to lower interest rates, thus stimulating investment spending.
   d) increases in government spending tend to stimulate investment spending by making business leaders more optimistic.

4. Which of the following is a true statement about the monetarists?
   a) They favor the use of discretionary monetary policy to guide the economy's performance.
   b) They believe that the money supply should be increased at a constant rate.
   c) They favor legislation to provide Fed policymakers with more power to guide the economy's performance.
   d) a and c

5. When monetarists call for a "monetary rule," what they really want is
   a) greater reliance on discretionary monetary policy and less reliance on discretionary fiscal policy.
   b) legislation to provide Fed policymakers with more power to guide the economy's performance.
   c) legislation that would require the Fed to increase the money supply at a constant rate.
   d) bigger paychecks for monetarist economists.

6. The two types of lags in monetary policy are the
   a) policy lag and the implementation lag.
   b) recognition lag and the impact lag.
   c) recognition lag and the policy lag.
   d) identification lag and the implementation lag.

7. The major reason monetarists oppose the use of discretionary monetary policy to guide the economy's performance is that they
   a) do not believe that changes in the money supply have any impact on output or employment.
   b) believe that lags cause monetary policy to have a destabilizing effect on the economy.
   c) believe that monetary policy is not as effective as fiscal policy.
   d) believe that rational expectations make monetary policy changes ineffective.

8. Neo-Keynesians believe that the economy is inherently unstable due to
   a) the instability created by government fiscal policy.
   b) fluctuations in the level of government spending.
   c) the volatility of investment spending.
   d) Federal Reserve monetary policies.

9. Which of the following is *not* a belief of the new classical economists?
   a) Wages and prices are highly flexible.
   b) Expectations are formed rationally.
   c) Unemployment is voluntary.
   d) Labor markets adjust very slowly to changes in demand.

10. According to the theory of rational expectations,
   a) households and businesses base their expectations only on past experience.
   b) people use all available information in developing their expectations about the future.
   c) it is reasonable for households and businesses to ignore the actions of policymakers.
   d) only policymakers have sufficient knowledge to develop accurate estimates of future price levels.

11. According to the policy ineffectiveness theorem,
   a) anticipated changes in monetary or fiscal policy will alter only the price level.
   b) fiscal policy is ineffective unless it is accompanied by monetary policy.
   c) monetary policy is ineffective unless it is accompanied by fiscal policy.
   d) unanticipated changes in monetary or fiscal policy will alter only the price level.

12. The new classical economists believe that any anticipated increase in the money supply will
   a) expand output and employment.
   b) be immediately offset by a reduction in aggregate supply.
   c) immediately cause potential GDP to expand.
   d) lead to an immediate reduction in the price level, with no change in output or employment.

13. According to neo-Keynesians, which of the following is true?
    a) When unemployment is caused by inadequate aggregate demand, expanding the money supply will reduce unemployment but intensify inflation.
    b) When inflation is caused by a supply shock, reducing the money supply will lower the rate of inflation but aggravate unemployment.
    c) When unemployment is caused by a reduction in aggregate supply, increasing the money supply will reduce unemployment but aggravate inflation.
    d) All of the above
    e) None of the above

14. Which of the following is *not* a supply-side remedy?
    a) Use tax credits to encourage investment.
    b) Reduce marginal tax rates to encourage people to work longer and harder.
    c) Increase tax rates on interest income in order to discourage saving and stimulate consumption spending.
    d) Eliminate government regulations that do not serve a valid purpose.

15. In the short run reductions in marginal tax rates probably increase
    a) only aggregate demand.
    b) only aggregate supply.
    c) both aggregate demand and aggregate supply but have a greater impact on demand.
    d) both aggregate demand and aggregate supply but have a greater impact on supply.

Problems and Questions for Discussion

1. Given that the economy has a self-correcting mechanism, what is the essence of the neo-Keynesian argument for government intervention to combat unemployment?

2. Why do the monetarists believe that fiscal policy cannot be used to stimulate the economy?

3. Discuss the lags involved in the implementation of monetary policy.

4. Neo-Keynesians blame the inherent instability of capitalist economies on the volatility of investment spending. Try to recall from Chapter 11 why investment spending tends to volatile.

5. What is the nature of the *monetarist* argument for a monetary rule?

6. The new classical economists sometimes argue that only random monetary policy can alter output and employment. Use their model to explain this conclusion. Does this mean that policymakers should replace Keynesian demand-management policies with random policies?

7. Explain the logic behind the policy ineffectiveness theorem of the new classical economists. Supplement your explanation with a graph.

8. Discuss the similarities and differences between the monetarists and the new classical economists with regard to the issue of demand-management policy.

9. List as many supply-side remedies as you can remember, and discuss the rationale for each.

10. Critics of the Reagan experiment with supply-side economics often argue that it was "oversold." What do they mean? What evidence might they summon to support their position?

Answer Key

Fill in the Blanks

1. activists
2. monetarists, new classical economists
3. recognition, impact
4. monetarists, new classical economists
5. Milton Friedman
6. new classical economists
7. policy ineffectiveness
8. monetary rule
9. fine tuning
10. supply-side

Multiple Choice

1. b	4. b	7. b	10. b	13. d
2. c	5. c	8. c	11. a	14. c
3. a	6. b	9. d	12. b	15. c

International Economics: Trade, Exchange Rates, and the Balance of Payments

C hapter 16 introduces the economic rationale for international trade and considers the consequences of barriers to free trade. You will learn the meaning of such concepts as "comparative advantage" and "absolute advantage" and see why these concepts are used to summon support for free trade. Arguments for and against free trade will be presented, and we will look closely at the impact of foreign competition. Chapter 17 considers the financial dimension of international trade and the role of exchange rates. You will see how exchange rates are determined and how changes in exchange rates influence international trade. You will also learn about the balance of payments accounts that nations use to keep track of their international transactions, and why a nation's balance of payments always balances.

International Trade

The first fifteen chapters of the text have included numerous examples involving our economic relationships with other nations. We've previewed the benefits of international trade, and we've considered the impact of trade on our GDP. We've seen how international influences can dominate the process of price determination in competitive markets and how requiring U.S. firms to provide their workers with health insurance could impair the ability of these firms to compete with producers in other nations. We've included these examples because, like it or not, the U.S. economy is increasingly an **open economy**—an economy that exchanges goods and services with other nations. (A **closed economy,** by contrast, does not exchange goods and services with other nations.)

The increased openness of the U.S. economy is a matter of some controversy. Many Americans see foreign competition as a destructive force that threatens their jobs and their way of life. Others view foreign competition as a blessing that provides quality products at prices lower than domestic producers charge. Economic policymakers must weigh these costs and benefits as they develop policies to promote or retard international trade. In this chapter we explore the theoretical basis for free, or unrestricted, international trade, and we'll take a closer look at the costs and benefits associated with it.

Interdependent Economies and U.S. Trade

Statistics show that the economies of the world are becoming more interdependent. Consumers in the United States are buying more foreign products, and foreign consumers are buying more U.S. goods. Producers around the world are using more imported parts and raw materials in the products they manufacture. In short, foreign trade is already more important than most Americans realize, and current signs indicate that it will gain even more importance in the future.

Import and Export Patterns

The Sony television sets, Nike tennis shoes, and Raleigh bicycles we see in U.S. stores are all **imports**—goods or services purchased from foreign producers.[1] In the last two decades trade between the United States and other nations has expanded significantly. More Americans are driving Saabs, Nissans, Peugeots, and Isuzus; are listening to CD players made in Japan; are drinking wine from France and Italy; and are wearing clothes from Korea, Romania, Taiwan, and other countries. As you can see from Exh. 16.1, imports almost tripled as a fraction of GDP between 1960 and 1994.

U.S. exports are expanding as well. **Exports** are goods and services produced domestically and sold to customers in other countries. For example, U.S. farmers export wheat and rice and a variety of other agricultural products while U.S. manufacturing firms export products such as earth-moving equipment, laptop computers, and jet airplanes. Exports of goods and services accounted for less than 5 percent of our gross domestic product in 1960; by 1994 that figure had climbed to more than 10 percent of GDP. That percent-

---

[1] The services component of imports includes such items as transportation charges for moving goods and passengers between nations and expenditures made by tourists while traveling in foreign countries.

EXHIBIT 16.1

Trends in U.S. Imports and Exports

	1960	1970	1980	1994
Exports of goods and services	$25.3 billion (4.9% of) GDP	$57.0 billion (5.6% of GDP)	$279.2 billion (10.3% of GDP)	$698 billion (10.4% of GDP)
Imports of goods and services	$22.8 billion (4.4% of GDP)	$55.8 billion (5.5% of GDP)	$293.9 billion (10.9% of GDP)	$804.4 billion (11.9% of GDP)

SOURCE: Developed from data in *The Economic Report of the President, 1995* and the *Survey of Current Business,* March 1995.

age is low when compared with Ireland (65 percent of GDP), Sweden (32 percent of GDP), and Canada (22 percent of GDP), but it is a significant fraction of GDP and one that undoubtedly will increase in the future.[2]

Interdependence and Attitudes Toward Trade

We are constantly reminded of the many ways that national economies are linked to one another. Consumers the world over felt the impact of the oil cutbacks that resulted from Iraq's invasion of Kuwait in August 1990. When there is a poor harvest in Brazil, we all pay higher prices for coffee. Consider, too, the many products of U.S. manufacture that require foreign parts or materials. Many of our automobiles, for example, have foreign-made engines and other components. U.S. steel producers rely on imported coke, and our refineries use imported oil to manufacture gasoline and other petroleum products.

Countries often react strongly, almost resentfully, to the actions of foreign nations with whom they trade. When Japanese automobile producers step up production, U.S. producers cry foul. When Federal Reserve policies drive up interest rates in the United States and attract investment funds, complaints ring out from other nations. With increasing frequency, economic events in one part of the world have global repercussions—repercussions that affect each of us.

---

[2] The percentage figures for Sweden and Canada are for 1993; the figure for Ireland is for 1992. The percentages are based on information in *The World Factbook 1994,* published by the Central Intelligence Agency of the United States.

Domestic workers often protest against imported products.

How should Americans react to this growing interdependence? Does the availability of Japanese automobiles and Taiwanese shoes and other foreign products make Americans better off? Or does the inflow of foreign products simply mean less demand for American products and fewer jobs in domestic manufacturing industries? Should we support U.S. steel and automobile producers and shoe manufacturers when they appeal to our government for protection from "cheap foreign labor"? To respond intelligently to these questions, it is necessary to have some understanding of international economics. We need to understand why countries trade. What are the benefits of trade? Does trade help one country at the expense of another, or is it mutually beneficial? What are the arguments for and against trade barriers? These are the questions we now take up.

The Basis for International Trade

Why do countries trade? The various nations of the world are not all equally blessed in terms of either natural resources or capital and labor endowments. Therefore different nations have different production abilities. Great Britain may be self-sufficient in petroleum products because of oil discoveries in the North Sea. If the British want oranges and grapefruit, however, they will probably have to trade for them, because Britain's climate is ill-suited to growing citrus fruits. Americans, by contrast, have no trouble buying domestically grown fruits and vegetables, but must rely on other nations for such items as tin, tea, and teakwood furniture. One reason why countries trade, then, is to acquire the products they cannot produce themselves. But that is not the sole—or even the most important—reason for trade.

The Opportunity Cost of Domestic Production

Virtually every country is capable of producing almost any product its citizens desire—if it is willing to expend the necessary resources. Lacking alternative sources of supply, the British probably could grow hothouse oranges and grapefruit, and Americans probably would find some way to produce tea domestically. The important point is that neither country chooses to expend its resources this way, because other countries can produce these products so much less expensively.

Think of the resources the British would need to use to produce hothouse oranges. More important, think of the other products that Britain could produce with those same resources. Whenever economists talk about the true cost of producing something, they mean the *opportunity cost*. As you will recall, the opportunity cost of anything is what you have to give up to obtain it. The opportunity cost of hothouse oranges would be whatever products the British would sacrifice to produce those oranges. By the same token, the cost of tea or coffee produced in the United States would be whatever other domestic products we could have produced with the same resources.

By making comparisons based on opportunity cost, we can determine which country is the low-cost producer of a particular product without becoming confused or misled as we would if we made comparisons in dollars or some other currency. Economic logic dictates that each country should specialize in the products it can produce at a relatively low opportunity cost and trade those products for the items that other countries can produce more cheaply. This logic is called the principle of **comparative advantage,** and it is the key to understanding how countries can benefit from trade.

The Principle of Comparative Advantage

The classic example of comparative advantage doesn't involve foreign countries; it has to do with a lawyer and the lawyer's secretary. The lawyer, Ms. Legal Wizard, not only is the best legal mind in the country but also types better than anyone else around. We could say that she has an **absolute advantage** over her secretary (and everyone else in the community) in both jobs. That means that the lawyer is more efficient at those jobs; she can accomplish more work in a given amount of time. If that is the case, why does the lawyer have her secretary, Mr. Average Typist, do the typing? By having the secretary do the typing, the lawyer frees her own time to do legal work.

Consider the high opportunity cost of having the lawyer do her own typing. It would mean the loss of the additional income she could have generated by handling more cases. The secretary, who has almost no talent for legal work, has a comparative advantage in typing because the amount of legal work he gives up to perform the typing duties is insignificant. The secretary does the typing not because he is a better typist than the lawyer (absolute advantage) but because he is better at typing than at legal work (comparative advantage). By allowing individuals to concentrate on the jobs they do the best—the jobs in which their absolute advantage is the greatest or their disadvantage the least—the firm is able to handle more clients, earn more money, and thereby raise the standard of living of all its members.

Comparative Advantage as a Basis for Trade

Countries can benefit from specialization and trade in much the same way that the lawyer and the secretary benefit from their relationship. Consider the possibility of trade between the United States and France. Even if the United States were more efficient than France in the production of everything, specialization and trade along the lines of comparative advantage would allow each country to achieve a higher standard of living than it could possibly attain if it remained self-sufficient.

In order to illustrate that conclusion as simply as possible, let's assume that the United States and France are the only two countries in the world and that they produce only two products: microcomputers and champagne. Exhibit 16.2 summarizes the production abilities of these two nations in terms of a hypothetical unit of resources, with each unit representing some combination of land, labor, capital, and entrepreneurship, some set amount of those resources. For instance, each resource unit might contain 10,000 hours of labor, 1,000 units of raw materials, the use of 10 machines for a year, and 500 hours of entrepreneurial talent. Although each unit contains the same quantities of these resources, the quality of these inputs would vary from nation to nation, giving rise to differences in productive abilities.

With each unit of resources, the United States can produce either 50 microcomputers or 100 cases of champagne. With the same unit, France can produce either 20 microcomputers or 80 cases of champagne. Because the United States can produce more microcomputers and more champagne per unit of resources, we know that it has an absolute advantage over France in the production of both products, just as the lawyer had an absolute advantage over her secretary in both typing and legal work. How is it possible for both countries

EXHIBIT 16.2

Production Possibilities per Unit of Economic Resources

	MICROCOMPUTERS	CASES OF CHAMPAGNE
United States	50	100
France	20	80

to benefit from trade when one of them is more efficient, or has an absolute advantage, in producing both products? To answer this question, we must explore the concept of comparative advantage.

In our example the United States has a comparative advantage in the production of microcomputers because the opportunity cost of producing that product is lower in the United States than in France. The United States must sacrifice two cases of champagne in order to free the resources necessary to produce one additional microcomputer. (Each resource unit can produce either 50 microcomputers or 100 cases of champagne, so each additional computer costs us two cases of champagne.) In France, however, the opportunity cost of each additional microcomputer is four cases of champagne because each unit of French resources can produce either 80 cases of champagne or 20 microcomputers. The United States can produce microcomputers at a lower opportunity cost and therefore has a comparative advantage in that product.

If we switch our attention to champagne production, we note that the French have a comparative advantage in this area. In the United States the production of one additional microcomputer forces the society to sacrifice two cases of champagne. The opportunity cost of producing one more case of champagne is therefore half a computer. In France the cost is lower. Each additional microcomputer requires the sacrifice of four cases of champagne. Therefore the opportunity cost of each case of champagne is one fourth of a computer. The French do indeed have a comparative advantage in the production of champagne.

The Benefits of Trade

Now that you understand how to determine a nation's comparative advantage, let's see how trade based on the principle of comparative advantage can result in a higher standard of living for both trading partners. In the absence of product specialization and trade, both France and the United States would produce some microcomputers and some champagne, the exact amounts of each depending on the strength of demand for the two products. Prior to trade, we can't say with precision what those amounts would be, but we know that one microcomputer would exchange for two cases of champagne in the United States and for four cases of champagne in France.

Suppose that the United States decides to specialize in the production of microcomputers and offers to trade one microcomputer to France for three cases of champagne. Would the French agree? Of course they would agree! Through trade they can acquire a microcomputer for three cases of champagne, whereas they would have to sacrifice four cases of champagne to produce one domestically. Under such circumstances they are better off to specialize in producing champagne and to trade for the microcomputers they desire.

As U.S. citizens, would we be better off with this arrangement? We certainly would be. We would be getting three cases of champagne for each microcomputer we traded, whereas we would be able to manufacture only two cases of champagne from the resources we used to produce each microcomputer. Clearly, trade based on the principle of comparative advantage will allow both countries to enjoy a higher standard of living.

The Production Possibilities Curve and the Gains from Trade

We can see the gains from trade more clearly by using the production possibilities curve introduced in Chapter 1. A production possibilities curve shows the combinations of goods that an economy is capable of producing with its present stock of economic resources and existing techniques of production.

Let's assume that the United States and France each have 100 units of economic resources to use in producing either microcomputers or champagne and that these resources are equally suited to the production of either product. When resources are assumed to be equally productive, the production possibilities curve appears as a straight rather than a bowed-out line (recall Chapter 1). In the United States these 100 resource units can be used to produce either 10,000 cases of champagne or 5,000 microcomputers or any other combination of champagne and microcomputers found on its production possibilities curve [see Exh. 16.3(a)]. In France the 100 resource units can be used to produce either 8,000 cases of champagne or 2,000 microcomputers or any other combination of champagne and microcomputers found on France's production possibilities curve [see Exh. 16.3(b)]. Recall that any combination of products we can plot either on or within the production possibilities curve (PPC) is available to the society. Combinations falling outside the PPC are beyond the economy's production capability and therefore unattainable unless we can trade for them.

Suppose that prior to trade the United States chooses to produce and consume 2,000 cases of champagne and 4,000 microcomputers, whereas France

EXHIBIT 16.3

Production Possibilities Curves and the Gains from Trade

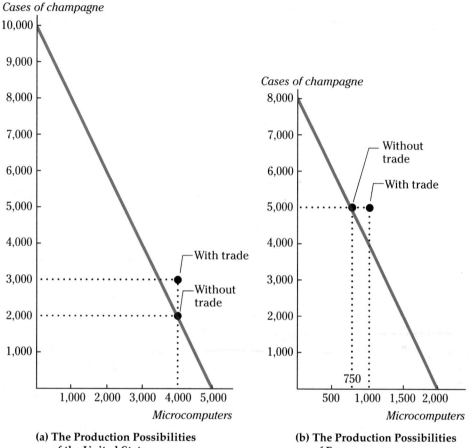

**(a) The Production Possibilities
of the United States**

**(b) The Production Possibilities
of France**

The two production possibilities curves show the combinations of champagne and microcomputers
that the United States (a) and France (b) can produce. Without trade, each nation is forced to select
a combination of the two products that lies either on the production possibilities curve or inside it.
For example, the United States might choose to produce and consume 2,000 cases of champagne
and 4,000 microcomputers, whereas France might select a combination of 5,000 cases of champagne
and 750 microcomputers. Through specialization and trade, each of these nations can enjoy a
higher standard of living. If the United States specializes in producing microcomputers and France
specializes in champagne, each of these nations can move to a point beyond its production
possibilities curve. For example, if the two countries agree on an exchange ratio of one
microcomputer for three cases of champagne, the United States can exchange 1,000
microcomputers for 3,000 cases of champagne. That will leave the United States with 4,000
microcomputers and 3,000 cases of champagne, whereas France will have 1,000 microcomputers
and 5,000 cases of champagne; both countries will be better off than they were without trade.

chooses a combination of 5,000 cases of champagne and 750 computers. Total world production would then be 7,000 cases of champagne (2,000 produced by the United States and 5,000 by France) and 4,750 microcomputers (4,000 produced by the United States and 750 by France).

Suppose next that the two countries decide to specialize along the lines of comparative advantage, agreeing to trade with each other at our hypothetical exchange ratio: one microcomputer = three cases of champagne. The United States has a comparative advantage in microcomputers, so it will use all its 100 resource units to produce microcomputers and will trade for champagne. The French will produce champagne, their product of comparative advantage, and will trade for microcomputers.

We know that the United States is producing 5,000 microcomputers and that France is producing 8,000 cases of champagne. What will be the result if the United States trades 1,000 microcomputers for some champagne? With an exchange ratio of one microcomputer to three cases of champagne, the United States will receive 3,000 cases of champagne in return for its 1,000 microcomputers and will still have 4,000 microcomputers left over. France will have 5,000 cases of champagne left over plus 1,000 microcomputers. The United States will have 1,000 more cases of champagne than it had prior to trade, and France will have 250 more microcomputers.

Trade and specialization have made it possible for each country to move beyond its PPC and to enjoy a combination of products that it could not obtain on its own. Moreover, total world production has increased from 7,000 to 8,000 cases of champagne and from 4,750 to 5,000 microcomputers. The principle of comparative advantage has allowed each of the trading partners to obtain more goods from each resource unit and to enjoy a higher standard of living.

The Transition to Greater Specialization: Winners and Losers

Trade based on comparative advantage clearly makes sense. And in the absence of **trade barriers**—legal restrictions on trade—we can be confident that the pursuit of self-interest will automatically lead producers to specialize in the products in which their country has a comparative advantage. Consider again our hypothetical world economy. Prior to trade, microcomputers were selling for twice as much as a case of champagne in the United States but four times as much as a case of champagne in France. Enterprising French and U.S. businesses would take advantage of these international price differentials to increase their profits. For instance, suppose that microcomputers were selling for $1,000 in the United States and that a case of champagne was selling for $500. In France, on the other hand, microcomputers were selling for 4,000 francs and a case of champagne for 1,000 francs. U.S. businesses could make a substantial profit by selling microcomputers in France and using the money to buy champagne for resale in the United States. French businesses could do the reverse; they could sell champagne in the United States and use the proceeds to buy computers for resale in France. Because French producers can sell champagne for less, ultimately they would force U.S. champagne producers out of business. The same fate would befall French computer manufacturers: They would be eliminated by competition from the United States.[3]

What would happen to the workers displaced from the French computer industry and the U.S. champagne industry? Our model assumes that all resources are equally suited for champagne production or computer manufacturing and that they move freely between those industries within each country but not between countries. Thus the economic resources—workers, factories, and equipment—no longer needed by the U.S. champagne industry would flow to the U.S. computer industry, and the resources released by the French computer industry would flow to the French champagne industry. With greater specialization, workers in both countries would become more productive, and they would be paid higher wages by their employers. In this way the benefits of trade would be shared by all members of the society; everyone would benefit from specialization and trade based on comparative advantage.

The transition to greater international specialization, however, is never painless. When a domestic industry is eliminated or reduced in size by foreign competition, difficult adjustments follow. Unemployed workers need time to find other jobs, and factories must be put to other uses. Some of these resources will never be reemployed, because firms are reluctant to invest money to retrain a fifty-five-year-old winemaker, for example, or remodel a thirty-year-old computer plant. Even though the total output of both countries will be greater than before trade (see Exh. 16.3), not every individual or group will be better off. Thus specialization has costs as well as benefits.

---

[3] Even in the absence of trade barriers, specialization may be less than complete. The United States might continue to produce some champagne, and France might continue to produce some microcomputers.

In order to conclude that foreign trade along the lines of comparative advantage will lead to complete specialization, we have to assume that (1) the products offered by French and U.S. manufacturers are identical—that French champagne is the same as U.S. champagne; (2) all economic resources are equally productive in both uses; (3) economic resources can move freely from one industry to the other but not between countries; (4) transportation costs are not large enough to outweigh the differences in production costs in the two nations; and (5) the computer and champagne industries are purely competitive. To the extent that these assumptions are not met, specialization will be less than complete.

Lower Prices through International Competition

Even when specialization is incomplete and several countries continue to produce the same products, international trade can benefit consumers by providing them with a wider variety of products from which to choose. Furthermore the availability of foreign products limits the pricing discretion of domestic producers and forces them to be more responsive to consumer demands.

Consider the U.S. automobile market. Foreign competition has not only given U.S. consumers more brands from which to choose but also spurred domestic manufacturers to develop small, fuel-efficient cars. In addition, competition from foreign producers has helped to keep automobile prices in the United States lower than they would be otherwise. A 1980 study by the Council of Economic Advisors concluded that if automobile imports were limited to 10 percent of the U.S. market, new-car prices would increase between 13 and 17 percent. Studies by the Federal Trade Commission and the International Automobile Dealers Association also predicted significant price hikes—

Competition from foreign automobile manufacturers has helped to hold down new-car prices in the United States.

up to $3,000 a car.[4] As you can see, international competition can be a powerful force in restraining the market power of domestic oligopolists and promoting a higher standard of living for consumers.

When we consider the benefits of trade in permitting greater specialization along the lines of comparative advantage and fostering greater competition, we can understand why economists generally agree on the desirability of **free trade**—trade that is not hindered by artificial restrictions or trade barriers of any type.

Types of Barriers to Trade

We have seen that free trade benefits consumers but often imposes substantial costs on particular groups in a society. Moreover, the benefits of free trade are widely diffused across a large number of people, each of whom is made a little better off, whereas the losses tend to be concentrated in a relatively small segment of the society. Workers who are forced out of jobs by foreign competition provide the best example.

Not surprisingly, the segment that is significantly harmed by foreign competition is likely to be more vocal than the group whose welfare is slightly improved. That's why politicians in the United States and elsewhere hear more often about the costs of free trade than about its benefits. As Michael Oldfather, former Chairman of the Kansas Council on Economic Education, has noted,

> [R]emoving import barriers on cars . . . might save every car-buying family a few hundred dollars a year. On the other hand, several thousand families would lose a great deal each (the families of U.S. automobile workers). Even though the total gains of car buyers would far exceed the total losses of car makers, it's not hard to guess whose voice will be the loudest.[5]

Virtually all the nations of the world impose trade barriers of one sort or another, partly in response to political pressure. These trade barriers are designed primarily to limit competition from imports, although export restrictions are sometimes established. The most common devices for limiting import competition are protective tariffs and import quotas.

---

[4] Murray L. Weidenbaum, with Michael C. Munger and Ronald J. Penoyer, *Toward a More Open Trade Policy* (Center for the Study of American Business, Formal Publication Number 53, January 1983), p. 5.

[5] Michael Oldfather, "Cost of any import ban outweighs gain," *Springfield* (MO) *News-Leader*, March 9, 1983, p. 7E.

Tariffs

A **tariff** is a tax on imported products. Its purpose is either to generate revenue for the taxing country through a *revenue tariff* or to protect domestic producers from foreign competition by means of a *protective tariff*. Historically, revenue tariffs were the major tool for financing government expenditures. Such tariffs served as the principal source of revenue for the U.S. government through the nineteenth century and remain the principal source in some less-developed countries.

Today most developed countries rely on other forms of taxation for revenue—income and sales taxes, for example. When developed countries, such as the United States, employ tariffs, their main purpose is to protect domestic producers. A tariff on a foreign product increases its price and makes it less competitive in the marketplace, thereby encouraging consumers to buy domestic products instead. In this way tariffs help to insulate domestic producers from foreign competition.

Quotas

Quotas restrict trade in a different way. An **import quota** specifies the maximum amount of a particular product that can be imported. The volume of imported wine, for example, might be limited to 50 million gallons per year, or the quantity of imported steel could be limited to 100,000 tons each year.

Import quotas can be either global or selective. A *global quota* limits the amount of a product that can be imported from the rest of the world. When the limit is reached, all further imports of that item are prohibited. A *selective quota* specifies the maximum amount of a product that can be imported from a particular country. For example, the United States might set a global quota of 500,000 imported automobiles per year and further specify selective quotas: 250,000 cars from Japan and 50,000 from France, perhaps, and the remaining 200,000 from other countries.

Domestic producers generally support import quotas over tariffs. Both trade barriers reduce competition from imported goods, but quotas are considered more effective. If consumers prefer foreign products to those offered by domestic producers, they may continue to buy relatively large amounts of these products in spite of the higher prices caused by the tariff. On the other hand, a quota will completely prohibit imports once the limit has been met.

Other Restrictions

Trade agreements (which are discussed later in the chapter) have helped to discourage the use of quotas and have reduced tariff rates significantly. But other forms of trade protection are more subtle and more difficult to legislate against. For example, health and safety laws are sometimes invoked to prevent or complicate the importation of certain products. The acquisition of import licenses can be made difficult or expensive, and government agencies can be required to purchase domestic products. The state of New York requires that state agencies buy American-made steel, for example, and New Jersey requires that all state cars be produced in the United States.[6]

In addition, new forms of trade interference have emerged, largely to bypass or take advantage of the rules in existing trade agreements. Among the most troubling is the **voluntary export restraint (VER),** an agreement under which an exporting country "voluntarily" limits its exports to a particular country, often under threat of the imposition of a quota. For example, in 1981 Japan signed a VER that limited its auto exports to the United States to 1.68 million units annually. Although VERs have essentially the same effect as quotas, they are not expressly prohibited by existing trade agreements, which discourage the use of unilaterally imposed quotas.

Another method of discouraging imports is to accuse a country of dumping. **Dumping** occurs when a product is sold to foreign consumers at a lower price than is charged domestic buyers. From an economic point of view, selling to different markets at different prices may make perfect sense. In fact, such price discrimination (recall Chapter 6) is a common practice of U.S. businesses. For example, airlines commonly charge a lower fare on routes where they face substantial competition and charge a much higher fare (for a trip of the same length) on routes where competition is absent. Economic logic notwithstanding, the United States has long held that dumping is an unfair form of competition (perhaps because in *rare* circumstances it can be used to drive a competitor out of business). As a consequence, U.S. laws prohibit dumping and call for additional tariffs to be imposed on products dumped in the U.S. market. (Existing trade agreements permit such "antidumping duties.") The U.S. Department of Commerce judges cases involving dumping in the United States and generally finds in favor of U.S. companies. As a consequence, the mere threat of a dumping case is often enough to convince foreign firms to raise their prices. As with VERs, the real loser is the consumer. The article on page 502, "U.S.'s Tough Trade Enforcement: Is It Fair?" examines the U.S. government's use of antidumping laws.

---

[6] Murray L. Weidenbaum, *Confessions of a One-Armed Economist* (Center for the Study of American Business, Formal Publication Number 56, August 1983), p. 25.

U.S.'s Tough Trade Enforcement: Is It Fair?

Just who is being unfair to whom? While President Clinton spent much of his time at the Tokyo summit meeting pleading for an even break on trade, some experts counter that fair play must begin at home.

They argue that Federal bureaucrats have been playing the same games that outrage American exporters, and point to the reversal of a string of recent Commerce Department rulings that foreign companies have been "dumping" their goods in the United States at prices that are unfair to American competitors.

In a decision last month, for example, Judge Nicholas Tsoucalas of the United States Court of International Trade—the appellate court in most anti-dumping suits—required the Government to give back penalties assessed against NSK, a Japanese ball-bearing maker.

"Commerce repeatedly ignores the law and disobeys the decisions of this court," he said.

Judge R. Kenton Musgrave of the same court sent the case of Bowe-Passat, a German manufacturer of dry-cleaning machinery, back for reconsideration in May.

The Commerce Department, he concluded, used the company's failure to dot every "i" and cross every "t" as an excuse to get tough. "This predatory 'gotcha' policy," he wrote, "does not promote co-operation or accuracy.". . .

"The Department of Commerce is on a holy crusade to find foreigners dumping" their goods, said James Bovard, author of the book "Fair Trade Fraud.". . .

Commerce Department officials declined to comment on the charges of bias. But people familiar with the department say that Congress, and, in particular, Senator Ernest F. Hollings, Democrat of South Carolina, chairman of the Senate Commerce Committee, have grown increasingly influential in the department's day-to-day thinking. . . .

Rule Increasingly Used

With hindsight, growing friction over anti-dumping cases is not difficult to explain. Modestly conceived as an antitrust measure to prevent foreigners from strangling domestic industries in the crib, dumping restrictions have grown ever broader in response to interest-group pressures.

Like most countries, the American law assumes that the practice of selling abroad below the price charged back home is inherently unfair. But the American law goes much further, adding a prohibition against sales at less than "fair market value," defined as the average cost of production, plus a 10 percent overhead, plus an 8 percent profit margin.

If the Commerce Department finds that dumping has occurred and another Federal agency, the United States International Trade Commission, decides that American competitors have been injured, penalties equal to the "dumping margin" are assessed.

Few economists see the logic in barring price-cutting where there is no intent to deliver a knockout punch. American consumers, after all, benefit from aggressive pricing. Fewer still would defend the cost-based definition of fair market value. Domestic industries routinely sell below average cost to minimize losses in bad years. Indeed, every American company that suffers losses is selling below average cost, and thus is "dumping" in its home market.

The dumping law is "just not sensible," concluded Seth Kaplan, director of economic research at Trade Resources Inc. in Washington.

Tit-for-Tat Law

But few would argue that Congress is disappointed with the impact. And the marketing handicap created by the anti-dumping law is widely justified as tit for tat: "The law is less biased against imports than the European Community and Canadian system," contends James Cannon, a lawyer at the Washington firm of Stewart & Stewart.

What is in dispute, though, is the fairness of the procedures used by the Commerce Department to assess dumping charges. . . .

One complaint is that the Commerce Department increasingly chooses to compare apples and oranges when it compares foreign and domestic prices. To determine foreign market value, the department takes an average price on sales back home over a six-month period. But to compute the difference between that value and the American price, the department can—and increasingly does—compare this average with specific individual sales—rather than an average across all sales—in America. . . .

Defendants in dumping cases are obliged to provide enormous amounts of information on the prices they charge and, frequently, on their costs of production. The information must be in English, must conform to the Commerce Department's accounting criteria, must be available in computer-readable form—and typically must be submitted within weeks of the request.

"It's time-consuming and it's expensive," concedes Mike Stein, a lawyer at Dewey Ballantine in Washington, which generally represents petitioners. But he says it is the only way to resolve complaints quickly and judiciously.

Hurdles for Foreigners

Cynics, however, see the ever-growing demands for information in ever-more-precisely specified formats as hurdles that foreign producers are not really meant to overcome. For if the Commerce Department is not satisfied with the response, it uses the "best information available"—what Tracy Murray, an economist at the University of Arkansas, notes is usually information provided by the domestic industry fighting for protection. . . .

—*Peter Passell*

SOURCE: Peter Passell, "U.S.'s Tough Trade Enforcement: Is It Fair?" July 20, 1993. Copyright © 1993 by The New York Times Company. Reprinted with permission.

Use Your Economic Reasoning

1. A product's fair market value is essentially its cost of production (average total cost), including a normal profit. Under what circumstances does economic theory suggest that a firm would to be willing to sell its product for a price that did not cover the firm's average cost? Does it seem reasonable to prohibit this practice?

2. Some critics argue that dumping cases are sometimes filed merely to harass foreign firms into raising their prices. Why might firms choose to raise their prices rather than fight in court?

3. When the U.S. government files dumping cases, it is likely to harm the interests of both U.S. consumers and U.S. exporters. Discuss.

Trade Barriers and Consumer Welfare

Economists generally condemn all forms of trade barriers. By reducing competitive pressures on domestic producers, such barriers allow firms with market power to charge higher prices yet be less responsive to the demands of consumers. Moreover, trade barriers interfere with the principle of comparative advantage: They prevent countries from concentrating on the things they do best and enjoying the best products produced by other countries.

Consider the impact of tariffs imposed by the United States on luggage imported from China and the Dominican Republic. These tariffs not only increase the prices consumers have to pay for imported luggage but also permit U.S. producers to charge more for their luggage. If imported luggage were not taxed, it would sell for less, and U.S. producers would be forced to reduce their prices in order to compete. Therefore U.S. producers desire tariffs even though tariffs are harmful to U.S. consumers.

Tariffs are less damaging to consumer welfare than quotas are, however. When increased demand causes the prices of domestic products to rise, comparable tariff-bearing foreign products become more competitive because the price differential between the foreign and domestic products is reduced. Because foreign products are now a more viable alternative for consumers, domestic producers may be restrained from raising prices further, lest they lose sales to foreign rivals. This is not the case with import quotas. When domestic producers are protected by quotas rather than tariffs, rising domestic prices cannot call forth additional units from foreign suppliers once the quotas have been met. As a consequence, domestic producers have more freedom under a quota system to increase prices without fear of losing their market share to foreign firms.

Another point in favor of import tariffs is that they provide governments with additional revenue, whereas quotas do not. This additional revenue can be used to reduce personal taxes or provide additional government services. Suppose, for example, that instead of using a voluntary export restraint (in effect, a "voluntary" quota) to restrain Japanese automobile exports, we chose to impose a tariff of $1,000 on each imported Japanese car. If two million cars were imported annually, that would amount to an additional *$2 billion* in revenue, not an insignificant sum. None of this is meant to suggest that tariffs are desirable, only that they are preferable to quotas.

The impact of trade barriers on the prices that consumers pay is only part of the story. When the United States erects trade barriers to keep out Japanese motorcycles or South Korean clothing or Canadian lumber, it interferes with the pursuit of comparative advantage. Not only do U.S. consumers get less for their dollars, the United States and the other nations of the world get less from their scarce resources. When we establish import quotas to protect high-cost U.S. motorcycle manufacturers, for example, we allow those firms to stay in business and use resources that could be put to better use in producing airplanes or machinery or other products in which the United States has a comparative advantage. We can acquire more motorcycles by producing aircraft and trading for motorcycles than by producing the motorcycles U.S. consumers demand. If we insist on protecting our motorcycle manufacturers and if Japan insists on protecting its aircraft producers, both societies lose. Their people will have to settle for fewer goods and services than free trade could produce. The price tag for this kind of protection is a lower standard of living for the average citizen.

Common Arguments for Protection

In spite of the costs imposed by trade barriers, they continue to exist. They exist because they serve the interests of certain powerful groups, even though they penalize society as a whole. Anyone who reads the newspaper or watches television is aware of the ongoing efforts of U.S. shoe manufacturers to maintain import protection against cheaper products from Taiwan and South Korea and Italy. Automobile producers, clothing manufacturers, and steel firms also lobby for protection. They argue that removing import restrictions would mean eliminating some producers and shrinking the output of others. The workers in these industries would have to look for new jobs, learn new skills, and perhaps even relocate to other parts of the country. These adjustments would be easy for some but difficult for others, particularly older workers. For these reasons employers and employees in industries that suffer from foreign competition have a strong personal interest in lobbying, or appealing to Congress for protection. Invariably the arguments that are used to justify protection mix some truth with at least an equal amount of misunderstanding or distortion. Let's consider three of the most popular arguments.

1. *Infant industries need protection from foreign competition.* The infant-industry argument suggests that new industries need protection until they become firmly established and able to compete with foreign producers. This argument makes little sense in a diversified and sophisticated economy like that of the United States but may have some relevance in less-developed countries. Even in that setting there are dangers. There is no assurance that the new industry will ever be able to compete internationally, and once protection has been granted, it is difficult to take away.

2. *Defense-related industries must be protected to ensure our military self-sufficiency.* This argument suggests that we must protect certain critical indus-

tries so that the United States will not be dependent on foreign countries for the things it needs to defend itself in time of war. The national-defense argument is commonly used to summon support for the protection of a long list of industries, including steel, munitions, rubber, and petrochemicals. There is no way to decide which industries are critical to our national defense and which are not. The longer the list, the more expensive protection becomes for U.S. consumers.

3. *U.S. workers need protection from cheap foreign labor.* The cheap-labor argument is heard often today. It claims that U.S. producers and their workers need protection from firms operating in countries with much lower wage rates than the United States, wage rates that constitute an unfair advantage that protection should offset.

There are two major flaws in this argument. First, low wages do not necessarily mean cheap labor. Labor is cheap only if the value of the output it produces is high relative to the wage rate. In many industries the United States is very competitive internationally, despite its high wage rates. Workers produce more output per hour than their foreign counterparts because U.S. workers tend to work with more and better machinery and tend to be better trained than workers in many other countries. (The article on page 508, "U.S. Productivity Gains Cut Costs . . . ," examines how increased productivity has enabled U.S. producers to compete with low-wage overseas firms.)

Second, we must remember that no country can have a comparative advantage in everything. The United States has a comparative *disadvantage* in the production of products whose manufacture requires large amounts of unskilled labor. On the other hand, we tend to have a comparative advantage in goods that are produced using highly skilled labor or large quantities of land or capital.

If we insist on protecting our labor-intensive industries, other nations have every right to protect their capital-intensive industries. Of course, such protectionism will deprive everyone of the benefits of comparative advantage, and we'll all be poorer for having resorted to protectionist measures.

Reducing Barriers: The Role of Trade Agreements

Arguments in favor of protecting domestic businesses and workers have always been with us. They were heard when our nation was in its infancy, and they are still common today. The protectionist sentiment was particularly high during the Great Depression. The job losses and business failures of that period led to pleas for protection from foreign competition. In 1930 Congress responded by passing the Smoot-Hawley Act, which raised import tariffs to an average of roughly 50 percent. Other countries retaliated, and the result was a lessening of trade, which may have contributed to a deepening of the Depression. Fortunately the remainder of the twentieth century has seen significant, though halting, progress toward eliminating trade barriers.

The Reciprocal Trade Agreements Act of 1934 began the work of undoing Smoot-Hawley. The 1934 act permitted the President to engage in negotiations with individual trading partners of the United States to reduce tariffs. Negotiations were on an item-by-item basis, so progress was slow. But by the end of World War II substantial progress had been made. U.S. tariff rates had been reduced from the 50 percent range to about half that level.

International Trade Agreements: GATT

Following the war, the United States led efforts to reduce trade barriers still further. In 1947 twenty-three countries signed the General Agreement on Tariffs and Trade (GATT), which established some basic rules for trade and created an organization to oversee trade negotiations. Under GATT rules, countries are discouraged from using import quotas. Instead, they are expected to use tariffs as their means of import protection. And although tariffs are viewed as the preferable form of import protection, the primary objective of GATT has been to reduce tariff rates. This has been accomplished through periodic negotiations known as "rounds." By 1994 those negotiations had reduced the average tariff applied by industrial nations to less than 5 percent, a far cry from the 50 percent rates of the Depression era.

Although GATT has resulted in steady downward movement of tariff and quota barriers, it has been less successful in dislodging subtle forms of protectionism, such as the use of health and safety regulations, to discourage imports. In addition, the desire to work within the rules of GATT (but still restrain competition) has led to an increased use of voluntary export restraints and accusations of dumping. It is these nontariff/nonquota forms of protectionism that constitute the modern threat to free trade.

The most recent round of GATT negotiations, initiated in Punta del Este, Uruguay, in 1986, did little to deter the use of VERs or dumping cases. However, the Uruguay Round, which concluded in 1993, will cut tariffs by about one third, force exporting nations to reduce agricultural subsidies, and strengthen patent protection to reduce pirating. The talks also resulted in the formation of a new organization, the World Trade Organization, to replace GATT and arbitrate trade disputes between nations.

U.S. Productivity Gains Cut Costs, Close Gap with Low-Wage Overseas Firms

U.S. companies have long complained that they can't beat low-wage foreign competitors without cutting their own workers' pay or heading for the border. Now, they're making liars of themselves.

Many American manufacturing and mining concerns—even old-line giants in the steel, coal, aluminum and machinery industries—are discovering that their American operations can keep pace with firms in developing nations where the pay is only one-third of the U.S. wage.

A major reason the gap has closed is that productivity gains have dropped labor costs to only a fraction of total costs, making U.S. producers less labor-intensive. Because labor has become only a small part of the equation for both domestic and foreign producers, the U.S. wage disadvantage—while still there—is a relatively minor factor.

Birmingham Steel Corp., for example, with a lofty average compensation of $55,000 a year, would seem easy prey for low-wage steel-

makers in Asia and South America. But it isn't.

The Birmingham, Ala., concern has reduced its labor cost to $42 a ton of steel from $51 over three years by hammering its productivity down to a mere 1.36 man-hours per ton. As a result, it costs Birmingham less in labor to make a ton of steel than it costs overseas competitors to ship a ton of steel to the U.S. "We don't care if their labor cost is zero," Chairman James A. Todd Jr. says. "If our cost of labor is less than their transportation cost, we have them licked."

Even giant USX Corp., in Pittsburgh, is closing in on low-wage foreigners. A decade ago, when its U.S. Steel unit's labor costs were 40% of total costs, it found itself far behind South Korean steelmakers, for example, which, according to a PaineWebber study, had labor costs of only 11% of total costs. But U.S. Steel has tripled its productivity and reduced its labor costs to only 20% of total costs. South Korea's labor cost, meanwhile, has risen to 17%. "Because productivity is up so

sharply, labor is less of an issue," concludes PaineWebber analyst Peter Marcus . . .

Of course, some of U.S. companies' newfound competitiveness reflects . . . rising wages overseas, particularly in developing countries. And . . . some productivity gains result from heavy investments in equipment.

Yet some U.S. manufacturers have pulled even with developing nations' costs without fresh capital investments. Cincinnati Milacron Inc., a machinery concern, for example, had virtually surrendered the market for low-end machines in the mid-1980s to the Japanese, Taiwanese and South Koreans; Milacron's costs were up to 50% higher and its wages at least double competitors'. But in the last two years, Milacron overhauled its assembly process, abolishing its stockroom and reducing job categories to one from seven. Without any additional capital investment, it cut labor hours by 50% and now exceeds Taiwan's productivity by a third.

As a result, Milacron's new Talon line low-end machine tools has pulled even with its foreign competitors. It has sold hundreds of the new machines so far and "each of these machines has been taken away from a Japanese or Taiwanese or Korean company," says Sandeep Malik, the Talon project manager. A few weeks ago, Milacron even sold one of its machines to a company in Singapore—in its low-wage competitors' backyard.

Cincinnati Milacron's competitor, Giddings & Lewis, Inc., of Fond du Lac, Wis., says it has reduced its direct labor to only about 10% of costs. Fully half of its workers are highly skilled professionals, up from only 25% a few years ago. With such a small proportion of its costs in labor and such a high percentage of its workers with skills that developing nations' workers lack, Giddings has proven wrong the notion that you can't compete against cheap foreign labor. "It creates a very different type of economics," says Dale Norton, the company's vice president for business development.

Warding Off Imports
In the coal industry, productivity gains have helped U.S. firms ward off an import surge from developing nations such as Colombia and Venezuela. At first glance, these nations are formidable: They have high-quality, low-sulfur coal, and they pay only $8 to $10 an hour in total compensation, compared

with $28 for U.S. coal companies.

But Cyprus Coal Co., a unit of Cyprus Minerals Co., isn't worried. The Englewood, Colo., company has boosted productivity by some 30% in the last three years. It now ships 18.5 million tons of coal annually with 2,050 workers; six years ago, it shipped 12.6 million tons with 2,300 employees. "They [South Americans] do with 250 people what we do

with 100," says Donald P. Brown, Cyprus Coal's president. "We can match them.". . .

—*Dana Milbank*

SOURCE: Dana Milbank, "U.S. Productivity Gains Cut Costs, Close Gap with Low-Wage Overseas Firms," December 23, 1992. Reprinted by permission of *The Wall Street Journal*, © 1992 Dow Jones & Co., Inc. All Rights Reserved Worldwide.

Use Your Economic Reasoning

1. Workers at Birmingham Steel earn roughly $31 an hour. If it takes them 1.36 hours to produce a ton of steel, what is the labor cost per ton of steel? Does your answer agree with the figure provided in the article? How will increasing the productivity of labor help to reduce this cost?

2. How are increases in the productivity of U.S. workers helping to offset higher U.S. wage rates?

3. Explain how transportion costs help to protect U.S. industries from producers in countries with lower wage rates.

4. Consider a hypothetical industry in which the United States pays its workers $20 per hour, whereas its foreign competitors pay only $10. Suppose, also, that workers in each country are able to produce two units of output per hour. If it costs foreign producers $4.50 a unit to ship their product to the United States, which producers will capture the U.S. market? Would the outcome change if U.S. productivity increased by 10 percent (to 2.2 units per hour)?

Regional Trade Agreements: NAFTA

The Uruguay Round, like all previous rounds of GATT negotiations, represented an attempt to decrease trade barriers worldwide. Recently, however, we have seen the emergence of regional trade agreements that attempt to eliminate or reduce trade barriers only among countries in a particular region or trading block. Members of the trading block face no trade barriers (or reduced barriers), but nonmembers do. For example, the European Union (formerly the European Economic Community) has eliminated most tariff barriers among member countries while continuing to impose tariffs on imports from nonmembers.[7] The North American Free Trade Agreement (NAFTA) attempts to create a similar trading block involving the United States, Canada, and Mexico. Under the agreement (signed by the United States and Canada in 1989 and joined by Mexico in 1993), tariffs among the countries are to be eliminated, in steps, over a ten-year period.

Both GATT and NAFTA are clearly steps in the direction of more open, or less-restricted, trade. But economists are generally more supportive of GATT than of NAFTA. If the world moves toward trading blocks rather than open trade among all nations, the principle of comparative advantage may be compromised. For example, the United States may find itself buying shoes from Mexico (because Mexico can produce shoes at a lower opportunity cost than the United States) but foregoing shoe imports from Taiwan (which may be able to produce shoes at a lower opportunity cost than Mexico), because Taiwan is outside our trading block and thus faces higher U.S. tariffs. If this occurs, the U.S. standard of living will be somewhat lower than it would have been under a system that provided equal access to all foreign producers.

The Case for Trade Adjustment Assistance

Both GATT and NAFTA were hotly debated in the United States. Supporters saw massive increases in U.S. GDP and employment; critics saw huge job losses. Although most objective analysis suggests that neither of these extreme outcomes is likely, it is clear that reductions in trade barriers will bring winners and losers. Unfortunately the losers are often those who can least afford to lose. For this reason many economists believe that efforts to reduce trade barriers should be accompanied by programs to retrain workers and otherwise assist those harmed by foreign competition.

The Trade Adjustment Act of 1962 took an important first step in this direction. Under this act workers losing their jobs because of increased competi-

---

[7] The EEC was created in 1957 by Belgium, France, West Germany, Italy, Luxemburg, and the Netherlands. They were later joined by Denmark, Greece, Ireland, Portugal, Spain, and the United Kingdom.

tion from imports become eligible for **trade adjustment assistance** in the form of higher unemployment compensation and funds for retraining. Businesses are granted money to modernize and better prepare to compete with foreign producers. About $3 billion worth of assistance was given in 1981, primarily to displaced automobile workers. The program was cut back during the Reagan and Bush administrations, which supported increased spending for job-training programs rather than assistance targeted specifically toward workers hurt by foreign competition. In the aftermath of the 1994 elections, it is difficult to know what, if any, assistance will be available to displaced workers. Although the Clinton administration has argued for a continuation of government-sponsored education and training programs, Republicans (who gained control of Congress) favor large cuts in such programs.

Even with government programs, the process of retraining and relocating workers is much more complicated than it appears. In some cases displaced workers have very poor educational backgrounds, which makes retraining difficult and expensive. Sometimes there are no additional industries in the area for which the workers can be retrained. Additional factors, such as age, family ties, and limited personal savings, often mean that relocation can be accomplished only at the cost of considerable personal hardship.

All of these problems complicate the transfer of labor to other industries and increase the human suffering associated with the removal of trade barriers. In fact, some critics argue that the case for free trade is commonly overstated because economists forget the assumptions of the model—that resources can shift easily from one industry to another, for example—seldom hold true in reality. This important criticism reinforces what we learned earlier in the chapter: Free trade tends to benefit consumers in general, but it usually imposes substantial costs on particular groups in the society. Such criticisms point to the need for adjustment assistance (perhaps available to any worker in need of retraining or relocation) and programs and policies designed to improve the mobility of the work force—better general education for high school students, for example—so that there will be a greater likelihood that workers released by one industry can find employment elsewhere without an unbearable delay. By approaching the problem this way, we can move closer to the ideal of free trade while minimizing the distress of workers who are displaced by foreign competition.

Summary

The economies of the world are becoming more interdependent. Americans are buying more *imports*—goods or services purchased from foreigners—and foreign consumers are buying more of our *exports*—products produced domestically and sold in other countries. Furthermore, many American-made products have foreign-made components. To know how to react to this growing interdependence, it is necessary to have some understanding of international economics—of why nations trade and how countries can benefit from trade.

One reason why nations trade is to acquire products that they cannot produce domestically. However, this is not the most important reason. Most countries can produce any product their citizens desire, *if* they are willing to expend the necessary resources. But trade may permit countries to acquire products much more cheaply—at a lower opportunity cost—than they can produce them domestically. This is the major benefit of international trade.

According to the theory of *comparative advantage,* each country should specialize in the products it can produce at a relatively low opportunity cost and trade for the items that other countries can produce more efficiently. This principle will permit each nation to achieve a higher standard of living than it could possibly attain if it remained self-sufficient.

Even when specialization is incomplete, trade can benefit consumers by providing them with a wider variety of products, limiting the pricing discretion of domestic producers, and forcing domestic producers to be more responsive to consumer demands.

Although free, or unrestricted, trade generally benefits consumers, it often imposes substantial costs on particular groups in any society—workers forced out of jobs by foreign competition, for instance. At least partly in response to pressure from these groups, countries erect *trade barriers*—legal restrictions on trade—to protect their domestic industries.

The most common devices for restricting imports are protective tariffs and import quotas. A *tariff* is a tax on imported products. A tariff on a foreign product increases its price and makes it less competitive in the marketplace, thereby encouraging consumers to buy domestic products instead. An *import quota* specifies the maximum amount of a particular product that can be imported.

Nations also employ a variety of other measures to limit import competition. For instance, stringent safety inspections may be imposed on foreign products to deter their importation, and government agencies may be required to purchase domestic products whenever possible. In addition, countries may negotiate *voluntary export restraints*—agreements under which a country voluntarily limits its exports to a particular country—or accuse foreign firms of illegal *dumping*—selling to foreign consumers at a lower price than they charge domestic buyers.

Economists tend to condemn all forms of trade barriers. Such barriers allow domestic producers to charge higher prices and to be less responsive to consumers. They also prevent countries from concentrating on the things they do best and trading for the best products produced by other countries.

In spite of the costs imposed by trade barriers, they continue to exist. Three common arguments are used to support trade barriers:

1. Infant industries need protection from foreign competition.
2. Defense-related industries must be protected to ensure our military self-sufficiency.
3. U.S. workers need protection from cheap foreign labor.

In the 1930s the U.S. government was particularly receptive to protectionist arguments. Since that time, tariff and quota barriers to trade have been reduced substantially. The General Agreement on Tariffs and Trade (GATT) has produced seven rounds of negotiations, which have reduced the average tariff applied by industrial countries to less than 5 percent. In addition, the North American Free Trade Agreement (NAFTA) will help to reduce trade barriers among the United States, Canada, and Mexico.

Although economists are generally supportive of the more open trade that GATT and NAFTA promote, there is no denying that the removal or lowering of trade barriers will hurt industries that are vulnerable to foreign competition. Therefore efforts to reduce trade barriers should be accompanied by programs to retrain workers and otherwise assist those harmed by foreign competition.

Glossary

Absolute advantage. One nation's ability to produce a product more efficiently—with fewer resources—than another nation.

Closed economy. An economy that does not exchange goods and services with other nations.

Comparative advantage. One nation's ability to produce a product at a lower opportunity cost than other nations.

Dumping. The sale of a product to foreign consumers at a lower price than is charged domestic buyers.

Exports. Goods and services produced domestically and sold to customers in other countries.

Free trade. Trade that is not hindered by artificial restrictions or trade barriers of any type.

Imports. Goods and services that are purchased from foreign producers.

Import quota. A law that specifies the maximum amount of a particular product that can be imported.

Open economy. An economy that exchanges goods and services with other nations.

Tariff. A tax on imported goods.

Trade adjustment assistance. Aid to workers and firms that have been harmed by import competition.

Trade barriers. Legal restrictions on trade.

Voluntary export restraint (VER). An agreement under which an exporting country voluntarily limits its exports to a particular country, often under threat of the imposition of a quota.

Study Questions

Fill in the Blanks

1. Economists advocate that countries specialize in the products they can produce at a lower _____ than other countries.

2. If country A can produce all products more efficiently than country B, country A is said to have a(n) _____ in the production of everything.

3. If country A can produce a given product at a lower opportunity cost than country B, country A is said to have a(n) _____ in the production of that product.

4. A _____ is a tax on imported products.

5. An _____ specifies the maximum amount of a particular product that can be imported.

6. The _____ argument suggests that new industries need protection until they are firmly established.

7. A _____ quota simply limits the amount of a product that can be imported from the rest of the world, whereas a _____ quota specifies the maximum amount of a product that can be imported from each country.

8. Aid to workers who have been harmed by foreign competition is called _____.

9. In most situations the (benefits/costs) _____ of free trade are widely diffused, whereas the (benefits/costs) _____ tend to be concentrated.

10. Most economists would like to see trade barriers eliminated. However, if they are forced to choose between tariffs and quotas, they would probably agree that _____ are less damaging to consumer welfare.

11. In 1930 Congress passed the _____ Act, which raised U.S. import tariffs to roughly 50 percent.

12. Nations may attempt to negotiate voluntary export restraints because the use of import quotas is discouraged by the _____ (trade agreement).

Multiple Choice

Use the following table in answering questions 1 through 4.

Production Possibilities per Unit of Economic Resources

	FOOD	CLOTHING
Country A	60	240
Country B	100	300

1. Which of the following statements is true?
   a) Country A has an absolute advantage in the production of both food and clothing.
   b) Country B has an absolute advantage in the production of both food and clothing.
   c) Country A has an absolute advantage in food, and country B has an absolute advantage in clothing.
   d) Country B has an absolute advantage in food, and country A has an absolute advantage in clothing.

2. In country A, the opportunity cost of a unit of food is
   a) 4 units of clothing.
   b) 60 units of clothing.
   c) 240 units of clothing.
   d) 1 unit of clothing.

3. According to the table,
    a) country A has a comparative advantage in food.
    b) country B has a comparative advantage in clothing.
    c) country A has a comparative advantage in clothing.
    d) country B has a comparative advantage in both food and clothing.

4. According to the principle of comparative advantage,
    a) country A should specialize in food, and country B should specialize in clothing.
    b) countries A and B should each continue to produce both food and clothing.
    c) country A should specialize in clothing, and country B should specialize in food.
    d) country B should specialize in clothing, and country A should specialize in food.

5. Which of the following is *not* a correct statement about trade barriers?
    a) Import tariffs are taxes on imports.
    b) Tariffs encourage consumers to buy domestic products.
    c) Quotas specify the maximum amount of a product that can be imported.
    d) Tariffs are probably more harmful to consumer welfare than quotas.

6. Which of the following is a true statement about trade barriers?
    a) They tend to enhance competition and benefit consumers.
    b) They benefit society as a whole but penalize small groups.
    c) They are needed to protect U.S. workers from cheap foreign labor.
    d) They serve the interests of certain powerful groups, even though they penalize society as a whole.

7. The purpose of trade adjustment assistance is to
    a) assist foreign countries when a tariff or quota is used to reduce imports from that country.
    b) assist domestic workers who are harmed when a quota is levied.
    c) assist domestic workers who are harmed when a tariff is reduced or a quota is eliminated.
    d) a and c

8. Which of the following is an accurate description of the impact of tariffs?
    a) They tend to raise the prices of imported products that are subject to the tariff.
    b) They tend to raise the prices of domestically produced products that are comparable to those being taxed.
    c) They permit inefficient industries to continue to exist.
    d) All of the above

9. Suppose that Britain can produce either 20 bicycles or 100 calculators with a unit of resources and that Taiwan can produce either 10 bicycles or 80 calculators. Which of the following statements is true?
    a) Taiwan has a comparative advantage in calculators.

b) Taiwan has an absolute advantage in bicycles.

c) Britain has a comparative advantage in calculators.

d) Taiwan has an absolute advantage in calculators.

10. Why do economists prefer tariffs to quotas?

a) Consumers may continue to buy imported products in spite of the tariff.

b) Tariffs do not really hinder trade; in fact, they may enhance trade.

c) As domestic products increase in price, foreign products become more competitive.

d) a and c

11. The General Agreement on Tariffs and Trade has *not* been very successful in

a) reducing tariff rates.

b) reducing the use of import quotas.

c) discouraging the filing of dumping cases.

d) all of the above

12. Dumping occurs whenever a firm

a) charges a lower price in foreign markets than it charges in its home markets.

b) sells a lower-quality product in foreign markets than it sells in its home market.

c) earns economic profits on its sales to foreign markets.

d) disposes of wastes by shipping them to disposal sites in foreign countries.

Problems and Questions for Discussion

1. Suppose that your roommate can make a bed in three minutes, whereas it takes you six minutes. Suppose also that your roommate can polish a pair of shoes in ten minutes, whereas it takes you fifteen minutes to do the same chore. What can we say about comparative advantage and absolute advantage in this example? How could the principle of comparative advantage be used to make you both better off? Does it make any difference how often each of these tasks must be performed?

2. Explain the difference between comparative advantage and absolute advantage. Why do economists emphasize the concept of comparative advantage (rather than absolute advantage) as the basis for trade?

3. How is the concept of opportunity cost related to the principle of comparative advantage?

4. The chapter mentions that politicians in the United States and elsewhere often hear more about the costs of free trade than the benefits. Why is that the case?

5. How can specialization and trade allow countries to consume beyond their own respective production possibilities curves?

6. How do trade barriers contribute to the inefficient use of a society's scarce resources?

7. Some economists have suggested that interference with free trade may be legitimate if it is used as a "bargaining chip" to convince another country to lower its trade barriers. Economist Robert Lawrence has criticized this approach because "it's something like a nuclear deterrent—it only applies if it isn't used." ("New Theory Backs Some Protectionism," *New York Times*, September 9, 1985, page D1.) Explain Mr. Lawrence's comment.

8. If resources (including labor) could move freely from one industry to the next, there would be less opposition to the removal of trade barriers. Please explain.

9. As Wisconsin University economist John Culbertson once suggested, "There is little comparative advantage in today's manufacturing industries, since they produce the same goods in the same ways in all parts of the world."("'Free Trade' Is Impoverishing the West," *New York Times*, July 28, 1985, page F3.) How could less-developed countries gain access to the same type of capital equipment employed by the United States? Could they operate it if they could obtain it? What are the implications of Mr. Culbertson's statement?

10. State the three most common arguments for trade protection. What are the limitations of each of these arguments?

11. Why are regional trade agreements, such as NAFTA, sometimes viewed as inferior to international agreements, such as GATT?

12. How can domestic firms use antidumping laws to stifle foreign competition?

Answer Key

Fill in the Blanks

1. opportunity cost	5. import quota	9. benefits, costs
2. absolute advantage	6. infant industry	10. tariffs
3. comparative advantage	7. global, selective	11. Smoot-Hawley
4. tariff	8. trade adjustment assistance	12. GATT

Multiple Choice

1. b	4. c	7. c	9. a	11. c
2. a	5. d	8. d	10. d	12. a
3. c	6. d			

CHAPTER 17

International Finance

LEARNING OBJECTIVES

1. Explain what is meant by an exchange rate and how exchange rates influence international transactions.
2. Describe the difference between a system of flexible exchange rates and a system of fixed exchange rates.
3. Illustrate graphically how the equilibrium exchange rate is determined, and identify the factors that can cause it to change.
4. Explain what it means for a currency to appreciate or depreciate in value.
5. Describe the policies that a nation may be required to pursue to maintain a fixed exchange rate, and why those policies may be unpopular.
6. Describe the current exchange rate system and the role of central banks in that system.
7. Describe the content of a country's balance of payments statement including its four major sections: the current account, capital account, statistical discrepancy, and official reserve transactions.

What are exchange rates, and how do they influence the prices we pay for imported products and even for travel? What do news commentators mean when they say that the dollar has "depreciated in value" or that the "appreciation of the yen" has made Japanese cars more expensive for Americans?

In Chapter 16 our simplified trade model assumed an arrangement whereby two countries exchanged their products directly. In reality, however, international transactions almost always involve money. Indeed, they usually involve two different types of money—the currencies of the two nations participating in the exchange. As we examine the financial dimension of international transactions, we'll learn how the dollars we spend on imported products are converted into the currencies desired by foreign producers, and we'll explore the systems used to determine exchange rates. We'll consider the factors that

519

can cause the exchange value of a nation's currency to change and examine the impact of those changes on the nation's economy. Finally, we will examine the U.S. balance of payments accounts and learn what it means to have a "current account deficit" and a "capital account surplus." In short, this chapter extends the analysis of Chapter 16, allowing us to gain a more complete understanding of international trade and our economic relationships with other nations.

The Meaning of Exchange Rates

If you want to buy a Japanese radio, you can pay for your purchase with cash or check or credit card. Ultimately, however, Japanese producers want to receive payment in yen, their domestic currency, because their workers and domestic suppliers expect to be paid in yen. That's why French perfume manufacturers seek payment in francs and Scottish producers of cashmere sweaters expect payment in pounds. The need to convert dollars into a foreign currency (or foreign currency into dollars) is the distinguishing feature of our trade with other nations.

The rate at which one currency can be exchanged for another currency is called the **exchange rate;** it is simply the price of one nation's currency stated in terms of another nation's currency. If you have traveled abroad, you know that the exchange rate is of more than passing interest. Suppose that you are having dinner at a quaint London restaurant where steak and kidney pie costs ten pounds (£10). How much is that in U.S. money? If the exchange rate is £1 to $3, you'll be spending $30.00; if it's £1 to $1.50, the same meal will cost you only $15.00.

U.S. importers also want to know the dollar cost of British goods. A wool sweater that sells for £25 will cost the importer $75 if the exchange rate is £1 to $3, but it will cost $100 if the exchange rate is £1 to $4. Whenever the pound is cheaper (whenever it takes fewer dollars to purchase each pound), U.S. tourists and importers will find British goods more attractive. If the pound becomes more expensive, fewer tourists will opt for British vacations, and fewer British products will be imported into the United States.

Exchange Rate Systems: Flexible Exchange Rates

Today exchange rates are determined primarily by market forces, by the interaction of the demand and supply of the various currencies. This is described as a system of **flexible,** or **floating, exchange rates,** since rates are free to move up or down with market forces.

To illustrate how the system works, assume that the United States and France are the only two countries in the world, so that we need to determine only one exchange rate, that between the U.S. dollar and the French franc. As you can see from Exh. 17.1, the demand curve for francs is downward sloping, just like the demand curves for jogging shoes and steak encountered in Chapter 3. The demand curve for francs is downward sloping because, ceteris paribus, as the price of the franc falls, Americans will tend to buy more French products. For example, if the dollar price of the franc fell from $0.30 per franc to $0.20 per franc, U.S. consumers would tend to buy more French wine, clothing, and Paris vacations. And, of course, to buy these products, they would demand more French francs. This assumes that the other factors affecting the demand for French francs remain unchanged. The factors that are assumed to be constant include the tastes and incomes of U.S. consumers, interest rates in the United States and France, and the overall price levels in

EXHIBIT 17.1

The Equilibrium Exchange Rate

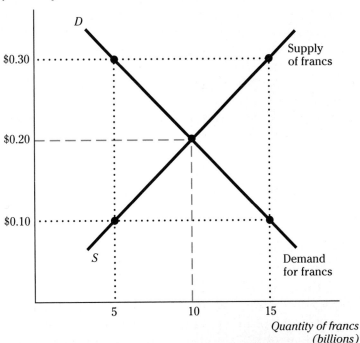

*Price of each franc
(in dollars)*

At the equilibrium exchange rate ($0.20 = 1 Fr), the quantity of francs demanded is exactly equal to the quantity supplied. If the dollar price of the franc is too high for equilibrium, the resulting surplus will tend to reduce the price of the franc. If the price is too low for equilibrium, the shortage of francs will tend to increase its price.

the two countries. If any of these factors changes, the entire demand curve will shift to a new position.

The French supply francs when they want to purchase dollars. If French residents want to buy U.S. products or to visit Disneyland or to invest in California real estate, they exchange their francs to buy dollars. The supply curve of francs is upward sloping because, other things being constant, as the value of the franc increases (which means that the dollar becomes less expensive), the French want to buy more U.S. products and will therefore supply more francs. This assumes that the tastes and incomes of French consumers remain unchanged, that French and U.S. interest rates remain constant, and that the price levels in the United States and France are unchanged.

The Equilibrium Exchange Rate

The intersection of the supply and demand curves for French francs determines the **equilibrium exchange rate**—the exchange rate at which the quantity of francs demanded is exactly equal to the quantity supplied. In our example these market forces will lead to an equilibrium exchange rate of $0.20 = 1 Fr. At that rate 10 billion francs are demanded and supplied.

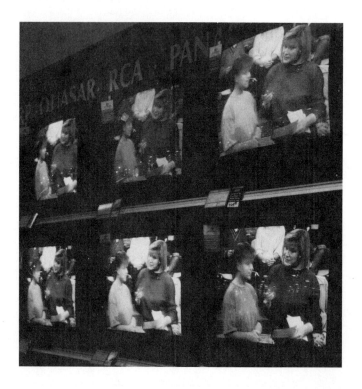

Because manufacturers desire payment in their domestic currency, U.S. importers must convert dollars into Japanese yen, South Korean won, and other currencies in order to purchase foreign televisions.

If the exchange rate were temporarily above or below the equilibrium level, pressures would exist to push it toward the equilibrium rate. For instance, if the exchange rate were $0.30 to 1 Fr, 15 billion francs would be supplied, but only 5 billion would be demanded. This surplus of francs would drive down the dollar price of the franc, just as a surplus drives down the price of wheat or cattle or anything else sold in a competitive market. At an exchange rate of $0.10 per franc, 15 billion francs would be demanded but only 5 billion supplied, and the resulting shortage would tend to push the price of the franc upward. These pressures would exist until the equilibrium exchange rate had been established.

Changes in the Equilibrium Exchange Rate.

Exchange rates can change frequently and sometimes quite dramatically. Any change that results in a shift of either the demand or the supply curve for a currency will cause the exchange rate to change. The factors that can shift the demand and supply curves include changes in tastes or income levels, changes in relative interest rates, and changes in price levels.

Changes in Tastes or Income Levels.
Suppose that the average income in the United States increased. This would cause U.S. consumers to demand more goods and services, including French goods and services. The result would be an increase in the demand for French francs: The demand curve for francs would shift to the right, as depicted in Exh. 17.2. The same thing would happen if Americans suddenly found French fashions more appealing or decided to switch from California wines to those imported from France.

When the demand curve for francs shifts to the right, the dollar price of the franc is driven up. For example, in Exh. 17.2 you can see that the dollar price of the franc has risen from $0.20 per franc to $0.30 per franc. The dollar has **depreciated** (lost value against the franc) because it now takes a larger fraction of a dollar to buy each franc. Conversely, the franc has **appreciated** (gained value) against the dollar because each franc now buys more dollars (cents) than before.

How would we represent the impact of an increase in French incomes or an increased desire to buy American fashions—Levi's blue jeans, for example? Either of these changes would increase the demand for U.S. products and consequently would increase the demand for U.S. dollars. And the French acquire more dollars by supplying more francs. Remember that! To acquire more dollars, the French must supply more francs! As a consequence, the supply curve of francs will shift to the right, as depicted in Exh. 17.3. Would these changes cause the dollar to appreciate or to depreciate? What about the franc? Take a moment and try to answer these questions before reading further.

EXHIBIT 17.2

An Increase in the Demand for Francs

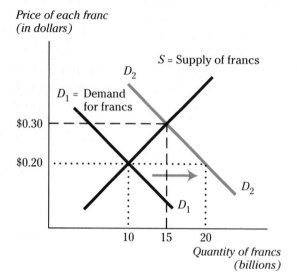

Price of each franc (in dollars)

An increase in U.S. incomes or an increased preference for French products would tend to increase the demand for francs. This would cause the franc to appreciate in value; each franc would buy more U.S. cents than before. When the franc appreciates, the dollar depreciates; it takes a larger fraction of a dollar to buy each franc.

EXHIBIT 17.3

An Increase in the Supply of Francs

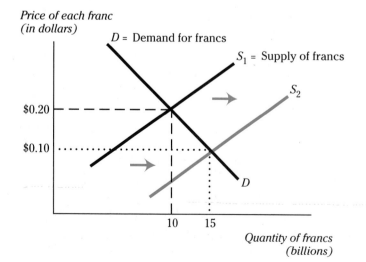

Price of each franc (in dollars)

An increase in French incomes or an increased preference for U.S. products would lead to an increase in the supply of francs. This would cause the franc to depreciate and the dollar to appreciate.

The correct answer is that an increase in the supply of francs would cause the dollar to appreciate in value. As you can see from Exh. 17.3, the dollar price of the franc has declined from $0.20 to only $0.10. The dollar must be more valuable—must have appreciated—because it now takes a smaller fraction of each dollar to buy a franc. Conversely, the franc has depreciated in value because each franc now buys fewer cents than before.

Changes in Relative Interest Rates. In the short run, one of the most important sources of changes in exchange rates is changes in relative interest rates. If French interest rates increased relative to those in the United States (as shown in Exh. 17.4), we could expect U.S. households and businesses to buy more French securities in order to earn the higher interest rates. This would shift the demand curve for francs to the right. At the same time, fewer French investors would be willing to buy U.S. securities, so the supply curve

EXHIBIT 17.4

The Impact of Higher French Interest Rates

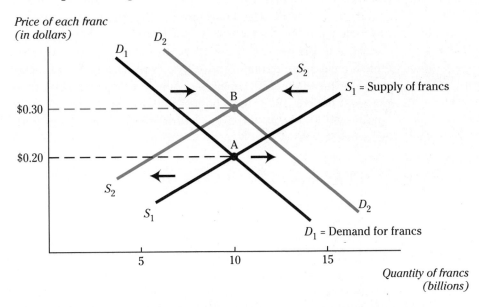

If French interest rates increase in relation to those in the United States, French securities become relatively more attractive. U.S. investors will demand more francs in order to buy French securities, whereas French investors will reduce their purchases of U.S. securities and thus supply fewer francs. These changes will tend to appreciate the franc and depreciate the dollar. (We move from equilibrium point *A* to point *B*.)

of francs would shift to the left. As the exhibit shows, these changes would cause the dollar price of the franc to rise from $0.20 to $0.30; the franc would appreciate, and the dollar would depreciate.

Changes in Relative Price Levels. Changes in relative price levels also influence exchange rates. To illustrate, imagine a U.S.-made automobile that sells for $20,000 in the United States and a comparable French auto that sells for 100,000 francs in France. At an exchange rate of $0.20 per franc, these vehicles will have the same sticker prices; the U.S. auto will sell for 100,000 francs in France and the French auto for $20,000 in the United States. Consumers in each country will choose between these vehicles on the basis of design features, available options, and other nonprice characteristics.

Now suppose that France experiences 20 percent inflation while inflation in the United States is only 10 percent. On average, prices in France will increase by 20 percent, so the price of the French auto will be pushed up to 120,000 francs. U.S. prices, including automobile prices, will rise by only 10 percent, so the U.S.-made automobile will now sell for $22,000. At an exchange rate of $0.20 per franc (or $1 = 5 Fr), U.S. automobiles now cost French consumers 110,000 francs, whereas French autos will be available for $24,000 in the United States. The same thing will happen to the prices of the other products traded by the two countries. Since U.S. products have become more attractive in price, the result will be an increase in the supply of francs (as French consumers demand more U.S. products) and a reduction in the demand for francs (as U.S. consumers demand fewer French products). As you can see from Exh. 17.5, these changes will cause the dollar price of the franc to fall from $0.20 to $0.10. The franc has depreciated in value, whereas the dollar has appreciated.

The Impact of Changes in Exchange Rates

How will Americans react when the dollar appreciates relative to the franc; will they be happy about the stronger dollar or unhappy? (When the dollar appreciates relative to another currency, it is described as getting stronger, whereas the other currency has weakened.) In truth, it depends on which Americans we are talking about. Consider U.S. exporting firms, for example. If the dollar appreciates as it did in Exh. 17.5, U.S. products will become more expensive for French consumers and thus less attractive. To illustrate, consider a computer that is selling for $20,000 in the United States. When the exchange rate is $0.20 per franc (or $1 = 5 Fr), that computer will cost French consumers 100,000 francs. But if the dollar appreciates so that it takes only $0.10 to buy each franc, that same $20,000 computer will cost French consumers 200,000 francs. Predictably, fewer French consumers will buy U.S. computers at the higher price, so U.S.

EXHIBIT 17.5

The Effect of a Rise in the French Price Level

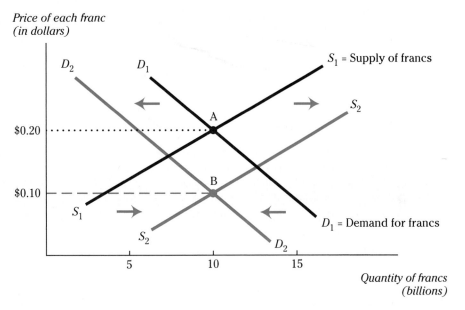

Price of each franc (in dollars)

If prices in France rise in relation to those in the United States, U.S. products will become more attractive. French consumers will supply more francs as they demand more U.S. products, and U.S. consumers will demand fewer francs as they demand fewer French products. The dollar price of the franc will fall from $0.20 to $0.10 (we move from equilibrium point *A* to point *B*).

exporters will find their sales suffering as a result of the appreciation of the dollar. And if U.S. exports suffer, some U.S. workers lose their jobs.

The other side of the story has to do with U.S. importers of French products. A stronger dollar means a weaker franc. And a weaker franc means that French products will be cheaper for Americans. Consider a bottle of French wine that costs 200 francs in France. When the exchange rate is $0.20 = 1 Fr, that bottle of wine will cost a U.S. importer $40. But if the franc depreciates so that the exchange rate is $0.10 = 1 Fr, that same bottle of wine will cost a U.S. consumer only $20. So the strong dollar will be welcomed by U.S. consumers and by U.S. businesses that import foreign products. The point is that whenever the exchange rate changes, there are winners and losers; some individuals and businesses will like the change, and others will not. (The article on page 528 looks at some of the consequences of a substantial weakening in the value of the Mexican peso.)

U.S. Firms Feel the Pain of Peso's Plunge

Ford Expects Mexico Sales to Slip; Mattel to Record Charge

Foreign-exchange traders and investors aren't the only Americans feeling the pain of the two-week plunge in the value of the Mexican peso.

For U.S. companies that are paid in pesos or that own substantial assets in Mexico, the recent 37% decline in the currency's value is a vivid example of just how quickly and substantially changes in the value of foreign currency can affect sales and profits.

That's because U.S. companies that receive pesos for payment suddenly are getting fewer dollars for those pesos. For instance, a U.S. company that sold widgets for 345 pesos early last month received about $100. Now, 345 pesos is worth between $60 and $65. Meanwhile, as the value of the peso declines, prices of U.S. exports will rise, making them less affordable for Mexican buyers.

Ford Motor Co.'s chairman and chief executive officer, Alexander Trotman, said yesterday that the cost of Ford autos "in peso terms has gone up enormously," Ford exported 27,000 to 28,000 vehicles to Mexico in 1994, up from a few hundred in 1992, as it took advantage of the North American Free Trade Agreement. Ford continues to build more than 200,000 vehicles in Mexico, but its Mexican output excludes such hot-selling vehicles as the Mustang sports coupe, which is imported from the U.S.

Toy Maker to Take Charge

Toy maker Mattel Inc. said yesterday that it will take an eight-cent-a-share charge for the fourth quarter because the peso's decline has reduced the value of its Mexican inventory and receivables. The charge means that despite a 35% jump in world-wide sales, Mattel's record earnings for the year will be on the "conservative" side of analysts' estimates.

Metalclad Corp., a Newport Beach, Calif., company with waste-oil recycling and landfill operations in Mexico, said the peso's plunge may wipe out its hopes for a profitable fiscal third quarter ending Feb. 28. And Pilgrim's Pride, a Pittsburg, Texas, chicken producer, expects to take a substantial write-down for its first quarter ended Dec. 31, as it marks down its $120 million in assets in Mexico.

For many big U.S. companies, however, the swings are just another day in the currency markets. Many companies say they do business in dollars or have otherwise hedged against currency changes, and won't feel any immediate financial impact. Further, Mexico is a relatively small international market.

Still, some are putting expansion plans on hold and even large companies expect exports to Mexico to fall off next year as Mexican buyers adjust to the higher prices of U.S. goods. After all, that's part of Mexico's goal in letting the peso's value fall in relation to the dollar. "The whole purpose of what they're doing is to try to reduce the level of imports" and increase Mexican exports, says Sidney Weintraub of the Center for Strategic and International Studies, a Washington think tank.

Impact on Texas

A drop in product sales to Mexico would be felt particularly in Texas, which exported about $20.38 billion in goods to its southern neighbor in 1993—nearly half the U.S. exports to Mexico. The state comptroller's office is predicting that exports will grow another 5% to 7% this year, but rise just 3% a year in 1996 and beyond, in part, because currency changes will curtail demand.

Several U.S. companies are pulling back while they wait to see what happens. Clorox Co. of Oakland, Calif., says it suspended exports to Mexico, although it continues to sell products it makes in a plant near Mexico City. David Rynne, chief financial officer for Tandem Computers Inc., says the maker of big computer systems has "aggressive" expansion plans for Latin America, but "we're not going to be doing anything [in Mexico]until we see the situation settling down.". . . .

Many U.S. companies say they remain optimistic about prospects for Mexico. Beyond the currency problems, they see an expanding economy and a burgeoning middle class for their products and services. Pilgrim's Pride, which had about $188 million in sales in Mexico in fiscal

1994, is pushing ahead with plans to expand its chicken business, even if its assets are worth less. "We're still making money in Mexico and we plan to continue to make money in Mexico," says Cliff Butler, chief financial officer.

SOURCE: "U.S. Firms Feel the Pain of Peso's Plunge," January 1, 1995. Reprinted by permission of *The Wall Street Journal*, © 1995 Dow Jones & Co., Inc. All Rights Reserved Worldwide.

Use Your Economic Reasoning

Prior to December 1994, the Mexican government had attempted to peg, or "fix," the value of the Mexican peso through central bank intervention in the exchange market. In December the government decided to allow the peso to float—to have its value determined by market forces. The result was a substantial decline in the value of the peso relative to other currencies.

1. The article argues that the purpose of allowing the peso to depreciate in value was to reduce Mexico's imports and increase its exports. How will a weaker peso contribute to those objectives?

2. Texans are particularly concerned about the peso's plunge. How can businesses in Texas be hurt by the drop in the peso's value?

3. What impact will the depreciation in the value of the peso have on the tourist trade between Mexico and the United States? Will it encourage Americans to visit Mexico? Will it encourage Mexicans to visit the United States?

4. What impact would you expect the peso's drop to have on Mexican emigration to the United States? Defend your conclusion.

Although changes in exchange rates are always unpopular with some groups, wide swings in exchange rate—whereby the dollar appreciates or depreciates substantially in a relatively short period of time—are particularly disruptive. For example, from the late 1970s to the mid-1980s, the dollar appreciated an average of approximately 80 percent. Then over the next half-dozen years, the dollar fell about as much as it had risen. This volatility creates a great deal of risk for firms trading internationally because they cannot know how much imports will cost (in their own country's currency) or how much they will receive for their exports.[1] In addition, wide swings in exchange rates can have a major impact on the competitiveness of exporting firms and firms facing import competition. This in turn can translate into undesirable volatility in the levels of domestic employment. These problems have caused some critics to argue for government intervention to "fix" or at least "manage" exchange rates. We will consider those possibilities next.

Exchange Rate Systems: Fixed Exchange Rates

Prior to the emergence of flexible exchange rates, the international monetary system was characterized by one form or another of **fixed exchange rates**—rates established by central governments rather than by market forces.

From the early 1800s to the end of the Great Depression, the international fixed exchange rate system was the **gold standard**; each country's currency was linked to gold. A central government agreed to buy and sell gold to anyone and everyone at a specified price stated in terms of that country's currency. For example, if the United States agreed to buy gold for $20 an ounce and France agreed to pay 100 Fr an ounce, the exchange rate of dollar to franc was $20 to 100 Fr, or $1 to 5 Fr. That rate would prevail until either the United States or France changed the price it was willing to pay for gold.

The gold standard fell apart following World War I for reasons that are beyond the scope of this chapter. From the end of World War I until after World War II, the international community experimented with a variety of temporary exchange rate systems, none of which gained acceptance. Then an international monetary conference held in 1944 at Bretton Woods, New

---

[1] Many exporters and importers protect themselves against exchange rate changes by buying and selling foreign currency in the "futures market." For example, if an importer wanted to protect itself against a change in the exchange rate, it would buy forward foreign exchange of the country whose products it was importing. This means that the importer buys foreign currency to be received in the future at an exchange rate agreed upon now. This service is not free, so it increases the cost of foreign trade. And, since most futures contracts cover only a few months, long-term importing and exporting agreements remain risky.

In 1944, a conference at Bretton Woods, New Hampshire, led to a new fixed exchange rate system. The British economist John Maynard Keynes (seated at the far left) represented Great Britain.

Hampshire, developed a new fixed exchange rate system in which the U.S. dollar played a prominent role. Under what became known as the **Bretton Woods system,** most governments agreed to maintain a fixed value for their currency in terms of the dollar; the United States agreed to redeem dollars (from foreign central banks) for gold at $35 an ounce. This linked all major currencies directly to the dollar and indirectly to one another. For example, if France and the United States agreed that $1.00 would exchange for 6 Fr and if the United States and Germany agreed that $1.00 would exchange for 2 DM (Deutsche marks), 3 Fr would exchange for 1 DM. Each government would then be committed to maintaining that exchange rate, even if market forces wanted to push the exchange rate elsewhere.

Fixed Exchange Rates and the Balance of Payments

To illustrate the consequences of fixed exchange rates, consider the demand and supply curves for francs represented in Exh. 17.6. Suppose that the governments of France and the United States have fixed the exchange rate at $0.20 per franc ($1 = 5 Fr) and that this initially represents the equilibrium exchange rate. Now suppose that an increase in the U.S. incomes causes the demand for francs to increase from D_1 to D_2. Under a system of flexible exchange rates, the dollar price of the franc would increase to $0.30 = 1 Fr. But that can't happen under system of fixed rates, bcause the governments are committed to maintaining an exchange rate of $0.20 = 1 Fr. At the fixed exchange rate of $0.20 = 1

EXHIBIT 17.6

Fixed Exchange Rates and the Balance of Payments

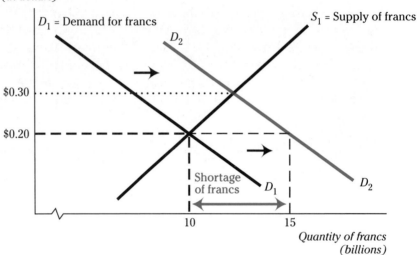

If the exchange rate is fixed at $0.20 = 1 franc, an increase in the demand for francs would lead to a shortage of the French currency. This shortage of francs represents a balance of payments deficit for the United States and a balance of payments surplus for France.

Fr, 15 billion francs will be demanded but only 10 billion supplied; there will be a shortage of 5 billion francs.

This shortage of francs represents a balance of payments deficit for the United States. A **balance of payments deficit** exists when a nation's foreign expenditures exceed its foreign receipts in a given year. In our hypothetical example the U.S. deficit is 5 billion francs (or $1 billion at an exchange rate of 5 francs per dollar). Of course, if the United States has a balance of payments deficit, France enjoys a **balance of payments surplus**; its foreign receipts exceed its foreign expenditures.

Under a system of flexible exchange rates, the shortage of francs would push the price of the franc up to $0.30, eliminating France's balance of payments surplus (and the U.S. balance of payments deficit). That's one of the desirable features of flexible exchange rates; they automatically eliminate balance of payments deficits and surpluses. But because the United States and

France are committed to maintaining an exchange rate of $0.20 = 1 Fr, that can't be allowed to happen. Instead, something must be done to maintain the agreed on rate.

Intervention in Foreign Exchange Markets. One approach to maintaining the fixed exchange rate would be for the Federal Reserve, the U.S. central bank, to use its accumulated reserves of francs to supply francs to the foreign exchange market. This would tend to shift the supply curve of francs to the right, as represented in Exh. 17.7, and allow the exchange rate to be maintained at $0.20 = 1 Fr. Alternatively, the French central bank could directly demand dollars. (Remember, in order to buy dollars, the central bank would need to supply francs.)

As long as the equilibrium exchange rate is sometimes above and sometimes below the fixed exchange rate (and relatively close to it), this type of intervention can go on indefinitely. Central banks will sometimes be required to

EXHIBIT 17.7

Intervention in Exchange Markets

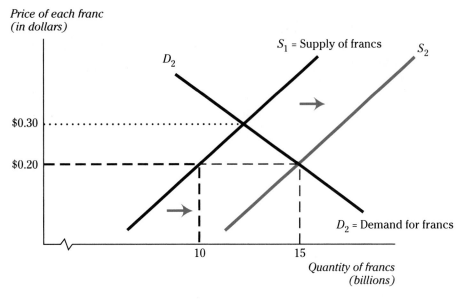

To maintain the exchange rate at $0.20 = 1 franc, the Federal Reserve must be willing to use its reserves of francs to buy dollars. By supplying francs to buy dollars, the Fed can shift the supply curve of francs to the right and maintain the fixed exchange rate.

use their reserves of foreign currencies, but during other periods they will be accumulating reserves. But when a more or less permanent change in demand or supply causes the equilibrium exchange rate to remain consistently above or below the fixed rate, something has to give. In our example the Federal Reserve cannot intervene forever; eventually its reserves of francs will run out. And the French central bank won't be willing to buy dollars forever, either. After all, the French are accumulating dollars without any guarantee that they will ever want to use them.

Intervention in the Domestic Economy. When persistent balance of payments problems exist, they can be eliminated by using fiscal and monetary policy to alter the demand and supply of foreign exchange. For example, the United States could eliminate its balance of payments deficit with France by increasing income taxes. This would reduce the disposable incomes of U.S. consumers and cause them to buy fewer French imports, shifting the demand curve for francs back to D_1 in Exh. 17.6. Reducing government spending in the United States could accomplish the same objective, since it would also tend to reduce the income levels in the United States. Alternatively, the country with a surplus (France) could employ an expansionary fiscal policy, cutting taxes and increasing government spending. This would tend to increase income levels and cause France to import more U.S. products, reducing the U.S. balance of payments deficit.

Monetary policy could be used in a similar manner. By reducing the money supply, the Fed could push up interest rates in the United States and slow spending for goods and services, including imported products. This would tend to reduce the demand for francs. In addition, the higher interest rates available in the United States would tend to attract money from French investors, who would need to buy dollars (supply francs) for that purpose. This would also help to reduce the U.S. balance of payments deficit. The alternative would be for France to expand its money supply. By driving down French interest rates, the French central bank would cause spending to increase, including spending for U.S. products. And the lower French interest rates would cause French investors to buy more U.S. securities.

Curing balance of payments problems by using monetary and fiscal policies can be tough medicine. In effect, the country with the deficit is forced to reduce employment and income as the price it must pay to eliminate the deficit. Alternatively, the country with the surplus is asked to accept the inflation that results as it expands its economy to eliminate the surplus. It was the unwillingness of either party to accept this harsh medicine that led to the breakdown of the Bretton Woods system—the fixed exchange rate system that existed from World War II until 1971.

The Current System: The Managed Float

As we've seen, neither fixed exchange rates nor flexible exchange rates provide nations with everything they want. Flexible exchange rates can lead to undesirable fluctuations in exchange rates, but fixed rates force countries to sacrifice domestic employment (or price stability) in order to stabilize exchange rates. Perhaps because neither of these systems is fully satisfactory, the system that has emerged can best be described as a system of managed exchange rates for major industrialized countries.

Managed exchange rates combine the flexible exchange rate system we described earlier in the chapter with intervention by central banks. Rather than completely fixing exchange rates (as in the fixed rate system), the purpose of central bank intervention is to limit or narrow exchange rate movements. In some instances, they may even attempt to reverse exchange rate changes they consider inappropriate or to hasten exchange rate changes they see as desirable. This system of quasiflexible exchange rates is sometimes described as **managed float.** (The article on page 536, "Japan Spares No Expense in Effort to Control Yen," looks at the Bank of Japan's intervention in the foreign exchange market.)

Like flexible exchange rates and fixed exchange rates, the managed float has also been subject to criticism. Even with intervention, exchange rates have proved to be quite volatile. This is not surprising when you recognize that the amounts central banks can spend to intervene in foreign exchange markets are small in comparison with the total amounts traded. For example, when central banks intervene they spend something on the order of one or two billion dollars a day. That compares with approximately $200 billion in foreign currency trading taking place on the average day. So while central banks may be effective in offsetting minor changes in supply and demand conditions or in slowing the pace of more fundamental changes, it is unlikely that central banks can preserve exchange rates that are significantly out of line with prevailing demand and supply conditions for the currencies in question. As a consequence, exchange rates have remained quite volatile and the search continues for an exchange rate system that can provide greater stability in exchange rates without the problems posed by the fixed rate systems of the past.

The U.S. Balance of Payments Accounts

Regardless of the exchange rate system adopted, countries will always want to keep track of their transactions with other nations. They want to know how dependent they are on imported products and how well their own exports are

Japan Spares No Expense in Effort to Control Yen

TOKYO

Japanese officials have contended for months that they cannot accept the Clinton Administration's demands for guaranteed increases in imports because the measures would amount to interference with the free play of the markets. Yet, in another realm, the Japanese Government has engaged in one of the heaviest waves of market intervention in memory in an attempt to manage the value of the yen and keep Japan's exports flowing.

Data on Japan's foreign exchange reserves show that since the beginning of last year, the Bank of Japan has used more than $35 billion in an effort to brake a sharp rise in the value of the yen against the dollar. . . .

Some economists say the intervention amounts to a policy of controlling Japan's trade flows, since the yen's rise—to 104.32 today in Tokyo trading—is expected to reduce the huge trade surplus by making Japanese goods more expensive overseas and by encouraging imports.

Some New Figures

Their concern was underscored by the release on Thursday of bilateral trade figures, which showed that the American merchandise trade deficit with Japan soared from $4.63 billion in February to $5.8 billion in March, the third-largest monthly deficit on record.

The critics have also said that the intervention flies in the face of a responsible interplay of supply and demand, a principle to which Japan's Government says it adheres.

"This has been a waste of money," said Kazuaki Harada, the chief economist at the Sanwa Research Institute. "The reason for the yen's rise is the trade surplus. And judging from the continuing large size of the surplus, I think we can expect an even stronger yen."

C. Fred Bergsten, head of the Institute for International Economics in Washington, agrees: "This is the most dramatic example of managed trade in the relationship between the U.S. and Japan over the last year or so. It's very clear that the yen would have strengthened well beyond 100 in the absence of this intervention."

The issue touches on one of the most sensitive aspects of the United States' troubled relationship with Japan—not just Japan's gaping surplus, but what methods are appropriate for tackling it.

The United States has said Japan must cut its trade surplus or relations cannot improve. The reform-minded Japanese Governments in office since last summer have said they share this goal. But they have asked for more time to devise a plan.

Nevertheless, the Bank of Japan, which operates under the influence of the Finance Ministry, has consistently sold yen to buy dollars, trying to counter heavy purchases of the yen by investors, corporations and speculators, both here and abroad. Those purchases have driven the yen's value to 104.25 yen to the dollar in New York today from 145 yen in 1990.

Japanese Government officials have said the bank's intervention has been aimed at calming jittery markets or smoothing out the many excessively volatile swings in trading. They have also said the yen's appreciation does not reflect underlying economic factors like the anemic economic growth rate or low Japanese interest rates. . . .

A Both Ways' Approach?

But a number of economists argue that the sustained nature of the Japanese intervention and the huge amounts involved make clear that the effort is an attempt to interfere with market forces and, ultimately, manage trade in Japan's favor.

"They are spending money like water," said Richard Koo, a senior economist at the Nomura Research Institute. "If you are saying you are in favor of free trade, that means that you should let the yen go. If you intervene as they have, you are saying you don't want the price-adjustment mechanism to work. You can't have it both ways." . . .

A Hard-Hit Sector

When the Clinton Administration took office, it vowed to attack the Japanese surpluses aggressively. After various Treasury officials hinted that they would not object to an appreciation of the yen, traders got the message. The dollar fell from 125 yen at the beginning of last year to lows of almost 100 yen last August and again earlier this month.

The yen's rise has hurt Japanese exporters badly, making it unprofitable for many of them to sell goods overseas. Economists here estimate that exporters break even at a level of about 115

yen to the dollar and begin to lose money below that.

In addition, the slump in exports has slowed the economy, which is already in the midst of its longest recession since World War II.

Many economists thus contend that Japan should take stronger measures to reduce its trade surplus to avoid the punishment of a rising yen. This could be done with a large increase in public works spending, tax reductions, interest rate reductions or some combination of these steps.

Toshihiro Kiribuchi, a former Finance Ministry official and now an executive at the Omron Corporation, an electronics manufacturer, said . . . that the ultimate solution

was not pouring more money into the currency market but aggressive economic policies to reduce the surplus.

"To stop this, the Japanese Government has to come forward with a very effective package of economic stimulus measures, lower interest rates and come up with more deregulation," Mr. Kiribuchi said, "Without these steps, the whole burden is placed on the shoulders of the Bank of Japan. But it cannot stop the dollar's decline alone."

—*James Sterngold*

SOURCE: James Sterngold, "Japan Spares No Expense in Effort to Control Yen," May 21, 1994. Copyright © 1994 by the New York Times Company. Reprinted with permission.

Use Your Economic Reasoning

1. When the exchange rate changes from 100 yen per dollar to 105 yen per dollar, has the yen appreciated or depreciated? What about the dollar?

2. Why is the Bank of Japan attempting to keep the yen from appreciating relative to the dollar? Who will benefit from these actions? Who will be harmed?

3. Construct a graph showing the demand and sup-

ply of yen. Now use your graph to show how intervention by the Bank of Japan could depress the dollar price of the yen. (*Hint:* Start with an equilibrium exchange rate of 2 cents per yen.)

4. Some economists are suggesting that Japan should increase its government spending or cut its tax rates. Why are these policies being recommended?

selling. And they're interested in where their residents are investing and in how much foreign money is being invested in their land. The answers to these questions and others are contained in a nation's balance of payments statement.

The U.S. **balance of payments (BOP) statement** is a record of all economic transactions between the United States and the rest of the world during a given year. Like other accounting statements, the BOP statement records credits and debits. Transactions that provide us with foreign exchange (the sale of exports, for example) are recorded as credits and are entered with a plus sign. Transactions that require us to use foreign exchange (such as the purchase of imports) are recorded as debits and are entered with a minus sign.

To simplify the recording of these debits and credits, the BOP statement is divided into four main sections: the current account, the capital account, the statistical discrepancy, and official reserve transactions. These categories are clearly indicated in Exh. 17.8, which depicts the U.S. balance of payments statement for 1994.

The Current Account

The first entries listed under the **current account** are merchandise exports and imports. The exports figure (a credit) reflects the value of the computers, airplanes, agricultural products, and other merchandise sold by U.S. firms to buyers in other countries. The figure for imports (a debit) reflects our purchases of Japanese automobiles, Brazilian coffee, Canadian lumber, and any other merchandise purchased from foreign sellers. As you can see from Exh. 17.8, in 1994 U.S. merchandise imports exceeded exports by $166.4 billion. This means that the United States experienced a **trade deficit** in 1994. If merchandise exports had exceeded merchandise imports, the United States would have enjoyed a **trade surplus.**

The next entries in the current account are the exports and imports of services. This category includes such items as shipping and banking services, insurance, and tourist expenditures. For example, if Colombian rose growers decide to use U.S. air carriers to ship their flowers to market, the transportation charge will be recorded as a credit in the services category of our balance of payments statement. On the other hand, when U.S. citizens vacation in Paris, their expenditures are recorded as a debit under services. Exhibit 17.8 reveals that in 1994 the value of service exports exceeded the value of service imports by $60 billion.

The final entries in the current account record investment income paid to and received from foreigners. This includes interest and dividend income earned by U.S. residents on investments in other countries (a credit) and interest and dividend income earned by foreign residents on investments in the United States (a debt). If you're earning interest on money in a Swiss bank account, that interest payment will be recorded as a credit in the U.S. balance

EXHIBIT 17.8

The U.S. Balance of Payments Accounts: 1994

Current Account

Merchandise exports	+ 502.7 *credit*	
Merchandise imports	− 669.1 *debit*	
Merchandise balance	− 166.4	
Service exports	+ 195.3	
Service imports	− 135.3	
Service balance	+ 60.0	
Receipts of investment income	+ 134.9	
Payments of investment income*	− 184.1	
Balance on investment income	− 49.2	
Balance on current account		− 155.6

Capital Account

Capital inflows	+ 275.7	
Capital outflows	− 130.8	
Balance on capital account		+ 144.9

Statistical Discrepancy

	− 33.5

Official Reserve Transactions

Decrease in U.S. reserve assets abroad	+ 5.3	
Increase in foreign reserve assets in the U.S.	+ 38.9	
Official reserve balance		+ 44.2

*The entries for investment income include unilateral transfers such as gifts and charitable contributions made to people and organizations in other countries and aid provided to foreign governments.

SOURCE: U.S. Department of Commerce *Survey of Current Business,* March 1995.

of payments. On the other hand, when General Motors makes dividend payments to British stockholders, that payment will be recorded as a debit. According to the exhibit, in 1994 U.S. interest and dividend payments exceeded receipts by roughly $49 billion.

The current account balance gives us the net result of all transactions involving merchandise, services, and payments of investment income. In 1994, the United States spent $155.6 billion more for these purposes than it received, so it had a current account deficit of that amount. (If it had earned more than it spent it would have enjoyed a current account surplus.)

The Capital Account

Like individuals, nations can spend more than they earn either by selling assets to raise money or by borrowing. For example, one of the ways that the United States can pay for a current account deficit is by selling some of its capital assets—real estate or factories or entire businesses—to foreigners. So if a group of Japanese businesspeople buys a quaint San Francisco hotel or a small Midwestern brewery, that transaction will be recorded as a credit under our **capital account.** The United States can also finance its current account deficit by borrowing money. This is accomplished when foreigners purchase U.S. stocks and bonds and bank accounts. Since these transactions also provide us with foreign funds, they too are recorded as credits under the capital account. Of course, while some U.S. residents are selling assets and borrowing money, others may be buying foreign assets and lending abroad. If a U.S. resident purchases an Italian winery or buys stock in a new Canadian company or opens a bank account in Japan, these transactions are recorded as debits under the capital account.

As you can see, the United States enjoyed a large capital account surplus in 1994. The $144.9 billion surplus was almost enough to finance the substantial current account deficit it experienced that year.

Statistical Discrepancy

If we compare the balance on current account and the balance on capital account, it appears that the United States experienced a balance of payments deficit of $10.7 billion in 1994. That is, the country's foreign spending exceeded its foreign earnings by $10.7 billion. But that figure understates the U.S. deficit. In collecting information for the balance of payments accounts, some transactions are missed or improperly recorded. The entry entitled **statistical discrepancy** reflects an adjustment to compensate for these transactions. After adjusting for the statistical discrepancy ($33.5 billion), the true size of the U.S. balance of payments deficit in 1994 is increased to $44.2 billion.

Official Reserve Transactions

Whenever a balance of payments deficit exists, it must be financed in some way. The primary method is through **official reserve transactions** by central banks.

The Federal Reserve and foreign central banks maintain reserves of foreign currencies that they can use to intervene in exchange markets. The Fed maintains reserves of Japanese yen and German marks, for example, whereas Germany's central bank, the Bundesbank, maintains reserves of yen and dollars. Exhibit 17.8 indicates that in 1994 the Fed reduced its holdings of reserve assets by $5.3 billion. (It was using its reserves of foreign currencies to buy dollars.) This entry is recorded as a credit because, like U.S. exports, it increases the supply of foreign currency and helps the U.S. finance its transactions with other countries. Over the same period, foreign central banks increased their holdings of reserve assets (dollars) held in the United States by $38.9 billion. By buying dollars (and supplying foreign currencies), these central banks in effect loaned U.S. residents another $38.9 billion to finance their expenditures abroad. The net effect of these two official reserve transactions is to provide a credit of $44.2 billion, exactly enough to finance the U.S. balance of payments deficit.

As you can see from this example, a nation's balance of payments statement always balances. The only question is *how* it will balance. If a country experiences a current account deficit, it must be offset by a capital account surplus or by official reserve transactions or by some combination of the two. If a country experiences a current account surplus, the surplus must be offset either by a capital account deficit or by official reserve transactions or some combination of the two.

The common wisdom is that a nation cannot run current account deficits indefinitely; ultimately it must learn to "live within its means." But the United States has recorded such deficits for roughly a decade. Clearly our capacity to spend more than we earn depends on our ability to attract foreign investment funds (to generate a surplus in the capital account). When foreigners no longer see the United States as an attractive place to invest, the dollar will tend to depreciate, and the current account deficit will shrink. And as long as foreign residents and central banks are willing to loan us the foreign exchange we need to finance our present spending habits, our current account deficits can continue.

SUMMARY

The feature that distinguishes international trade from trade within a nation is the need to convert the currency of one nation to the currency of some other nation. The rate at which one currency is exchanged for some other currency is called the *exchange rate.* The exchange rate plays a critical role in determining each country's level of imports and exports. Whenever the dollar is cheaper—that is, whenever it takes fewer pounds or yen or francs to purchase each dollar—importers find U.S. goods more attractive, and Americans will find British and Japanese and French goods more expensive. On the other hand, if the dollar becomes more expensive, U.S. goods will become less attractive and foreign goods a better buy.

Under a system of *flexible,* or *floating, exchange rates,* exchange rates are determined by market forces, by the interaction of demand and supply. At the *equilibrium exchange rate,* the quantity demanded of a currency is equal to the quantity supplied, and there is neither a shortage nor a surplus of the currency.

The equilibrium exchange rate will change in response to changes in the demand or supply of the currency being exchanged. When the exchange value of a nation's currency increases relative to other currencies, the currency has *appreciated* in value; when its exchange value declines, it has *depreciated* in value. Factors that will shift the demand and supply curves of currencies include changes in the tastes and income levels in the trading countries, changes in relative income levels in the trading countries, and changes in relative prices in the trading countries.

The alternative to flexible exchange rates is a system of fixed exchange rates. *Fixed exchange rates* are established by central governments rather than by market forces. Under a system of fixed exchange rates, nations are expected to use central bank intervention or monetary and fiscal policies to maintain the established rate. The *gold standard* and the *Bretton Woods system* are examples of fixed exchange rate systems.

Neither fixed nor flexible exchange rates provide nations with everything they desire. Flexible exchange rates can lead to undesirable fluctuations in exchange rates, whereas fixed rates may force countries to sacrifice domestic employment or price stability in order to stabilize exchange rates. Because neither system is fully satisfactory, most nations have turned to a system of managed exchange rates. *Managed exchange rates* combine the flexible exchange rate system with occasional intervention by central banks.

Regardless of the exchange rate system, countries want to keep track of their transactions with other nations. This is facilitated through a balance of payments statement. A *balance of payments statement* is a record of all economic transactions between a given country and the rest of the world.

Each country's balance of payments statement is divided into four parts: the current account, the capital account, the statistical discrepancy, and official reserve transactions. The *current account* is the portion of the balance of payments statement that records the exports and imports of goods and services. The *capital account* records the purchase and sale of capital assets, including factories and businesses, as well as stocks, bonds, and bank accounts. The *statistical discrepancy* adjusts for missing or improperly recorded transactions. The *official reserve transactions* is a record of the purchase or sale of reserve assets—including reserve currencies—by central banks. These reserve transactions commonly reflect central bank intervention in exchange markets.

When all transactions have been completed, each country's balance of payments statement must balance. If a country has a deficit on current account, that deficit (after adjustment for any statistical discrepancy) must be offset by a surplus on capital account or official reserve transactions.

Glossary

Appreciation of currency. An increase in the exchange value of a currency relative to other currencies.

Balance of payments deficit. Total payments to other countries exceed total receipts from other countries for an unfavorable balance of payments.

Balance of payments (BOP) statement. A record of all economic transactions between a particular country and the rest of the world during some specified period of time.

Balance of payments surplus. Total receipts from other countries exceed total payments to other countries for a favorable balance of payments.

Bretton Woods system. A fixed exchange rate system whereby nations agreed to fix a value on their currency in terms of the dollar, and the United States agreed to redeem dollars from other central banks for gold.

Capital account. The portion of a nation's balance of payments statement that records the purchase and sale of capital assets.

Current account. The portion of a nation's balance of payments statement that records the exports and imports of goods and services.

Depreciation of currency. A decrease in the exchange value of a currency relative to other currencies.

Equilibrium exchange rate. The exchange rate at which the quantity of a currency demanded is equal to the quantity supplied.

Exchange rate. The price of one nation's currency stated in terms of another nation's currency.

Fixed exchange rate. An exchange rate established by central governments rather than by market forces.

Flexible exchange rate. An exchange rate that is determined by market forces, by the supply and demand for the currency. Also described as a floating exchange rate.

Floating exchange rate. See flexible exchange rate.

Gold standard. A fixed exchange rate system whereby the value of each country's currency is directly tied to gold.

Managed exchange rates. Exchange rates that are determined by market forces with some intervention by central banks. Also described as a managed float.

Managed float. See managed exchange rates.

Official reserve transactions. The purchase and sale of reserve assets by central banks.

Statistical discrepancy. The entry in a nation's balance of payments statement that adjusts for missing or improperly recorded transactions.

Trade deficit. Merchandise imports exceed merchandise exports for an unfavorable balance of trade.

Trade surplus. Merchandise exports exceed merchandise imports for a favorable balance of trade.

Study Questions

Fill in the Blanks

1. The price of one currency in terms of another currency is called the _____ _____.

2. Another term for foreign currency is _____.

3. When imports exceed exports, a country is experiencing a _____ _____; when exports exceed imports, a country is experiencing a _____.

4. The _____ refers to merchandise imports and exports, whereas the _____ refers to all economic transactions between nations.

5. There are essentially two types of exchange rate systems: those involving _____ exchange rates and those involving _____ exchange rates.

6. Under a system of flexible exchange rates, if it takes more French francs than before to buy a U.S. dollar, we can say that the dollar has _____ and that the franc has _____.

7. If per capita incomes increased in the United States due to an economic expansion, U.S. imports of foreign products would probably (increase/decrease) _____.

8. If a country's exports of goods and services exceeded its imports of goods and services, it would experience a _____ account _____ _____ (deficit/surplus).

9. If interest rates are higher in the United States than they are abroad, foreign investors will tend to invest more money in the United States, and the dollar will tend to (appreciate/depreciate) _____ in value.

10. If the dollar appreciates in value, it will be (harder/easier) _____ for U.S. producers to sell their products abroad.

Multiple Choice

1. If total merchandise exports by the United States exceed merchandise total imports, the United States is experiencing a
   a) balance of payments deficit.
   b) balance of payments surplus.
   c) trade deficit.
   d) trade surplus.

2. Which of the following is not a source of foreign exchange for the United States?
   a) Foreign tourists visiting the United States
   b) U.S. exports to France
   c) U.S. imports from Japan
   d) German investments in the United States

3. For which of the following transactions must the United States acquire foreign exchange?
   a) Buying Japanese automobiles
   b) Investing in French companies
   c) Paying dividends to Arabs on their U.S. investments
   d) All of the above

4. If Americans decide to buy more Japanese automobiles,
   a) the demand curve for Japanese yen will shift to the left.
   b) the demand curve for American dollars will shift to the right.
   c) the demand curve for Japanese yen will shift to the right.
   d) the supply curve of Japanese yen will shift to the right.

5. The Bretton Woods system
   a) preceded the gold standard.
   b) was identical to the gold standard.
   c) was established after World War II.
   d) lasted until 1982.

6. If German interest rates increased relative to those in the United States,
   a) Americans would tend to demand fewer German marks.
   b) Germans would tend to supply more marks.
   c) the mark would tend to appreciate relative to the dollar.
   d) the dollar would tend to appreciate relative to the mark.

7. If the price level in Japan increases more rapidly than the price level in the United States,
   a) the Japanese will tend to supply more yen, appreciating the dollar relative to the yen.
   b) the Japanese will tend to supply fewer yen, appreciating the dollar relative to the yen.
   c) U.S. consumers will tend to demand more yen, depreciating the dollar relative to the yen.
   d) U.S. consumers will tend to demand more yen, appreciating the dollar relative to the yen.

8. If the German central bank intervenes in the foreign exchange market by buying dollars for marks, the intervention would tend to
   a) depreciate the dollar relative to the mark.
   b) appreciate the mark relative to the dollar.
   c) depreciate both the mark and the dollar.
   d) appreciate the dollar.

9. The purchase of a French company by a U.S. business would be recorded in the U.S. balance of payments accounts as a
   a) credit in the current account.
   b) debit in the current account.
   c) credit in the capital account.
   d) debit in the capital account.

10. Interest payments to foreign residents would be recorded in the U.S. balance of payments accounts as a
    a) credit in the current account.
    b) debit in the current account.
    c) credit in the capital account.
    d) debit in the capital account.

11. If the British decide to purchase more U.S. products,
    a) the demand curve for the British pound will shift to the right.
    b) the supply curve of the British pound will shift to the right.

    c) the supply curve of the American dollar will shift to the right.

    d) the supply curve of the American dollar will shift to the left.

12. If a $40,000 U.S. computer costs a German importer 120,000 DM, the exchange rate must be

    a) 1 Deutsche mark to 3 dollars.

    b) 1 Deutsche mark to 1/4 dollar.

    c) 1 dollar to 1/3 Deutsche mark.

    d) 1 dollar to 3 Deutsche marks.

13. Under a system of flexible exchange rates, if U.S. citizens started buying more British goods,

    a) the dollar would tend to appreciate relative to the pound.

    b) the price of the pound (in dollars) would begin to fall.

    c) the dollar would tend to depreciate relative to the pound.

    d) the price of the dollar (in pounds) would begin to rise.

14. If the yen price of the dollar (the price of a dollar stated in terms of Japanese yen) declined,

    a) Japanese cars would cost Americans fewer dollars.

    b) Japanese tourists would find American meals less expensive.

    c) American cars would cost Japanese consumers more yen.

    d) American tourists would be encouraged to tour Japan.

15. The existing exchange rate system is best described as a

    a) gold standard.

    b) system of fixed exchange rates.

    c) system of flexible exchange rates.

    d) managed float.

Problems and Questions for Discussion

1. If you were visiting London, which exchange rate would you prefer: $4 to £1 or $3 to £1? Why?

2. Suppose that we are operating under a system of flexible exchange rates. If Americans demand more British automobiles, will the dollar tend to appreciate or depreciate? Show this result graphically. What about the pound?

3. How was the Bretton Woods system different from the gold standard? What did the two systems have in common?

4. We sometimes read about balance of payments deficits or surpluses, but a nation's balance of payments statement must always balance. Clarify this apparent contradiction.

5. Japan's central bank has often intervened to buy dollars and prevent the dollar from depreciating relative to the yen. What is the rationale for such intervention?

6. Japan's central bank is in a better position to keep the dollar from depreciating than is the U.S. central bank (the Fed). Why? (*Hint:* How would the Fed go about trying to appreciate the dollar?)

7. If a nation is experiencing persistent balance of payments deficits, how could monetary and fiscal policies be used to remedy this problem? Why might a nation be reluctant to use such remedies?

8. Suppose that the Fed pursues a restrictive monetary policy to combat inflation in the United States. What impact would these policies be likely to have on the current account balance, the capital account balance, and the exchange value of the dollar relative to other currencies?

9. Federal government deficits are thought to drive up domestic interest rates. How could this indirectly hurt our merchandise exports?

10. If the German economy entered a recession, what impact would this have on the exchange rate between the German mark and the U.S. dollar? Why would it have this impact?

Answer Key

Fill in the Blanks

1. exchange rate
2. foreign exchange
3. trade deficit;
   trade surplus
4. balance of trade,
   balance of payments
5. fixed, flexible
6. appreciated, depreciated
7. increase
8. current, surplus
9. appreciate
10. harder

Multiple Choice

1. d
2. c
3. d
4. c
5. c
6. c
7. a
8. d
9. d
10. b
11. b
12. d
13. c
14. b
15. d

Index

Index